BEOWULF

AN INTRODUCTION TO THE STUDY OF THE POEM WITH A DISCUSSION OF THE STORIES OF OFFA AND FINN

BY

R. W. CHAMBERS

WITH A SUPPLEMENT BY

C. L. WRENN

*Rawlinson and Bosworth Professor
of Anglo-Saxon in the University of Oxford*

THIRD EDITION

CAMBRIDGE
AT THE UNIVERSITY PRESS
1959

PUBLISHED BY
THE SYNDICS OF THE CAMBRIDGE UNIVERSITY PRESS

Bentley House, 200 Euston Road, London, N.W.1
American Branch: 32 East 57th Street, New York 22, N.Y.

First Edition   1921
Second Edition 1932
Third Edition   1959

Printed in Great Britain at the University Press, Cambridge
(Brooke Crutchley, University Printer)

TO

PROF. WILLIAM WITHERLE LAWRENCE

Dear Prof. Lawrence,

When, more than four years ago, I asked you to allow me to dedicate this volume to you, it was as a purely personal token of gratitude for the help I had received from what you have printed, and from what you have written to me privately.

Since then much has happened: the debt is greater, and no longer purely personal. We in this country can never forget what we owe to your people. And the self-denial which led them voluntarily to stint themselves of food, that we in Europe might be fed, is one of many things about which it is not easy to speak. Our heart must indeed have been hardened if we had not considered the miracle of those loaves. But I fear that to refer to that great debt in the dedication to this little book may draw on me the ridicule incurred by the poor man who dedicated his book to the Universe.

Nevertheless, as a fellow of that College which has just received from an American donor the greatest benefaction for medical research which has ever been made in this country of ours, I may rejoice that the co-operation between our nations is being continued in that warfare against ignorance and disease which some day will become the only warfare waged among men.

> Sceal hring-naca   ofer heafu bringan
> lāc ond luf-tācen.   Ic þā lēode wāt
> ge wið fēond ge wið frēond   fæste geworhte,
> æghwæs untæle   ealde wīsan.

R. W. C.

PREFACE TO THE THIRD EDITION

INEVITABLE protraction and interruptions in the preparation of the first edition made it structurally less satisfying than expected, as Chambers well knew. Yet he decided, rightly, I believe, to reprint it with the minimum of change for the second edition, preferring to add a fifth part to cover recent work up to 1930, with some additional notes and the corresponding additions to the bibliography, rather than re-write or re-cast the whole book. For this third edition I have followed this plan as exactly as was possible, by adding a supplementary sixth part to cover the period between the second and third editions, adding a little to his "Additional Notes", and including a corresponding supplementary bibliography. Though rather less elaborately than was done by Miss Husbands for the second edition, I have enlarged the index so as to make it inclusive for the whole volume.

In the re-presentation of this uniquely and permanently valuable work to the public, a choice had to be made between a thorough revision and reshaping of the book so as to bring the whole into efficient form with corrected details and the addition of all the new material at the appropriate places, or reprinting the book which its maker had left, with separately made substantial additions. After much thought, it was decided to retain Chambers's practice. Both *pietas* and economy influenced the decision. For to have rewritten and reshaped the book would have raised the price of this work to a point beyond the reach of many of those who would value it most.

In a very rare degree Raymond Chambers expressed his wide and humane learning in an individual style which outstandingly conveyed the flavour of a personality beloved by all who in any way came in contact with it: he could combine the impression of *curiosa felicitas* with one of spontaneous wit and wisdom. Some of his general ideas and many of his detailed suggestions are now questioned by the newer experts: yet no one could revise and correct Chambers's book without a subjective introduction of his own notions and style.

I think that any attempt at revision would have made this volume into something other than its maker's book and thereby have reduced disastrously its unique charm and value. All new and divergent views, therefore, will be found only in the supplementary matter I have added to bring the work factually up-to-date: and in making my new Part VI and the supplementary bibliography I have tried always to respect Chambers's methods and attitudes.

The book as now published may seem to have suffered in structure: but its all-inclusive index should mitigate this inconvenience. The omission of the former illustrations, some of which are now perhaps out-of-date, was a concession to economy. But I am confident that most who knew Chambers and his book will agree that I have chosen the better course.

Amid the constantly changing approaches to the study of *Beowulf* I have felt constrained to leave this, the greatest single study of the greatest piece of Anglo-Saxon literature, as far as possible unchanged. For me, as for our greatest lexicographer, when he was revising Henry Sweet's *Anglo-Saxon Reader,* "Reverence for the opinion of a great master has restrained the correcting hand[1]."

C. L. W.

Oxford
November 5, 1958

[1] Prefatory Note to the ninth edition.

PREFACE TO THE SECOND EDITION

I HAVE again to thank a large number of friends for help generously and willingly rendered.

I am peculiarly indebted to Docent Birger Nerman and Prof. Sune Lindqvist for sending me photographs of the discoveries made when Ottar's mound was opened: I have thus been able to supplement the short account of that important discovery, given in the first edition of this book.

As before, I have been indebted to the advice of Prof. W. W. Lawrence of Columbia, and of my colleague Mrs Elsie Blackman, who have both read the additional sections in manuscript.

I have to thank Prof. Bruce Dickins for advice and help on many points—also Prof. Norman Baynes, and various friends who have called my attention to references and allusions which I might otherwise have overlooked: Prof. Knut Liestøl, Miss E. C. Batho, Dr A. H. Smith, Miss Audrey M. Cambridge, and Mr H. Gordon Ward. Miss W. Husbands has supplied an elaborate index, which will, I trust, make the book easier to use.

I have made no attempt to recast the section on Finnesburh. The work of Prof. Rudolf Imelmann, the elaborate study of Prof. R. A. Williams on the Finn episode, and the papers of Prof. Kemp Malone have all to be considered. I recognize also that very few critics agree with the tentative solution which I put forward, and that Prof. Malone, especially, has scored some palpable hits (see p. 551). Possibly some day I may return to the problem: the fact that I leave that section unaltered does not mean that I am satisfied with it, but that I do not see my way at present to any satisfactory solutions. As Mr Bruce Dickins has put it

> "In the Fragment, we have at least a shred of an original poem; in the Episode a mere abstract as obscure in its brevity as abstracts so often are; and who shall say that the versions represented by them agreed in more than general outline? How accurately could one reconstruct the Old Norse *Atlamál*, if nothing but stanzas 49–52, plus a brief abstract of the *Atlakvitha*, had survived?"

In the first edition, I marked in the bibliography those books which I had not seen by the sign ‡. I have to thank friends who have either sent me copies of these books, or told me where I could find them. As the plates are stereotyped, however, the sign ‡ remains in this edition. In the Addenda to the bibliography there are a number of items which I have had to take at second hand without seeing them: but I have not this time differentiated these by any mark. I trust that these omissions may be held to cancel out.

R. W. C.

June, 1931.

PREFACE TO THE FIRST EDITION

I HAVE to thank various colleagues who have read proofs of this book, in whole or in part: first and foremost my old teacher, W. P. Ker; also Robert Priebsch, J. H. G. Grattan, Ernest Classen and two old students, Miss E. V. Hitchcock and Mrs Blackman. I have also to thank Prof. W. W. Lawrence of Columbia; and though there are details where we do not agree, I think there is no difference upon any important issues. If in these details I am in the right, this is largely due to the helpful criticism of Prof. Lawrence, which has often led me to reconsider my conclusions, and to re-state them more cautiously, and, I hope, more correctly. If, on the other hand, I am in the wrong, then it is thanks to Prof. Lawrence that I am not still more in the wrong.

From Axel Olrik, though my debt to him is heavy, I find myself differing on several questions. I had hoped that what I had to urge on some of these might have convinced him, or, better still, might have drawn from him a reply which would have convinced me. But the death of that great scholar has put an end to many hopes, and deprived many of us of a warm personal friend. It would be impossible to modify now these passages expressing dissent, for the early pages of this book were printed off some years ago. I can only repeat that it is just because of my intense respect for the work of Dr Olrik that, where I cannot agree with his conclusions, I feel bound to go into the matter at length. Names like those of Olrik, Bradley, Chadwick and Sievers carry rightly such authority as to make it the duty of those who differ, if only on minor details, to justify that difference if they can.

From Dr Bradley especially I have had help in discussing various of these problems: also from Mr Wharton of the British Museum, Prof. Collin of Christiania, Mr Ritchie Girvan of Glasgow, and Mr Teddy. To Prof. Brøgger, the Norwegian state-antiquary, I am indebted for permission to reproduce photographs of the

Viking ships[1]: to Prof. Finnur Jónsson for permission to quote from his most useful edition of the *Hrólfs Saga* and the *Bjarka Rímur*, and, above all, to Mr Sigfús Blöndal, of the Royal Library of Copenhagen, for his labour in collating with the manuscript the passages quoted from the *Grettis Saga*.

Finally, I have to thank the Syndics of the University Press for undertaking the publication of the book, and the staff for the efficient way in which they have carried out the work, in spite of the long interruption caused by the war.

R. W. C.

April 6, 1921

[1] Omitted in the Third Edition.

GENEALOGICAL TABLES

The names of the corresponding characters in Scandinavian legend are added in italics; first the Icelandic forms, then the Latinized names as recorded by Saxo Grammaticus.

(1) THE DANISH ROYAL FAMILY

Scyld Scēfing [*Skjǫldr, Skyoldus*]

Bēowulf [not the hero of the poem]

Healfdene [*Halfdan, Haldanus*]

Heorogār [*no Scandinavian parallel*]

Hrōðgār [*Hróarr*[1], *Roe*], mar. Wealhþēow

Hālga [*Helgi, Helgo*]

a daughter [*Signy*]

Heoroweard [*Hjǫrvarðr, Hiarwarus: but not recognized as belonging to this family*]

Hrēðrīc [*Hrærekr, Rœricus: not recognized as a son of Hroarr*]

Hrōðmund

Frēawaru mar. Ingeld

Hrōðulf [*Hrólfr Kraki, Roluo*]

(2) THE GEAT ROYAL FAMILY

Hrēðel

Wǣgmund

Herebeald Hæðcyn Hygelāc, *mar.* Hygd a daughter, *mar.* Ecgþēow Wēohstān

a daughter, *mar.* Eofor

Heardrēd

Bēowulf

Wiglāf

(3) THE SWEDISH ROYAL FAMILY

Ongenþēow

Onela [*Áli, not recognized as belonging to this family*]

Ōhthere [*Óttarr*]

Eanmund

Ēadgils [*Aðils*[2], *Athislus*]

---

[1] The exact equivalent to *Hrōðgār* is found in O.N., in the form *Hróðgeirr*. The by-form *Hróarr*, which is used of the famous Danish king, is due to a number of rather irregular changes, which can however be paralleled. The Primitive Germanic form of the name would have been **Hrōþugaisaz*: for the loss of the *g* at the beginning of the second element we may compare *Aðils* with *Ēadgils* (Noreen, *Altisländische Grammatik*, 1903, § 223); for the loss of *ð* before *w* compare *Hrólfr* with *Hrōðwulf* (Noreen, § 222); for the absence of *R*- umlaut in the second syllable, combined with loss of the *g*, compare O.N. *nafarr* with O.E. *nafugār* (Noreen, § 69).

[2] Corresponding to O.N. *Aðils* we should expect O.E. *Ǣðgils, Ǣðgisl*. The form *Ēadgils* may be due to confusion with the famous Eadgils, king of the Myrgingas, who is mentioned in *Widsith*. The name comes only once in *Beowulf* (l. 2392) and may owe its form there to a corruption of the scribe. That the O.E. form is corrupt seems more likely than that the O.N. *Aðils*, so well known and so frequently recorded, is a corruption of *Auðgisl*.

CONTENTS

PART II

DOCUMENTS ILLUSTRATING THE STORIES IN *BEOWULF*, AND THE *OFFA*-SAGA

PART III

THE FIGHT AT FINNSBURG

PART IV

APPENDIX

PART V

RECENT WORK ON *BEOWULF* TO 1930

PART VI

RECENT WORK ON *BEOWULF* TO 1958

PART I

CHAPTER I

THE HISTORICAL ELEMENTS

Section I. The Problem.

The unique MS of *Beowulf* may be, and if possible should be, seen by the student in the British Museum. It is a good specimen of the elegant script of Anglo-Saxon times: "a book got up with some care," as if intended for the library of a nobleman or of a monastery. Yet this MS is removed from the date when the poem was composed and from the events which it narrates (so far as these events are historic at all) by periods of time approximately equal to those which separate us from the time when Shakespeare's *Henry V* was written, and when the battle of Agincourt was fought.

To try to penetrate the darkness of the five centuries which lie behind the extant MS by fitting together such fragments of illustrative information as can be obtained, and by using the imagination to bridge the gaps, has been the business of three generations of scholars distributed among the ten nations of Germanic speech. A whole library has been written around our poem, and the result is that this book cannot be as simple as either writer or reader might have wished.

The story which the MS tells us may be summarized thus: Beowulf, a prince of the Geatas, voyages to Heorot, the hall of Hrothgar, king of the Danes; there he destroys a monster Grendel, who for twelve years has haunted the hall by night and slain all he found therein. When Grendel's mother in revenge makes an attack on the hall, Beowulf seeks her out and kills her also in her home beneath the waters. He then returns to his land with honour and is rewarded by his king Hygelac. Ultimately he himself becomes king of the Geatas, and fifty years later slays a dragon and is slain by it. The poem closes with an account of the funeral rites.

Fantastic as these stories are, they are depicted against a background of what appears to be fact. Incidentally, and in a number of digressions, we receive much information about the Geatas, Swedes and Danes: all which information has an appearance of historic accuracy, and in some cases can be proved, from external evidence, to be historically accurate.

SECTION II. THE GEATAS—THEIR KINGS AND THEIR WARS.

Beowulf's people have been identified with many tribes: but there is strong evidence that the Geatas are the Götar (O.N. *Gautar*), the inhabitants of what is now a portion of Southern Sweden, immediately to the south of the great lakes Wener and Wetter. The names *Geatas* and *Gautar* correspond exactly[1], according to the rules of O.E. and O.N. phonetic development, and all we can ascertain of the Geatas and of the Gautar harmonizes well with the identification[2].

We know of one occasion only when the Geatas came into violent contact with the world outside Scandinavia. Putting together the accounts which we receive from Gregory of Tours and from two other (anonymous) writers, we learn that a piratical raid was made upon the country of the Atuarii (the O.E. *Hetware*) who dwelt between the lower Rhine and what is now the Zuyder Zee, by a king whose name is spelt in a variety of ways, all of which readily admit of identification with that of the Hygelac of our poem[3]. From the land of the Atuarii this king carried much spoil to his ships; but, remaining on shore, he was overwhelmed and slain by the army which the

---

[1] It must be remembered that the sound changes of the Germanic dialects have been worked out so minutely that it is nearly always possible to decide quite definitely whether two names do or do not exactly correspond. Only occasionally is dispute possible [e.g. whether *Hrothgar* is or is not phonetically the exact equivalent of *Hroarr*].

[2] See below, pp. 8–10.

[3] *Chochilaicus*, which appears to be the correct form, corresponds to *Hygelac* (in the primitive form *Hugilaikaz*) as *Chlodovechus* to *Hludovicus*.

Frankish king Theodoric had sent under his son to the rescue of these outlying provinces; the plunderers' fleet was routed and the booty restored to the country. The bones of this gigantic king of the "Getae" [presumably = Geatas] were long preserved, it was said, on an island near the mouth of the Rhine.

Such is the story of the raid, so far as we can reconstruct it from monkish Latin sources. The precise date is not given, but it was after 515, probably after 520, but before 530.

Now this disastrous raid of Hygelac is referred to constantly in *Beowulf*: and the mention there of Hetware, Franks and the Merovingian king as the foes confirms an identification which would be satisfactory even without these additional data[1].

Our authorities are:

(1) Gregory of Tours (d. 594):

His ita gestis, Dani cum rege suo nomine Chlochilaico evectu navale per mare Gallias appetunt. Egressique ad terras, pagum unum de regno Theudorici devastant atque captivant, oneratisque navibus tam de captivis quam de reliquis spoliis, reverti ad patriam cupiunt ; sed rex eorum in litus resedebat donec naves alto mare conpraehenderent, ipse deinceps secuturus. Quod cum Theudorico nuntiatum fuisset, quod scilicet regio ejus fuerit ab extraneis devastata, Theudobertum, filium suum, in illis partibus cum valido exercitu et magno armorum apparatu direxit. Qui, interfecto rege, hostibus navali proelio superatis opprimit, omnemque rapinam terrae restituit.

The name of the vanquished king is spelt in a variety of ways: *Chlochilaichum, Chrochilaicho, Chlodilaichum, Hrodolaicum.*

See *Gregorii episcopi Turonensis Historia Francorum*, p. 110, in *Monumenta Germaniae Historica (Scriptores rerum merovingicarum, I).*

(2) The *Liber Historiae Francorum* (commonly called the *Gesta Francorum):*

In illo tempore Dani cum rege suo nomine Chochilaico cum navale hoste per alto mare Gallias appetent, Theuderico paygo [i.e. pagum] Attoarios vel alios devastantes atque captivantes plenas naves de captivis alto mare intrantes rex eorum ad litus maris resedens. Quod cum Theuderico nuntiatum fuisset, Theudobertum filium suum cum magno exercitu in illis partibus dirigens. Qui consequens eos, pugnavit cum eis caede magna atque prostravit, regem eorum interficit, preda tullit, et in terra sua restituit.

The *Liber Historiae Francorum* was written in 727, but although so much later than Gregory, it preserves features which are wanting in the earlier historian, such as the mention of the Hetware (*Attoarii*). Note too that the name of the invading king is given in a form which

---

[1] The passages in *Beowulf* referring to this expedition are:

1202 *etc.* Frisians (adjoining the Hetware) and Franks mentioned as the foes.

2354 *etc.* Hetware mentioned.

2501 *etc.* Hugas (= Franks) and the Frisian king mentioned.

2914 *etc.* Franks, Frisians, Hugas, Hetware and "the Merovingian" mentioned.

approximates more closely to *Hygelac* than that of any of the MSS of Gregory: variants are *Chrochilaico, Chohilaico, Chochilago*, etc.

See *Monumenta Germaniae Historica (Scriptores rerum merovingicarum, II*, 274).

(3) An anonymous work *On monsters and strange beasts*, appended to two MSS of Phaedrus.

Et sunt [monstra] mirae magnitudinis: ut rex Huiglaucus qui imperavit Getis et a Francis occisus est. Quem equus a duodecimo anno portare non potuit. Cujus ossa in Reni fluminis insula, ubi in Oceanum prorumpit, reservata sunt et de longinquo venientibus pro miraculo ostenduntur.

This treatise was first printed (from a MS of the tenth century, in private possession) by J. Berger de Xivrey (*Traditions tératologiques,* Paris, 1836, p. 12). It was again published from a second MS at Wolfenbüttel by Haupt (see his *Opuscula* II, 223, 1876). This MS is in some respects less accurate, reading *Huncglacus* for *Huiglaucus,* and *gentes* for *Getis*. The treatise is assigned by Berger de Xivrey to the sixth century, on grounds which are hardly conclusive (p. xxxiv). Haupt would date it not later than the eighth century (II, 220).

The importance of this reference lies in its describing Hygelac as king of the Getae, and in its fixing the spot where his bones were preserved as near the mouth of the Rhine[1].

But if *Beowulf* is supported in this matter by what is almost contemporary evidence (for Gregory of Tours was born only some twenty years after the raid he narrates) we shall probably be right in arguing that the other stories from the history of the Geatas, their Danish friends, and their Swedish foes, told with what seems to be such historic sincerity in the different digressions of our poem, are equally based on fact. True, we have no evidence outside *Beowulf* for Hygelac's father, king Hrethel, nor for Hygelac's elder brothers, Herebeald and Hæthcyn; and very little for Hæthcyn's deadly foe, the Swedish king Ongentheow[2].

And in the last case, at any rate, such evidence might

---

[1] The identification of Chochilaicus with Hygelac is the most important discovery ever made in the study of *Beowulf*, and the foundation of our belief in the historic character of its episodes. It is sometimes attributed to Grundtvig, sometimes to Outzen. It was first vaguely suggested by Grundtvig (*Nyeste Skilderie af Kjøbenhavn*, 1815, col. 1030): the importance of the identification was worked out by him fully, two years later (*Danne-Virke*, II, 285). In the meantime the passage from Gregory had been quoted by Outzen in his review of Thorkelin's *Beowulf* (*Kieler Blätter*, III, 312). Outzen's reference was obviously made independently, but he failed to detect the real bearing of the passage upon *Beowulf*. Credit for the find accordingly belongs solely to Grundtvig.

[2] Ongentheow is mentioned in *Widsith* (l. 31) as a famous king of the Swedes. Many of the kings mentioned in the same list can be proved to be historical, and the reference in *Widsith* therefore supports Ongentheow's historic character, but is far, in itself, from proving it.

fairly have been expected. For there are extant a very early
Norse poem, the *Ynglinga tal*, and a much later prose account,
the *Ynglinga saga*, enumerating the kings of Sweden. The
Ynglinga tal traces back these kings of Sweden for some thirty
reigns. Therefore, though it was not composed till some four
centuries after the date to which we must assign Ongentheow,
it should deal with events even earlier than the reign of that
king: for, unless the rate of mortality among early Swedish
kings was abnormally high, thirty reigns should occupy a period
of more than 400 years. Nothing is, however, told us in the
Ynglinga tal concerning the deeds of any king Angantyr—
which is the name we might expect to correspond to Ongentheow[1].

But on the other hand, the son and grandson of Ongentheow,
as recorded in *Beowulf*, *do* meet us both in the *Ynglinga tal*
and in the *Ynglinga saga*.

According to *Beowulf*, Ongentheow had two sons, Onela and
Ohthere: Onela became king of Sweden and is spoken of in
terms of highest praise[2]. Yet to judge from the account given
in *Beowulf*, the Geatas had little reason to love him. He had
followed up the defeat of Hygelac by dealing their nation a
second deadly blow. For Onela's nephews, Eadgils and Eanmund (the sons of Ohthere), had rebelled against him, and had
taken refuge at the court of the Geatas, where Heardred, son of
Hygelac, was now reigning, supported by Beowulf. Thither
Onela pursued them, and slew the young king Heardred.
Eanmund also was slain[3], then or later, but Eadgils escaped.

It is not clear from the poem what part Beowulf is supposed
to have taken in this struggle, or why he failed to ward off
disaster from his lord and his country. It is not even made
clear whether or no he had to make formal submission to the
hated Swede: but we are told that when Onela withdrew he
succeeded to the vacant throne. In later days he took his
revenge upon Onela. "He became a friend to Eadgils in his
distress; he supported the son of Ohthere across the broad
water with men, with warriors and arms: he wreaked his

---

[1] Strictly *Anganþér*. See Heusler, *Heldennamen in mehrfacher Lautgestalt*
Z.f.d.A. LII, 101.

[2] ll. 2382–4.   [3] ll. 2612–9.

vengeance in a chill journey fraught with woe: he deprived the king [Onela] of his life."

This story bears in its general outline every impression of true history: the struggle for the throne between the nephew and the uncle, the support given to the unsuccessful candidate by a rival state, these are events which recur frequently in the wild history of the Germanic tribes during the dark ages, following inevitably from the looseness of the law of succession to the throne.

Now the *Ynglinga tal* contains allusions to these events, and the *Ynglinga saga* a brief account of them, though dim and distorted[1]. We are told how Athils (= Eadgils) king of Sweden, son of Ottar (= Ohthere), made war upon Ali (=Onela). By the time the *Ynglinga tal* was written it had been forgotten that Ali was Athils' uncle, and that the war was a civil war. But the issue, as reported in the *Ynglinga tal* and *Ynglinga saga,* is the same as in *Beowulf*:

> "King Athils had great quarrels with the king called Ali of Upp-land; he was from Norway. They had a battle on the ice of Lake Wener; there King Ali fell, and Athils had the victory. Concerning this battle there is much said in the *Skjoldunga saga*."

From the *Ynglinga saga* we learn more concerning King Athils: not always to his credit. He was, as the Swedes had been from of old, a great horse-breeder. Authorities differed as to whether horses or drink were the death of him[2]. According to one account he brought on his end by celebrating, with immoderate drinking, the death of his enemy Rolf (the *Hrothulf* of *Beowulf*). According to another:

> "King Athils was at a sacrifice of the goddesses, and rode his horse through the hall of the goddesses: the horse tripped under him and fell and threw the king; and his head smote a stone so that the skull broke and the brains lay on the stones, and that was his death. He died at Uppsala, and there was laid in mound, and the Swedes called him a mighty king."

---

[1] Whether it be accuracy or accident, these names Ottar and Athils come just at that place in the list of the *Ynglinga tal* which, when we reckon back the generations, we find to correspond to the beginning of the sixth century. And this is the date when we know from *Beowulf* that they should have been reigning.

[2] But the accounts are quite inconsistent. Saxo (ed. Holder, pp. 56–7) implies a version in which Athils was deposed, if not slain, by Bothvar Bjarki, which is quite at variance with other information given by Saxo.

There has therefore never been reason to doubt the existence of the king of Sweden known in *Beowulf* as Eadgils: Swedish philologists and antiquaries have identified beyond reasonable doubt his grave mound, and those of his father, grandfather and great grandfather. These investigations led to one of the most instructive and romantic of modern discoveries.

The Swedish Kings.

The account in the *Ynglinga saga* of the fight between Onela and Eadgils is as follows:

Aðils konungr átti deilur miklar við konung þann, er Áli hét inn upplenzki : hann var ór Nóregi. þeir áttu orrostu á Vænis ísi ; þar fell Áli konungr en Aðils hafði sigr ; frá þessarri orrostu er langt sagt í Skjǫldunga sǫqu. (*Ynglinga saga* in *Heimskringla,* ed. Jónsson, Kjøbenhavn, 1893, I, 56.)

The *Skjoldunga saga* here mentioned is an account of the kings of Denmark. It is preserved only in a Latin abstract.

Post haec ortis inter Adilsum illum Sveciae regem et Alonem Opplandorum regem in Norvegia, inimicitiis, praelium utrinque indicitur: loco pugnae statuto in stagno Waener, glacie jam obducto. Ad illud igitur se viribus inferiorem agnoscens Rolphonis privigni sui opem implorat, hoc proposito praemio, ut ipse Rolpho tres praeciosissimas res quascunque optaret ex universo regno Sveciae praemii loco auferret : duodecim autem pugilum ipsius quilibet 3 libras auri puri, quilibet reliquorum bellatorum tres marcas argenti defecati. Rolpho domi ipse reses pugilos suos duodecim Adilso in subsidium mittit, quorum etiam opera is alioqui vincendus, victoriam obtinuit. Illi sibi et regi propositum praemium exposcunt, negat Adilsus, Rolphoni absenti ullum deberi praemium, quare et Dani pugiles sibi oblatum respuebant, cum regem suum eo frustrari intelligerent, reversique rem, ut gesta est, exponunt. (See *Skjoldungasaga í Arngrim Jonssons Udtog, udgiven af Axel Olrik,* Kjøbenhavn, 1894, p. 34 [116].)

There is also a reference to this battle on the ice in the *Kálfsvísa,* a mnemonic list of famous heroes and their horses. It is noteworthy that in this list mention is made of Vestein, who is perhaps the Wihstan of our poem, and of Biar, who has been thought (very doubtfully) to correspond to the O.E. Beaw.

Dagr reið Drǫsle   en Dvalenn Móðne...
Ále Hrafne   es til íss riþo,
enn annarr austr   und Aþilse
grár hvarfaþe   geire undaþr.
Bjǫrn reið Blakke   en Biarr Kerte,
Atle Glaume   en Aþils Slungne...

   Lieder der Edda, ed. Symons and Gering, I, 221-2.

"Ale was on Hrafn when they rode to the ice: but another horse, a grey one, with Athils on his back, fell eastward, wounded by the spear." This, as Olrik points out, appears to refer to a version of the story in which Athils had his fall from his horse, not at a ceremony at Uppsala, but after the battle with Ali. (*Heltedigtning,* I, 203-4.)

---

[1] See below, p. 344, pp. 356-7, and particularly the section, in Appendix II, on *Beowulf* as a source of early Northern History.

For various theories as to the early history of the Swedish royal house, as recorded in *Beowulf*, see Weyhe, *König Ongentheows Fall*, in *Engl. Stud.* XXXIX, 14-39: Schück, *Studier i Ynglingatal* (1905-7): Stjerna, *Vendel och Vendelkråka*, in *A.f.n.F.* XXI, 71, *etc.*

The Geatas.

The identification of Geatas and Götar has been accepted by the great majority of scholars, although Kemble wished to locate the Geatas in Schleswig, Grundtvig in Gotland, and Haigh in England. Leo was the first to suggest the Jutes: but the "Jute-hypothesis" owes its currency to the arguments of Fahlbeck (*Beovulfsqvädet såsom källa för nordisk fornhistoria* in the *Antiqvarisk Tidskrift för Sverige*, VIII, 2, 1). Fahlbeck's very inconclusive reasons were contested at the time by Sarrazin (23 *etc.*) and ten Brink (194 *etc.*) and the arguments against them have lately been marshalled by H. Schück (*Folknamnet Geatas i den fornengelska dikten Beowulf*, Upsala, 1907). It is indeed difficult to understand how Fahlbeck's theory came to receive the support it has had from several scholars (e.g. Bugge, *P.B.B.* XII, 1 *etc.*; Weyhe, *Engl. Stud.* XXXIX, 38 *etc.*; Gering). For his conclusions do not arise naturally from the O.E. data: his whole argument is a piece of learned pleading, undertaken to support his rather revolutionary speculations as to early Swedish history. These speculations would have been rendered less probable had the natural interpretation of Geatas as Götar been accepted. The Jute-hypothesis has recently been revived, with the greatest skill and learning, by Gudmund Schütte (*Journal of English and Germanic Philology*, XI, 574 *etc.*). But here again I cannot help suspecting that the wish is father to the thought, and that the fact that that eminent scholar is a Dane living in Jutland, has something to do with his attempt to locate the Geatas there. No amount of learning will eradicate patriotism.

The following considerations need to be weighed:

(1) *Geatas* etymologically corresponds exactly with O.N. *Gautar,* the modern Götar. The O.E. word corresponding to Jutes (the Iutae of Bede) should be, not *Geatas,* but in the Anglian dialect *Eote, Iote,* in the West Saxon *Iete, Yte.*

Now it is true that in one passage in the O.E. translation of Bede (I, 15) the word "Iutarum" *is* rendered *Geata:* but in the other (IV, 16) "Iutorum" is rendered *Eota, Ytena.* And this latter rendering is supported (*a*) by the *Anglo-Saxon Chronicle* (*Iotum, Iutna*) and (*b*) by the fact that the current O.E. word for Jutes was *Yte, Ytan,* which survived till after the Norman conquest. For the name *Ytena land* was used for that portion of Hampshire which had been settled by the Jutes: William Rufus was slain, according to Florence of Worcester, in *Ytene* (which Florence explains as *prouincia Jutarum*).

From the purely etymological point of view the Götar-hypothesis, then, is unimpeachable: but the Jute-hypothesis is unsatisfactory, since it is based upon one passage in the O.E. Bede, where *Jutarum* is incorrectly rendered *Geata,* whilst it is invalidated by the other passage in the O.E. Bede, by the *Chronicle* and by Florence of Worcester, where *Jutorum* is correctly translated by *Ytena,* or its Anglian or Kentish equivalent *Eota, Iotna.*

(2) It is obvious that the Geatas of *Beowulf* were a strong and independent power—a match for the Swedes. Now we learn from Procopius that in the sixth century the Götar were an independent

and numerous nation. But we have no equal evidence for any similar preponderant Jutish power in the sixth century. The *Iutae* are indeed a rather puzzling tribe, and scholars have not even been able to agree where they dwelt.

The Götar on the other hand are located among the great nations of Scandinavia both by Ptolemy (*Geog.* II, 11, 16) in the second century and by Procopius (*Bell. Gott.* II, 15) in the sixth. When we next get clear information (through the Christian missionaries) both Götar and Swedes have been united under one king. But the Götar retained their separate laws, traditions, and right of confirmation of the king, and they were constantly asserting themselves during the Middle Ages. The title of the king of Sweden, *rex Sveorum Gothorumque*, commemorates the old distinction.

From the historical point of view, then, the Götar comply with what we are told in *Beowulf* of the power of the Geatas much better than do the Jutes.

(3) Advocates of the Jute-hypothesis have claimed much support from the geographical argument that the Swedes and Geatas fight *ofer sæ* (e.g. when Beowulf and Eadgils attack Onela, 2394). But the term *sæ* is just as appropriate to the great lakes Wener and Wetter, which separated the Swedes from the Götar, as it is to the Cattegatt. And we have the evidence of Scandinavian sources that the battle between Eadgils and Onela actually *did* take place on the ice of lake Wener (see above, p. 6). Moreover the absence of any mention of ships in the fighting narrated in ll. 2922–2945 would be remarkable if the contending nations were Jutes and Swedes, but suits Götar and Swedes admirably: since they could attack each other by land as well as by water.

(4) There is reason to think that the old land of the Götar included a great deal of what is now the south-west coast of Sweden[1]. Hygelac's capital was probably not far from the modern Göteborg. The descriptions in *Beowulf* would suit the cliffs of southern Sweden well, but they are quite inapplicable to the sandy dunes of Jutland.

Little weight can, however, be attached to this last argument, as the cliffs of the land of the Geatas are in any case probably drawn from the poet's imagination.

(5) If we accept the identification Beowulf = Bjarki (see below, pp. 60-1) a further argument for the equation of Geatas and Götar will be found in the fact that Bjarki travels to Denmark from Gautland just as Beowulf from the land of the Geatas; Bjarki is the brother of the king of the Gautar, Beowulf the nephew of the king of the Geatas.

(6) No argument as to the meaning of *Geatas* can be drawn from the fact that Gregory calls Chlochilaicus (Hygelac) a Dane. For it is clear from *Beowulf* that, whatever else they may have been, the Geatas were not Danes. Either, then, Gregory must be misinformed, or he must be using the word *Dane* vaguely, to cover any kind of Scandinavian pirate.

(7) Probably what has weighed most heavily (often perhaps not consciously) in gaining converts to the "Jute-hypothesis" has been the conviction that "in ancient times each nation celebrated in song its own heroes alone." Hence one set of scholars, accepting the identification of the Geatas with the Scandinavian Götar, have argued that *Beowulf* is therefore simply a translation from a Scandinavian Götish original. Others, accepting *Beowulf* as an English poem, have

[1] See Schück, *Folknamnet Geatas*, 22 etc.

argued that the Geatas who are celebrated in it must therefore be one of the tribes that settled in England, and have therefore favoured the "Jute theory." But the *a priori* assumption that each Germanic tribe celebrated in song its own national heroes only is demonstrably incorrect[1].

But in none of the accounts of the warfare of these Scandinavian kings, whether written in Norse or monkish Latin, is there mention of any name corresponding to that of Beowulf, as king of the Geatas. Whether he is as historic as the other kings with whom in our poem he is brought into contact, we cannot say.

It has been generally held that the Beowulf of our poem is compounded out of two elements: that an historic Beowulf, king of the Geatas, has been combined with a mythological figure Beowa[2], a god of the ancient Angles: that the historical achievements against Frisians and Swedes belong to the king, the mythological adventures with giants and dragons to the god. But there is no conclusive evidence for either of these presumed component parts of our hero. To the god Beowa we shall have to return later: here it is enough to note that the current assumption that there *was* a king Beowulf of the Geatas lacks confirmation from Scandinavian sources.

And one piece of evidence there is, which tends to show that Beowulf is not an historic king at all, but that his adventures have been violently inserted amid the historic names of the kings of the Geatas. Members of the families in *Beowulf* which we have reason to think historic bear names which alliterate the one with the other. The inference seems to be that it was customary, when a Scandinavian prince was named in the Sixth Century, to give him a name which had an initial letter similar to that of his father: care was thus taken that metrical difficulties should not prevent the names of father and son being linked together in song[3]. In the case of Beowulf himself, however, this rule breaks down. Beowulf seems an intruder

---

[1] See below, p. 98 and Appendix (E); The "Jute-Question."

[2] See below, pp. 45 *etc.*

[3] Olrik (*Heltedigtning*, I, 22 *etc.*). The Danish house—Healfdene, Heorogar, Hrothgar, Halga, Heoroweard, Hrethric, Hrothmund, Hrothulf: the Swedish—Ongentheow, Onela, Ohthere, Eanmund, Eadgils: the Geatic—Hrethel, Herebeald, Hæthcyn, Hygelac, Heardred. The same principle is strongly marked in the Old English pedigrees.

into the house of Hrethel. It may be answered that since he
was only the offspring of a daughter of that house, and since
that daughter had three brothers, there would have been no
prospect of his becoming king, when he was named. But
neither does his name fit in with that of the other great house
with which he is supposed to be connected. Wiglaf, son of
Wihstan of the Wægmundingas, was named according to the
familiar rules: but Beowulf, son of Ecgtheow, seems an intruder
in that family as well.

This failure to fall in with the alliterative scheme, and the
absence of confirmation from external evidence, are, of course,
not in themselves enough to prove that the reign of Beowulf
over the Geatas is a poetic figment. And indeed our poem *may*
quite possibly be true to historic fact in representing him as
the last of the great kings of the Geatas; after whose death
his people have nothing but national disaster to expect[1]. It
would be strange that this last and most mighty and mag-
nanimous of the kings of the Geatas should have been forgotten
in Scandinavian lands: that outside *Beowulf* nothing should be
known of his reign. But when we consider how little, outside
Beowulf, we know of the Geatic kingdom at all, we cannot
pronounce such oblivion impossible.

What tells much more against Beowulf as a historic Geatic
king is that there is always apt to be something extravagant
and unreal about what the poem tells us of his deeds, con-
trasting with the sober and historic way in which other kings,
like Hrothgar or Hygelac or Eadgils, are referred to. True, we
must not disqualify Beowulf forthwith because he slew a
dragon[2]. Several unimpeachably historical persons have done
this: so sober an authority as the *Anglo-Saxon Chronicle*
assures us that fiery dragons were flying in Northumbria as
late as A.D. 793[3].

---

[1] ll. 3018 *etc.*

[2] As is done, e.g., by Schück (*Studier i Beowulf-sagan*, 27).

[3] "Dragon fights are more frequent, not less frequent, the nearer we come
to historic times": Olrik, *Heltedigtning*, I, 313. The dragon survived much later
in Europe than has been generally recognized. He was flying from Mount
Pilatus in 1649. (See J. J. Scheuchzer, *Itinera per Helvetiae Alpinas regiones*,
1723, III, p. 385.) The same authority quotes accounts of dragons authenticated by priests, his own contemporaries, and supplies many bloodcurdling
engravings of the same.

But (and this is the serious difficulty) even when Beowulf
is depicted in quite historic circumstances, there is still something unsubstantial about his actions.   When, in the midst of
the strictly historical account of Hygelac's overthrow, we are
told that Beowulf swam home bearing thirty suits of armour,
this is as fantastic as the account of his swimming home from
Grendel's lair with Grendel's head and the magic swordhilt.
We may well doubt whether there is any more kernel of historic
fact in the one feat than in the other[1].   Again, we are told how
Beowulf defended the young prince Heardred, Hygelac's son.
Where was he, then, when Heardred was defeated and slain?
To protect and if necessary avenge his lord upon the battle-
field was the essential duty of the Germanic retainer.   Yet
Beowulf has no part to play in the episode of the death of
Heardred.   He is simply ignored till it is over.   True, we
are told that in later days he *did* take vengeance, by supporting the claims of Eadgils, the pretender, against Onela, the
slayer of Heardred.   But here again difficulties meet us: for
the Scandinavian authorities, whilst they agree that Eadgils
overthrew Onela by the use of foreign auxiliaries, represent
these auxiliaries as Danish retainers, dispatched by the Danish
king Hrothulf.   The chief of these Danish retainers is Bothvar
Bjarki, who, as we shall see later, has been thought to stand
in some relation to Beowulf.   But Bothvar is never regarded
as king of the Geatas: and the fact remains that *Beowulf* is at
variance with our other authorities in representing Eadgils as
having been placed on the throne by a Geatic rather than by
a Danish force.   Yet this Geatic expedition against Onela is,
with the exception of the dragon episode, the only event which
our poem has to narrate concerning Beowulf's long reign of
fifty years.   And in other respects the reign is shadowy.
Beowulf, we are told, came to the throne at a time of utter
national distress; he had a long and prosperous reign, and
became so powerful that he was able to dethrone the mighty[2]
Swedish king Onela, and place in his stead the miserable
fugitive[3] Eadgils.   Yet, after this half century of success, the

---

[1] Cf. on this point Klaeber in *Anglia,* xxxvi (1912) p. 190.
[2] l. 2382.   [3] l. 2393.

kingdom is depicted upon Beowulf's death as being in the same tottering condition in which it stood at the time when he is represented as having come to the throne, after the fall of Heardred.

The destruction one after the other of the descendants of Hrethel sounds historic: at any rate it possesses verisimilitude. But the picture of the childless Beowulf, dying, after a glorious reign, in extreme old age, having apparently made no previous arrangements for the succession, so that Wiglaf, a youth hitherto quite untried in war, steps at once into the place of command on account of his valour in slaying the dragon—this is a picture which lacks all historic probability.

I cannot avoid a suspicion that the fifty years' reign of Beowulf over the Geatas may quite conceivably be a poetic fiction[1]; that the downfall of the Geatic kingdom and its absorption in Sweden were very possibly brought about by the destruction of Hygelac and all his warriors at the mouth of the Rhine.

Such an event would have given the Swedes their opportunity for vengeance: they may have swooped down, destroyed Heardred, and utterly crushed the independent kingdom of the Geatas before the younger generation had time to grow up into fighting men.

To the fabulous achievements of Beowulf, his fight with Grendel, Grendel's dam, and the dragon, it will be necessary to return later. As to his other feats, all we can say is that the common assumption that they rest upon an historic foundation does not seem to be capable of proof. But that they have an historic background is indisputable.

Section III.   Heorot and the Danish Kings.

Of the Danish kings mentioned in *Beowulf*, we have first Scyld Scefing, the foundling, an ancient and probably a mythical figure, then Beowulf, son of Scyld, who seems an intruder among the Danish kings, since the Danish records know nothing

---

[1] Of course, even if Beowulf's reign over the Geatas is not historic, this does not exclude the possibility of his having *some* historic foundation.

of him, and since his name does not alliterate with those of
either his reputed father or his reputed son.   Then comes the
"high" Healfdene, to whom four children were born: Heorogar,
Hrothgar, Halga "the good," and a daughter who was wedded
to the Swedish king.   Since Hrothgar is represented as an elder
contemporary of Hygelac, we must date[1] Healfdene and his sons,
should they be historic characters, between A.D. 430 and 520.

Now it is noteworthy that just after A.D. 500 the Danes
first become widely known, and the name "Danes" first meets
us in Latin and Greek authors.   And this cannot be explained
on the ground that the North has become more familiar to
dwellers in the classical lands: on the contrary far less is
known concerning the geography of the North Sea and the
Baltic than had been the case four or five centuries before.
Tacitus and Ptolemy knew of many tribes inhabiting what is
now Denmark, but not of the Danes: the writers in Ravenna
and Constantinople in the sixth century, though much less
well informed on the geography of the North, know of the
Danes as amongst the most powerful nations there.   *Beowulf*
is, then, supported by the Latin and Greek records when it
depicts these rulers of Denmark as a house of mighty kings, the
fame of whose realm spread far and wide.   We cannot tell to
what extent this realm was made by the driving forth of alien
nations from Denmark, to what extent by the coming together
(under the common name of Danes) of many tribes which had
hitherto been known by other distinct names.

The pedigree of the house of Healfdene can be constructed
from the references in *Beowulf*.   Healfdene's three sons,
Heorogar, Hrothgar, Halga, are presumably enumerated in
order of age, since Hrothgar mentions Heorogar, but not Halga,
as his senior[2].   Heorogar left a son Heoroweard[3], but it is in
accordance with Teutonic custom that Hrothgar should have
succeeded to the throne if, as we may well suppose, Heoroweard
was too young to be trusted with the kingship.

[1] Attempts at working out the chronology of *Beowulf* have been made by
Gering (in his translation) and by Heusler (*Archiv*, CXXIV, 9–14).   On the
whole the chronology of *Beowulf* is self-consistent, but there are one or two
discrepancies which do not admit of solution.

[2] l. 468.   [3] l. 2161.

The younger brother Halga is never mentioned during Beowulf's visit to Heorot, and the presumption is that he is already dead.

The Hrothulf who, both in *Beowulf* and *Widsith*, is linked with King Hrothgar, almost as his equal, is clearly the son of Halga: for he is Hrothgar's nephew[1], and yet he is not the son of Heorogar[2]. The mention of how Hrothgar shielded this Hrothulf when he was a child confirms us in the belief that his father Halga had died early. Yet, though he thus belongs to the youngest branch of the family, Hrothulf is clearly older than Hrethric and Hrothmund, the two sons of Hrothgar, whose youth, in spite of the age of their father, is striking. The seat of honour occupied by Hrothulf[3] is contrasted with the undistinguished place of his two young cousins, sitting among the *giogoth*[4]. Nevertheless Hrothgar and his wife expect their son, not their nephew, to succeed to the throne[5]. Very small acquaintance with the history of royal houses in these lawless Teutonic times is enough to show us that trouble is likely to be in store.

So much can be made out from the English sources, *Beowulf* and *Widsith*. Turning now to the Scandinavian records, we find much confusion as to details, and as to the characters of the heroes: but the relationships are the same as in the Old English poem.

Heorogar is, it is true, forgotten; and though a name Hiarwarus is found in Saxo corresponding to that of Heoroweard, the son of Heorogar, in *Beowulf*, this Hiarwarus is cut off from the family, now that his father is no longer remembered. Accordingly the Halfdan of Danish tradition (Haldanus in Saxo's Latin: = O.E. Healfdene) has only two sons, Hroar

---

[1] *Widsith*, l. 46.

[2] *Beowulf*, l. 2160. Had Hrothulf been a son of Heorogar he could not have been passed over in silence here. Neither can Hrothulf be Hrothgar's sister's son: for since the sister married the Swedish king, Hrothulf would in that case be a Swedish prince, and presumably would be living at the Swedish court, and bearing a name connected by alliteration with those of the Swedish, not the Danish house. Besides, had he been a Swedish prince, he must have been heard of in connection with the dynastic quarrels of the Swedish house.

[3] ll. 1163–5.   [4] ll. 1188–91.

[5] ll. 1180 *etc.*

(Saxo's Roe, corresponding to O.E. Hrothgar) and Helgi (Saxo's Helgo: = O.E. Halga). Helgi is the father of Rolf Kraki (Saxo's Roluo: = O.E. Hrothulf), the type of the noble king, the Arthur of Denmark.

And, just as Arthur holds court at Camelot, or Charlemagne is at home *ad Ais, à sa capele*, so the Scandinavian traditions represent Rolf Kraki as keeping house at Leire (*Lethra, Hleiðar garðr*).

Accounts of all these kings, and above all of Rolf Kraki, meet us in a number of Scandinavian documents, of which three are particularly important:

(1) Saxo Grammaticus (the lettered), the earlier books of whose *Historia Danica* are a storehouse of Scandinavian tradition and poetry, clothed in a difficult and bombastic, but always amusing, Latin. How much later than the English these Scandinavian sources are, we can realize by remembering that when Saxo was putting the finishing touches to his history, King John was ruling in England.

There are also a number of other Danish-Latin histories and genealogies.

(2) The Icelandic *Saga of Rolf Kraki*, a late document belonging to the end of the middle ages, but nevertheless containing valuable matter.

(3) The Icelandic *Skjoldunga saga*, extant only in a Latin summary of the end of the sixteenth century.

SECTION IV.   LEIRE AND HEOROT.

The village of Leire remains to the present day. It stands near the north coast of the island of Seeland, some five miles from Roskilde and three miles from the sea, in a gentle valley, through the midst of which flows a small stream. The village itself consists of a tiny cluster of cottages: the outstanding feature of the place is formed by the huge grave mounds scattered around in all directions.

The tourist, walking amid these cottages and mounds, may feel fairly confident that he is standing on the site of Heorot.

There are two distinct stages in this identification: it must be proved (*a*) that the modern Leire occupies the site of the Leire (*Lethra*) where Rolf Kraki ruled, and (*b*) that the Leire of Rolf Kraki was built on the site of Heorot.

(*a*) That the modern Leire occupies the site of the ancient Leire has indeed been disputed[1], but seems hardly open to

---

[1] Doubts are expressed, for example, in Trap's monumental topographical work (*Kongeriket Danmark*, II, 328, 1898).

doubt, in view of the express words of the Danish chroniclers[1].
It is true that the mounds, which these early chroniclers
probably imagined as covering the ashes of 'Haldanus' or 'Roe,'
and which later antiquaries dubbed with the names of other
kings, are now thought to belong, not to the time of Hrothgar,
but to the Stone or Bronze Ages. But this evidence that
Leire was a place of importance thousands of years before
Hrothgar or Hrothulf was born, in no wise invalidates the
overwhelming evidence that it was their residence also.

The equation of the modern Leire with the Leire of Rolf
Kraki we may then accept. We cannot be quite so sure of
our thesis (*b*): that the ancient Leire was identical with the
site where Hrothgar built Heorot. But it is highly probable:
for although Leire is more particularly connected with the
memory of Rolf Kraki himself, we are assured, in one of the
mediæval Danish chronicles, that Leire was the royal seat of
Rolf's predecessors as well: of Ro (Hrothgar) and of Ro's
father: and that Ro "enriched it with great magnificence[2]."
Ro also, according to this chronicler, heaped a mound at
Leire over the grave of his father, and was himself buried at
Leire under another mound.

Now since the Danish tradition represents Hrothgar as
enriching his royal town of Leire, whilst English tradition
commemorates him as a builder king, constructing a royal hall
"greater than the sons of men had ever heard speak of"—it
becomes very probable that the two traditions are reflections of
the same fact, and that the site of that hall was Leire. That
Heorot, the picturesque name of the hall itself, should, in
English tradition, have been remembered, whilst that of the
town where it was built had been forgotten, is natural[3]. For

---

[1] For example Sweyn Aageson (c. 1200) had no doubt that the little village
of Leire near Roskilde was identical with the Leire of story: *Rolf Kraki, occisus
in Lethra, qvae tunc famosissima Regis extitit curia, nunc autem Roskildensi
vicina civitati, inter abjectissima ferme vix colitur oppida.* Svenonis Aggonis
Historia Regum Daniae, in Langebek, I, 45.

[2] *Ro...patrem vero suum Dan colle apud Lethram tumulavit Sialandie ubi
sedem regni pro eo pater constituit, qvam ipse post eum divitiis multiplicibus
ditavit.* In the so-called *Annales Esromenses,* in Langebek, I, 224. Cf. Olrik,
Heltedigtning, I, 188, 194. For further evidence, see Appendix (G) below.

[3] We must not think of Heorot as an isolated country seat. The Royal Hall
would stand in the middle of the Royal Village, as in the case of the halls of Attila
(Priscus in Möller's *Fragmenta,* IV, 85) or Cynewulf (*A.S. Chronicle,* Anno 755).

though the names of heroes survived in such numbers, after the settlement of the Angles in England, it was very rarely indeed, so far as we can judge, that the Angles and Saxons continued to have any clear idea concerning the *places* which had been familiar to their forefathers, but which they themselves had never seen.

Further, the names of both Hrothgar and Hrothulf are linked with Heorot in English tradition in the same way as those of Roe and Rolf are with Leire in Danish chronicles.

Yet there is some little doubt, though not such as need seriously trouble us, as to this identification of the site of Heorot with Leire. Two causes especially have led students to doubt the connection of Roe (Hrothgar) with Leire, and to place elsewhere the great hall Heorot which he built.

In the first place, Rolf Kraki came to be so intimately associated with Leire that his connection overshadowed that of Roe, and Saxo even goes so far in one place as to represent Leire as having been *founded* by Rolf[1]. In that case Leire clearly could not be the place where Rolf's predecessor built his royal hall. But that Saxo is in error here seems clear, for elsewhere he himself speaks of Leire as being a Danish stronghold when Rolf was a child[2].

In the second place, Roe is credited with having founded the neighbouring town of Roskilde (Roe's spring)[3] so that some have wished to locate Heorot there, rather than at Leire, five miles to the west. But against this identification of Heorot with Roskilde it must be noted that Roe is said to have built Roskilde, not as a capital for himself, but as a market-place for the merchants: there is no suggestion that it was his royal town, though in time it became the capital, and its cathedral is still the Westminster Abbey of Denmark.

What at first sight looks so much in favour of our equating

---

[1] *Lethram pergitur, quod oppidum, a Roluone constructum eximiisque regni opibus illustratum, ceteris confinium prouinciarum urbibus regie fundacionis et sedis auctoritate prestabat.* Saxo, Book II (ed. Holder, p. 58).

[2] *His cognitis Helgo filium Roluonem Lethrica arce conclusit, heredis saluti consulturus* (p. 52).

[3] *A Roe Roskildia condita memoratur.* Saxo, Book II (ed. Holder, p. 51). Roe's spring, after being a feature of the town throughout the ages, is now (owing perhaps to its sources having been tapped by a neighbouring mineral-water factory) represented only by a pump in a market-garden.

Roskilde with Heorot—the presence in its name of the element *Ro* (Hrothgar)—is in reality the most suspicious thing about the identification. There are other names in Denmark with the element *Ro*, in places where it is quite impossible to suppose that the king's name is commemorated. Some other explanation of the name has therefore to be sought, and it is very probable that Roskilde meant originally not "Hrothgar's spring," but "the horses' spring," and that the connection with King Ro is simply one of those inevitable pieces of popular etymology which take place so soon as the true origin of a name is forgotten[1].

Leire has, then, a much better claim than Roskilde to being the site of Heorot: and geographical considerations confirm this. For Heorot is clearly imagined by the poet of *Beowulf* as being some distance inland; and this, whilst it suits admirably the position of Leire, is quite inapplicable to Roskilde, which is situated on the sea at the head of the Roskilde fjord[2]. Of course we must not expect to find the poet of *Beowulf*, or indeed any epic poet, minutely exact in his geography. At the same time it is clear that at the time *Beowulf* was written there were traditions extant, dealing with the attack made upon Heorot by the ancestral foes of the Danes, a tribe called the Heathobeardan. These accounts of the fighting around Heorot must have preserved the general impression of its situation, precisely as from the *Iliad* we know that Troy is neither on the sea nor yet very remote from it. A poet would draw on his imagination for details, but would hardly alter a feature like this.

In these matters absolute certainty cannot be reached: but we may be fairly sure that the spot where Hrothgar built his "Hart-Hall" and where Hrothulf held that court to which the North ever after looked for its pattern of chivalry was

---

[1] I owe this paragraph to information kindly supplied me by Dr Sofus Larsen, librarian of the University Library, Copenhagen.

[2] It was once believed that, in prehistoric times, the sea came up to Leire also (Forchhammer. Steenstrup and Worsaae: *Undersøgelser i geologisk-anti-qvarisk Retning*, Kjøbenhavn, 1851). A most exact scrutiny of the geology of the coast-line has proved this to be erroneous. (Danmarks geologiske Undersøgelse I.R. 6. *Beskrivelse til Kaartbladene Kjøbenhavn og Roskilde*, af K. Rørdam, Kjøbenhavn, 1899.)

Leire, where the grave mounds rise out of the waving corn-fields[1].

SECTION V. THE HEATHOBEARDAN.

Now, as *Beowulf* is the one long Old English poem which happens to have been preserved, we, drawing our ideas of Old English story almost exclusively from it, naturally think of Heorot as the scene of the fight with Grendel.

But in the short poem of *Widsith*, almost certainly older than *Beowulf*, we have a catalogue of the characters of the Old English heroic poetry. This catalogue is dry in itself, but is of the greatest interest for the light it throws upon Old Germanic heroic legends and the history behind them. And from *Widsith* it is clear that the rule of Hrothgar and Hrothulf at Heorot and the attack of the Heathobeardan upon them, rather than any story of monster-quelling, was what the old poets more particularly associated with the name of Heorot. The passage in *Widsith* runs:

> "For a very long time did Hrothgar and Hrothwulf, uncle and nephew, hold the peace together, after they had driven away the race of the Vikings and humbled the array of Ingeld, had hewed down at Heorot the host of the Heathobeardan."

The details of this war can be reconstructed, partly from the allusions in *Beowulf*, partly from the Scandinavian accounts. The Scandinavian versions are less primitive and historic. They have forgotten all about the Heathobeardan as an independent tribe, and, whilst remembering the names of the leading chieftains on both sides, they see in them members of two rival branches of the Danish royal house.

We gather from *Beowulf* that for generations a blood feud has raged between the Danes and the Heathobeardan. Nothing is told us in *Beowulf* about the king Healfdene, except that he

---

[1] The presence at Leire of early remains makes it tempting to suppose that it may have been from very primitive times a stronghold or sacred place. It is impossible here to examine these conjectures, which would connect Heorot ultimately with the "sacred place on the isle of the ocean" mentioned by Tacitus. The curious may be referred to Much in *P.B.B.* XVII, 196–8; Mogk in *Pauls Grdr.* (2) III, 367; Kock in the Swedish *Historisk Tidskrift*, 1895, 162 *etc.*; and particularly to the articles by Sarrazin: *Die Hirsch Halle* in *Anglia*, XIX, 368–91, *Neue Beowulfstudien* (*Der Grendelsee*) in *Engl. Stud.* XLII, 6–15.

was fierce in war and that he lived to be old. From the Scandinavian stories it seems clear that he was concerned in the
Heathobard feud. According to some later Scandinavian
accounts he was slain by Frothi (= Froda, whom we know
from *Beowulf* to have been king of the Heathobeardan) and
this may well have been the historic fact[1]. How Hroar and
Helgi (Hrothgar and Halga), the sons of Halfdan (Healfdene),
evaded the pursuit of Frothi, we learn from the Scandinavian
tales; whether the Old English story knew anything of their
hair-breadth escapes we cannot tell. Ultimately, the saga tells
us, Hroar and Helgi, in revenge for their father's death, burnt
the hall over the head of his slayer, Frothi[2]. To judge from
the hints in *Beowulf*, it would rather seem that the Old English
tradition represented this vengeance upon Froda as having
been inflicted in a pitched battle. The eldest brother Heorogar
—known only to the English story—perhaps took his share in
this feat. But, after his brothers Heorogar and Halga were
dead, Hrothgar, left alone, and fearing vengeance in his turn,
strove to compose the feud by wedding his daughter Freawaru
to Ingeld, the son of Froda. So much we learn from the
report which Beowulf gives, on his return home, to Hygelac,
as to the state of things at the Danish court.

Beowulf is depicted as carrying a very sage head upon his
young shoulders, and he gives evidence of his astuteness by
predicting[3] that the peace which Hrothgar has purchased will
not be lasting. Some Heathobard survivor of the fight in
which Froda fell, will, he thinks, see a young Dane in the
retinue of Freawaru proudly pacing the hall, wearing the
treasures which his father had won from the Heathobeardan.
Then the old warrior will urge on his younger comrade "Canst
thou, my lord, tell the sword, the dear iron, which thy father
carried to the fight when he bore helm for the last time, when
the Danes slew him and had the victory? And now the son

---

[1] This seems to me much more probable than, as Olrik supposes, that Froda
fell in battle against Healfdene (*Skjoldungasaga*, 162 [80]).

[2] *Saga of Rolf Kraki*, cap. IV.

[3] Olrik wishes to read the whole of this account, not as a prediction in the
present future tense, but as a narrative of past events in the historic present.
(*Heltedigtning*, I, 16: II, 38.) Considering the rarity of the historic present
idiom in Old English poetry, this seems exceedingly unlikely.

of one of these slayers paces the hall, proud of his arms, boasts
of the slaughter and wears the precious sword which thou by
right shouldst wield[1]."

Such a reminder as this no Germanic warrior could long
resist. So, Beowulf thinks, the young Dane will be slain;
Ingeld will cease to take joy in his bride; and the old feud
will break out afresh.

That it did so we know from *Widsith*, and from the same
source we know that this Heathobard attack was repulsed by
the combined strength of Hrothgar and his nephew Hrothulf.

But the tragic figure of Ingeld, hesitating between love for
his father and love for his wife, between the duty of vengeance
and his plighted word, was one which was sure to attract the
interest of the old heroic poets more even than those of the
victorious uncle and nephew. In the eighth century Alcuin,
the Northumbrian, quotes Ingeld as the typical hero of song.
Writing to a bishop of Lindisfarne, he reproves the monks for
their fondness for the old stories about heathen kings, who are
now lamenting their sins in Hell: "in the Refectory," he says,
"the Bible should be read: the lector heard, not the harper:
patristic sermons rather than pagan songs. For what has
Ingeld to do with Christ[2]?" This protest testifies eloquently
to the popularity of the Ingeld story, and further evidence is
possibly afforded by the fact that few heroes of story seem to
have had so many namesakes in Eighth Century England.

What is emphasized in *Beowulf* is not so much the struggle
in the mind of Ingeld as the stern, unforgiving temper of the
grim old warrior who will not let the feud die down; and this
is the case also with the Danish versions, preserved to us in
the Latin of Saxo Grammaticus. In two songs (translated by
Saxo into "delightful sapphics") the old warrior Starcatherus
stirs up Ingellus to his revenge:

"Why, Ingeld, buried in vice, dost thou delay to avenge thy father?
Wilt thou endure patiently the slaughter of thy righteous sire?...

---

[1] ll. 2047–2056.

[2] *Verba dei legantur in sacerdotali convivio; ibi decet lectorem audiri, non
citharistam, sermones patrum, non carmina gentilium. Quid Hinieldus cum
Christo?* See Jaffé's *Monumenta Alcuiniana* (*Bibliotheca Rer. Germ.* VI),
Berlin, 1873, p. 357; *Epistolae*, 81.

Whilst thou takest pleasure in honouring thy bride, laden with gems, and bright with golden vestments, grief torments us, coupled with shame, as we bewail thine infamies.

Whilst headlong lust urges thee, our troubled mind recalls the fashion of an earlier day, and admonishes us to grieve over many things.

For we reckon otherwise than thou the crime of the foes, whom now thou holdest in honour; wherefore the face of this age is a burden to me, who have known the old ways.

By nought more would I desire to be blessed, if, Froda, I might see those guilty of thy murder paying the due penalty of such a crime[1]."

Starkath came to be one of the best-known figures in Scandinavian legend, the type of the fierce, unrelenting warrior. Even in death his severed head bit the earth: or according to another version "the trunk fought on when the head was gone[2]." Nor did the Northern imagination leave him there. It loved to follow him below, and to indulge in conjectures as to his bearing in the pit of Hell[3].

Who the Heathobeardan were is uncertain. It is frequently argued that they are identical with the Longobardi; that the words *Heatho-Bard* and *Long-Bard* correspond, just as we get sometimes *Gar-Dene*, sometimes *Hring-Dene*. (So Heyne; Bremer in *Pauls Grdr.* (2) III, 949 *etc.*) The evidence for this is however unsatisfactory (see Chambers, *Widsith*, 205). Since the year 186 A.D. onwards the Longobardi were dwelling far inland, and were certainly never in a position from which an attack upon the Danes would have been practicable. If, therefore, we accept the identification of Heatho-Bard and Long-Bard, we must suppose the Heathobeardan of *Beowulf* to have been not the Longobardi of history, but a separate portion of the people, which had been left behind on the shores of the Baltic, when the main body went south. But as we have no evidence for any such offshoot from the main tribe, it is misleading to speak of the Heathobeardan as identical with the Longobardi: and although the similarity of one element in the name suggests some primitive relationship, that relationship may well have been exceedingly remote[4].

[1] Saxo, Book VI (ed. Holder, 205, 212–13).
The contrast between this lyrical outburst, and the matter-of-fact speech in which the old warrior in *Beowulf* eggs on the younger man, is thoroughly characteristic of the difference between Old English and Old Scandinavian heroic poetry. This difference is very noticeable whenever we have occasion to compare a passage in *Beowulf* with any parallel passage in a Scandinavian poem, and should be carefully pondered by those who still believe that *Beowulf* is, in its present form, a translation from the Scandinavian.

[2] Saxo, Book VIII (ed. Holder, p. 274); *Helga kviþa Hundingsbana.* II, 19. See also Bugge, *Helge-digtene*, 157.

[3] *Þáttr Þorsteins Skelks* in *Flateyjarbók* (ed. Vigfússon and Unger), I, 416.

[4] Similarly, there is certainly a primitive connection between the names of the Geatas (Gautar) and of the Goths: but they are quite distinct peoples: we should not be justified in speaking of the Geatas as identical with the Goths.

It has further been proposed to identify the Heathobeardan with the Heruli[1]. The Heruli came from the Scandinavian district, overran Europe, and became famous for their valour, savagery, and value as light-armed troops. If the Heathobeardan are identical with the Heruli, and if what we are told of the customs of the Heruli is true, Freawaru was certainly to be pitied. The Heruli were accustomed to put to death their sick and aged: and to compel widows to commit suicide.

The supposed identity of the Heruli with the Heathobeardan is however very doubtful. It rests solely upon the statement of Jordanes that they had been driven from their homes by the Danes (*Dani... Herulos propriis sedibus expulerunt*). This is inconclusive, since the growth of the Danish power is likely enough to have led to collisions with more than one tribe. In fact *Beowulf* tells us that Scyld "tore away the mead benches from *many* a people." On the other hand the dissimilarity of names is not conclusive evidence against the identification, for the word *Heruli* is pretty certainly the same as the Old English *Eorlas*, and is a complimentary nick-name applied by the tribe to themselves, rather than their original racial designation.

Nothing, then, is really known of the Heathobeardan, except that evidence points to their having dwelt somewhere on the Baltic[2].

The Scandinavian sources which have preserved the memory of this feud have transformed it in an extraordinary way. The Heatho-beardan came to be quite forgotten, although maybe some trace of their name remains in *Hothbrodd*, who is represented as the foe of Roe (Hrothgar) and Rolf (Hrothulf). When the Heathobeardan were forgotten, Froda and Ingeld were left without any subjects, and naturally came to be regarded, like Healfdene and the other kings with whom they were associated in story, as Danish kings. Accordingly the tale developed in Scandinavian lands in two ways. Some documents, and especially the Icelandic ones[3], represent the struggle as a feud between two branches of the Danish royal house. Even here there is no agreement who is the usurper and who the victim, so that sometimes it is Froda and sometimes Healfdene who is represented as the traitor and murderer.

But another version[4]—the Danish—whilst making Froda and Ingeld into Danish kings, separates their story altogether from that of Healfdene and his house: in this version the quarrel is still thought of as being between two nations, not as between the rightful heir to the throne and a treacherous and relentless usurper. Accordingly the feud is such as may be, at any rate temporarily, laid aside: peace between the contending parties is not out of the question. This version therefore preserves much more of the original character of the story, for it remains the tale of a young prince who, willing to marry into the house of his ancestral foes and to forgive and forget the old feud, is stirred by his more unrelenting henchman into taking vengeance for his father. But, owing to the prince having come to be represented as a Dane, patriotic reasons have suggested to the

---

[1] Müllenhoff (*Beovulf.* 29–32) followed by Much (*P.B.B.* XVII, 201) and Heinzel (*A.f.d.A.* XVI, 271). The best account of the Heruli is in Procopius (*Bell. Gott.* II, 14, 15).

[2] See also Olrik, *Heltedigtning*, I, 21, 22: Sarrazin in *Engl. Stud.* XLII. 11: Bugge. *Helgi-digtene.* 151-63: 181: Chambers, *Widsith*, p. 82 (note), pp. 205-6.

[3] *Saga of Rolf Kraki: Skjoldungasaga.*

[4] Best represented in Saxo.

Danish poets and historians a quite different conclusion to the story.
Instead of being routed, Ingeld, in Saxo, is successful in his revenge.
See Neckel, *Studien über Froði* in *Z.f.d.A.* XLVIII, 182: Heusler, *Zur
Skiöldungendichtung* in *Z.f.d.A.* XLVIII, 57: Olrik, *Skjoldungasaga*, 1894,
112 [30]; Olrik, *Heltedigtning*, II, 11 *etc.*: Olrik, *Sakses Oldhistorie*,
222–6: Chambers, *Widsith*, pp. 79–81.

SECTION VI. HROTHULF.

Yet, although the Icelandic sources are wrong in representing Froda and Ingeld as Danes, they are not altogether
wrong in representing the Danish royal house as divided
against itself. Only they fail to place the blame where it
really lay. For none of the Scandinavian sources attribute
any act of injustice or usurpation to Rolf Kraki. He is the
ideal king, and his title to the throne is not supposed to be
doubtful.

Yet we saw that, in *Beowulf*, the position of Hrothulf is
represented as an ambiguous one[1], he is the king's too powerful
nephew, whose claims may prejudice those of his less distinguished young cousins, the king's sons, and the speech of
queen Wealhtheow is heavy with foreboding. "I know," she
says, "that my gracious Hrothulf will support the young princes
in honour, if thou, King of the Scyldings, shouldst leave the
world sooner than he. I ween that he will requite our children,
if he remembers all which we two have done for his pleasure
and honour, being yet a child[2]." Whilst Hrethric and Hrothmund, the sons of King Hrothgar, have to sit with the juniors,
the *giogoth*[3], Hrothulf is a man of tried valour, who sits side
by side with the king: "where the two good ones sat, uncle
and nephew: *as yet* was there peace between them, and each
was true to the other[4]."

Again we have mention of "Hrothgar and Hrothulf.
Heorot was filled full of friends: *at that time* the mighty Scylding
folk in no wise worked treachery[5]." Similarly in *Widsith* the
mention of Hrothgar and Hrothulf together seems to stir the
poet to dark sayings. "*For a very long time* did Hrothgar and
Hrothulf, uncle and nephew, hold the peace together[6]."

[1] See above, p. 15.   [2] ll. 1180–87.   [3] ll. 1188–91.
[4] ll. 1163–5.   [5] ll. 1017–19.   [6] ll. 45–6.

The statement that "as yet" or "for a very long time" or "at that time" there was peace within the family, necessarily implies that, at last, the peace *was* broken, that Hrothulf quarrelled with Hrothgar, or strove to set aside his sons[1].

Further evidence is hardly needed; yet further evidence we have: by rather complicated, but quite unforced, fitting together of various Scandinavian authorities, we find that Hrothulf deposed and slew his cousin Hrethric.

Saxo Grammaticus tells us how Roluo (Rolf = O.N. Hrolfr, O.E. Hrothulf) slew a certain Røricus (or Hrærek = O.E. Hrethric) and gave to his own followers all the plunder which he found in the city of Røricus. Saxo is here translating an older authority, the *Bjarkamál* (now lost), and he did not know who Røricus was: he certainly did not regard him as a son or successor of Roe (Hrothgar) or as a cousin of Roluo (Hrothulf). "Roluo, who laid low Røricus *the son of the covetous Bøkus*" is Saxo's phrase (*qui natum Bøki Røricum stravit avari*). This would be a translation of some such phrase in the *Bjarkamál* as *Hræreks bani hnøggvanbauga,* "the slayer of Hrærek Hnoggvanbaugi[2]."

But, when we turn to the genealogy of the Danish kings[3], we actually find a *Hrærekr Hnauggvanbaugi* given as a king of Denmark about the time of Roluo. This *Røricus* or *Hrærekr* who was slain by Roluo was then, himself, a king of the Danes, and must, therefore, have preceded Roluo on the throne. But in that case Røricus *must* be son of Roe, and identical with his namesake Hrethric, the son of Hrothgar, in *Beowulf*. For no one but a son of King Roe could have had such a claim to the throne as to rule between that king and his all powerful nephew Roluo[3].

It is difficult, perhaps, to state this argument in a way which will be convincing to those who are not acquainted with Saxo's method of working. To those who realize how he treats

---

[1] For a contrary view see Clarke, *Sidelights*, 100.

[2] Saxo has mistaken a title *hnøggvanbaugi* for a father's name. (*hins*) *hnøggva Baugs* "(son of the) covetous Baug."

[3] *Langfeðgatal* in Langebek, I, 5. The succession given in *Langfeðgatal* is Halfdan, Helgi and Hroar, Rolf, Hrærek: it should, of course, run Halfdan, Helgi and Hroar, Hrærek, Rolf. Hrærek has been moved from his proper place in order to clear Rolf of any suspicion of usurpation.

his sources, it will be clear that Rǿricus is the son of Roe, and is slain by Roluo. Translating the words into their Old English equivalents, Hrethric, son of Hrothgar, is slain by Hrothulf.

The forebodings of Wealhtheow were justified.

Hrethric is then almost certainly an actual historic prince who was thrust from the throne by Hrothulf. Of Hrothmund[1], his brother, Scandinavian authorities seem to know nothing. He is very likely a poetical fiction, a duplicate of Hrethric. For it is very natural that in story the princes whose lives are threatened by powerful usurpers should go in pairs. Hrethric and Hrothmund go together like Malcolm and Donalbain. Their helplessness is thus emphasized over against the one mighty figure, Rolf or Macbeth, threatening them[2].

Yet this does not prove Hrothmund unhistoric. On the contrary it may well happen that the facts of history will coincide with the demands of well-ordered narrative, as was the case when Richard of Gloucester murdered *two* young princes in the Tower.

Two other characters, who meet us in *Beowulf*, seem to have some part to play in this tragedy.

It was a maxim of the old Teutonic poetry, as it is of the British Constitution, that the king could do no wrong: the real fault lay with the adviser. If Ermanaric the Goth slew his wife and his son, or if Irminfrid the Thuringian unwisely challenged Theodoric the Frank to battle, this was never supposed to be due solely to the recklessness of the monarch himself—it was the work of an evil counsellor—a Bikki or an Iring. Now we have seen that there is mischief brewing in Heorot—and we are introduced to a counsellor Unferth, the *thyle* or official spokesman and adviser of King Hrothgar. And Unferth is evil. His jealous temper is shown by the hostile and inhospitable reception which he gives to Beowulf. And Beowulf's reply gives us a hint of some darker stain: "though

---

[1] l. 1189.

[2] See Olrik, *Episke Love* in *Danske Studier*, 1908, p. 79. Compare the remark of Goethe in *Wilhelm Meister*, as to the necessity of there being *both* a Rosencrantz *and* a Guildenstern (*Apprenticeship*, Book V, chap. v).

thou hast been the slayer of thine own brethren—thy flesh and
blood: for that thou shalt suffer damnation in hell, good though
thy wit may be[1]." One might perhaps think that Beowulf in
these words was only giving the "countercheck quarrelsome,"
and indulging in mere reckless abuse, just as Sinfjotli (the
Fitela of *Beowulf*) in the *First Helgi Lay* hurls at his foes all
kinds of outrageous charges assuredly not meant to be taken
literally. But, as we learn from the *Helgi Lay* itself, the
uttering of such unfounded taunts was not considered good
form; whilst it seems pretty clear that the speech of Beowulf
to Unferth is intended as an example of justifiable and spirited
self-defence, not, like the speech of Sinfjotli, as a storehouse of
things which a well-mannered warrior should *not* say.

Besides, the taunt of Beowulf is confirmed, although but
darkly, by the poet himself, in the same passage in which he
has recorded the fears of Wealhtheow lest perhaps Hrothulf
should not be loyal to Hrothgar and his issue: "Likewise
there Unferth the counsellor sat at the foot of the lord of the
Scyldingas: each of them [i.e. both Hrothgar and Hrothulf]
trusted to his spirit: that his courage was great, *though he had
not done his duty by his kinsmen at the sword-play*[2]."

But, granting that Unferth has really been the cause of the
death of his kinsmen, some scholars have doubted whether we
are to suppose that he literally slew them himself. For, had
that been the case, they urge, he could not be occupying a place
of trust with the almost ideal king Hrothgar. But the record
of the historians makes it quite clear that murder of kin did
happen, and that constantly[3]. Amid the tragic complexities
of heroic life it often could not be avoided. The *comitatus*-
system, by which a man was expected to give unflinching
support to any chief whose service he had entered, must often
have resulted in slaughter between men united by very close
bonds of kin or friendship. Turning from history to saga, we find
some of the greatest heroes not free from the stain. Sigmund,

---

[1] ll. 587–9.   [2] ll. 1165–8.

[3] Perhaps such murder of kin was more common among the aristocratic
houses than among the bulk of the population (Chadwick, *H.A.* 348). In some
great families it almost becomes the rule, producing a state of things similar
to that in present day Afghanistan, where it has become a proverb that a man
is "as great an enemy as a cousin" (Pennell, *Afghan Frontier*, 30).

Gunnar, Hogni, Atli, Hrothulf, Heoroweard, Hnæf, Eadgils,
Hæthcyn, Ermanaric and Hildebrand were all marred with this
taint, and indeed were, in many cases, rather to be pitied
than blamed. I doubt, therefore, whether we need try and
save Unferth's character by suggesting that the stern words
of the poet mean only that he had indirectly caused the death
of his brethren by failing them, in battle, at some critical
moment[1]. I suspect that this, involving cowardice or incom-
petence, would have been held the more unpardonable offence,
and *would* have resulted in Unferth's disgrace. But a man
might well have slain his kin under circumstances which,
while leaving a blot on his record, did not necessitate his
banishment from good society. All the same, the poet evidently thinks it a weakness on the part of Hrothgar and
Hrothulf that, after what has happened, they still put their
trust in Unferth.

Here then is the situation. The king has a counsellor:
that counsellor is evil. Both the king and his nephew trust
the evil counsellor. A bitter feud springs up between the king
and his nephew. That the feud was due to the machinations
of the evil adviser can hardly be doubted by those who have
studied the ways of the old Germanic heroic story. But it
is only an inference: positive proof we have none.

Lastly, there is Heoroweard. Of him we are told in
Beowulf very little. He is son of Heorogar (or Heregar),
Hrothgar's elder brother, who was apparently king before him,
but died young[2]. It is quite natural, as we have seen, that,
if Heoroweard was too young for the responsibility when his
father died, he should not have succeeded to the throne. What
is not so natural is that he does not inherit his father's arms,
which one might reasonably have supposed Hrothgar would
have preserved, to give to him when he came of age. Instead,
Hrothgar gives them to Beowulf[3]. Does Hrothgar deliberately
avoid doing honour to Heoroweard, because he fears that
any distinction conferred upon him would strengthen a rival

---

[1] This is proposed by Cosijn (*Aanteekeningen,* 21) and again independently
by Lawrence in *M.L.N.* xxv, 157.
[2] ll. 467–9.   [3] ll. 2155–62.

whose claims to the throne might endanger those of his own sons? However this may be, in any future struggle for the throne Heoroweard may reasonably be expected to play some part.

Turning now to Saxo, and to the *Saga of Rolf Kraki,* we find that Rolf owed his death to the treachery of one whose name corresponds exactly to that of Heoroweard—Hiarwarus (Saxo), Hjǫrvarthr *(Saga).* Neither Saxo nor the *Saga* thinks of Hiarwarus as the cousin of Rolf Kraki: they do not make it really clear *what* the cause of his enmity was. But they tell us that, after a banquet, he and his men treacherously rose upon Rolf and his warriors. The defence which Rolf and his men put up in their burning hall: the loyalty and defiance of Rolf's champions, invincible in death—these were amongst the most famous things of the North; they were told in the *Bjarkamál,* now unfortunately extant in Saxo's paraphrase only.

But the triumph of Hiarwarus was brief. Rolf's men all fell around him, save the young Wiggo, who had previously, in the confidence of youth, boasted that, should Rolf fall, he would avenge him. Astonished at the loyalty of Rolf's champions, Hiarwarus expressed regret that none had taken quarter, declaring that he would gladly accept the service of such men. Whereupon Wiggo came from the hiding-place where he had taken refuge, and offered to do homage to Hiarwarus, by placing his hand on the hilt of his new lord's sword: but in doing so he drove the point through Hiarwarus, and rejoiced as he received his death from the attendants of the foe he had slain. It shows how entirely the duty of vengeance was felt to outweigh all other considerations, that this treacherous act of Wiggo is always spoken of with the highest praise.

For the story of the fall of Rolf and his men see Saxo, Book II (ed. Holder, pp. 55–68): *Saga of Rolf Kraki,* caps. 32–34: *Skjoldunga Saga* (ed. Olrik, 1894, 36–7 [118–9]).

How the feud between the different members of the Danish family forms the background to *Beowulf* was first explained in full detail by Ludvig Schrøder *(Om Bjovulfs-drapen. Efter en række foredrag på folke-höjskolen i Askov,* Kjøbenhavn, 1875). Schrøder showed how the bad character of Unferth has its part to play: "It is a *weakness* in Hrothgar that he entrusts important office to such a man—a weakness which will carry its punishment." Independently the domestic feud was demonstrated again by Sarrazin (*Rolf Krake und sein vetter im Beowulfliede*: *Engl. Stud.* XXIV, 144–5). The story has been fully worked out by Olrik (*Heltedigtning*, 1903, I, 11–18 *etc.*).

These views have been disputed by Miss Clarke (*Sidelights*, 102), who seems to regard as "hypotheses" of Olrik data which have been ascertained facts for more than a generation. Miss Clarke's contentions, however, appear to me to be based upon a misunderstanding of Olrik.

Section VII. King Offa.

The poem, then, is mainly concerned with the deeds of Geatic and Danish kings: only once is reference made to a king of Anglian stock—Offa.

The *Anglo-Saxon Chronicle* tells us of several kings named Offa, but two only concern us here. Still remembered is the historic tyrant-king who reigned over Mercia during the latter half of the eighth century, and who was celebrated through the Middle Ages chiefly as the founder of the great abbey of St Albans. This Offa is sometimes referred to as Offa *the Second*, because he had a remote ancestor, Offa I, who, if the Mercian pedigree can be trusted, lived twelve generations earlier, and therefore presumably in the latter half of the fourth century. Offa I, then, must have ruled over the Angles whilst they were still dwelling in Angel, their continental home, in or near the modern Schleswig.

Now the Offa mentioned in *Beowulf* is spoken of as related to Garmund and Eomer (MS *geomor*). This, apart from the abundant further evidence, is sufficient to identify him with Offa I, who was, according to the pedigree, the son of Wærmund and the grandfather of Eomer.

This Offa I, king of Angel, is referred to in *Widsith*. *Widsith* is a composite poem: the passage concerning Offa, though not the most obviously primitive portion of it, is, nevertheless, early: it may well be earlier than *Beowulf*. After a list of famous chieftains we are told:

Offa ruled Angel, Alewih the Danes; he was the boldest of all these men, yet did he not in his deeds of valour surpass Offa. But Offa gained, first of men, by arms the greatest of kingdoms whilst yet a boy; no one of equal age ever did greater deeds of valour in battle with his single sword: he drew the boundary against the Myrgingas at Fifeldor. The boundaries were held afterwards by the Angles and the Swæfe as Offa struck it out.

Much is obscure here: more particularly our ignorance as
to the Myrgingas is to be regretted: but there is reason for
thinking that they were a people dwelling to the south of the
old continental home of the Angles.

After the lapse of some five centuries, we get abundant
further information concerning Offa. The legends about him,
though carried to England by the Anglian conquerors, must
also have survived in the neighbourhood of his old kingdom of
Angel: for as Angel was incorporated into the Danish kingdom,
so these stories became part of the stock of Danish national
legend. Offa came to be regarded as a Danish king, and his
story is told at length by the two earliest historians of Denmark,
Sweyn Aageson and Saxo Grammaticus. In Saxo the story
runs thus:

Wermund, king of Denmark, had a son Uffo [Offa], tall
beyond the measure of his age, but dull and speechless. When
Wermund grew blind, his southern neighbour, the king of
Saxony, laid claim to Denmark on the ground that he was no
longer fit to rule, and, relying upon Uffo's incapacity, suggested
that the quarrel should be decided by their two sons in single
combat. Wermund, in despair, offered himself to fight, in
spite of his blindness: this offer the envoys of the Saxon king
refused with insult, and the Danes knew not what to say.
Thereupon Uffo, who happened to be present, suddenly asked
leave to speak. Wermund could not believe that it was really
his son who had spoken, but when they all assured him that
it *was*, he gave the permission. "In vain," then said Uffo,
"does the king of Saxony covet the land of Denmark, which
trusts to its true king and its brave nobles: neither is a son
wanting to the king nor a successor to the kingdom." And
he offered to fight not only the Saxon prince, but any chosen
champion the prince might bring with him.

The Saxon envoys accepted the offer and departed. The
blind king was at last convinced, by passing his hands over him,
that the speaker had been in truth his son. But it was found
difficult to arm him; for his broad chest split the rings of
every coat of mail: the largest, his father's, had to be cleft
down the side and fastened with a clasp. Likewise no sword

was so well tempered that he did not shatter it by merely brandishing it, till the old king directed his men how they might find his ancient sword, *Skrep* (= ? stedfast) which he had buried, in despair, thinking his son unworthy of it. The sword, when found, was so frail from age that Uffo did not test it: for Wermund told him that, if he broke it, there was no other left strong enough for him.

So Uffo and his two antagonists were taken to the place of combat, an island in the river Eider. Crowds lined either bank, and Wermund stood prepared to throw himself into the river should his son be slain. Uffo held back at first, till he had discovered which of his antagonists was the more dangerous, since he feared the sword would only be good for one blow. Then, having by his taunts induced the champion to come to close quarters, he clove him asunder with one stroke. Wermund cried out that he had heard the sound of his son's sword, and asked where the blow had fallen: his attendants assured him that it had pierced, not any particular part, but the man's whole structure.

So Wermund drew back from the edge, desiring life now as keenly as before he had longed for death. Finally Uffo smote his second antagonist through, thus opening a career which after such a beginning we may well believe to have been glorious.

The story is told again by Sweyn Aageson in a slightly varying form. Sweyn's story has some good traits of its own —as when it makes Uffo enter the lists girt with *two* swords, intending to use his father's only in an emergency. The worthless sword breaks, and all the Danes quake for fear: whereupon Uffo draws the old sword and achieves the victory. But above all Sweyn Aageson tells us the *reason* of Uffo's dumbness and incapacity, which Saxo leaves obscure: it was the result of shame over the deeds of two Danes who had combined to avenge their father upon a single foe. What is the incident referred to we can gather from Saxo. Two Danes, Keto and Wigo, whose father Frowinus had been slain by a hostile king Athislus, attacked Athislus together, two to one, thus breaking the laws of the duel. Uffo had wedded the sister of

Keto and Wigo, and it was in order to wipe out the stain left upon his family and his nation by their breach of duelling etiquette that he insisted upon fighting single-handed against two opponents.

That this incident was also known in England is rendered probable by the fact that Freawine and Wig, who correspond to Saxo's Frowinus and Wiggo, are found in the genealogy of English kings, and that an Eadgils, king of the Myrgingas, who is almost certainly the Athislus of Saxo[1], also appears in Old English heroic poetry. It is probable then that the two tales were connected in Old English story: the two brethren shamefully combine to avenge their father: in due time the family of the slain foe take up the feud: Offa saves his country and his country's honour by voluntarily undertaking to fight one against two.

About the same time that the Danish ecclesiastics were at work, a monk of St Albans was committing to Latin the English stories which were still current concerning Offa. The object of the English writer was, however, local rather than national. He wrote the *Vitae duorum Offarum* to celebrate the historic Offa, king of Mercia, the founder of his abbey, and that founder's ancestor, Offa I: popular tradition had confused the two, and much is told concerning the Mercian Offa that seems to belong more rightly to his forefather. The St Albans writer drew upon contemporary tradition, and it is evident that in certain cases, as when he gives two sets of names to some of the chief actors in the story, he is trying to harmonize two distinct versions: he makes at least one error which seems to point to a written source[2]. In one of the MSS the story is illustrated by a series of very artistic drawings, which might possibly be from the pen of Matthew Paris himself[3]. These drawings depict a version of the story which in some respects differs from the Latin text which they accompany.

The story is located in England. Warmundus is represented as a king of the Western Angles, ruling at Warwick.

---

[1] See *Widsith*, ed. Chambers, pp. 92–4.
[2] See Rickert, " The Old English Offa Saga " in *Mod. Phil.* II, esp. p. 75.
[3] The common ascription of the *Lives of the Offas* to Matthew Paris is erroneous: they are somewhat earlier.

Offa, his only son, was blind till his seventh, dumb till his thirtieth year. Accordingly an ambitious noble, Riganus, otherwise called Aliel, claims to be recognized heir, in hope of gaining the throne for his son, Hildebrand (Brutus). Offa gains the gift of speech in answer to prayer; to the joy of his father and the councillors he vindicates his right, much as in the Danish story. He is knighted with a chosen body of companions, armed, and leads the host to meet the foe. He dashes across the river which separates the two armies, although his followers hang back. This act of cowardice on their part is not explained: it is apparently a reminiscence of an older version in which Offa fights his duel single handed by the river, and his host look on. The armies join battle, but after a long struggle draw away from each other with the victory undecided. Offa remaining in front of his men is attacked by Brutus (or Hildebrand) and Sueno, the sons of the usurper, and slays them both (a second reminiscence of the duel-scene). He then hurls himself again upon the foe, and wins the victory.

Widsith shows us that the Danish account has kept closer to the primitive story than has later English tradition. *Widsith* confirms the Danish view that the quarrel was with a foreign, not with a domestic foe, and the combat a duel, not a pitched battle: above all, *Widsith* confirms Saxo in representing the fight as taking place on the Eider—*bī Fīfeldore*[1], whilst the account recorded by the monk of St Albans had localised the story in England.

[1] The identification of *Fifeldor* with the Eider has been doubted, notably by Holthausen, though he seems less doubtful in his latest edition (third edit. II, 178). The reasons for the identification appear to me the following. Place names ending in *dor* are exceedingly rare. When, therefore, two independent authorities tell us that Offa fought at a place named *Fifel-dor* or *Egi-dor*, it appears unlikely that this can be a mere coincidence: it seems more natural to assume that the names are corruptions of one original. But further, the connection is not limited to the second element in the name. For the Eider (*Egidora*, *Ægisdyr*) would in O.E. be *Egor-dor*: and *Egor-dor* stands to *Fifel-dor* precisely as *egor-stream* (Boethius, *Metra*, xx, 118) does to *fifel-stream* (*Metra*, xxvi, 26), "*egor*" and "*fifel*" *being interchangeable synonyms*. See note to *Widsith*, l. 43 (p. 204). It is objected that the interchange of *fifel* and *egor*, though frequent in common nouns, would be unusual in the name of a place. The reply is that the Old English scop may not have regarded it as a place-name. He may have substituted *fifel-dor* for the synonymous *egor-dor*, "the monster gate," without realizing that it was the name of a definite place, just as he would have substituted *fifel-stream* for *egor-stream*, "the monster stream, the sea," if alliteration demanded the change.

In *Beowulf* too we hear of Offa as a mighty king, "the best of all mankind betwixt the seas." But, although his wars are referred to, we are given no details of them. The episode in *Beowulf* relates rather to his wife Thryth, and his dealings with her. The passage is the most obscure in the whole poem, but this at least is clear: Thryth had an evil reputation for cruelty and murder: she wedded Offa, and he put a stop to her evil deeds: she became to him a good and loyal wife.

Now in the *Lives of the two Offas* quite a long space is devoted to the matrimonial entanglements of both kings. Concerning Offa I, a tale is told of how he succoured a daughter of the king of York, who had been turned adrift by her father; how when his years were advancing his subjects pressed him to marry: and how his mind went back to the damsel whom he had saved, and he chose her for his wife. Whilst the king was absent on his wars, a messenger whom he had sent with a letter to report his victories passed through York, where the wicked father of Offa's queen lived. A false letter was substituted, commanding that the queen and her children should be mutilated and left to die in the woods, because she was a witch and had brought defeat upon the king's arms. The order was carried out, but a hermit rescued and healed the queen and her children, and ultimately united them to the king.

This is a popular folk-tale which is scattered all over Europe, and which has many times been clothed in literary form: in France in the romance of the *Manekine*, in English in the metrical romance of *Emaré*, and in Chaucer's *Man of Lawes Tale*. From the name of the heroine in the last of these versions, the tale is often known as the *Constance*-story. But it is clear that this tale is not identical with the obscure story of the wife of Offa, which is indicated in *Beowulf*.

When, however, we turn to the *Life of Offa II*, we do find a very close parallel to the Thryth story.

This tells how in the days of Charles the Great a certain beautiful but wicked girl, related to that king, was condemned to death on account of her crimes, but, from respect for her birth, was exposed instead in a boat without sails or tackle, and driven ashore on the coast of King Offa's land. Drida, as she said her name was, deceived the king by a tale of injured innocence, and he committed her to the safe keeping of his mother, the Countess Marcellina. Later, Offa fell in love with Drida, and married her, after which she became known as *Quendrida*. But Drida continued her evil courses and compassed the death of St Æthelbert, the vassal king of East Anglia. In the end she was murdered by robbers—a just punishment for her crimes—and her widowed husband built the Abbey of St Albans as a thank-offering for her death.

The parallel here is too striking to be denied: for Drida is but another way of spelling Thryth, and the character of the murderous queen is the same in both stories. There are, however, striking differences: for whereas Thryth ceases from her evil deeds and becomes a model wife to Offa, Drida continues on her course of crime, and is cut off by violence in the midst of her evil career. How are we to account for the parallels and for the discrepancies?

As a matter of historical fact, the wife of Offa, king of Mercia, *was* named (not indeed Cwœnthryth, which is the form which should correspond to Quendrida, but) Cynethryth. The most obvious and facile way of accounting for the likeness between what we are told in *Beowulf* of the queen of Offa I, and what we are elsewhere told of the queen of Offa II, is to suppose that Thryth in *Beowulf* is a mere fiction evolved from the historic Cynethryth, wife of Offa II, and by poetic licence represented as the wife of his ancestor, Offa I. It was in this way she was explained by Professor Earle:

> The name [Thrytho] was suggested by that of Cynethryth, Offa's queen....The vindictive character here given to Thrytho is a poetic and veiled admonition addressed to Cynethryth[1].

Unfortunately this, like many another facile theory, is open to fatal objections. In the first place the poem of *Beowulf* can, with fair certainty, be attributed to a date *earlier* than that at which the historic Offa and his spouse lived. Of course, it may be said that the Offa episode in *Beowulf* is an interpolation of a later date. But this needs proof.

There are metrical and above all syntactical grounds

---

[1] *The Deeds of Beowulf*, LXXXV.

which have led most scholars to place *Beowulf* very early[1]. If we wish to regard the *Offa-Thryth*-episode as a later interpolation, we ought first to prove that it is later in its syntax and metre. We have no right to assume that the episode is an interpolation merely because such an assumption may suit our theory of the development of *Beowulf*. So until reasons are forthcoming for supposing the episode of Thryth to be later than the rest of the poem, we can but note that what we know of the date of *Beowulf* forbids us to accept Earle's theory that Thryth is a reflection of, or upon, the historic Cynethryth.

But there are difficulties in the way of Earle's theory even more serious than the chronological one. We know nothing very definitely about the wife of Offa II, except her name, but from a reference in a letter of Alcuin it seems clear that she was a woman of marked piety: it is not likely that she could have been guilty of deliberate murder of the kind represented in the *Life of Offa II*. The St Albans *Life* depends, so far as we know, upon the traditions which were current four centuries after her death. There may be, there doubtless are, some historic facts concerning Offa preserved in it: but we have no reason to think that the bad character of Offa's queen is one of them. Indeed, on purely intrinsic grounds we might well suppose the reverse. As a matter of history we know that Offa *did* put to death Æthelberht, the vassal king of East Anglia. When in the *Life* we find Offa completely exonerated, and the deed represented as an assassination brought about by the malice and cruelty of his queen, it seems intrinsically likely that we are dealing with an attempt of the monks to clear their founder by transferring his cruel deeds to the account of his wife.

So far, then, from Thryth being a reflection of an historic cruel queen Cynethryth, it is more probable that the influence has been in the reverse direction; that the pious Cynethryth has been represented as a monster of cruelty because she has not unnaturally been confused with a mythical Thryth, the wife of Offa I.

To this it may be objected that we have no right to assume remarkable coincidences, and that such a coincidence is in-

---

[1] See below, pp. 105–12, and Appendix (D) below.

volved by the assumption that there was a story of a mythical
Thryth, the wife of Offa I, and that this existed prior to, and
independently of, the actual wedding of Offa II to a Cynethryth.   But the exceeding frequency of the element *thryth* in
the names of women robs this objection of all its point.   Such
a coincidence, far from being remarkable, would be the most
natural in the world.   If we look at the Mercian pedigree we
find that almost half the ladies connected with it have that
element *thryth* in their names.   The founder of the house,
Wihtlæg, according to Saxo Grammaticus[1], wedded Hermuthruda, the old English form of which would be Eormenthryth.

It is to this lady Hermuthruda that we must now devote
our attention.   She belongs to a type which is common in
folk-tale down to the time of Hans Andersen—the cruel princess
who puts her lovers to death unless they can vanquish her in
some way, worsting her in a contest of wits, such as the guessing
of riddles, or a contest of strength, such as running, jumping,
or wrestling.   The stock example of this perilous maiden is,
of course, for classical story Atalanta, for Germanic tradition
the Brunhilt of the *Nibelungen Lied*, who demands from her
wooer that he shall surpass her in all three feats; if he fails in
one, his head is forfeit[2].

Of this type was Hermuthruda: "in the cruelty of her
arrogance she had always loathed her wooers, and inflicted
upon them the supreme punishment, so that out of many
there was not one but paid for his boldness with his head[3],"
words which remind us strongly of what our poet says of Thryth.

Hamlet (Amlethus) is sent by the king of Britain to woo
this maiden for him: but she causes Hamlet's shield and the
commission to be stolen while he sleeps: she learns from the
shield that the messenger is the famous and valiant Hamlet,
and alters the commission so that her hand is requested, not
for the king of Britain, but for Hamlet himself.   With this
request she complies, and the wedding is celebrated.   But when
Wihtlæg (Vigletus) conquers and slays Hamlet, she weds the
conqueror, thus becoming ancestress of Offa.

[1] Wihtlæg appears in Saxo as *Vigletus* (Book IV, ed. Holder, p. 105).
[2] *Nibelungen Lied*, ed. Piper, 328.   [3] Book IV (ed. Holder, p. 102).

It may well be that there is some connection between the Thryth of *Beowulf* and the Hermuthruda who in Saxo weds Offa's ancestor—that they are both types of the wild maiden who becomes a submissive though not always happy wife. If so, the continued wickedness of Drida in the *Life of Offa II* would be an alteration of the original story, made in order to exonerate Offa II from the deeds of murder which, as a matter of history, did characterize his reign.

CHAPTER II

THE NON-HISTORICAL ELEMENTS

SECTION I. THE GRENDEL FIGHT.

WHEN we come to the story of Beowulf's struggle with
Grendel, with Grendel's mother, and with the dragon, we are
faced by difficulties much greater than those which meet us
when considering that background of Danish or Geatic history
in which these stories are framed.

In the first place, it is both surprising and confusing that,
in the prologue, before the main story begins, *another* Beowulf
is introduced, the son of Scyld Scefing. Much emphasis is
laid upon the upbringing and youthful fame of this prince, and
the glory of his father. Any reader would suppose that the
poet is going on to tell of *his* adventures, when suddenly the
story is switched off, and, after brief mention of this Beowulf's
son, Healfdene, we come to Hrothgar, the building of Heorot,
Grendel's attack, and the voyage of Beowulf the Geat to the
rescue.

Now "Beowulf" is an exceedingly rare name. The presence
of the earlier Beowulf, Scyld's son, seems then to demand
explanation, and many critics, working on quite different lines,
have arrived independently at the conclusion that either the
story of Grendel and his mother, or the story of the dragon,
or both stories, were originally told of the son of Scyld, and
only afterwards transferred to the Geatic hero. This has
indeed been generally accepted, almost from the beginning of

Beowulf criticism[1]. Yet, though possible enough, it does not admit of any demonstration.

Now Beowulf, son of Scyld, clearly corresponds to a Beow or Beaw in the West Saxon genealogy. In this genealogy Beow is always connected with Scyld and Scef, and in some versions the relations are identical with those given in *Beowulf*: Beow, son of Scyld, son of Scef, in the genealogies[2], corresponding to Beowulf, son of Scyld Scefing, in our poem. Hence arose the further speculation of many scholars that the hero who slays the monsters was originally called, not Beowulf, but Beow, and that he was identical with the hero in the West Saxon pedigree; in other words, that the original story was of a hero Beow (son of Scyld) who slew a monster and a dragon: and that this adventure was only subsequently transferred to Beowulf, prince of the Geatas.

This is a theory based upon a theory, and some confirmation may reasonably be asked, before it is entertained. As to the dragon-slaying, the confirmatory evidence is open to extreme doubt. It is dealt with in Section VII (Beowulf-Frotho), below. As to Grendel, one such piece of confirmation there is. The conquering Angles and Saxons seem to have given the names of their heroes to the lands they won in England: some such names—'Wade's causeway,' 'Weyland's smithy'—have survived to modern times. The evidence of the Anglo-Saxon charters shows that very many which have now been lost existed in England prior to the Conquest. Now in a Wiltshire charter of the year 931, we have *Bēowan hammes hecgan* mentioned not far from a *Grendles mere*. This has been claimed as evidence that the story of Grendel, with Beow as his adversary, was localized in Wiltshire in the reign of Athelstan, and perhaps had been localized there since the settlement four centuries previously. Until recently this was accepted as definitely

---

[1] Kemble, *Beowulf, Postscript* IX; followed by Müllenhoff, *etc.* So, lately, Chadwick (*H.A.* 126): cf. also Sievers ('Beowulf und Saxo' in the *Berichte d. k. sächs. Gesell. d. Wissenschaften*, 1895, pp. 180–88); Bradley in *Encyc. Brit.* III, 761; Boer, *Beowulf*, 135. See also Olrik, *Danmarks Heltedigtning*, I, 246. For further discussion see below, Appendix (A).

[2] *Beo—Scyld—Scef* in Ethelwerd: *Beowius—Sceldius—Sceaf* in William of Malmesbury. But in the *Anglo-Saxon Chronicle* five generations intervene between Sceaf and his descendant Scyldwa, father of Beaw.

proving that the Beowulf-Grendel story was derived from an
ancient Beow-myth. Yet one such instance of name-associa-
tion is not conclusive. We cannot leave out of consideration
the possibility of its being a mere chance coincidence, especially
considering how large is the number of place names recorded
in Old English charters. Of late, people have become more
sceptical in drawing inferences from proper names, and quite
recently there has been a tendency entirely to overlook the
evidence of the charter, by way of making compensation for
having hitherto overrated it.

All that can be said with certainty is that it *is* remarkable
that a place named after Beowa should be found in the immediate proximity of a "Grendel's lake," and that this fact
supports the possibility, though it assuredly does not prove,
that in the oldest versions of the tale the monster queller was
named Beow, not Beowulf. But it is only a possibility: it is
not grounded upon any real evidence.

These crucial references occur in a charter given by Athelstan at
Luton, concerning a grant of land at Ham in Wiltshire to his thane
Wulfgar. [See Birch, *Cartularium Saxonicum*, 1887, vol. II, p. 363.]
...Ego Æðelstanus, rex Anglorum...quandam telluris particulam
meo fideli ministro Wulfgaro...in loco quem solicolae *æt Hamme*
vocitant tribuo...Praedicta siquidem tellus his terminis circumcincta
clarescit....

ðonne norð ofer dūne on mēos-hlinc westeweardne; ðonne adūne on
ðā yfre on bēowan hammes hecgan, on brēmeles sceagan ēasteweardne;
ðonne on ðā blācan grǣfan; ðonne norð be ðēm ondhēafdan tō ðǣre
scortan dīc būtan ānan æcre; ðonne tō fugelmere tō ðān wege; ondlong
weges tō ottes forda; ðonon tō wudumere; ðonne tō ðǣre rūwan
hecgan; ðæt on langan hangran; ðonne on grendles mere; ðonon on
dyrnan geat....

Ambiguous as this evidence is, I do not think it can be dismissed
as it is by Lawrence (*Pub. Mod. Lang. Assoc. Amer.* XXIV, 252) and
Panzer (*Beowulf*, 397), who both say "How do we know that it is
not the merest chance?" It *may* of course be chance: but this does
not justify us in basing an argument upon the assumption that it
is the merest chance. Lawrence continues: "Suppose one were to
set up a theory that there was a saga-relation between Scyld and
Bikki, and offered as proof the passage in the charter for the year
917 in which there are mentioned, as in the same district, *scyldes
treow* and *bican sell*....How much weight would this carry?"

The answer surely is that the occurrence of the two names together
in the charter would, by itself, give no basis whatever for starting
such a theory: but if, on other grounds, the theory were likely, then
the occurrence of the two names together would certainly have some
corroborative value. Exactly how much, it is impossible to say,
because we cannot estimate the element of chance, and we cannot

be certain that the *grendel* and the *beowa* mentioned are identical
with our Grendel and our Beowulf.

Miller has argued [*Academy*, May 1894, p. 396] that *grendles* is
not a proper name here, but a common noun signifying "drain," and
that *grendles mere* therefore means "cesspool."

Now "grindle" is found in modern dialect and even in Middle
English[1] in the sense of "a narrow ditch" or "gutter," but I doubt
if it can be proved to be an Old English word. Evidence would
rather point to its being an East Anglian corruption of the much more
widely spread *drindle*, or *dringle*, used both as a verb "to go slowly,
to trickle," and as "a small trickling stream." And even if an O.E.
grendel as a common noun meaning "gutter" were authenticated, it
seems unlikely to me that places were named "the fen," "the mere,"
"the pit," "the brook"—"of the gutter." There is no ground whatever for supposing the existence of an O.E. *grendel* = "sewer," or
anything which would lead us to suppose *grendles mere* or *gryndeles
sylle* to mean "cesspool[2]." It is probable, considering what we
know of the way in which the English settlers gave epic names to the
localities around their settlements, that these places were named
after Grendel because they seemed the sort of place where his story
might be localized—like "Weyland's smithy" or "Wade's causeway":
and that the meaning is "Grendel's fen," "mere," "pit" or "brook."

Again, both Panzer and Lawrence suggest that the Beowa who
gave his name to the *ham* may have been, not the hero, but "an
ordinary mortal called after him"..."some individual who lived in
this locality." But, among the numerous English proper names
recorded, can any instance be found of any individual named Beowa?

[1] "Item there is vii acres lond lying by the high weye toward the grendyll":
Bury Wills, ed. S. Tymms (Camden Soc. XLIX, 1850, p. 31).

[2] I should hardly have thought it worth while to revive this old "cesspool"
theory, were it not for the statement of Dr Lawrence that "Miller's argument
that the word *grendel* here is not a proper name at all, that it means 'drain,'
has never, to my knowledge, been refuted." (*Pub. Mod. Lang. Assoc. Amer.*
XXIV, 253.)

Miller was a scholar whose memory should be reverenced, but the letter
to the *Academy* was evidently written in haste. The only evidence which
Miller produced for *grendel* standing alone as a common noun in Old English
was a charter of 963 (Birch, 1103: vol. III, p. 336): *þanon forð eft on grendel:
þanon on clyst: grendel* here, he asserted, meant "drain": and consequently
gryndeles sylle and *grendles mere* in the other charters must mean "cesspool."
But the locality of this charter of 963 is known (Clyst St Mary, a few miles
east of Exeter), and the two words exist there as names of streams to this day
—"thence again along the Greendale brook, thence along the river Clyst."
The Grindle or Greendale brook is no sewer, but a stream some half dozen
miles in length which "winds tranquilly through a rich tract of alluvial soil"
(*Journal of the Archaeol. Assoc.* XXXIX, 273), past three villages which bear
the same name, Greendale, Greendale Barton and Higher Greendale, under
Greendale Bridge and over the ford by Greendale Lane, to its junction with the
Clyst. Why the existence of this charming stream should be held to justify
the interpretation of *Grendel* or *Gryndel* as "drain" and *grendles mere* as "cesspool" has always puzzled me. Were a new Drayton to arise he might, in a
new *Polyolbion*, introduce the nymph complaining of her hard lot at the hands
of scholars in the Hesperides. I hope, when he next visits England, to conduct
Dr Lawrence to make his apologies to the lady. Meantime a glance at the
"six inch" ordnance map of Devon suffices to refute Miller's curious hypothesis.

And was it in accordance with the rules of Old English nomenclature to give to mortals the names of these heroes of the genealogies[1]?

Recent scepticism as to the "Beow-myth" has been largely due to the fact that speculation as to Beow had been carried too far. For example, because Beow appeared in the West Saxon genealogy, it had been assumed that the Beow-myth belonged essentially to the Angles and Saxons. Yet Beow would seem to have been also known among Scandinavians. For in somewhat later days Scandinavian genealogists, when they had made the acquaintance of the Anglo-Saxon pedigrees, noted that Beow had a Scandinavian counterpart in a hero whom they called Bjar[2]. That something was known in the north of this Bjar is proved by the *Kálfsvísa*, that same catalogue of famous heroes and their horses which we have already found giving us the counterparts of Onela and Eadgils. Yet this dry reference serves to show that Bjar must once have been sufficiently famous to have a horse specially his own[3]. Whether the fourteenth century Scandinavian who made Bjar the Northern equivalent of Beow was merely guessing, we unfortunately cannot tell. Most probably he was, for there is reason to think that the hero corresponding to Beow was named, not *Bjár*, but *Byggvir*[4]: a correspondence intelligible to modern philologists as in agreement with phonetic law, but naturally not obvious to an Icelandic genealogist. But however this may be, the assumption that Beow was peculiarly the hero of Angles and Saxons seems hardly justified.

---

[1] It is often asserted that the same Beowa appears as a witness to a charter (Müllenhoff, *Beovulf*, p. 8: Haak, *Zeugnisse zur altenglischen Heldensage*, 53). But this rests upon a misprint of Kemble (*C.D.S.* v, 44). The name is really *Beoba* (Birch, *Cart. Sax.* I, 212).

[2] *Beaf er ver kollum Biar*, in the descent of Harold Fairhair from Adam, in *Flateyjarbók*, ed. Vigfússon and Unger, Christiania, 1859, I, 27. [The genealogy contains many names obviously taken from a MS of the O.E. royal pedigrees, not from oral tradition, as is shown by the miswritings, e.g., *Beaf* for *Beaw*, owing to mistaking the O.E. *w* for *f*.] "This is no proof," Dr Lawrence urges, "of popular acquaintance with Bjár as a Scandinavian figure." (*Pub. Mod. Lang. Assoc. Amer.* XXIV, 246.) But how are we to account for the presence of his name among a mnemonic list of some of the most famous warriors and their horses—mention along with heroes like Sigurd, Gunnar, Atli, Athils and Ali, unless Bjar was a well-known figure?

[3] *en Bjárr [reið] Kerti. Kortr*, "short" (Germ. *Kurz*), if indeed we are so to interpret it, is hardly an Icelandic word, and seems strange as the name of a horse. Egilsson (*Lex. Poet.* 1860) suggests *kertr*, "erect," "with head high" (cf. Kahle in *I.F.* XIV, 164).   [4] See Appendix (A) below.

Again, since Beow is an ancestor of Woden, it was further assumed that he was an ancient god, and that in the story of his adventures we had to deal with a nature-myth of a divine deliverer who saved the people from Grendel and his mother, the personified powers of the stormy sea. It is with the name of Müllenhoff, its most enthusiastic and ablest advocate, that this "mythological theory" is particularly associated. That Grendel is fictitious no one, of course, would deny. But Müllenhoff and his school, in applying the term "mythical" to those portions of the *Beowulf* story for which no historical explanation could be found, meant that they enshrined *nature-myths*. They thought that those elements in heroic poetry which could not be referred back to actual fact must be traced to ancient stories in which were recorded the nation's belief about the sun and the gods: about storms and seasons.

The different mythological explanations of Beowulf-Beowa and Grendel have depended mainly upon hazardous etymological explanations of the hero's name. The most popular is Müllenhoff's interpretation. Beaw is the divine helper of man in his struggle with the elements. Grendel represents the stormy North Sea of early spring, flooding and destroying the habitations of men, till the god rescues them: Grendel's mother represents the depths of the ocean. But in the autumn the power of the god wanes: the dragon personifies the coming of the wild weather: the god sinks in his final struggle to safeguard the treasures of the earth for his people[1]. Others, remembering that Grendel dwells in the fen, see in him rather a demon of the sea-marsh than of the sea itself: he is the pestilential swamp[2], and the hero a wind which drives him away[3]. Or, whilst Grendel still represents the storms, his antagonist is a "Blitzheros[4]." Others, whilst hardly ranking Beowulf as

---

[1] Müllenhoff derived Beaw from the root *bhū*, "to be, dwell, grow": Beaw therefore represented settled dwelling and culture. Müllenhoff's mythological explanation (*Z.f.d.A.* VII, 419, *etc., Beovulf.* 1, *etc.*) has been largely followed by subsequent scholars, e.g., ten Brink (*Pauls Grdr.* II, 533: *Beowulf*, 184), Symons (*Pauls Grdr.* (2), III, 645–6) and, in general outline, E. H. Meyer (*Mythol. der Germanen*, 1903, 242). [2] Uhland in *Germania*, II, 349.
[3] Laistner (*Nebelsagen*, 88, *etc.*, 264, *etc.*), Kögel (*Z.f.d.A.* XXXVII, 274: *Geschichte d. deut. Litt.* I, 1, 109), and Golther (*Handbuch der germ. Mythologie*, 1895, 173) see in Grendel the demon of combined storm and pestilence.
[4] E. H. Meyer (*Germ. Mythol.* 1891, 299).

a god, still see an allegory in his adventures, and Grendel must
be a personification either of an inundation[1], or of the terror
of the long winter nights[2], or possibly of grinding at the mill,
the work of the enslaved foe[3].

Such explanations were till recently universally current:
the instances given above might be increased considerably.

Sufficient allowance was not made for the influence upon
heroic poetry of the simple popular folk-tale, a tale of wonder
with no mythological or allegorical meaning. Now, of late
years, there has been a tendency not only to recognize but
even to exaggerate this influence: to regard the hero of the
folk-tale as the original and essential element in heroic poetry[4].
Though this is assuredly to go too far, it is but reasonable to
recognize the fairy tale element in the O.E. epic.

We have in *Beowulf* a story of giant-killing and dragon-
slaying. Why should we construct a legend of the gods or
a nature-myth to account for these tales? Why must Grendel
or his mother represent the tempest, or the malaria, or the
drear long winter nights? We know that tales of giant-killers
and dragon-slayers have been current among the people of
Europe for thousands of years. Is it not far more easy to
regard the story of the fight between Beowulf and Grendel
merely as a fairy tale, glorified into an epic[5]?

Those students who of late years have tried thus to elucidate
the story of Beowulf and Grendel, by comparison with folk-
tales, have one great advantage over Müllenhoff and the
"mythological" school. The weak point of Müllenhoff's view
was that the nature-myth of Beow, which was called in to
explain the origin of the Beowulf story as we have it, was
itself only an assumption, a conjectural reconstruction. But
the various popular tales in which scholars have more recently
tried to find parallels to *Beowulf* have this great merit, that

---

[1] Mogk (*Pauls Grdr.* (2), III, 302) regards Grendel as a "water-spirit."
[2] Boer (*Ark. f. nord. Filol.* XIX, 19).
[3] This suggestion is made (very tentatively) by Brandl, in *Pauls Grdr.* (2),
II, i, 992.
[4] This view has been enunciated by Wundt in his *Völkerpsychologie*, II, i,
326, *etc.*, 382. For a discussion see A. Heusler in *Berliner Sitzungsberichte*,
XXXVII, 1909, pp. 939–945.
[5] Cf. Lawrence in *Pub. Mod. Lang. Assoc. Amer.* XXIV, 265, *etc.*, and Panzer's
"Beowulf" throughout.

they do indubitably exist. And as to the first step—the parallel between *Beowulf* and the *Grettis saga*—there can, fortunately, be but little hesitation.

Section II. The Scandinavian Parallels— Grettir and Orm.

The *Grettis saga* tells the adventures of the most famous of all Icelandic outlaws, Grettir the strong. As to the historic existence of Grettir there is no doubt: we can even date the main events of his life, in spite of chronological inconsistencies, with some precision. But between the year 1031, when he was killed, and the latter half of the thirteenth century, when his saga took form, many fictitious episodes, derived from folk-lore, had woven themselves around his name. Of these, one bears a great, if possibly accidental, likeness to the Grendel story: the second is emphatically and unmistakably the same story as that of Grendel and his mother. In the first, Grettir stops at a farm house which is haunted by Glam, a ghost of monstrous stature. Grettir awaits his attack alone, but, like Beowulf, lying down. Glam's entry and onset resemble those of Grendel: when Grettir closes with him he tries to get out. They wrestle the length of the hall, and break all before them. Grettir supports himself against anything that will give him foothold, but for all his efforts he is dragged as far as the door. There he suddenly changes his tactics, and throws his whole weight upon his adversary. The monster falls, undermost, so that Grettir is able to draw, and strike off his head; though not till Glam has laid upon Grettir a curse which drags him to his doom.

The second story—the adventure of Grettir at Sandhaugar (Sandheaps)—begins in much the same way as that of Grettir and Glam. Grettir is staying in a haunted farm, from which first the farmer himself and then a house-carl have, on two successive Yuletides, been spirited away. As before, a light burns in the room all night, and Grettir awaits the attack alone, lying down, without having put off his clothes. As before, Grettir and his assailant wrestle down the room, breaking all in their way. But this time Grettir is pulled out of the hall, and dragged to the brink of the neighbouring gorge. Here, by a final effort, he wrenches a hand free, draws, and hews off the arm of the ogress, who falls into the torrent below.

Grettir conjectures that the two missing men must have been pulled by the ogress into the gulf. This, after his experience, is surely a reasonable inference: but Stein, the priest, is unconvinced. So they go together to the river, and find the side of the ravine a sheer precipice: it is ten fathom down to the water below the fall. Grettir lets down a rope: the priest is to watch it. Then Grettir dives in: "the priest saw the soles of his feet, and then knew no more what had become of him." Grettir swims under the fall and gets into the cave, where he sees a giant sitting by a fire: the giant aims a blow at him with a weapon with a wooden handle ("such a weapon men then called a *hefti-sax*"). Grettir hews it asunder. The giant then grasps at another sword hanging on the wall of the cave, but before he can use it Grettir wounds him. Stein, the priest, seeing the water stained with blood from this wound, concludes that Grettir is dead, and departs home, lamenting the loss of such a man. "But Grettir let little space come between his blows till the giant lay dead." Grettir finds the bones of the two dead men in the cave, and bears them away with him to convince the priest: but when he reaches the rope and shakes it, there is no reply, and he has to climb up, unaided. He leaves the bones in the church porch, for the confusion of the priest, who has to admit that he has failed to do his part faithfully.

Now if we compare this with *Beowulf*, we see that in the Icelandic story much is different: for example, in the *Grettis saga* it is the female monster who raids the habitation of men, the male who stays at home in his den. In this the *Grettis saga* probably represents a corrupt tradition: for, that the female should remain at home whilst the male searches for his prey, is a rule which holds good for devils as well as for men[1].

---

[1] The tradition of "the devil and his dam" resembles that of Grendel and his mother in its coupling together the home-keeping female and the roving male. See E. Lehmann, "Fandens Oldemor" in *Dania*, VIII, 179–194; a paper which has been undeservedly neglected in the *Beowulf* bibliographies. But the

The change was presumably made in order to avoid the difficulty
—which the *Beowulf* poet seems also to have realized—that
after the male has been slain, the rout of the female is felt to
be a deed of less note—something of an anti-climax[1].

The sword on the wall, also, which in the *Beowulf*-story is
used by the hero, is, in the *Grettir*-story, used by the giant in
his attack on the hero.

But that the two stories are somehow connected cannot be
disputed. Apart from the general likeness, we have details
such as the escape of the monster after the loss of an arm, the
fire burning in the cave, the *hefti-sax*, a word which, like its old
English equivalent (*hæft-mēce, Beowulf*, 1457), is found in this
story only, and the strange reasoning of the watchers that the
blood-stained water must necessarily be due to the hero's
death[2].

Now obviously such a series of resemblances cannot be
the result of an accident. Either the *Grettir*-story is derived
directly or indirectly from the *Beowulf* epic, more or less as we
have it, or both stories are derived from one common earlier
source. The scholars who first discovered the resemblance
believed that both stories were independently derived from
one original[3]. This view has generally been endorsed by later
investigators, but not universally[4]. And this is one of the
questions which the student cannot leave open, because our
view of the origin of the *Grendel*-story will have to depend
largely upon the view we take as to its connection with the
episode in the *Grettis saga*.

If this episode be derived from *Beowulf*, then we have an
interesting literary curiosity, but nothing further. But if it is

---

devil beats his dam (cf. *Piers Plowman*, C-text, xxi, 284): conduct of which one
cannot imagine Grendel guilty. See too Lehmann in *Arch. f. Religionswiss.*
viii, 411–30: Panzer, *Beowulf*, 130, 137, *etc.*: Klaeber in *Anglia*, xxxvi, 188.

[1] Cf. *Beowulf*, ll. 1282–7.

[2] There are other coincidences which *may* be the result of mere chance.
In each case, before the adventure with the giants, the hero proves his strength
by a feat of endurance in the ice-cold water. And, at the end of the story, the
hero in each case produces, as evidence of his victory, a trophy with a runic
inscription: in *Beowulf* an engraved sword-hilt; in the *Grettis saga* bones and
a "rune-staff."

[3] Vigfússon, *Corp. Poet. Boreale*, ii, 502: Bugge, *P.B.B.* xii, 58.

[4] Boer, for example, believes that *Beowulf* influenced the *Grettis saga*
(*Grettis saga*, Introduction, xliii); so, tentatively, Olrik (*Heltedigtning*, i, 248).

independently derived from a common source, then the episode in the *saga*, although so much later, may nevertheless contain features which have been obliterated or confused or forgotten in the *Beowulf* version. In that case the story, as given in the *Grettis saga*, would be of great weight in any attempt to reconstruct the presumed original form of the *Grendel*-story.

The evidence seems to me to support strongly the view of the majority of scholars—that the *Grettir*-episode is not derived from *Beowulf* in the form in which that poem has come down to us, but that both come from one common source.

It is certain that the story of the monster invading a dwelling of men and rendering it uninhabitable, till the adventurous deliverer arrives, did not originate with Hrothgar and Heorot. It is an ancient and widespread type of story, of which one version is localized at the Danish court. When therefore we find it existing, independently of its Danish setting, the presumption is in favour of this being a survival of the old independent story. Of course it is *conceivable* that the Hrothgar-Heorot setting might have been first added, and subsequently stripped off again so clean that no trace of it remains. But it seems going out of our way to assume this, unless we are forced to do so[1].

Again, it is certain that these stories—like all the subject matter of the Old English epic—did not originate in England, but were brought across the North Sea from the old home. And that old home was in the closest connection, so far as the passage to and fro of story went, with Scandinavian lands. Nothing could be intrinsically more probable than that a story, current in ancient Angel and carried thence to England, should also have been current in Scandinavia, and thence have been carried to Iceland.

Other stories which were current in England in the eighth century were also current in Scandinavia in the thirteenth. Yet this does not mean that the tales of Hroar and Rolf, or of Athils and Ali, were borrowed from English epic accounts of Hrothgar and Hrothulf, or Eadgils and Onela. They were part of the common inheritance—as much so as the strong verbs

---

[1] For this argument and the following, cf. Schück, *Studier i Beowulfssagan*, 21.

or the alliterative line. Why then, contrary to all analogy, should we assume a literary borrowing in the case of the *Beowulf-Grettir*-story? The compiler of the *Grettis saga* could not possibly have drawn his material from a MS of *Beowulf*[1]: he could not have made sense of a single passage. He conceivably *might* have drawn from traditions *derived* from the Old English epic. But it is difficult to see how. Long before his time these traditions had for the most part been forgotten in England itself. One of the longest lived of all, that of Offa, is heard of for the last time in England at the beginning of the thirteenth century. That a Scandinavian sagaman at the end of the century could have been in touch, in any way, with Anglo-Saxon epic tradition seems on the whole unlikely. The Scandinavian tradition of Offa, scholars are now agreed[2], was not borrowed from England, and there is no reason why we should assume such borrowing in the case of Grettir.

The probability is, then, considerable, that the *Beowulf*-story and the *Grettir*-story are independently derived from one common original.

And this probability would be confirmed to a certainty if we should find that features which have been confused and half obliterated in the O.E. story become clear when we turn to the Icelandic. This argument has lately been brought forward by Dr Lawrence in his essay on "The Haunted Mere in *Beowulf*[3]." Impressive as the account of this mere is, it does not convey any very clear picture. Grendel's home seems sometimes to be in the sea: and again it seems to be amid marshes, moors and fens, and again it is "where the mountain torrent goes down under the darkness of the cliffs —the water below the ground (i.e. beneath overhanging rocks)."

This last account agrees admirably with the landscape depicted in the *Grettis saga*, and the gorge many fathoms deep through which the stream rushes, after it has fallen over the precipice; not so the other accounts. These descriptions are

---

[1] Even assuming that a MS of *Beowulf* had found its way to Iceland, it would have been unintelligible. This is shown by the absurd blunders made when Icelanders borrowed names from the O.E. genealogies.

[2] Cf. Olrik, *A. f. n. F.*, VIII (N.F. IV), 368–75; and Chadwick, *Origin*, 125–6.

[3] *Pub. Mod. Lang. Assoc. Amer.* XXVII, 208 *etc.*

best harmonized if we imagine an original version in which the monsters live, as in the *Grettis saga*, in a hole under the waterfall. This story, natural enough in a Scandinavian country, would be less intelligible as it travelled South. The Angles and Saxons, both in their old home on the Continent and their new one in England, were accustomed to a somewhat flat country, and would be more inclined to place the dwelling of outcast spirits in moor and fen than under waterfalls, of which they probably had only an elementary conception. "The giant must dwell in the fen, alone in the land[1]."

Now it is in the highest degree improbable that, after the landscape had been blurred as it is in *Beowulf*, it could have been brought out again with the distinctness it has in the *Grettis saga*. To preserve the features so clearly the *Grettir*-story can hardly be derived from *Beowulf*: it must have come down independently.

But if so, it becomes at once of prime importance. For by a comparison of *Beowulf* and *Grettir* we must form an idea of what the original story was, from which both were derived

Another parallel, though a less striking one, has been found in the story of Orm Storolfsson, which is extant in a short saga about contemporary with that of Grettir, *Ormsþáttr Stórólfssonar*[2], in two ballads from the Faroe Islands[3] and two from Sweden[4].

It is generally asserted that the *Orm*-story affords a close parallel to the episodes of Grendel and his mother. I cannot find close resemblance, and I strongly suspect that the repetition of the assertion is due to the fact that the *Orm*-story has not been very easily accessible, and has often been taken as read by the critics.

But, in any case, it has been proved that the *Orm*-tale borrows largely from other sagas, and notably from the *Grettis saga* itself[5]. Before arguing, therefore, from any parallel, it must first be shown that the feature in which Orm resembles

---

[1] *Cotton. Gnomic Verses*, ll. 42–3.   [2] *Fornmannasǫgur*, III, 204–228.
[3] Hammershaimb, *Færöiske Kvæder*, II, 1855, Nos. 11 and 12.
[4] A. I. Arwidsson, *Svenska Fornsänger*, 1834–42, Nos. 8 and 9.
[5] Boer, *Beowulf*, 177–180.

Beowulf is not derived at second hand from the *Grettis saga.* One such feature there is, namely Orm's piety, which he certainly does not derive from Grettir. In this he with equal certainty resembles Beowulf. According to modern ideas, indeed, there is more of the Christian hero in Beowulf than in Orm.

Now Orm owes his victory to the fact, among other things, that, at the critical moment, he vows to God and the holy apostle St Peter to make a pilgrimage to Rome should he be successful. In this a parallel is seen to the fact that Beowulf is saved, not only by his coat of mail, but also by the divine interposition[1]. But is this really a parallel? Beowulf is too much of a sportsman to buy victory by making a vow when in a tight place. *Gǣð ā wyrd swā hīo scel*[2] is the exact antithesis of Orm's pledge.

However, I have given in the Second Part the text of the *Orm*-episode, so that readers may judge for themselves the closeness or remoteness of the parallel.

The parallel between Grettir and Beowulf was noted by the Icelander Gudbrand Vigfússon upon his first reading *Beowulf* (see *Prolegomena to Sturlunga saga*, 1878, p. xlix: *Corpus Poeticum Boreale*, II, 501: *Icelandic Reader*, 1879, 404). It was elaborately worked out by Gering in *Anglia*, III, 74–87, and it is of course noticed in almost every discussion of *Beowulf*. The parallel with Orm was first noted by Schück (*Svensk Literaturhistoria*, Stockholm, 1886, *etc.*, I, 62) and independently by Bugge (*P.B.B.* XII, 58–68).

The best edition of the *Grettis saga* is the excellent one of Boer (Halle, 1900), but the opinions there expressed as to the relationship of the episodes to each other and to the Grendel story have not received the general support of scholars.

SECTION III. BOTHVAR BJARKI.

We have seen that there are in *Beowulf* two distinct elements, which never seem quite harmonized: firstly the historic background of the Danish and Geatic courts, with their chieftains, Hrothgar and Hrothulf, or Hrethel and Hygelac: and secondly the old wives' fables of struggles with ogres and dragons. In the story of Grettir, the ogre fable appears—unmistakably connected with the similar story as given in *Beowulf*, but with

---

[1] ll. 1553–6.　　　　[2] l. 455.

no faintest trace of having ever possessed any Danish heroic setting.

Turning back to the *Saga of Rolf Kraki*, we *do* find against that Danish setting a figure, that of the hero Bothvar Bjarki, bearing a very remarkable resemblance to Beowulf.

Bjarki, bent on adventure, leaves the land of the Gautar (Götar), where his brother is king, and reaches Leire, where Rolf, the king of the Danes, holds his court; [just as Beowulf, bent on adventure, leaves the land of the Geatas (Götar) where his uncle is king, and reaches Heorot, where Hrothgar and Hrothulf (Rolf) hold court].

Arrived at Leire, Bjarki takes under his protection the despised coward Hott, whom Rolf's retainers have been wont to bully. The champions at the Danish court [in *Beowulf* one of them only—Unferth] prove quarrelsome, and they assail the hero during the feast, in the *Saga* by throwing bones at him, in *Beowulf* only by bitter words. The hero in each case replies, in kind, with such effect that the enemy is silenced.

But despite the fame and splendour of the Danish court, it has long been subject to the attacks of a strange monster[1] —a winged beast whom no iron will bite [just as Grendel is immune from swords[2]]. Bjarki [like Beowulf[3]] is scornful at the inability of the Danes to defend their own home: "if one beast can lay waste the kingdom and the cattle of the king." He goes out to fight with the monster *by night*, accompanied only by Hott. He tries to draw his sword, but the sword is fast in its sheath: he tugs, the sword comes out, and he slays the beast with it. This seems a most pointless incident: taken in connection with the supposed invulnerability of the foe, it looks like the survival of some episode in which the hero was unwilling [as in Beowulf's fight with Grendel[4]] or unable [as in Beowulf's fight with Grendel's mother[5]] to slay the foe

---

[1] The attacks have taken place at Yule for two successive years, exactly as in the *Grettis saga*. [In *Beowulf* it is, of course, "twelve winters" (l. 147).] Is this mere accident, or does the *Grettis saga* here preserve the original time limit, which has been exaggerated in *Beowulf*? If so, we have another point of resemblance between the *Saga of Rolf Kraki* and the earliest version of the *Beowulf*-story.

[2] *Beowulf*, ll. 801–5.   [3] Cf. *Beowulf*, ll. 590–606.
[4] *Beowulf*, l. 679.   [5] *Beowulf*, ll. 1508–9, 1524.

with his sword. Bjarki then compels the terrified coward
Hott to drink the monster's blood. Hott forthwith becomes
a valiant champion, second only to Bjarki himself. The beast
is then propped up as if still alive: when it is seen next morning
the king calls upon his retainers to play the man, and Bjarki
tells Hott that now is the time to clear his reputation. Hott
demands first the sword, Gullinhjalti, from Rolf, and with this
he slays the dead beast a second time. King Rolf is not
deceived by this trick; yet he rejoices that Bjarki has not only
himself slain the monster, but changed the cowardly Hott
into a champion; he commands that Hott shall be called
Hjalti, after the sword which has been given him. We are
hardly justified in demanding logic in a wild tale like this, or
one might ask how Rolf was convinced of Hott's valour by
what he knew to be a piece of stage management on the part
of Bjarki. But, however that may be, it is remarkable that in
Beowulf also the monster Grendel, though proof against all
ordinary weapons, is smitten *when dead* by a magic sword
of which the *golden hilt*[1] is specially mentioned.

In addition to the undeniable similarity of the stories of
these heroes, a certain similarity of name has been claimed.
That *Bjarki* is not etymologically connected with *Bēowulf* or
Bēow is clear: but if we are to accept the identification of
Beowulf and Beow, remembering that the Scandinavian equivalent of the latter is said to be *Bjár*, the resemblance to *Bjarki*
is obvious. Similarity of sound might have caused one name
to be substituted for another[2]. This argument obviously
depends upon the identification *Bēow = Bjár*, which is extremely doubtful: it will be argued below that it is more likely
that *Bēow = Byggvir*[3].

But force remains in the argument that the name Bjarki
(little bear) is very appropriate to a hero like the Beowulf of

---

[1] It is only in this adventure that Rolf carries the sword *Gullinhjalti*.
His usual sword, as well known as Arthur's Excalibur, was *Skofnungr*. For
Gyldenhilt, whether descriptive, or proper noun, see *Beowulf*, 1677.
[2] Cf. Symons in *Pauls Grdr.* (2) III. 649: Züge aus dem anglischen Mythus
von Béaw-Biar (Biarr oder Bjár?; s. Symons Lieder der Edda, I, 222) wurden
auf den dänischen Sagenhelden (Boðvarr) Bjarki durch Ähnlichkeit der Namen
veranlasst, übertragen. Cf. too, Heusler in *A.f.d.A.* xxx, 32.
[3] See p. 87 and Appendix (A) below.

our epic, who crushes or hugs his foe to death instead of using
his sword; even if we do not accept explanations which would
interpret the name "Beowulf" itself as a synonym for "Bear."

It is scarcely to be wondered at, then, that most critics
have seen in Bjarki a Scandinavian parallel to Beowulf. But
serious difficulties remain. There is in the Scandinavian story
a mass of detail quite unparallelled in *Beowulf*, which over-
shadows the resemblances. Bjarki's friendship, for example,
with the coward Hott or Hjalti has no counterpart in *Beowulf*.
And Bjarki becomes a retainer of King Rolf and dies in his
service, whilst Beowulf never comes into direct contact with
Hrothulf at all; the poet seems to avoid naming them together.
Still, it is quite intelligible that the story should have developed
on different lines in Scandinavia from those which it followed
in England, till the new growths overshadowed the original
resemblance, without obliterating it. After nearly a thousand
years of independent development discrepancies must be expected. It would not be a reasonable objection to the identity
of *Gullinhjalti* with *Gyldenhilt*, that the word *hilt* had grown to
have a rather different meaning in Norse and in English;
subsequent developments do not invalidate an original resemblance if the points of contact are really there.

But, allowing for this independent growth in Scandinavia,
we should naturally expect that the further back we traced the
story the greater the resemblance would become.

This brings us to the second, serious difficulty: that, when we
turn from the *Saga of Rolf Kraki*—belonging in its present form
perhaps to the early fifteenth century—to the pages of Saxo
Grammaticus, who tells the same tale more than two centuries
earlier, the resemblance, instead of becoming stronger, almost
vanishes. Nothing is said of Bjarki coming from Gautland, or
indeed of his being a stranger at the Danish court: nothing is
said of the monster having paid previous visits, visits repeated
till king Rolf, like Hrothgar, has to give up all attempt at
resistance, and submit to its depredations. The monster,
instead of being a troll, like Grendel, becomes a commonplace
bear. All Saxo tells us is that "He [Biarco, i.e. Bjarki] met
a great bear in a thicket and slew it with a spear, and bade his

comrade Ialto [i.e. Hjalti] place his lips to the beast and drink its blood as it flowed, that he might become stronger."

Hence the Danish scholar, Axel Olrik, in the best and most elaborate discussion of Bjarki and all about him, has roundly denied any connection between his hero and Beowulf. He is astonished at the slenderness of the evidence upon which previous students have argued for relationship. "Neither Beowulf's wrestling match in the hall, nor in the fen, nor his struggle with the firedrake has any real identity, but when we take a little of them all we can get a kind of similarity with the latest and worst form of the Bjarki saga[1]." The development of Saxo's bear into a winged monster, "the worst of trolls," Olrik regards as simply in accordance with the usual heightening, in later Icelandic, of these early stories of struggles with beasts, and of this he gives a parallel instance.

Some Icelandic ballads on Bjarki (the *Bjarka rímur*), which were first printed in 1904, were claimed by Olrik as supporting his contention. These ballads belong to about the year 1400. Yet, though they are thus in date and dialect closely allied to the *Saga of Rolf Kraki* and remote from Saxo Grammaticus, they are so far from supporting the tradition of the *Saga* with regard to the monster slain, that they represent the foe first as a man-eating she-wolf, which is slain by Bjarki, then as a grey bear [as in Saxo], which is slain by Hjalti after he has been compelled to drink the blood of the she-wolf. We must therefore give up the winged beast as mere later elaboration; for if the Bjarki ballads in a point like this support Saxo, as against the *Saga* which is so closely connected with them by its date and Icelandic tongue, we must admit Saxo's version here to represent, beyond dispute, the genuine tradition.

Accordingly the attempt which has been made to connect Bjarki's winged monster with Beowulf's winged dragon goes overboard at once. But such an attempt ought never to have been made at all. The parallel is between Bjarki and the Beowulf-Grendel episode, not between Bjarki and the Beowulf-dragon episode, which ought to be left out of consideration. And the monstrous bear and the wolf of the *Rímur* are not so

[1] *Heltedigtning*, I, 1903, 135–6.

dissimilar from Grendel, with his bear-like hug, and Grendel's
mother, the 'sea-wolf[1].'

The likeness between Beowulf and Bjarki lies, not in the
wingedness or otherwise of the monsters they overthrow, but
in the similarity of the position—in the situation which places
the most famous court of the North, and its illustrious king,
at the mercy of a ravaging foe, till a chance stranger from
Gautland brings deliverance. And here the *Rímur* support, not
Saxo, but the *Saga*, though in an outworn and faded way.
In the *Rímur* Bjarki is a stranger come from abroad: the
bear has made previous attacks upon the king's folds.

Thus, whilst we grant the wings of the beast to be a later
elaboration, it does not in the least follow that other features
in which the *Saga* differs from Saxo—the advent of Bjarki from
Gautland, for instance—are also later elaboration.

And we must be careful not to attach too much weight to
the account of Saxo merely because it is earlier in date than
that of the *Saga*. The presumption is, of course, that the
earlier form will be the more original: but just as a late manuscript will often preserve, amidst its corruptions, features
which are lost in much earlier manuscripts, so will a tradition.
Saxo's accounts are often imperfect[2]. And in this particular
instance, there is a want of coherency and intelligibility in
Saxo's account, which in itself affords a strong presumption
that it *is* imperfect.

What Saxo tells us is this:

> At which banquet, when the champions were rioting with every
> kind of wantonness, and flinging knuckle-bones at a certain Ialto
> [Hjalti] from all sides, it happened that his messmate Biarco [Bjarki]
> through the bad aim of the thrower received a severe blow on the head.
> But Biarco, equally annoyed by the injury and the insult, sent the
> bone back to the thrower, so that he twisted the front of his head
> to the back and the back to the front, punishing the cross-grain of
> the man's temper by turning his face round about.

But who were this "certain Hjalti" and Bjarki? There seems
to be something missing in the story. The explanation [which
Saxo does not give us, but the *Saga* does] that Bjarki has
come from afar and taken the despised Hott-Hjalti under his

---

[1] *Beowulf*, 1518.
[2] See Heusler in *Z.f.d.A.* XLVIII, 62.

protection, seems to be necessary. Why was Hjalti chosen as the victim, at whom missiles were to be discharged? Obviously [though Saxo does not tell us so], because he was the butt of the mess. And if Bjarki had been one of the mess for many hours, his messmates would have known him too well to throw knuckle-bones either at him or his friend. This is largely a matter of personal feeling, but Saxo's account seems to me pointless, till it is supplemented from the *Saga*[1].

And there is one further piece of evidence which seems to clinch the whole matter finally, though its importance has been curiously overlooked, by Panzer and Lawrence in their arguments for the identification, and by Olrik in his arguments to the contrary.

We have seen above how Beowulf "became a friend" to Eadgils, helping him in his expedition against King Onela of Sweden, and avenging, in "chill raids fraught with woe," *cealdum cearsīðum*, the wrongs which Onela had inflicted upon the Geatas. We saw, too, that this expedition was remembered in Scandinavian tradition. "They had a battle on the ice of Lake Wener; there King Ali fell, and Athils had the victory. Concerning this battle there is much said in the *Skjoldunga saga*." The *Skjoldunga saga* is lost, but the Latin extracts from it give some information about this battle[2]. Further, an account of it *is* preserved in the *Bjarka rímur*, probably derived from the lost *Skjoldunga saga*. And the *Bjarka rímur* expressly mention Bjarki as helping Athils in this battle against Ali on the ice of Lake Wener[3].

Olrik does not seem to allow for this at all, though of course aware of it. The other parallels between Bjarki and Beowulf he believes to be mere coincidence. But is this likely?

To recapitulate: In old English tradition a hero comes from the land of the Geatas to the royal court of Denmark, where Hrothgar and Hrothulf hold sway. This hero is received in none too friendly wise by one of the retainers, but

---

[1] Cf. on this Heusler, *Z.f.d.A.* XLVIII, 64–5.
[2] Cf. *Skjoldunga saga*, cap. XII; and see Olrik, *Heltedigtning*, I, 201–5; *Bjarka rímur*, VIII.
[3] Similarly *Skáldskaparmál*, 41 (44)

puts his foe to shame, is warmly welcomed by the king, and
slays by night a monster which has been attacking the Danish
capital and against which the warriors of that court have been
helpless. The monster is proof against all swords, yet its
dead body is mutilated by a sword with a golden hilt. Subsequently this same hero helps King Eadgils of Sweden to
overthrow Onela.

We find precisely the same situation in Icelandic tradition
some seven centuries later, except that not Hrothgar and
Hrothulf, but Hrothulf (Rolf) alone is represented as ruling the
Danes, and the sword with the golden hilt has become a sword
named "Golden-hilt." It is *conceivable* for a situation to have
been reconstructed in this way by mere accident, just as it is
conceivable that one player may have the eight or nine best
trumps dealt him. But it does not seem advisable to base
one's calculations, as Olrik does, upon such an accident
happening.

The parallel of Bjarki and Beowulf seems to have been first noted
by Gisli Brynjulfsson (*Antiquarisk Tidsskrift*, 1852–3, p. 130). It has
been often discussed by Sarrazin (*Beowulf Studien*, 13 *etc.*, 47: *Anglia*,
IX, 195 *etc.*: *Engl. Stud.* XVI, 79 *etc.*, XXIII, 242 *etc.*, XXXV, 19 *etc.*).
Sarrazin's over-elaborated parallels form a broad target for doubters:
it must be remembered that a case, though it may be discredited, is
not invalidated by exaggeration. The problem is of course noted
in the Beowulf studies of Müllenhoff (55), Bugge (*P.B.B.* XII, 55)
and Boer (*Die Beowulfsage*, II, in *Arkiv f. nord. filol.* XIX, 44 *etc.*) and
discussed at length and convincingly by Panzer (364–386) and Lawrence (*Pub. Mod. Lang. Assoc. Amer.* XXIV, 1909, 222 *etc.*). The
usual view which accepts some relationship is endorsed by all these
scholars, as it is by Finnur Jónsson in his edition of the *Hrólfs Saga
Kraka og Bjarkarimur* (København, 1904, p. xxii).

Ten Brink (185 *etc.*) denied any original connection, on the ground
of the dissimilarity between *Beowulf* and the story given by Saxo.
Any resemblances between *Beowulf* and the *Hrólfs Saga* he attributed
to the influence of the English *Beowulf*-story upon the *Saga*.

For Olrik's emphatic denial of any connection at all, see *Danmarks
Heltedigtning*, I, 134 *etc.* (This seems to have influenced Brandl, who
expresses some doubt in *Pauls Grdr.* (2) II. 1. 993.) For arguments to
the contrary, see Heusler in *A.f.d.A.* XXX, 32, and especially Panzer
and Lawrence as above.

The parallel of *Gullinhjalti* and *gyldenhilt* was first noted tentatively
by Kluge (*Engl. Stud.* XXII, 145).

Section IV. Parallels from Folklore.

Hitherto we have been dealing with parallels to the Grendel story in written literature: but a further series of parallels, although much more remote, is to be found in that vast store of old wives' tales which no one till the nineteenth century took the trouble to write down systematically, but which certainly go back to a very ancient period. One particular tale, that of the Bear's Son[1] (extant in many forms), has been instanced as showing a resemblance to the *Beowulf*-story. In this tale the hero, a young man of extraordinary strength, (1) sets out on his adventures, associating with himself various companions; (2) makes resistance in a house against a supernatural being, which his fellows have in vain striven to withstand, and succeeds in mishandling or mutilating him. (3) By the blood-stained track of this creature, or guided by him in some other manner, the hero finds his way to a spring, or hole in the earth, (4) is lowered down by a cord and (5) overcomes in the underworld different supernatural foes, amongst whom is often included his former foe, or very rarely the mother of that foe: victory can often only be gained by the use of a magic sword which the hero finds below. (6) The hero is left treacherously in the lurch by his companions, whose duty it was to have drawn him up...

Now it may be objected, with truth, that this is not like the *Beowulf*-story, or even particularly like the *Grettir*-story. But the question is not merely whether it resembles these stories as we possess them, but whether it resembles the story which must have been the common origin of both. And we have only to try to reconstruct from *Beowulf* and from the *Grettis saga* a tale which can have been the common original of both, to see that it must be something extraordinarily like the folk-tale outlined above.

[1] Bärensohn. Jean l'Ours. The name is given to the group because the hero is frequently (though by no means always) represented as having been brought up in a bear's den. The story summarized above is a portion of Panzer's "Type A." See Appendix (H), below.

For example, it is true that the departure of the Danes
homeward because they believe that Beowulf has met his
death in the water below, bears only the remotest resemblance
to the deliberate treachery which the companions in the folk-
tale mete out to the hero. But when we compare the *Grettir-*
story, we see there that a real breach of trust is involved, for
there the priest Stein leaves the hero in the lurch, and abandons
the rope by which he should have drawn Grettir up. This can
hardly be an innovation on the part of the composer of the
Grettis saga, for he is quite well disposed towards Stein, and has
no motive for wantonly attributing treachery to him. The
innovation presumably lies in the *Beowulf*-story, where Hrothgar
and his court are depicted in such a friendly spirit that no disreputable act can be attributed to them, and consequently
Hrothgar's departure home must not be allowed in any way
to imperil or inconvenience the hero. A comparison of the
Beowulf-story with the *Grettir*-story leads then to the conclusion that in the oldest version those who remained above
when the hero plunged below *were* guilty of some measure of
disloyalty in ceasing to watch for him. In other words we
see that the further we track the *Beowulf*-story back, the
more it comes to resemble the folk-tale.

And our belief that there is some connection between the
folk-tale and the original of *Beowulf* must be strengthened
when we find that, by a comparison of the folk-tale, we are
able to explain features in *Beowulf* which strike us as difficult
and even absurd : precisely as when we turn to a study of
Shakespeare's sources we often find the explanation of things
that puzzle us : we see that the poet is dealing with an unmanageable source, which he cannot make quite plausible.
For instance : when Grendel enters Heorot he kills and eats
the first of Beowulf's retinue whom he finds : no one tries to
prevent him. The only explanation which the poet has to
offer is that the retinue are all asleep[1]—strange somnolence on
the part of men who are awaiting a hostile attack, which they
expect will be fatal to them all[2]. And Beowulf at any rate is
not asleep. Yet he calmly watches whilst his henchman is

[1] ll. 704, 729.   [2] ll. 691–6.

both killed and eaten: and apparently, but for the accident that the monster next tackles Beowulf himself, he would have allowed his whole bodyguard to be devoured one after another.

But if we suppose the story to be derived from the folk-tale, we have an explanation. For in the folk-tale, the companions and the hero await the foe singly, in succession: the turn of the hero comes last, after all his companions have been put to shame. But Beowulf, who is represented as having specially voyaged to Heorot in order to purge it, cannot leave the defence of the hall for the first night to one of his comrades. Hence the discomfiture of the comrade and the single-handed success of the hero have to be represented as simultaneous. The result is incongruous: Beowulf *has* to look on whilst his comrade is killed.

Again, both Beowulf and Grettir plunge in the water with a sword, and with the deliberate object of shedding the monster's blood. Why then should the watchers on the cliff above assume that the blood-stained water must necessarily signify the *hero's* death, and depart home? Why did it never occur to them that this deluge of blood might much more suitably proceed from the monster?

But we can understand this unreason if we suppose that the story-teller had to start from the deliberate and treacherous departure of the companions, whilst at the same time it was not to his purpose to represent the companions as treacherous. In that case some excuse *must* be found for them: and the blood-stained water was the nearest at hand[1].

Again, quite independently of the folk-tale, many *Beowulf* scholars have come to the conclusion that in the original version of the story the hero did not wait for a second attack from the mother of the monster he had slain, but rather, from a natural and laudable desire to complete his task, followed the monster's tracks to the mere, and finished him and his mother below. Many traits have survived which may conceivably point to an original version of the story in which Beowulf (or the figure corresponding to him) at once plunged down

---

[1] In the *Beowulf* it was even desirable, as explained above, to go further, and completely to exculpate the Danish watchers.

in order to combat the foe corresponding to Grendel. There
are unsatisfactory features in the story as it stands. For why,
it might be urged, should the wrenching off of an arm have
been fatal to so tough a monster? And why, it has often been
asked, is the adversary under the water sometimes male, sometimes female? And why is it apparently the blood of Grendel,
not of his mother, which discolours the water and burns up the
sword, and the head of Grendel, not of his mother, which is
brought home in triumph? These arguments may not carry
much weight, but at any rate when we turn to the folk-tale we
find that the adventure beneath the earth *is* the natural
following up of the adventure in the house, not the result of
any renewed attack.

In addition, there are many striking coincidences between
individual versions or groups of the folk-tale on the one hand
and the *Beowulf-Grettir* story on the other: yet it is very
difficult to know what value should be attached to these
parallels, since there are many features of popular story
which float around and attach themselves to this or that tale
without any original connection, so that it is easy for the same
trait to recur in *Beowulf* and in a group of folk-tales, without
this proving that the stories as a whole are connected[1].

The hero of the Bear's son folk-tale is often in· his youth
unmanageable or lazy. This is also emphasized in the stories
both of Grettir and of Orm: and though such a feature was
uncongenial to the courtly tone of *Beowulf*, which sought to
depict the hero as a model prince, yet it *is* there[2], even though
only alluded to incidentally, and elsewhere ignored or even
denied[3].

Again, the hero of the folk-tale is very frequently (but not
necessarily) either descended from a bear, nourished by a bear,
or has some ursine characteristic. We see this recurring in
certain traits of Beowulf such as his bear-like method of hugging

---

[1] From the controversial point of view Panzer has no doubt weakened his
case by drawing attention to so many of these, probably accidental, coincidences.
It gives the critic material for attack (cf. Boer, *Beowulf*, 14)

[2] ll. 2183 *etc.*

[3] ll. 408–9.

his adversary to death. Here again the courtly poet has not emphasized his hero's wildness[1].

Again, there are some extraordinary coincidences in names, between the *Beowulf-Grettir* story and the folk-tale. These are not found in *Beowulf* itself, but only in the stories of Grettir and Orm. Yet, as the *Grettir*-episode is presumably derived from the same original as the *Beowulf*-episode, any *original* connection between it and the folk-tale involves such connection for *Beowulf* also. We have seen that in *Grettis saga* the priest Stein, as the unfaithful guardian of the rope which is to draw up the hero, seems to represent the faithless companions of the folktale. There is really no other way of accounting for him, for except on this supposition he is quite otiose and unnecessary to the *Grettir*-story: the saga-man has no use for him. And his name confirms this explanation, for in the folktale one of the three faithless companions of the hero is called the Stone-cleaver, *Steinhauer*, *Stenklǿver*, or even, in one Scandinavian version, simply *Stein*[2].

Again, the struggle in the *Grettis saga* is localized at Sandhaugar in Barthardal in Northern Iceland. Yet it is difficult to say why the saga-teller located the story there. The scenery, with the neighbouring river and mighty waterfall, is fully described: but students of Icelandic topography assert that the neighbourhood does *not* at all lend itself to this description[3]. When we turn to the story of Orm we find it localized on the island Sandey. We are forced to the conclusion that the name belongs to the story, and that in some early version this was localized at a place called Sandhaug, perhaps at one of the numerous places in Norway of that name. Now turning to one of the Scandinavian versions of the folk-tale, we find that the descent into the earth and the consequent struggle is localized in *en stor sandhaug*[4].

---

[1] It comes out strongly in the *Bjarki*-story.

[2] It can hardly be argued that Stein is mentioned because he was an historic character who in some way came into contact with the historic Grettir: for in this case his descent would have been given, according to the usual custom in the sagas. (Cf. note to Boer's edition of *Grettis saga*, p. 233.)

[3] P. E. K. Kaalund, *Bidrag til en historisk-topografisk Beskrivelse af Island*, Kjøbenhavn, 1877, II, 151.

[4] The localization in *en stor sandhaug* is found in a version of the story to which Panzer was unable to get access (see p. 7 of his *Beowulf*, Note 2). A copy

On the other hand, it must be remembered that if a collection
is made of some two hundred folk-tales, it is bound to contain,
in addition to the essential kernel of common tradition, a vast
amount of that floating material which tends to associate
itself with this or that hero of story. Individual versions or
groups of versions of the tale may contain features which occur
also in the *Grendel*-story, without that being any evidence for
primitive connection. Thus we are told how Grendel forces
open the door of Heorot. In a Sicilian version of the folk-tale
the doors spring open of themselves as the foe appears. This
has been claimed as a parallel. But, as a sceptic has observed,
the extraordinary thing is that of so slight a similarity (if it
is entitled to be called a similarity) we should find only one
example out of two hundred, and have to go to Sicily for that[1].

> The parallel between the *Beowulf*-story and the "Bear's son"
> folk-tale had been noted by Laistner (*Das Rätsel der Sphinx*, Berlin,
> 1889, ii, 22 *etc.*): but the prevalent belief that the *Beowulf*-story was
> a nature-myth seems to have prevented further investigation on these
> lines till Panzer independently (p. 254) undertook his monumental
> work.

Yet there are other features in the folk-tale which are
entirely unrepresented in the *Beowulf-Grettir* story. The hero
of the folk-tale rescues captive princesses in the underworld
(it is because they wish to rob him of this prize that his companions leave him below); he is saved by some miraculous
helper, and finally, after adopting a disguise, puts his treacherous
comrades to shame and weds the youngest princess. None of
these elements[2] are to be found in the stories of Beowulf,
Grettir, Orm or Bjarki, yet they are essential to the fairy tale[3].

is to be found in the University Library of Christiania, in a small book entitled
Nor, en Billedbog for den norske Ungdom. Christiania, 1865. (*Norske Folke-
Eventyr...fortalte af P. C. Asbjrnsen,* pp. 65–128.)
    The *sandhaug* is an extraordinary coincidence, if it *is* a mere coincidence.
It cannot have been imported into the modern folk-tale from the *Grettis saga,*
for there is no superficial resemblance between the two tales.
    [1] Cf. Boer, *Beowulf,* 14.
    [2] Yet both Beowulf and Orm are saved by divine help.
    [3] Panzer exaggerates the case against his own theory when he quotes only
six versions as omitting the princesses (p. 122). Such unanimity as this is
hardly to be looked for in a collection of 202 kindred folk-tales. In addition
to these six, the princesses are altogether missing, for example, in the versions
which Panzer numbers 68, 69, 77: they are only faintly represented in other
versions (e.g. 76). Nevertheless the rescue of the princesses may be regarded
as the most essential element in the tale.

So that to speak of *Beowulf* as a version of the fairy tale is undoubtedly going too far. All we can say is that some early story-teller took, from folk-tale, those elements which suited his purpose, and that a tale, containing many leading features found in the "Bear's son" story, but omitting many of the leading motives of that story, came to be told of Beowulf and of Grettir[1].

SECTION V. SCEF AND SCYLD.

Our poem begins with an account of the might, and of the funeral, of Scyld Scefing, the ancestor of that Danish royal house which is to play so large a part in the story. After Scyld's death his retainers, following the command he had given them, placed their beloved prince in the bosom of a ship, surrounded by many treasures brought from distant lands, by weapons of battle and weeds of war, swords and byrnies. Also they placed a golden banner high over his head, and let the sea bear him away, with soul sorrowful and downcast. Men could not say for a truth, not the wisest of councillors, who received that burden.

Now there is much in this that can be paralleled both from the literature and from the archaeological remains of the North. Abundant traces have been found, either of the burial or of the burning of a chief within a ship. And we are told by different authorities of two ancient Swedish kings who, sorely wounded, and unwilling to die in their beds, had themselves placed upon ships, surrounded by weapons and the bodies of the slain. The funeral pyre was then lighted on the vessel, and the ship sent blazing out to sea. Similarly the dead body of Baldr was put upon his ship, and burnt.

> Haki konungr fekk svá stór sár, at hann sá, at hans lífdagar mundu eigi langir verða; þá lét hann taka skeið, er hann átti, ok lét hlaða dauðum mǫnnum, ok vápnum, lét þá flytja út til hafs ok leggja stýri

---

[1] I cannot agree with Panzer when (p. 319) he suggests the possibility of the *Beowulf* and the *Grettir*-story having been derived independently from the folk-tale. For the two stories have many features in common which do not belong to the folk-tale: apart from the absence of the princesses we have the *hæft-mēce* and the strange conclusion drawn by the watchers from the blood-stained water.

í lag ok draga upp segl, en leggja eld í tyrviᵭ ok gera bál á skipinu;
veᵭr stóᵭ af landi; Haki var þá at kominn dauᵭa eᵭa dauᵭr, er hann
var lagiᵭr á bálit; siglᵭi skipit síᵭan loganda út í haf, ok var þetta
allfrægt lengi síᵭan.

(King Haki was so sore wounded that he saw that his days could
not be long. Then he had a warship of his taken, and loaded with
dead men and weapons, had it carried out to sea, the rudder shipped,
the sail drawn up, the fir-tree wood set alight, and a bale-fire made
on the ship. The wind blew from the land. Haki was dead or
nearly dead, when he was placed on the pyre. Then the ship sailed
blazing out to sea; and that was widely famous for a long time after.)

    Ynglinga Saga, Kap. 23, in *Heimskringla*, udg. af Finnur Jónsson,
Kǿbenhavn, 1893, vol. I, p. 43.

The *Skjoldunga Saga* gives a story which is obviously connected
with this. King Sigurd Ring in his old age asked in marriage the lady
Alfsola: but her brothers scorned to give her to an aged man. War
followed; and the brothers, knowing that they could not withstand
the hosts of Sigurd, poisoned their sister before marching against him.
In the battle the brothers were slain, and Sigurd badly wounded.

    Qui, Alfsola funere allato, magnam navim mortuorum cadaveribus
oneratam solus vivorum conscendit, seque et mortuam Alfsolam in
puppi collocans navim pice, bitumine et sulphure incendi jubet: atque
sublatis velis in altum, validis a continente impellentibus ventis,
proram dirigit, simulque manus sibi violentas intulit; sese...more
majorum suorum regali pompa Odinum regem (id est inferos) invisere
malle, quam inertis senectutis infirmitatem perpeti....

    Skjoldungasaga i Arngrim Jónssons udtog, udgiven af Axel Olrik,
Kjǿbenhavn, 1894, Cap. XXVII, p. 50 [132].

So with the death of Baldr.

    En æsirnir tóku lík Baldrs ok fluttu til sævar. Hringhorni hét skip
Baldrs; hann var allra skipa mestr, hann vildu goᵭin framm setja ok
gera þar á bálfǫr Baldrs...þá var borit út á skipit lík Baldrs,...Óᵭinn
lagᵭi á bálit gullhring þann, er Draupnir heitir...hestr Baldrs var leiddr
á bálit meᵭ ǫllu reiᵭi.

(But the gods took the body of Baldr and carried it to the sea-shore.
Baldr's ship was named Hringhorni: it was the greatest of all ships
and the gods sought to launch it, and to build the pyre of Baldr on
it....Then was the body of Baldr borne out on to the ship....Odin laid
on the pyre the gold ring named Draupnir...and Baldr's horse with
all his trappings was placed on the pyre.)

    Snorra Edda : Gylfaginning, 48; udg. af Finnur Jónsson, Kǿben-
havn, 1900.

We are justified in rendering *setja skip fram* by "launch": Olrik
(*Heltedigtning*, I, 250) regards Baldr's funeral as a case of the burning
of a body in a ship on land. But it seems to me, as to Mr Chadwick
(*Origin*, 287), that the natural meaning is that the ship was launched
in the sea.

But the case of Scyld is not exactly parallel to these. The
ship which conveyed Scyld out to sea was *not* set alight. And
the words of the poet, though dark, seem to imply that it was
intended to come to land somewhere: "None could say who
received that freight."

Further, Scyld not merely departed over the waves—he had in the first instance come over them: "Not with less treasure did they adorn him," says the poet, speaking of the funeral rites, "than did those who at the beginning sent him forth alone over the waves, being yet a child."

Scyld Scefing then, like Tennyson's Arthur, comes from the unknown and departs back to it.

The story of the mysterious coming over the water was not confined to Scyld. It meets us in connection with King Scef, who was regarded, at any rate from the time of Alfred, and possibly much earlier, as the remotest ancestor of the Wessex kings. Ethelwerd, a member of the West Saxon royal house, who compiled a bombastic Latin chronicle towards the end of the tenth century, traces back the pedigree of the kings of Wessex to Scyld *and his father Scef*. "This Scef," he says, "came to land on a swift boat, surrounded by arms, in an island of the ocean called Scani, when a very young child. He was unknown to the people of that land, but was adopted by them as if of their kin, well cared for, and afterwards elected king[1]." Note here, firstly, that the story is told, not of Scyld Scefing, but of Scef, father of Scyld. Secondly, that although Ethelwerd is speaking of the ancestor of the West Saxon royal house, he makes him come to land and rule, not in the ancient homeland of continental Angeln, but in the "island of Scani," which signifies what is now the south of Sweden, and perhaps also the Danish islands[2]—that same land of *Scedenig* which is mentioned in *Beowulf* as the realm of Scyld. The tone of the narrative is, so far as we can judge from Ethelwerd's dry summary, entirely warlike: Scef is surrounded by weapons.

In the twelfth century the story is again told by William of Malmesbury. "Sceldius was the son of Sceaf. He, they say, was carried as a small boy in a boat without any oarsman to a certain isle of Germany called Scandza, concerning which

---

[1] Ipse Scef cum uno dromone advectus est in insula Oceani, quae dicitur Scani, armis circundatus, eratque valde recens puer, & ab incolis illius terrae ignotus; attamen ab eis suscipitur, & ut familiarem diligenti animo eum custodierunt, & post in regem eligunt.
Ethelwerdus, III, 3, in Savile's *Rerum Anglicarum Scriptores post Bedam* Francofurti, 1601, p. 842.

[2] See Chadwick, *Origin*, 259–60

Jordanes, the historian of the Goths, speaks. He was sleeping,
and a handful of corn was placed at his head, from which he
was called 'Sheaf.' He was regarded as a wonder by the folk
of that country and carefully nurtured; when grown up he
ruled in a town then called Slaswic, and now Haithebi—that
region is called ancient Anglia[1]."

William of Malmesbury was, of course, aware of Ethelwerd's
account, and may have been influenced by it. Some of his
variations may be his own invention. The substitution of the
classical form *Scandza* for Ethelwerd's *Scani* is simply a change
from popular to learned nomenclature, and enables the historian
to show that he has read something of Jordanes. The alteration by which Malmesbury makes Sceaf, when grown up,
rule at Schleswig in ancient Angel, may again be his own work
—a variant added in order to make Sceaf look more at home
in an Anglo-Saxon pedigree.

But William of Malmesbury was, as we shall see later,
prone to incorporate current ballads into his history, and
after allowing for what he may have derived from Ethelwerd,
and what he may have invented, there can be no doubt that
many of the additional details which he gives are genuine
popular poetry. Indeed, whilst the story of Scyld's *funeral*
is very impressive in *Beowulf*, it is in William's narrative that
the story of the child coming over the sea first becomes poetic.

Now since even the English historians connected this tale
with the Danish territory of *Scani*, *Scandza*, we should expect
to find it again on turning to the records of the Danish royal
house. And we do find there, generally at the head of the
pedigree[2], a hero—Skjold—whose name corresponds, and whose
relationship to the later Danish kings shows him to be the same
as the *Scyld Scefing* of *Beowulf*. But neither Saxo Grammaticus, nor any other Danish historian, knows anything of

---

[1] Sceldius [fuit filius] Sceaf. Iste, ut ferunt, in quandam insulam Germaniae
Scandzam, de qua Jordanes, historiographus Gothorum, loquitur, appulsus navi
sine remige, puerulus, posito ad caput frumenti manipulo, dormiens, ideoque
Sceaf nuncupatus, ab hominibus regionis illius pro miraculo exceptus et sedulo
nutritus: adulta aetate regnavit in oppido quod tunc Slaswic, nunc vero
Haithebi appellatur. Est autem regio illa Anglia vetus dicta....
William of Malmesbury, *De Gestis Regum Anglorum*. Lib. II, § 116, vol. I,
p. 121, ed. Stubbs, 1887.
[2] Although Saxo Grammaticus has provided some even earlier kings.

Skjold having come in his youth or returned in his death over the ocean.

How are we to harmonize these accounts?

Beowulf and Ethelwerd agree in representing the hero as "surrounded by arms"; William of Malmesbury mentions only the sheaf; the difference is weighty, for presumably the spoils which the hero brings with him from the unknown, or takes back thither, are in harmony with his career. *Beowulf* and Ethelwerd seem to show the warrior king, William of Malmesbury seems rather to be telling the story of a semi-divine foundling, who introduces the tillage of the earth[1].

In *Beowulf* the child is Scyld Scefing, in Ethelwerd and William of Malmesbury he is Sceaf, father of Scyld.

Beowulf, Ethelwerd and William of Malmesbury agree in connecting the story with *Scedenig, Scani* or *Scandza*, yet the two historians and the *Anglo-Saxon Chronicle* all make Sceaf the ancestor of the West Saxon house. Yet we have no evidence that the English were regarded as having come from Scandinavia.

The last problem admits of easy solution. In heathen times the English traced the pedigree of most of their kings to Woden, and stopped there. For higher than that they could not go. But a Christian poet or genealogist, who had no belief in Woden as a god, would regard the All Father as a man—a mere man who, by magic powers, had made the heathen believe he was a god. To such a Christian pedigree-maker Woden would convey no idea of finality; he would feel no difficulty in giving this human Woden any number of ancestors. Wishing to glorify the pedigree of his king, he would add any other distinguished and authentic genealogies, and the obvious place for these would be at the end of the line, i.e., above Woden. Hence we have in some quite early (not West Saxon) pedigrees, five names given as ancestors of Woden. These five names end in Geat or Geata, who was apparently regarded as a god, and was possibly Woden under another name[2]. Somewhat later, in the *Anglo-Saxon Chronicle*, under

---

[1] Cf. Müllenhoff in *Z.f.d.A.* vii, 413.

[2] In *Grímnismál*, 54, Odin gives *Gautr* as one of his names.

the year 855, we have a long version of the West Saxon pedigree
with yet nine further names above Geat, ending in Sceaf.
Sceaf is described as a son of Noah, and so the pedigree is
carried back to Adam, 25 generations in all beyond Woden[1].
But it is rash to assume with Müllenhoff that, because Sceaf
comes at the head[2] of this English pedigree, Sceaf was therefore
essentially an English hero. *All* these later stages above
Woden look like the ornate additions of a later compiler.
Some of the figures, Finn, Sceldwa, Heremod, Sceaf himself,
we have reason to identify with the primitive heroes of other
nations.

The genealogist who finally made Sceaf into a son born to
Noah in the ark, and then carried the pedigree nine stages
further back through Noah to Adam, merely made the last of
a series of accretions. It does not follow that, because he made
them ancestors of the English king, this compiler regarded
Noah, Enoch and Adam as Englishmen. Neither need he
have so regarded Sceaf or Scyld[3] or Beaw. In fact—and this
has constantly been overlooked—the authority for Sceaf, Scyld
and Beaw as Anglo-Saxon heroes is but little stronger than the
authority for Noah and Adam in that capacity. The pedigree
in Ethelwerd stops at Scef, but otherwise there is no version
which goes beyond Geat except that which goes up to Adam.
Scyld, Beaw, Sceaf, Noah and Adam as heroes of English
mythology are all alike doubtful.

We must be careful, however, to define what we mean when
we regard these stages of the pedigree as doubtful. They
are doubtful in so far as they are represented as standing
above Woden in the Anglo-Saxon pedigree, because it is incredible that, in primitive and heathen times, Woden was
credited with a dozen or more forefathers. The *position* of
these names in the pedigree is therefore doubtful. But it is
only their connection with the West Saxon house that is unauthentic. It does not follow that the names are, *per se*,
unauthentic. On the contrary, it is because the genealogist
had such implicit belief in the authenticity of the generations

---

[1] See below.   [2] Excluding, of course, the Hebrew names.
[3] *Scyld* appears as *Scyldwa*, *Sce(a)ldwa* in the *Chronicle*. The forms
correspond.

from Noah to Adam that he could not rest satisfied with his West Saxon pedigree till he had incorporated these names. They are not West Saxon, but they are part of a tradition much more ancient than any pedigree of the West Saxon kings. And the argument which applies to the layer of Hebrew names between Noah and Adam applies equally to the layer of Germanic names between Woden and Sceaf. From whatever branch of the Germanic race the genealogist may have taken them, the fact that he placed them where he did in the pedigree is a proof of his veneration for them. But we must not without evidence claim them as West Saxon or Anglo-Saxon: we must not be surprised if evidence points to some of them being connected with other nations—as Heremod, for example, with the Danes[1].

More difficult are the other problems. William of Malmesbury tells the story of Sceaf, with the attributes of a culture-hero: *Beowulf*, four centuries earlier, tells it of Scyld, a warrior hero: Ethelwerd tells it of Sceaf, but gives him the warrior attributes of Scyld[2] instead of the sheaf of corn.

The earlier scholars mostly agreed[3] in regarding Malmesbury's attribution of the story to Sceaf as the original and correct version of the story, in spite of its late date. As a representative of these early scholars we may take Müllenhoff[4]. Müllenhoff's love of mythological interpretation found ample scope in the story of the child with the sheaf, which he, with considerable reason, regarded as a "culture-myth." Müllenhoff believed the carrying over of the attributes of a god to a line of his supposed descendants to be a common feature of myth— the descendants representing the god under another name. In accordance with this view, Scyld could be explained as an "hypostasis" of his father or forefather Sceaf, as a figure further explaining him and representing him, so that in the end the tale of the boat arrival came to be told, in *Beowulf*, of Scyld instead of Sceaf.

---

[1] See Part II.   [2] *armis circundatus*.

[3] For a list of the scholars who have dealt with the subject, see *Widsith*, p. 119.

[4] *Beowulf*, p. 6 etc.

Recent years have seen a revolt against most of Müllenhoff's
theories. The view that the story originally belonged to Sceaf
has come to be regarded with a certain amount of impatience
as "out of date." Even so fine a scholar as Dr Lawrence has
expressed this impatience:

> "That the graceful story of the boy sailing in an open boat to the
> land of his future people was told originally of Sceaf...needs no detailed
> refutation at the present day.
> "The attachment of the motive to Sceaf must be, as an examination
> of the sources shows, a later development[1]."

Accordingly the view of recent scholars has been this:
That the story belongs essentially to Scyld. That, as the hero
of the boat story is obviously of unknown parentage, we must
interpret *Scefing* not as "son of Sceaf" but as "with the sheaf"
(in itself a quite possible explanation). That this stage of the
story is preserved in *Beowulf*. That subsequently *Scyld
Scefing*, standing at the head of the pedigree, came to be misunderstood as "Scyld, son of Sceaf." That consequently the
story, which must be told of the earlier ancestor, was thus
transferred from Scyld to his supposed father Sceaf—the
version which is found in Ethelwerd and William of Malmesbury.

One apparent advantage of this theory is that the oldest
version, that of *Beowulf*, is accepted as the correct and original
one, and the much later versions of the historians Ethelwerd
and William of Malmesbury are regarded as subsequent corruptions. This on the surface seems eminently reasonable.
But let us look closer. *Scyld Scefing* in *Beowulf* is to be interpreted "Scyld with the Sheaf." But *Beowulf* nowhere
mentions the sheaf as part of Scyld's equipment. On the
contrary, we gather that the hero is connected rather with
prowess in war. It is the same in Ethelwerd. It is not till
William of Malmesbury that the sheaf comes into the story.
So that the interpretation of *Scefing* as "with the sheaf"
assumes the accuracy of William of Malmesbury's story even in
a point where it receives no support from the *Beowulf* version.
In other words this theory does the very thing to avoid doing
which it was called into being[2].

---

[1] *Pub. Mod. Lang. Assoc. Amer.* XXIV, 259 *etc.*

[2] This objection to the Scyld-theory has been excellently expressed by Olrik
—at a time, too, when Olrik himself accepted the story as belonging to Scyld

Besides this, there are two fundamental objections to the
theory that Sceaf is a late creation, a figure formed from the
misunderstanding of the epithet *Scefing* applied to *Scyld*.
One portion of the poem of *Widsith* consists of a catalogue of
ancient kings, and among these occurs *Sceafa*, ruling the Langobards. Now portions of *Widsith* are very ancient, and this
catalogue in which Sceafa occurs is almost certainly appreciably
older than *Beowulf* itself.

Secondly, the story of the wonderful foundling who comes
over the sea from the unknown and founds a royal line, must
ex hypothesi be told of the first in the line, and we have seen
that it is Sceaf, not Scyld, who comes at the head of the
Teutonic names in the genealogy in the *Anglo-Saxon Chronicle*.

Now we can date this genealogy fairly exactly. It occurs
under the year 855, and seems to have been drawn up at the
court of King Æthelwulf. In any case it cannot be later than the
latter part of Alfred's reign. This takes us back to a period when
the old English epic was still widely popular. A genealogist at
Alfred's court must have known much about Old English story.

These facts are simply not consistent with the belief that
Sceaf is a late creation, a figure formed from a misunderstanding
of the epithet *Scefing*, applied to Scyld[1].

---

rather than Sceaf. "Binz," says Olrik, "rejects William of Malmesbury as
a source for the Scyld story. But he has not noticed that in doing so he saws
across the branch upon which he himself and the other investigators are sitting.
For if William is not a reliable authority, and even a more reliable authority
than the others, then 'Scyld with the sheaf' is left in the air." *Heltedigtning*,
I, 238–9, note.

[1] The discussion of Skjold by Olrik (*Danmarks Heltedigtning*, I, 223–271)
is perhaps the most helpful of any yet made, especially in emphasizing the
necessity of differentiating the stages in the story. But it must be taken in
connection with the very essential modifications made by Dr Olrik in his second
volume (pp. 249–65, especially pp. 264–5). Dr Olrik's earlier interpretation
made Scyld the original hero of the story: *Scefing* Olrik interpreted, not as
"with the sheaf," but as "son of Scef." To the objection that any knowledge
of Scyld's parentage would be inconsistent with his unknown origin, Olrik
replied by supposing that Scyld was a foundling whose origin, though unknown
to the people of the land to which he came, was well known to the poet. The
poet, Dr Olrik thought, regarded him as a son of the Langobardic king, Sceafa,
a connection which we are to attribute to the Anglo-Saxon love of framing
genealogies. But this explanation of Scyld Scefing as a human foundling does
not seem to me to be borne out by the text of *Beowulf*. "The child is a poor
foundling," says Dr Olrik, "*he suffered distress from the time when he was first
found as a helpless child*. Only as a grown man did he get compensation for
his childhood's adversity" (p. 228). But this is certainly not the meaning of
egsode eorl[as]. It is "*He inspired the earl[s] with awe*."

To arrive at any definite conclusion is difficult. But the following may be hazarded.

It may be taken as proved that the Scyld or Sceldwa of the genealogists is identical with the Scyld Scefing of *Beowulf.* For Sceldwa according to the genealogy is also ultimately a *Sceafing,* and is the father of Beow; Scyld is *Scefing* and is father of Beowulf[1].

It is equally clear that the Scyld Scefing of *Beowulf* is identical with the Skjold of the Danish genealogists and historians. For Scyld and Skjold are both represented as the founder and head of the Danish royal house of Scyldingas or Skjoldungar, and as reigning in the same district. Here, however, the resemblance ceases. *Beowulf* tells us of Scyld's marvellous coming and departure. The only Danish authority who tells us much of Skjold is Saxo Grammaticus, who records how as a boy Skjold wrestled successfully with a bear and overcame champions, and how later he annulled unrighteous laws, and distinguished himself by generosity to his court. But the Danish and English accounts have nothing specifically in common, though the type they portray is the same—that of a king from his youth beloved by his retainers and feared by neighbouring peoples, whom he subdues and makes tributary. It looks rather as if the oldest traditions had had little to say about this hero beyond the typical things which might be said of any great king; so that Danes and English had each supplied the deficiency in their own way.

Now this is exactly what we should expect. For Scyld-Skjold is hardly a personality: he is a figure evolved out of the name *Scyldingas, Skjoldungar,* which is an old epic title for the Danes. Of this we may be fairly certain: the Scyldingas did not get their name because they were really descended from Scyld, but Scyld was created in order to provide an eponymous father to the Scyldingas[2]. In just the same way

---

[1] See below (App. C) for instances of ancestral names extant both in weak and strong forms, like *Scyld. Sceldwa* (the identity of which no one doubts) or *Sceaf. Sceafa* (the identity of which has been doubted).

[2] "As for the name *Scyldungas-Skjöldungar,* we need not hesitate to believe that this originally meant 'the people' or 'kinsmen of the shield.' Similar appellations are not uncommon, e.g., *Rondingas, Helmingas, Brondingas...*

tradition also evolved a hero Dan, from whom the Danes were supposed to have their name. Saxo Grammaticus has combined both pedigrees, making Skjold a descendant of Dan; but usually it was agreed that nothing came before Skjold, that he was the beginning of the Skjoldung line[1]. At first a mere name, we should expect that he would have no characteristic save that, like every respectable Germanic king, he took tribute from his foes and gave it to his friends. He differs therefore from those heroic figures like Hygelac or Guthhere (Gunnar) which, being derived from actual historic characters, have, from the beginning of their story, certain definite features attached to them. Scyld is, in the beginning, merely a name, the ancestor of the Scyldings. Tradition collects round him gradually.

Hence it will be rash to attach much weight to any feature which is found in one account of him only. Anything we are told of Scyld in English sources alone is not to be construed as evidence as to his original story, but only as to the form that story assumed in England. When, for example, *Beowulf* tells us that Scyld is *Scefing*, or that he is father of Beowulf, it will be very rash of us to assume that these relationships existed in the Danish, but have been forgotten. This is, I think, universally admitted[2]. Yet the very scholars who emphasize this, have assumed that the marvellous arrival as a child, in a boat, surrounded by weapons, is an essential feature of Scyld's story. Yet the evidence for this is no better and no worse than the evidence for his relationship to Sceaf or Beow—it rests solely on the English documents. Accordingly it only shows what was told about Scyld in England.

Of course the boat arrival *might* be an original part of the story of *Scyld-Skjold*, which has been forgotten in his native

---

probably these names meant either 'the people of *the* shield, *the* helmet,' *etc.*, or else the people who used shields, helmets, *etc.*, in some special way. In the former case we may compare the Ancile of the Romans and the Palladion of the Greeks; in either case we may note that occasionally shields have been found in the North which can never have been used except for ceremonial purposes." Chadwick, *Origin*, p. 284: cf. Olrik, *Heltedigtning*, I, 274.

[1] Sweyn Aageson, *Skiold Danis primum didici praefuisse*, in Langebek, *S.R.D.* I, 44.

[2] Olrik, *Heltedigtning*, I, 246; Lawrence, *Pub. Mod. Lang. Assoc.* XXIV, 254.

country, but remembered in England. But I cannot see that we have any right to assert this, without proof.

What we can assert to have been the original feature of Scyld is this—that he was the eponymous hero king of the Danes. Both *Beowulf* and the Scandinavian authorities agree upon that. The fact that his name (in the form *Sceldwa*) appears in the genealogy of the kings of Wessex is not evidence against a Danish origin. The name appears in close connection with that of Heremod, another Danish king, and is merely evidence of a desire on the part of the genealogist of the Wessex kings to connect his royal house with the most distinguished family he knew: that of the Scyldingas, about whom so much is said in the prologue to *Beowulf*.

Neither do the instances of place-names in England, such as *Scyldes treow*, *Scildes well*, prove Scyld to have been an English hero. They merely prove him to have been a hero who was celebrated in England—which the Prologue to *Beowulf* alone is sufficient to show to have been the case. For place-names commemorating heroes of alien tribes are common enough[1] on English ground.

So much at least is gained. Whatever Müllenhoff[2] and his followers constructed upon the assumption that Scyld was an essentially Anglo-Saxon hero goes overboard. Scyld is the ancestor king of the Danish house—more than this we can hardly with safety assert.

Now let us turn to the figure of Sceaf. This was not necessarily connected with Scyld from the first.

The story of Sceaf first meets us in its completeness in the pages of William of Malmesbury. And William of Malmesbury is a twelfth century authority; by his time the Old English courtly epics had died out—for they could not have long survived the Norman Conquest and the overthrow of Old English court life. But the popular tradition[3] remained, and

---

[1] It is odd that Binz, who has recorded so many of these, should have argued on the strength of these place-names that the Scyld story is not Danish but an ancient possession of the tribes of the North Sea coast (p. 150). For Binz also records an immense number of names of heroes of alien stock— Danish, Gothic or Burgundian—as occurring in England (*P.B.B.* xx, 202 etc.).

[2] *Beowulf*, p. 7.   [3] Chadwick, *Origin*, p. 278

a good many of the old stories, banished from the hall, must
have lingered on at the cross-roads—tales of Wade and Weyland, of Offa and Sceaf. For songs, sung by minstrels at the
cross roads, William of Malmesbury is good evidence, and he
owns to having drawn information from similar popular
sources[1]. William's story, then, is evidence that in his own
day there was a tradition of a mythical king Sheaf who came
as a child sleeping in a ship with a sheaf of corn at his head.
How old this tradition may be, we cannot say. Ethelwerd
knew the story, though he has nothing to say of the sheaf.
But we have seen that when we get back to the ninth century,
and the formation of the *Anglo-Saxon Chronicle*, at a court
where we may be sure the old English heroic stories were still
popular, it is Sceaf and not Sceldwa who is regarded as the
beginning of things—the king whose origin is so remote that
he is the oldest Germanic ancestor one can get back to[2]: "he
was born in Noah's ark."

Whether or no Noah's ark was chosen as Sceaf's birthplace
because legend represented him as coming in a boat over the
water, we cannot tell. But the place he occupies, with only
the Biblical names before him, as compared with Sceldwa the
son of Heremod, clearly marks Sceaf rather than Sceldwa as
the hero who comes from the unknown. Turning now to the
catalogue of kings in *Widsith*, probably the oldest extant piece
of Anglo-Saxon verse, some generations more ancient than
Beowulf, we find a King Sceafa, who ruled over the Langobards.
Finally, in *Beowulf* itself, although the story is told of Scyld,
nevertheless this Scyld is characterized as *Scefing*. If this
means "with the sheaf," then the *Beowulf*-story stands convicted
of imperfection, of needing explanation outside itself from the

---

[1] The scandals about King Edgar (*infamias quas post dicam magis resper-
serunt cantilenae*: see *Gesta Regum Anglorum.* II, § 148, ed. Stubbs, vol. I, p. 165);
the story of Gunhilda, the daughter of Knut, who, married to a foreign King
with great pomp and rejoicing, *nostro seculo etiam in triviis cantitata*, was un-
justly suspected of unchastity till her English page, in vindication of her honour,
slew the giant whom her accusers had brought forward as their champion
(*Gesta,* II, § 188, ed. Stubbs, I, pp. 229, 230); the story of King Edward and
the shepherdess, learnt from *cantilenis per successiones temporum detritis*
(*Gesta,* II, § 138, ed. Stubbs, I, 155). Macaulay in the *Lays of Ancient Rome*
has selected William as a typical example of the historian who draws upon
popular song. Cf. Freeman's *Historical Essays.*

[2] Olrik, *Heltedigtning,* I, 245.

account which William of Malmesbury wrote four centuries
later. If it means " son of Sceaf," why should a father be given
to Scyld, when the story demands that he should come from
the unknown? Was it because, if the boat story was to be
attributed to Scyld, it was felt that this could only be made
plausible by giving him some relation to Sceaf?

When we find an ancient king bearing the extraordinary
name of "Sheaf," it is difficult not to connect this with the
honour done to the sheaf of corn, survivals of which have been
found in different parts of England. In Herrick's time, the
sheaves of corn were still kissed as they were carried home on
the Hock-cart, whilst

> Some, with great
> Devotion, stroke the home-borne wheat.

Professor Chadwick argues, on the analogy of Prussian and
Bulgarian harvest customs, that the figure of the "Harvest
Queen" in the English ceremony is derived from a corn figure
made from the last sheaf, and that the sheaf was once regarded
as a religious symbol[1]. But the evidence for this is surely
even stronger than would be gathered from Professor Chadwick's
very cautious statement. I suppose there is hardly a county
in England from Kent to Cornwall and from Kent to Northumberland, where there is not evidence for honour paid to the
last sheaf—an honour which cannot be accounted for as merely
expressing the joy of the reapers at having got to the end of
their task. In Kent "a figure composed of some of the best
corn" was made into a human shape: "this is afterwards
curiously dressed by the women, and adorned with paper
trimmings cut to resemble a cap, ruffles, handkerchief, etc., of
the finest lace. It is brought home with the last load of corn[2]."
In Northumberland and Durham a sheaf known as the "Kern
baby" was made into the likeness of a human figure, decked
out and brought home in triumph with dancing and singing[3].
But the most striking form of the sheaf ceremony is found
in the honour done to the "Neck" in the West of England.

---

[1] *Origin*, pp. 279–281.   [2] Brand, *Popular Antiquities*, 1813, I, 443.
[3] Henderson, *Folklore of the Northern Counties*, 87–89.

...After the wheat is all cut, on most farms in the north of Devon, the harvest people have a custom of "crying the neck." I believe that this practice is seldom omitted on any large farm in that part of the country. It is done in this way. An old man, or someone else well acquainted with the ceremonies used on the occasion (when the labourers are reaping the last field of wheat), goes round to the shocks and sheaves, and picks out a little bundle of all the best ears he can find; this bundle he ties up very neat and trim, and plats and arranges the straws very tastefully. This is called "the neck" of wheat, or wheaten-ears. After the field is cut out, and the pitcher once more circulated, the reapers, binders, and the women, stand round in a circle. The person with "the neck" stands in the centre, grasping it with both his hands. He first stoops and holds it near the ground, and all the men forming the ring take off their hats, stooping and holding them with both hands towards the ground. They then all begin at once in a very prolonged and harmonious tone to cry "the neck!" at the same time slowly raising themselves upright, and elevating their arms and hats above their heads; the person with "the neck" also raising it on high. This is done three times. They then change their cry to "wee yen!"—"way yen!"—which they sound in the same prolonged and slow manner as before, with singular harmony and effect, three times. This last cry is accompanied by the same movements of the body and arms as in crying "the neck."...

...After having thus repeated "the neck" three times, and "wee yen" or "way yen" as often, they all burst out into a kind of loud and joyous laugh, flinging up their hats and caps into the air, capering about and perhaps kissing the girls. One of them then gets "the neck," and runs as hard as he can down to the farm-house, where the dairy-maid, or one of the young female domestics, stands at the door prepared with a pail of water. If he who holds "the neck" can manage to get into the house, in any way, unseen or openly, by any other way than the door at which the girl stands with the pail of water, then he may lawfully kiss her; but, if otherwise, he is regularly soused with the contents of the bucket. On a fine still autumn evening, the "crying of the neck" has a wonderful effect at a distance, far finer than that of the Turkish muezzin, which Lord Byron eulogizes so much, and which he says is preferable to all the bells in Christendom. I have once or twice heard upwards of twenty men cry it, and sometimes joined by an equal number of female voices. About three years back, on some high grounds, where our people were harvesting, I heard six or seven "necks" cried in one night, although I know that some of them were four miles off[1].

The account given by Mrs Bray of the Devonshire custom, in her letters to Southey, is practically identical with this[2]. We have plenty of evidence for this ceremony of "Crying the Neck" in the South-Western counties—in Somersetshire[3], in Cornwall[4], and in a mutilated form in Dorsetshire[5].

---

[1] Hone's *Every Day Book*, 1827, p. 1170.
[2] *The Tamar and the Tavy*, I, 330 (1836).
[3] Raymond, *Two men o' Mendip*, 1899, 259.
[4] Miss M. A. Courtney, *Glossary of West Cornwall*; T. Q. Couch, *Glossary of East Cornwall*, s.v. Neck (*Eng. Dial. Soc.* 1880); Jago, *Ancient Language of Cornwall*, 1882, s. v. Anek.   [5] *Notes and Queries*, 4th Ser. XII, 491 (1873).

On the Welsh border the essence of the ceremony consisted in tying the last ears of corn—perhaps twenty—with
ribbon, and severing this "neck" by throwing the sickle at
it from some distance. The custom is recorded in Cheshire[1],
Shropshire[2], and under a different name in Herefordshire[3].
The term "neck" seems to have been known as far afield as
Yorkshire and the "little England beyond Wales"—the English-
speaking colony of Pembrokeshire[4].

Whether we are to interpret the expression "the Neck,"
applied to the last sheaf, as descended from a time when "the
corn spirit is conceived in human form, and the last standing
corn is a part of its body—its neck[5]......" or whether it is merely
a survival of the Scandinavian word for sheaf—*nek* or *neg*[6], we
have here surely evidence of the worship of the sheaf. "In
this way 'Sheaf' was greeted, before he passed over into a
purely mythical being[7]."

I do not think these "neck" customs can be traced back
beyond the seventeenth century[8]. Though analogous usages
are recorded in England (near Eton) as early as the sixteenth
century[9], it was not usual at that time to trouble to record
such things.

The earliest document bearing upon the veneration of the
sheaf comes from a neighbouring district, and is contained in
the Chronicle of the Monastery of Abingdon, which tells how
in the time of King Edmund (941–946) a controversy arose as
to the right of the monks of Abingdon to a certain portion of
land adjoining the river. The monks appealed to a judgment
of God to vindicate their claim, and this took the shape of

---

[1] Holland's *Glossary of Chester* (*Eng. Dial. Soc.*), s.v. *Cutting the Neck*.
[2] Burne, *Shropshire Folk Lore*, 1883, 371.
[3] "to cry the Mare." Blount, *Glossographia*, 4th edit. 1674, s.v. *mare*.
Cf. *Notes and Queries*, 5th Ser. VI, 286 (1876).
[4] Wright, *Eng. Dial. Dict.*, s.v. *neck*.
[5] Frazer, *Spirits of the Corn*, 1912, I, 268. The word was understood as = "neck" by the peasants, because "They'm taied up under the
chin laike" (*Notes and Queries*, 5th Ser. X, 51). But this may be false
etymology.
[6] Wright, *Eng. Dial. Dict.* Cf. *Notes and Queries*, 5th Ser. X, 51.
[7] *Heltedigtning*, II, 252.
[8] The earliest record of the term "cutting the neck" seems to be found in
Randle Holme's *Store House of Armory*, 1688 (II 73). It may be noted that
Holme was a Cheshire man.
[9] Mannhardt, *Mythologische Forschungen*, Strassburg, 1884, 326 *etc.*

placing a sheaf, with a taper on the top, upon a round shield, and letting it float down the river, the shield by its movements hither and thither indicating accurately the boundaries of the monastic domain. At last the shield came to the field in debate, which, thanks to the floods, it was able to circumnavigate[1].

Professor Chadwick, who first emphasized the importance of this strange ordeal[2], points out that although the extant MSS of the *Chronicle* date from the thirteenth century, the mention of a *round* shield carries the superstition back to a period before the Norman Conquest. Therefore this story seems to give us evidence for the use of the sheaf and shield together as a magic symbol in Anglo-Saxon times. "An ordeal by letting the sheaf sail down the river on a shield was only possible at a time when the sheaf was regarded as a kind of supernatural being which could find the way itself[3]."

But a still closer parallel to the story of the corn-figure coming over the water is found in Finnish mythology in the person of Sämpsä Pellervoinen. Finnish mythology seems remote from our subject, but if the figure of Sämpsä was borrowed from Germanic mythology, as seems to be thought[4], we are justified in laying great weight upon the parallel.

Readers of the *Kalewala* will remember, near the beginning, the figure of Sämpsä Pellervoinen, the god of Vegetation. He does not seem to do much. But there are other Finnish

---

[1] Quod dum servi Dei propensius actitarent, inspiratum est eis salubre consilium et (ut pium est credere) divinitus provisum. Die etenim statuto mane surgentes monachi sumpserunt scutum rotundum, cui imponebant manipulum frumenti, et super manipulum cereum circumspectae quantitatis et grossitudinis. Quo accenso scutum cum manipulo et cereo, fluvio ecclesiam praetercurrenti committunt, paucis in navicula fratribus subsequentibus. Praecedebat itaque eos scutum et quasi digito demonstrans possessiones domui Abbendoniae de jure adjacentes nunc huc, nunc illuc divertens; nunc in dextra nunc in sinistra parte fiducialiter eos praeibat, usquedum veniret ad rivum prope pratum quod Beri vocatur, in quo cereus medium cursum Tamisiae miraculose deserens se declinavit et circumdedit pratum inter Tamisiam et Gifteleia, quod hieme et multociens aestate ex redundatione Tamisiae in modum insulae aqua circumdatur. *Chronicon Monasterii de Abingdon*, ed. Stevenson, 1858, vol. I, p. 89.

[2] Chadwick, *Origin*, 278.

[3] Olrik, *Heltedigtning*, II, 251.

[4] But is this so? "The word Sämpsä (now sämpsykka) 'small rush, *scirpus silvaticus*, forest rush,' is borrowed from the Germanic family (Engl. semse; Germ. simse)." Olrik, 253. But the Engl. "semse" is difficult to track. See also note by A. Mieler in *Finnisch-Ugrische Forschungen*, x, 43, 1910.

poems in his honour, extant in varying versions[1]. It is difficult
to get a collected idea from these fragmentary records, but it
seems to be this: Ahti, the god of the sea, sends messengers to
summon Sämpsä, so that he may bring fertility to the fields.
In one version, first the Winter and then the Summer are sent
to arouse Sämpsä, that he may make the crops and trees grow.
Winter—

> Took a foal swift as the spring wind,
> Let the storm wind bear him forward,
> Blew the trees till they were leafless,
> Blew the grass till it was seedless,
> Bloodless likewise the young maidens.

Sämpsä refuses to come. Then the Summer is sent with better
results. In another version Sämpsä is fetched from an island
beyond the sea:

> It is I who summoned Sämpsä
> From an isle amid the ocean,
> From a skerry bare and treeless.

In yet another variant we are told how the boy Sämpsä

> Took six grains from off the corn heap,
> Slept all summer mid the corn heap,
> In the bosom of the corn boat.

Now "It's a long, long way to" Ilomantsi in the east of
Finland, where this last variant was discovered. But at least
we have evidence that, within the region influenced by Germanic
mythology, the spirit of vegetation was thought of as a boy
coming over the sea, or sleeping in a boat with corn[2].

To sum up:

Sceafa, when the Catalogue of Kings in *Widsith* was drawn
up—before *Beowulf* was composed, at any rate in its present
form—was regarded as an ancient king. When the West
Saxon pedigree was drawn up, certainly not much more than
a century and a half after the composition of *Beowulf*, and
perhaps much less, Sceaf was regarded as the primitive figure
in the pedigree, before whom no one lived save the Hebrew
patriarchs. That he was originally thought of as a child,

---

[1] Kaarle Krohn, "Sampsa Pellervoinen" in *Finnisch-Ugrische Forschungen*,
IV, 231 etc., 1904.
[2] Cf. Olrik, *Heltedigtning*, II, 252 etc..

coming across the water, with the sheaf of corn, is, in view of the Finnish parallel, exceedingly probable, and acquires some confirmation from the Chronicler's placing him in Noah's ark. But the definite evidence for this is late.

Scyld, on the other hand, is in the first place probably a mere eponym of the power of the Scylding kings of Denmark. He may, at a very early date, have been provided with a ship funeral, since later two Swedish kings, both apparently of Danish origin, have this ship funeral accorded to them, and in one case it is expressly said to be "according to the custom of his ancestors." But it seems exceedingly improbable that his original story represented him as coming over the sea in a boat. For, if so, it remains to be explained why this motive has entirely disappeared among his own people in Scandinavia, and has been preserved only in England. Would the Danes have been likely to forget utterly so striking a story, concerning the king from whom their line derived its name? Further, in England, *Beowulf* alone attributes this story to Scyld, whilst later historians attribute it to Sceaf. In view of the way in which the story of William of Malmesbury is supported by folk-lore, to regard that story as merely the result of error or invention seems perilous indeed.

On the other hand, all becomes straightforward if we allow that Scyld and Sceaf were both ancient figures standing at the head of famous dynasties. Their names alliterate. What more likely than that their stories should have influenced each other, and that one king should have come to be regarded as the parent or ancestor of the other? Contamination with Scyld would account for Sceaf's boat being stated to have come to land in Scani, Scanza—that Scedeland which is mentioned as the seat of Scyld's rule. Yet this explanation is not necessary, for if Sceaf were an early Longobard king, he would be rightly represented as ruling in Scandinavia[1].

---

[1] I do not understand why Olrik (*Heltedigtning*, I, 235) declares the coming to land in Scani (Ethelwerd) to be inconsistent with Sceaf as a Longobardic king (*Widsith*). For, according to their national historian, the Longobardi came from "Scadinavia" [Paul the Deacon, I, 1–7]. It is a more serious difficulty that Paul knows of no Longobardic king with a name which we can equate with Sceaf.

SECTION VI. BEOW

The Anglo-Saxon genealogies agree that the son of Sceldwa (Scyld) is Beow (Beaw, Beo). In *Beowulf*, he is named not Beow, but Beowulf.

Many etymologies have been suggested for *Bēow*. But considering that Beow is in some versions a grandson, in all a descendant of Sceaf, it can hardly be an accident that his name is identical with the O.E. word for grain, *bēow*. The Norse word corresponding to this is *bygg*[1].

Recent investigation of the name is best summed up in the words of Axel Olrik:

"New light has been cast upon the question of the derivation of the name Beow by Kaarle Krohn's investigation of the debt of Finnish to Norse mythology, together with Magnus Olsen's linguistic interpretation. The Finnish has a deity Pekko, concerning whom it is said that he promoted the growth of barley: the Esths, closely akin to the Finns, have a corresponding Peko, whose image—the size of a three-year-old child—was carried out into the fields and invoked at the time of sowing, or else was kept in the corn-bin by a custodian chosen for a year. This Pekko is plainly a personification of the barley; the form corresponding phonetically in Runic Norse would be **beggw-* (from which comes Old Norse *bygg*).

"So in Norse there was a grain **beggw-* (becoming *bygg*) and a corn-god **Beggw-* (becoming *Pekko*). In Anglo-Saxon there was a grain *béow* and an ancestral *Béow*. And all four are phonetically identical (proceeding from a primitive form **beuwa*, 'barley'). The conclusion which it is difficult to avoid is, that the corn-spirit 'Barley' and the ancestor 'Barley' are one and the same. The relation is the same as that between King Sheaf and the worship of the sheaf: the worshipped corn-being gradually sinks into the background, and comes to be regarded as an epic figure, an early ancestor.

"We have no more exact knowledge of the mythical ideas connected either with the ancestor Beow or the corn-god Pekko. But we know enough of the worship of Pekko to show that he dwelt in the corn-heap, and that, in the spring, he was fetched out in the shape of a little child. That reminds us not a little of Sämpsä, who lay in the corn-heap on the ship, and came to land and awoke in the spring[2]."

[1] So, corresponding to O.E. *tríewe* we have Icel. *tryggr*; to O.E. *glēaw*, Icel. *glǫggr*; O.E. *scúwa*, Icel. *skugg-*.

[2] Olrik, *Heltedigtning*, II, 1910, pp. 254–5.

An account of the worship of Pekko will be found in *Finnisch-Ugrische Forschungen*, VI, 1906, pp. 104–111: *Über den Pekokultus bei den Setukesen*, by M. J. Eisen. See also Appendix (A) below.

Pellon-Pecko is mentioned by Michael Agricola, Bishop of Åbo, in his translation of the Psalter into Finnish, 1551. It is here that we are told that he "promoted the growth of barley."

But it may be objected that this is "harking back" to the old mythological interpretations. After refusing to accept Müllenhoff's assumptions, are we not reverting, through the names of Sceaf and Beow, and the worship of the sheaf, to very much the same thing?

No. It is one thing to believe that the ancestor-king Beow may be a weakened form of an ancient divinity, a mere name surviving from the figure of an old corn-god Beow; it is quite another to assume, as Müllenhoff did, that what we are told about Beowulf was originally told about Beow *and that therefore we are justified in giving a mythological meaning to it.*

All we know, conjecture apart, about Beow is his traditional relationship to Scyld, Sceaf and the other figures of the pedigree. That Beowulf's dragon fight belonged originally to him is only a conjecture. In confirmation of this conjecture only one argument has been put forward: an argument turning upon Beowulf, son of Scyld—that obscure figure, apparently equivalent to Beow, who meets us at the beginning of our poem.

Beowulf's place as a son of Scyld and father of Healfdene is occupied in the Danish genealogies by Frothi, son of Skjold, and father of Halfdan. It has been urged that the two figures are really identical, in spite of the difference of name. Now Frothi slays a dragon, and it has been argued that this dragon fight shows similarities which enable us to identify it with the dragon fight attributed in our poem to Beowulf the Geat.

The argument is a strong one—if it really is the case that the dragon slain by Frothi was the same monster as that slain by Beowulf the Geat.

Unfortunately this parallel, which will be examined in the next section, is far from certain. We must be careful not to argue in a circle, identifying Beowulf and Frothi because they slew the same dragon, and then identifying the dragons because they were slain by the same hero.

Whilst, therefore, we admit that it is highly probable that Beow (grain) the descendant of Sceaf (sheaf) was originally a corn divinity or corn fetish, we cannot follow Müllenhoff in his bold attribution to this "culture hero" of Beowulf's adventures with the dragon or with Grendel.

SECTION VII. THE HOUSE OF SCYLD AND DANISH
PARALLELS: HEREMOD-LOTHERUS AND BEOWULF-FROTHO.

Scyld, although the source of that Scylding dynasty which
our poem celebrates, is *not* apparently regarded in *Beowulf* as
the earliest Danish king. He came to the throne after an
interregnum; the people whom he grew up to rule had long
endured cruel need, "being without a prince[1]." We hear in
Beowulf of one Danish king only whom we can place chronologically before Scyld—viz. Heremod[2]. The way in which
Heremod is referred to would fit in very well with the supposition[3] that he was the last of a dynasty; the immediate
predecessor of Scyld; and that it was the death or exile of
Heremod which ushered in the time when the Danes were
without a prince.

Now there is a natural tendency in genealogies for each king
to be represented as the descendant of his predecessor, whether
he really was so or no; so that in the course of time, and
sometimes of a very short time, the first king of a new dynasty
may come to be reckoned as son of a king of the preceding line[4].
Consequently, there would be nothing surprising if, in another
account, we find Scyld represented as a son of Heremod. And
we *do* find the matter represented thus in the West Saxon
genealogy, where Sceldwa or Scyld is son of Heremod.
Turning to the Danish accounts, however, we do not find any
Hermóðr (which is the form we should expect corresponding to
Heremōd) as father to Skjold (Scyld). Either no father of
Skjold is known, or else (in Saxo Grammaticus) he has a father
Lotherus. But, although the names are different, there is
some correspondence between what we are told of Lother and
what we are told of Heremod. A close parallel has indeed
been drawn by Sievers between the whole dynasty: on the one
hand Lotherus, his son Skioldus, and his descendant Frotno,

---

[1] l. 15.
[2] That Heremod is a Danish king is clear from ll. 1709 *etc.* And as we have
all the stages in the Scylding genealogy from Scyld to Hrothgar, Heremod
must be placed earlier.
[3] Of Grein in *Eberts Jahrbuch*, IV, 264.
[4] A good example of this is supplied by the Assyrian records, which make
Jehu a son of Omri—whose family he had destroyed.

as given in Saxo: and on the other hand the corresponding
figures in *Beowulf*, Heremod, Scyld, and Scyld's son, Beowulf
the Dane.

The fixed and certain point here is the identity of the
central figure, Skioldus-Scyld. All the rest is very doubtful;
not that there are not many parallel features, but because the
parallels are of a commonplace type which might so easily
recur accidentally.

The story of Lother, as given by Saxo, will be found below:
the story of Heremod as given in *Beowulf* is hopelessly obscure
—a mere succession of allusions intended for an audience who
knew the tale quite well. Assuming the stories of Lother and
Heremod to be different versions of one original, the following
would seem to be the most likely reconstruction[1], the more
doubtful portions being placed within round brackets thus ( ):

> The old Danish prince [Dan in Saxo] has two sons, one a weakling
> [*Humblus,* Saxo] the other a hero [*Lotherus,* Saxo: *Heremod, Beowulf*]
> (who was already in his youth the hope of the nation). But after
> his father's death the elder was (through violence) raised to the throne:
> and Lother-Heremod went into banishment. (But under the rule of
> the weakling the kingdom went to pieces, and thus) many a man
> longed for the return of the exile, as a help against these evils. So
> the hero conquers and deposes the weaker brother. But then his
> faults break forth, his greed and his cruelty: he ceases to be the
> darling and becomes the scourge of his people, till they rise and either
> slay him or drive him again into exile.

If the stories of Lother and Heremod *are* connected, we may
be fairly confident that Heremod, not Lother, was the name of
the king in the original story.

For Scandinavian literature does know a Hermoth (*Hermóðr*), though no such adventures are attributed to him as
those recorded of Heremod in *Beowulf*. Nevertheless it is
probable that this Hermoth and Heremod in *Beowulf* are one
and the same, because both heroes are linked in some way or
other with Sigemund. How these two kings, Heremod and
Sigemund, came to be connected, we do not know, but we find
this connection recurring again and again[2]. This *may* be

---

[1] This reconstruction is made by Sievers in the *Berichte d. k. sächs. Gesellschaft der Wissenschaften,* 1895, pp. 180–88.

[2] The god *Hermóðr* who rides to Hell to carry a message to the dead Baldr
is here left out of consideration. His connection with the king *Hermóðr* is
obscure.

mere coincidence: but I doubt if we are justified in assuming it to be so[1].

It has been suggested[2] that both Heremod and Sigemund were originally heroes specially connected with the worship of Odin, and hence grouped together. The history of the Scandinavian Sigmund is bound up with that of the magic sword which Odin gave him, and with which he was always victorious till the last fight when Odin himself shattered it.

And we are told in the Icelandic that Odin, whilst he gave a sword to Sigmund, gave a helm and byrnie to Hermoth.

Again, whilst in one Scandinavian poem Sigmund is represented as welcoming the newcomer at the gates of Valhalla, in another the same duty is entrusted to Hermoth.

It is clear also that the *Beowulf*-poet had in mind some kind of connection, though we cannot tell what, between Sigemund and Heremod.

We may take it, then, that the Heremod who is linked with Sigemund in *Beowulf* was also known in Scandinavian literature as a hero in some way connected with Sigmund: whether or no the adventures which Saxo records of Lotherus were really told in Scandinavian lands in connection with Hermoth, we cannot say. The wicked king whose subjects rebel against him is too common a feature of Germanic story for us to feel sure, without a good deal of corroborative evidence, that the figures of Lotherus and Heremod are identical.

The next king in the line, Skioldus in Saxo, is, as we have seen, clearly identical with Scyld in *Beowulf*. But beyond the name, the two traditions have, as we have also seen, but little in common. Both are youthful heroes[3], both force neighbouring kings to pay tribute[4]; but such things are commonplaces[5].

We must therefore turn to the next figure in the pedigree: the son of Skjold in Scandinavian tradition is Frothi (Frotho

---

[1] On this see Dederich, *Historische u. geographische Studien*, 214; Heinzel in *A.f.d.A.* xv, 161; Chadwick, *Origin*, 148; Chadwick, *Cult of Othin*, 51.

[2] Chadwick, *Cult of Othin*, pp. 50, *etc.*

[3] *puerulus...pro miraculo exceptus* (William of Malmesbury). Cf. *Beowulf*, l. 7. In Saxo, Skjold distinguishes himself at the age of fifteen.

[4] *omnem Alemannorum gentem tributaria ditione perdomuit.* Cf. *Beowulf*, l. 11.

[5] See above, p. 77.

in Saxo)[1], the son of Scyld in *Beowulf* is Beowulf the Dane. And Frothi is the father of Halfdan (Haldanus in Saxo) as Beowulf the Dane is of Healfdene. The Frothi of Scandinavian tradition corresponds then in position to Beowulf the Dane in Old English story[2].

Now of Beowulf the Dane we are told so little that we have really no means of drawing a comparison between him and Frothi. But a *theory* that has found wide acceptance among scholars assumes that the dragon fight of Beowulf the Geat was originally narrated of Beowulf the Dane, and only subsequently transferred to the Geatic hero. Theoretically, then, Beowulf the Dane kills a dragon. Now certainly Frotho kills a dragon: and it has been generally accepted[3] that the parallels between the dragon slain by Frotho and that slain by Beowulf the Geat are so remarkable as to exclude the possibility of mere accidental coincidence, and to lead us to conclude that the dragon story was originally told of that Beowulf who corresponds to Frothi, i.e. Beowulf the Dane, son of Scyld and father of Healfdene; not Beowulf, son of Ecgtheow, the Geat.

But are the parallels really so close? We must not forget that here we are building theory upon theory. That the Frotho of Saxo is the same figure as Beowulf the Dane in Old English, is a theory, based upon his common relationship to Skiold-Scyld before him and to Haldanus-Healfdene coming after him: that Beowulf the Dane was the original hero of the dragon fight, and that that dragon fight was only subsequently transferred to the credit of Beowulf the Geat, is again a theory. Only if we can find real parallels between the dragon-slaying of Frotho and the dragon-slaying of Beowulf will these theories have confirmation.

---

[1] This relationship of Frothi and Skjold is preserved by Sweyn Aageson: Skiold Danis primum didici praefuisse....A quo primum...Skioldunger sunt Reges nuncupati. Qui regni post se reliquit haeredes Frothi videlicet & Haldanum. Svenonis Aggonis *Hist. Regum Dan.* in Langebek, *S.R.D.* I, 44.

In Saxo Frotho is not the son, but the great grandson of Skioldus—but this is a discrepancy which may be neglected, because it seems clear that the difference is due to Saxo having inserted two names into the line at this point—those of Gram and Hadding. There seems no reason to doubt that Danish tradition really represented Frothi as son of Skjold.

[2] Those who accept the identification would regard *Fróði* (O.E. *Frōda*, 'the wise') as a title which has ousted the proper name.

[3] Boer, *Ark. f. nord. filol.*, XIX, 67, calls this theory of Sievers "indisputable."

Parallels have been pointed out by Sievers which he regards as so close as to justify a belief that both are derived ultimately from an old lay, with so much closeness that verbal resemblances can still be traced.

Unfortunately the parallels are all commonplaces. That Sievers and others have been satisfied with them was perhaps due to the fact that they started by assuming as proved that the dragon fight of Beowulf the Geat belonged originally to Beowulf the Dane[1], and argued that since Frotho in Saxo occupies a place corresponding exactly to that of Beowulf the Dane in *Beowulf*, a comparatively limited resemblance between two dragons coming, as it were, at the same point in the pedigree, might be held sufficient to identify them.

But, as we have seen, the assumption that the dragon fight of Beowulf the Geat belonged originally to Beowulf the Dane is only a theory that will have to stand or fall as we can prove that the dragon fight of Frotho is really parallel to that of Beowulf the Geat, and therefore must have belonged to the connecting link supplied by the Scylding prince Beowulf the Dane. In other words, the theory that the dragon in *Beowulf* is to be identified with the dragon which in Saxo is slain by Frotho the Danish prince, father of Haldanus-Healfdene, is one of the main arguments upon which we must base the theory that the dragon in *Beowulf* was originally slain by the Danish Beowulf, father of Healfdene, not by Beowulf the Geat. We cannot then turn round, and assert that the fact that they were both slain by a Danish prince, the father of Healfdene, is an argument for identifying the dragons.

Turning to the dragon fight itself, the following parallels have been noted by Sievers:

(1)   A native (*indigena*) comes to Frotho, and tells him of the treasure-guarding dragon. An informer (*melda*) plays the same part in *Beowulf*[2].

But a dragon is not game which can be met with every day. He is a shy beast, lurking in desert places. Some informant has very frequently to guide the hero to his

---

[1] Sievers, p. 181.
[2] *Beowulf*, 2405.   Cf. 2215, 2281.

foe[1]. And the situation is widely different. Frotho knows
nothing of the dragon till directed to the spot: Beowulf's
land has been assailed, he knows of the dragon, though he
needs to be guided to its *exact* lair.

(2) Frotho's dragon lives on an island. Beowulf's lives
near the sea, and there is an island (*ēalond*, 2334) in the neighbourhood.

But *ēalond* in *Beowulf* probably does not mean "island"
at all: and in any case the dragon did not live upon the *ēalond*.
Many dragons have lived near the sea. Sigemund's dragon
did so[2].

(3) The hero in each case attacks the dragon single-handed.

But what hero ever did otherwise? On the contrary,
Beowulf's exploit differs from that of Frotho and of most
other dragon slayers in that he is unable to *overcome* his foe
single-handed, and needs the support of Wiglaf.

(4) Special armour is carried by the dragon slayer in each
case.

But this again is no uncommon feature. The Red Cross
Knight also needs special armour. Dragon slayers constantly
invent some ingenious or even unique method. And again
the parallel is far from close. Frotho is advised to cover his
shield and his limbs with the hides of bulls and kine: a sensible precaution against fiery venom. Beowulf constructs a
shield of iron[3]: which naturally gives very inferior protection[4].

(5) Frotho's informant tells him that he must be of good
courage[5]. Wiglaf encourages Beowulf[6].

But the circumstances under which the words are uttered
are entirely different, nor have the words more than a general
resemblance. That a man needs courage, if he is going to
tackle a dragon, is surely a conclusion at which two minds
could have arrived independently.

(6) Both heroes waste their blows at first on the scaly
back of the dragon.

---

[1] So Regin guides Sigurd: Una the Red Cross Knight. The list might be
indefinitely extended. Similarly with giants: "Then came to him a husbandman of the country, and told him how there was in the country of Constantine,
beside Brittany, a great giant".... *Morte d'Arthur*, Book v, cap. v.

[2] *Beowulf*, 895.   [3] l. 2338.   [4] ll. 2570 etc.

[5] intrepidum mentis habitum retinere memento.   [6] ll. 2663 etc.

But if the hero went at once for the soft parts, there would be no fight at all, and all the fun would be lost. Sigurd's dragon-fight is, for this reason, a one-sided business from the first. To avoid this, Frotho is depicted as beginning by an attack on the dragon's rough hide (although he has been specially warned by the *indigena* not to do so):

> ventre sub imo
> esse locum scito quo ferrum mergere fas est,
> hunc mucrone petens medium rimaberis anguem[1].

(7) The hoard is plundered by both heroes.

But it is the nature of a dragon to guard a hoard[2]. And, having slain the dragon, what hero would neglect the gold?

(8) There are many verbal resemblances: the dragon spits venom[3], and twists himself into coils[4].

Some of these verbal resemblances may be granted as proved: but they surely do not prove the common origin of the two dragon fights. They only tend to prove the common origin of the school of poetry in which these two dragon fights were told. That dragons dwelt in mounds was a common Germanic belief, to which the Cottonian Gnomic verses testify. Naturally, therefore, Frotho's dragon is *montis possessor*: Beowulf's is *beorges hyrde*. The two phrases undoubtedly point back to a similar gradus, to a similar traditional stock phraseology, and to similar beliefs: that is all. As well argue that two kings must be identical, because each is called *folces hyrde*.

These commonplace phrases and commonplace features are surely quite insufficient to prove that the stories are identical —at most they only prove that they bear the impress of one and the same poetical school. If a parallel is to carry weight there must be something individual about it, as there is, for example, about the arguments by which the identity of Beowulf and Bjarki have been supported. That a hero comes from

---

[1] Cf. *Beowulf*, 2705: *forwrāt Wedra helm wyrm on middan.*
[2] Cf. *Cotton. Gnomic verses*, ll. 26–7: *Draca sceal on hlǣwe: frōd, frǣtwum wlanc.*
[3] virusque profundens: *wearp wæl-fȳre*, 2582.
[4]
    implicitus gyris serpens crebrisque reflexus
    orbibus et caudae sinuosa volumina ducens
    multiplicesque agitans spiras.
Cf. *Beowulf*, 2567–8, 2569, 2561 (*hring-boga*), 2827 (*wōhbogen*).

Geatland (Gautland) to the court where Hrothulf (Rolf) is
abiding; that the same hero subsequently is instrumental in
helping Eadgils (Athils) against Onela (Ali)—here we have
something tangible. But when two heroes, engaged upon
slaying a dragon, are each told to be brave, the parallel is too
general to be a parallel at all. "There is a river in Macedon:
and there is also moreover a river at Monmouth, and there is
salmons in both."

And there is a fundamental difference, which would serve
to neutralize the parallels, even did they appear much less
accidental than they do.

Dragon fights may be classified into several types: two
stand out prominently. There is the story in which the young
hero begins his career by slaying a dragon or monster and
winning, it may be a hoard of gold, it may be a bride. This
is the type of story found, for instance, in the tales of Sigurd,
or Perseus, or St George. On the other hand there is the hero
who, at the end of his career, seeks to ward off evil from himself
and his people. He slays the monster, but is himself slain by
it. The great example of this type is the god Thor, who in
the last fight of the gods slays the Dragon, but dies when he
has reeled back nine paces from the "baleful serpent[1]."

Now the story of the victorious young Frotho is of the one
type: that of the aged Beowulf is of the other. And this
difference is essential, fundamental, dominating the whole
situation in each case: giving its cheerful and aggressive tone
to the story of Frotho, giving the elegiac and pathetic note
which runs through the whole of the last portion of *Beowulf*[2].
It is no mere detail which could be added or subtracted by
a narrator without altering the essence of the story.

In face of this we must pronounce the two stories essentially
and originally distinct. If, nevertheless, there were a large
number of striking and specific similarities, we should have to
allow that, though originally distinct, the one dragon story had
influenced the other in detail. For, whilst each poet who
retold the tale would make alterations in detail, and might

---

[1] *Volospá*, 172–3 in *Corpus Poeticum Boreale*, I, 200.
[2] Cf. on this Olrik, *Heltedigtning*, I, 305–15.

import such detail from one dragon story into another, what we know of the method of the ancient story tellers does not allow us to assume that a poet would have altered the whole drift of a story, either by changing the last death-struggle of an aged, childless prince into the victorious feat of a young hero, or by the reverse process.

Those, there ore, who hold the parallels quoted above to be convincing, may believe that one dragon story has influenced another, originally distinct[1]. To me, it does not appear that even this necessarily follows from the evidence.

It seems very doubtful whether any of the parallels drawn by Sievers between the stories of Lotherus and Heremod[2], Skioldus and Scyld, Frotho and Beowulf, are more than the resemblances inevitable in poetry which, like the Old Danish and the Old English, still retains so many traces of the common Germanic frame in which it was moulded.

Indeed, of the innumerable dragon-stories extant, there is probably not one which we can declare to be really identical with that of Beowulf. There is a Danish tradition which shows many similarities[3], and I have given this below, in Part II ; but rather as an example of a dragon-slaying of the *Beowulf* type, than because I believe in any direct connection between the two stories.

---

[1] Panzer, *Beowulf*, 313.

[2] A further and more specific parallel between Lotherus and Heremod has been pointed out by Sarrazin (*Anglia*, xix, 392). It seems from *Beowulf* that Heremod went into exile (ll. 1714-15), and apparently *mid Eotenum* (l. 902) which (in view of the use of the word *Eotena, Eotenum*, in the *Finnsburg* episode) very probably means "among the Jutes." A late Scandinavian document tells us that *Lotherus...superatus in Jutiam profugit* (Messenius, *Scondia illustrata*, printed 1700, but written about 1620).

[3] Pointed out by Panzer. A possible parallel to the old man who hides his treasure is discussed by Bugge and Olrik in *Dania*, i, 233-245 (1890-92).

CHAPTER III

THEORIES AS TO THE ORIGIN, DATE, AND STRUCTURE OF THE POEM

SECTION I. IS "BEOWULF" TRANSLATED FROM A SCANDINAVIAN ORIGINAL?

OUR poem, the first original poem of any length in the English tongue, ignores England. In one remarkable passage (ll.1931–62) it mentions with praise Offa I, the great king who ruled the Angles whilst they were still upon the Continent. But, except for this, it deals mainly with heroes who, so far as we can identify them with historic figures, are Scandinavian.

Hence, not unnaturally, the first editor boldly declared *Beowulf* to be an Anglo-Saxon version of a Danish poem; and this view has had many supporters. The poem *must* be Scandinavian, said one of its earliest translators, because it deals mainly with Scandinavian heroes and "everyone knows that in ancient times each nation celebrated in song its own heroes alone[1]." And this idea, though not so crudely expressed, seems really to underlie the belief which has been held by numerous scholars, that the poem is nothing more than a translation of a poem in which some Scandinavian minstrel had glorified the heroes of his own nation.

But what do we mean by "nation"? Doubtless, from the point of view of politics and war, each Germanic tribe, or offshoot of a tribe, formed an independent nation: the Longobardi had no hesitation in helping the "Romans" to cut the throats of their Gothic kinsmen: Penda the Mercian was willing to ally with the Welshmen in order to overthrow his

---

[1] Cf. Ettmüller, *Scopas and Boceras*, 1850, p. ix; *Carmen de Beovvulfi rebus gestis*, 1875, p. iii.

fellow Angles of Northumbria. But all this, as the history of the ancient Greeks or of the ancient Hebrews might show us, is quite compatible with a consciousness of racial unity among the warring states, with a common poetic tradition and a common literature. For purposes of poetry there was only one nation—the Germanic—split into many dialects and groups, but possessed of a common metre, a common style, a common standard of heroic feeling: and any deed of valour performed by any Germanic chief might become a fit subject for the poetry of any Germanic tribe of the heroic age.

So, if by "nation" we mean the whole Germanic race, then Germanic poetry is essentially "national." The Huns were the only non-Germanic tribe who were received (for poetical purposes) into Germania. Hunnish chiefs seem to have adopted Gothic manners, and after the Huns had disappeared it often came to be forgotten that they were not Germans. But with this exception the tribes and heroes of Germanic heroic poetry are Germanic.

If, however, by "nation" we understand the different warring units into which the Germanic race was, politically speaking, divided, then Germanic poetry is essentially "international."

This is no theory, but a fact capable of conclusive proof. The chief actors in the old Norse Volsung lays are not Norsemen, but Sigurd the Frank, Gunnar the Burgundian, Atli the Hun. In Continental Germany, the ideal knight of the Saxons in the North and the Bavarians in the South was no native hero, but Theodoric the Ostrogoth. So too in England, whilst *Beowulf* deals chiefly with Scandinavian heroes, the *Finnsburg* fragment deals with the Frisian tribes of the North Sea coast: *Waldere* with the adventures of Germanic chiefs settled in Gaul, *Deor* with stories of the Goths and of the Baltic tribes, whilst *Widsith*, which gives us a catalogue of the old heroic tales, shows that amongst the heroes whose names were current in England were men of Gothic, Burgundian, Frankish, Lombard, Frisian, Danish and Swedish race. There is nothing peculiar, then, in the fact that *Beowulf* celebrates heroes who were not of Anglian birth.

In their old home in Schleswig the Angles had been in the exact centre of Germania: with an outlook upon both the North Sea and the Baltic, and in touch with Scandinavian tribes on the North and Low German peoples on the South. That the Angles were interested in the stories of all the nations which surrounded them, and that they brought these stories with them to England, is certain. It is a mere accident that the one heroic poem which happens to have been preserved at length is almost exclusively concerned with Scandinavian doings. It could easily have happened that the history of the *Beowulf* MS and the *Waldere* MS might have been reversed: that the *Beowulf* might have been cut up to bind other books, and the *Waldere* preserved intact: in that case our one long poem would have been localized in ancient Burgundia, and would have dealt chiefly with the doings of Burgundian champions. But we should have had no more reason, without further evidence, to suppose the *Waldere* a translation from the Burgundian than we have, without further evidence, to suppose *Beowulf* a translation from the Scandinavian.

To deny that *Beowulf*, as we have it, is a translation from the Scandinavian does not, of course, involve any denial of the Scandinavian origin of the *story* of Beowulf's deeds. The fact that his achievements are framed in a Scandinavian setting, and that the closest parallels to them have to be sought in Scandinavian lands, makes it probable on *a priori* grounds that the story had its origin there. On the face of it, Müllenhoff's belief that the story was indigenous among the Angles is quite unlikely. It would seem rather to have originated in the Geatic country. But stories, whether in prose or verse, would spread quickly from the Geatas to the Danes and from the Danes to the Angles.

After the Angles had crossed the North Sea, however, this close intimacy ceased, till the Viking raids again reminded Englishmen, in a very unpleasant way, of their kinsmen across the sea. Now linguistic evidence tends to show that *Beowulf* belongs to a time prior to the Viking settlement in England, and it is unlikely that the Scandinavian traditions embodied in *Beowulf* found their way to England just at the time when communication with Scandinavian lands seems to have been suspended. We must conclude then that all this Scandinavian tradition probably spread to the Angles whilst they were still in their old continental home, was brought across to England by the settlers in the sixth century, was handed on by English bards from generation to generation, till the poem of *Beowulf* as we know it was formed in England.

Of course, if evidence can be produced that *Beowulf* is translated from some Scandinavian original, which was brought over in the seventh century or later, that is another matter. But the evidence produced so far is not merely inconclusive, but ludicrously inadequate.

It has been urged[1] by Sarrazin, the chief advocate of the translation theory, that the description of the country round Heorot, and especially of the journey to the Grendel-lake, shows such local knowledge as to point to its having been composed by some Scandinavian poet familiar with the locality. Heorot can probably, as we have seen, be identified with Leire: and the Grendel-lake Sarrazin identifies with the neighbouring Roskilde fjord. But it is hardly possible to conceive a greater contrast than that between the Roskilde fjord and the scenery depicted in ll. 1357 *etc.*, 1408 *etc.* Seen, as Sarrazin saw it, on a May morning, in alternate sun and shadow, the Roskilde fjord presents a view of tame and peaceful beauty. In the days of Hrothgar, when there were perhaps fewer cultivated fields and more beech forests, the scenery may have been less tame, but can hardly have been less peaceful. The only trace of accurate geography is that Heorot is represented as not on the shore, and yet not far remote from it (ll. 307 *etc.*). But, as has been pointed out above, we know that traditions of the attack by the Heathobeardan upon Heorot were current in England: and these would be quite sufficient to keep alive, even among English bards, some remembrance of the strategic situation of Heorot with regard to the sea. A man need not have been near Troy, to realize that the town was no seaport and yet near the sea.

---

[1] *P.B.B.* **xi**, 167–170.

Again, it has been claimed by Sarrazin that the language of *Beowulf* shows traces of the Scandinavian origin of the poem. Sarrazin's arguments on this head have been contested energetically by Sievers[1]. After some heated controversy Sarrazin made a final and (presumably) carefully-weighed statement of his case. In this he gave a list of twenty-nine words upon which he based his belief[2]. Yet of these twenty-nine, twenty-one occur in other O.E. writings, where there can be no possible question of translation from the Scandinavian: some of these words, in fact, are amongst the commonest of O.E. poetical expressions. There remain eight which do not happen to be found elsewhere in the extant remains of O.E. poetry. But these are mostly compounds like *heaðo-lāc, feorh-sēoc*: and though the actual compound is not elsewhere extant in English, the component elements are thoroughly English. There is no reason whatever to think that these eight rare words are taken from Old Norse. Indeed, three of them do not occur in Old Norse at all.

Evidence to prove *Beowulf* a translation from a Scandinavian original is, then, wanting. On the other hand, over and above the difficulty that the *Beowulf* belongs just to the period when intimate communication between the Angles and Scandinavians was suspended, there is much evidence against the translation theory. The earliest Scandinavian poetry we possess, or of which we can get information, differs absolutely from *Beowulf* in style, metre and sentiment: the manners of *Beowulf* are incompatible with all we know of the wild heathendom of Scandinavia in the seventh or eighth century[3]. *Beowulf*, as we now have it, with its Christian references and its Latin loan-words, *could* not be a translation from the Scandinavian. And the proper names in *Beowulf* which Sarrazin claimed were Old Norse, not Old English, and had been taken

---

[1] Sarrazin, *Der Schauplatz des ersten Beowulfliedes* (*P.B.B.* XI. 170 *etc.*): Sievers, *Die Heimat des Beowulfdichters* (*P.B.B.* XI, 354 *etc.*); Sarrazin, *Altnordisches im Beowulfliede* (*P.B.B.* XI, 528 *etc.*); Sievers, *Altnordisches im Beowulf?* (*P.B.B.* XII, 168 *etc.*)   [2] *Beovulf-Studien.* 68.
[3] Sarrazin has countered this argument by urging that since the present day Swedes and Danes have better manners than the English, they therefore presumably had better manners already in the eighth century. I admit the premises, but deny the deduction.

over from the Old Norse original, are in all cases so correctly
transliterated as to necessitate the assumption that they were
brought across early, at the time of the settlement of Britain
or very shortly after, and underwent phonetic development
side by side with the other words in the English language.
Had they been brought across from Scandinavia at a later date,
much confusion must have ensued in the forms.

Somewhat less improbable is the suggestion "that the poet
had travelled on the continent and become familiar with the
legends of the Danes and Geats, or else had heard them from
a Scandinavian resident in England[1]." But it is clear from
the allusive manner in which the Scandinavian tales are told,
that they must have been familiar to the poet's audience.
If, then, the English audience knew them, why must the poet
himself have travelled on the continent in order to know them?
There is, therefore, no need for this theory, and it is open to
many of the objections of the translation theory: for example
it fails, equally with that theory, to account for the uniformly
correct development of the proper names.

The obvious conclusion is that these Scandinavian traditions
were brought over by the English settlers in the sixth century.
Against this only one cavil can be raised, and that will not
bear examination. It has been objected that, since Hygelac's
raid took place about 516, since Beowulf's accession was some
years subsequent, and since he then reigned fifty years, his
death cannot be put much earlier than 575, and that this
brings us to a date when the migration of the Angles and
Saxons had been completed[2]. But it is forgotten that all the
historical events mentioned in the poem, which we can date,
occur before, or not very long after, the raid of Hygelac, c. 516.
The poem asserts that fifty years after these events Beowulf
slew a dragon and was slain by it. But this does not make the
dragon historic, nor does it make the year 575 the historic
date of the death of Beowulf. We cannot be sure that there
was any actual king of the Geatas named Beowulf; and if
there was, the last known historic act with which that king is
associated is the raising of Eadgils to the Swedish throne,

---

[1] Sedgefield, *Beowulf* (1st ed.), p. 27.   [2] Schück, *Studier i Beovulfsagan*, 41.

c. 530: the rest of Beowulf's long reign, since it contains no event save the slaying of a dragon, has no historic validity.

It is noteworthy that, whereas there is full knowledge shown in our poem of those events which took place in Scandinavian lands during the whole period from about 450 to 530 —the period during which hordes of Angles, Saxons and Jutes were landing in Britain—there is no reference, not even by way of casual allusion, to any continental events which we can date with certainty as subsequent to the arrival of the latest settlers from the continent. Surely this is strong evidence that these tales were brought over by some of the last of the invaders, not carried to England by some casual traveller a century or two later.

SECTION II. THE DIALECT, SYNTAX, AND METRE OF " BEOWULF " AS EVIDENCE OF ITS LITERARY HISTORY.

A full discussion of the dialect, metre and syntax of *Beowulf* forms no part of the scheme of this study. It is only intended in this section to see how far such investigations throw light upon the literary history of the poem.

Dialect.

Beowulf is written in the late West Saxon dialect. Imbedded in the poem, however, are a large number of forms, concerning which this at least can be said—that they are not normal late West Saxon. Critics have classified these forms, and have drawn conclusions from them as to the history of the poem: arguing from sporadic "Mercian" and "Kentish" forms that *Beowulf* is of Mercian origin and has passed through the hands of a Kentish transcriber.

But, in fact, the evidence as to Old English dialects is more scanty and more conflicting than philologists have always been willing to admit. It is exceedingly difficult to say with any certainty what forms are "Mercian" and what "Kentish." Having run such forms to earth, it is still more difficult to say what arguments are to be drawn from their *occasional* appearance in any text. Men from widely different parts of the country would be working together in the scriptorium of one and the same monastery, and this fact alone may have often led to confusion in the dialectal forms of works transcribed.

A thorough investigation of the significance of all the abnormal forms in *Beowulf* has still to be made. Whether it would repay the labour of the investigator may well be questioned. In the meantime we may accept the view that the poem was in all probability originally written in some non-West-Saxon dialect, and most probably in an Anglian dialect, since this is confirmed by the way in which the Anglian hero Offa is dragged into the story.

> Ten Brink's attempt to decide the dialect and transmission of *Beowulf* will be found in his *Beowulf*, pp. 237–241: he notes the difficulty that the "Kentish" forms from which he argues are nearly all such as occur also sporadically in West Saxon texts. A classification of the forms by P. G. Thomas will be found in the *Modern Language Review*, I, 202 etc. How difficult and uncertain all classification must be has been shown by Frederick Tupper (*Pub. Mod. Lang. Assoc. Amer.* XXVI, 235 etc.; *J.E.G.P.* XI, 82–9).

" Lichtenheld's Test."

Somewhat more definite results can be drawn from certain syntactical usages. There can be no doubt that as time went on, the use of *se, sēo, þæt* became more and more common in O.E. verse. This is largely due to the fact that in the older poems the *weak adjective + noun* appears frequently where we should now use the definite article: *wīsa fengel*—"the wise prince"; *se wīsa fengel* is used where some demonstrative is needed—"that wise prince." Later, however, *se, sēo, þæt* comes to be used in the common and vague sense in which the definite article is used in Modern English.

We consequently get with increasing frequency the use of the *definite article + weak adjective + noun*: whilst the usage *weak adjective + noun* decreases. Some rough criterion of date can thus be obtained by an examination of a poet's usage in this particular. Of course it would be absurd—as has been done—to group Old English poems in a strict chronological order according to the proportion of forms with and without the article. Individual usage must count for a good deal:

also the scribes in copying and recopying our text must to a considerable extent have obliterated the earlier practice. Metre and syntax combine to make it probable that, in line 9 of our poem, the scribe has inserted the unnecessary article *þāra* before *ymbsittendra*: and in the rare cases where we have an O.E. poem preserved in two texts, a comparison proves that the scribe has occasionally interpolated an article. But this later tendency to level out the peculiarity only makes it the more remarkable that we should find such great differences between O.E. poems, all of them extant in copies transcribed about the year 1000.

How great is the difference between the usage of *Beowulf* and that of the great body of Old English poetry will be clear from the following statistics.

The proportion of phrases containing the weak adjective + noun with and without the definite article in the certain works of Cynewulf is as follows[1]:

	With article	Without article
Juliana	27	3
Christ (II) ...	28	3
Elene	66	9

In *Guthlac* (A) (c. 750) the proportions are:

	With article	Without article
Guthlac (A) ...	42	6

Contrast this with the proportion in our poem:

	With article	Without article
Beowulf	13	65

The nearest approach to the proportions of *Beowulf* is in the (certainly very archaic)

	With article	Without article
Exodus	10	14

On the other hand, certain late texts show how fallible this criterion is. Anyone dating *Maldon* solely by "Lichtenheld's Test" would assuredly place it much earlier than 991.

---

[1] The brief *Fata Apostolorum* is doubted by Sievers (*Anglia*, XIII, 24).

It is easy to make a false use of grammatical statistics: and this test should only be applied with the greatest caution. But the difference between *Beowulf* and the works of Cynewulf is too striking to be overlooked. In *Beowulf*, to every five examples without the article (e.g. *heaðo-stēapa helm*) we have *one* with the article (e.g. *se hearda helm*): in Cynewulf to every five examples without the article we have *forty* with it.

A further test of antiquity is in the use of the weak adjective with the instrumental—a use which rapidly diminishes.

There are eighteen such instrumental phrases in *Beowulf* (3182 lines)[1]. In *Exodus* (589 lines) there are six examples[2] —proportionally more than in *Beowulf*. In Cynewulf's undoubted works (c. 2478 lines) there is one example only, *beorhtan reorde*[3].

This criterion of the absence of the definite article before the weak adjective is often referred to as Lichtenheld's Test (see article by him in *Z.f.d.A.* XVI, 325 *etc.*). It has been applied to the whole body of O.E. poetry by Barnouw (*Textcritische Untersuchungen*, 1902). The data collected by Barnouw are most valuable, but we must be cautious in the conclusions we draw, as is shown by Sarrazin (*Eng. Stud.* XXXVIII, 145 *etc.*), and Tupper (*Pub. Mod. Lang. Assoc.* XXVI, 274).

Exact enumeration of instances is difficult. For example, Lichtenheld gave 22 instances of definite article + weak adjective + noun in *Beowulf*[4]. But eight of these are not quite certain; *se gōda mǣg Hygelāces* may be not "the good kinsman of Hygelac," but "the good one—the kinsman of Hygelac," for there is the half line pause after *gōda*. These eight examples therefore should be deducted[5]. One instance, though practically certain, is the result of conjectural emendation[6]. Of the remaining thirteen[7] three are variations of the same phrase.

The statistics given above are those of Brandl (*Sitzungsberichte d. k. Preuss. Akad. d. Wissenschaften*, 1905, p. 719) which are based upon those of Barnouw.

"*Morsbach's Test.*"

Sievers' theories as to O.E. metre have not been accepted by all scholars in their entirety. But the statistics which he

---

[1] Two of these occur twice: *hātan heolfre*, 1423, 849: *nīowan stefne*, 1789, 2594; the rest once only, 141, 561, 963, 977, 1104, 1502, 1505, 1542, 1746 2102, 2290, 2347, 2440, 2482, 2492, 2692. See Barnouw, 51.
[2] 74, 99, 122, 257, 390, 412.   [3] *Christ*, 510.
[4] Lichtenheld omits 2011, *se mǣra mago Healfdenes*, inserting instead 1474, where the same phrase occurs, but with a vocative force.
[5] 758, 813, 2011, 2587, 2928, 2971, 2977, 3120.   [6] 1199.
[7] 102, 713, 919, 997, 1016, 1448, 1984, 2255, 2264, 2675, 3024, 3028, 3097.

collected enable us to say, with absolute certainty, that some given types of verse were not acceptable to the ear of an Old English bard.

Sceptics may emphasize the fact that Old English texts are uncertain, that nearly all poems are extant in one MS only, that the MS in each case was written down long after the poems were composed, and that precise verbal accuracy is therefore not to be expected[1]. All the more remarkable then becomes the fact, for it is a fact, that there are certain types of line which never occur in *Beowulf*, and that there are other types which are exceedingly rare. Again, there are certain types of line which *do* occur in *Beowulf* as we have it, though they seem contrary to the principles of O.E. scansion. When we find that such lines consistently contain some word which had a different metrical value when our extant MS of *Beowulf* was transcribed, from that which it had at the earlier date when *Beowulf* was composed, and that the earlier value makes the line metrical, the conclusion is obvious. *Beowulf* must have been composed at a time or in a dialect when the earlier metrical values held good.

But we reach a certain date beyond which, if we put the language back into its older form, it will no longer fit into the metrical structure. For example, words like *flōd*, *feld*, *eard* were originally "u-nouns": with nom. and acc. sing. *flōdu*, etc. But the half-line *ofer fealone flōd* (1950) becomes exceedingly difficult if we put it in the form *ofer fealone flōdu*[2]: the half-line *fīfelcynnes eard* becomes absolutely impossible in the form *fīfelcynnes eardu*[3].

It can, consequently, with some certainty be argued that these half-lines were composed after the time when *flōdu*, *eardu* had become *flōd*, *eard*. Therefore, it has been further argued, *Beowulf* was composed after that date. But are we justified in this further step—in assuming that because a certain number of half-lines in *Beowulf* must have been composed after a certain date, therefore *Beowulf* itself must have been composed after that date?

---

[1] Saintsbury in *Short History of English Literature*, I. 3.
[2] Morsbach, 270.　　　　　　　　[3] Morsbach, 271.

From what we know of the mechanical way in which the Old English *scribe* worked, we have no reason to suppose that he would have consistently altered what he found in an older copy, so as to make it metrical according to the later speech into which he was transcribing it. But if we go back to a time when poems were committed to memory by a *scop*, skilled in the laws of O.E. metre, the matter is very different. A written poem may be copied word for word, even though the spelling is at the same time modernized, but it is obvious that a poem preserved orally will be altered slightly from time to time, if the language in which it is written is undergoing changes which make the poem no longer metrically correct.

Imagine the state of things at the period when final *u* was being lost after a long syllable. This loss of a syllable would make a large number of the half-lines and formulas in the old poetry unmetrical. Are we to suppose that the whole of O.E. poetry was at once scrapped, and entirely new poems composed to fit in with the new sound laws? Surely not; old formulas would be recast, old lines modified where they needed it, but the old poetry would go on[1], with these minor verbal changes adapting it to the new order of things. We can see this taking place, to a limited extent, in the transcripts of Middle English poems. In the transmission of poems by word of mouth it would surely take place to such an extent as to baffle later investigation[2].

Consequently I am inclined to agree that this test is hardly final except "on the assumption that the poems were written down from the very beginning[3]." And we are clearly not justified in making any such assumption. A small number of such lines would accordingly give, not so much a means of fixing a period before which *Beowulf* cannot have been composed, as merely

---

[1] Chadwick, *Heroic Age*, 4.

[2] "Thus in place of the expression *to widan feore* we find occasionally *widan feore* in the same sense, and even in *Beowulf* we meet with *widan feorh*, which is not improbably the oldest form of the phrase. Before the loss of the final -*u* it [*widan feorhu*] would be a perfectly regular half verse, but the operation of this change would render it impossible and necessitate the substitution of a synonymous expression. In principle, it should be observed, the assumption of such substitutions seems to be absolutely necessary, unless we are prepared to deny that any old poems or even verses survived the period of apocope." Chadwick, *Heroic Age*, pp. 46–7.   [3] *Heroic Age*, 46.

one before which *Beowulf* cannot have been fixed by writing in its present form.

If, however, more elaborate investigation were to show that the *percentage* of such lines is *just as great* in *Beowulf* as it is in poems certainly written after the sound changes had taken place, it might be conceded that the test was a valid one, and that it proved *Beowulf* to belong to a period after these sound changes occurred.

This would then bring us to our second difficulty. At what date exactly did these sound changes take place? The chief documents available are the proper names in Bede's History, and in certain Latin charters, the glosses, and a few early runic inscriptions. Most important, although very scanty, are the charters, since they bear a date. With these we proceed to investigate:

A. The dropping of the *u* after a long accented syllable (*flódu* becoming *flód*), or semi-accented syllable (*Stánfòrdu* becoming *Stánfòrd*).

There is evidence from an Essex charter that this was already lost in 692 or 693 (*uuidmundesfelt*)[1]. From this date on, examples without the *u* are forthcoming in increasing number[2]. One certain example only has been claimed for the preservation of *u*. In the runic inscription on the "Franks casket" *flodu* is found for *flod*. But the spelling of the Franks casket is erratic: for example *giuþeasu* is also found for *giuþeas*, "the Jews." Now *u* here is impossible[3], and we must conclude perhaps that the inscriber of the runes intended to write *giuþea su[mæ]*[3] or *giuþea su[na]*[4], "some of the Jews," "the sons of the Jews," and that having reached the end of his line at *u*, he neglected to complete the word: or else perhaps that he wrote *giuþeas* and having some additional space added a *u* at the end of his line, just for fun. Whichever explanation we

---

[1] Birch, *Cart. Sax.* No. 81. See Morsbach, 260.

[2] The most important examples being *breguntford* (Birch, *Cart. Sax.* No. 115, dating between 693 and 731; perhaps 705): *heffled* in the life of St Gregory written by a Whitby monk apparently before 713: *-gar* on the Bewcastle Column, earlier than the end of the first quarter of the eighth century and perhaps much earlier: and many names in *ford* and *feld* in the Moore MS of Bede's *Ecclesiastical History* (a MS written about 737).

[3] An English Miscellany presented to Dr Furnivall, 370.

[4] Grienberger, *Anglia*, XXVII, 443.

adopt, it will apply to *flodu*, which equally comes at the end
of a line, and the *u* of which may equally have been part of
some following word which was never completed[1].

Other linguistic data of the Franks casket would lead us to
place it somewhere in the first half of the eighth century, and
we should hardly expect to find *u* preserved as late as this[2].
For we have seen that by 693 the *u* was already lost after a
subordinate accent in the Essex charter. Yet it is arguable
that the *u* was retained later after a long accented syllable
(*flódu*) than after a subordinate accent (*uuídmùndesfèlt*); and,
besides, the casket is Northumbrian, and the sound changes
need not have been simultaneous all over the country.

We cannot but feel that the evidence is pitifully scanty.
All we can say is that *perhaps* the *flodu* of the Franks casket
shows that *u* was still preserved after a fully accented syllable
as late as 700. But the *u* in *flodu* may be a deliberate archaism
on the part of the writer, may be a local dialectal survival,
may be a mere miswriting.

B. The preservation of *h* between consonant and vowel.

Here there is one clear example which we can date: the
archaic spelling of the proper name *Welhisc*. *Signum manus
uelhisci* occurs in a Kentish charter of 679[3]. The same charter
shows *h* already lost between vowels: *uuestan ae* (*ae* dative of
ēa, "river," cf. Gothic *ahwa*).

Not much can be argued from the proper name *Welhisc*, as
to the current pronunciation in Kent in 679, for an old man
may well have continued to spell his name as it was spelt when
he was a child, even though the current pronunciation had
changed[4]. But we have further evidence in the glosses, which
show *h* sometimes preserved and sometimes not. These
glosses are mechanical copies of an original which was presumably compiled between 680 and 720. We are therefore
justified in arguing that at that date *h* was still preserved, at
any rate occasionally.

---

[1] i.e. *flodu ahof* might stand for *flōd u[p] āhōf*, as is suggested by Chadwick, *Heroic Age*, 69.

[2] In the Franks casket *b* already appears as *f*, and the *u* of *sefu*, "seven," has been lost.   [3] Birch, *Cart. Sax.* No. 45.

[4] Chadwick, *Heroic Age*, 67: "In personal names we must clearly allow for traditional orthography." Morsbach admits this in another connection (p. 259).

Of "Morsbach's test" we can then say that it establishes something of an argument that *Beowulf* was composed after the date when final *u* after a long syllable, or *h* between consonant and vowel, was lost, and that this date was probably within a generation or so of the year 700 A.D. But there are too many uncertain contingencies involved to make the test at all a conclusive one.

Morsbach's *Zur Datierung des Beowulf-epos* will be found in the Göttingen *Nachrichten*, 1906, pp. 252–77. These tests have been worked out for the whole body of Old English poetry in the *Chronologische Studien* of Carl Richter, Halle, 1910.

SECTION III.   THEORIES AS TO THE STRUCTURE OF "BEOWULF."

Certain peculiarities in the structure of *Beowulf* can hardly fail to strike the reader. (1) The poem is not a biography of Beowulf, nor yet an episode in his life: it is two distinct episodes: the Grendel business and the dragon business, joined by a narrow bridge. (2) Both these stories are broken in upon by digressions: some of these concern Beowulf himself, so that we get a fairly complete idea of the life of our hero: but for the most part these digressions are not strictly apposite. (3) Even apart from these digressions, the narrative is often hampered: the poet begins his story, diverges and returns. (4) The traces of Christian thought and knowledge which meet us from time to time seem to belong to a different world from that of the Germanic life in which our poem has its roots.

Now in the middle of the nineteenth century it was widely believed that the great epics of the world had been formed from collections of original shorter lays fitted together (often unskilfully) by later redactors. For a critic starting from this assumption, better material than the *Beowulf* could hardly be found. And it *was* with such assumptions that Carl Müllenhoff, the greatest of the scholars who have dissected the *Beowulf*, set to work. He attended the lectures of Lachmann, and formed, a biographer tells us, the fixed resolve to do for one epic what his admired master had done for another[1].

Müllenhoff claimed for his theories that they were simple[2] and straightforward : and so they were, if we may be allowed to assume as a basis that the *Beowulf* is made up out of shorter lays, and that the only business of the critic is to define the scope of these lays. In the story of Beowulf's fight with Grendel (ll.194–836 : Müllenhoff's Sect. I) and with the dragon (ll. 2200–3183 : Müllenhoff's Sect. IV) Müllenhoff saw the much interpolated remains of two original lays by different authors. But, before it was united to the dragon story, the Grendel story, Müllenhoff held, had already undergone many interpolations and additions. The story of Grendel's mother (ll. 837–1623 : Sect. II) was added, Müllenhoff held, by one continuator as a sequel to the story of Grendel, and ll. 1–193 were added by another hand as an introduction. Then this Grendel story was finally rounded off by an interpolator (A) who added the account of Beowulf's return home (Sect. III, ll. 1629–2199) and at the same time inserted passages into the poem throughout. Finally came Interpolator B, who was the first to combine the Grendel story, thus elaborated, with the dragon story. Interpolator B was responsible for the great bulk of the interpolations : episodes from other cycles and "theologizing" matter.

Ten Brink, like Müllenhoff, regarded the poem as falling into four sections : the Grendel fight, the fight with Grendel's mother, the return home, the dragon fight. But Müllenhoff had imagined the epic composed out of one set of lays : incoherences, he thought, were due to the bungling of successive interpolators. Ten Brink assumed that in the case of all three fights, with Grendel, with Grendel's mother, and with the dragon, there had been two *parallel* versions, which a later redactor had combined together, and that it was to this combination that the frequent repetitions in the narra-

---

[1] Lübke's preface to Müllenhoff's *Beovulf*. Both the tendencies specially associated with Müllenhoff's name—the "mythologizing" and the "dissecting"— are due to the influence of Lachmann. It must be frankly admitted that on these subjects Müllenhoff did not begin his studies with an open mind.
[2] "Es ist einfach genug"—*Beovulf*, 110.

tive were due: he believed that not only were the different episodes of the poem originally distinct, but that each episode was compounded of two originally distinct lays, combined together.

Now it cannot be denied that the process postulated by Müllenhoff *might* have taken place: a lay on Grendel and a lay on the dragon-fight might have been combined by some later compiler. Ten Brink's theory, too, is inherently not improbable: that there should have been two or more versions current of a popular story is probable enough: that a scribe should have tried to fit these two parallel versions together is not without precedent: very good examples of such attempts at harmonizing different versions can be got from an examination of the MSS of *Piers Plowman*.

It is only here and there that we are struck by an inherent improbability in Müllenhoff's scheme. Thus the form in which Müllenhoff assumes the poem to have existed before Interpolator A set to work on it, is hardly a credible one. The "original poet" has brought Beowulf from his home to the Danish court, to slay Grendel, and the "continuator" has taken him to the haunted lake: Beowulf has plunged down, slain Grendel's mother, come back to land. Here Müllenhoff believed the poem to have ended, until "Interpolator A" came along, and told how Beowulf returned in triumph to Hrothgar, was thanked and rewarded, and then betook himself home, and was welcomed by Hygelac. That it would have been left to an interpolator to supply what from the old point of view was so necessary a part of the story as the return to Hrothgar is an assumption perilous indeed. "An epic poem only closes when everything is really concluded: not, like a modern novel, at a point where the reader can imagine the rest for himself[1]."

Generally speaking, however, the theories of the "dissecting school" are not in themselves faulty, if we admit the assumptions on which they rest. They fail however in two ways. An examination of the short lay and the long epic, so far as these are represented in extant documents, does not bear out

[1] Möller, *V.E.* 140: cf. Schücking, *B.R.* 14.

well the assumptions of the theorizers. Secondly, the minute scrutiny to which the poem has been subjected in matters of syntax, metre, dialect and tradition has failed to show any difference between the parts attributed to the different authors, such as we must certainly have expected to find, had the theories of the "dissecting school" been correct.

That behind our extant *Beowulf*, and connecting it with the events of the sixth century, there must have been a number of older lays, may indeed well be admitted: also that to these lays our poem owes its plot, its traditions of metre and its phraseology, and perhaps (but this is a perilous assumption) continuous passages of its text. But what Müllenhoff and ten Brink go on to assume is that these original oral lays were simple in outline and treated a single well-defined episode in a straightforward manner; that later redactors and scribes corrupted this primitive simplicity; but that the modern critic, by demanding it, and using its presence or absence as a criterion, can still disentangle from the complex composite poem the simpler elements out of which it was built up.

Here are rather large assumptions. What right have we to postulate that this primitive "literature without letters[1]," these short oral ballads and lays, dealt with a single episode without digression or confusion: whilst the later age,—the civilized, Christianized age of written literature during which *Beowulf* in the form in which we now have it was produced, —is assumed to have been tolerant of both?

No doubt, here and there, in different literatures, groups of short lays can be found which one can imagine might be combined into an orderly narrative poem, without much hacking about. But on the other hand a short lay will often tell, in less than a hundred lines, a story more complex than that of the *Iliad* or the *Odyssey*. Its shortness may be due, not to any limitation in the scope of the plot, but rather to the passionate haste with which it rushes through a long story. It is one thing to admit that there must have been short lays on the story of Beowulf: it is another to assume that these lays were of such a character that nothing was needed but compilers

[1] Earle, *Deeds of Beowulf,* xlix (an excellent criticism of Müllenhoff).

with a taste for arrangement and interpolation in order to turn them into the extant epic of *Beowulf.*

When we find nearly five hundred lines spent in describing the reception of the hero in Hrothgar's land, we may well doubt whether this passage can have found its way into our poem through any such process of fitting together as Müllenhoff postulated. It would be out of scale in any narrative shorter than the *Beowulf* as we have it. It suggests to us that the epic is developed out of the lay, not by a process of fitting together, but rather by a retelling of the story in a more leisurely way.

A comparison of extant short lays or ballads with extant epics has shown that, if these epics were made by stringing lays together, such lays must have been different from the great majority of the short lays now known. "The lays into which this theory dissects the epics, or which it assumes as the sources of the epics, differ in two ways from extant lays: they deal with short, incomplete subjects and they have an epic breadth of style[1]."

It has been shown by W. P. Ker[2] that a comparison of such fragments as have survived of the Germanic short lay (*Finnsburg, Hildebrand*) does not bear out the theory that the epic is a conglomeration of such lays. "It is the change and development in style rather than any increase in the complexity of the themes that accounts for the difference in scale between the shorter and the longer poems."

A similar conclusion is reached by Professor Hart: "It might be illuminating to base a *Liedertheorie* in part, at least, upon a study of existing *Lieder*, rather than wholly upon an attempt to dismember the epic in question. Such study reveals indeed a certain similarity in kind of Ballad and Epic, but it reveals at the same time an enormous difference in degree, in stage of development. If the *Beowulf*, then, was made up of a series of heroic songs, strung together with little or no modification, these songs must have been something very different from the popular ballad[3]."

---

[1] Heusler, *Lied u. Epos,* 26.   [2] *Epic and Romance,* Chap. II, § 2.
[3] *Ballad and Epic,* 311–12.

And subsequent investigations into the history and folk-lore of our poem have not confirmed Müllenhoff's theory: in some cases indeed they have hit it very hard. When a new light was thrown upon the story by the discovery of the parallels between *Beowulf* and the *Grettis saga*, it became clear that passages which Müllenhoff had condemned as otiose interpolations were likely to be genuine elements in the tale. Dr Olrik's minute investigations into the history of the Danish kings have shown from yet another point of view how allusions, which were rashly condemned by Müllenhoff and ten Brink as idle amplifications, are, in fact, essential.

How the investigation of the metre, form, and syntax of *Beowulf* has disclosed an archaic strictness of usage has been explained above (Sect. II). This usage is in striking contrast with the practice of later poets like Cynewulf. How far we are justified in relying upon such differences of usage as criteria of *exact* date is open to dispute. But it seems clear that, had Müllenhoff's theories been accurate, we might reasonably have expected to have been able to differentiate between the earlier and the later strata in so composite a poem.

The composite theory has lately been strongly supported by Schücking[1]. Schücking starts from the fact, upon which we are all agreed, that the poem falls into two main divisions: the story of how Beowulf at Heorot slew Grendel and Grendel's mother, and the story of the dragon, which fifty years later he slew at his home. These are connected by the section which tells how Beowulf returned from Heorot to his own home and was honourably received by his king, Hygelac.

It is now admitted that the ways of Old English narrative were not necessarily our ways, and that we must not postulate, because our poem falls into two somewhat clumsily connected sections, that therefore it is compounded out of two originally distinct lays. But, on the other hand, as Schücking rightly urges, instances *are* forthcoming of two O.E. poems having been clumsily connected into one[2]. Therefore, whilst no one would now urge that *Beowulf* is put together out of two older

---

[1] *Beowulfs Rückkehr*, 1905. [2] e.g. *Genesis.*

lays, *merely* because it can so easily be divided into two sections, this fact does suggest that a case exists for examination.

Now if a later poet had connected together two old lays, one on the Grendel and Grendel's mother business, and one on the dragon business, we might fairly expect that this connecting link would show traces of a different style. It is accordingly on the connecting link, the story of *Beowulf's Return* and reception by Hygelac, that Schücking concentrates his attention, submitting it to the most elaborate tests to see if it betrays metrical, stylistic or syntactical divergences from the rest of the poem.

Various tests are applied, which admittedly give no result, such as the frequency of the repetition in the *Return* of half verse formulas which occur elsewhere in *Beowulf*[1], or the way in which compound nouns fit into the metrical scheme[2]. Metrical criteria are very little more helpful[3]. We have seen that the antiquity of *Beowulf* is proved by the cases where metre demands the substitution of an older uncontracted form for the existing shorter one. Schücking argues that no instance occurs in the 267 lines of the *Return*. But, even if this were the case, it might well be mere accident, since examples only occur at rare intervals anywhere in *Beowulf*. As a matter of fact, however, examples are to be found in the *Return*[4] (quite up to the normal proportion), though two of the clearest come in a portion of it which Schücking rather arbitrarily excludes.

Coming to syntax in its broadest sense, and especially the method of constructing and connecting sentences, Schücking enumerates several constructions which are found in the *Return*, but not elsewhere in *Beowulf*. Syntax is a subject to which he has given special study, and his opinion upon it must be of value. But I doubt whether anyone as expert in the subject as Schücking could not find in every passage of like length in *Beowulf* some constructions not to be exactly paralleled elsewhere in the poem.

---

[1] Chap. IV pp. 29–33.   [2] Chap. V, pp. 34–41.
[3] Chap. VI, cf. esp. p. 50.
[4] In the portion which Schücking excludes, we twice have *gæð = gáið* (2034, 2055). Elsewhere in the *Return* we have *dōn = dōan* (2166) whilst *frēa* (1934), *Hondsciŏ* (2076) need to be considered.

The fact that we find here, and here only, passages introduced by the clauses *ic sceal forð sprecan*[1], and *tō lang ys tō reccenne*[2], is natural when we realize that we have here the longest speech in the whole poem, which obviously calls for such apologies for prolixity.

The fact that no parentheses occur in the *Return* does not differentiate it from the rest of *Beowulf*: for, as Schücking himself points out elsewhere, there are three other passages in the poem, longer than the *Return*, which are equally devoid of parentheses[3].

There remain a few *hapax legomena*[4], but very inconclusive.

There are, in addition, examples which occur only in the *Return*, and in certain other episodic passages. These episodic passages also, Schücking supposes, may have been added by the same reviser who added the *Return*. But this is a perilous change of position. For example, a certain peculiarity is found only in the *Return* and the introductory genealogical section[5]; or in the *Return* and the *Finn Episode*[6]. But when Schücking proceeds to the suggestion that the *Introduction* or the *Finn Episode* may have been added by the same reviser who added *Beowulf's Return*, he knocks the bottom out of some of his previous arguments. The argument from the absence of parentheses (whatever it was worth) must go: for according to Schücking's own punctuation, such parentheses are found both in the *Introduction* and in the *Finn Episode*. If these are by the author of the *Return*, then doubt is thrown upon one of the alleged peculiarities of that author; we find the author of the *Return* no more averse *on the whole* to parentheses than the author or authors of the rest of the poem.

Peculiar usages of the moods and tenses are found twice in the *Return*[7], and once again in the episode where Beowulf

<hr>

[1] 2069. [2] 2093.

[3] *Satzverknüpfung im Beowulf*, 139.

[4] *þȳlæs* = "lest" (1918); *ac* in direct question (1990); *þā* occurring unsupported late in the sentence (2192); *forþām* (1957) [see Sievers in *P.B.B.* xxix, 313]; *swā* = "since," "because" (2184). But Schücking admits in his edition two other instances of *forþām* (146 and 2645), so this can hardly count.

[5] *hȳrde ic* as introducing a statement, 62, 2163, 2172; *sið ðan ǣrest*, 6, 1947.

[6] A similar use of *þā*, 1078, 1988; cf. 1114, 1125, 2135.

[7] *hæbbe*, 1928; *gēong*, 2019.

recalls his youth[1]. Supposing this episode to be also the work of the author of the *Return*, we get peculiar constructions used three times by this author, which cannot be paralleled elsewhere in *Beowulf*[2].

Now a large number of instances like this last might afford basis for argument; but they must be in bulk in order to prove anything. By the laws of chance we might expect, in any passage of three hundred lines, taken at random anywhere in *Beowulf*, to find something which occurred only in one other passage elsewhere in the poem. We cannot forthwith declare the two passages to be the work of an interpolator. One swallow does not make a summer.

And the arguments as to style are not helped by arguments as to matter. Even if it be granted—which I do not grant—that the long repetition narrating Beowulf's contest with Grendel and Grendel's mother is tedious, there is no reason why this tedious repetition should not as well be the work of the original poet as of a later reviser. Must we find many different authors for *The Ring and the Book*? It must be granted that there are details (such as the mention of Grendel's glove) found in the Grendel struggle as narrated in *Beowulf's Return*, but not found in the original account of the struggle. Obviously the object is to avoid monotony, by introducing a new feature: but this might as well have been aimed at by the old poet retelling the tale as by a new poet retelling it.

To me, the fact that so careful and elaborate a study of the story of *Beowulf's Return* fails to betray any satisfactory evidence of separate authorship, is a confirmation of the verdict of "not proven" against the "dividers[3]." But there can be no doubt that Schücking's method, his attempt to prove differences in treatment, grammar, and style, is the right one. If any satisfactory results are to be attained, it must be in this way.

---

[1] *þurfe*, 2495. [2] Schücking, Chap. VIII.
[3] Cf. Brandl in Herrigs *Archiv*, cxv, 421 (1905).

SECTION IV. ARE THE CHRISTIAN ELEMENTS INCOMPATIBLE
WITH THE REST OF THE POEM?

Later students (like the man in Dante, placed between
two equally enticing dishes) have been unable to decide in
favour of either of the rival theories of Müllenhoff and ten
Brink, and consequently the unity of the poem, which always
had its champions, has of late years come to be maintained
with increasing conviction and certainty.

Yet many recent critics have followed Müllenhoff so far at
least as to believe that the Christian passages are inconsistent
with what they regard as the "essentially heathen" tone of
the rest of the poem, and are therefore the work of an interpolator[1].

Certainly no one can escape a feeling of incongruity, as he
passes from ideas of which the home lies in the forests of ancient
Germany, to others which come from the Holy Land. But that
both sets of ideas could not have been cherished, in England,
about the year 700, by one and the same poet, is an assumption
which calls for examination.

As Christianity swept northward, situations were created
which to the modern student are incongruous. But the
Teutonic chief often had a larger mind than the modern student:
he needed to have, if he was to get the best at the same time
both from his wild fighting men and from his Latin clerks.
It is this which gives so remarkable a character to the great
men of the early centuries of converted Teutonism: men, like
Theodoric the Great or Charles the Great, who could perform
simultaneously the duties of a Germanic king and of a Roman
Emperor: kings like Alfred the Great or St Olaf, who combined
the character of the tough fighting chieftain with that of the
saintly churchman. I love to think of these incongruities: to
remember that the warrior Alfred, surrounded by *thegn* and
gesith, listening to the "Saxon songs" which he loved, was yet
the same Alfred who painfully translated Gregory's *Pastoral*

---

[1] e.g. Blackburn in *Pub. Mod. Lang. Assoc. Amer.* XII, 204–225; Bradley
in the *Encyc. Brit.* III, 760; Chadwick, *H.A.* 49; Clarke, *Sidelights*, 10.

Care under the direction of foreign clerics. It is well to remember that Charles the Great, the catholic and the orthodox,
collected ancient lays which his successors thought too heathen
to be tolerated; or that St Olaf (who was so holy that, having
absent mindedly chipped shavings off a stick on Sunday, he
burnt them, as penance, on his open hand) nevertheless allowed
to be sung before him, on the morning of his last fight, one of
the most wild and utterly heathen of all the old songs—the
Bjarkamál.

It has been claimed that the account of the funeral rites of
Beowulf is such as "no Christian poet could or would have
composed[1]." Lately this argument has been stated more at
length:

> "In the long account of Beowulf's obsequies—beginning with the
> dying king's injunction to construct for him a lofty barrow on the
> edge of the cliff, and ending with the scene of the twelve princes
> riding round the barrow, proclaiming the dead man's exploits—we
> have the most detailed description of an early Teutonic funeral which
> has come down to us, and one of which the accuracy is confirmed in
> every point by archaeological or contemporary literary evidence[2].
> Such an account must have been composed within living memory of
> a time when ceremonies of this kind were still actually in use[3]."

Owing to the standing of the scholar who urges it, this
argument is coming to rank as a dogma[4], and needs therefore
rather close examination.

Professor Chadwick *may* be right in urging that the custom
of burning the dead had gone out of use in England even before
Christianity was introduced[5]: anyhow it is certain that, wher-
ever it survived, the practice was disapproved by ecclesiastics,
and was, indeed, formally censured and suppressed by the
church abroad.

The church equally censured and endeavoured to suppress
the ancient "heathen lays"; but without equal success. Now,
in many of these lays the heathen rites of cremation must
certainly have been depicted, and, in this way, the memory
of the old funeral customs must have been kept fresh, long

---

[1] Chadwick, in *Cambridge History,* I, 30.
[2] We may refer especially to the account of Attila's funeral given by
Jordanes. [Mr Chadwick's note.]   [3] Chadwick in *The Heroic Age,* 53.
[4] It is adopted, e.g., by Clarke, *Sidelights,* 8.
[5] Yet this is very doubtful: see Leeds, *Archæology,* 27, 74.

after the last funeral pyre had died out in England. Of course there were then, as there have been ever since, puritanical people who objected that heathen lays and heathen ways were no fit concern for a Christian man. But the protests of such purists are just the strongest evidence that the average Christian did continue to take an interest in these things. We have seen that the very monks of Lindisfarne had to be warned by Alcuin. I cannot see that there is any such *a priori* impossibility that a poet, though a sincere Christian enough, would have described a funeral in the old style, modelling his account upon older lays, or upon tradition derived from those lays.

The church might disapprove of the practice of cremation, but we have no reason to suppose that mention of it was tabooed. And many of the old burial customs seem to have kept their hold, even upon the converted. Indeed, when the funeral of Attila is instanced as a type of the old heathen ceremony, it seems to be forgotten that those Gothic chieftains who rode their horses round the body of Attila were themselves probably Arian Christians, and that the historian who has preserved the account was an orthodox cleric.

Saxo Grammaticus, ecclesiastic as he was, has left us several accounts[1] of cremations. He mentions the "pyre built of ships" and differs from the poet of *Beowulf* chiefly because he allows those frankly heathen references to gods and offerings which the poet of *Beowulf* excludes. Of course, Saxo was merely translating. One can quite believe that a Christian poet composing an account of a funeral in the old days, would have omitted the more frankly heathen features, as indeed the *Beowulf* poet does. But Saxo shows us how far into Christian times the ancient funeral, in all its heathendom, was remembered; and how little compunction an ecclesiastic had in recording it. The assumption that no Christian poet would have composed the account of Beowulf's funeral or of Scyld's funeral ship, seems then to be quite unjustified.

The further question remains: Granting that he *would*, could he? Is the account of Beowulf's funeral so true to old custom that it must have been composed by an eye-witness of

[1] Notably in Book VIII (ed. Holder. 264) and Book III (ed. Holder, 74).

the rite of cremation? Is its "accuracy confirmed in every point by archaeological or contemporary literary evidence"?

As to the archaeological evidence, the fact seems to be that the account is archaeologically so inexact that it has given great trouble to one eminent antiquary, Knut Stjerna. That the pyre should be hung with arms, which are *burnt* with the hero (ll. 3139–40), and that then a second supply of unburnt treasures should be *buried* with the cremated bones (ll. 3163–8), is regarded by Stjerna as extraordinary[1].

Surely, any such inexactitude is what we should expect in a late poet, drawing upon tradition. He would know that in heathen times bodies were burnt, and that weapons were buried; and he might well combine both. It is not necessary to suppose, as Stjerna does, that the poet has combined two separate accounts of Beowulf's funeral, given in older lays, in one of which the hero was burnt, and in the other buried. But the fact that an archaeological specialist finds the account of Beowulf's funeral so inexact that he has to assume a confused and composite source, surely disposes of the argument that it is so exact that it must date back to heathen times.

As to confirmation from literary documents, the only one instanced by Chadwick is the account of the funeral of Attila. The parallel here is by no means so close as has been asserted. The features of Attila's funeral are: the lying in state, during which the chosen horsemen of the nation rode round the body singing the dead king's praises; the funeral feast; and the burial (not burning) of the body. Now the only feature which recurs in *Beowulf* is the praise of the dead man by the mounted thanes. Even here there is an essential difference. Attila's men rode round the dead body of their lord *before* his funeral. Beowulf's retainers ride and utter their lament around (not the body but) the grave mound of their lord, ten days after the cremation.

And this is perhaps no accidental discrepancy: it may well correspond to a real difference in practice between the Gothic custom of the time of the migrations and the Anglo-Saxon

---

[1] 'Fasta fornlämningar i Beowulf,' in *Ant. Tidskrift för Sverige*, XVIII, 4, 64.

practice as it prevailed in Christian times[1]. For many documents, including the *Dream of the Rood*, tend to show that the
sorhlēoð, the lament of the retainers for their dead lord, survived
into Christian times, but as a ceremony which was subsequent
not merely to the funeral, but even to the building of the tomb.

So that, here again, so far from the archaeological accuracy
of the account of Beowulf's funeral being confirmed by the
account of that of Attila, we find a discrepancy such as we
might expect if a Christian poet, in later times, had tried to
describe a funeral of the old heathen type.

Of course, the evidence is far too scanty to allow of much
positive argument. Still, *so far as it goes*, and that is not far,
it rather tends to show that the account of the funeral customs
is not quite accurate, representing what later Christian times
knew by tradition of the rite of cremation, rather than showing
the observation of that rite by an eye-witness.

We must turn, then, to some other argument, if we wish to
prove that the Christian element is inconsistent with other
parts of the poem.

A second argument that *Beowulf* must belong either to
heathen times, or to the very earliest Christian period in
England, has been found in the character of the Christian
allusions: they contain no "reference to Christ, to the Cross,
to the Virgin or the Saints, to any doctrine of the church in
regard to the Trinity, the Atonement, *etc.*[2]" "A pious Jew
would have no difficulty in assenting to them all[3]." Hence it
has been argued[4] that they are the work of an interpolator who,
working upon a poem "essentially heathen," was not able to
impose upon it more than this "vague and colourless Christianity." I cannot see this. If passages had to be rewritten
at all, it was just as easy to rewrite them in a tone emphatically
Christian as in a tone mildly so. The difficulties which the
interpolator would meet in removing a heathen phrase, and
composing a Christian half-line in substitution, would be
metrical, rather than theological. For example, in a second

[1] See Schücking, *Das angelsächsische Totenklaglied*, in *Engl. Stud.* xxxix, 1–13.
[2] Blackburn, in *Pub. Mod. Lang. Assoc. Amer.* Cf. Hart, *Ballad and Epic*, 175
[3] Clark Hall, xlvii.   [4] Blackburn, as above, p. 126.

half-line the interpolator could have written *ond hālig Crist* or *ylda nergend* just as easily as *ond hālig god*, or *ylda waldend*: he could have put in an allusion to the Trinity or to the Cross as easily as to the Lord of Hosts or the King of Glory. It would depend upon the alliteration which was the more convenient. And surely, if he was a monk deliberately sitting down to turn a heathen into a Christian poem, he would, of two alternatives, have favoured the more dogmatically Christian.

The vagueness which is so characteristic of the Christian references in *Beowulf* can then hardly be due to the poem having originally been a heathen one, worked over by a Christian.

Others have seen in this vagueness a proof "that the minstrels who introduced the Christian element had but a vague knowledge of the new faith[1]": or that the poem was the work of "a man who, without having, or wanting to have, much definite instruction, had become Christian because the Court had newly become Christian[2]." But, vague as it is, does the Christianity of *Beowulf* justify such a judgment as this? Do not the characters of Hrothgar or of Beowulf, of Hygd or of Wealhtheow, show a Christian influence which, however little dogmatic, is anything but superficial? This is a matter where individual feeling rather than argument must weigh: but the *Beowulf* does not seem to me the work of a man whose adherence to Christianity is merely nominal[3].

And, so far as the absence of dogma goes, it seems to have been overlooked that the Christian references in the *Battle of Maldon*, written when England had been Christian for over three centuries, are precisely of the same vague character as those in *Beowulf*.

Surely the explanation is that to a devout, but not theo-

---

[1] Chadwick, in *Cambridge History*, I, 30.
[2] Clark Hall, xlvii. See, to the contrary, Klaeber in *Anglia*, xxxvi, 196.
[3] This point is fully developed by Brandl, 1002–3. As Brandl points out, if we want to find a parallel to the hero Beowulf, saving his people from their temporal and ghostly foes, we must look, not to the other heroes of Old English heroic poetry, such as Waldhere or Hengest, but to Moses in the Old English *Exodus*. [Since this was written the essentially Christian character of *Beowulf* has been further, and I think finally, demonstrated by Klaeber, in the last section of his article on *Die Christlichen Elemente im Beowulf*, in *Anglia*, xxxvi; see especially 194–199.]

logically-minded poet, writing battle poetry, references to God as the Lord of Hosts or the Giver of Victory came naturally —references to the Trinity or the Atonement did not. This seems quite a sufficient explanation; though it may be that in *Beowulf* the poet has consciously avoided dogmatic references, because he realized that the characters in his story were not Christians[1]. That, at the same time, he allows those characters with whom he sympathizes to speak in a Christian spirit is only what we should expect. Just so Chaucer allows his pagans—Theseus for instance—to use Christian expressions about God or the soul, whilst avoiding anything strikingly doctrinal.

Finally I cannot admit that the Christian passages are "poetically of no value[2]." The description of Grendel nearing Heorot is good:

> Ðā cōm of mōre under mist-hleoþum
> Grendel gongan—

but it is heightened when the poet adds:

> Godes yrre bær.

Yet here again it is impossible to argue: it is a matter of individual feeling.

When, however, we come to the further statement of Dr Bradley, that the Christian passages are not only interpolations poetically worthless, but "may be of any date down to that of the extant MS" (i.e. about the year 1000 A.D.), we have reached ground where argument *is* possible, and where definite results can be attained. For Dr Bradley, at the same time that he makes this statement about the character of the Christian passages, also quotes the archaic syntax of *Beowulf* as proving an early date[3]. *But this archaic syntax is just as prominent a feature of the Christian passages as of any other parts of the poem.* If these Christian passages are really the work of a "monkish copyist, whose piety exceeded his poetic powers[4]," how do they come to show an antique syntax and a strict technique surpassing those of Cynewulf or the *Dream*

---

[1] Cf. *Beowulf*, ll. 180 etc.
[2] Bradley, in *Encyc. Brit.*
[3] Bradley, in *Encyc. Brit.* III, 760–1.
[4] Blackburn, 218.

of the Rood? Why do they not betray their origin by metrical inaccuracies such as we find in poems undoubtedly interpolated, like *Widsith* or the *Seafarer*?

Dr Bradley is "our chief English seer in these matters," as Dr Furnivall said long ago; and it is only with the greatest circumspection that one should differ from any of his conclusions. Nevertheless, I feel that, before we can regard any portion of *Beowulf* as later than the rest, discrepancies need to be demonstrated.

Until such discrepancies between the different parts of *Beowulf* can be demonstrated, we are justified in regarding the poem as homogeneous: as a production of the Germanic world enlightened by the new faith. Whether through external violence or internal decay, this world was fated to rapid change, and perished with its promise unfulfilled. The great merit of *Beowulf* as a historic document is that it shows us a picture of a period in which the virtues of the heathen "Heroic Age" were tempered by the gentleness of the new belief; an age warlike, yet Christian: devout, yet tolerant.

PART II

DOCUMENTS ILLUSTRATING THE STORIES IN *BEOWULF,* AND THE *OFFA*-SAGA.

A. The early Kings of the Danes according to Saxo Grammaticus

Saxo, Book I, ed. Ascensius, fol. iii b ; ed. Holder, p. 10, l. 25.

Uerum a Dan, ut fert antiquitas, regum nostrorum stemmata, ceu quodam deriuata principio, splendido successionis ordine profluxerunt. Huic filii Humblus et Lotherus fuere, ex Grytha, summæ inter Teutones dignitatis matrona, suscepti. Lecturi regem ueteres affixis humo saxis insistere, suffragiaque promere consueuerant, subiectorum lapidum firmitate facti constantiam ominaturi. Quo ritu Humblus, decedente patre, nouo patriæ beneficio rex creatus, sequentis fortunæ malignitate, ex rege priuatus euasit. Bello siquidem a Lothero captus, regni depositione spiritum mercatus est; hæc sola quippe uicto salutis conditio reddebatur. Ita fraternis iniuriis imperium abdicare coactus, documentum hominibus præbuit, ut plus splendoris, ita minus securitatis, aulis quam tuguriis inesse. Ceterum iniuriæ tam patiens fuit, ut honoris damno tanquam beneficio gratulari crederetur, sagaciter, ut puto, regiæ conditionis habitum contemplatus. Sed nec Lotherus tolerabiliorem regem quam militem egit, ut prorsus insolentia ac scelere regnum auspicari uideretur; siquidem illustrissimum quemque uita aut opibus spoliare, patriamque bonis ciuibus uacuefacere probitatis loco duxit, regni æmulos ratus, quos nobilitate pares habuerat. Nec diu scelerum impunitus, patriæ consternatione perimitur; eadem spiritum eripiente, quæ regnum largita fuerat.

Cuius filius Skyoldus naturam ab ipso, non mores sortitus, per summam tenerioris ætatis industriam cuncta paternæ contagionis uestigia ingeniti erroris deuio præteribat. Igitur ut a paternis uitiis prudenter desciuit, ita auitis uirtutibus feliciter respondit, remotiorem pariter ac præstantiorem hereditarii moris portionem amplexus. Huius adolescentia inter paternos uenatores immanis beluæ subactione insignis extitit, mirandoque rei euentu futuræ eius fortitudinis habitum ominata est. Nam cum a tutoribus forte, quorum summo studio educabatur, inspectandæ uenationis licentiam impetrasset, obuium sibi insolitæ granditatis ursum, telo uacuus, cingulo, cuius usum habebat, religandum curauit, necandumque comitibus præbuit. Sed et complures spectatæ fortitudinis pugiles per idem tempus uiritim ab eo superati produntur, e quibus Attalus et Scatus clari illustresque fuere. Quindecim annos natus, inusitato corporis incremento perfectissimum humani roboris specimen præferebat, tantaque indolis eius experimenta fuere, ut ab ipso ceteri Danorum reges communi quodam uocabulo Skioldungi nuncuparentur...

Saxo then relates the adventures of Gram, Hadingus and Frotho, whom he represents as respectively son, grandson and great-grandson of Skioldus. That Gram and Hadingus are interpolated in the family is shewn by the fact that the pedigree of Sweyn Aageson passes direct from Skiold to his son Frothi.

Saxo, Book II, ed. Ascensius, fol. xi b; ed. Holder, p. 38, l. 4.

Hadingo filius Frotho succedit, cuius uarii insignesque casus fuere. Pubertatis annos emensus, iuuenilium præferebat complementa uirtutum, quas ne desidiæ corrumpendas præberet, abstractum uoluptatibus animum assidua armorum intentione torquebat. Qui cum, paterno thesauro bellicis operibus absumpto, stipendiorum facultatem, qua militem aleret, non haberet, attentiusque necessarii usus subsidia circunspiceret, tali subeuntis indigenæ carmine concitatur:

Insula non longe est præmollibus edita cliuis,
Collibus æra tegens et opimæ conscia prædæ.
Hic tenet eximium, montis possessor, aceruum

Implicitus giris serpens crebrisque reflexus
Orbibus, et caudæ sinuosa uolumina ducens,
Multiplicesque agitans spiras, uirusque profundens.
Quem superare uolens clypeo, quo conuenit uti,
Taurinas intende cutes, corpusque bouinis
Tergoribus tegito, nec amaro nuda ueneno
Membra patere sinas; sanies, quod conspuit, urit.
Lingua trisulca micans patulo licet ore resultet,
Tristiaque horrifico minitetur uulnera rictu,
Intrepidum mentis habitum retinere memento.
Nec te permoueat spinosi dentis acumen,
Nec rigor, aut rapida iactatum fauce uenenum.
Tela licet temnat uis squamea, uentre sub imo
Esse locum scito, quo ferrum mergere fas est;
Hunc mucrone petens medium rimaberis anguem.
Hinc montem securus adi, pressoque ligone
Perfossos scrutare cauos; mox ære crumenas
Imbue, completamque reduc ad littora puppim.

Credulus Frotho solitarius in insulam traiicit: ne comitatior beluam adoriretur, quam athletas aggredi moris fuerat. Quæ cum aquis pota specum repeteret, impactum Frothonis ferrum aspero cutis horrore contempsit. Sed et spicula, quæ in eam coniecta fuerant, eluso mittentis conatu læsionis irrita resultabant. At ubi nil tergi duritia cessit, uentris curiosius annotati mollities ferro patuit. Quæ se morsu ulcisci cupiens, clypeo duntaxat spinosum oris acumen impegit. Crebris deinde linguam micatibus ducens, uitam pariter ac uirus efflauit.

Repertæ pecuniæ regem locupletem fecere...

Saxo, Book II, ed. Ascensius, fol. xv b; ed. Holder, p. 51, l. 4.

His, uirtute paribus, æqua regnandi incessit auiditas. Imperii cuique cura extitit; fraternus nullum respectus astrinxit. Quem enim nimia sui caritas ceperit, aliena deserit: nec sibi quisquam ambitiose atque aliis amice consulere potest. Horum maximus Haldanus, Roe et Scato fratribus interfectis, naturam scelere polluit: regnum parricidio carpsit. Et ne ullum crudelitatis exemplum omitteret, comprehensos eorum fautores prius

uinculorum pœna coercuit, mox suspendio consumpsit. Cuius
ex eo maxime fortuna ammirabilis fuit, quod, licet omnia
temporum momenta ad exercenda atrocitatis officia contulisset,
senectute uitam, non ferro, finierit. Huius filii Roe et Helgo fuere. A Roe Roskildia condita
memoratur: quam postmodum Sueno, furcatæ barbæ cogno-
mento clarus, ciuibus auxit, amplitudine propagauit. Hic
breui angustoque corpore fuit: Helgonem habitus procerior
cepit. Qui, diuiso cum fratre regno, maris possessionem sortitus,
regem Sclauiæ Scalcum maritimis copiis lacessitum oppressit.
Quam cum in prouinciam redegisset, uarios pelagi recessus uago
nauigationis genere perlustrabat.

Saxo, Book II, ed. Ascensius, fol. xvi a; ed. Holder, p. 53, l. 16.

Huic filius Roluo succedit, uir corporis animique dotibus
uenustus, qui staturæ magnitudinem pari uirtutis habitu com-
mendaret.

Ibid., ed. Ascensius, fol. xvii a; ed. Holder, p. 55, l. 40.

Per idem tempus Agnerus quidam, Ingelli filius, sororem
Roluonis, Rutam nomine, matrimonio ducturus, ingenti conuiuio nuptias instruit. In quo cum pugiles, omni petulantiæ
genere debacchantes, in Ialtonem quendam nodosa passim ossa
coniicerent, accidit, ut eius consessor, Biarco nomine, iacientis
errore uehementem capite ictum exciperet. Qui dolore pariter
ac ludibrio lacessitus, osse inuicem in iacientem remisso, frontem
eius in occuput reflexit, idemque loco frontis intorsit, transuer-
sum hominis animum uultus obliquitate mulctando. Ea res
contumeliosam ioci insolentiam temperauit, pugilesque regia
abire coegit. Qua conuiuii iniuria permotus, sponsus ferro cum
Biarcone decernere statuit, uiolatæ hilaritatis ultionem duelli
nomine quæsiturus. In cuius ingressu, utri prior feriendi copia
deberetur diutule certatum est. Non enim antiquitus in edendis
agonibus crebræ ictuum uicissitudines petebantur: sed erat cum
interuallo temporis etiam feriendi distincta successio; rarisque
sed atrocibus plagis certamina gerebantur, ut gloria potius
percussionum magnitudini, quam numero deferretur. Prælato
ob generis dignitatem Agnero, tanta ui ictum ab eo editum

constat, ut, prima cassidis parte conscissa, supremam capitis
cuticulam uulneraret, ferrumque mediis galeæ interclusum
foraminibus dimitteret. Tunc Biarco mutuo percussurus, quo
plenius ferrum libraret, pedem trunco annixus, medium Agneri
corpus præstantis acuminis mucrone transegit. Sunt qui
asserant, morientem Agnerum soluto in risum ore per summam
doloris dissimulationem spiritum reddidisse. Cuius ultionem
pugiles auidius expetentes, simili per Biarconem exitio mulctati
sunt. Utebatur quippe præstantis acuminis inusitatæque longi-
tudinis gladio, quem Lφui uocabat. Talibus operum meritis
exultanti nouam de se siluestris fera uictoriam præbuit. Ursum
quippe eximiæ magnitudinis obuium sibi inter dumeta factum
iaculo confecit: comitemque suum Ialtonem, quo uiribus maior
euaderet, applicato ore egestum belluæ cruorem haurire iussit.
Creditum namque erat, hoc potionis genere corporei roboris
incrementa præstari. His facinorum uirtutibus clarissimas op-
timatum familiaritates adeptus, etiam regi percarus euasit;
sororem eius Rutam uxorem asciuit, uictique sponsam uictoriæ
præmium habuit. Ab Atislo lacessiti Roluonis ultionem armis
exegit, eumque uictum bello prostrauit. Tunc Roluo magni
acuminis iuuenem Hiarthwarum nomine, sorore Sculda sibi in
matrimonium data, annuoque uectigali imposito, Suetiæ præ-
fectum constituit, libertatis iacturam affinitatis beneficio
leniturus.

   Hoc loci quiddam memoratu iucundum operi inseratur.
Adolescens quidam Wiggo nomine, corpoream Roluonis magnitudinem attentiori contemplatione scrutatus, ingentique eiusdem admiratione captus, percontari per ludibrium cœpit, quisnam esset iste Krage, quem tanto staturæ fastigio prodiga rerum
natura ditasset; faceto cauillationis genere inusitatum pro-
ceritatis habitum prosecutus. Dicitur enim lingua Danica
'krage' truncus, cuius semicæsis ramis fastigia conscenduntur,
ita ut pes, præcisorum stipitum obsequio perinde ac scalæ
beneficio nixus, sensimque ad superiora prouectus, petitæ cel-
situdinis compendium assequatur. Quem uocis iactum Roluo
perinde ac inclytum sibi cognomen amplexus, urbanitatem dicti
ingentis armillæ dono prosequitur. Qua Wiggo dexteram
excultam extollens, læua per pudoris simulationem post tergum

reflexa, ridiculum corporis incessum præbuit, præfatus, exiguo lætari munere, quem sors diutinæ tenuisset inopiæ. Rogatus, cur ita se gereret, inopem ornamenti manum nulloque cultus beneficio gloriantem ad aspectum reliquæ uerecundo paupertatis rubore perfundi dicebat. Cuius dicti calliditate consentaneum priori munus obtinuit. Siquidem Roluo manum, quæ ab ipso occultabatur, exemplo reliquæ in medium accersendam curauit. Nec Wiggoni rependendi beneficii cura defuit. Siquidem arctissima uoti nuncupatione pollicitus est, si Roluonem ferro perire contingeret, ultionem se ab eius interfectoribus exacturum. Nec prætereundum, quod olim ingressuri curiam proceres famulatus sui principia alicuius magnæ rei uoto principibus obligare solebant, uirtute tirocinium auspicantes.

Interea Sculda, tributariæ solutionis pudore permota, diris animum commentis applicans, maritum, exprobrata condicionis deformitate, propulsandæ seruitutis monitu concitatum atque ad insidias Roluoni nectendas perductum atrocissimis nouarum rerum consiliis imbuit, plus unumquenque libertati quam necessitudini debere testata. Igitur crebras armorum massas, diuersi generis tegminibus obuolutas, tributi more per Hiarthwarum in Daniam perferri iubet, occidendi noctu regis materiam præbituras. Refertis itaque falsa uectigalium mole nauigiis, Lethram pergitur, quod oppidum, a Roluone constructum eximiisque regni opibus illustratum, ceteris confinium prouinciarum urbibus regiæ fundationis et sedis auctoritate præstabat. Rex aduentum Hiarthwari conuiualis impensæ deliciis prosecutus ingenti se potione proluerat, hospitibus præter morem ebrietatis intemperantiam formidantibus. Ceteris igitur altiorem carpentibus somnum, Sueones, quibus scelesti libido propositi communem quietis usum ademerat, cubiculis furtim delabi cœpere. Aperitur ilico telorum occlusa congeries, et sua sibi quisque tacitus arma connectit. Deinde regiam petunt, irruptisque penetralibus in dormientium corpora ferrum destringunt. Experrecti complures, quibus non minus subitæ cladis horror quam somni stupor incesserat, dubio nisu discrimini restitere, socii an hostes occurrerent, noctis errore incertum reddente. Eiusdem forte silentio noctis Hialto, qui inter regios proceres spectatæ probitatis merito præeminebat, rus egressus, scorti se complexibus dederat. Hic cum obortum pugnæ fragorem stupida procul aure sensisset, fortitudinem luxuriæ prætulit, maluitque funestum Martis discrimen appetere, quam blandis Veneris illecebris indulgere. Quanta hunc militem regis caritate flagrasse putemus, qui, cum ignorantiæ simulatione excusationem absentiæ præstare posset, salutem suam manifesto periculo obicere, quam uoluptati seruare satius existimauit? Discedentem pellex percunctari cœpit, si ipso careat, cuius ætatis uiro nubere debeat. Quam Hialto, perinde ac secretius allocuturus, propius accedere iussam, indignatus amoris sibi successorem requiri, præciso naso deformem reddidit, erubescendoque uulnere libidinosæ percunctationis dictum mulctauit, mentis lasciuiam oris iactura temperandam existimans. Quo facto, liberum quæsitæ rei iudicium a se ei relinqui dixit. Post hæc, repetito ocius oppido, confertissimis se globis immergit, aduersasque acies mutua uulnerum inflictione prosternit. Cumque dormientis adhuc Biarconis cubiculum præteriret, expergisci iussum, tali uoce compellat:

Saxo's translation of the *Bjarkamál* follows. The part which concerns students of *Beowulf* most is the account of how Roluo deposed and slew Røricus.

Saxo, Book II, ed. Ascensius, fol. xix a; ed. Holder, p. 62, l. 1.

At nos, qui regem uoto meliore ueremur,
Iungamus cuneos stabiles, tutisque phalangem
Ordinibus mensi, qua rex præcepit, eamus
Qui natum Bøki Røricum strauit auari,
Implicuitque uirum leto uirtute carentem.
Ille quidem præstans opibus, habituque fruendi
Pauper erat, probitate minus quam fœnore pollens;
Aurum militia potius ratus, omnia lucro
Posthabuit, laudisque carens congessit aceruos
Æris, et ingenuis uti contempsit amicis.
Cumque lacessitus Roluonis classe fuisset,
Egestum cistis aurum deferre ministros
Iussit, et in primas urbis diffundere portas,

Dona magis quam bella parans, quia militis expers
Munere, non armis, tentandum credidit hostem;
Tanquam opibus solis bellum gesturus, et usu
Rerum, non hominum, Martem producere posset.
Ergo graues loculos et ditia claustra resoluit,
Armillas teretes et onustas protulit arcas,
Exitii fomenta sui, ditissimus æris,
Bellatoris inops, hostique adimenda relinquens
Pignora, quæ patriis præbere pepercit amicis.
Annellos ultro metuens dare, maxima nolens
Pondera fudit opum, ueteris populator acerui.
Rex tamen hunc prudens, oblataque munera spreuit,
Rem pariter uitamque adimens; nec profuit hosti
Census iners, quem longo auidus cumulauerat æuo.
Hunc pius inuasit Roluo, summasque perempti
Cepit opes, inter dignos partitus amicos,
Quicquid auara manus tantis congesserat annis;
Irrumpensque opulenta magis quam fortia castra,
Præbuit eximiam sociis sine sanguine prædam.
Cui nil tam pulchrum fuit, ut non funderet illud,
Aut carum, quod non sociis daret, æra fauillis
Assimulans, famaque annos, non fœnore mensus.
Unde liquet, regem claro iam funere functum
Præclaros egisse dies, speciosaque fati
Tempora, præteritos decorasse uiriliter annos.
Nam uirtute ardens, dum uiueret, omnia uicit,
Egregio dignas sortitus corpore uires.
Tam præceps in bella fuit, quam concitus amnis
In mare decurrit, pugnamque capessere promptus
Ut ceruus rapidum bifido pede tendere cursum.

Saxo, Book II, ed. Ascensius, fol. xxi a; ed. Holder, p. 67, l. 1.

Hanc maxime exhortationum seriem idcirco metrica ratione
compegerim, quod earundem sententiarum intellectus Danici
cuiusdam carminis compendio digestus a compluribus anti-
quitatis peritis memoriter usurpatur.

Contigit autem, potitis uictoria Gothis, omne Roluonis

agmen occumbere, neminemque, excepto Wiggone, ex tanta
iuuentute residuum fore. Tantum enim excellentissimis regis
meritis ea pugna a militibus tributum est, ut ipsius cædes
omnibus oppetendæ mortis cupiditatem ingeneraret, eique morte
iungi uita iucundius duceretur.

Lætus Hiartuarus prandendi gratia positis mensis conuiuium
pugnæ succedere iubet, uictoriam epulis prosecuturus. Quibus
oneratus magnæ sibi ammirationi esse dixit, quod ex tanta
Roluonis militia nemo, qui saluti fuga aut captione consuleret,
repertus fuisset. Unde liquidum fuisse quanto fidei studio
regis sui caritatem coluerint, cui superstites esse passi non
fuerint. Fortunam quoque, quod sibi ne unius quidem eorum
obsequium superesse permiserit, causabatur, quam libentissime
se talium uirorum famulatu usurum testatus. Oblato Wiggone
perinde ac munere gratulatus, an sibi militare uellet, perquirit.
Annuenti destrictum gladium offert. Ille cuspidem refutans,
capulum petit, hunc morem Roluoni in porrigendo militibus
ense extitisse præfatus. Olim namque se regum clientelæ
daturi, tacto gladii capulo obsequium polliceri solebant. Quo
pacto Wiggo capulum complexus, cuspidem per Hiartuarum
agit, ultionis compos, cuius Roluoni ministerium pollicitus
fuerat. Quo facto, ouans irruentibus in se Hiartuari militibus
cupidius corpus obtulit, plus uoluptatis se ex tyranni nece
quam amaritudinis ex propria sentire uociferans. Ita conuiuio
in exequias uerso, uictoriæ gaudium funeris luctus insequitur.
Clarum ac semper memorabilem uirum, qui, uoto fortiter
expleto, mortem sponte complexus suo ministerio mensas
tyranni sanguine maculauit. Neque enim occidentium manus
uiuax animi uirtus expauit, cum prius a se loca, quibus Roluo
assueuerat, interfectoris eius cruore respersa cognosceret.
Eadem itaque dies Hiartuari regnum finiuit ac peperit. Fraudulenter enim quæsitæ res eadem sorte defluunt, qua petuntur,
nullusque diuturnus est fructus, qui scelere ac perfidia partus
fuerit. Quo euenit ut Sueones, paulo ante Daniæ potitores,
ne suæ quidem salutis potientes existerent. Protinus enim a
Syalandensibus deleti læsis Roluonis manibus iusta exsoluere
piacula. Adeo plerunque fortunæ sæuitia ulciscitur, quod dolo
ac fallacia patratur.

B. HRÓLFS SAGA KRAKA, CAP. 23

(ed Finnur Jónsson, København, 1904, p. 65 ff.)

Síðan fór Bǫðvarr leið sína til Hleiðargarðs. Hann kemr til konungs atsetu. Bǫðvarr leiðir síðan hest sinn á stall hjá konungs hestum hinum beztu ok spyrr engan at; gekk síðan inn í hǫllina, ok var þar fátt manna. Hann sez utarliga, ok sem hann hefir verit þar litla hríð, heyrir hann þrausk nǫkkut utar í hornit í einhverjum stað. Bǫðvarr lítr þangat ok sér, at mannshǫnd kemr upp úr mikilli beinahrúgu, er þar lá; hǫndin var svǫrt mjǫk. Bǫðvarr gengr þangat til ok spyrr, hverr þar væri í beinahrúgunni; þá var honum svarat ok heldr óframliga: "Hǫttr heiti ek, Bokki sæll." "Hví ertu hér, segir Bǫðvarr, eða hvat gerir þú?" Hǫttr segir: "ek geri mér skjaldborg, Bokki sæll." Boðvarr sagði: "vesall ertu þinnar skjaldborgar." Bǫðvarr þrífr til hans ok hnykkir honum upp úr beinahrúgunni. Hǫttr kvað þá hátt við ok mælti: "nú viltu mér bana, ger eigi þetta, svá sem ek hefi nú vel um búiz áðr, en þú hefir nú rótat í sundr skjaldborg minni, ok hafða ek nú svá gert hana háva utan at mér, at hún hefir hlíft mér við ǫllum hǫggum ykkar, svá at engi hǫgg hafa komit á mik lengi, en ekki var hún enn svá búin, sem ek ætlaði hún skyldi verða." Bǫðvarr mælti: "ekki muntu fá skjaldborgina lengr." Hǫttr mælti ok grét: "skaltu nú bana mér, Bokki sæll?" Bǫðvarr bað hann ekki hafa hátt, tók hann upp síðan ok bar hann út úr hǫllinni ok til vats nǫkkurs, sem þar var í nánd, ok gáfu fáir at þessu gaum, ok þó hann upp allan. Síðan gekk Bǫðvarr til þess rúms, sem hann hafði áðr tekit, ok leiddi eptir sér Hǫtt ok þar setr hann Hǫtt hjá sér, en hann er svá hræddr, at skelfr á honum leggr ok liðr, en þó þykkiz hann skilja, at þessi maðr vill hjálpa sér. Eptir þat kveldar ok drífa menn í hǫllina ok sjá Hrólfs kappar, at Hǫttr er settr á bekk upp, ok þykkir þeim sá maðr hafa gert sik ærit djarfan, er þetta hefir til tekit. Ilt tillit hefir Hǫttr, þá *er* hann sér kunningja sína, því *at* hann hefir ilt eitt af þeim reynt; hann vill lifa gjarnan ok fara aptr í beinahrúgu sína, en Bǫðvarr heldr honum, svá *at* hann náir ekki í burtu at fara, því *at* hann þóttiz ekki jafnberr fyrir hǫggum þeira, ef hann næði þangat at komaz sem hann er nú. Hirðmenn hafa nú sama vanda, ok kasta fyrst beinum smám um þvert gólfit til Bǫðvars ok Hattar. Bǫðvarr lætr, sem hann sjái eigi þetta. Hǫttr er svá hræddr, at hann tekr eigi mat né drukk, ok þykkir honum þá ok þá sem hann muni vera lostinn; ok nú mælti Hǫttr til Bǫðvars : " Bokki sæll, nú ferr at þér stór hnúta, ok mun þetta ætlat okkr til nauða." Bǫðvarr bað hann þegja; hann setr við holan lófann ok tekr svá við hnútunni; þar fylgir leggrinn með; Bǫðvarr sendi aptr hnútuna ok setr á þann, sem kastaði ok rétt framan í hann með svá harðri svipan, at hann fekk bana; sló þá miklum ótta yfir hirðmennina. Kemr nú þessi fregn fyrir Hrólf konung ok kappa hans upp í kastalann, at maðr mikilúðligr sé kominn til hallarinnar ok hafi drepit einn hirðmann hans, ok vildu þeir láta drepa manninn. Hrólfr konungr spurðiz eptir, hvárt hirðmaðrinn hefði verit saklauss drepinn. " Því var næsta," sǫgðu þeir. Kómuz þá fyrir Hrólf konung ǫll sannindi hér um. Hrólfr konungr sagði þat skyldu fjarri, at drepa skyldi manninn—'' hafi þit hér illan vanda upp tekit, at berja saklausa menn beinum; er mér í því óvirðing, en yðr stór skǫmm, at gera slíkt; hefi ek jafnan rætt um þetta áðr, ok hafi þit at þessu engan gaum gefit, ok hygg ek, at þessi maðr muni ekki alllítill fyrir sér, er þér hafið nú á leitat, ok kallið hann til mín, svá *at* ek viti, hverr hann er.'' Bǫðvarr gengr fyrir konung ok kveðr hann kurteisliga. Konunga spyrr hann at nafni. "Hattargriða kalla mik hirðmenn yðar, en Bǫðvarr heiti ek.'' Konungr mælti : '' hverjar bætr viltu bjóða mér fyrir hirðmann minn?'' Bǫðvarr segir: "til þess gerði hann, sem hann fekk." Konungr mælti: "viltu vera minn maðr ok skipa rúm hans?'' Bǫðvarr segir : '' ekki neita ek, at vera yðarr maðr, ok munu vit ekki skiljaz svá búit, vit Hǫttr, ok dveljaz nær þér báðir, heldr en þessi hefir setit, elligar vit fǫrum burt báðir." Konungr mælti : " eigi sé ek at honum sæmd en ek spara ekki mat við hann." Bǫðvarr gengr nú til þess rúms, sem honum líkaði, en ekki vill hann þat skipa, sem hinn hafði áðr; hann kippir upp í einhverjum stað þremr mǫnnum, ok síðan settuz þeir Hǫttr þar niðr ok innar í hǫllinni en þeim var skipat. Heldr þótti mǫnnum ódælt við Bǫðvar, ok er þeim hinn mesti íhugi at honum. Ok sem leið at jólum, gerðuz menn ókátir. Bǫðvarr spyrr Hǫtt, hverju þetta sætti; hann segir honum, at dýr eitt hafi þar komit tvá vetr í samt, mikit ok ógurligt—"ok hefir vængi á bakinu ok flýgr þat jafnan; tvau haust hefir þat nú hingat vitjat ok gert mikinn skaða; á þat bíta ekki vápn, en kappar konungs koma ekki heim, þeir sem at eru einna mestir." Bǫðvarr mælti: "ekki er hǫllin svá vel skipuð, sem ek ætlaði, ef eitt dýr skal hér eyða ríki ok fé konungsins." Hǫttr sagði: "þat er ekki dýr, heldr er þat hit mesta trǫll." Nú kemr jólaaptann; þá mælti konungr: "nú vil ek, at menn sé kyrrir ok hljóðir í nótt, ok banna ek ǫllum mínum mǫnnum at ganga í nǫkkurn háska við dýrit, en fé ferr eptir því sem auðnar; menn mína vil ek ekki missa." Allir heita hér góðu um, at gera eptir því, sem konungr bauð. Bǫðvarr leyndiz í burt um nóttina; hann lætr Hǫtt fara með sér, ok gerir hann þat nauðugr ok kallaði hann sér stýrt til bana. Bǫðvarr segir, at betr mundi til takaz. Þeir ganga í burt frá hǫllinni, ok verðr Bǫðvarr at bera hann; svá er hann hræddr. Nú sjá þeir dýrit; ok því næst æpir Hǫttr slíkt, sem hann má, ok kvað dyrit mundu gleypa hann. Bǫðvarr bað bikkjuna hans þegja ok kastar honum niðr í mosann, ok þar liggr hann ok eigi með ǫllu óhræddr; eigi þorir hann heim at fara heldr. Nú gengr Bǫðvarr móti dýrinu; þat hæfir honum, at sverðit er fast í umgjǫrðinni, er hann vildi bregða því. Bǫðvarr eggjar nú fast sverðit ok þá bragðar í umgjǫrðinni, ok nú fær hann brugðit umgjǫrðinni, svá at sverðit gengr úr slíðrunum, ok leggr þegar undir bægi dýrsins ok svá fast, at stóð í hjartanu, ok datt þá dýrit til jarðar dautt niðr. Eptir þat ferr hann þangat sem Hǫttr liggr. Bǫðvarr tekr hann upp ok berr þangat, sem dýrit liggr dautt. Hǫttr skelfr ákaft. Bǫðvarr mælti: "nú skaltu drekka blóð dýrsins." Hann er lengi tregr, en þó þorir hann víst eigi annat. Bǫðvarr lætr hann drekka tvá sopa stóra; hann lét hann ok eta nǫkkut af dýrshjartanu; eptir þetta tekr Bǫðvarr til hans, ok áttuz þeir við lengi. Bǫðvarr mælti: "hclzt ertu nú sterkr orðinn, ok ekki vænti ek, et þú hræðiz nú hirðmenn Hrólfs konungs." Hǫttr sagði: "eigi mun ek þá hræðaz ok eigi þik upp frá þessu." "Vel er þá orðit, Hǫttr félagi; fǫru vit nú til ok reisum upp dýrit ok búum svá um, at aðrir ætli at kvikt muni vera."

þeir gera nú svá. Eptir þat fara þeir heim ok hafa kyrt um sik, ok veit engi maðr, hvat þeir hafa iðjat. Konungr spyrr um morguninn, hvat þeir viti til dýrsins, hvárt þat hafi nǫkkut þangat vitjat um nóttina; honum var sagt, at fé alt væri heilt í grindum ok ósakat. Konungr bað menn forvitnaz, hvárt engi sæi líkindi til, at þat hefði heim komit. Varðmenn gerðu svá ok kómu skjótt aptr ok sǫgðu konungi, at dýrit færi þar ok heldr geyst at borginni. Konungr bað hirðmenn vera hrausta ok duga nú hvern eptir því, sem hann hefði hug til, ok ráða af óvætt þenna; ok svá var gert, sem konungr bauð, at þeir bjuggu sik til þess. Konungr horfði á dýrit ok mælti síðan: "enga sé ek fǫr á dýrinu, en hverr vill nú taka kaup einn ok ganga í móti því?" Bǫðvarr mælti: "þat væri næsta hrausts manns forvitnisbót. Hǫttr félagi, rektu nú af þér illmælit þat, at menn láta, sem engi krellr né dugr muni í þer vera; far nú ok drep þú dýrit; máttu sjá, at engi er allfúss til annarra." "Já," sagði Hǫttr, "ek mun til þessa ráðaz." Konungr mælti: "ekki veit ek, hvaðan þessi hreysti er at þér komin, Hǫttr, ok mikit hefir um þik skipaz á skammri stundu." Hǫttr mælti: "gef mér til sverðit Gullinhjalta er þú heldr á, ok skal ek þá fella dýrit eða fá bana." Hrólf konungr mælti: "þetta sverð er ekki beranda nema þeim manni, sem bæði er góðr drengr ok hraustr." Hǫttr sagði: "svá skaltu til ætla, at mér sé svá háttat." Konungr mælti: "hvat má vita, nema fleira hafi skipz um hagi þína, en sjá þykkir, en fæstir menn þykkjaz þik kenna, at þú sér enn sami maðr; nú tak við sverðinu ok njót manna bezt, ef þetta er til unnit." Síðan gengr Hǫttr at dýrinu alldjarfliga ok hǫggr til þess, þá *er* hann kemr í hǫggfæri, ok dýrit fellr niðr dautt. Bǫðvarr mælti: "sjáið nú, herra, hvat hann hefir til unnit." Konungr segir: "víst hefir hann mikit skipaz, en ekki hefir Hǫttr einn dýrit drepit, heldr hefir þú þat gert." Bǫðvarr segir: "vera má, at svá sé." Konungr segir: "vissa ek, þá *er* þú komt hér, at fáir mundu þínir jafningjar vera, en þat þykki mér þó þitt verk frægiligast, at þú hefir gert hér annan kappa, þar *er* Hǫttr er, ok óvænligr þótti til mikillar giptu; ok nú vil ek *at* hann heiti eigi Hǫttr lengr ok skal hann heita Hjalti upp frá þessu; skaltu heita eptir sverðinu Gullinhjalta."

Then Bothvar went on his way to Leire, and came to the king's dwelling.

Bothvar stabled his horse by the king's best horses, without asking leave; and then he went into the hall, and there were few men there. He took a seat near the door, and when he had been there a little time he heard a rummaging in a corner. Bothvar looked that way and saw that a man's hand came up out of a great heap of bones which lay there, and the hand was very black. Bothvar went thither and asked who was there in the heap of bones.

Then an answer came, in a very weak voice, "Hott is my name, good fellow."

"Why art thou here?" said Bothvar, "and what art thou doing?"

Hott said, "I am making a shield-wall for myself, good fellow."

Bothvar said, "Out on thee and thy shield-wall!" and gripped him and jerked him up out of the heap of bones.

Then Hott cried out and said, "Now thou wilt be the death of me: do not do so. I had made it all so snug, and now thou hast scattered in pieces my shield-wall; and I had built it so high all round myself that it has protected me against all your blows, so that for long no blows have come upon me, and yet it was not so arranged as I meant it should be."

Then Bothvar said, "Thou wilt not build thy shield-wall any longer."

Hott said, weeping, "Wilt thou be the death of me, good fellow?" Bothvar told him not to make a noise, and then took him up and bore him out of the hall to some water which was close by, and washed him from head to foot. Few paid any heed to this.

Then Bothvar went to the place which he had taken before, and led Hott with him, and set Hott by his side. But Hott was so afraid that he was trembling in every limb, and yet he seemed to know that this man would help him.

After that it grew to evening, and men crowded into the hall: and Rolf's warriors saw that Hott was seated upon the bench. And it seemed to them that the man must be bold

enough who had taken upon himself to put him there. Hott
had an ill countenance when he saw his acquaintances, for he
had received naught but evil from them. He wished to save
his life and go back to his bone-heap, but Bothvar held him
tightly so that he could not go away. For Hott thought that,
if he could get back into his bone-heap, he would not be as
much exposed to their blows as he was.

Now the retainers did as before; and first of all they tossed
small bones across the floor towards Bothvar and Hott. Bothvar pretended not to see this. Hott was so afraid that he
neither ate nor drank; and every moment he thought he would
be smitten.

And now Hott said to Bothvar, "Good fellow, now a great
knuckle bone is coming towards thee, aimed so as to do us sore
injury." Bothvar told him to hold his tongue, and put up
the hollow of his palm against the knuckle bone and caught it,
and the leg bone was joined on to the knuckle bone. Then
Bothvar sent the knuckle bone back, and hurled it straight at
the man who had thrown it, with such a swift blow that it was
the death of him. Then great fear came over the retainers.

Now news came to King Rolf and his men up in the castle
that a stately man had come to the hall and killed a retainer,
and that the retainers wished to kill the man. King Rolf
asked whether the retainer who had been killed had given any
offence. "Next to none," they said: then all the truth of the
matter came up before King Rolf.

King Rolf said that it should be far from them to kill the
man: "You have taken up an evil custom here in pelting men
with bones without quarrel. It is a dishonour to me and a
great shame to you to do so. I have spoken about it before,
and you have paid no attention. I think that this man whom
you have assailed must be a man of no small valour. Call
him to me, so that I may know who he is."

Bothvar went before the king and greeted him courteously.
The king asked him his name. "Your retainers call me Hott's
protector, but my name is Bothvar."

The king said, "What compensation wilt thou offer me for
my retainer?"

Bothvar said, "He only got what he asked for."

The king said, "Wilt thou become my man and fill his place?"

Bothvar said, "I do not refuse to be your man, but Hott and I must not part so. And we must sit nearer to thee than this man whom I have slain has sat; otherwise we will both depart together." The king said, "I do not see much credit in Hott, but I will not grudge him meat." Then Bothvar went to the seat that seemed good to him, and would not fill that which the other had before. He pulled up three men in one place, and then he and Hott sat down there higher in the hall than the place which had been given to them. The men thought Bothvar overbearing, and there was the greatest ill will among them concerning him.

And when it drew near to Christmas, men became gloomy. Bothvar asked Hott the reason of this. Hott said to him that for two winters together a wild beast had come, great and awful, "And it has wings on its back, and flies. For two autumns it has attacked us here and done much damage. No weapon will wound it: and the champions of the king, those who are the greatest, come not back."

Bothvar said, "This hall is not so well arrayed as I thought, if one beast can lay waste the kingdom and the cattle of the king." Hott said, "It is no beast: it is the greatest troll."

Now Christmas-eve came; then said the king, "Now my will is that men to-night be still and quiet, and I forbid all my men to run into any peril with this beast. It must be with the cattle as fate will have it: but I do not wish to lose my men." All men promised to do as the king commanded. But Bothvar went out in secret that night; he caused Hott to go with him, but Hott did that only under compulsion, and said that it would be the death of him. Bothvar said that he hoped that it would be better than that. They went away from the hall, and Bothvar had to carry Hott, so frightened was he. Now they saw the beast; and thereupon Hott cried out as loud as he could, and said that the beast would swallow him. Bothvar said, "Be silent, thou dog," and threw him down in the mire. And there he lay in no small fear; but he did not dare to go home, any the more.

Now Bothvar went against the beast, and it happened that his sword was fast in his sheath when he wished to draw it. Bothvar now tugged at his sword, it moved, he wrenched the scabbard so that the sword came out. And at once he plunged it into the beast's shoulder so mightily that it pierced him to the heart, and the beast fell down dead to the earth. After that Bothvar went where Hott lay. Bothvar took him up and bore him to where the beast lay dead. Hott was trembling all over. Bothvar said, "Now must thou drink the blood of the beast." For long Hott was unwilling, and yet he did not dare to do anything else. Bothvar made him drink two great sups; also he made him eat somewhat of the heart of the beast.

After that Bothvar turned to Hott, and they fought a long time.

Bothvar said, "Thou hast now become very strong, and I do not believe that thou wilt now fear the retainers of King Rolf."

Hott said, "I shall not fear them, nor thee either, from now on."

"That is good, fellow Hott. Let us now go and raise up the beast, and so array him that others may think that he is still alive." And they did so. After that they went home, and were quiet, and no man knew what they had achieved.

In the morning the king asked what news there was of the beast, and whether it had made any attack upon them in the night. And answer was made to the king, that all the cattle were safe and uninjured in their folds. The king bade his men examine whether any trace could be seen of the beast having visited them. The watchers did so, and came quickly back to the king with the news that the beast was making for the castle, and in great fury. The king bade his retainers be brave, and each play the man according as he had spirit, and do away with this monster. And they did as the king bade, and made them ready.

Then the king faced towards the beast and said, "I see no sign of movement in the beast. Who now will undertake to go against it?"

Bothvar said, "That would be an enterprise for a man of true valour. Fellow Hott, now clear thyself of that ill-repute, in that men hold that there is no spirit or valour in thee. Go now and do thou kill the beast; thou canst see that there is no one else who is forward to do it."

"Yea," said Hott, "I will undertake this."

The king said, "I do not know whence this valour has come upon thee, Hott; and much has changed in thee in a short time."

Hott said, "Give me the sword Goldenboss, Gullinhjalti, which thou dost wield, and I will fell the beast or take my death." Rolf the king said, "That sword cannot be borne except by a man who is both a good warrior and valiant." Hott said, "So shalt thou ween that I am a man of that kind." The king said, "How can one know that more has not changed in thy temper than can be seen? Few men would know thee for the same man. Now take the sword and have joy of it, if this deed is accomplished." Then Hott went boldly to the beast and smote at it when he came within reach, and the beast fell down dead. Bothvar said, "See now, my lord, what he has achieved." The king said, "Verily, he has altered much, but Hott has not killed the beast alone, rather hast thou done it." Bothvar said, "It may be that it is so." The king said, "I knew when thou didst come here that few would be thine equals. But this seems to me nevertheless thy most honourable work, that thou hast made here another warrior of Hott, who did not seem shaped for much luck. And now I will that he shall be called no longer Hott, but Hjalti from this time; thou shalt be called after the sword Gullinhjalti (Goldenboss)."

C. Extracts from *Grettis Saga*

(ed. G. Magnússon, 1853; R. C. Boer, 1900)

(a) *Glam episode* (caps. 32–35)

Þórhallr hét maðr, er bjó á Þórhallsstǫ́um í Forsæludal. Forsæludalr er upp af Vatnsdal. Þórhallr var Grímsson, Þórhallssonar, Friðmundarsonar, er nam Forsæludal. Þórhallr átti þá konu, er Guðrún hét. Grímr hét sonr þeira, en Þuríðr dóttir; þau váru vel á legg komin. Þórhallr var vel auðigr

maðr, ok mest at kvikfé, svá at engi maðr átti jafnmart gan-
ganda fé, sem hann. Ekki var hann hǫfðingi, en þó skilríkr
bóndi. Þar var reimt mjǫk, ok fekk hann varla sauðamann,
svá at honum þœtti duga. Hann leitaði ráðs við marga vitra
menn, hvat hann skyldi til bragðs taka; en engi gat þat ráð til
gefit, er dygði. Þórhallr reið til þings hvert sumar. Hann
átti hesta góða. Þat var eitt sumar á alþingi, at Þórhallr
gekk til búðar Skapta lǫgmanns, Þóroddssonar. Skapti var
manna vitrastr, ok heilráðr, ef hann var beiddr. Þat skildi
með þeim feðgum: Þóroddr var forspár ok kallaðr undir-
hyggjumaðr af sumum mǫnnum, en Skapti lagði þat til með
hverjum manni, sem hann ætlaði at duga skyldi, ef eigi væri
af því brugðit; því var hann kallaðr betrfeðrungr. Þórhallr
gekk í búð Skapta; hann fagnaði vel Þórhalli, því hann vissi,
at hann var ríkr maðr at fé, ok spurði hvat at tíðendum væri.

Þórhallr mælti: "Heilræði vilda ek af yðr þiggja."

"Í litlum fœrum em ek til þess," sagði Skapti; "eða hvat
stendr þik?"

Þórhallr mælti: "Þat er svá háttat, at mér helz lítt á
sauðamǫnnum. Verðr þeim heldr klakksárt, en sumir gera
engar lyktir á. Vill nú engi til taka, sá er kunnigt er til, hvat
fyrir býr."

Skapti svarar: "Þar mun liggja meinvættr nǫkkur, er
menn eru tregari til at geyma síðr þíns fjár en annarra manna.
Nú fyrir því, at þú hefir at mér ráð sótt, þá skal ek fá þér sauðamann, þann er Glámr heitir, ættaðr ór Svíþjóð, ór Sylgsdǫlum,
er út kom í fyrra sumar, mikill ok sterkr, ok ekki mjǫk við
alþýðu skap."

Þórhallr kvaz ekki um þat gefa, ef hann geymdi vel fjárins;
Skapti sagði ǫðrum eigi vænt horfa, ef hann geymdi eigi fyrir
afls sakir ok áræðis; Þórhallr gekk þá út. Þetta var at þing-
lausnum.

Þórhalli var vant hesta tveggja ljósbleikra, ok fór sjálfr at
leita; af því þykkjaz menn vita, at hann var ekki mikilmenni.
Hann gekk upp undir Sleðás ok suðr með fjalli því, er Ár-
mannsfell heitir. Þá sá hann, hvar maðr fór ofan ór Goðaskógi
ok bar hrís á hesti. Brátt bar saman fund þeira; Þórhallr
spurði hann at nafni, en hann kvez Glámr heita. Þessi maðr

var mikill vexti ok undarligr í yfirbragði, bláeygðr ok opineygðr, úlfgrár á hárslit. Þórhalli brá nǫkkut í brún, er hann sá þenna mann; en þó skildi hann, at honum mundi til þessa vísat. "Hvat er þér bezt hent at vinna?" segir Þórhallr. Glámr kvað sér vel hent at geyma sauðfjár á vetrum. "Viltu geyma sauðfjár míns?" segir Þórhallr; "gaf Skapti þik á mitt vald."

"Svá mun þér hentust mín vist, at ek fari sjálfráðr; því ek em skapstyggr, ef mér líkar eigi vel," sagði Glámr. "Ekki mun mér mein at því," segir Þórhallr, "ok vil ek, at þú farir til mín."

"Gera má ek þat," segir Glámr; "eða eru þar nǫkkur vandhœfi á?"

"Reimt þykkir þar vera," sagði Þórhallr.

"Ekki hræðumz ek flykur þær," sagði Glámr, "ok þykkir mér at ódauflig[r]a."

"Þess muntu við þurfa," segir Þórhallr, "ok hentar þar betr, at vera eigi alllítill fyrir sér."

Eptir þat kaupa þeir saman, ok skal Glámr koma at vetrnóttum. Síðan skildu þeir, ok fann Þórhallr hesta sína, þar sem hann hafði nýleitat. Reið Þórhallr heim, ok þakkaði Skapta sinn velgerning.

Sumar leið af, ok frétti Þórhallr ekki til sauðamanns, ok engi kunni skyn á honum. En at ánefndum tíma kom hann á Þórhallsstaði. Tekr bóndi við honum vel, en ǫllum ǫðrum gaz ekki at honum, en húsfreyju þó minst. Hann tók við fjárvarðveizlu, ok varð honum lítit fyrir því; hann var hljóðmikill ok dimmraddaðr, ok féit stǫkk allt saman, þegar hann hóaði. Kirkja var á Þórhallsstǫðum; ekki vildi Glámr til hennar koma; hann var ósǫngvinn ok trúlauss, stirfinn ok viðskotaillr; ǫllum var hann hvimleiðr.

Nú leið svá þar til er kemr atfangadagr jóla. Þá stóð Glámr snemma upp ok kallaði til matar síns.

Húsfreyja svarar: "Ekki er þat háttr kristinna manna, at mataz þenna dag, þvíat á morgin er jóladagr hinn fyrsti," segir hon, "ok er því fyrst skylt at fasta í dag."

Hann svarar: "Marga hindrvitni hafi þér, þá er ek sé til enskis koma. Veit ek eigi, at mǫnnum fari nú betr at, heldr

en þá, er menn fóru ekki með slíkt. Þótti mér þá betri
siðr, er menn váru heiðnir kallaðir; ok vil ek mat minn en
engar refjur."
Húsfreyja mælti: "Víst veit ek, at þér mun illa faraz í
dag, ef þú tekr þetta illbrigði til."
Glámr bað hana taka mat í stað; kvað henni annat skyldu
vera verra. Hon þorði eigi annat, en at gera, sem hann vildi.
Ok er hann var mettr, gekk hann út, ok var heldr gustillr.
Veðri var svá farit, at myrkt var um at litaz, ok flǫgraði ór
drífa, ok gnýmikit, ok versnaði mjǫk sem á leið daginn. Heyrðu
menn til sauðamanns ǫndverðan daginn, en miðr er á leið daginn.
Tók þá at fjúka, ok gerði á hríð um kveldit; kómu menn til
tíða, ok leið svá fram at dagsetri; eigi kom Glámr heim. Var
þá um talat, hvárt hans skyldi eigi leita; en fyrir því, at hríð
var á ok niðamyrkr, þá varð ekki af leitinni. Kom hann eigi
heim jólanóttina; biðu menn svá fram um tíðir. At œrnum
degi fóru menn í leitina, ok fundu féit víða í fǫnnum, lamit af
ofviðri eða hlaupit á fjǫll upp. Þvínæst kómu þeir á traðk
mikinn ofarliga í dalnum. Þótti þeim því líkt, sem þar hefði
glímt verit heldr sterkliga, þvíat grjótit var víða upp leyst, ok
svá jǫrðin. Þeir hugðu at vandliga ok sá, hvar Glámr lá, skamt
á brott frá þeim. Hann var dauðr, ok blár sem Hel, en digr sem
naut. Þeim bauð af honum óþekt mikla, ok hraus þeim mjǫk
hugr við honum. En þó leituðu þeir við at fœra hann til
kirkju, ok gátu ekki komit honum, nema á einn gilsþrǫm þar
skamt ofan frá sér; ok fóru heim við svá búit, ok sǫgðu bónda
þenna atburð. Hann spurði, hvat Glámi mundi hafa at bana
orðit. Þeir kváðuz rakit hafa spor svá stór, sem keraldsbotni
væri niðr skelt þaðan frá, sem traðkrinn var, ok upp undir bjǫrg
þau, er þar váru ofarliga í dalnum, ok fylgðu þar með blóðdrefjar
miklar. Þat drógu menn saman, at sú meinvættr, er áðr
hafði [þar] verit, mundi hafa deytt Glám; en hann mundi fengit
hafa henni nǫkkurn áverka, þann er tekit hafi til fulls,
þvíat við þá meinvætti hefir aldri vart orðit síðan. Annan
jóladag var enn til farit at fœra Glám til kirkju. Váru eykir
fyrir beittir, ok gátu þeir hvergi fœrt hann, þegar sléttlendit
var ok eigi var forbrekkis at fara. Gengu nú frá við svá búit.
Hinn þriðja dag fór prestr með þeim, ok leituðu allan daginn,

ok Glámr fannz eigi. Eigi vildi prestr optar til fara; en sauðamaðr fannz, þegar prestr var eigi í ferð. Létu þeir þá fyrir vinnaz, at fœra hann til kirkju; ok dysjuðu hann þar, sem þá var hann kominn. Lítlu síðar urðu menn varir við þat, at Glámr lá eigi kyrr. Varð mǫnnum at því mikit mein, svá at margir fellu í óvit, ef sá hann, en sumir heldu eigi vitinu. Þegar eptir jólin þóttuz menn sjá hann heima þar á bœnum. Urðu menn ákafliga hræddir; stukku þá margir menn í brott. Þvínæst tók Glámr at ríða húsum á nætr, svá at lá við brotum. Gekk hann þá náliga nætr ok daga. Varla þorðu menn at fara upp í dalinn, þóat ætti nóg ørendi. Þótti mǫnnum þar í heraðinu mikit mein at þessu.

Um várit fekk Þórhallr sér hjón ok gerði bú á jǫrðu sinni. Tók þá at minka aptrgangr, meðan sólargangr var mestr. Leið svá fram á miðsumar. Þetta sumar kom út skip í Húnavatni; þar var á sá maðr, er Þorgautr hét. Hann var útlendr at kyni, mikill ok sterkr; hann hafði tveggja manna afl; hann var lauss ok einn fyrir sér; hann vildi fá starfa nǫkkurn, því(at) hann var félauss. Þórhallr reið til skips ok fann Þorgaut; spurði ef hann vildi vinna fyrir honum; Þorgautr kvað þat vel mega vera, ok kvez eigi vanda þat.

"Svá skaltu við búaz," segir Þórhallr, "sem þar sé ekki veslingsmǫnnum hent at vera, fyrir aptrgǫngum þeim, er þar hafa verit um hríð, en ek vil ekki þik á tálar draga."

Þorgautr svarar: "Eigi þykkjumz ek upp gefinn, þóat ek sjá smáváfur; mun þá eigi ǫðrum dælt, ef ek hræðumz; ok ekki bregð ek vist minni fyrir þat."

Nú semr þeim vel kaupstefnan, ok skal Þorgautr gæta sauðfjár at vetri.

Leið nú af sumarit. Tók Þorgautr við fénu at vetrnáttum. Vel líkaði ǫllum við hann. Jafnan kom Glámr heim ok reið húsum. Þat þótti Þorgauti allkátligt, ok kvað, "þrælinn þurfa mundu nær at ganga, ef ek hræðumz." Þórhallr bað hann hafa fátt um; "er bezt, at þit reynið ekki með ykkr."

Þorgautr mælti: "Sannliga er skekinn þróttr ór yðr; ok dett ek eigi niðr milli dœgra við skraf þetta."

Nú fór svá fram um vetrinn allt til jóla. Atfangakveld jóla fór sauðamaðr til fjár.

þá mælti húsfreyja: "þurfa þœtti mér, at nú fœri eigi at fornum brǫgðum."

Hann svarar: "Ver eigi hrædd um þat, húsfreyja," sagði hann; "verða mun eitthvert sǫguligt, ef ek kem ekki aptr." Síðan gekk hann aptr til fjár síns. Veðr var heldr kalt, ok fjúk mikit. því var þorgautr vanr, at koma heim, þá er hálfrǫkkvat var; en nú kom hann ekki heim í þat mund. Kómu tíðamenn, sem vant var. þat þótti mǫnnum eigi ólíkt á horfaz sem fyrr. Bóndi vildi leita láta eptir sauðamanni, en tíðamenn tǫlduz undan, ok sǫgðuz eigi mundu hætta sér út í trǫllahendr um nætr; ok treystiz bóndi eigi at fara, ok varð ekki af leitinni. Jóladag, er menn váru mettir, fóru menn til ok leituðu sauðamanns. Gengu þeir fyrst til dysjar Gláms, þvíat menn ætluðu af hans vǫldum mundi orðit um hvarf sauðamanns. En er þeir kómu nær dysinni, sáu þeir þar mikil tíðendi, ok þar fundu þeir sauðamann, ok var hann brotinn á háls, ok lamit sundr hvert bein í honum. Síðan fœrðu þeir hann til kirkju, ok varð engum manni mein at þorgauti síðan. En Glámr tók at magnaz af nýju. Gerði hann nú svá mikit af sér, at menn allir stukku brott af þórhallsstǫðum, útan bóndi einn ok húsfreyja. Nautamaðr hafði þar verit lengi hinn sami. Vildi þórhallr hann ekki lausan láta fyrir góðvilja sakir ok geymslu. Hann var mjǫk við aldr, ok þótti honum mikit fyrir, at fara á brott; sá hann ok, at allt fór at ónytju, þat er bóndi átti, ef engi geymdi. Ok einn tíma eptir miðjan vetr var þat einn morgin, at húsfreyja fór til fjóss, at mjólka kýr eptir tíma. þá var alljóst, þvíat engi treystiz fyrr úti at vera annarr en nautamaðr; hann fór út, þegar lýsti. Hon heyrði brak mikit í fjósit, ok beljan ǫskurliga; hon hljóp inn œpandi ok kvaz eigi vita, hver ódœmi um væri í fjósinu. Bóndi gekk út ok kom til nautanna, ok stangaði hvert annat. þótti honum þar eigi gott, ok gekk innar at hlǫðunni. Hann sá, hvar lá nautamaðr, ok hafði hǫfuðit í ǫðrum bási en fœtr í ǫðrum; hann lá á bak aptr. Bóndi gekk at honum ok þreifaði um hann; finnr brátt, at hann er dauðr ok sundr hryggrinn í honum. Var hann brotinn um báshelluna. Nú þótti bónda eigi vært, ok fór í brott af bœnum með allt þat, sem hann mátti í brott flytja. En allt kvikfé þat, sem eptir var, deyddi Glámr. Ok þvínæst fór

hann um allan dalinn ok eyddi alla bœi upp frá Tungu. Var
Þórhallr þá meÞ vinum sínum þat [sem] eptir var vetrarins.
Engi maÞr mátti fara upp í dalinn meÞ hest eÞr hund, þvíat þat
var þegar drepit. En er váraÞi, ok sólargangr var sem mestr,
létti heldr aptrgǫngunum. Vildi Þórhallr nú fara aptr til lands
síns. UrÞu honum ekki auÞfengin hjón, en þó gerÞi hann bú
á ÞórhallsstǫÞum. Fór allt á sama veg sem fyrr; þegar at
haustaÞi, tóku at vaxa reimleikar. Var þá mest sótt at
bóndadóttur; ok svá fór, at hon léz af því. Margra ráÞa var
í leitat, ok varÞ ekki at gǫrt. Þótti mǫnnum til þess horfaz, at
eyÞaz mundi allr Vatnsdalr, ef eigi yrÞi bœtr á ráÞnar.

Nú er þar til at taka, at Grettir Ásmundarson sat heima
at Bjargi um haustit, síÞan þeir VígabarÞi skildu á Þóreyjar-
gnúpi. Ok er mjǫk var komit at vetrnóttum, reiÞ Grettir
heiman norÞr yfir hálsa til VíÞidals, ok gisti á AuÞunarstǫÞum.
Sættuz þeir AuÞunn til fulls, ok gaf Grettir honum øxi góÞa,
ok mæltu til vináttu meÞ sér. AuÞunn bjó lengi á AuÞunarstǫÞum ok var kynsæll maÞr. Hans sonr var Egill, er átti
ÚlfheiÞi, dóttur Eyjólfs GuÞmundarsonar, ok var þeira sonr
Eyjólfr, er veginn var á alþingi. Hann var faÞir Orms, kapiláns
Þorláks biskups. Grettir reiÞ norÞr til Vatnsdals ok kom á
kynnisleit í Tungu. Þar bjó þá Jǫkull BárÞarson, móÞurbróÞir
Grettis; Jǫkull var mikill maÞr ok sterkr ok hinn mesti ofsa-
maÞr. Hann var siglingamaÞr, ok mjǫk ódæll, en þó mikil-
hœfr maÞr. Hann tók vel viÞ Gretti, ok var hann þar þrjár
nætr. Þá var svá mikit orÞ á aptrgǫngum Gláms, at mǫnnum
var ekki jafntíÞrœtt sem þat. Grettir spurÞi inniliga at þeim
atburÞum, er hǫfÞu orÞit; Jǫkull kvaÞ þar ekki meira af sagt
en til væri hœft; "eÞa er þér forvitni á, frændi! at koma
þar?"

Grettir sagÞi, at þat var satt.

Jǫkull baÞ hann þat eigi gera, "því þat er gæfuraun mikil;
en frændr þínir eiga mikit í hættu, þar sem þú ert," sagÞi hann;
"þykkir oss nú engi slíkr af ungum mǫnnum sem þú; en illt
mun af illum hljóta, þar sem Glámr er. Er ok miklu betra,
at fáz viÞ mennska menn en viÞ óvættir slíkar."

Grettir kvaÞ sér hug á, at koma á ÞórhallsstaÞi, ok sjá, hversu
þar væri um gengit.

Jǫkull mælti: "Sé ek nú, at eigi tjáir at letja þik; en satt er þat sem mælt er, at sitt er hvárt, gæfa eða gervigleikr."

"Þá er ǫðrum vá fyrir dyrum, er ǫðrum er inn um komit; ok hygg at, hversu þér mun fara sjálfum, áðr lýkr," kvað Grettir.

Jǫkull svarar: "Vera kann, at vit sjáim báðir nǫkkut fram, en hvárrgi fái við gǫrt."

Eptir þat skildu þeir, ok líkaði hvárigum annars spár. Grettir reið á Þórhallsstaði, ok fagnaði bóndi honum vel. Hann spurði, hvert Grettir ætlaði at fara; en hann segiz þar vilja vera um nóttina, ef bónda líkaði, at svá væri. Þórhallr kvaz þǫkk fyrir kunna, at hann væri þar, "en fám þykkir slœgr til at gista hér um tíma; muntu hafa heyrt getit um, hvat hér er at væla. En ek vilda gjarna, at þú hlytir engi vandræði af mér. En þóat þú komiz heill á brott, þá veit ek fyrir víst, at þú missir hests þíns; því engi heldr hér heilum sínum fararskjóta, sá er kemr."

Grettir kvað gott til hesta, hvat sem af þessum yrði.

Þórhallr varð glaðr við, er Grettir vildi þar vera, ok tók við honum báðum hǫndum. Var hestr Grettis læstr í húsi sterkliga. Þeir fóru til svefns, ok leið svá af nóttin, at ekki kom Glámr heim.

Þá mælti Þórhallr: "Vel hefir brugðit við þína kvámu, þvíat hverja nótt er Glámr vanr at ríða húsum eða brjóta upp hurðir, sem þú mátt merki sjá."

Grettir mælti: "Þá mun vera annathvárt, at hann mun ekki lengi á sér sitja, eða mun af venjaz meirr en eina nótt. Skal ek vera hér nótt aðra ok sjá, hversu ferr."

Síðan gengu þeir til hests Grettis, ok var ekki við hann glez. Allt þótti bónda at einu fara. Nú er Grettir þar aðra nótt, ok kom ekki þrællinn heim. Þá þótti bónda mjǫk vænkaz. Fór hann þá at sjá hest Grettis. Þá var upp brotit húsit, er bóndi kom til, en hestrinn dreginn til dyra útar, ok lamit í sundr í honum hvert bein.

Þórhallr sagði Gretti, hvar þá var komit, ok bað hann forða sér: "þvíat víss er dauðinn, ef þú bíðr Gláms."

Grettir svarar: "Eigi má ek minna hafa fyrir hest minn, en at sjá þrælinn."

Bóndi sagði, at þat var eigi bati, at sjá hann, "þvíat hann er ólíkr nǫkkurri mannligri mynd; en góð þykki mér hver sú stund, er þú vilt hér vera."

Nú líðr dagrinn; ok er menn skyldu fara til svefns, vildi Grettir eigi fara af klæðum, ok lagðiz niðr í setit gegnt lokrekkju bónda. Hann hafði rǫggvarfeld yfir sér, ok knepti annat skautit niðr undir fœtr sér, en annat snaraði hann undir hǫfuð sér, ok sá út um hǫfuðsmáttina. Setstokkr var fyrir framan setit, mjǫk sterkr, ok spyrndi hann þar í. Dyraumbúningrinn allr var frá brotinn útidyrunum, en nú var þar fyrir bundinn hurðarflaki, ok óvendiliga um búit. Þverþilit var allt brotit frá skálanum, þat sem þar fyrir framan hafði verit, bæði fyrir ofan þvertréit ok neðan. Sængr allar váru ór stað fœrðar. Heldr var þar óvistuligt. Ljós brann í skálanum um nóttina. Ok er af mundi þriðjungr af nótt, heyrði Grettir út dynur miklar. Var þá farit upp á húsin, ok riðit skálanum ok barit hælunum, svá at brakaði í hverju tré. Því gekk lengi; þá var farit ofan af húsunum ok til dyra gengit. Ok er upp var lokit hurðunni, sá Grettir, at þrællinn rétti inn hǫfuðit, ok sýndiz honum afskræmiliga mikit ok undarliga stórskorit. Glámr fór seint ok réttiz upp, er hann kom inn í dyrnar; hann gnæfaði ofarliga við ræfrinu; snýr at skálanum ok lagði handleggina upp á þvertréit, ok gægðiz inn yfir skálann. Ekki lét bóndi heyra til sín, þvíat honum þótti œrit um, er hann heyrði, hvat um var úti. Grettir lá kyrr ok hrœrði sik hvergi. Glámr sá, at hrúga nǫkkur lá í setinu, ok réz nú innar eptir skálanum ok þreif í feldinn stundarfast. Grettir spyrndi í stokkinn, ok gekk því hvergi. Glámr hnykti í annat sinn miklu fastara, ok bifaðiz hvergi feldrinn. Í þriðja sinn þreif hann í með báðum hǫndum svá fast, at hann rétti Gretti upp ór setinu; kiptu nú í sundr feldinum í millum sín. Glámr leit á slitrit, er hann helt á, ok undraðiz mjǫk, hverr svá fast mundi togaz við hann. Ok í því hljóp Grettir undir hendr honum, ok þreif um hann miðjan, ok spenti á honum hrygginn sem fastast gat hann, ok ætlaði hann, at Glámr skyldi kikna við. En þrællinn lagði at handleggjum Grettis svá fast, at hann hǫrfaði allr fyrir orku sakir. Fór Grettir þá undan í ýms setin. Gengu þá frá stokkarnir, ok allt brotnaði, þat sem fyrir varð. Vildi

Glámr leita út, en Grettir fœrði við fœtr, hvar sem hann mátti. En þó gat Glámr dregit hann fram ór skálanum. Áttu þeir þá allharða sókn, þvíat þrællinn ætlaði at koma honum út ór bœnum; en svá illt sem var at eiga við Glám inni, þú sá Grettir, at þó var verra, at fáz við hann úti; ok því brauz hann í móti af ǫllu afli at fara út. Glámr fœrðiz í aukana, ok knepti hann at sér, er þeir kómu í anddyrit. Ok er Grettir sér, at hann fekk eigi við spornat, hefir hann allt eitt atriðit, at hann hleypr sem harðast í fang þrælnum ok spyrnir báðum fótum í jarðfastan stein, er stóð í dyrunum. Við þessu bjóz þrællinn eigi; hann hafði þá togaz við at draga Gretti at sér; ok því kiknaði Glámr á bak aptr, ok rauk ǫfugr út á dyrnar, svá at herðarnar námu uppdyrit, ok ræfrit gekk í sundr, bæði viðirnir ok þekjan frerin; fell hann svá opinn ok ǫfugr út ór húsunum, en Grettir á hann ofan. Tunglskin var mikit úti ok gluggaþykkn; hratt stundum fyrir, en stundum dró frá. Nú í því, er Glámr fell, rak skýit frá tunglinu, en Glámr hvesti augun upp í móti. Ok svá hefir Grettir sagt sjálfr, at þá eina sýn hafi hann sét svá, at honum brygði við. Þá sigaði svá at honum af ǫllu saman, mœði ok því, er hann sá at Glámr gaut sínum sjónum harðliga, at hann gat eigi brugðit saxinu, ok lá náliga í milli heims ok heljar. En því var meiri ófagnaðarkraptr með Glámi en flestum ǫðrum aptrgǫngumǫnnum, at hann mælti þá á þessa leið: "Mikit kapp hefir þú á lagit, Grettir," sagði hann, "at finna mik. En þat mun eigi undarligt þykkja, þóat þú hljótir ekki mikit happ af mér. En þat má ek segja þér, at þú hefir nú fengit helming afls þess ok þroska, er þér var ætlaðr, ef þú hefðir mik ekki fundit. Nú fæ ek þat afl eigi af þér tekit, er þú hefir áðr hrept; en því má ek ráða, at þú verðr aldri sterkari en nú ertu, ok ertu þó nógu sterkr, ok at því mun mǫrgum verða. Þú hefir frægr orðit hér til af verkum þínum; en heðan af munu falla til þín sektir ok vígaferli, en flest ǫll verk þín snúaz þér til ógæfu ok hamingjuleysis. Þú munt verða útlægr gǫrr, ok hljóta jafnan úti at búa einn samt. Þá legg ek þat á við þik, at þessi augu sé þér jafnan fyrir sjónum, sem ek ber eptir; ok mun þér erfitt þykkja, einum at vera; ok þat mun þér til dauða draga."

Ok sem þrællinn hafði þetta mælt, þá rann af Gretti ómegin,

þat sem á honum hafði verit. Brá hann þá saxinu ok hjó hǫfuð af Glámi ok setti þat við þjó honum. Bóndi kom þá út, ok hafði klæz, á meðan Glámr lét ganga tǫluna; en hvergi þorði hann nær at koma, fyrr en Glámr var fallinn. Þórhallr lofaði guð fyrir, ok þakkaði vel Gretti, er hann hafði unnit þenna óhreina anda. Fóru þeir þá til, ok brendu Glám at kǫldum kolum. Eptir þat [báru þeir ǫsku hans í eina hít ok] grófu þar niðr, sem sízt váru fjárhagar eða mannavegir. Gengu heim eptir þat, ok var þá mjǫk komit at degi. Lagðiz Grettir niðr, þvíat hann var stirðr mjǫk. Þórhallr sendi menn á næstu bœi eptir mǫnnum; sýndi ok sagði, hversu farit hafði. Ǫllum þótti mikils um vert um þetta verk, þeim er heyrðu. Var þat þá almælt, at engi væri þvílíkr maðr á ǫllu landinu fyrir afls sakir ok hreysti ok allrar atgervi, sem Grettir Ásmundarson.

Þórhallr leysti Gretti vel af garði ok gaf honum góðan hest ok klæði sœmilig, því[at] þau váru ǫll sundr leyst, er hann hafði áðr borit. Skildu þeir með vináttu. Reið Grettir þaðan í Ás í Vatnsdal, ok tók Þorvaldr við honum vel ok spurði inniliga at sameign þeira Gláms; en Grettir segir honum viðskipti þeira, ok kvaz aldri í þvílíka aflraun komit hafa, svá langa viðreign sem þeir hǫfðu saman átt.

Þorvaldr bað hann hafa sik spakan, "ok mun þá vel duga, en ella mun þér slysgjarnt verða."

Grettir kvað ekki batnat hafa um lyndisbragðit, ok sagðiz nú miklu verr stiltr en áðr, ok allar mótgerðir verri þykkja. Á því fann hann mikla muni, at hann var orðinn maðr svá myrkfælinn, at hann þorði hvergi at fara einn saman, þegar myrkva tók. Sýndiz honum þá hvers kyns skrípi; ok þat er haft síðan fyrir orðtœki, at þeim ljái Glámr augna eðr gefi glámsýni, er mjǫk sýniz annan veg, en er. Grettir reið heim til Bjargs, er hann hafði gǫrt ørendi sín, ok sat heima um vetrinn.

(b) *Sandhaugar episode* (caps. 64–66)

Steinn hét prestr, er bjó at Eyjardalsá í Bárðardal. Hann var búþegn góðr ok ríkr at fé. Kjartan hét son hans, rǫskr maðr ok vel á legg kominn. Þorsteinn hvíti hét maðr, er bjó at Sandhaugum, suðr frá Eyjardalsá. Steinvǫr hét kona hans, ung ok glaðlát. Þau áttu bǫrn, ok váru þau ung í þenna tíma. Þar þótti mǫnnum reimt mjǫk sakir trǫllagangs. Þat bar til, tveim vetrum fyrr en Grettir kom norðr í sveitir, at Steinvǫr húsfreyja at Sandhaugum fór til jólatíða til Eyjardalsár eptir vana, en bóndi var heima. Lǫgðuz menn niðr til svefns um kveldit; ok um nóttina heyrðu menn brak mikit í skálann, ok til sængr bónda. Engi þorði upp at standa at forvitnaz um, þvíat þar var fáment mjǫk. Húsfreyja kom heim um morguninn, ok var bóndi horfinn, ok vissi engi, hvat af honum var orðit. Liðu svá hin næstu misseri. En annan vetr eptir, vildi húsfreyja fara til tíða; bað hon húskarl sinn heima vera. Hann var tregr til; en bað hana ráða. Fór þar allt á sǫmu leið, sem fyrr, at húskarl var horfinn. Þetta þótti mǫnnum undarligt. Sáu menn þá blóðdrefjar nǫkkurar í útidyrum. Þóttuz menn þat vita, at óvættir mundu hafa tekit þá báða. Þetta fréttiz víða um sveitir. Grettir hafði spurn af þessu. Ok með því at honum var mjǫk lagit at koma af reimleikum eða aptrgǫngum, þá gerði hann ferð sína til Bárðardals, ok kom atfangadag jóla til Sandha[u]ga. Hann duldiz ok nefndiz Gestr. Húsfreyja sá, at hann var furðu mikill vexti, en heimafólk var furðu hrætt við hann. Hann beiddiz þar gistingar. Húsfreyja kvað honum mat til reiðu, "en ábyrgz þik sjálfr."

Hann kvað svá vera skyldu. "Mun ek vera heima," segir hann, "en þú far til tíða, ef þú vilt."

Hon svarar: "Mér þykkir þú hraustr, ef þú þorir heima at vera."

"Eigi læt ek mér at einu getit," sagði hann.

"Illt þykkir mér heima at vera," segir hon, "en ekki komumz ek yfir ána."

"Ek skal fylgja þér yfir," segir Gestr.

Síðan bjóz hon til tíða, ok dóttir hennar með henni, lítil vexti. Hláka mikil var úti, ok áin í leysingum; var á henni jakafǫr.

Þá mælti húsfreyja: "Ófœrt er yfir ána, bæði mǫnnum ok hestum."

"Vǫð munu á vera," kvað Gestr; "ok verið eigi hræddar."

"Ber þú fyrst meyna," kvað húsfreyja, "hon er léttari."
"Ekki nenni ek at gera tvær ferðir at þessu," segir Gestr,
"ok mun ek bera þik á handlegg mér."
Hon signdi sik ok mælti: "þetta er ófœra; eða hvat gerir
þú þá af meyjunni?"

"Sjá mun ek ráð til þess," segir hann; ok greip þær upp
báðar ok setti hina yngri í kné móður sinnar, ok bar þær svá
á vinstra armlegg sér; en hafði lausa hina hœgri hǫnd ok óð
svá út á vaðit. Eigi þorðu þær at œpa, svá váru þær hræddar.
En áin skall þegar upp á brjósti honum. þá rak at honum
jaka mikinn; en hann skaut við hendi þeiri, er laus var, ok hratt
frá sér. Gerði þá svá djúpt, at strauminn braut á ǫxlinni.
Óð hann sterkliga, þar til er hann kom at bakkanum ǫðrum
megin, ok fleygir þeim á land. Síðan sneri hann aptr, ok var
þá hálfrøkkvit, er hann kom heim til Sandhauga; ok kallaði
til matar. Ok er hann var mettr, bað hann heimafólk fara
innar í stofu. Hann tók þá borð ok lausa viðu, ok rak um
þvera stofuna, ok gerði bálk mikinn, svá at engi heimamaðr
komz fram yfir. Engi þorði í móti honum at mæla, ok í engum
skyldi kretta. Gengit var í hliðvegginn stofunnar inn við
gaflhlaðit; ok þar þverpallr hjá. þar lagðiz Gestr niðr ok fór
ekki af klæðunum. Ljós brann í stofunni gegnt dyrum. Liggr
Gestr svá fram á nóttina.

Húsfreyja kom til Eyjardalsár til tíða, ok undruðu menn um
ferðir hennar yfir ána. Hon sagðiz eigi vita, hvárt hana hefði
yfir flutt maðr eða trǫll. Prestr kvað mann víst vera mundu,
þóat fárra maki sé; "ok látum hljótt yfir," sagði hann; "má
vera, at hann sé ætlaðr til at vinna bót á vandræðum þínum."
Var húsfreyja þar um nóttina.

Nú er frá Gretti þat at segja, at þá er dró at miðri nótt,
heyrði hann út dynur miklar. þvínæst kom inn í stofuna
trǫllkona mikil. Hon hafði í hendi trog, en annarri skálm,
heldr mikla. Hon litaz um, er hon kom inn, ok sá, hvar Gestr
lá, ok hljóp at honum, en hann upp í móti, ok réðuz á grimmliga
ok sóttuz lengi í stofunni. Hon var sterkari, en hann fór
undan kœnliga. En allt þat, sem fyrir þeim varð, brutu þau,
jafnvel þverþilit undan stofunni. Hon dró hann fram yfir
dyrnar, ok svá í anddyrit; þar tók hann fast í móti. Hon

vildi draga hann út ór bœnum, en þat varð eigi fyrr en þau leystu frá allan útidyraumbúninginn ok báru hann út á herðum sér. Þœfði hon þá ofan til árinnar ok allt fram at gljúfrum. Þá var Gestr ákafliga móðr, en þó varð annathvárt at gera: at herða sik, ella mundi hon steypa honum í gljúfrin. Alla nóttina sóttuz þau. Eigi þóttiz hann hafa fengiz við þvílíkan ófagnað fyrir afls sakir. Hon hafʻi haldit honum svá fast at sér, at hann mátti hvárigri hendi taka til nǫkkurs, útan hann helt um hana miðja k[ett]una. Ok er þau kómu á árgljúfrit, bregðr hann flagðkonunni til sveiflu. Í því varð honum laus hin hœgri hǫndin. Hann þreif þá skjótt til saxins, er hann var gyrðr með, ok bregðr því; hǫggr þá á ǫxl trǫllinu, svá at af tók hǫndina hœgri, ok svá varð hann lauss. En hon steyptiz í gljúfrin ok svá í fossinn. Gestr var þá bæði stirðr ok móðr, ok lá þar lengi á hamrinum. Gekk hann þá heim, er lýsa tók, ok lagðiz í rekkju. Hann var allr þrútinn ok blár.

Ok er húsfreyja kom frá tíðum, þótti henni heldr raskat um hýbýli sín. Gekk hon þá til Gests ok spurði, hvat til hefði borit, er allt var brotit ok bœlt. Hann sagʻi allt, sem farit hafði. Henni þótti mikils um vert, ok spurði, hverr hann var. Hann sagði þá til hit sanna, ok bað sœkja prest ok kvaz vildu finna hann. Var ok svá gǫrt. En er Steinn prestr kom til Sandhauga, varð hann brátt þess víss, at þar var kominn Grettir Ásmundarson, er Gestr nefndiz. Prestr spurði, hvat hann ætlaði af þeim mǫnnum mundi vera orðit, er þar hǫfðu horfit. Grettir kvaz ætla, at í gljúfrin mundu þeir hafa horfit. Prestr kvaz eigi kunna at leggja trúnað á sagnir hans, ef engi merki mætti til sjá. Grettir segir, at síðar vissi þeir þat gǫrr. Fór prestr heim. Grettir lá í rekkju margar nætr. Húsfreyja gerði við hann harðla vel; ok leið svá af jólin. Þetta er sǫgn Grettis, at trǫllkonan steypðiz í gljúfrin við, er hon fekk sárit; en Bárðardalsmenn segja, at hana dagaði uppi, þá er þau glímdu, ok spryngi, þá er hann hjó af henni hǫndina, ok standi þar enn í konu líking á bjarginu. Þeir dalbúarnir leyndu þar Gretti.

Um vetrinn eptir jól var þat einn dag, at Grettir fór til Eyjardalsár. Ok er þeir Grettir funduz ok prestr, mælti Grettir: "Sé ek þat, prestr," segir hann, "at þú leggr lítinn trúnaðˇ á sagnir mínar. Nú vil ek at þú farir með mér til árinnar, ok sjáir, hver líkendi þér þykkir á vera."

Prestr gerði svá. En er þeir kómu til fossins, sáu þeir skúta upp undir bergit; þat var meitilberg svá mikit, at hvergi mátti upp komaz, ok nær tíu faðma ofan at vatninu. Þeir hǫfðu festi með sér.

Þá mælti prestr: "Langt um ófœrt sýniz mér þér niðr at fara."

Grettir svarar: "Fœrt er víst; en þeim mun bezt þar, sem ágætismenn eru. Mun ek forvitnaz, hvat í fossinum er, en þú skalt geyma festar."

Prestr bað hann ráða, ok keyrði niðr hæl á berginu, ok bar at grjót, [ok sat þar hjá].

Nú er frá Gretti at segja, at hann lét stein í festaraugat ok lét svá síga ofan at vatninu. "Hvern veg ætlar þú nú," segir prestr, "at fara?"

"Ekki vil ek vera bundinn," segir Grettir, "þá er ek kem í fossinn; svá boðar mér hugr um."

Eptir þat bjó hann sik til ferðar, ok var fáklæddr, ok gyrði sik með saxinu, en hafði ekki fleiri vápn. Síðan hljóp hann af bjarginu ok niðr í fossinn. Sá prestr í iljar honum, ok vissi síðan aldri, hvat af honum varð. Grettir kafaði undir fossinn, ok var þat torvelt, þvíat iða var mikil, ok varð hann allt til grunns at kafa, áðr en hann kœmiz upp undir fossinn. Þar var forberg nǫkkut, ok komz hann inn þar upp á. Þar var hellir mikill undir fossinum, ok fell áin fram af berginu. Gekk hann þá inn í hellinn, ok var þar eldr mikill á brǫndum. Grettir sá, at þar sat jǫtunn ǫgurliga mikill; hann var hræðiligr at sjá. En er Grettir kom at honum, hljóp jǫtunninn upp ok greip flein einn ok hjó til þess, er kominn var, þvíat bæði mátti hǫggva ok leggja með [honum]. Tréskapt var í; þat kǫlluðu menn þá heptisax, er þannveg var gǫrt. Grettir hjó á móti með saxinu, ok kom á skaptit, svá at í sundr tók. Jǫtunninn vildi þá seilaz á bak sér aptr til sverðs, er þar hekk í hellinum. Í því hjó Grettir framan á brjóstit, svá at náliga tók af alla bring- spelina ok kviðinn, svá at iðrin steyptuz ór honum ofan í ána, ok keyrði þau ofan eptir ánni. Ok er prestr sat við festina, sá hann, at slyðrur nǫkkurar rak ofan eptir strengnum blóðugar allar. Hann varð þá lauss á velli, ok þóttiz nú vita, at Grettir mundi dauðr vera. Hljóp hann þá frá festarhaldinu ok fór heim. Var þá komit at kveldi, ok sagði prestr vísliga, at Grettir væri dauðr; ok sagði, at mikill skaði væri eptir þvílíkan mann.

Nú er frá Gretti at segja; hann lét skamt hǫggva í milli, þar til er jǫtunninn dó. Gekk Grettir þá innar eptir hellinum. Hann kveikti ljós ok kannaði hellinn. Ekki er frá því sagt, hversu mikit fé hann fekk í hellinum; en þat ætla menn, at verit hafi nǫkkut. Dvaldiz honum þar fram á nóttina. Hann fann þar tveggja manna bein, ok bar þau í belg einn. Leitaði hann þá ór hellinum ok lagðiz til festarinnar, ok hristi hana, ok ætlaði, at prestr mundi þar vera. En er hann vissi, at prestr var heim farinn, varð hann þá at handstyrkja upp festina, ok komz hann svá upp á bjargit. Fór hann þá heim til Eyjardalsár ok kom í forkirkju belginum þeim, sem beinin váru í, ok þar með rúnakefli því, er vísur þessar váru forkunnliga vel á ristnar:

"Gekk ek í gljúfr et dǫkkva
gein veltiflug steina,
við hjǫrgæþi hríþar
hlunns úrsvǫlum munni,
fast lá framm á brjósti
flugstraumr í sal naumu
heldr kom á herþar skáldi
hǫrþ fjón Braga kvónar."

Ok en þessi:

"Ljótr kom mér í móti
mellu vinr ór helli;
hann fekz, heldr at sǫnnu
harþfengr, við mik lengi;
harþeggjat lét ek hǫggvit
heptisax af skepti;
Gangs klauf brjóst ok bringu
bjartr gunnlogi svarta[1]."

---

[1] See Finnur Jónsson, *Den Norsk-Islandske Skjaldedigtning*, B. ii. 473–4.

þar sagði svá, at Grettir hafi bein þessi ór hellinum haft. En er prestr kom til kirkju um morgininn, fann hann keflit ok þat sem fylgdi, ok las rúnarnar. En Grettir hafði farit heim til Sandhauga.

En þá er prestr fann Gretti, spurði hann inniliga eptir atburðum; en hann sagði alla sǫgu um ferð sína, ok kvað prest ótrúliga hafa haldit festinni. Prestr lét þat á sannaz. Þóttuz menn þat vita, at þessar óvættir mundu valdit hafa manna-hvǫrfum þar í dalnum. Varð ok aldri mein af aptrgǫngum eða reimleikum þar í dalnum síðan. Þótti Grettir þar gǫrt hafa mikla landhreinsan. Prestr jarðaði bein þessi í kirkju-garði.

Translation of Extracts from *Grettis Saga*

The *Grettis saga* was first printed in the middle of the eighteenth century, in Iceland (Marcússon, *Nockrer Marg-frooder Sogu-/alter*, 1756, pp. 81–163). It was edited by Magnússon and Thordarson, Copenhagen, 1853, with a Danish translation, and again by Boer (*Altnordische Saga-bibliothek*, Halle, 1900). An edition was also printed at Reykjavik in 1900, edited by V. Ásmundarson.

There are over forty MSS of the saga: *Cod. Arn. Mag.* 551 *a* (quoted in the notes below as A) forms the basis of all three modern editions. Boer has investigated the relationship of the MSS (*Die handschriftliche über-lieferung der Grettissaga*, *Z.f.d.Ph.* XXXI, 40–60), and has published, in an appendix to his edition, the readings of five of the more important, in so far as he considers that they can be utilized to amend the text supplied by A.

The reader who consults the editions of both Magnússon and Boer will be struck by the differences in the text, although both are following the same MS. Many of these differences are, of course, due to the fact that the editors are normalizing the spelling, but on different principles: many others, however, are due to the extraordinary difficulty of the MS itself. Mr Sigfús Blöndal, of the Royal Library of Copenhagen, has examined *Cod. Arn. Mag.* 551 *a* for me, and he writes:

"It is the very worst MS I have ever met with. The writing is small, almost every word is abbreviated, and, worst of all, the writing is in many places effaced, partly by smoke (I suppose the MS needs must have been lying for years in some smoky and damp *baðstofa*) rendering the parchment almost as black as shoe-leather, but still more owing to the use of chemicals, which modern editors have been obliged to use, to make sure of what there really was in the text. By the use of much patience and a lens, one can read it, though, in most places Unfortunately, this does not apply to the *Glámur* episode, a big portion of which belongs to the very worst part of the MS, and the readings of that portion are therefore rather uncertain."

The Icelandic text given above agrees in the main with that in the excellent edition of Boer, to whom, in common with all students of the

Grettis saga. I am much indebted: but I have frequently adopted in pre-
ference a spelling or wording nearer to that of Magnússon. In several of
these instances (notably the spelling of the verses attributed to Grettir)
I think Prof Boer would probably himself agree.

The words or letters placed between square brackets are those which
are not to be found in *Cod. Arn. Mag.* 551 *a.*

To Mr Blöndal, who has been at the labour of collating with the MS,
for my benefit, both the passages given above, my grateful thanks are due.

There are English translations of the *Grettis saga* by Morris and E.
Magnússon (1869, and in Morris' *Works*, 1911, vol. VII) and by G. A. Hight
(*Everyman's Library*, 1914).

For a discussion of the relationship of the *Grettis saga* to other stories,
see also Boer, *Zur Grettissaga*, in *Z.f.d.Ph.* XXX, 1–71.

(*a*) *Glam episode* (p. 146 above)

There was a man called Thorhall, who lived at Thorhall's
Farm in Shadow-dale. Shadow-dale runs up from Water-dale.
Thorhall was son of Grim, son of Thorhall, son of Frithmund,
who settled Shadow-dale. Thorhall's wife was called Guthrun:
their son was Grim, and Thurith their daughter—they were
grown up.

Thorhall was a wealthy man, and especially in cattle, so p. 147
that no man had as much live stock as he. He was not a
chief, yet a substantial yeoman. The place was much haunted,
and he found it hard to get a shepherd to suit him. He sought
counsel of many wise men, what device he should follow, but
he got no counsel which was of use to him. Thorhall rode each
summer to the All-Thing; he had good horses. That was one
summer at the All-Thing, that Thorhall went to the booth of
Skapti Thoroddsson, the Law-man.

Skapti was the wisest of men, and gave good advice if he
was asked. There was this difference between Skapti and his
father Thorodd: Thorodd had second sight, and some men
called him underhanded; but Skapti gave to every man that
advice which he believed would avail, if it were kept to: so he
was called 'Better than his father.' Thorhall went to the booth
of Skapti. Skapti greeted Thorhall well, for he knew that he
was a prosperous man, and asked what news he had.

Thorhall said, "I should like good counsel from thee."
"I am little use at that," said Skapti. "But what is thy
need?"

Thorhall said, "It happens so, that it is difficult for me to keep my shepherds: they easily get hurt, and some will not serve their time. And now no one will take on the task, who knows what is before him."

Skapti answered, "There must be some evil being about, if men are more unwilling to look after thy sheep than those of other folk. Now because thou hast sought counsel of me, I will find thee a shepherd, who is named Glam, a Swede, from Sylgsdale, who came out to Iceland last summer. He is great and strong, but not much to everybody's taste."

Thorhall said that he would not mind that, if he guarded the sheep well. Skapti said that if Glam had not the strength and courage to do that, there was no hope of anyone else. Then Thorhall went out; this was when the All-Thing was nearly ending.

Thorhall missed two light bay horses, and he went himself to look for them—so it seems that he was not a great man. He went up under Sledge-hill and south along the mountain called Armannsfell.

Then he saw where a man came down from Gothashaw, bearing faggots on a horse. They soon met, and Thorhall asked him his name, and he said he was called Glam. Glam
p. 148 was tall and strange in bearing, with blue[1] and glaring eyes, and wolf-grey hair. Thorhall opened his eyes when he saw him, but yet he discerned that this was he to whom he had been sent.

"What work art thou best fitted for?" said Thorhall.

Glam said he was well fitted to watch sheep in the winter.

"Wilt thou watch my sheep?" said Thorhall. "Skapti gave thee into my hand."

"You will have least trouble with me in your house if I go my own way, for I am hard of temper if I am not pleased," said Glam.

"That will not matter to me," said Thorhall, "and I wish that thou shouldst go to my house."

"That may I well do," said Glam, "but are there any difficulties?"

---

[1] ms A, followed by Magnússon, makes Glam *bláeygðr*, "blue-eyed": Boer reads *gráeygðr*, considering grey a more uncanny colour.

"It is thought to be haunted," said Thorhall.

"I am not afraid of such phantoms," said Glam, "and it seems to me all the less dull."

"Thou wilt need such a spirit," said Thorhall, "and it is better that the man there should not be a coward."

After that they struck their bargain, and Glam was to come at the winter-nights [14th–16th of October]. Then they parted, and Thorhall found his horses where he had just been searching. Thorhall rode home and thanked Skapti for his good deed.

Summer passed, and Thorhall heard nothing of his shepherd, and no one knew anything of him; but at the time appointed he came to Thorhall's Farm. The yeoman greeted him well, but all the others could not abide him, and Thorhall's wife least of all. Glam undertook the watching of the sheep, and it gave him little trouble. He had a great deep voice, and the sheep came together as soon as he called them. There was a church at Thorhall's Farm, but Glam would not go to it. He would have nothing to do with the service, and was godless; he was obstinate and surly and abhorred by all.

Now time went on till it came to Yule eve. Then Glam rose early and called for meat. The yeoman's wife answered, "That is not the custom of Christian men to eat meat today, because tomorrow is the first day of Yule," said she, "and therefore it is right that we should first fast today."

He answered, "Ye have many superstitions which I see are good for nothing. I do not know that men fare better now than before, when they had nought to do with such things. It seemed to me a better way when men were called heathen; and I want my meat and no tricks." p. 149

The yeoman's wife said, "I know for a certainty that it will fare ill with thee today, if thou dost this evil thing."

Glam bade her bring the meat at once, else he said it should be worse for her. She dared not do otherwise than he willed, and when he had eaten he went out, foul-mouthed.

Now it had gone so with the weather that it was heavy all round, and snow-flakes were falling, and it was blowing loud, and grew much worse as the day went on. The shepherd was heard early in the day, but less later. Then wind began to drive the snow, and towards evening it became a tempest. Then men came to the service, and so it went on to nightfall. Glam did not come home. Then there was talk whether search ought not to be made for him, but because there was a tempest and it was pitch dark, no search was attempted. That Yule night he did not come home, and so men waited till after the service [next, i.e. Christmas, morning]. But when it was full day, men went to search, and found the sheep scattered in the snow-drifts[1], battered by the tempest, or strayed up into the mountains. Then they came on a great space beaten down, high up in the valley. It looked to them as if there had been somewhat violent wrestling there, because the stones had been torn up for a distance around, and the earth likewise. They looked closely and saw where Glam lay a little distance away. He was dead, and blue like Hel and swollen like an ox. They had great loathing of him, and their souls shuddered at him. Nevertheless they strove to bring him to the church, but they could get him no further than the edge of a ravine a little below, and they went home leaving matters so, and told the yeoman what had happened. He asked what appeared to have been the death of Glam. They said that, from the trodden spot, up to a place beneath the rocks high in the valley, they had tracked marks as big as if a cask-bottom had been stamped down, and great drops of blood with them. So men concluded from this, that the evil thing which had been there before must have killed Glam, but Glam must have done it damage which had been enough, in that nought has ever happened since from that evil thing.

The second day of Yule it was again essayed to bring Glam to the church.

Beasts of draught were harnessed, but they could not move him where it was level ground and not down hill, so they departed, leaving matters so.

The third day the priest went with them, and they searched
p. 150 all day, but Glam could not be found. The priest would go no

---

[1] ms A has *fon^m* or *fen^m*, it is difficult to tell which. Magnússon reads *fenum*, "morasses."

more, but Glam was found when the priest was not in the company. Then they gave up trying to carry him to the church, and buried him where he was, under a cairn.

A little later men became aware that Glam was not lying quiet. Great harm came to men from this, so that many fell into a swoon when they saw him, and some could not keep their wits. Just after Yule, men thought they saw him at home at the farm. They were exceedingly afraid, and many fled away. Thereupon Glam took to riding the house-roofs at nights, so that he nearly broke them in. He walked almost night and day. Men hardly dared to go up into the dale, even though they had business enough. Men in that country-side thought great harm of this.

In the spring Thorhall got farm-hands together and set up house on his land. Then the apparition began to grow less frequent whilst the sun's course was at its height; and so it went on till midsummer. That summer a ship came out to Hunawater. On it was a man called Thorgaut. He was an outlander by race, big and powerful; he had the strength of two men. He was in no man's service, and alone, and he wished to take up some work, since he had no money. Thorhall rode to the ship, and met Thorgaut. He asked him if he would work for him. Thorgaut said that might well be, and that he would make no difficulties.

"But thou must be prepared," said Thorhall, "that it is no place for weaklings, by reason of the hauntings which have been going on for a while, for I will not let thee into a trap."

Thorgaut answered, "It does not seem to me that I am undone, even though I were to see some little ghosts. It must be no easy matter for others if I am frightened, and I will not give up my place for that."

So now they agreed well, and Thorgaut was to watch the sheep when winter came.

Now the summer passed on. Thorgaut took charge of the sheep at the winter-nights. He was well-pleasing to all. Glam ever came home and rode on the roofs. Thorgaut thought it sporting, and said that the thrall would have to come nearer in order to scare him. But Thorhall bade him keep quiet: "It is best that ye should not try your strength together." Thorgaut said, "Verily, your courage is shaken out of you: I shall not drop down with fear between day and night over such talk."

Now things went on through the winter up to Yule-tide. On Yule evening the shepherd went out to his sheep. Then p. 151 the yeoman's wife said, "It is to be hoped that now things will not go in the old way."

He answered, "Be not afraid of that, mistress; something worth telling will have happened if I do not come back."

Then he went to his sheep. The weather was cold, and it snowed much. Thorgaut was wont to come home when it was twilight, but now he did not come at that time. Men came to the service, as was the custom. It seemed to people that things were going as they had before. The yeoman wished to have search made for the shepherd, but the church-goers excused themselves, and said they would not risk themselves out in the hands of the trolls by night. And the yeoman did not dare to go, so the search came to nothing.

On Yule-day, when men had eaten, they went and searched for the shepherd. They went first to Glam's cairn, because men thought that the shepherd's disappearance must have been through his bringing-about. But when they came near the cairn they saw great things, for there they found the shepherd with his neck broken and not a bone in him whole. Then they carried him to the church, and no harm happened to any man from Thorgaut afterwards; but Glam began to increase in strength anew. He did so much that all men fled away from Thorhall's Farm, except only the yeoman and his wife.

Now the same cattle-herd had been there a long time. Thorhall would not let him go, because of his good-will and good service. He was far gone in age and was very unwilling to leave: he saw that everything went to waste which the yeoman had, if no one looked after it. And once after mid-winter it happened one morning that the yeoman's wife went to the byre to milk the cows as usual. It was quite light, because no one dared to go out before, except the cattle-herd: he went

out as soon as it dawned.   She heard great cracking in the byre
and a hideous bellowing.   She ran back, crying out, and said
she did not know what devilry was going on in the byre.

The yeoman went out, and came to the cattle, and they were
goring each other.   It seemed to him no good to stay there, and
he went further into the hay-barn.   He saw where the cattle-
herd lay, and he had his head in one stall and his feet in the
next.   He lay on his back.   The yeoman went to him and felt
him.   He soon found that he was dead, and his back-bone broken
in two ; it had been broken over the partition slab.

Now it seemed no longer bearable to Thorhall, and he left his
farm with all that he could carry away; but all the live-stock
left behind Glam killed.   After that he went through all the p. 152
dale and laid waste all the farms up from Tongue.   Thorhall
spent what was left of the winter with his friends.   No man
could go up into the dale with horse or hound, because it was
slain forthwith.   But when spring came, and the course of the
sun was highest, the apparitions abated somewhat.   Now
Thorhall wished to go back to his land.   It was not easy for
him to get servants, but still he set up house at Thorhall's Farm.

All went the same way as before.   When autumn came on
the hauntings began to increase.   The yeoman's daughter was
most attacked, and it fared so that she died.   Many counsels
were taken, but nothing was done.   Things seemed to men to
be looking as if all Water-dale must be laid waste, unless some
remedies could be found.

Now the story must be taken up about Grettir, how he sat
at home at Bjarg that autumn, after he had parted from Barthi-
of-the-Slayings at Thorey's Peak.   And when it had almost
come to the winter-nights, Grettir rode from home, north over
the neck to Willow-dale, and was a guest at Authun's Farm.
He was fully reconciled to Authun, and gave him a good axe,
and they spake of their wish for friendship one with the other.
(Authun dwelt long at Authun's Farm, and much goodly offspring had he.   Egil was his son, who wedded Ulfheith, daughter
of Eyjolf Guthmundson; and their son was Eyjolf, who was
slain at the All-Thing.   He was father of Orm, chaplain to

Bishop Thorlak.)   Grettir rode north to Water-dale and came
on a visit to Tongue.   At that time Jokul Barthson lived
there, Grettir's uncle.   Jokul was a man great and strong and
very proud.   He was a seafaring man, and very over-bearing,
yet of great account.   He received Grettir well, and Grettir was
there three nights.

There was so much said about the apparitions of Glam
that nothing was spoken of by men equally with that.
Grettir inquired exactly about the events which had happened.
Jokul said that nothing more had been spoken than had
verily occurred.   "But art thou anxious, kinsman, to go
there?"

Grettir said that that was the truth.   Jokul begged him not
to do so, "For that is a great risk of thy luck, and thy kinsmen
have much at stake where thou art," said he, "for none of the
young men seems to us to be equal to thee; but ill will come of
ill where Glam is, and it is much better to have to do with mortal
men than with evil creatures like that."

Grettir said he was minded to go to Thorhall's Farm and
p. 153 see how things had fared there.   Jokul said, "I see now that it
is of no avail to stop thee, but true it is what men say, that
good-luck is one thing, and goodliness another."

"Woe is before one man's door when it is come into another's
house.   Think how it may fare with thee thyself before the end,"
said Grettir.

Jokul answered, "It may be that both of us can see somewhat
into the future, but neither can do aught in the matter."

After that they parted, and neither was pleased with the
other's foreboding.

Grettir rode to Thorhall's Farm, and the yeoman greeted
him well.   He asked whither Grettir meant to go, but Grettir
said he would stay there over the night if the yeoman would
have it so.   Thorhall said he owed him thanks for being there,
"But few men find it a profit to stay here for any time.   Thou
must have heard what the dealings are here, and I would fain
that thou shouldst have no troubles on my account; but though
thou shouldst come whole away, I know for certain that thou

wilt lose thy steed, for no one who comes here keeps his horse whole."

Grettir said there were plenty of horses, whatever should become of this one.

Thorhall was glad that Grettir would stay there, and welcomed him exceedingly.

Grettir's horse was strongly locked in an out-house. They went to sleep, and so the night passed without Glam coming home. Then Thorhall said, "Things have taken a good turn against thy coming, for every night Glam has been wont to ride the roofs or break up the doors, even as thou canst see."

Grettir said, "Then must one of two things happen. Either he will not long hold himself in, or the wonted haunting will cease for more than one night. I will stay here another night and see how it goes."

Then they went to Grettir's horse, and he had not been attacked. Then everything seemed to the yeoman to be going one way. Now Grettir stayed for another night, and the thrall did not come home. Then things seemed to the yeoman to be taking a very hopeful turn. He went to look after Grettir's horse. When he came there, the stable was broken into, and the horse dragged out to the door, and every bone in him broken asunder.

Thorhall told Grettir what had happened, and bade him save his own life—"For thy death is sure if thou waitest for Glam."

Grettir answered, "The least I must have in exchange for my horse is to see the thrall."

The yeoman said that there was no good in seeing him: "For he is unlike any shape of man; but every hour that thou p. 154 wilt stay here seems good to me."

Now the day went on, and when bed-time came Grettir would not put off his clothes, but lay down in the seat over against the yeoman's sleeping-chamber. He had a shaggy cloak over him, and wrapped one corner of it down under his feet, and twisted the other under his head and looked out through the head-opening. There was a great and strong partition beam in front of the seat, and he put his feet against it. The doorframe was all broken away from the outer door, but now boards, fastened together carelessly anyhow, had been tied in front. The panelling which had been in front was all broken away from the hall, both above and below the cross-beam; the beds were all torn out of their places, and everything was very wretched[1].

A light burned in the hall during the night: and when a third part of the night was past, Grettir heard a great noise outside. Some creature had mounted upon the buildings and was riding upon the hall and beating it with its heels, so that it cracked in every rafter. This went on a long time. Then the creature came down from the buildings and went to the door. When the door was opened Grettir saw that the thrall had stretched in his head, and it seemed to him monstrously great and wonderfully huge. Glam went slowly and stretched himself up when he came inside the door. He towered up to the roof. He turned and laid his arm upon the cross-beam and glared in upon the hall. The yeoman did not let himself be heard, because the noise he heard outside seemed to him enough. Grettir lay quiet and did not move.

Glam saw that a heap lay upon the seat, and he stalked in up the hall and gripped the cloak wondrous fast. Grettir pressed his feet against the post and gave not at all. Glam pulled a second time much more violently, and the cloak did not move. A third time he gripped with both hands so mightily that he pulled Grettir up from the seat, and now the cloak was torn asunder between them.

Glam gazed at the portion which he held, and wondered much who could have pulled so hard against him; and at that moment Grettir leapt under his arms and grasped him round

---

[1] Immediately inside the door of the Icelandic dwelling was the *anddyri* or vestibule. For want of a better word, I translate *anddyri* by "porch": but it is a porch inside the building. Opening out of this 'porch' were a number of rooms. Chief among which were the *skáli* or "hall," and the *stufa* or "sitting room," the latter reached by a passage (*gǫng*). These were separated from the "porch" by panelling. In the struggle with Glam, Grettir is lying in the hall (*skáli*), but the panelling has all been broken away from the great cross-beam to which it was fixed. Grettir consequently sees Glam enter the outer door; Glam turns to the *skáli*, and glares down it, leaning over the cross-beam: then enters the hall, and the struggle begins. See Guðmundsson (V.), *Privatboligen på Island i Sagatiden*, 1889.

the middle, and bent his back as mightily as he could, reckoning
that Glam would sink to his knees at his attack.   But the thrall
laid such a grip on Grettir's arm that he recoiled at the might
of it.   Then Grettir gave way from one seat to another.   The
beams[1] started, and all that came in their way was broken.
Glam wished to get out, but Grettir set his feet against any p. 155
support he could find; nevertheless Glam dragged him forward
out of the hall.   And there they had a sore wrestling, in that
the thrall meant to drag him right out of the building; but
ill as it was to have to do with Glam inside, Grettir saw that it
would be yet worse without, and so he struggled with all his
might against going out.   Glam put forth all his strength, and
dragged Grettir towards himself when they came to the porch.
And when Grettir saw that he could not resist, then all at once
he flung himself against the breast of the thrall, as powerfully
as he could, and pressed forward with both his feet against
a stone which stood fast in the earth at the entrance.   The
thrall was not ready for this, he had been pulling to drag
Grettir towards himself; and thereupon he stumbled on his back
out of doors, so that his shoulders smote against the cross-
piece of the door, and the roof clave asunder, both wood and
frozen thatch.   So Glam fell backwards out of the house and
Grettir on top of him.   There was bright moonshine and
broken clouds without.   At times they drifted in front of the
moon and at times away.   Now at the moment when Glam
fell, the clouds cleared from before the moon, and Glam
rolled up his eyes; and Grettir himself has said that that
was the one sight he had seen which struck fear into him.
Then such a sinking came over Grettir, from his weariness
and from that sight of Glam rolling his eyes, that he had
no strength to draw his knife and lay almost between life and
death.

---

[1] The partition beams (*set-stokkar*) stood between the middle of the *skáli* or
hall and the planked daïs which ran down each side.   The strength of the
combatants is such that the *stokkar* give way.   Grettir gets no footing to withstand Glam till they reach the outer-door.   Here there is a stone set in the
ground, which apparently gives a better footing for a push than for a pull.
So Grettir changes his tactics, gets a purchase on the stone, and at the same
time pushes against Glam's breast, and so dashes Glam's head and shoulders
against the lintel of the outer-door.

But in this was there more power for evil in Glam than in most other apparitions, in that he spake thus: "Much eagerness hast thou shown, Grettir," said he, "to meet with me. But no wonder will it seem if thou hast no good luck from me. And this can I tell thee, that thou hast now achieved one half of the power and might which was fated for thee if thou hadst not met with me. Now no power have I to take that might from thee to which thou hast attained. But in this may I have my way, that thou shalt never become stronger than now thou art, and yet art thou strong enough, as many a one shall find to his cost. Famous hast thou been till now for thy deeds, but from now on shall exiles and manslaughters fall to thy lot, and almost all of thy labours shall turn to ill-luck and unhappiness. Thou shalt be outlawed and doomed ever to dwell alone, away from men; and then lay I this fate on thee, that these eyes of mine be ever before thy sight, and it shall seem grievous unto thee to be alone, and that shall drag thee to thy death."

And when the thrall had said this, the swoon which had
p. 156 fallen upon Grettir passed from him. Then he drew his sword and smote off Glam's head, and placed it by his thigh.

Then the yeoman came out: he had clad himself whilst Glam was uttering his curse, but he dare in no wise come near before Glam had fallen. Thorhall praised God for it, and thanked Grettir well for having vanquished the unclean spirit.

Then they set to work and burned Glam to cold cinders. After, they put the ashes in a skin-bag and buried them as far as possible from the ways of man or beast. After that they went home, and by that time it was well on to day. Grettir lay down, for he was very stiff. Thorhall sent people to the next farm for men, and showed to them what had happened. To all those who heard of it, it seemed a work of great account; and that was then spoken by all, that no man in all the land was equal to Grettir Asmundarson for might and valour and all prowess. Thorhall sent Grettir from his house with honour, and gave him a good horse and fit clothing; for all the clothes which he had worn before were torn asunder. They parted great friends. Grettir rode thence to Ridge in Water-dale, and Thorvald greeted him well, and asked closely as to his meeting

with Glam.   Grettir told him of their dealings, and said that
never had he had such a trial of strength, so long a struggle had
theirs been together.

Thorvald bade him keep quiet, "and then all will be well,
otherwise there are bound to be troubles for thee."

Grettir said that his temper had not bettered, and that he
was now more unruly than before, and all offences seemed worse
to him.   And in that he found a great difference, that he had
become so afraid of the dark that he did not dare to go anywhere
alone after night had fallen.   All kinds of horrors appeared to
him then.   And that has since passed into a proverb, that Glam
gives eyes, or gives "glam-sight" to those to whom things seem
quite other than they are.   Grettir rode home to Bjarg when
he had done his errand, and remained at home during the
winter.

(b)   Sandhaugar episode (p. 156 above)

There was a priest called Stein who lived at Eyjardalsá
(Isledale River) in Barthardal.   He was a good husbandman
and rich in cattle.   His son was Kjartan, a doughty man and
well grown.   There was a man called Thorstein the White who
lived at Sandhaugar (Sandheaps), south of Isledale river; his p. 157
wife was called Steinvor, and she was young and merry.   They
had children, who were young then.

People thought the place was much haunted by reason of
the visitation of trolls.   It happened, two winters before Grettir
came North into those districts, that the good-wife Steinvor at
Sandhaugar went to a Christmas service, according to her
custom, at Isledale river, but her husband remained at home.
In the evening men went to bed, and during the night they heard
a great rummage in the hall, and by the good-man's bed.   No
one dared to get up to look to it, because there were very few
men about.   The good-wife came home in the morning, but her
husband had vanished, and no one knew what had become of
him.

The next year passed away.   But the winter after, the good-
wife wished again to go to the church-service, and she bade her

manservant remain at home. He was unwilling, but said she must have her own way. All went in the same manner as before, and the servant vanished. People thought that strange. They saw some splashes of blood on the outer door, and men thought that evil beings must have taken away both the good-man and the servant.

The news of this spread wide throughout the country. Grettir heard of it; and because it was his fortune to get rid of hauntings and spirit-walkings, he took his way to Barthardal, and came to Sandhaugar on Yule eve. He disguised himself[1], and said his name was Guest. The good-wife saw that he was great of stature; and the farm-folk were much afraid of him. He asked for quarters for the night. The good-wife said that he could have meat forthwith, but "You must look after your own safety."

He said it should be so. "I will be at home," said he, "and you can go to the service if you will."

She answered, "You are a brave man, it seems to me, if you dare to remain at home."

"I do not care to have things all one way[2]," said he.

"It seems ill to me to be at home," said she, "but I cannot get over the river."

"I will see you over," said Guest.

Then she got ready to go to the service, and her small daughter with her. It was thawing, the river was in flood, and there were ice floes in it. Then the good-wife said, "It is impossible for man or horse to get across the river."

"There must be fords in it," said Guest, "do not be afraid."

p. 158 "Do you carry the child first," said the good-wife, "she is the lighter."

"I do not care to make two journeys of it," said Guest, "and I will carry thee on my arm."

She crossed herself and said, "That is an impossible way; what will you do with the child?"

---

[1] So MS 551 a. Magnússon reads *dvaldist þar* "he stayed there."

[2] Meaning that an attack by the evil beings would at least break the monotony.

"I will see a way for that," said he; and then he took them both up, and set the child on her mother's knee and so bore them both on his left arm. But he had his right hand free, and thus he waded out into the ford.

They did not dare to cry out, so much afraid were they. The river washed at once up against his breast; then it tossed a great icefloe against him, but he put out the hand that was free and pushed it from him. Then it grew so deep that the river dashed over his shoulder; but he waded stoutly on, until he came to the bank on the other side, and threw Steinvor and her daughter on the land.

Then he turned back, and it was half dark when he came to Sandhaugar and called for meat; and when he had eaten, he bade the farm folk go to the far side of the room. Then he took boards and loose timber which he dragged across the room, and made a great barrier so that none of the farm folk could come over it. No one dared to say anything against him or to murmur in any wise. The entrance was in the side wall of the chamber by the gable-end, and there was a dais there. Guest lay down there, but did not take off his clothes: a light was burning in the room over against the door: Guest lay there far into the night.

The good-wife came to Isledale river to the service, and men wondered how she had crossed the river. She said she did not know whether it was a man or a troll who had carried her over. The priest said, "It must surely be a man, although there are few like him. And let us say nothing about it," said he, "it may be that he is destined to work a remedy for your evils." The good-wife remained there through the night.

Now it is to be told concerning Grettir that when it drew towards midnight he heard great noises outside. Thereupon there came into the room a great giantess. She had in one hand a trough and in the other a short-sword, rather a big one. She looked round when she came in, and saw where Guest lay, and sprang at him; but he sprang up against her, and they struggled fiercely and wrestled for a long time in the room. She was the

stronger, but he gave way warily; and they broke all that was
before them, as well as the panelling of the room. She dragged
him forward through the door and so[1] into the porch, and he
p. 159 struggled hard against her. She wished to drag him out of the
house, but that did not happen until they had broken all the
fittings of the outer doorway and forced them out on their
shoulders. Then she dragged him slowly down towards the
river and right along to the gorge.

By that time Guest was exceedingly weary, but yet, one or
other it had to be, either he had to gather his strength together,
or else she would have hurled him down into the gorge. All
night they struggled. He thought that he had never grappled
with such a devil in the matter of strength. She had got such
a grip upon him that he could do nothing with either hand,
except to hold the witch by the middle; but when they came to
the gorge of the river he swung the giantess round, and thereupon got his right hand free. Then quickly he gripped his
knife that he wore in his girdle and drew it, and smote the
shoulder of the giantess so that he cut off her right arm.
So he got free: but she fell into the gorge, and so into the
rapids below.

Guest was then both stiff and tired, and lay long on the
rocks; then he went home when it began to grow light, and lay
down in bed. He was all swollen black and blue.

And when the good-wife came from the service, it seemed to
her that things had been somewhat disarranged in her house.
Then she went to Guest and asked him what had happened, that
all was broken and destroyed[2]. He told her all that had taken
place. She thought it very wonderful, and asked who he was.
He told her the truth, and asked her to send for the priest, and
said he wished to meet him; and so it was done.

Then when Stein the priest came to Sandhaugar, he knew
soon that it was Grettir Asmundarson who had come there,
and who had called himself Guest.

The priest asked Grettir what he thought must have become
of those men who had vanished. Grettir said he thought they

---

[1] A passage (*gǫng*) had to be traversed between the door of the room (*stufa*)
and the porch (*anddyri*).

[2] MSS *bœlt*. Boer reads *bolat* "hewn down."

must have vanished into the gorge. The priest said that he
could not believe Grettir's saying, if no signs of it were to be
seen. Grettir said that they would know more accurately
about it later. Then the priest went home. Grettir lay many
days in bed. The good-wife looked after him well, and so the
Christmas-time passed.

Grettir's account was that the giantess fell into the gulf
when she got her wound; but the men of Barthardal say that
day came upon her whilst they wrestled, and that she burst
when he smote her hand off, and that she stands there on the
cliff yet, a rock in the likeness of a woman[1].

The dwellers in the dale kept Grettir in hiding there. But
after Christmas time, one day that winter, Grettir went to
Isledale river. And when Grettir and the priest met, Grettir
said, "I see, priest, that you place little belief in my words. p. 160
Now will I that you go with me to the river and see what the
likelihood seems to you to be."

The priest did so. But when they came to the waterfall
they saw that the sides of the gorge hung over[2]: it was a sheer cliff
so great that one could in nowise come up, and it was nearly
ten fathoms[3] from the top to the water below. They had a rope
with them. Then the priest said, "It seems to me quite impossible for thee to get down."

Grettir said, "Assuredly it is possible, but best for those who
are men of valour. I will examine what is in the waterfall,
and thou shalt watch the rope."

---

[1] A night-troll, if caught by the sunrise, was supposed to turn into stone.

[2] *Skúta* may be acc. of the noun *skúti*, "overhanging precipice, cave"; or
it may be the verb, "hang over." Grettir and his companion see that the sides
of the ravine are precipitous (*skúta upp*) and so clean-cut (*meitil-berg*: *meitill*,
"a chisel") that they give no hold to the climber. Hence the need for the rope.
The translators all take *skúta* as acc. of *skúti*, which is quite possible: but they
are surely wrong when they proceed to identify the *skúti* with the *hellir* behind
the waterfall. For this cave behind the waterfall is introduced in the *saga* as
something which Grettir discovers *after* he has dived beneath the fall, the fall
in front naturally hiding it till then.

The verb *skúta* occurs elsewhere in *Grettis saga*, of the glaciers overhanging
a valley. Boer's attempt to reconstruct the scene appears to me wrong: cf.
Ranisch in *A.f.d.A.* xxviii, 217.

[3] The old editions read *fimm tigir faðma* "fifty fathoms": but according
to Boer's collation the best MS (A) reads **X**, whilst four of the five others
collated give XV (*fimtán*). The editors seem dissatisfied with this: yet sixty
to ninety feet seems a good enough height for a dive.

The priest said it should be as he wished, drove a peg into the cliff, piled stones against it, and sat by it[1].

Now it must be told concerning Grettir that he knotted a stone into the rope, and so let it down to the water.

"What way," said the priest, "do you mean to go?"

"I will not be bound," said Grettir, "when I go into the water, so much my mind forebodes me."

After that he got ready for his exploit, and had little on; he girded himself with his short sword, and had no other weapon.

Then he plunged from the cliff down into the waterfall. The priest saw the soles of his feet, and knew no more what had become of him. Grettir dived under the waterfall, and that was difficult because there was a great eddy, and he had to dive right to the bottom before he could come up behind the waterfall. There was a jutting rock and he climbed upon it. There was a great cave behind the waterfall, and the river fell in front of it from the precipice. He went into the cave, and there was a big fire burning. Grettir saw that there sat a giant of frightful size. He was terrible to look upon: but when Grettir came to him, the giant leapt up and seized a pike, and hewed at the new-comer: for with the pike he could both cut and stab. It had a handle of wood: men at that time called a weapon made in such a way a *heptisax*. Grettir smote against it with his short sword, and struck the handle so that he cut it asunder. Then the giant tried to reach back for a sword which hung behind him in the cave. Thereupon Grettir smote him in the breast, and struck off almost all the lower part of his chest and his belly, so that the entrails gushed out of him down into the river, and were swept along the current.

And as the priest sat by the rope he saw some lumps, clotted p. 161 with blood, carried down stream. Then he became unsteady, and thought that now he knew that Grettir must be dead: and he ran from keeping the rope and went home. It was then evening, and the priest said for certain that Grettir was dead, and added that it was a great loss of such a man.

Now the tale must be told concerning Grettir. He let little space go between his blows till the giant was dead. Then he

---

[1] *ok sat þar hjá*, not in MS A, nor in Boer's edition.

went further into the cave; he kindled a light and examined it.
It is not said how much wealth he took in the cave, but men
think that there was something. He stayed there far into the
night. He found there the bones of two men, and put them
into a bag. Then he left the cave and swam to the rope and
shook it, for he thought that the priest must be there. But
when he knew that the priest had gone home, then he had to
draw himself up, hand over hand, and so he came up on to the
cliff.

Then he went home to Isledale river, and came to the church
porch, with the bag that the bones were in, and with a rune-
staff, on which these verses were exceedingly well cut:

> There into gloomy gulf I passed,
> O'er which from the rock's throat is cast
> The swirling rush of waters wan,
> To meet the sword-player feared of man.
> By giant's hall the strong stream pressed
> Cold hands against the singer's breast;
> Huge weight upon him there did hurl
> The swallower of the changing whirl[1].

And this rhyme too:

> The dreadful dweller of the cave
> Great strokes and many 'gainst me drave;
> Full hard he had to strive for it,
> But toiling long he wan no whit;
> For from its mighty shaft of tree
> The heft-sax smote I speedily;
> And dulled the flashing war-flame fair
> In the black breast that met me there.

These verses told also that Grettir had taken these bones out p. 162
of the cave. But when the priest came to the church in the
morning he found the staff, and what was with it, and read the
runes; but Grettir had gone home to Sandhaugar.

But when the priest met Grettir he asked him closely as to
what had happened: and Grettir told him all the story of his
journey. And he added that the priest had not watched the
rope faithfully. The priest said that that was true enough.

Men thought for certain that these monsters must have
caused the loss of men there in the dale; and there was never
any loss from hauntings or spirit-walkings there afterwards.

[1] The two poems are given according to the version of William Morris.

Grettir was thought to have caused a great purging of the land.
The priest buried these bones in the churchyard.

D. EXTRACTS FROM *BJARKA RÍMUR*

(*Hrólfs saga Kraka og Bjarkarímur* udgivne ved F. Jónsson,
København, 1904)

58. Flestir ǫmuðu Hetti heldr,
hann var ekki í máli sneldr,
einn dag fóru þeir út af hǫll,
svó ekki vissi hirðin ǫll.

59. Hjalti talar er felmtinn fær,
"fǫrum við ekki skógi nær,
hér er sú ylgr sem etr upp menn,
okkr drepr hún báða senn."

60. Ylgrin hljóp úr einum runn,
ógurlig með gapanda munn,
hǫrmuligt varð Hjalta viðr,
á honum skalf bæði leggr og liðr.

61. Ótæpt Bjarki að henni gengr,
ekki dvelr hann við það lengr,
hǫggur svó að í hamri stóð,
hljóp úr henni ferligt blóð.

62. "Kjóstu Hjalti um kosti tvó,"
kappinn Bǫðvar talaði svó,
"drekk nú blóð eða drep eg þig hér,
dugrinn líz mér engi í þér."

63. Ansar Hjalti af ærnum móð,
"ekki þori eg að drekka blóð,
nýtir flest ef nauðigr skal,
nú er ekki á betra val."

64. Hjalti gjǫrir sem Bǫðvar biðr,
að blóði frá eg hann lagðist niðr,
drekkur síðan drykki þrjá,
duga mun honum við einn að rjá.

IV, 58–64.

4. Hann hefr fengið hjartað snjalt
af hǫrðum móði,
fekk hann huginn og aflið alt
af ylgjar blóði.

5. Í grindur vandist gráhjǫrn einn
í garðinn Hleiðar,
var sá margur vargrinn beinn
og víða sveiðar.

6. Bjarka er kent, að hjarðarhunda
hafi hann drepna,
ekki er hónum allvel hent
við ýta kepna.

7. Hrólfur býst og hirð hans ǫll
að húna stýri,
"Sá skal mestr í minni hǫll
er mætir dýri."

8. Beljandi hljóp bjǫrninn framm
úr bóli krukku,
veifar sínum vónda hramm,
svó virðar hrukku.

9. Hjalti sér og horfir þá á,
er hafin er róma,
hafði hann ekki í hǫndum þá
nema hnefana tóma.

10. Hrólfur fleygði að Hjalta þá
þeim hildar vendi,
kappinn móti krummu brá
og klótið hendi.

11. Lagði hann síðan bjǫrninn brátt
við bóginn hægra,
bessi fell í brúðar átt
og bar sig lægra.

12. Vann hann það til frægða fyst
og fleira síðar,
hans var lundin lǫngum byst
í leiki gríðar.

13. Hér með fekk hann Hjalta nafn
hins hjartaprúða,
Bjarki var eigi betri en jafn
við býti skrúða.

v, 4–13.

23. Aðals var glaðr afreksmaðr,
austur þangað kómu,
fyrðar þeir með fránan geir
flengja þegar til rómu.

24. Ýtar býta engum frið,
unnu vel til mála,
þar fell Áli og alt hans lið
ungr í leiki stála.

25. Hestrinn beztur Hrafn er kendr,
hafa þeir tekið af Ála,
Hildisvín er hjálmrinn vendr,
hann kaus Bjarki í mála.

26. Qðling það þá eigi drafl
eiga um nǫkkur skipti,
það mun kosta kóngligt afl,
hann kappann gripunum svipti.

27. Ekki þótti Bǫðvar betr,
í burtu fóru þeir Hjalti,
létust áðr en liðinn er vetr
leita að Fróða malti.

28. Síðan ríða seggir heim
og sǫgðu kóngi þetta,
hann kveðst mundu handa þeim
heimta slíkt af létta.

viii, 23–28.

TRANSLATION OF EXTRACTS FROM *BJARKA RÍMUR*

58.　Most [of Rolf's retainers] much tormented Hott [Hjalti];
he was not cunning in speech. One day Hjalti and Bothvar went
out of the hall, in such wise that none of the retainers knew
thereof.

59. Hjalti spake in great terror, "Let us not go near the wood; here is the she-wolf who eats up men; she will kill us both together."

60. The she-wolf leapt from a thicket, dread, with gaping jaws. A great terror was it to Hjalti, and he trembled in every limb.

61. Without delay or hesitation went Bjarki towards her, and hewed at her so that the axe went deep; a monstrous stream of blood gushed from her.

62. "Choose now, Hjalti, of two things"—so spake Bothvar the champion—"Drink now the blood, or I slay thee here; it seems unto me that there is no valour in thee."

63. Hjalti replied stoutly enough, "I cannot bring myself to drink blood; but if I needs must, it avails most [to submit], and now is there no better choice."

64. Hjalti did as Bothvar bade: he stooped down to the blood; then drank he three sups: that will suffice him to wrestle with one man.

iv, 58–64.

4. He [Hjalti] has gained good courage and keen spirit; he got strength and all valour from the she-wolf's blood.

5. A grey bear visited the folds at Hleithargarth; many such a ravager was there far and wide throughout the country.

6. The blame was laid upon Bjarki, because he had slain the herdsmen's dogs; it was not so suited for him to have to strive with men[1].

7. Rolf and all his household prepared to hunt the bear; "He who faces the beast shall be greatest in my hall."

8. Roaring did the bear leap forth from out its den, swinging its evil claws, so that men shrank back.

9. Hjalti saw, he turned and gazed where the battle began; nought had he then in his hands—his empty fists alone.

---

[1] On his first arrival at Leire, Bjarki had been attacked by, and had slain, the watch-dogs (*Rímur*, iv, 41): this naturally brings him now into disfavour, and he has to dispute with men.

10. Rolf tossed then to Hjalti his wand of war [his sword]; the warrior put forth his hand towards it, and grasped the pommel.

11. Quickly then he smote the bear in the right shoulder; Bruin fell to the earth, and bore himself in more lowly wise.

12. That was the beginning of his exploits: many followed later; his spirit was ever excellent amid the play of battle.

13. Herefrom he got the name of Hjalti the stout-hearted: Bjarki was no more than his equal.

v, 4–13.

23. Joyful was the valiant Athils when they [Bjarki and Rolf's champions] came east to that place [Lake Wener]; troops with flashing spears rode quickly forthwith to the battle.

24. No truce gave they to their foes: well they earned their pay; there fell Ali and all his host, young in the game of swords.

25. The best of horses, Hrafn by name, they took from Ali; Bjarki chose for his reward the helm Hildisvin.

26. The prince [Athils] bade them have no talk about the business; he deprived the champions[1] of their treasures—that will be a test of his power.

27. Ill-pleased was Bothvar: he and Hjalti departed; they declared that before the winter was gone they would seek for the treasure [the malt of Frothi].

28. Then they rode home and told it to the king [Rolf]; he said it was their business to claim their due outright.

viii, 23–28.

E.   EXTRACT FROM *ÞÁTTR ORMS STÓRÓLFSSONAR*

(*Fornmanna Sǫgur*, Copenhagen, 1827, iii. 204 *etc.*;
Flateyarbók, Christiania, 1859–68, i. 527 *etc.*)

7. Litlu síðarr enn þeir Ormr ok Ásbjǫrn hǫfðu skilit, fýstist Ásbjǫrn norðr í Sauðeyjar, fór hann við 4 menn ok 20 á skipi, heldr norðr fyrir Mæri, ok leggr seint dags at Sauðey

---

[1] Reading *kappana*.

hinni ytri, gánga á land ok reisa tjald, eru þar um nóttina, ok
verða við ekki varir; um morgininn árla rís Ásbjǫrn upp,
klæðir sik, ok tekr vópn sín, ok gengr uppá land, en biðr menn
sína bíða sín; en er nokkut svá var liðit frá því, er Ásbjǫrn hafði
í brott gengit, verða þeir við þat varir, at ketta ógrlig var
komin í tjaldsdyrnar, hon var kolsvǫrt at lit ok heldr grimmlig,
þvíat eldr þótti brenna or nǫsum hennar ok munni, eigi var hon
ok vel eyg; þeim brá mjǫk við þessa sýn, ok urðu óttafullir.
Ketta hleypr þá innar at þeim, ok grípr hvern at ǫðrum, ok
svá er sagt at suma gleypti hon, en suma rifi hon til dauðs með
klóm ok tǫnnum, 20 menn drap hon þar á lítilli stundu, en 3
kvómust út ok undan ok á skip, ok héldu þegar undan landi;
en Ásbjǫrn gengr þar til, er hann kemr at hellinum Brúsa, ok
snarar þegar inn í; honum varð nokkut dimt fyrir augum, en
skuggamikit var í hellinum; hann verðr eigi fyrr var við, enn
hann er þrifinn álopt, ok færðr niðr svá hart, at Ásbirni þótti
furða í, verðr hann þess þá varr, at þar er kominn Brúsi jǫtun,
ok sýndist heldr mikiligr. Brúsi mælti þá: þó lagðir þú mikit
kapp á at sækja híngat; skaltu nú ok eyrindi hafa, þvíat þú
skalt hér lífit láta með svá miklum harmkvælum, at þat skal
aðra letja at sækja mik heim með ófriði; fletti hann þá Ásbjǫrn
klæðum, þvíat svá var þeirra mikill afla munr, at jǫtuninn varð
einn at ráða þeirra í milli; bálk mikinn sá Ásbjǫrn standa um
þveran hellinn ok stórt gat á miðjum bálkinum; járnsúla stór
stóð nokkut svá fyrir framan bálkinn. Nú skal prófa þat, segir
Brúsi, hvárt þú ert nokkut harðari enn aðrir menn. Lítit mun
þat at reyna, segir Ásbjǫrn....

Síðan lét Ásbjǫrn líf sitt með mikilli hreysti ok dreingskap.

8. Þat er at segja at þeir þrír menn, er undan kómust,
sóttu knáliga róðr, ok léttu eigi fyrr enn þeir kómu at landi,
sǫgðu þau tíðindi er gerzt hǫfðu í þeirra fǫrum, kvóðust ætla
Ásbjǫrn dauðan, en kunnu ekki frá at segja, hversu at hefði
borizt um hans líflát; kvómu þeir sér i skip með kaupmǫnnum,
ok fluttust svá suðr til Danmerkr; spurðust nú þessi tíðindi
víða, ok þóttu mikil. Þá var orðit hǫfðíngja skipti í Noregi,
Hakon jarl dauðr, en Ólafr Tryggvason í land kominn, ok bauð
ǫllum rétta trú. Ormr Stórólfsson spurði út til Íslands um

farar ok líflát Ásbjarnar, er mǫnnum þótti sem vera mundi;
þótti honum þat allmikill skaði, ok undi eigi lengr á Íslandi,
ok tók sér far í Reyðarfirði, ok fór þar utan; þeir kvómu nor-
ðarliga við Noreg, ok sat hann um vetrinn í Þrándheimi; þá
hafði Ólafr ráðit 3 vetr Noregi. Um vórit bjóst Ormr at fara
til Sauðeya, þeir vóru því nærr margir á skipi, sem þeir Ásbjǫrn
hǫfðu verit; þeir lǫgðu at minni Sauðey síð um kveldit, ok
tjǫlduðu á landi, ok lágu þar um náttina....

9. Nú gengr Ormr þar til er hann kemr at hellinum, sér
hann nú bjargit þat stóra, ok leizt úmátuligt nokkurum manni
þat í brott at færa; þó dregr hann á sik glófana Menglaðarnauta,
tekr síðan á bjarginu ok færir þat burt or dyrunum, ok þikist
Ormr þá aflraun mesta sýnt hafa; hann gekk þá inní hellinn,
ok lagði málajárn í dyrnar, en er hann var inn kominn, sá hann
hvar kettan hljóp með gapanda ginit. Ormr hafði boga ok
ǫrvamæli, lagði hann þá ǫr á streing, ok skaut at kettunni
þremr ǫrum, en hon hendi allar með hvoptunum, ok beit í
sundr, hefir hon sik þá at Ormi, ok rekr klærnar framan í fángit,
svá at Ormr kiknar við, en klærnar gengu í gegnum klæðin svá
at í beini stóð; hon ætlar þá at bíta í andlit Ormi, finnr hann
þá at honum mun eigi veita, heitir þá á sjálfan guð ok hinn
heilaga Petrum postula, at gánga til Róms, ef hann ynni
kettuna ok Brúsa, son hennar; síðan fann Ormr at mínkaðist
afl kettunnar, tekr hann þá annarri hendi um kverkr henni, en
annarri um hrygg, ok gengr hana á bak, ok brýtr ísundr í henni
hrygginn, ok gengr svá af henni dauðri. Ormr sá þá, hvar
bálkr stórr var um þveran hellinn; hann gengr þá innar at,
en er hann kemr þar, sér hann at fleinn mikill kemr utar í gegnum
bálkinn, hann var bæði digr ok lángr; Ormr grípr þá í móti
fleininum, ok leggr af út; Brúsi kippir þá at sér fleininum ok
var hann fastr svá at hvergi gekk; þat undraðist Brúsi, ok
gægdist upp yfir bálkinn, en er Ormr sér þat, þrífr hann í
skeggit á Brúsa báðum hǫndum, en Brúsi bregzt við í ǫðrum
stað, sviptast þeir þá fast um bálkinn. Ormr hafði vafit skegg-
inu um hǫnd sér, ok rykkir til svá fast, at hann rífr af Brúsa
allan skeggstaðinn, hǫkuna, kjaptana báða, vángafyllurnar upp
alt at eyrum, gekk hér með holdit niðr at beini. Brúsi lét þá

síga brýnnar, ok grettist heldr greppiliga. Ormr stǫkkr þá
innar yfir bálkinn, grípast þeir þá til ok glíma lengi, mæddi
Brúsa þá fast blóðrás, tekr hann þá heldr at gángast fyrir, gefr
Ormr þá á, ok rekr Brúsa at bálkinum ok brýtr hann þar um
á bak aptr. Snemma sagði mér þat hugr, sagði Brúsi, at ek
munda af þér nokkut erfitt fá, þegar ek heyrða þín getit, enda
er þat nú fram komit, muntu nú vinna skjótt um, ok hǫggva
hǫfuð af mér, en þat var satt, at mjǫk pínda ek Ásbjǫrn prúða,
þá er ek rakta or honum alla þarmana, ok gaf hann sik ekki
við, fyrrenn hann dó. Illa gerðir þú þat, segir Ormr, at pína
hann svá mjǫk jafnrǫskvan mann, skaltu ok hafa þess nokkurar
menjar. Hann brá þá saxi ok reist blóðǫrn á baki honum, ok
skar ǫll rifin frá hryggnum, ok dró þar út lúngun; lét Brúsi
svá líf sitt með litlum dreingskap; síðan bar Ormr eld at, ok
brendi upp til ǫsku bæði Brúsa ok kettuna, ok er hann hafði
þetta starfat, fór hann burt or hellinum með kistur tvær fullar
af gulli ok silfri, en þat sem meira var fémætt, gaf hann í vald
Menglaðar, ok svá eyna; skildu þau með mikilli vináttu, kom
Ormr til manna sinna í nefndan tíma, héldu síðan til meginlands.
Sat Ormr í Þrándheimi vetr annan.

TRANSLATION OF EXTRACT FROM *ÞÁTTR ORMS STÓRÓLFSSONAR*

7.

A little after Orm and Asbiorn had parted, Asbiorn wished
to go north to Sandeyar[1]; he went aboard with twenty-four
men, went north past Mæri, and landed late in the day at the
outermost of the Sandeyar[1]. They landed and pitched a tent,
and spent the night there, and met with nothing.

Early in the morning Asbiorn arose, clothed himself, took
his arms, went inland, and bade his men wait for him.

But when some time had passed from Asbiorn's having gone
away, they were aware that a monstrous[2] cat had come to the

---

[1] The MSS have either *Sandeyar* or *Saudeyar* (*Sauðeyar*). But that *Sandeyar* is the correct form is shown by the name Sandø, which is given still to the
island of Dollsey, where Orm's fight is localized (Panzer, 403).

[2] Literally "she-cat," *ketta*; but the word may mean "giantess." It is used
in some MSS of the *Grettis saga* of the giantess who attacks Grettir at Sandhaugar.

door of the tent: she was coal-black in colour and very fierce, for it seemed as if fire was burning from her nostrils and mouth, and her eyes were nothing fair: they were much startled at this sight, and full of fear. Then the cat leapt within the tent upon them, and gripped one after the other, and so it is said that some she swallowed and some she tore to death with claws and teeth. Twenty men she killed in a short time, and three escaped aboard ship, and stood away from the shore.

But Asbiorn went till he came to the cave of Brusi, and hastened in forthwith. It was dim before his eyes, and very shadowy in the cave, and before he was aware of it, he was caught off his feet, and thrown down so violently that it seemed strange to him. Then was he aware that there was come the giant Brusi, and he seemed to him a great one.

Then said Brusi, "Thou didst seek with great eagerness to come hither—now shalt thou have business, in that thou shalt here leave thy life with so great torments that that shall stay others from attacking me in my lair."

Then he stripped Asbiorn of his clothes, forasmuch as so great was their difference in strength that the giant could do as he wished. Asbiorn saw a great barrier standing across the cave, and a mighty opening in the midst of it; a great iron column stood somewhat in front of the barrier. "Now it must be tried," said Brusi, "whether thou art somewhat hardier than other men." "Little will that be to test," said Asbiorn....

[Asbiorn then recites ten stanzas, Brusi tormenting him the while. The first stanza is almost identical with No. 50 in the *Grettis saga*.]

Then Asbiorn left his life with great valour and hardihood.

8.

Now it must be told concerning the three men who escaped; they rowed strongly, and stopped not until they came to land. They told the tidings of what had happened in their journey, and said that they thought that Asbiorn was dead, but that they could not tell how matters had happened concerning his death. They took ship with merchants, and so went south to

Denmark: now these tidings were spread far and wide, and seemed weighty.

There had been a change of rulers in Norway: jarl Hakon was dead, and Olaf Tryggvason come to land: and he proclaimed the true faith to all. Orm Storolfson heard, out in Iceland, about the expedition of Asbiorn, and the death which it seemed to men must have come upon him. It seemed to him a great loss, and he cared no longer to be in Iceland, and took passage at Reytharfirth and went abroad. They reached Norway far to the north, and he stayed the winter at Thrandheim: Olaf at that time had reigned three years in Norway.

In the spring Orm made ready for his journey to Sandeyar, and there were nearly as many in the ship as the company of Asbiorn had been.

They landed at Little Sandey late in the evening, and pitched a tent on the land, and lay there the night....

9.

Now Orm went till he came to the cave. He saw the great rock, and thought it was impossible for any man to move it. Then he drew on the gloves that Menglath had given him, and grasped the rock and moved it away from the door; this is reckoned Orm's great feat of strength. Then he went into the cave, and thrust his weapon against the door. When he came in, he saw a giantess (she-cat) springing towards him with gaping jaws. Orm had a bow and quiver; he put the arrow on the string, and shot thrice at the giantess. But she seized all the arrows in her mouth, and bit them asunder. Then she flung herself upon Orm, and thrust her claws into his breast, so that Orm stumbled, and her claws went through his clothes and pierced him to the bone. She tried then to bite his face, and Orm found himself in straits: he promised then to God, and the holy apostle Peter, to go to Rome, if he conquered the giantess and Brusi her son. Then Orm felt the power of the giantess diminishing: he placed one hand round her throat, and the other round her back, and bent it till he broke it in two, and so left her dead.

Then Orm saw where a great barrier ran across the cave: he went further in, and when he came to it he saw a great shaft coming out through the barrier, both long and thick. Orm gripped the shaft and drew it away; Brusi pulled it towards himself, but it did not yield. Then Brusi wondered, and peeped up over the barrier. But when Orm saw that, he gripped Brusi by the beard with both hands, but Brusi pulled away, and so they tugged across the barrier. Orm twisted the beard round his hand, and tugged so violently that he pulled the flesh of Brusi away from the bone—from chin, jaws, cheeks, right up to the ears. Brusi knitted his brows and made a hideous face. Then Orm leapt in over the barrier, and they grappled and wrestled for a long time. But loss of blood wearied Brusi, and he began to fail in strength. Orm pressed on, pushed Brusi to the barrier, and broke his back across it. "Right early did my mind misgive me," said Brusi, "even so soon as I heard of thee, that I should have trouble from thee: and now has that come to pass. But now make quick work, and hew off my head. And true it is that much did I torture the gallant Asbiorn, in that I tore out all his entrails—yet did he not give in, before he died." "Ill didst thou do," said Orm, "to torture him, so fine a man as he was, and thou shalt have something in memory thereof." Then he drew his knife, and cut the "blood eagle" in the back of Brusi, shore off his ribs and drew out his lungs. So Brusi died in cowardly wise. Then Orm took fire, and burned to ashes both Brusi and the giantess. And when he had done that, he left the cave, with two chests full of gold and silver.

And all that was most of value he gave to Menglath, and the island likewise. So they parted with great friendship, and Orm came to his men at the time appointed, and then they sailed to the mainland. Orm remained a second winter at Thrandheim.

F. A Danish Dragon-slaying of the Beowulf-type

Paa den Tid, da kong Gram Guldkølve regierede i Leire, vare der ved Hoffet to Ministre, Bessus og Henrik. Og da der paa samme Tid indkom idelige klager fra Indbyggerne i Vendsyssel, at et grueligt Udyr, som Bønderne kaldte Lindorm, ødelagde baade Mennesker og Kreaturer, gav Bessus det Raad, at Kongen skulde sende Henrik did hen, efterdi ingen i det ganske Rige kunde maale sig med ham in Tapperhed og Mod. Da svarede

Henrik, at han vel vilde paatage sig dette, dog tilføiede han, at han ansaae det for umuligt at slippe fra saadan Kamp med Livet. Og belavede han sig da strax til Reisen, tog rørende Afsked med sin Herre og Konge og sagde iblandt andet: "Herre! om jeg ikke kommer tilbage, da sørg for min kone og for mine Børn!" Da han derefter var kommen over til Vendsyssel, lod han sig af Bønderne vise det Sted, hvor Uhyret havde sit Leie, og fik da at vide, at Ormen endnu den samme Dag havde været ude af Hulen og borttaget en Hyrde og en Oxe, og at den efter Sædvane nu ikke vilde komme ud, førend om tre Timer, naar den skulde ned til Vandet for at drikke efter Maaltidet. Henrik iførte sig da sin fulde Rustning, og eftersom Ingen vovede at staae ham bi i dette Arbeide, lagde han sig ganske alene ved Vandet, dog saaledes, at Vinden ikke bar fra ham henimod Dyret. Da udsendte han først en vældig Piil fra sin Bue, men uagtet den rammede nøie det sted, hvortil han havde sigtet, tørnede den dog tilbage fra Ormens haarde Skæl. Herover blev Uhyret saa optændt af Vrede, at det strax gik henimod ham, agtende ham kun et ringe Maaltid; men Henrik havde iforveien hos en Smed ladet sig giøre en stor Krog med Gjenhold, hvilken han jog ind i Beestets aabne Gab, saa at det ikke kunde blive den qvit, ihvormeget det end arbeidede, og ihvorvel Jern-stangen brast i Henriks Hænder. Da slog det ham med sin vældige Hale til Jorden, og skiøndt han havde fuldkommen Jernrustning paa, kradsede det dog med sine forfærdelige Kløer saa at han, næsten dødeligt saaret, faldt i Besvimelse. Men da han, efterat Ormen i nogen Tid havde haft ham liggende under sin Bug, endelig kom lidt til sin Samling igien, greb han af yderste Evne en Daggert, af hvilke han førte flere med sig i sit Bælte, og stak Dyret dermed i underlivet, hvor Skællene vare blødest, saa at det tilsidst maate udpuste sin giftige Aande, medens han selv laae halv knust under dens Byrde. Da Bønderne i Vendsyssel som stode i nogen Afstand, under megen Frygt og lidet Haab omsider mærkede, at Striden sagtnede, og at begge Parter holdte sig rolige, nærmede de sig og fandt Hr. Henrik næsten livløs under det dræbte Udyr. Og efterat de i nogen Tid havde givet ham god Pleie, vendte han tilbage for at dø hos sin Konge, til hvem han gientagende anbefalede sin

Slægt. Fra ham nedstammer Familien Lindenroth, som til
Minde om denne vældige Strid fører en Lindorm i sit Vaaben.
MS 222. 4°. Stamme och Slectebog over den høiadelige
Familie af Lindenroth, in *Danmarks Folkesagn*, samlede af
J. M. Thiele, 1843, ɪ, 125–7.

A DANISH DRAGON-SLAYING OF THE BEOWULF-TYPE.

Translation.

In the days when King Gram Guldkølve ruled in Leire,
there were two ministers at court, Bessus and Henry. And at
that time constant complaints came to the court from the inhabitants of Vendsyssel, that a dread monster, which the peasants
called a Drake, was destroying both man and beast. So Bessus
gave counsel, that the king should send Henry against the
dragon, seeing that no one in the whole kingdom was his equal
in valour and courage. Henry answered that assuredly he would
undertake it; but he added that he thought it impossible to
escape from such a struggle with his life. And he made himself
ready forthwith for the expedition, took a touching farewell
of his lord and king, and said among other things: "My lord,
if I come not back, care thou for my wife and my children."
Afterwards, when he crossed over to Vendsyssel, he caused
the peasants to show him the place where the monster had its
lair, and learnt how that very day the drake had been out of
its den, and had carried off a herdsman and an ox; how, according to its wont, it would now not come out for three hours,
when it would want to go down to the water to drink after its
meal. Henry clothed himself in full armour, and inasmuch as
no one dared to stand by him in that task, he lay down all alone
by the water, but in such wise that the wind did not blow from
him toward the monster. First of all he sent a mighty arrow
from his bow: but, although it exactly hit the spot at which
he had aimed, it darted back from the dragon's hard scales.
At this the monster was so maddened, that it attacked him
forthwith, reckoning him but a little meal. But Henry had
had a mighty barbed crook prepared by a smith beforehand,
which he thrust into the beast's open mouth so that it could

not get rid of it, however much it strove, although the iron rod broke in Henry's hands. Then it smote him to the ground with its mighty tail, and although he was in complete armour, clutched at him with its dread claws, so that he fell in a swoon, wounded almost to death. But when he came somewhat to his senses again, after the drake for some time had had him lying under its belly, he rallied his last strength and grasped a dagger, of which he carried several with him in his belt, and smote it therewith in the belly, where the scales were weakest. So the monster at last breathed out its poisoned breath, whilst he himself lay half crushed under its weight. When the Vendsyssel peasants, who stood some distance away, in great fear and little hope, at last noticed that the battle had slackened, and that both combatants were still, they drew near and found Henry almost lifeless under the slain monster. And after they for some time had tended him well, he returned to die by his king, to whom he again commended his offspring. From him descends the family Lindenroth, which in memory of this mighty contest carries a drake on its coat of arms.

This story resembles the dragon fight in *Beowulf*, in that the hero faces the dragon as protector of the land, with forebodings, and after taking farewell; he attacks the dragon in its lair, single-handed; his first attack is frustrated by the dragon's scales; in spite of apparatus specially prepared, he is wounded and stunned by the dragon, but nevertheless smites the dragon in the soft parts and slays him; the watchers draw near when the fight is over. Yet these things merely prove that the two stories are of the same type; there is no evidence that this story is descended from *Beowulf*.

G. The Old English Genealogies.

I. *THE MERCIAN GENEALOGY.*

Of the Old English Genealogies, the only one which, in its stages *below* Woden, immediately concerns the student of *Beowulf* is the Mercian. This contains three names which also occur in *Beowulf*, though two of them in a corrupt form—Offa, Wermund (Garmund, *Beowulf*), and Eomær (Geomor, *Beowulf*).

This Mercian pedigree is found in its best form in *MS Cotton Vesp. B. VI*, fol. 109 b,[1] and in the sister MS at Corpus Christi College, Cambridge (*C.C.C.C.* 183)[2]. Both these MSS are of

[1] See Sweet, *Oldest English Texts*, 1885, p. 170.
[2] See *Catalogue of MSS. in the Library of Corpus Christi College, Cambridge* by Montague Rhodes James, Camb., 1912, p. 437.

the 9th century. They contain lists of popes and bishops, and pedigrees of kings. By noting where these lists stop, we get a limit for the final compilation of the document. It must have been drawn up in its present form between 811 and 814[1]. But it was obviously compiled from lists already existing, and some of them were even at that date old. For the genealogy of the Mercian kings, from Woden, is not traced directly down to this period 811–814, but in the first place only as far as Æthelred (reigning 675–704), son of Penda: that is to say, it stops considerably more than a century before the date of the document in which it appears. Additional pedigrees are then appended which show the subsequent stages down to and including Cenwulf, king of Mercia (reigning 796–821). It is difficult to account for such an arrangement except on the hypothesis that the genealogy was committed to writing in the reign of Æthelred, the monarch with whose name it terminates in its first form, and was then brought up to date by the addition of the supplementary names ending with Cenwulf. This is confirmed when we find that precisely the same arrangement holds good for the accompanying Northumbrian pedigree, which terminates with Ecgfrith (670–685), the contemporary of Æthelred of Mercia, and is then brought up to date by additional names.

Genealogies which draw from the same source as the *Vespasian* genealogies, and show the same peculiarities, are found in the *Historia Brittonum* (§§ 57–61). They show, even more emphatically than do the *Vespasian* lists, traces of having been originally drawn up in the time of Æthelred of Mercia (675–704) or possibly of his father Penda, and of having then been brought up to date in subsequent revisions[2].

One such revision must have been made about 796[3]: it is a

---

[1] See *Publications of the Palæographical Society*, 1880, where a facsimile of part of the *Vespasian MS* is given. (Pt. 10, Plate 165: subsequently Ser. I, Vol. II.)

[2] So Zimmer, *Nennius Vindicatus*, Berlin, 1893, pp. 78 etc., and Duchesne (*Revue Celtique*, xv, 196). Duchesne sums up these genealogies as "un recueil constitué, vers la fin du VII⁰ siècle, dans le royaume de Strathcluyd, mais complété par diverses retouches, dont la dernière est de 796."

[3] This is shown by one of the supplementary Mercian pedigrees being made to end, both in the *Vespasian* genealogy and the *Historia Brittonum*, in Ecgfrith, who reigned for a few months in 796. See Thurneysen (*Z.f.d.Ph.* xxviii, 101).

modification of this revision which is found in the *Historia Brittonum.* Another was that which, as we have seen, must have been made between 811–814, and in this form is found in *MS Cotton Vespasian B. VI, MS C.C.C.C.* 183, both of the 9th century, and in the (much later) *MS Cotton Tiberius B. V.* The genealogy up to Penda is also found in the *A.-S. Chronicle* under the year 626 (accession of Penda).

This Mercian list, together with the Northumbrian and other pedigrees which accompany it, can claim to be the earliest extant English historical document, having been written down in the 7th century, and recording historic names which (allowing thirty years for a generation) cannot be later than the 4th century A.D. In most similar pedigrees the earliest names are meaningless to us. But the Mercian pedigree differs from the rest, in that we are able from *Beowulf, Widsith,* Saxo Grammaticus, Sweyn Aageson and the *Vitae Offarum,* to attach stories to the names of Wermund and Offa. How much of these stories is history, and how much fiction, it is difficult to say—but, with them, extant English history and English poetry and English fiction alike have their beginning.

MS Cotton Vesp. B. VI.		MS C.C.C.C. 183.	
Aeðilred	Peding	Æðelred	Pending
Penda	Pypbing	Penda	Pybbing
Pypba	Crioding	Pybba	Creoding
Crioda	Cynewalding	Creoda	Cynewalding
Cynewald	Cnebbing	Cynewald	Cnebbing
Cnebba	Icling	Cnebba	Icling
Icil	Eamering	Icel	Eomæring
Eamer	Angengeoting	Eomær	Angengeoting
Angengeot	Offing	Angengiot	Offing
Offa	Uærmunding	Offa	Wærmunding
Uermund	Uihtlaeging	Wærmund	Wihtlæging
Uihtlaeg	Wioðulgeoting	Wihtlæg	Wioþolgeoting
Weoðulgeot	Wodning	Weoþolgiot	Wodning
Woden	Frealafing	Woden	Frealafing

Historia Brittonum[1].	*Anglo-Saxon Chronicle.*	
MS Harl 3859.	MSS Cotton Tib. A. VI. and B. I.[2]	
Penda	Penda	Pybbing
Pubba	Pybba	Creoding
	Creoda	Cynewalding
	Cynewald	Cnebbing
	Cnebba	Iceling
	Icel	Eomæring
Eamer	Eomær	Angelþeowing
Ongen	Angelþeow	Offing
Offa	Offa	Wærmunding
Guerdmund	Wærmund	Wihtlæging
Guithleg	Wihtlæg	Wodening
Gueagon		
Guedolgeat		
[U]Uoden		

II. THE STAGES ABOVE WODEN

(1) WODEN TO GEAT.

The stages above Woden are found in two forms: a short
list which traces the line from Woden up to Geat: and a longer
list which carries the line from Geat to Sceaf and through Noah
to Adam.

The line from Woden to Geat is found in the *Historia
Brittonum*, not with the other genealogies, but in § 31, where
the pedigree of the Kentish royal family is given, when the
arrival of Hengest in Britain is recounted.   Notwithstanding
the dispute regarding the origin and date of the *Historia Brittonum*, there is a pretty general agreement that this *Woden to
Geat* pedigree is one of the more primitive elements, and is not
likely to be much later than the end of the 7th century[3].   The
original nucleus of the *Historia Brittonum* was revised by

---

[1] Ed. Mommsen, p. 203.

[2] Anno 626: a similar genealogy will be found in these MSS and in the
Parker MS, anno 755 (accession of Offa II).

[3] Zimmer (*Nennius Vindicatus*, p. 84) argues that this *Geta-Woden* pedigree belongs to a portion of the *Historia Brittonum* written down A.D. 685.
Thurneysen (*Z.f.d.Ph.* XXVIII, 103–4) dates the section in which it occurs
679; Duchesne (*Revue Celtique*, XV, 196) places it more vaguely between the
end of the sixth and the beginning of the eighth century; van Hamel (*Hoops
Reallexikon* s.v. *Nennius*) between much the same limits, and clearly before 705.

Nennius in the 9th century, or possibly at the end of the 8th[1].
The earliest MS of the *Historia*, that of Chartres, belongs to
the 9th or 10th century—this is fragmentary and already interpolated; the received text is based upon *MS Harleian* 3859,
dating from the end of the 11th century[2], or possibly somewhat
later.

I give the pedigree in four forms:

A. The critical text of the *Historia Brittonum* as edited by
Th. Mommsen (*Monumenta Germaniae Historica, Auct. Antiq.,
Chronica Minora*, III, Berolini, 1898, p. 171).

B. *MS Harl.* 3859, upon which Mommsen's text is based,
fol. 180.

C. The *Chartres MS.*

D. Mommsen's critical text of the later revision, *Nennius
interpretatus*, which he gives parallel to the *Historia Brittonum*.

A	B	C	D
Hors et Hengist	Hors & Hengist	Cors et Haecgens	Hors et Hengist
filii Guictgils	filii Guictgils	filii Guictils	filii Guictgils
Guigta	Guitta	Guicta	Guigta
Guectha	Guectha	Gueta	Guectha
VVoden	VVoden	VVoden	Voden
Frealaf	Frealaf	Frelab	Frealaf
Fredulf	Fredulf	Freudulf	Fredolf
Finn	Finn	Fran	Finn
			Frenn
Fodepald	Fodepald	Folcpald	Folcvald
Geta	Geta	G[e]uta	Gaeta
qui fuit, ut aiunt,	qui fuit, ut aiunt,	qui sunt [sic], ut	Vanli
filius dei	filius dei	aiunt, filius dei	Saxi
			Negua

MS Cotton Vespasian B. VI (9th century) contains a number
of Anglo-Saxon genealogies and other lists revised up to the
period 811–14[3]. The genealogy of the kings of Lindsey in this
list has the stages from Woden to Geat. This genealogy is also
found in the sister list in the 9th century MS at Corpus Christi
College, Cambridge (*MS C.C.C.C.* 183).

[1] Zimmer (p. 275) says A.D. 796; Duchesne (p. 196) A.D. 800; Thurneysen
(*Zeitschr. f. Celtische Philologie*, I, 166) A.D. 826; Skene (*Four Ancient Books of
Wales*, 1868, I, 38) A.D. 858; van Hamel (p. 304) A.D. 820–859. See also Chad-
wick, *Origin*, 38.

[2] Bradshaw, *Investigations among Early Welsh, Breton and Cornish MSS.*
in *Collected Papers*, 466.   [3] See above, p. 196.

A similar list is to be found in the *Anglo-Saxon Chronicle* (entered under the year 547). But there it is appended to the genealogy of the Northumbrian kings. This genealogy has been erased in the oldest MS (Parker, end of the 9th century) to make room for later additions, but is found in *MSS Cotton Tiberius A. VI* and *B. I.*

Cotton (*Vespasian*) MS.	Corpus MS.	A.-S. Chronicle
UUoden Frealafing	Woden Frealafing	Woden Freoþolafing
Frealaf Frioðulfing	Frealaf Frioþowulsing (*sic*)	Freoþelaf Freoþulfing
Frioðulf Finning	Freoþowulf Godwulfing	Friþulf Finning
Finn Goduulfing		Finn Godulfing
Godulf Geoting	Godwulf Geating	Godulf Geating

The *Fodepald* or *Folcpald* who, in the *Historia Brittonum*, appears as the father of Finn, is clearly the *Folcwalda* who appears as Finn's father in *Beowulf* and *Widsith*. The Old English *w* (p) has been mistaken for *p*, just as in *Pinefred* for *Winefred* in the *Life of Offa II*. In the *Vespasian MS* and in other genealogies Godwulf is Finn's father. It has been very generally held that Finn and his father Godwulf are mythical heroes, quite distinct from the presumably historic Finn, son of Folcwalda, mentioned in *Beowulf* and *Widsith*: and that by confusion *Folcwald* came to be written instead of *Godwulf* in the genealogy, as given in the *Historia Brittonum*. I doubt whether there is sufficient justification for this distinction between a presumed historic Finn Folcwalding and a mythical Finn Godwulfing. Is it not possible that Godwulf was a traditional, probably historic, king of the Frisians, father of Finn, and that *Folcwalda*[1] was a *title* which, since it alliterated conveniently, in the end supplanted the proper name in epic poetry?

III. THE STAGES ABOVE WODEN.

(2) WODEN TO SCEAF.

The stages above Geat are found in the genealogy of the West-Saxon kings only[2]. This is recorded in the *Chronicle*

[1] Cf. *Bretwalda*.

[2] The genealogies have recently been dealt with by E. Hackenberg, *Die Stammtafeln der angelsächsischen Königreiche*, Berlin, 1918; and by Brandl, (Herrig's *Archiv*, CXXXVII, 1–24). Most of Brandl's derivations seem to me to depend upon very perilous conjectures. Thus he derives *Scēfing* from the Gr.-Lat. *scapha*, "a skiff": a word which was not adopted into Old English. This seems to be sacrificing all probability to the desire to find a new interpretation:

under the year 855 (notice concerning Æthelwulf) and it was probably drawn up at the court of that king. Though it doubtless contains ancient names, it is apparently not so ancient as the *Woden-Geat* list. It became very well known, and is also found in Asser and the *Textus Roffensis*. It was copied by later historians such as William of Malmesbury, and by the Icelandic genealogists[1].

The principal versions of this pedigree are given in tabular form below (pp. 202–3); omitting the merely second-hand reproductions, such as those of Florence of Worcester.

H. Extract from the Chronicle Roll.

This roll was drawn up in the reign of Henry VI, and its compiler must have had access to a document now lost.

There are many copies of the roll extant—the "Moseley" Roll at University College, London (formerly in the Phillipps collection); at Corpus Christi College, Cambridge (No. 98 A); at Trinity College, Cambridge; and in the Bibliothèque Nationale, Paris[2]; and one which recently came into the market in London.

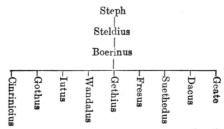

Steph
|
Steldius
|
Boerinus
|

Cinrinicius — Gothus — Iutus — Wandalus — Gethius — Fresus — Suethedus — Dacus — Geate

[*continued on* p. 204

and, even so, it is not quite successful. For Riley in the *Gentleman's Magazine*, August, 1857, p. 126, suggested the derivation of the name of Scef from the *schiff* or *skiff* in which he came.

[1] For a list of the Icelandic versions, see Heusler, *Die gelehrte Urgeschichte im altisländischen Schrifttum*, pp. 18–19, in the *Abhandlungen d. preuss. Akad., Phil. Hist. Klasse*, 1908, Berlin.

[2] The names are given as in the Trinity Roll (T), collated with Corpus (C) and Moseley (M). For Paris (P) I follow Kemble's report (*Postscript to Preface*, 1837, pp. vii, viii: *Stammtafel der Westsachsen*, pp. 18, 31). All seem to agree in writing *t* for *c* in Steph and Steldius, and in Boerinus, *obviously, as Kemble pointed out, r is written by error for p = Beowinus* [*or Beowius*]; Cinrinicius T, Cinrinicus C, Cininicus P, Siuruncius M; Suethedus TCP, Suechedius M; Gethius T, Thecius M, Ehecius CP; Geate T, Geathe CM, Geathus P.

WEST-SAXON GENEALOGY—STAGES ABOVE WODEN

CHRONICLE PARKER MS	ASSER	TEXTUS ROFFENSIS I	ÆTHELWERD	CHRONICLE MSS Corr. Tib. A. VI [& B. I]
Woden Friþowalding	Uuoden	Woden	Uuothen	Woden Frealafing
Friþuwald Freawining	Frithowald	Friþewold	Frithouuald	
Frealaf Friþuwulfing	Frealaf	Frealaf	Frealaf	Frealaf Fin[n]ing
Friþuwulf Finning	Frithuwulf	Friþewulf	Frithouulf	
Fin Godwulfing	Fingodwulf	Finn	Fin	Finn Godwulfing [Godulfing]
Godwulf Geating		Godwulf	Goduulfe	Godulf Geat[t]ing
Geat Tætwaing	Geata*…	Geata*…	Geat	Geata [Geatt] Tætwaing
Tætwa Beawing	Caetuua	Teþwa	Tetuua	Tætwa Beawing
Beaw Sceldwaing	Beauu	Beaw	Beo	Beaw Sceldweaing [Scealdwaing]
Sceldwea Heremoding	Sceldwea	Sealdwa	Scyld	Scyldwa [Scealdwa] Heremoding
Heremod Itermoning	Heremod	Heremod		Heremod Itermoning
Itermon Hraþraing	Itermod	Iterman		Itermon Haðraing
	Hathra	Haþra		Haðra Hwalaing
	Huala	Hwala		Hwala Bedwiging
	Beduuig	Bedwig		Bedwig Sceafing, [i]d est filius Nóe, se wæs geboren on þære earce Nóes
	Seth	Scyf, se wæs in ðam arken geboran [but son of Sem, not Noe]		
	Noe, etc.			

se wæs geboren in þære earce Noe etc.

* quem Getam iamdudum pagani pro deo venerabantur

* ðeneða hæþena wuþedon for god

Scef. Ipse Scef cum uno dromone aduectus est in insula oceani, quae dicitur Scani, armis circumdatus, eratque ualde recens puer, et ab incolis illius terrae ignotus; attamen ab eis suscipitur et ut familiarem diligenti animo eum custodierunt et post in regem eligunt; de cuius prosapia ordinem trahit Athulf [i.e. Æthelwulf] rex.

CHRONICLE MS COTT. TIB. B. IV Woden Frealafing	TEXTUS ROFFENSIS II Woden Frealafing	MS COTT. TIB. B. V Woden Frealafing	LANGFEÐGATAL Langebek, I, 3 Woden þan kollvm ver Oden	FLATEYARBÓK Christiania, 1860, I, 27 Voden, er ver kollum Odinn
Frealaf Finning	Frealaf Finning	Frealaf Finning	Frealaf	Frialafr, e.v.k. Bors
Fin Godulfing	Finn Godulfing	Finn Godulfing	Finn	Burri, e.v.k. Finn
Godulf Gating	Godulf Eating	Godulf Eating	Godvlfi	Godolfr
Geat Tætwaing	Eata Tebwafing	Eat Beawing	Eat	
Tætwa Beawing	Tebwa Beawing			
Beaw Scealdwaing	Beaw Scealdwaging	Beaw Scealdwaging	Beaf	Beaf, e.v.k. Biar
Scealdhwa Heremoding	Scealwa Heremoding	Scealwa Heremoding	Scealdna	Skialldin, e.v.k. Skiolld
Heremod Itermoning	Heremod Hermanning	Heremod Itermanning	Heremotr	Heremoth, e.v.k. Hermod
Itermon Haðrahing	Hernan Haþraing	Iterman Haðraing	Itermann	Trinaan
Haþra	Haðra Hwalaing	Haðra Bedwiging	Athra	Atra
Hwala Beowung	Hwala Bedwining			
Beowi Sceafing, id est filius	Bedwig Sceafing	Bedwig Sceafing	Bedvig	Beduigg
Noe, se wæs geboren on	Se Scef wæs Noes sunu	se Scef wæs Nóes sunu	Seskef vel	Seseph
þære arce Nones...	and he wæs innan ðære	and he wæs innan	Sescef	
	earce geboren	þære earce geboren		

WILLIAM OF MALMESBURY. Wodenius fuit filius Fridewaldi, Fridewaldus Frelafii, Frelafius Finni, Finnus Godulfi, Godulfus Getii, Getius Tetii, Tetius Beowii, Beowius Sceldii, Sceldius Sceaf. Iste, ut ferunt, in quandam insulam Germaniae Scandzam... appulsus, navi sine remige, puerulus, posito ad caput frumenti manipulo, dormiens, ideoque Sceaf nuncupatus, ab hominibus regionis illius pro miraculo exceptus et sedulo nutritus, adulta aetate regnavit in oppido quod tunc Slaswic, nunc vero Haithebi appellatur... Sceaf fuit filius Heremodii, Heremodius Stermonii, Stermonius Hadrae, Hadra Gwalae, Gwala Bedwigii, Bedwegius Strephii; hic, ut dicitur, fuit filius Noae in arca natus.

The following marginal note occurs:

Iste Steldius *primus* inhabitator Germanie fuit. Que Germania sic dicta erat, quia instar ram*crum* germin *ncium* ab arbore, sic nome*n* regnaq*ue* germania nuncupa*n*tur. In nouem filiis diuisa a radi*ce* Boerini geminaueru*n*t. Ab istis nouem filii Boerini descenderu*n*t nouem gentes septentrionalem p*artem* inhabitantes, qui quondam regnu*m* Britan*n*ie inuaseru*n*t et optinueru*n*t, videlicet Saxones, Angli, Iuthi, Daci, Norwagences, Gothi, Wandali, Geathi et Fresi[1].

I. Extract from the Little Chronicle of the Kings of Leire

From the *Annales Lundenses*. These Annals are comparatively late, going up to the year 1307; but the short *Chronicle of the Kings of Leire*, which is incorporated in them, is supposed to date from the latter half of the 12th century. The text is given in Langebek, *Scriptores Rerum Danicarum*, I, 224–6 (under the name of *Annales Esromenses*) from *Cod. Arn. Mag.* 841. There is a critical edition by Gertz, *Scriptores Minores historiæ Danicæ*, Copenhagen, 1917, based upon *Cod. Arn. Mag.* 813. The text given below is mainly that of Langebek, with corrections from Gertz's fine edition. See below, p. 216.

Erat ergo Dan rex in Dacia[2] per triennium. Anno tandem tertio cognouit uxorem suam Daniam, genuitque ex ea filium nomine Ro. Qui post patris obitum hereditarie possidebat regnum. Patrem uero suum Dan colle apud Lethram tumulauit Sialandiæ, ubi sedem regni pro eo pater constituit, quam ipse post eum diuitiis multiplicibus ditauit. Tempore illo ciuitas magna erat in medio Sialandiæ, ubi adhuc mons desertus est, nomine Hekebiarch, ubi sita erat ciuitas quæ Høkekoping nuncupata est; ad quam ut mox Ro rex uidit, quod mercatores a nauibus in uia currus conducentes multum expenderent, a loco illo ciuitatem amoueri jussit ad portum, ubi tenditur Isæfiorth, et circa fontem pulcherrimum domos disponere. Ædificauit ibi Ro ciuitatem honestam, cui nomen partitiuum imposuit post se et Fontem, partem capiens fontis partemque sui, Roskildam Danice uocans, quæ hoc nomine uoca[bi]tur[3] in æternum. Uixit autem rex Ro ita pacifice, ut nullus ei aciem opponeret, nec ipse usquam expeditionem direxit[4]. Erat autem uxor eius

[1] I follow the spelling of the Moseley roll in this note.
[2] *Dacia* = "Denmark": *Dacia* and *Dania* were identified.
[3] *uocabitur*, Gertz; *uocatur* all MSS.
[4] This account of the peaceful reign of Ro is simply false etymology from Danish *ro*, "rest."

fecunda sobole, ex qua genuit duos filios, nomen primi Helhgi et secundi Haldan[1]. Cumque cepissent pueri robore confortari et crescere, obiit pater eorum Ro, et sepultus est tumulo quodam Læthræ, post cuius obitum partiti sunt regnum filii, quod in duas partes diuidentes, alter terras, alter mare possidebat. Rexit itaque terras Haldanus, et genuit filium nomine Siwardum, cognomine Album, qui patrem suum Haldanum Læthræ tumulauit mortuum. Helgi autem rex erat marinus, et multos ad se traxit malificos, nauali bello bene adeptus diuersas partes, quasdam pace, quasdam cum piratica classe[2] petisse perhibetur...

The Chronicle then tells how Rolf was born, the son of Helgi and Yrse or Ursula: also of the death and burial of Helgi.

Filius autem eius et Ursulæ puer crescebat Rolf et fortitudine uigebat. Mater uero eius Ursula, uelo uiduitatis deposito, data est regi Suethiæ Athislo, qui ex ea filiam sibi genuit, Rolf uero ex matre eius sororem nomine Skuld. Interea dum hæc de rege marino Helgi agerentur, frater eius, rex Daciæ, mortuus est Haldanus. Post quem[3] rex Sweciæ Athisl a Danis suscepit tributum.

*　　*　　*　　*

Interea...confortabatur filius Helgi, Rolff, cognomine Krake. Quem post mortem Snyo[4] Dani [in][5] regem assumpserunt. Qui Sialandiæ apud Lethram, sicut antecessores sui, sæpissime moratus est. Sororem suam nomine Sculd secum habuit, Athisli regis filiam, et suæ matris Ursulæ, de qua superius dictum est; quam fraterno amore dilexit. Cui provinciam Hornshæræth Sialandiæ ad pascendas puellas suas in expensam dedit, in qua uillam ædificauit, nomine Sculdelef, unde nomen suscepit. Hoc tempore erat quidam Comes Scaniæ, nomine Hiarwarth, Teotonicus genere, Rolf tributarius, qui ad eum procos misit, ut

---

[1] Note that Ro (Hrothgar), the son of Haldanus (Healfdene), is here represented as his father. Saxo Grammaticus, combining divergent accounts, as he often does, accordingly mentions two Roes—one the brother of Haldanus, the other his son. See above, pp. 131–2.

[2] *cum piratica classe*, Langebek; the MSS have *cum pietate* (!) with or without *classe*.

[3] *post quem*, Holder-Egger, Gertz; *postquam*, all MSS.

[4] Snyo: the viceroy whom Athisl had placed over the Danes.

[5] *in* added by Gertz; omitted in all MSS.

sororem suam Sculd Hiarwardo daret uxorem. Quo nolente, propria ipsius uoluntate puellæ clanculo eam raptam sociauit sibi. Unde conspirauerunt inter se deliberantes Hiarwart et Sculd, quomodo Rolf interficeretur, et Hiarwardus superstes regni heres efficeretur. Non post multum vero temporis animosus ad uxoris exhortationem Hiarwart Sialandiam classe petiit. Genero suo Rolff tributum attulisse simulauit. Die quadam dilucescente ad Læthram misit, ut uideret tributum, Rolff nunciauit. Qui cum uidisset non tributum sed exercitum armatum, uallatus est Rolff militibus, et a Hyarwardo interfectus est. Hyarwardum autem Syalandenses et Scanienses, qui cum eo erant, in regem assumpserunt. Qui breui tempore, a mane usque ad primam, regali nomine potitus est. Tunc uenit Haky, frater Haghbardi, filius Hamundi; Hyarwardum interfecit et Danorum rex effectus est. Quo regnante, uenit quidam nomine Fritleff a partibus Septentrionalibus et filiam sibi desponsauit Rolff Crake, ex qua filium nomine Frothe genuit, cognomine Largus.

K. THE STORY OF OFFA IN SAXO GRAMMATICUS

Book IV, ed. Ascensius, fol. xxxii b; ed. Holder, pp. 106–7.

Cui filius Wermundus succedit. Hic prolixis tranquillitatis otiis felicissima temporum quiete decursis, diutinam domesticæ pacis constantiam inconcussa rerum securitate tractabat. Idem prolis expers iuuentam exegit; senior uero filium Uffonem sero fortunæ munere suscitauit, cum nullam ei sobolem elapsa tot annorum curricula peperissent. Hic Uffo coæuos quosque corporis habitu supergressus, adeo hebetis ineptique animi principio iuuentæ existimatus est, ut priuatis ac publicis rebus inutilis uideretur. Siquidem ab ineunte ætate nunquam lusus aut ioci consuetudinem præbuit; adeoque humanæ delectationis uacuus fuit, ut labiorum continentiam iugi silentio premeret, et seueritatem oris a ridendi prorsus officio temperaret. Uerum ut incunabula stoliditatis opinione referta habuit, ita post modum conditionis contemptum claritate mutauit; et quantum inertiæ spectaculum fuit, tantum prudentiæ et fortitudinis exemplum euasit.

Book IV, ed. Ascensius, fol. xxxiv b; ed. Holder, pp. 113–7.

Cumque Wermundus ætatis uitio oculis orbaretur, Saxoniæ
rex, Daniam duce uacuam ratus, ei per legatos mandat, regnum,
quod præter ætatis debitum teneat, sibi procurandum committat,
ne nimis longa imperii auiditate patriam legibus armisque destituat. Qualiter enim regem censeri posse, cui senectus animum,
cæcitas oculum pari caliginis horrore fuscauerit? Quod si abnuat,
filiumque habeat, qui cum suo ex prouocatione confligere
audeat, uictorem regno potiri permittat. Si neutrum probet,
armis secum, non monitis agendum cognoscat, ut tandem inuitus
præbeat, quod ultroneus exhibere contemnat. Ad hæc Wermundus, altioribus suspiriis fractus, impudentius se ætatis
exprobratione lacerari respondit, quem non ideo huc infelicitatis
senectus prouexerit, quod pugnæ parcus timidius iuuentam
exegerit. Nec aptius sibi cæcitatis uitium obiectari, quod
plerunque talem ætatis habitum talis iactura consequi soleat,
potiusque condolendum calamitati quam insultandum uideatur.
Iustius autem Saxoniæ regi impatientiæ notam afferri posse,
quem potius senis fatum operiri, quam imperium poscere
decuisset, quod aliquanto præstet defuncto succedere, quam
uiuum spoliare. Se tamen, ne tanquam delirus priscæ libertatis
titulos externo uideatur mancipare dominio, propria manu
prouocationi pariturum. Ad hæc legati, scire se inquiunt,
regem suum conserendæ cum cæco manus ludibrium perhorrere,
quod tam ridiculum decernendi genus rubori quam honestati
propinquius habeatur. Aptius uero per utriusque pignus et
sanguinem amborum negotio consuli. Ad hæc obstupefactis
animo Danis, subitaque responsi ignorantia perculsis, Uffo, qui
forte cum ceteris aderat, responsionis a patre licentiam flagita-
bat, subitoque uelut ex muto uocalis euasit. Cumque Wermundus, quisnam talem a se loquendi copiam postularet,
inquireret, ministrique eum ab Uffone rogari dixissent, satis
esse perhibuit, ut infelicitatis suæ uulneribus alienorum fastus
illuderet, ne etiam a domesticis simili insultationis petulantia
uexaretur. Sed satellitibus Uffonem hunc esse pertinaci
affirmatione testantibus, "Liberum ei sit," inquit, "quisquis
est, cogitata profari." Tum Uffo, frustra ab eorum rege regnum
appeti, inquit, quod tam proprii rectoris officio quam fortissi-

morum procerum armis industriaque niteretur: præterea, nec regi filium nec regno successorem deesse. Sciantque, se non solum regis eorum filium, sed etiam quemcunque ex gentis suæ fortissimis secum adsciuerit, simul pugna aggredi constituisse. Quo audito legati risere, uanam dicti animositatem existimantes. Nec mora, condicitur pugnæ locus, eidemque stata temporis meta præfigitur. Tantum autem stuporis Uffo loquendi ac prouocandi nouitate præsentibus iniecit, ut, utrum uoci eius an fiduciæ plus admirationis tributum sit, incertum extiterit.

Abeuntibus autem legatis, Wermundus, responsionis auctore laudato, quod uirtutis fiduciam non in unius, sed duorum prouocatione statuerit, potius se ei, quicunque sit, quam superbo hosti regno cessurum perhibuit. Uniuersis autem filium eius esse testantibus, qui legatorum fastum fiduciæ sublimitate contempserit, propius eum accedere iubet: quod oculis nequeat, manibus experturus. Corpore deinde eius curiosius contrectato, cum ex artuum granditate lineamentisque filium esse cognosset, fidem assertoribus habere cœpit, percontarique eum, cur suauissimum uocis habitum summo dissimulationis studio tegendum curauerit, tantoque ætatis spatio sine uoce et cunctis loquendi commerciis degere sustinuerit, ut se linguæ prorsus officio defectum natiuæque taciturnitatis uitio obsitum credi permitteret? Qui respondit, se paterna hactenus defensione contentum, non prius uocis officio opus habuisse, quam domesticam prudentiam externa loquacitate pressam animaduerteret. Rogatus item ab eo, cur duos quam unum prouocare maluit, hunc iccirco dimicationis modum a se exoptatum respondit, ut Athisli regis oppressio, quæ, quod a duobus gesta fuerat, Danis opprobrio extabat, unius facinore pensaretur, nouumque uirtutis specimen prisca ruboris monumenta conuelleret. Ita antiquæ crimen infamiæ recentis famæ litura respergendum dicebat. Quem Wermundus iustam omnium æstimationem fecisse testatus, armorum usum, quod eis parum assueuisset, prædiscere iubet. Quibus Uffo oblatis, magnitudine pectoris angustos loricarum nexus explicuit; nec erat ullam reperire, quæ eum iusto capacitatis spatio contineret. Maiore siquidem corpore erat, quam ut alienis armis uti posset. Ad ultimum, cum paternam quoque

loricam uiolenta corporis astrictione dissolueret, Wermundus
eam a læuo latere dissecari, fibulaque sarciri præcepit, partem,
quæ clypei præsidio muniatur, ferro patere parui existimans.
Sed et gladium, quo tuto uti possit, summa ab eo cura
conscisci iussit. Oblatis compluribus, Uffo manu capulum
stringens, frustatim singulos agitando comminuit; nec erat
quisquam ex eis tanti rigoris gladius, quem non ad primæ con-
cussionis motum crebra partium fractione dissolueret. Erat
autem regi inusitati acuminis gladius, Skrep dictus, qui quodlibet
obstaculi genus uno ferientis ictu medium penetrando diffin-
deret, nec adeo quicquam prædurum foret, ut adactam eius
aciem remorari potuisset. Quem ne posteris fruendum relin-
queret, per summam alienæ commoditatis inuidiam in profunda
defoderat, utilitatem ferri, quod filii incrementis diffideret,
ceteris negaturus. Interrogatus autem, an dignum Uffonis
robore ferrum haberet, habere se dixit, quod, si pridem a se
terræ traditum recognito locorum habitu reperire potuisset,
aptum corporis eius uiribus exhiberet. In campum deinde
perduci se iubens, cum, interrogatis per omnia comitibus,
defossionis locum acceptis signorum indiciis comperisset, ex-
tractum cauo gladium filio porrigit. Quem Uffo nimia uetustate
fragilem exesumque conspiciens, feriendi diffidentia percontatur,
an hunc quoque priorum exemplo probare debeat, prius habitum
eius, quam rem ferro geri oporteat, explorandum testatus.
Refert Wermundus, si præsens ferrum ab ipso uentilando
collideretur, non superesse, quod uirium eius habitui responderet.
Abstinendum itaque facto, cuius in dubio exitus maneat.

Igitur ex pacto pugnæ locus expetitur. Hunc fluuius
Eidorus ita aquarum ambitu uallat, ut earum interstitio repug-
nante, nauigii duntaxat aditus pateat. Quem Uffone sine
comite petente, Saxoniæ regis filium insignis uiribus athleta
consequitur, crebris utrinque turbis alternos riparum anfractus
spectandi auiditate complentibus. Cunctis igitur huic spectaculo
oculos inferentibus, Wermundus in extrema pontis parte se
collocat, si filium uinci contigisset, flumine periturus. Maluit
enim sanguinis sui ruinam comitari, quam patriæ interitum
plenis doloris sensibus intueri. Uerum Uffo, geminis iuuenum
congressibus lacessitus, gladii diffidentia amborum ictus umbone

uitabat, patientius experiri constituens, quem e duobus atten-
tius cauere debuisset, ut hunc saltem uno ferri impulsu contingeret. Quem Wermundus imbecillitatis uitio tantam recipien-
dorum ictuum patientiam præstare existimans, paulatim in
occiduam pontis oram mortis cupiditate se protrahit, si de
filio actum foret, fatum precipitio petiturus. Tanta sanguinis
caritate flagrantem senem fortuna protexit. Uffo siquidem
filium regis ad secum auidius decernendum hortatus, claritatem
generis ab ipso conspicuo fortitudinis opere æquari iubet, ne
rege ortum plebeius comes uirtute præstare uideatur. Athletam
deinde, explorandæ eius fortitudinis gratia, ne domini sui terga
timidius subsequeretur, admonitum fiduciam a regis filio in se
repositam egregiis dimicationis operibus pensare præcepit,
cuius delectu unicus pugnæ comes adscitus fuerit. Obtemper-
antem illum propiusque congredi rubore compulsum, primo
ferri ictu medium dissecat. Quo sono recreatus Wermundus,
filii ferrum audire se dixit, rogatque, cui potissimum parti ictum
inflixerit. Referentibus deinde ministris, eum non unam corporis partem, sed totam hominis transegisse compagem,
abstractum præcipitio corpus ponti restituit, eodem studio
lucem expetens, quo fatum optauerat. Tum Uffo, reliquum
hostem prioris exemplo consumere cupiens, regis filium ad
ultionem interfecti pro se satellitis manibus parentationis loco
erogandam impensioribus uerbis sollicitat. Quem propius
accedere sua adhortatione coactum, infligendi ictus loco curiosius denotato, gladioque, quod tenuem eius laminam suis
imparem uiribus formidaret, in aciem alteram uerso, penetrabili
corporis sectione transuerberat. Quo audito Wermundus
Screp gladii sonum secundo suis auribus incessisse perhibuit.
Affirmantibus deinde arbitris, utrunque hostem ab eius filio
consumptum, nimietate gaudii uultum fletu soluit. Ita genas,
quas dolor madidare non poterat, lætitia rigauit. Saxonibus
igitur pudore mœstis, pugilumque funus summa cum ruboris
acerbitate ducentibus, Uffonem Dani iocundis excepere tri-
pudiis. Quieuit tum Athislanæ cædis infamia, Saxonumque
obprobriis expirauit.

Ita Saxoniæ regnum ad Danos translatum, post patrem
Uffo regendum suscepit, utriusque imperii procurator effectus,

qui ne unum quidem rite moderaturus credebatur. Hic a
compluribus Olauus est dictus, atque ob animi moderationem
Mansueti cognomine donatus. Cuius sequentes actus uetus-
tatis uitio solennem fefellere notitiam. Sed credi potest,
gloriosos eorum processus extitisse, quorum tam plena laudis
principia fuerint.

L. From Skiold to Offa in Sweyn Aageson

In Langebek, *Scriptores*, i, 44–7; Gertz, i, 97.

CAP. I.

De primo Rege Danorum.

Skiold Danis primum didici præfuisse. Et ut eius alludamus
uocabulo, idcirco tali functus est nomine, quia uniuersos regni
terminos regiæ defensionis patrocinio affatim egregie tuebatur.
A quo primum, modis Islandensibus, "Skioldunger" sunt reges
nuncupati. Qui regni post se reliquit hæredes, Frothi uidelicet
et Haldanum. Successu temporum fratribus super regni
ambitione inter se decertantibus, Haldan, fratre suo interempto,
regni monarchiam obtinuit. Hic filium, scilicet Helghi, regni
procreauit hæredem, qui ob eximiam uirtutum strenuitatem,
pyraticam semper exercuit. Qui cum uniuersorum circum-
iacentium regnorum fines maritimos classe pyratica depopulatus,
suo subiugasset imperio, "Rex maris" est cognominatus. Huic
in regno successit filius Rolf Kraki, patria virtute pollens,
occisus in Lethra, quæ tunc famosissima Regis extitit curia,
nunc autem Roskildensi uicina ciuitati, inter abiectissima ferme
uix colitur oppida. Post quem regnauit filius eius Rökil cog-
nomento dictus "Slaghenback." Cui successit in regno hæres,
agilitatis strenuitate cognominatus, quem nostro uulgari
"Frothi hin Frökni" nominabant. Huius filius et hæres regni
extitit Wermundus, qui adeo prudentiæ pollebat uirtute, ut
inde nomen consequeretur. Unde et "Prudens" dictus est.
Hic filium genuit Uffi nomine, qui usque ad tricesimum ætatis
suæ annum fandi possibilitatem cohibuit, propter enormitatem
opprobrii, quod tunc temporis Danis ingruerat, eo quod in

14—2

ultionem patris duo Dani in Sueciam profecti, patricidam suum
una interemerunt.   Nam et tunc temporis ignominiosum extitit
improperium, si solum duo iugularent; præsertim cum soli
strenuitati tunc superstitiosa gentilitas operam satagebat im-
pendere.   Præfatus itaque Wermundus usque ad senium
regni sui gubernabat imperium; adeo tandem ætate consumptus,
ut oculi eius præ senio caligarent.   Cuius debilitatis fama cum
apud transalpinas[1] partes percrebuisset, elationis turgiditate
Teotonica intumuit superbia, utpote suis nunquam contenta
terminis.   Hinc furoris sui rabiem in Danos exacuit Imperator,
se iam Danorum regno conquisito sceptrum nancisci augustius
conspicatus.   Delegantur itaque spiculatores, qui turgidi principis jussa reportent præfato Danorum regi, scilicet Wermundo,
duarum rerum præfigentes electionem, quarum pars tamen
neutra extitit eligenda.   Aut enim regnum jussit Romano
resignare imperio, et tributum soluere, aut athletam inuestigare,
qui cum Imperatoris campione monomachiam committere
auderet.   Quo audito, regis extitit mens consternata; totiusque
regni procerum legione corrogata, quid facto opus sit, diligenti
inquisitione percontabatur.   Perplexam se namque regis autu-
mabat autoritas, utpote cui et ius incumbebat decertandi, et qui
regno patrocinari tenebatur.   Uultum cœcitas obnubilauerat,
et regni heres elinguis factus, desidia torpuerat, ita ut in eo,
communi assertione, nulla prorsus species salutis existeret.
Nam ab infantia præfatus Uffo uentris indulgebat ingluuiei,
et Epicuræorum more, coquinæ et cellario alternum officiose
impendebat obsequium.   Corrogato itaque cœtu procerum,
totiusque regni placito[2] celebrato, Alamannorum regis ambitionem explicuit, quid in hac optione haud eligenda facturus sit,
indagatione cumulata senior sciscitatur.   Et dum uniuersorum
mens consternaretur angustia, cunctique indulgerent silentio,
præfatus Uffo in media concione surrexit.   Quem cum cohors
uniuersa conspexisset, satis nequibat admirari, ut quid elinguis
uelut orationi gestus informaret.   Et quia omne rarum dignum
nouimus admiratione, omnium in se duxit intuitum.   Tandem
sic orsus cœpit: "Non nos minæ moueant lacessentium, cum

---

[1] A scribal error for *transalbinas*, " beyond the Elbe."
[2] Assembly.

"ea Teotonicæ turgiditati innata sit conditio, ut uerborum
"ampullositate glorientur, minarumque uentositate pusill-
"animes et imbecilles calleant comminatione consternare.
"Me etenim unicum et uerum regni natura produxit heredem,
"cui profecto nouistis incumbere, ut monomachiæ me discrimini
"audacter obiiciam, quatenus uel pro regno solus occumbam,
"uel pro patria solus uictoriam obtineam. Ut ergo minarum
"cassetur ampullositas, hæc Imperatori referant mandata, ut
"Imperatoris filius et heres imperii, cum athleta præstantissimo,
"mihi soli non formidet occurrere." Dixit, et hæc verba
dictauit voce superba. Qui dum orationem complesset, a
collateralibus senior sciscitabatur, cuiusnam hæc fuisset oratio?
Cum autem a circumstantibus intellexisset, quod filius suus,
prius veluti mutus, hunc effudisset sermonem, palpandum
eum jussit accersiri. Et cum humeros lacertosque, et clunes,
suras atque tibias, cæteraque membra organica crebro palpasset:
"Talem," ait, "me memini in flore extitisse iuuentutis." Quid
multa? Terminus pugnæ constituitur et locus. Talique res-
ponso percepto, ad propria legati repedabant.

CAP. II.

De duello Uffonis.

Superest ergo, ut arma nouo militi congrua corrogentur.
Allatisque ensibus, quos in regno præstantiores rex poterat
inuestigare, Uffo singulos dextra uibrans, in partes confregit
minutissimas. "Hæccine arma sunt," inquit, "quibus et
uitam et regni tuebor honorem?" Cuius cum pater uiuidam experiretur uirtutem, "Unicum adhuc," ait, "et regni et uitæ nostræ superest asylum." Ad tumulum itaque ducatum postulauit,
in quo prius mucronem experientissimum occultauerat. Et
mox intersigniis per petrarum notas edoctus, gladium jussit
effodi præstantissimum. Quem illico dextra corripiens, "Hic
est," ait, "fili, quo numerose triumphaui, et qui mihi infallibile
semper tutamen extitit." Et hæc dicens, eundem filio contra-
didit. Nec mora; terminus ecce congressioni præfixus arctius

instabat. Tandem, confluentibus undique phalangis innumera-
bilibus, in Egdoræ fluminis mediamne[1] locus pugnæ constituitur:
ut ita pugnatores ab utriusque cœtus adminiculo segregati
nullius opitulatione fungerentur. Teotonicis ergo ultra fluminis ripam in Holsatia considentibus, Danis uero citra amnem
dispositis, rex pontis in medio sedem elegit, quatenus, si uni-
genitus occumberet, in fluminis se gurgitem præcipitaret, ne
pariter nato orbatus et regno cum dolore superstes canos dedu-
ceret ad inferos. Deinde emissis utrinque pugilibus, in medio
amne conuenerunt. Ast ubi miles noster egregius Uffo, duos
sibi conspexit occurrere, tanquam leo pectore robusto infremuit,
animoque constanti duobus electis audacter se opponere non
detrectauit, illo cinctus mucrone, quem patrem supra memi-
nimus occuluisse, et alterum dextra strictum gestans. Quos
cum primum obuios habuisset, sic singillatim utrumque alloquitur, et quod raro legitur accidisse, athleta noster elegantissimus, cuius memoria in æternum non delebitur, ita aduersarios
animabat ad pugnam: "Si te," inquit, "regni nostri stimulat
"ambitio, ut nostræ opis, potentiæque, opumque capessere uelis
"opulentias, comminus te clientem decet præcedere, ut et
"regni tui terminos amplifices, et militibus tuis conspicientibus,
"strenuitatis nomen nanciscaris." Campionem uero hunc in
modum alloquitur: "Uirtutis tuæ experientiam jam locus est
"propagare, si comminus accesseris, et eam, quam pridem
"Alamannis gloriam ostendisti, Danis quoque propalare non
"cuncteris. Nunc ergo famam tuæ strenuitatis poteris ampliare,
"et egregiæ munificentiæ dono ditari, si et dominum præcedas,
"et clypeo defensionis eum tuearis. Studeat, quæso, Teotonicis
"experta strenuitas variis artis pugillatoriæ modis Danos
"instruere, ut tandem optata potitus uictoria, cum triumphi
"ualeas exultatione ad propria remeare." Quam quum complesset exhortationem, pugilis cassidem toto percussit conamine,
ita ut, quo feriebat, gladius in duo dissiliret. Cuius fragor per
uniuersum intonuit exercitum. Unde cohors Teotonicorum
exultatione perstrepebat: sed contra Dani desperationis con-
sternati tristitia, gemebundi murmurabant. Rex uero, ut
audiuit, quod filii ensis dissiliuisset, in margine se pontis jussit

[1] Island.

locari. Uerum Uffo, subito exempto, quo cinctus erat, gladio,
pugilis illico coxam cruentauit, nec mora, et caput pariter
amputauit.   Sic ergo ludus fortunæ ad instar lunæ uarius,
nunc his, nunc illis successibus illudebat, et quibus iamiam
exultatione fauebat ingenti, eos nouercali mox uultu, toruoque
conspexit intuitu. Hoc cognito, senior jam confidentius priori
se jussit sede locari. Nec jam anceps diu extitit uictoria.
Siquidem Uffo ualide instans, ad ripam amnis pepulit hæredem
imperii, ibique eum haud difficulter gladio iugulauit. Sicque
duorum solus uictor existens, Danis irrogatam multis retro
temporibus infamiam gloriosa uirtute magnifice satis aboleuit.
Atque ita Alamannis cum improperii uerecundia, cassatisque
minarum ampullositatibus, cum probris ad propria remeantibus,
postmodum in pacis tranquillitate præcluis Uffo regni sui
regebat imperium.

M. Note on the Danish Chronicles

The text of Saxo Grammaticus, given above, is based upon
the magnificent first edition printed by Badius Ascensius
(Paris, 1514).   Even at the time when this edition was printed,
manuscripts of Saxo had become exceedingly scarce, and we
have now only odd leaves of MS remaining.   One fragment,
however, discovered at Angers, and now in the Royal Library
at Copenhagen, comes from a MS which had apparently
received additions from Saxo himself, and therefore affords
evidence as to his spelling.

Holder's edition (Strassburg, 1886) whilst following in the
main the 1514 text of Badius Ascensius, is accordingly revised
to comply with the spelling of the Copenhagen fragments, and
with any other traces of MS authority extant.   I doubt the
necessity for such revision.   If the text were extant in MS,
one might feel bound to follow the spelling of the MS, as in the
case of the old English MSS of the *Vitae Offarum* below: but
seeing that Saxo, with the exception of a few pages, is extant
only in a 16th century printed copy, the spelling of which is
almost identical with that now current in Latin text books, it
seems a pity to restore conjecturally mediæval spellings likely

to worry a student. Accordingly I have followed the printed text of 1514, modernizing a very few odd spellings, and correcting some obvious printers errors[1]. A translation of the first nine books of Saxo by Prof. O. Elton has been published by the Folk-Lore Society (No. xxxiii, 1893). Saxo completed his history in the early years of the 13th century. His elder contemporary, Sweyn Aageson, had already written a *Brief History of the Kings of Denmark*. Sweyn's *History* must have been completed not long after 1185, to which date belongs the last event he records. The extracts given from it (pp. 211–15) are taken from Langebek's collection, with modifications of spelling. Langebek follows the first edition (Stephanius, 1642); the ms used in this edition had been destroyed in 1728. *Cod. Arn. Mag.* 33, recently printed by Gertz, although very corrupt, is supposed to give the text of Sweyn's *History* in a form less sophisticated than that of the received text (see Gertz, *Scriptores Minores Historiæ Danicæ*, 1917, p. 62). The *Little Chronicle of the Kings of Leire* is probably earlier than Sweyn's *History*. Gertz dates it c. 1170, and thinks it was written by someone connected with the church at Roskilde. It covers only the early traditional history. See above, pp. 17, 204.

For comparison, the following lists, as given in the roll of kings known as *Langfeðgatal*, in the *Little Chronicle*, in Sweyn, and in Saxo may be useful:

Langfeðgatal	Little Chronicle	*Sweyn*	*Saxo*	Names as given in *Beowulf*
	Dan		Dan	
			{Humblus	
			{Lotherus	? = Heremod
Skioldr...		Skiold	Skioldus	Scyld

---

[1] I have substituted *u* for *v*, and have abandoned spellings like *theutones, thezauro, orrifico, charitas, phas* (for *fas*), *atlethas, choercuit, iocundum, charum, fœlicissima, nanque, hæreditarii exoluere*.

The actual reading of the 1514 text is abandoned by substituting: p. 130, l. 3 *ingeniti* for *ingenitis* (1514); p. 132, l. 22, *iacientis* for *iacentis*; p. 134, l. 2, *diutinæ* for *diutiuæ*; p. 136, l. 11, *fudit* for *fugit*; p. 136, l. 20, *ut* for *aut*; p. 137, l. 8, *ammirationi* for *ammirationis*; p. 137, l. 16, *offert* for *affert*; p. 137, l. 17, *Roluoni* for *Rouolni*; p. 137, l. 27, *ministerio* for *ministros*; p. 127, l. 33 *diuturnus* for *diuturnius*; p. 206, l. 22, *diutinam* for *diutina*; p. 207 l. 3, *ei* for *eique*; p. 207, l. 5, *destituat* for *deficiat*; p. 209, l. 2, *latere* for *latera*; p. 209, l. 5, *conscisci* for *concissi*; p. 209, l. 14, *defoderat* for *defodera*.

Langfeðgatal	Little Chronicle	Sweyn	Saxo	Names as given in Beowulf
			Gram	
			Hadingus	
		⎰Frothi	Frotho I	? =Beowulf I
Halfdan		⎱Haldanus	⎧Haldanus I	Healfdene
	Ro		⎨Roe I	
			⎩Scato	
⎰Hroar	⎰Haldan		⎰Roe II	Hrothgar
⎱Helgi	⎱Helgi	Helghi	⎱Helgo	Halga
Rolf Kraki	Rolf Krake	Rolf Kraki	Roluo Krage	Hrothulf
	Hiarwarth		Hiarthuarus	Heoroweard
			. . . .	
Hrærekr		Rökil	Røricus	Hrethric

N. The *Life of Offa I*, with extracts from the *Life of Offa II*. Edited from two mss in the Cottonian Collection

The text is given from *MS Cotton Nero D. I* (quoted in the footnotes as A), collated with *MS Claudius E. IV* (quoted as B). Minor variations of B are not usually noted. The two mss agree closely.

The *Nero* ms is the more elaborate of the two, and is adorned with very fine drawings. *Claudius*, however, offers occasionally a better text; it has been read by a corrector whose alterations—contrary to what is so often the case in mediæval mss—seem to be authoritative.

The *Lives of the Offas* were printed by Wats in his edition of Matthew Paris (1639–40) from ms A. Miss Rickert has printed extracts from the two lives, in *Mod. Phil.* II, 14 *etc.*, following ms A, "as Wats sometimes takes liberties with the text."

INCIPIT HISTORIA DE OFFA PRIMO QUI STRENUITATE SUA SIBI ANGLIE MAXIMAM PARTEM SUBEGIT. CUI SIMILLIMUS FUIT SECUNDUS OFFA¹.

l. 2a   Inter occidentalium Anglorum reges illustrissimos, precipua commendacionis laude celebratur Rex Warmundus, ab hiis qui historias Anglorum non solum relatu proferre, set eciam scriptis inserere consueuerant. Is fundator erat cuiusdam urbis a seipso denominate, que lingua Anglicana Warwic, id est curia Warmundi, nuncupatur. Qui usque ad annos seniles absque liberis extitit, preter unicum filium; quem, ut estimabat, regni sui heredem et successorem puerilis debilitatis incomodo laborantem, constituere non ualebat. Licet enim idem unicus filius eius, Offa uel Offanus nomine, statura fuisset procerus,

¹ *Above this heading B has* Gesta Offe Regis merciorum.

corpore integer, *et* elegantissime forme iuuenis existeret, per-
ma*n*sit *tamen* a natiuitate uisu priuatus usq*ue* ad annu*m*
septimu*m*, mutus au*t*em *et* u*er*ba hu*m*ana no*n* proferens usq*ue*
ad annu*m* etatis sue tricesimum. Huius debilitatis incomodum
no*n* solum rex, s*ed* eciam regni proceres, supra q*u*am dici potest
moleste sustinuerunt. Cum eni*m* imineret p*at*ri etas senilis, *et*
ignoraret diem mortis sue, nesciebat q*u*em alium sibi[1] constitueret heredem *et* regni successore*m*. Quidam au*tem* pri-
mari*us* regni, cui nomen Riganus[2], cu*m* quoda*m* suo complice
Mitunno no*m*ine, ambic*i*osus cu*m* ambic*i*oso, seductor cu*m*
proditore uidens regem decrepitu*m*, *et* sine spe prolis procreande
senio fatiscente*m*, de se p*re*sumens, cepit ad regie dignitatis
culmen aspirare, conte*m*ptis aliis regni primatib*us*, se solum
p*re* ceter*is* ad h*o*c dignu*m* reputando.

Iccirco diebus singulis regi molestus nimis, proterue eum
aggreditur, ut se h*e*redis loco adoptaret. Aliq*u*ando cor regis
blande alliciens, interi*m* aspere minis *et* terroribus prouocans,
persuadere no*n* cessat regi q*uo*d optabat[3]. Suggerebat eciam
regi per uiros potentes, *com*plices cupiditatis *et* malicie sue, se
regni sui su*m*mu*m* apicem, uiolentia *et* terrorib*us* et ui extor-
quere, nisi arbitrio uoluntatis sue rex ip*s*e pareret, faciendo
uirtute*m* de necessitate. Super h*o*c itaq*ue* *et* aliis regni negociis,
euocato semel concilio, proteruus ille a rege reprobatus discessit
a curie p*re*sentia, iracundie calore freme*n*s in semetip*s*o, pro
repulsa q*u*am sustinuit.

Nec mora, accitis m*u*ltis qui cont*ra* regis i*m*perium partem
sua*m* *con*fouebant, infra paucos dies, copiosum i*m*mo infinitum
excercitum congregauit: *et* sub spe uictorie uirilit*er* optinende,
regem *et* suos ad hostile p*re*lium prouocauit. Rex au*tem* con-
fectus senio, time*n*s rebellare, declinauit aliquocie*n*s impet*us*
aduersario*rum*. Tandem uero, co*n*uocatis i*n* unum *p*rincipib*us*
et magnatib*us* suis, deliberare cepi*t* q*u*o fa*c*to opus h*a*be*r*et.
Dum igit*ur* tractarent i*n* co*m*mune per aliq*u*ot dies, secu*m*
deliberantes instantissime nece*s*citatis articulum, affuit int*er*

---

[1] A *repeats* sibi *after* constitueret.
[2] Hic Riganus binomin[i]s fuit. Vocaba*tur* enim alio nomine Aliel. Rigan*us* uero a ri*g*ore. Huic erat fili*us* Hildebrand*us*, miles strenuus, ab ense sic d*i*ctus. Hunc uoluit p*a*ter promouere: *Contemporary rubric in* A, *inserted in the middle of the sketch representing Riganus demanding the kingdom from Warmundus.*
[3] optat, B.

ol. 2b sermoci|nantes natus *et* unigenitus regis, eo usq*ue* elinguis *et*
absq*ue* sermone, *sed* aure purgata, singulorum uerba discernens.
Cum aut*em* p*a*tris seni*um*, *et* se ip*sum* ad regni negocia q*u*asi
inutilem *et* min*us* efficacem despici *et* reprobari ab om*n*ib*us*
perpenderet, contritus est *et* humiliatus in semetip*so*, usq*ue* in
lac*r*imarum aduberem profusionem. *Et* exitus aq*u*arum de-
dux*er*unt oculi eius; *et* estuabat dolore cordis intrinsecus
amarissimo. Et q*u*am uerbis no*n* pot*er*at, deo affec*tu* int*r*inseco
p*r*ecordial*iter* suggerebat, ingemiscens, reponensq*ue* lacrimabilem
q*u*erelam coram ip*so*, orabat ut a spiritu sanc*to* reciperet con-
solaci*onem*, a p*a*tre luminu*m* fortitudinem, *et* a filio p*a*tris
unigenito sapi*enc*ie salutaris donatiuum. In breui igitur,
co*n*t*r*iti cordis uota prospiciens, is, cui nuda *et* aperta sunt omnia,
resoluit os adolescentis in u*er*ba discreta *et* manifeste articulata.
Sicq*ue* de regni principatu tumide *et* minaciter contra se *et*
p*a*trem su*u*m perstrepentes, subito *et* ex insp*er*ato alloquitur:
"Quid adhuc me *et* p*a*tre meo sup*er*stite contra leges *et* iura
"uobis uendicatis regni iudicium enormiter co*n*t*r*ectare: *et* me
"excluso, herede geneali, alium degen*er*em facinorosu*m* *ec*iam
"in minas *et* diffiduciaci*onem* sup*er*be nimis prorumpente*m*,
"subrogare ut uos no*n* immerito iniquitatis *et* prodic*i*onis arguere
"valeam*us*. Quid, inquam, ext*er*i, qu*id* ex*tr*anei contra nos
"agere debeant, cu*m* nos affines *et* domestici n*os*tri a p*a*tria q*u*am
"hactenus gen*er*is n*os*t*r*i successio iure possedit hereditario,
"uelitis expellere?" Et dum hec Offanus uel Offa (hoc eni*m*
nomen adolescentulo erat) qui ia*m* n*un*c primo et*er*no nomine
cum bened[*i*]c[*i*]onis memoria meruit intitulari, ore facundo,
s*er*mone rethorico, uultu sereno prosequeret*ur*, omniu*m* audien-
tium plus q*u*am dici potest attonitoru*m* oculos facies *et* corda
in se conu*er*tit. Et prosequens inceptum s*er*monem, co*n*tinuan-
do rati*o*nem, ait (intuens ad superna): "Deum testor, om*n*esq*ue*
"celestis curie primates, quod tanti sceleris *et* discidii incentores,
"(n*is*i qui ceperint titubare, uiriliter erigantur in uirtute*m*
"p*r*istinam roborati) indem*p*nes (pro ut desides *et* formidolosi
"promeruer*un*t) ac impunitos, no*n* paciar. Fideles autem, ac
"strenuos, omni honore prosequ*ar* [et] co*n*fouebo."
    Audito *igitur* adolescentis sermone, q*u*em mutum estimabant
vanu*m* *et* inutilem, co*n*st*er*nati admodum *et* conterriti, ab ei*us*

presencia discesser*unt*, q*ui* co*n*tra p*a*trem suu*m* *et* ips*u*m, mota sedic*i*one, ausu temerario co*n*spirau*e*rant. Rigan*us* t*amen*, contumax *et* superbus, comi*t*ante Mittunno cu*m* aliis complicibus suis, qui iam iram in odium co*n*uert*er*ant, minas minis recessit cumulando, rege*m*que delirum cu*m* filio suo inutili ac vano murione, frontose diffiduciauit. Eco*n*tra, naturales ac fideles regis, ipsius

Fol. 3*a* minas paruipende*n*tes, i*m*mo | uilipendentes, inestimabili gaudio perfusi, regis *et* filii sui pedibus incuruati, sua suor*um*que corpora ad uindicandam regis iniuriam exponunt gratanter uni*ue*rsi. Nec mora, rex in sua *et* filii sui presentia generali edicto eos qui parti sue fauebant iubet assistere, uolens co*m*muni eor*um* consilio edoceri, q*ua*liter in agendis suis procedere *et* negocia sua exequi habeat conuenienter. Qui super hiis diebus aliquot deliberantes, i*n*primis consul*un*t regi ut filium suu*m* morib*us* *et* etate ad h*oc* maturu*m*, militari cingulo faciat insigniri: vt ad bellum procedens, hostibus suis horrori fieret *et* formidini. Rex aute*m* sano et salubri co*n*silio suor*um* obtemperans, celebri[1] ad hoc co*n*dicto die, cu*m* sollempni *et* regia pompa, gladio filium suum accinxit; adiunctis tirocinio suo strenuis adolescentib*us* gen*er*osis, quos rex ad dec*us* *et* gloriam filii sui militarib*us* indui fecit, *et* honorari.

Cum aute*m* post hec[2], aliq*u*andiu cu*m* sociis suis decertans, instrumenta tiro Offanus experiretur, omnes eum strenuissimu*m* *et* singulos sup*er*antem uehemen*ter*[3] admirabant*ur*. Rex igit*ur* in*d*e maiore*m* assumens audaciam, *et* in spem erectus alacriorem, co*m*municato cu*m* suis consilio, co*n*tra hostes regni sui insidiatores, i*m*mo iam manifeste co*n*tra regnum suu*m* insurgentes, *et* inito c*er*tami*n*e adu*er*santes, resu*m*pto s*p*iri*t*u bellum instaurari precep*it*. Potentissim*us* aute*m* ille, q*ui* regnu*m* sibi usurpare moliebatur, cu*m* filiis suis iuuenib*us* duob*us*, uidelicet tironib*us* strenuissimis Otta *et* Milione nominatis, ascita quoq*ue* non minima multitudine, n*i*chilomin*us* audac*ter* ad rebellandum, se suosq*ue* p*re*munire cepit, alacer *et* imp*er*territ*us*. Et preliandi diem *et* locum, hinc in*d*e rex *et* eius emulus det*er*minarunt.

Congregato itaq*ue* utrobiq*ue* copiosissimo *et* formidabili nimis excercitu, parati ad congressum, fixerunt tentoria e regione, n*i*chilq*ue* int*er*erat nisi fluui*us* torrens in medio, qui

---

[1] celebri, B; celibri, A.　　[2] hoc, B.　　[3] uehcementer, A.

utrumq*ue* excercitum sequestrabat. Et aliq*u*andiu hinc in*de*
meticulosi *et* co*n*sternati, rapidi fluminis alueum in*ter*positu*m*
(qui uix erat homini uel equo transmeabil*is*) transire distulerunt.
Tela tamen sola, cu*m* crebris comminacio*n*ibus *et* conuiciis,
transuolarunt. Tande*m* indignatus Offa *et* egre ferens probrose
more dispendia, electis de excercitu suo robustiorib*us* *et* bello
magis strenuis, q*u*os *eciam* credebat fideliores, subitus *et* im-
prouisus flumen raptim *per*transiens, *facto* impetu uehementi[1]
et repentino, hostes ei obuiam occurre*n*tes, preocupatos ta*m*en
circa ripam flum*in*is, plurimos de aduersario*rum* excercitu con-
*tr*iuit, *et* *in* ore gladii trucidauit. Primosq*ue* om*n*es *tr*ibunos
et primicerios potenter dissipauit. Cum ta*m*en sui commilitones,
forte uolentes *pr*escire in Offa *pr*euio Martis fortuna*m*, segni*ter*
amne*m* *tr*ansmearent, q*u*i latus suu*m* tenebantur suffulcire,
1. 3 *b* *cl*[2] pocius|circumuallando roborare, et resu*m*pto spi*ritu* uiuidiore,
reliquos om*n*es, hinc in*de* ad modu*m* nauis uelificantis *et* equora
uelocit*er* sulcantis, impetuosissime diuisit, ense *ter*ribilit*er*
fulminante, *et* hostiu*m* cruore sepius inebriato, donec sue om*n*es
acies ad ip*su*m illese *et* indempnes transmeare*n*t. Quo cum
*per*uenirent sui commilitones, congregati circa ip*su*m domi*n*um
suu*m*, excercitum magnu*m* et fortem conflauerunt. Duces
autem co*n*trarii excercitus, sese densis agminib*us* *et* consertis
aciebus, uiolent*er* opponu*n*t aduentantib*us*. Et congressu
inito cruentissimo, acclamatu*m* *est* utrobiq*ue* et exhortatu*m*,
ut res agatur pro capite, *et* certamen pro sua *et* uxoru*m* suaru*m*,
et liberoru*m* suoru*m*, *et* possessionu*m* libe*r*acione, in*e*ant iustissi-
mu*m*, auxilio diuino protegente. Perstrepunt igitur tube cu*m*
lituis, clamor exhortantiu*m*, equoru*m* hinnit*us*, morientiu*m*
et uulneratoru*m* gemitus, fragor lancearum, gladioru*m* tinnit*us*,
ictuu*m* tumultus, aera per*tur*bare uidebant*ur*. Aduersarii
tandem Offe legiones deiciunt, *et* *in* fugam dissipatas co*n*uertunt.

Quod cum uideret Offa strenuissim*us*, *et* ex hostiu*m* cede
cruent*us*, hausto spi*ritu* alacriori, in hostes, more leonis *et*
leene sublatis catulis, irruit truculent*er*, gladium suu*m* cruore
hostili inebriando. Quod cu*m* uider*e*nt tr*u*cida*n*di, fugitiui *et*
meticulosi pudore confusi, reuersi su*n*t sup*er* hostes, et ut famam
*r*edim*er*ent, ferociores in obstantes fulminant *et* debacant*ur*.

<hr/>

[1] ueheementi, A.   [2] eciam, B.

Multoque tempore truculenter nimis decertatum est, et utrobique suspensa est uictoria; tandem post multorum ruinam, hostes fatigati pedem retulerunt, ut respirarent et pausarent post conflictum.

Similiter eciam et excercitus Offani. Quod tamen moleste nimis tulit Offanus, cuius sanguis in ulcionem estuabat, et indefessus propugnator cessare erubescebat. Hic casu Offe obuiant duo filii diuitis illius, qui regnum patris eius sibi attemptauit usurpare. Nomen primogenito Brutus [sive Hildebrandus][1] et iuniori Sueno. Hii probra et uerba turpia in Offam irreuerenter ingesserunt, et iuueni pudorato in conspectu excercituum, non minus sermonibus quam armis, molesti extiterunt. Offa igitur, magis lacessitus, et calore audacie scintillans, et iracundia usque ad fremitum succensus, in impetu spiritus sui in eosdem audacter irruit. Et eorum alterum, videlicet Brutum, unico gladii ictu percussit, amputatoque galee cono, craneum usque ad cerebri medullam perforauit, et in morte singultantem sub equinis pedibus potenter precipitauit. Alterum uero, qui hoc uiso fugam iniit, repentinus insequens, uulnere letali sauciatum, contempsit et prostratum. Post hec[2] deseuiens in ceteros contrarii excercitus duces, gladius Offe quicquid obuiam habuit prosternendo deuorauit, excercitu ipsius tali exemplo recencius in hostes insurgente, et iam gloriosius triumphante.

Pater, uero, predictorum iuuenum, perterritus et dolore intrinseco sauciatus, subterfugiens amnem oppositum, nitebatur|

Fol. 4a pertransire: sed interfectorum sanguine torrens fluuius, eum loricatum et armorum pondere grauatum et multipliciter fatigatum, cum multis de suo excercitu simili incomodo prepeditis, ad ima submersit, et sine uulneribus, miseras animas exalarunt proditores, toti posteritati sue probra relinquentes. Amnis autem a Rigano ibi submerso sorciebatur uocabulum, et Riganburne, vt facti uiuat perpetuo memoria, nuncupatur. [Hiic alio nomine Auene dicitur.][3]

Reliqui autem omnes de excercitu Rigani [qui et Aliel dicebatur][3] qui sub ducatu Mitunni regebantur, in abissum desperacionis demersi, et timore effeminati, cum eorum duce in quo

---

[1] *Added in margin in* A; *not in* B.   [2] hec *omitted,* B.
[3] *Added in margin in* A; *not in* B.

magis Rigan*us* confidebat, in noctis crepusculo trucidati, c*um*
uictoria gloriosa campu*m* Offe strenuissimo (*in* nulla parte
corporis sui deformit*er* mutilato, nec *eciam* uel letaliter uel
periculose uul*n*erato, licet ea die multis se letiferis opposuiss*et*
p*er*iculis) reliquerunt[1].

Sicq*ue* Offe circa iuuentutis sue primicias, a Domino data
est uictoria in bello nimis ancipiti, ac cruentissimo, *et* int*er*
alienigenas uirtutis *et* indust*ri*e sue nomen celebre ipsius
uentilatum, *et* odor longe lateq*ue* bonitatis ac ciuilitatis, nec no*n*
et st*r*enuitatis ei*us* circumfusus, nomen ei*us* ad sidera subleuauit.

Porro in crastinu*m* post uictoria*m*, hostiu*m* spolia int*er*-
fecto*rum* *et* fugitiuoru*m* magnifice co*n*tempnens, nec sibi uol*c*ns
aliq*ua*tenus usurpare, ne q*uo*modolib*et* auaricie turpit*er* redar-
gueretur, militibus suis stipendiariis, *et* naturalib*us* suis homini-
b*us* (precipue[2] hiis quos nou*er*at indigere) liberalit*er* dereliq*u*it.
Solos t*amen* magnates, quos ipsemet *in* prelio cep*er*at, sibi
retinuit incarcerandos, redime*n*dos, uel iudicialiter puniendos.
Iussitq*ue* ut int*er*fecto*rum* duces *et* principes, quor*um* fama
titulos magnificauit, *et* p*re*cipue eor*um* qui in p*re*lio magnifice
ac fidelit*er* se habuerant (licet ei[3] adu*er*sarentur) seorsum honorifice i*n*tumulare*n*t*ur*, f*a*ctis eis obsequiis, c*um* lamentacionib*us*.
Ex*c*ercitus au*tem* popularis cadau*er*a, in arduo *et* eminenti loco,
ad post*er*itatis memoriam, t*ra*di iussit sepulture ignobiliori.
Vnde locus ille hoc nom*in*e Anglico Qualmhul[4], a strage uidelicet *et* sepultura interfectorum m*er*ito meruit intitulari.

Multor*um* eciam et magnor*um* lapidum super eos struem
ex*c*ercitus Offe, uoce p*re*conia iussus, congessit eminentem.
Totaq*ue* circumiacens planicies[5] ab ip*s*o cruentissimo c*er*tamine
et notabili sepultura nomen *et* titulum indelebilem est sortita,
et Blodiweld[6] a sa*n*guine interfecto*rum* deno*m*inabat*ur*.

Deletis igitur *et* confusis hostib*us*, Offa cum ingenti t*ri*umpho
ac tripudio *et* gloria reu*er*tit*ur* ad propria. Pater uero War-
mu*n*d*us*, q*u*i sese recep*er*at in locis tucioribus rei euentu*m*
expectans, s*ed* iam fausto nuncio c*er*tificatus, comperiensq*ue*
et securus de carissimi filii sui uictoria, cum ingenti leticia ei

---

[1] dereliquerunt, B.   [2] precipue *omitted*, B.   [3] ei *omitted*, B.
[4] Qualmhul *vel* Qualmweld *in margin*, A.
[5] planies, A: planicies, *perhaps corrected from* planies, B.   [6] blodifeld, B.

procedit obuius[1]: et in amplexus eius diutissime commoratus,

Fol. 4b *conceptum* | interius de filii sui palma gaudium *tegere* non uolens
set nec ualens, hui*us* cum lac*r*imis exul*t*a*ci*onis prorupit in
vocem: "Euge fili dulcissime, quo affectu, quaue mentis
"leticia, laudes tuas prout dign*um* est prosequar? Tu eni*m* es
"spes mea *et* subditor*um* iubilus ex in*s*perato *et* exultac*i*o. In
"te spes inopinata meis reuixit temporibus; in sinu tuo leticia
"mea, i*m*mo spes pocius toci*us* regni est reposita. Tu pop*u*li
"toci*us* firmamentum, tu pacis *et* lib*er*tatis mee basis *et* stabile,
"deo aspirante, fundamentum. Tibi debetur ruina proterui
"proditoris illi*us*, q*u*ondam publici hostis n*os*tri, qui regni
"fastigium quod m*i*hi *et* de genere meo propagatis iure debetur
"h*er*editario, tam impudent*er* q*u*am imprudenter, con*t*ra leges
"*et* ius gentium usurpare moliebatur. S*ed* uultus d*o*m*i*ni super
"eu*m* *et* complices suos facientes mala, ut perderet de terra
"memoriam eor*um*, Deus ulcionu*m* Domin*us* dissipau*i*t con-
"silium ipsius. Ip*sum* q*uoq*ue Riganu*m* in superbia rigente*m*,
"*et* immitem Mitunnu*m* co*m*militone*m* ipsius, cum excercitu
"eor*um* proiecit in flumen rapacissimu*m*. Descendunt q*u*asi
"plu*m*bum i*n* aq*u*is uehem*en*tib*us*; deuorauit gladi*us* tuus
"hostes n*os*tros fulmina*n*s *et* cruentat*us*, hostili sanguine magni-
"fice in*e*briatus; non degen*er* es fili mi genealis, s*ed* patrissans,
"patrum tuor*um* uestigia sequ*er*is magnificorum. Sepult*us* i*n*
"inferno n*os*ter hostis *et* adu*er*sarius, fructus viarum suar*um*
"condignos iam colligit, quos uiu*us* promerebatur. Luctum
"*et* miseriam q*u*am senectuti mee malignus ille inf*er*re dis-
"posuerat, u*er*sa uice, clementia diuina conuertit in tripudium[2].
"Quamobre*m* in *p*resenti accipe, quod tuis m*er*itis exigentib*us*
"debetur, eciam si filius meus non esses, *et* si m*i*hi iure heredi-
"tario non succederes; ecce iam, cedo, *et* regnum Anglor*um*
"uoluntatis tue arbitrio deinceps committo; etas enim mea
"fragilis *et* iam decrepita, regni ceptrum ulterius sustinere no*n*
"sufficit. Iccirco te fili desid*er*atissime, uicem meam supplere
"te co*n*uenit, *et* corpus meu*m* senio co*n*fectum, donec morientis
"oculos clauseris, quieti t*r*adere liberiori, vt a curis *et* secularib*us*
"sollicitudinibus, quib*us* discerpor lib*er*atus, p*r*ecibus uacem *et*
"*contem*placioni. Armis hucusq*ue* materialib*us* dimicaui: restat

---

[1] Gloria *t*riumphi, *in margin*, A.   [2] tripudium, B; tripuduum, A.

"ut de cetero uita mea que superest, militia sit super terram
"*contra* hostes spi*ri*tuales.

"Ego u*er*o pro incolumitate tua *et* regni statu, q*u*od stren-
"uitati tue, O anime mee dimidiu*m*, ia*m* co*m*misi, preces quales
"mea sci[t][1] simplicitas *et* potest i*m*becillitas, Deo fundam
"indefessas. S*ed* q*ui*a temp*us* perbreue amodo m*i*hi restat,
"*et* corpori meo solum s*up*erest sepulchru*m*, aure*m* benigna*m*
"meis accomoda salutaribus consiliis, *et* cor credulu*m* meis
"monitis *in*clina magnificis. Uerum ips*os* qui nobiscum co*n*tra
.1. 5 a "hostes publicos, Riganum videlicet *et* Mitunnu*m* | *et* eor*um*
"complices emulos no*s*tros fidelit*er* stet*er*u*n*t, *et* periculoso dis-
"crimini pro nobis se opposuer*un*t, p*ate*rno amore t*i*bi commendo,
"diligendos, honorandos, promouendos. Eos aut*em* qui decre-
"pite sen*e*ctutis mee membra[2] debilia *contemptui ha*b*ere ausi
"s*un*t, asserentes u*er*ba mea *et* regalia p*r*ecepta e*ss*e senilia
"delirame*n*ta, p*r*esumentes temer*e* apice regali me priuato te
"exheredare, suspectos habe *et* co*n*temptibiles, si qui sint elapsi
"ab hoc bello, *et* a tuo gladio deuorante, eciam cu*m* eor*um*
"post*er*itate: ne cu*m* in ramusculos uir*us* pullulet, a radice
"aliquid c*on*simile t*i*bi generetur in posterum. No*n* enim recolo
"me talem eor*um* promeruisse, q*u*i me *et* te filium meu*m* gratis
"oderunt, persecuc*i*onem. Similit*er* eos, quos d*i*cti proditores
"pro eo q*u*od nobis fideliter adheserant, exulare coeger*u*nt, uel
"qui impot*en*tes rabiem eor*um* fugiendo resist*er*e, ad horam
"declinau*er*unt, cu*m* omni mansuetudin*e* studeas reuocare,
"*et* honores eor*um* cu*m* possessionib*us* ex innata t*i*bi regali
"munificentia, graci*us* ampliare. Laus industrie tue *et* fame
"p*r*econia, *et* strenuitatis tue titulus, q*ue* adolescenciam tuam
"diuinit*us* illustraru*n*t, in posterum de te maiora prom*i*ttunt.
"Desid*er*anti animo sicient*er* affecto, ips*um*que Deu*m*, qui te
"t*i*bi, sua mera graci*a* reddidit *et* restaurauit, dep*r*ecor affectuose,
"vt has iuuentutis tue primicias, h*oc* *in*opinato triumpho subar-
"ratas, melior semp*er* ac splendidior op*er*um glor*i*a subsequatur.
"Et procul dubio post morte*m* meam (que non longe abest,
"iubente Dom*i*no) fame tue magnitudo per orbem uniu*er*sum
"dilatabitur, *et* felix suscipiet incrementu*m*. Et q*ue* Deo placita
"sunt, opere felici consumabis, q*ue* diuinitus pr*os*perabuntu*r*."

[1] scis, A, B.   [2] menbra, A.

Hec autem filius deuotus *et* mansuet*us*, licet magnific*us*
triumphator exaudiss*et et* intenta aure intellexiss*et*, flexis genib*us*
et iunctis manib*us*, *et* exundantib*us* oculis, p*a*tri suo grates[1]
rettulit accumulatas. Rex itaq*ue* per fines Anglie missis nunciis
expeditissimis, q*ui* ma*n*data regia detuler*unt*, tocius dicionis
sue conuocat nobilitatem. Que conuocata ex reg*is* precepto,
et persuasione, Offano filio suo unigenito ligiam fecerunt fideli-
tatem *et* homagiu*m* in p*a*tris presencia. Quod *et* om*n*es, animo
uolenti, i*m*mo gaudenti, co*m*munit*er* perfec*er*unt.

Rex igitur q*uem* pocius prona voluntas, q*uam* uigor prouexit
corporalis, per climata regni sui proficiscitur secur*us et* leta-
bundus, nullo cont*r*adicente, uel impediente, ut regni munici*ones*
et varias possessiones, diu per inimicos suos alienatas *et* iniuste
ac uiolent*er* possessas, ad sue dici*on*is reacciperet iure potestate*m*.
Que om*n*ia sibi sunt s*in*e difficultate uel more dispendio restituta.
Statimq*ue* p*a*t*er* filium eorum possessionib*us* corporaliter in-
uestiuit; *et* p*a*t*er*no contulit affect*u* ac gratuito, proc*er*ib*us*

Fol. 5*b* congauden|tib*us* super hoc uniuersis. Post hec autem, Rex
filio suo Offano erarium suum adaperiens, aurum suu*m et*
argentu*m*, uasa co*n*cupiscibilia, gemmas, oloserica omnia, sue
subdidit potestati. Sicq*ue* subactis *et* subt*r*actis hostib*us*[2]
cunctis, aliquandiu per uniu*er*sum regnu*m* uiguit pax *et* securitas
diu desiderabilis.

Rex igitur filii sui prosperitate gauisus, qui *eciam* diatim de
bono i*n* melius gradatim ascendit, aliquo tempore uite sue metas
distulit naturales: iubilus quoq*ue* in corde senis conceptus
languores seniles plurimu*m* mitigauit. Tandem Rex plenus
dierum, cu*m* benedic*cione* omniu*m*, qui ip*sum eciam* a remotis[3]
partib*us* per famam cognouerunt[4], nature debita persoluens
decessit. Et decedens, filio suo apice*m* regni sui pacatum *et*
quietu*m* reliquit: Offan*us* autem oculos p*a*tris sui pie claudens,
lamentaciones mensurnas cum magnis eiulatibus, lac*r*imis *et*
specialib*us* planctib*us* (prout moris tu*n*c erat principibus magnificis) lugubriter pro tanto funere continuauit. Obsequiisq*ue*
cu*m* exequiis, magnifice tam in ecc*lesi*a q*uam* in locis forinsecis
conpletis, apparatu regio *et* loco celeberrimo *et* nominatissimo,

---

[1] gracias, B.   [2] hosstibus, A.
[3] romotis, A.   [4] cong*n*ou*er*unt, A.

regibus *con*digno, videlicet *in* eminenciori ec*clesia* penes Glouer-
niam urbem egregiam, eidem exhiberi iubet sepulturam.
Offanus aut*em* cum morib*us* o*m*nibus foret redimitus, elegans
cor*po*re, armis strenuus, munificus *et* benignus, post obitum
p*at*ris sui magnifici Warmundi[1], cui*us* mores tractatus exigit
speciales, plenarie o*m*nium principum Regni do*m*inium suscipit,
et debitu*m* cum omni deuoc*i*one, *et* mera uoluntate, famulatu*m*.
Cum igitur cui*us*dam solempnitatis arrid*er*et serenitas, Offanus
cu*m* sollempni tripudio o*m*nib*us* applaudentibus *et* faustum
omen acclama*n*tibus, Anglie diademate feliciter est insignit*us*.

Adquiescens *igitur* senior*um* consiliis *et* sapientum persua-
sionib*us*, cepit tocius regni irrep*r*ehensibili*ter*, immo laudabiliter,
habenas[2] modernanter *et* sapien*ter* gubernare. Sic igitur,
subactis hostib*us* regni uniue*r*sis, uiguit pax secura *et* firmata
i*n* finib*us* Anglor*um*, p*er* te*m*pora longa; precipue *tamen* p*er*
spacium te*m*p*o*ris quinquennale. Erat au*tem* iam triginta
q*u*atuor annos etatis attingens, annis prospere pubescentib*us*.

Et cum Rex, more iuuenili, venatus gra*cia* per nemora fre-
quen*ter*, cu*m* suis ad h*o*c conuocatis uenatorib*us* *et* canibus
sagacib*us*, expeditus peragrasset, contigit die quada*m* quod
aere turbato, longe a suor*um* caterua semotus, solus p*er* nemoris
opaca penitus ipsorum locor*um*, necnon *et* fortune ignar*us*, casu
deambulabat. Du*m* aut*em* sic per ignota diuerticula *in*caucius
oberraret, *et* per inuia, uocem lacrimabilem *et* miserabiliter
q*u*erulam haut longe a se audiuit. Cui*us* sonitu*m* secutus,
l. 6 a *inter* densos frutices | virginem singularis forme *et* regii apparat*us*,
s*ed* decore uenustissimam, ex insperato repperit. Rex uero rei
euentum admirans, que ibi ageret et querele causas, eam blande
alloq*u*ens, cepit sciscitari. Que ex imo pectoris flebilia trahens
suspiria, regi respondit (nequaquam in auctorem s*ed* in seipsam
reatum retorquens): "Peccatis meis" inquit "exigentib*us* in-
"fortunii huius calamitas m*i*hi accidit." Erat aut*em* reguli
cui*us*dam filia q*ui* Eboracensibus preerat. Hui*us* incompara-
bilis pulchritudinis singularem eminentiam pa*ter* admirans,
amatorio demone seductus, cepit eam incestu libidinoso con-
cupiscere, *et* ad amorem illicitu*m* sepe sollicitare ipsam puellam,

---

[1] Warmandi, A.
[2] habenas *repeated after* regni *above in* A, *but cancelled in* B.

minis, pollicitis, blanditiis, atque muneribus adolescentule temptans emollire constantiam. Illa autem operi nephario nullatenus adquiescens, cum pater tamen minas minis exaggeraret[1], et promissa promissis accumularet, munera muneribus adaugeret, iuxta illud poeticum:

Imperium, promissa, preces, confudit in unum: elegit magis incidere in manus hominum, et eciam ferarum qualiumcunque, vel gladii subire sententiam, quam Dei offensam incurrere, pro tam graui culpa manifestam. Pater itaque ipsam sibi parere constanter renuentem, euocatis quibusdam maligne mentis hominibus quos ad hoc elegerat, precepit eam in desertum solitudinis remote duci, uel pocius trahi, et crudelissima morte condempnatam, bestiis ibidem derelinqui. Qui cum in locum horroris et vaste solitudinis peruenissent, trahentes eam seductores illi, Deo ut creditur inspirante, miserti pulchritudinis[2] illius eam ibidem sine trucidacione et membrorum mutilacione, uiuam, sed tamen sine aliquorum uictualium alimento (exceptis talibus qui de radicibus et frondibus uel herbis colligi, urgente ultima fame, possunt) dimiserunt.

Cum hac rex aliquandiu habens sermonem, comitem itineris sui illam habuit, donec solitarii cuiusdam habitacionem reperissent, ubi nocte superueniente quiescentes pernoctauerunt. In crastinum autem solitarius ille uiarum et semitarum peritus, regem cum comite sua usque ad fines domesticos, et loca regi non ignota[3] conduxit. Ad suos itaque rex rediens, desolate illius quam nuper inuenerat curam gerens, familiaribus et domesticis generis sui sub diligenti custodia commisit.

Post hec aliquot annis elapsis, cum rex celibem agens uitam, mente castus et corpore perseueraret, proceres dicionis sue, non solum de tunc presenti, sed de futuro sibi periculo precauentes, et nimirum multum solliciti, dominum suum de uxore ducenda unanimiter conuenerunt: ne sibi et regno successorem et heredem non habens, post obitum ipsius iminens periculum generaret. Etatis enim iuuenilis pubertas, morum maturitas, et urgens regni necessitas, necnon et honoris dignitas, itidem Fol. 6b postularunt. | Et cum super hoc negocio, sepius regem sollici-

---

[1] exaggeret, B.   [2] pulcritudinis, B; pulchritudini, A.   [3] ingnota, A.

tarentur, *et* alloquerentur, ip*s*e multociens ioculando, *et* talia
ue*r*ba asserendo interludia fuisse uanitatis, procerum suoru*m*
constantiam dissimulando differendo*que* delusit. Quod quidam
adue*r*tentes, co*m*municato cu*m* aliis consilio, regem ad nubendu*m*
incuntabiliter urgere ceperunt. Rex uero more optimi principis,
cui*us* primordia iam bene subarrauerat, nolens uoluntati
magnatu*m* suor*um* resistere, diu secum de thori socia, libra
profunde ra*ti*onis, studiose cepit deliberare. Cu*m*q*ue* hoc in
mente sua sollicicius tractaret, uen*i*t forte i*n* mente*m* suam
illius iuuencule memoria, q*u*am dudum inter uenandum i*n*uenit
uagabundam, solam, feris *et* predonibus miserabiliter expositam:
quam ad tuciora ducens, familiaribus gene*r*is sui co*m*mise*r*at
alendam, ac carius custodiendam. Que, ut rex audiuit, mori-
b*us* laudabiliter redimita, decoris existens ex*p*ectabilis, omnibus
sibi cognitis amabilem exhibuit *et* laudabilem; hec igit*ur* sola,
relictis multis, *eciam* regalis stematis sibi oblatis, complacuit;
illamq*ue* solam i*n* matrimoniu*m* sibi adoptauit.

Cum aute*m* eam duxisset in uxorem, non inte*r*ueniente
m*u*lta mora, elegantissime forme utriusq*ue* sexus liberos ex
eadem procreauit. Itaq*ue* cum p*r*ius e*ss*et rex propria seueritate
subditis suis formidabilis, magnates eius, necnon *et* populus
eius uniue*r*sus, heredum *et* successor*um* apparentia animati,
regni robur *et* leticiam geminar*un*t. Rex q*uoque* ab uniue*r*sis
suis, *et* no*n* solum prope positis, i*m*mo alienigenis *et* remotis,
extit*it* honori, uene*r*acioni, ac dileccioni. Et cu*m* inter se in
Britannia, (q*ue* tunc temporis in plurima regna multiphariam
diuisa fuisset) reg*u*li sibi finitimi hostilite*r* se impete*r*ent, solus
Rex Offa pace regni sui potitus felicite*r*, se sibiq*ue* s*u*bditos in
pace regebat *et* libertate. Unde *et* adiacencium prouinciarum
reges ei*us* mendicabant auxilium, *et* i*n* necce*ss*itatis articulo,
consiliu*m*.

Rex itaq*ue* Northamhimbror*um*, a barbara Scotor*um*
gente, *et* *eciam* aliquib*us* suor*um*, grauite*r* *et* usq*ue* *ferme* ad
inte*r*neci*o*nem percussus,*et* proprie defensionis auxilio destitutus,
ad Offam regem potentem legatos destinat; *et* pacificum sup-
plicans, ut p*r*esidii eius solacio cont*r*a hostes suos roboretur.
Tali mediante condici*o*ne, ut Offe filiam sibi matrimoni*o*
copularet, *et* non se proprii regni, **sed** Offam, primarium **ac**

principem preferre*t*, *et* se cu*m* suis om*n*ibu*s* ip*s*i subiugaret.
Nichil itaq*ue* dotis cum Offe filia rogitauit, hoc sane contentus
premio, ut a regni s*u*i finibus bar*b*aros illos potenter *et* frequenter
experta fugaret strenuitate.

Cum autem legatorum uerba rex Offa succepisset, consilio
Fol. 7 *a* suorum fretus sup|plicantis uoluntati ac precibus adquieuit,
si *tame*n rex ille pactum huiusmodi, tactis sac*r*osanc*t*is euuan-
geliis[1], *et* obsidum tradic*i*one, fideliter tenendum confirmaret.
Sic igitur Rex Offa, super hiis condic*i*onibu*s* sub c*er*ta forma
confirmatus, *et* ad plenum certificatus, in partes illas cu*m* equi-
tum numerosa multitudine proficiscitur. Cum autem illuc
peruenisse*t*, timore eius consternata pars aduersa cessit, fuge
presidio se saluando. Quam *tame*n rex Offa audacter prosecutus,
non prius destitit fugare fugientem, donec eam ex integro
contriuisset; se*d* nec eo contentus, ulteri*us* progreditur, bar-
baros expugnaturus. Interea ad patriam suam nunciu*m*
imperitum destinau*i*t, ad primates et precipuos regni sui,
quib*us* tocius dicionis sue regimen commendau*er*at, et liter*as*
regii sigilli sui munimine co*n*signatas[2], eidem nunc*i*o commisit,
deferendas. Q*ui* autem destinatus fuit, iter arripiens u*er*sus
Offe regnum, ut casu accidit int*er* eundu*m*, hospitandi *gracia*
aulam regiam introiuit illi*us* regis, cuius filiam Offa sibi *matri-
mo*nio copulau*er*at. Rex au*tem* ille, cum de statu *et* causa
itineris sui subdole requirendo cognouisset, uultus sui serenitate
animi u*er*suciam mentitus, specie ten*us* illum amantissime suscepit: *et* uelamen sceleris sui querens, a conspectu publico sub
quodam dileccionis pretexu, ad regii thalami secreta penetralia
ip*s*um nunciu*m* nichil sinist*r*i suspicantem introduxit: magnoq*ue*
studio elaborauit, ut ip*s*um, uino estuanti madentem, redderet
temulentum, et ip*s*o nuncio uel dormiente uel aliquo alio modo
ignorante, mandata *domi*ni sui regis Offe tacit*us* ac subdolus
apertis *et* explicatis liter*i*s perscrutabatur; cepitq*ue* perniciose
immutare et p*er*uertere sub Offe nomine sigillu*m* adultera*n*s,
fallacesq*ue* *et* perniciosas literas loco inuentarum occultauit.
Forma autem adulterina*rum* [*litera*rum][3] hec est q*ue* sub-
scribitur[4]:

¹ euuangelii, B.   ² co*n*singnatas, A.
³ *from B, written over erasure.*   ⁴ s*c*rib*itu*r, B.

[1]"Rex Offa, maioribus et precipuis regni sui, salutis et
"prosperitatis augmentum. Uniuersitati uestre notum facio, in
"itinere quod arripui infortunia et aduersa plurima tam michi
"quam subditis meis accidisse, et maiores excercitus mei, non
"ignauia propria, uel hostium oppugnantium uirtute, set pocius
"peccatis nostris iusto Dei iudicio interisse. Ego autem instantis
"periculi causam pertractans, et consciencie mee intima per-
"scrutatus, in memetipso nichil aliud conicio altissimo displicere,
"nisi quod perditam et maleficam illam absque meorum consensu
"uxorem imperito et infelici duxi matrimonio. Ut ergo de
"malefica memorata, uoluntati uestre ad plenum quam temere
"offendi satisfiat, asportetur cum liberis ex ea genitis ad loca
ɔl. 7 b "deserta, hominibus incognita[2], | feris et auibus aut siluestribus
"predonibus frequentata: ubi cum pueris suis puerpera, trun-
"cata manus et pedes, exemplo pereat inaudito."

Nuncius autem mane facto, uino quo maduerat digesto,
compos iam sui effectus, discessit: et post aliquot dies per-
ueniens ad propria, magnatibus qui regno regis Offe preerant
literas domini sui sigillo signatas exposuit. In quarum auditu
perlecta mandati serie, in stuporem et uehementissimam
admiracionem uniuersi, plus quam dici possit, rapiuntur. Et
super hiis, aliquot diebus communicato cum magnatibus consilio deliberantes, periculosum ducebant[3] mandatis ac iussionibus
regiis non obtemperare. Misera igitur seducta, deducta est in
remotissimum et inhabitabilem locum horroris et uaste solitudinis: cum qua eciam liberi eius miseri et miserabiles queruli
et uagientes, absque misericordia, ut cum ea traherentur occidendi, iudicium acceperunt.

Nec mora, memorati apparitores matrem cum pignoribus
suis in desertum uastissimum trahebant. Matri uero propter
eius formam admirabilem parcentes, liberos eius, nec forme,
nec sexui, etati uel condicioni parcentes, detruncarunt men-
bratim, immo pocius frustatim[4] crudeliter in bestialem feritatem
seuientes. Completaque tam crudeli sentencia, cruenti apparitores ocius reuertuntur. Nec mora, solitarius quidam uitam
in omni sanctitate, uigiliis assiduis, ieiuniis crebris, et continuis

---

[1] Epistola, *in margin,* A.   [2] incongnita, A.
[3] dicebant, B.   [4] frustratim, A, B

or*ati*onib*us*, ducens heremiticam, circa noctis crepusculum eo
per*transiens*, mulieris cuiusdam luctus lacrimabiles *et* querelas
usq*ue* ad intima cordis *et* ossuum[1] medullas penetratiuas, quas
D*omi*nus ex mortuorum corporib*us* licet lac*er*atis elicuit,
audiuit. Infantulorumq*ue* uagitus lugubres nimis cu*m* doloris
ululatibus quasi in materno sinu audiendo similiter annotauit.
Misericordia autem sanc*tus* Dei motus, usq*ue* ad lacrimaru*m*
aduberem effusionem, quo ipsa uox ip*sum* uocabat, Domino
ducente peruenit. Et cu*m* illuc peruenisset, nec aliud q*uam*
corp*or*a humana in frusta detruncata reperisset, cognouit[2] in
sp*iritu* ipsa alicuius innocentis corp*us*, uel aliquorum i*n*nocentiu*m*
corpuscula extitisse, que tam inhumanam sentenciam subierunt.
Nec sine martirii palma, ipsos quorum hee fuerunt exuuie, ab
hoc[3] seculo transmigrasse suspicabatur. Auxiliu*m* tam*en* pro
Dei amore *et* caritatis intuitu postulatu*m* non denegans, se pro
illorum reparac*i*one prostrauit in deuotissima*m* cum lacrimis
orac*i*onem, maxime propter uocem celitus emissam, quam profecto cognouit[2] p*er* D*eum* lingu*as* cadauerum protulisse. Piis
igitur sanc*tus* com*m*otus uisc*er*ibus, igneq*ue* succe*n*sus caritatis,
ex cognic*i*one[4] ei*us*, quam, ut ia*m* d*ictu*m, dudu*m* uiderat,
Fol. 8 a hab*ui*t, fact*us* hilarior, pro ipsis | flexis genib*us*, inundantibus
oculis, iunctisq*ue* palmis orauit, dicens: "D*omi*ne Jesu Chr*ist*e,
"q*ui* Lazarum quatriduanu*m* ac fetidum resuscitasti, immo
"qui omniu*m* n*ost*roru*m* corpora i*n* ex*t*remo examine suscitabis,
"ue*st*ram oro mis*er*icordiam, ut non habens ad me peccatorem,
"sed ad horum innocentum pressuras respectu*m* piissimu*m*,
"corpuscula hec iubeas resuscitari, ad laudem *et* gloriam tuam
"i*n* sempiternum, vt omn*es* qui mortis horum causam *et* forma*m*
"audierint, te glorificent Deum *et* Dominum mundi Saluatorem."
 Sic igitur sanc*tus* iste, D*omi*ni de fidei sue[5] uirtute i*n* Domino
presumens *et* confidens, int*er* orandum, membra p*re*cisa recolli-
gens, *et* sibi particulas adaptans *et* coniungens, *et* i*n* quantum
potuit redintegrans, in parcium quamplurimu*m*, set in integri-
tatem pocius delecta*tus*, Domino rei consummac*i*onem q*ui*
mortificat *et* uiuificat com*m*endauit. Coniuncta igitur corpora,
signo crucis triumphali consignauit. Mira fidei uirtus et

---

[1] ossium, B. [2] congnouit, A. [3] hoc *omitted*, B.
[4] co*n*gnic*i*one, A. [5] sui, A.

efficacia, signo crucis uiuifice et orationis ac fidei serui Dei
uirtute, non solum matris orbate animus reparatur, sed et filiorum
corpuscula in pristinum et integrum nature sunt reformata
decorem, necnon et anime mortuorum ad sua pristina domicilia
sunt reuerse. Ad mansiuncule igitur sue septa (a qua elongatus
fuerat, gracia lignorum ad pulmentaria dequoquenda colligen-
dorum) ipse senex: qui prius detruncati fuerant, Domino
iubente integri uiui et alacres sunt reuersi, ducem sanctum suum
sequentes pedetentim. Ubi more patris, ipsam desolatam cum
liberis sibi ipsis restitutis, alimentis quibus potuit, et que ad
manum habuit, pie ac misericorditer confouebat.

Nesciens ergo quo migraret regina, cum suis infantulis intra
uastissimam heremum cum memorato solitario, diu moram
ibidem orationibus, uigiliis, ac aliis sanctis operibus eius intenta
et iamiam conuenienter informata, et edulio siluestri sustentata,
continuabat. Post duorum uero mensium curricula, Rex Offa
uictoriosissimus domum letus remeauit, spolia deuictorum suis
magnatibus regali munificentia gloriose distribuendo; ueruntamen, ne lacrime gaudia regis, et eorum qui cum eo aduenerant,
miserabiliter interrumperent, consiliarii regii que de regina et
liberis eius acciderant, diu sub silencio caute dissimulando, et
causas absencie eius fictas annectendo, concelabant. Tandem
cum rex uehementer admiraretur ubinam regina delituisset,
que ipsi regi ab ancipiti bello reuertenti occurrisse gaudenter
teneretur, et in osculis et amplexibus ceteris gaudentius trium-
phatorem aduentantem suscepisse, sciscitabatur instantius, et
toruius et proteruius, quid de ipsa fieret uel euenisset. Suspi-
f. 8b cabatur enim eam morbo detentam, ipsamque cum liberis | suis,
regis et aliorum hominum, ut quieti uacaret, frequentiam
declinasse. Tandem cum iratus nullatenus se uelle amplius
ignorare, cum iuramento, quid de uxore sua et liberis euenisset,
uultu toruo asseruisset, unus ex edituis omnia que acciderant,
de tirannico eius mandato, et mandati plenaria execucione,
seriatim enarrauit.

Hiis auditis, risus in luctum, gaudium in lamenta, iubilus
in singultus flebiliter conuertuntur, totaque regia ululatibus
personuit et meroribus. Lugensque rex diu tam immane infortunium, induit se sacco cilicino, aspersum cinere, ac multipliciter

deformatum. Tandem monitu suorum, qui dicebant non uiro*rum* magnifico*rum* sed pocius effeminato*rum*, dolorem inter-iecto solacio nolle temperare[1], *esse* propriu*m* et *con*suetudine*m*, rex cepit respirare, *et* dolori modu*m* imponere. Consilio igitur pe*ri*torum, qui nouerant regem libent*er* i*n* tempore pro*s*pero in studio uenatico plurimu*m* delectari, conuoca*n*tur uenatores, ut rex spaciaturus uenando, dolorem suu*m* diminueret *et* luctu*m* solacio demulceret. Qui int*er* uenandum dum p*er* siluaru*m* abdita, Deo misericordiaru*m* *et* tociu*s* consolac[i]onis ducente, felicit*er* solus per inuia oberrauit, *et* tandem ad heremitoriu*m* memorati h*er*emite directe peruenit, eiusqu*e* exiguu*m* domicilium subintrans, humaniss[im]e *et* cu*m* su*m*mo gaudio receptus *est*. Et cu*m* humili residens sedili, membra[2] fatigata quieti daret ad horam, recolens quali*ter* uxore*m* sua*m* ibidem quonda*m* diuinitus reperisset, *et* feliciter educasset, *et* educatam duxisset i*n* uxorem, *et* quam elegantem ex ea prolem pr*o*tulisset, eruperunt lacrime cu*m* gemitibus, *et* in querelas lugubres ora resoluens, hospiti suo sinistru*m* de uxore sua qu*i*[3] infausto sidere nup*er* euen*er*at qua*m* *et* ip*s*e q*u*ondam viderat, enarrauit. At senex sereno uultu, factus ex intrinsecus concepto gaudio alacrior, consolatus est rege*m*, et in uocem exultac*io*nis eminus prorumpens: "Eia "do*m*ine mi rex, eia, ait; uere Deus misericordiaru*m*, Dominu*s*, "famulos suos quasi p*a*ter filios in omni t*r*ibulacione p*os*t pres-"suras consolatur, percutit *et* medetur, deicit ut gloriosius eleuet "pregrauatum. Uiuit uxor tua, cum lib*er*is tuis in o*m*ni sospi-"tate restauratis: non meis m*er*itis, s*ed* p*o*ciu*s* tuis, integritati, "sanitati *et* leticie pleniu*s* qui trucidabantur restituunt*ur*. Re-"cognosce[4] q*u*anta fecit t*i*bi Dominu*s*, *et* in laudes et gr*a*ciaru*m* "acciones tot*us* exurge." Tunc prosiliens sanct*us* pre gaudio, euocauit reginam, que in int*er*iori diu*er*ticulo, pueros suos balneo micius m*a*terno studio *con*fouebat. Que cu*m* ad regem intro-

Fol. 9 *a* isset, uix se | gaudio capiens, pedibus mariti sui pr*o*uoluta, in lacrimis exultac*io*nis inundauit. In cuius amplexus desidera-tissimos rue*n*s rex, ipsam in maius q*u*am dici possit gaudium suscepit. Interi*m* senex, pueros elegantissimos *et* ex ablucione elegantiores, uestit, comit, *et* p*a*terno more *et* affectu componit, *et* ad pr*e*sentiam p*a*tris *et* matris introducit. Quos p*a*ter intra

---

[1] obtemperare, B.   [2] menbra, A.   [3] qui, AB; quae, Wats.   [4] recongnosce, A.

brachia suscipiens, *et* ad pectus arctioribu*s* amplexibu*s* applicans,
roseis uultibu*s* infantu*m* oscula *im*primit *mu*ltiplicata; quos
*tam*en rore lac*r*imarum, p*r*e nimia mentis exultacione, made-
fecit. Et cu*m* diucius eoru*m* colloquiis pasceretu*r*, co*n*ue*r*sus
rex ad senem, ait: "O p*at*er s*an*cte, p*at*er dulcissime[1], me*n*tis
"mee reparator, *et* gaudii cordis mei restaurator, qua merita
"ue*st*ra, caritatis officia, pietatisq*ue* beneficia, p*r*osequar re-
"munerac[*i*]one? Accipe *er*go, licet m*u*lto maiora exigant
"merita tua, q*ui*cquid erarium meu*m* ualet effund*er*e; me, meos,
"et mea, tue expono uoluntati." At s*an*ct*u*s, "Domi*n*e mi rex,
"non decet me peccatorem co*n*ue*r*su*m* ad Domi*n*um, ad insanias
"quas reliqui falsas respicere. Tu uero pocius pro a*n*imabu*s*
"p*at*ris tui *et* matris tue, quibu*s* quandoq*ue* caru*s* fueram ac
"familiaris, *et* tua, *et* uxoris tue, *et* libe*r*oru*m* tuoru*m* corporali
"sanitate, *et* salute sp*ir*ituali, regni tui soliditate, *et* successoru*m*
"tuoru*m* p*r*osp*er*itate, Deo gratus, qui tot in te congessit bene-
"ficia, cenobium quodda*m* fundare, u*e*l aliquod dirutu*m* studeas
"restaurare: in quo digne *et* laudabiliter Deo in perpetuum
"seruiatur; *et* tui memoria cu*m* p*r*ecibu*s* ad Domi*n*um fusis, cu*m*
"benediccionibu*s* semp*er* recenter recolatur." Et co*n*ue*r*sus ad
reginam, ait, "Et tu, filia, q*u*amuis mulier, no*n* *tam*en mulie-
"b*r*iter, ad hoc regem accendas *et* admoneas diligenter, filiosq*ue*
"tuos instrui facias, ut[2] *et* Domi*n*um Deu*m*, qui eos uite reparauit,
"studeant gratant*er* honorare, *et* eidem fidelit*er* famulando
"fundandi cenobii possessiones ampliare, *et* tueri libertates."

Descensus ad secu*n*du*m* Offa*m*.

Sanctus autem ad cellam reue*r*sus, post paucu*m* temporis ab
incolatu hu*iu*s mundi migrauit ad Domi*n*um, m*er*cedem eter*n*am
pro labore temporali recepturus. Rex au*tem*, cito monita ipsius
salubria da*n*s obliuioni *et* incurie, ex tunc ocio ac paci uacauit:
prolemq*ue* copiosam utriusq*ue* sexus expectabilis pulch*r*itudinis
procreauit. Unde semen regium a latere *et* descensu felix suscepit incrementu*m*. Qui co*m*pleto uite sue tempore, post etatem
bonam q*u*ieuit in pace, *et* regaliter sepultus, appositus *est* ad
patres suos; in eo multu*m* redarguendu*s*, quod cenobium[3] uotiuo
affec*tu* repromissu*m*, thesauris parcendo no*n* construxit. Post

---

[1] sancte *et* dulcissime, B.   [2] ut *added above line*, A, B.
[3] scenobium, A; *the* s *is erased in* B.

uictorias enim a Domino[1] sibi collatas, amplexibus et ignauie
necnon auaricie plus equo indulsit. Prosperitas enim secularis,
Fol. 9b animos, licet uir|iles, solet frequenter effcminare. Ueruntamen
hoc onus humeris filii sui moriturus apposuit: qui cum deuota
assercione, illud sibi suscepit. Sed nec ipse Deo auerso pol-
licita, prout patri suo promiserat, compleuit; set filio suo huius
uoti obligacionem in fine uite sue dereliquit. Et sic memorati
uoti uinculum, sine efficacia complementi de patre in filium
descendens, usque ad tempora Pineredi filii Tuinfreth suspende-
batur. Quibus pro pena negligentie, tale euenit infortunium,
ut omnes principes, quos Offa magnificus edomuerat, a subiec-
cione ipsius Offe et posteritatis sue procaciter recesserunt, et
ipsum morientem despexerunt. Quia ut predictum est, ad mortem uergens, deliciis et senii ualitudine marcuit eneruatus.

De ortu secundi Offe.

Natus est igitur memorato Tuinfred[o][2] (et qui de stemate
regum fuit) filius, videlicet Pineredus, usque ad annos adoles-
centie inutilis, poplitibus contractis, qui nec oculorum uel aurium
plene officio naturali fungeretur. Unde patri suo Tuinfredo et
matri sue Marcelline, oneri fuit non honori, confusioni et non
exultacioni. Et licet unicus eis fuisset, mallent prole caruisse,
quam talem habuisse. Ueruntamen memorie reducentes euentum Offe magni, qui in tenera etate penitus erat inutilis, et
postea, Deo propicio, penitus sibi restitutus, mirabili strenuitate
omnes suos edomuit aduersarios, et bello prepotens, gloriose
multociens de magnis hostibus triumphauit: spem conceperunt,
quod eodem medico medente (Christo uidelicet, qui eciam mor-
tuos suscitat, propiciatus) posset similiter uisitari et sibi restitui.
Pater igitur eius et mater ipsum puerum inito salubri consilio,
in templo presentarunt Domino, votiua deuocione firmiter pro-
mittentes: "Ut si ipsum Deus restauraret, quod parentes eius
"negligenter omiserunt, ipse puer cum se facultas offerret fide-
"liter adimpleret": videlicet de cenobio[3], cuius mencio prelibata
est, honorifice construendo: uel de diruto restaurando. Et
cum hec tam puer quam pater et mater deuotissime postularent,
exaudita est oratio eorum a Deo, qui se nunquam difficilem
exhibet precibus iustis supplicantium, hoc modo.

[1] deo, B [2] tuinfreth, B. [3] scenobio, A; s *erased* B.

Quomodo prosperabatur.

Erat in eadem regione (Merciorum uidelicet) quidam tirannus,
pocius destruens et dissipans regni nobilitatem, quam regens,
nomine Beormredus[1]. Hic generosos, quos regius sanguis pre-
claros [fecerat][2], usque ad internecionem subdole persequebatur,
relegauit, et occulta nece perdidit iugulandos. Sciebat enim,
quod uniuersis de regno merito extitit odiosus; et ne aliquis loco
ipsius subrogaretur (et presertim de sanguine regio propagatus)
uehementer formidabat. Tetendit insuper laqueos Tuinfredo et
uxori eius, ut ipsos de terra expelleret, uel pocius perderet truci-
10a datos. | Puerum autem Pinefredum[3] spreuit, nec ipsum querere
ad perdendum dignabatur; reputans eum inutilem et ualitudin-
arium. Fugientes igitur memoratus Tuinfredus et uxor eius et
familia a facie persequentis, sese in locis tucioribus receperunt,
ne generali calumpnie inuoluerentur. Quod comperiens Pine-
fredus adolescens, quasi a graui sompno expergefactus, erexit se:
et compagibus neruorum laxatis, et miraculose protensis, sese de
longa desidia redarguens, fecit alices, brachia, crura, pedes, ex-
tendendo. Et aliquociens oscitans, cum loqui conaretur, solu-
tum est uinculum lingue eius, et loquebatur recte, uerba proferens ore facundo prompcius articulata. Quid plura? de con-
tracto, muto, et ceco, fit elegans corpore, eloquens sermone, acie
perspicax oculorum. Qui tempore modico in tantam floruit ac
uiguit strenuitatem, ut nullus in regno Merciorum, ipsi in mori-
bus et probitate multiplici ualuit comparari, unde ipsi Mercii,
secundum Offam, et non Pinefredum, iam nominantes (quia a
Deo respectus et electus fuisset, eodem modo quo et rex Offa
filius regis Warmundi) ceperunt ipsi quasi Domino uniuersaliter
adherere; ipsumque iam factum militem, contra regem Beorm-
redum et eius insidias, potenter ac prudenter protegere, dantes
ei dextras, et fedus cum ipso, prestitis iuramentis, ineuntes.
Quod audiens Beormredus, doluit, et dolens timuit sibi vehe-
menter. Penituitque eum amarissime, ipsum Pinefredum[3] (qui
iam Offa nominabatur) cum ceteris fraudulenter non intere-
misse....

* * * *

---

[1] de tirannide Beormredi regis Mercie, B.
[2] fecerat, *wanting in* A; *added in margin*, B.
[3] Pinefredum, B; Penefredum, A, *but with* i *above* *in first case.*

Fol. 11 *a*   Qualiter Offa rex uxorem duxerit.

Diebus itaque sub eisdem, regnante in Francia Karolo rege
magno ac uictoriosissimo, quedam puella, facie uenusta, sed
mente nimis inhonesta, ipsi regi consanguinea, pro quodam quod
patrauerat crimine flagiciosissimo, addicta est iudicialiter morti
ignominiose; uerum, ob regie dignitatis reuerentiam, igni uel
ferro tradenda non iudicatur, sed in nauicula armamentis ca-
rente, apposito uictu tenui, uentis et mari, eorumque ambiguis
casibus exponitur condempnata. Que diu uariis[1] procellis exagi-
tata, tandem fortuna trahente, litori Britonum est appulsa, et
cum in terra subiecta potestati regis Offe memorata cimba ap-
plicuisset, conspectui regis protinus presentatur. Interogata
autem quenam esset, respondens, patria lingua affirmauit, se
Karolo regi Francorum fuisse consanguinitate propinquam,

Fol. 11 *b* Dridamque nominatam, sed per tirannidem | quorundam igno-
bilium (quorum nuptias ne degeneraret, spreuit) tali fuisse discrimini adiudicatam, abortisque lacrimis addidit dicens, "Deus
"autem qui innocentes a laqueis insidiantium liberat, me
"captiuam ad alas tue protecionis, o regum serenissime, feliciter
"transmisit, vt meum infortunium, in auspicium fortunatum
"transmutetur, et beatior in exilio quam in natali patria, ab
"omni predicer posteritate."

Rex autem uerborum suorum ornatum et eloquentiam, et
corporis puellaris cultum et elegantiam considerans[2], motus pietate, precepit ut ad comitissam Marcellin[am][3] matrem suam
tucius duceretur alenda, ac mitius sub tam honeste matrone
custodia, donec regium mandatum audiret, confouenda. Puelle
igitur infra paucos dies, macie et pallore per alimenta depulsis,
rediit decor pristinus, ita ut mulierum pulcherima censeretur.
Sed cito in uerba iactantie et elacionis (secundum patrie sue
consuetudinem) prorumpens, domine sue comitisse, que materno
affectu eam dulciter educauerat, molesta nimis fuit, ipsam procaciter contempnendo. Sed comitissa, pro amore filii sui regis,
omnia pacienter tolerauit: licet et ipsa dicta puella, inter comitem
et comitissam uerba discordie seminasset. Una igitur dierum,
cum rex ipsam causa uisitacionis adiens, uerbis consolatoriis

[1] uariis *repeated*, A; *second* variis *cancelled.* B.
[2] considerans, B, *inserted in margin*; *omitted*, A.
[3] Marcelline, A; Marcell, B.

alloqueretur, incidit *in* retia amoris illius; erat enim iam spe*cies*
illius concupiscibilis. Clandestino *igitur* ac repentino *ma*tri-
monio ip*s*am sibi, *incon*sultis p*a*tre *et m*atre, necno*n et* magnatib*us*
suis uniu*ers*is, copulauit. Unde ut*er*q*ue* parentu*m*, dolore ac
tedio *in* etate senili *con*tabescens, dies uite abreuiando, sue mortis
horam lugubrit*er* anticiparu*nt*; sciebant eni*m* ipsam mulier-
culam fuisse *et* regalibus amplexibus prorsus indignam; perpen-
debantq*ue* iamiam ueracissime, *non* sine causa exilio lacrimabili,
ipsam, ut pre*dic*tu*m est*, fuisse conde[*m*]pnatam. Cum aut*em*
annos longeue senectutis vixisset[1] comes T*uinfredus*, *et* p*re*
senectute caligass*ent* oculi ei*us*, data filio suo regi bened*i*cione,
nature debita persoluit; cui*us* corpus magnifice, pr*out* decuit,
tradidit sepulture. Anno q*uoque* sub eode*m* uxor ei*us* comitissa
M*arcellina*, m*a*te*r* uidelic*et* regis, valedicens filio, ab huius incolatu seculi feliciter transmigrauit....

19*a* De s*an*c*to* Ælberto[2] cui tercia filia regis Offe
tradenda fuit nuptui.

Erat quoq*ue* quida*m* iuuenis, cui rex Offa regnu*m* Orientalium
Anglor*um*, q*uo*d eu*m* iure sanguinis *con*tingebat, *con*cesserat,
nomi*ne* Ælbertus. De cui*us* virtutibus[3] quida*m* uersificator,
solitus regum laudes *et* gesta describere, eleganter ait;

Ælbertus iuuenis fuerat rex, fortis ad arma,
Pace pius, pulch*er* corpore, me*n*te sagax.

Cumq*ue* Hu*m*bertus Archiep*iscopus* Lichefeldensis, *et* Vnwona
Ep*iscopus* Legrecestre*n*sis, uiri s*an*c*ti et* discreti, et de nobili
stirpe M*e*rcior*um* oriundi, speciales essent regis *con*siliarii, *et*
semp*er* q*ue* honesta era*n*t *et* iusta atq*ue* utilia, regi Offe sug-
gessissent, i*n*uidebat eis regina uxor Offe, q*ue* prius Drida, postea
u*ero* Quendrida, id est regina Drida, q*uia* regi ex insp*er*ato
nupsit, est appellata: sicut *in* precedentibus pleni*us* enarrat*ur*.
Mulier auara et subdola, superbiens, eo q*uo*d ex stirpe Karoli
origine*m* duxerat, et i*n*exorabili odio uiros memoratos p*er*seque-
batur, tende*n*s eis muscipulas muliebres. Porro cu*m* ipsi reges
supra*dic*tos regi Offe in sp*iri*tu consilii salubrit*er* reconciliassent,
et ut eidem regi federe m*a*trimoniali speciali*us* *con*iungerent*ur*,
diligent*er* *et* efficaciter procurassent, ips*a* mulier f*a*cta eor*um*

---

[1] vixsset, B, *inserted in margin; omitted*, A.   [2] Alberto, *etc. passim*, B.
[3] virtutibus, *in margin, later hand*, A; *in* B, *over erasure*.

nitebat*ur* i*n* irritu*m* reuocare, nec poter*at*, quib*us* acriter in-
uidebat. Ip*s*as eni*m* puellas filias suas, ultramarinis, alienigenis, in regis supplantacione*m* et regni Merc*i*oru*m* pernicie*m*,
credidit tr*a*didisse marita*n*das. Cui*us* rei pr*e*scii d*i*c*t*i Epi*s*copi,
muliebre co*n*siliu*m* prudencie repagulis impediebant. Uerum et
adhuc tercia filia regis Offe i*n* thalamo regine remansit mari-
tanda, Ælfleda no*m*ine. Procurantib*us* igitur supr*a*d*i*c*t*is epi*s*-
cop*i*s, inclinatu*m* est[1] cor regis ad co*n*sensum, lic*et* co*n*tr*a*diceret
regina, ut *et*[2] hec regi Ælberto nuptui trad*e*r*etur*: ut *et* sic speciali*us* regi O*ffe* teneretur i*n* fidelitate dilecionis obligatus.
Uoca*tus* igi*tur* rex Ælbert*us*, a rege O*ffa*, ut filia*m* sua*m* despon-

Fol. 19*b* saret, affuit festiu*us* | et gaudens, ob honorem sibi a tanto rege
oblatum. Cui amicabiliter rex occurrens aduentanti, recepit
ip*su*m in osculo *et* p*a*terno amplexu, dicens: "Prospere ueneris
"fili *et* gene*r*, ex h*o*c, iuuenis amantissime, te in filiu*m* adopto
"specialem." S*e*d hec postq*ua*m efferate regine plenius in-
notuer*it*[3], plus accensa est liuore ac furore, dole*n*s eu*m* pietatis
i*n* manu[4] regis *et* suoru*m* fidelium prosperari. Vide*n*sq*ue* sue
nequ*i*cie argumenta minime pr*e*ualere, nec hanc saltem terciam
filiam sua*m*, ad uolu*n*tatem suam alic*u*i transmarino amico suo,
i*n* regni subuersione*m* (q*u*od certissime sperauerat) dare nuptui,
cu*m* no*n* pr*e*ualuisset i*n* d*i*ctos ep*i*scop*o*s h*ui*us rei auctores
emin*us* malignari, i*n* Ælbertum regem uir*us* sue malicie truculent*er* euomuit, hoc mod*o*.

Fraus muliebr*i*s crudelissima.

Rex hui*us* rei ignarus tanta*m* latitasse fraude*m* no*n* credebat,
immo pociu*s* credebat hec ip*s*i omn*i*a placitu*r*a. Cum igit*ur* rex
piissimu*s* ipsam supe*r* premissis[5] secreciu*s* conueniret, co*n*silium
qu*e*rens qu*a*lit*er* *et* q*u*ando forent co*m*plenda, hec respondit:
"Ecce tradidit De*us* hodie inimicu*m* tuum, t*i*bi caute, si sapis,
"trucidandu*m*, qui sub specie superficiali, uenenu*m* prodicio*n*is
"i*n* te *et* regnum tuum exercende, nequ*i*ter, ut fertur, occultauit.
"Et te cupit iam senescentem, cu*m* sit iuuenis *et* elegans, de
"regno supplanta*n*do precipitare; *et* posterum suoru*m*, immo *et*
"multorum, ut iactitat, quos regnis *et* possessionibus uiolent*er*

---

[1] est *in margin.* A.   [2] *et omitted,* B.   [3] innotuerunt, B.
[4] in pietatis manu, B.   [5] premissimis, A.

"*et* iniuste spoliasti, iniurias uindicare. In cui*us* rei fidem,
"michi a meis amicis significatu*m* est, quod regis Karoli multis
"mun*er*ibus *et* nu*n*ciis ocultis int*er*meantib*us*, implorat ad hoc
"patrociniu*m*: se sponde*n*s ei fore tributarium. Illo igitur, dum
"se t*i*bi fortuna p*re*bet fauorabile*m*, extincto latent*er*, regnu*m*
"ei*us* in ius tuu*m et* successor*um* tuor*um* transeat in et*er*num."
  Cui rex mente nimiu*m* p*er*turbatus, *et* de u*er*bis quib*us* credidit in*esse* ueraciter falsitate*m et* fraude*m*, cum indignacione
ipsam i*n*crepando, respondit: "Quasi una de stultis mulierib*us*
"locuta es! Absit a me, absit, tam detestabile f*actum*! Quo
"perpetrato, mi*h*i meisq*ue* successorib*us* foret obprobriu*m* sem-
"piternu*m*, et peccatu*m* i*n* gen*us* meu*m* cum graui uind*i*cta
"diuci*us* propagabile." Et hiis di*c*tis, rex iratus ab ea recessit;
detestans ta*n*tos ac tales occultos laq*ue*os in muliere latitasse.
  Interea mentis p*er*turbacione paulati*m* deposita, *et* hiis
ciuilit*er* dissimulatis, reges co*n*sederunt ad me*n*sam pransuri:
ubi regalib*us* esculentis *et* poculentis refecti, in ti*m*panis, citharis,
et choris, diem totu*m* i*n* i*n*genti gaudio expleu*er*unt. S*ed* regina
malefica, int*er*im a ferali p*ro*posito no*n* recedens, iussit i*n* dolo
thalamu*m* more regio pallis sericis *et* auleis sollemp*niter* adornari,
i*n* quo rex Ælbertus nocturnu*m* caperet sompnu*m*; iuxta stratu*m*
quoq*ue* regium sedile p*re*parari fecit, cultu nobilissimo ex-
tructu*m*, *et* cortinis undiq*ue* redimitu*m*. Sub qu*o* ecia*m* fossam
20 *a* p*re*parari fecit profunda*m*, | ut nephandu*m* propositum perdu-
ceret ad eff*ectu*m.

  De martirio S*ancti* Ælberti, regis innocentissimi.

  Regina uero uultu sereno co*n*ceptum scelus pallians, intrauit
i*n* palatiu*m*, ut tam regem Offanu*m* qua*m* rege*m* Ælbertu*m*
exhilararet. Et int*er* iocandu*m*, co*n*uersa ad Ælbertu*m*, ni*h*il
sinistri[1] suspicantem, ait, "Fili, ueni uisendi causa puellam t*i*bi
"nuptu copulanda*m*, te i*n* thalamo meo sicient*er* expectante*m*,
"ut s*er*monib*us* gratissimis amores subarres profut*ur*os." Sur-
ge*n*s igi*tur* rex Ælbertus, secut*us* est reginam i*n* thalamu*m* i*n*-
grediente*m*: rege Offano remanente, q*u*i nil m*a*li formidabat.
Ingresso igi*tur* rege Æl*berto* cum regina, exclusi su*n*t om*n*es qui
eundem e uestigio seq*ue*bant*ur* sui co*m*militones. Et cu*m*
puellam exp*e*ctasset, ait regina: "Sede fili du*m* ueniat aduocata."

  [1] sinistrum, B.

Et cum in memorato sedili residisset, cum ipsa sella in fosse corruit profunditatem. In qua, subito a lictoribus quos regina non procul absconderat, rex innocens suffocatus expirauit. Nam ilico cum corruisset, proiecerunt super eum regina et sui complices nephandissimi puluinaria cum uestibus et cortinis, ne clamans ab aliquibus audiretur. Et sic elegantissimus iuuenis rex et martir Ælbertus, innocenter et sine noxa extinctus, accepit coronam uite, [quam]¹ ad instar Johannis Baptiste mulieris laqueis irretitus, meruit optinere.

Puella uero regis filia Ælfleda uirguncula uenustissima, cum hec audisset, non tantum matris detestata facinora, sed tocius seculi pompam relinquens, habitum suscepit religionis, ut uirgo martiris uestigia sequeretur. [P]orro² ad augmentum³ muliebris tirannidis⁴, decollatum est corpusculum exanime quia adhuc palpitans uidebatur. Clam igitur delatum est corpus cum capite, usque ad partes remociores ad occultandum sub profundo terre, et dum spiculator cruentus ista ferret, caput obiter amissum est feliciter: nox enim erat, et festinabat lictor, et aperto ore sacci, caput cecidit euolutum, ignorante hoc portitore. Corpus autem ab ipso carnifice sine aliquo teste conscio ignobiliter est humatum. Contigit autem, Deo sic disponente, ut quidam cecus eadem via graderetur, baculo semitam pretemptante. Habens autem caput memoratum pro pedum offendiculo, mirabatur quidnam esset: erat enim pes eius irretitus in cincinnis capitis flauis et prolixis. Et palpans cercius cognouit⁵ esse caput hominis decollati. Et datum est ei in spiritu intelligere, quod alicuius sancti caput esset, ac iuuenis. Et cum maduissent manus eius sanguine, apposuit et sanguinem faciei sue: et loco ubi quandoque oculi eius extiterant, et ilico restitutus est ei uisus; et quod habuerat pro pedum offendiculo, factum est ei felix luminis restitucio. Sed et in eodem loco quo caput sanctum iacuerat, fons erupit lucidissimus. Quod cum celebriter⁶ fuerat diuulgatum, compertum est hoc fuisse caput sancti adolescentis Ælberti, quem regina in thalamo nequiter fecit sugillari ac decollari. Corpus autem ubinam locorum occultatum fuerat, penitus ignoratur. Hoc cum constaret Humberto Archiepiscopo,

¹ quam *in margin,* A; *over erasure,* B.   ² *Space for cap. left vacant,* A.
³ aucmentum. A.   ⁴ facinoris, B.
⁵ congnouit, A.   ⁶ celeriter, B.

facta capside ex auro *et* argento, illud iussit in tesauro recondi *precioso* in Ecclesia Herefordensi.

De *predicti* facinoris ulcione.

Cuius tandem detestabilis sceleris a regina perpetrati, ad *commilitonum beati regis et Martiris* aures cum[1] *peruenisset*, fama *celerius* ante lucem aurore diei sequentis clanculo recesserunt, ne de ipsis simile fieret iudicium metuentes. Unde dolens regina, in thalamo ficta infirmitate decubans, quasi uulpecula latitabat.

Rex *uero* Offa *cum* de commisso facinore certitudinem comperisset, sese lugens, in cenaculo interiori recludens, pe[r][2] tres dies cibum penit*us* non gustauit, animam suam lacrimis, lamentacionibus, et ieiunio uehementer affligens. Et execrans mulieris impietatem, eam iussit omnibus uite sue diebus inclusam in loco remotam secreciori peccata sua deplorare, si forte sibi celitus collata gracia, penitendo tanti commissi facinoris maculam posset abolere. Rex autem ipsam postea ut sociam lateris in lecto suo dormire quasi suspectam non permisit[3].

De morte illius facinorose regine.

In loco igitur sibi deputato, commorante regina annis aliquot, insidiis latronum preuenta, auro *et* argento quo multum habundabat spoliata[4], in puteo suo proprio precipitata, spiritum exalauit; iusto dei iudicio sic condempnata, ut sicut regem Ælbertum innocentem in foueam fecit precipitari, *et* precipitatum suffocari, sic in putei profunditate submersa, uitam miseram terminaret.

O. Widsith, ll. 18, 24–49

18. Ætla wēold Hūnum, Eormanrīc ʒotum,
       *   *   *   *   *   *   *
     þēodrīc wēold Froncum, þyle Rondinʒum,
25. Breoca Brondinʒum, Billinʒ Wernum.
     Ōswine wēold Ēowum *ond* Ȳtum ʒefwulf,

---

[1] cum *in* A *is inserted after* peruenisset, *instead of before: and this was probably the original reading in* B, *although subsequently corrected.*
[2] per, B.   [3] *corrected to* nullatenus dormire quasi suspectam permisit, B.
[4] Justa Vindicta, A, *in margin.*

16—2

Fin Folcwaldinȝ Frēsna cynne.
Siȝehere lenȝest Sǣ-Denum wēold,
Hnæf Hōcinȝum, Helm Wulfinȝu*m*,
30. Wald Wōinȝum, Wōd þyrinȝu*m*,
Sǣferð Sycȝum, Swēom Onȝendþēow,
Sceafthere Ymbrum, Scēafa Lonȝ-Beardu*m*,
Hūn Hætwerum, *ond* Holen Wrosnum.
Hrinȝweald wæs hāten Herefarena cyning.
35. Offa wēold Ongle, Alewīh Denu*m*:
sē wæs þāra manna mōdȝast ealra;
nōhwæþre hē ofer Offan eorlscype fremede,
ac Offa ȝeslōȝ ǣrest monna
cniht wesende cynerīca mǣst;
40. nǣniȝ efen-eald him eorlscipe māran
on ōrette āne sweorde:
merce ȝemǣrde wið Myrȝinȝu*m*
bī Fīfeldore; hēoldon forð siþþan
Enȝle *ond* Swǣfe, swā hit Offa ȝeslōȝ.
45. Hrōþwulf *ond* Hrōðȝār hēoldon lenȝest
sibbe ætsomne suhtorfædran,
siþþan hȳ forwrǣcon wīcinȝa cynn
ond Inȝeldes ord forbīȝdan,
forhēowan æt Heorote Heaðo-Beardna þrym.

PART III

THE FIGHT AT FINNSBURG

SECTION I. THE *FINNSBURG FRAGMENT*

THE *Finnsburg Fragment* was discovered two centuries ago in the library of Lambeth Palace by George Hickes. It was written on a single leaf, which was transcribed and published by Hickes: but the leaf is not now to be found. This is to be regretted for reasons other than sentimental, since Hickes' transcript is far from accurate[1].

The *Fragment* begins and breaks off in the middle of a line: but possibly not much has been lost at the beginning. For the

---

[1] Mr Mackie, in an excellent article on the *Fragment* (*J.E.G.Ph.* XVI, 251) objects that my criticism of Hickes' accuracy "is not altogether judicial." Mackie urges that, since the MS is no longer extant, we cannot tell how far the errors are due to Hickes, and how far they already existed in the MS from which Hickes copied.

But we must not forget that there are other transcripts by Hickes, of MSS which *are* still extant, and from these we can estimate his accuracy. It is no disrespect to the memory of Hickes, a scholar to whom we are all indebted, to recognize frankly that his transcripts are not sufficiently accurate to make them at all a satisfactory substitute for the original MS. Hickes' transcript of the *Cottonian Gnomic Verses* (*Thesaurus*, I, 207) shows an average of one error in every four lines: about half these errors are mere matters of spelling, the others are serious. Hickes' transcript of the *Calendar* (*Thesaurus*, I, 203) shows an average of one error in every six lines. When, therefore, we find in the *Finnsburg Fragment* inaccuracies of exactly the type which Hickes often commits, it would be "hardly judicial" to attribute these to the MS which he copied, and to attribute to Hickes in this particular instance an accuracy to which he has really no claim.

Mr Mackie doubts the legitimacy of emending *Garulf* to *Garulf*[e]: but we must remember that Hickes (or his printer) was systematically careless as to the final *e*: cf. *Calendar*, 15, 23, 41, 141, 144, 171, 210; *Gnomic Verses*, 45. Other forms in the *Finnsburg Fragment* which can be easily paralleled by Hickes' miswritings in the *Calendar* and *Gnomic Verses* are

Confusion of *u* and *a* (*Finn.* 3, 27, perhaps 44) cf. *Gn.* 66.

,, ,, *c* ,, *e* (*Finn.* 12) cf. *Cal.* 136, *Gn.* 44.

,, ,, *e* ,, *æ* (*Finn.* 41) cf. *Cal.* 44, 73, *Gn.* 44.

,, ,, *e* ,, *a* (*Finn.* 22) cf. *Cal.* 74.

,, ,, *eo* ,, *ea* (*Finn.* 28) cf. *Cal.* 121.

,, ,, letters involving long down stroke, e.g., *f*, *s*, *r*, *þ*, *w*, *p* (*Finn.* 2, 36) cf. *Cal.* 97, 142, 180, 181, *Gn.* 9.

Addition of *n* (*Finn.* 22) cf. *Cal.* 161.

first lines of the fragment, as preserved, reveal a well-loved opening motive—the call to arms within the hall, as the watcher sees the foes approach. It was with such a call that the *Bjarkamál*, the poem on the death of Rolf Kraki, began: "a good call to work" as a fighting king-saint thought it[1]. It is with a similar summons to business that the *Finnsburg Fragment* begins. The watchman has warned the king within the hall that he sees lights approaching—so much we can gather from the two and a half words which are preserved from the watchman's speech, and from the reply made by the "war-young" king: "This is not the dawn which is rising, but dire deeds of woe; to arms, my men." And the defending warriors take their posts: at the one door Sigeferth and Eaha: at the other Ordlaf and Guthlaf, and Hengest himself[2].

Then the poet turns to the foes, as they approach for the attack. The text as reported by Hickes is difficult: but it seems that Garulf[3] is the name of the warrior about to lead the assault on the hall. Another warrior, Guthere, whether a friend, kinsman, or retainer[4] we do not know, is dissuading him, urging him not to risk so precious a life in the first brunt. But Garulf pays no heed; he challenges the champion on guard: "Who is it who holds the door?"

"Sigeferth is my name," comes the reply, "Prince I am of the Secgan: a wandering champion known far and wide: many a woe, many a hard fight have I endured: from me canst thou have what thou seekest."

So the clash of arms begins: and the first to fall is Garulf, son of Guthlaf: and many a good man round him. "The swords flashed as if all Finnsburg were afire."

---

[1] *Heimskringla*, chap. 220.

[2] It has been suggested that the phrase "Hengest himself" indicates that Hengest is the "war-young king." But surely the expression merely marks Hengest out as a person of special interest. If we *must* assume that he is one of the people who have been speaking, then it would be just as natural to identify him with the watcher who has warned the king, as with the king himself. The difficulties which prevent us from identifying Hengest with the king are explained below.

[3] Garulf must be an assailant, since he falls at the beginning of the struggle, whilst we are told that for five days none of the defenders fell.

[4] Very possibly Guthere is uncle of Garulf. For Garulf is said to be son of Guthlaf (l. 35) and a *Guth*ere would be likely to be a brother of a *Guth*laf. Further, as Klaeber points out (*Engl. Stud.* XXXIX, 307) it is the part of the uncle to protect and advise the nephew.

Never, we are told, was there a better defence than that of
the sixty champions within the hall. "Never did retainers repay
the sweet mead better than his bachelors did unto Hnæf. For five
days they fought, so that none of the men at arms fell: but they
held the doors." After a few more lines the piece breaks off.

There are many textual difficulties here. But these, for the
most part, do not affect the actual narrative, which is a story
of clear and straightforward fighting. It is when we try to fit
this narrative into relationship with the *Episode* in *Beowulf* that
our troubles begin. Within the *Fragment* itself one difficulty
only need at present be mentioned. Guthlaf is one of the
champions defending the hall. Yet the leader of the assault,
Garulf, is spoken of as Guthlaf's son. Of course it is possible
that we have here a tragic incident parallel to the story of
Hildebrand and Hadubrand: father and son may have been
separated through earlier misadventures, and now find themselves engaged on opposite sides. This would harmonize with
the atmosphere of the *Finnsburg* story, which is one of slaughter
breaking out among men near of kin, so that afterwards an uncle
and a nephew are burnt on the same pyre. And it has been
noted [1] that Garulf rushes to the attack only after he has asked
"Who holds the door?" and has learnt that it is Sigeferth:
Guthlaf had gone to the opposite door. Can Garulf's question
mean that he knows his father Guthlaf to be inside the hall,
and wishes to avoid conflict with him? Possibly; but I do not
think we can argue much from this double appearance of the
name Guthlaf. It is possible that the occurrence of Guthlaf as
Garulf's father is simply a scribal error. For, puzzling as the
tradition of *Finnsburg* everywhere is, it is peculiarly puzzling in
its proper names, which are mostly given in forms that seem
to have undergone some alteration. And even if *Gūðlāfes sunu*
be correctly written, it is possible that the Guthlaf who is father
of Garulf is not to be identified with the Guthlaf whom Garulf
is besieging within the hall [2].

[1] Koegel, *Geschichte d. deut. Litt.* I, i, 165.

[2] Klaeber (*Engl. Stud.* xxxix, 308) reminds us that, as there are two warriors
named Godric in the *Battle of Maldon* (l. 325), so there may be two warriors
named Guthlaf here. But to this it might possibly be replied that "Godric"
was, in England, an exceedingly common name, "Guthlaf" an exceedingly
rare one.

One or other of these rather unsatisfactory solutions must unfortunately be accepted. For no theory is possible which will save us from admitting that, according to the received text, Guthlaf is fighting on the one side, and a "son of Guthlaf" on the other.

Section II. The Episode in *Beowulf*

Further details of the story we get in the *Episode* of *Finnsburg*, as recorded in *Beowulf* (ll. 1068–1159).

Beowulf is being entertained in the court of the king of the Danes, and the king's harper tells the tale of Hengest and Finn. Only the main events are enumerated. There are none of the dramatic speeches which we find in the *Fragment*. It is evident that the tale has been reduced in scope, in order that it may be fitted into its place as an episode in the longer epic.

The tone, too, is quite different. Whereas the *Fragment* is inspired by the lust and joy of battle, the theme of the *Episode*, as told in *Beowulf*, is rather the pity of it all; the legacy of mourning and vengeance which is left to the survivors:

> For never can true reconcilement grow
> Where wounds of deadly hate have struck so deep.

It is on this note that the *Episode* in *Beowulf* begins: with the tragic figure of Hildeburh. Hildeburh is closely related to both contending parties. She is sister to Hnæf, prince of the "Half-Danes," and she is wedded to Finn, king of the Frisians. Whatever may be obscure in the story, it is clear that a fight has taken place between the men of Hnæf and those of Finn, and that Hnæf has been slain: probably by Finn directly, though perhaps by his followers[1]. A son of Finn has also fallen.

With regard to the peoples concerned there are difficulties. Finn's Frisians are presumably the main Frisian race, dwelling in and around the district still known as Friesland; for in the Catalogue of Kings in *Widsith* it is said that "Finn Folcwalding

---

[1] Finn is called the *bana*, "slayer" of Hnæf. But this does not necessarily mean that he slew him with his own hand; it would be enough if he were in command of the assailants at the time when Hnæf was slain. Cf. *Beowulf*, l. 1968.

ruled the kin of the Frisians[1]." Hnæf and his people are called
Half-Danes, Danes and Scyldings; Hnæf is therefore presumably
related to the Danish royal house. But, in no account which
has come down to us of that house, is Hnæf or his father Hoc
ever mentioned as king or prince of Denmark, and their connection with the family of Hrothgar, the great house of Scyldings
who ruled Denmark from the capital of Leire, remains obscure.
In *Widsith*, the people ruled over by Hnæf are called "children
of Hoc" (*Hōcingum*), and are mentioned immediately after the
"Sea-Danes[2]."

Then there is a mysterious people called the *Eotens*, upon
whom is placed the blame of the struggle: "Verily Hildeburh
had little reason to praise the good faith of the Eotens." This
is the typical understatement of Old English rhetoric: it can
only point to deliberate treachery on the part of the Eotens.
Our interpretation of the poem will therefore hinge largely upon
our interpretation of this name. There have been two views as
to the Eotens. The one view holds them to be Hnæf's Danes,
and consequently places on Hnæf the responsibility for the aggression. This theory is, I think, quite wrong, and has been
the cause of much confusion: but it has been held by scholars
of great weight[3]. The other view regards the Eotens as subjects

---

[1] The idea that Finn's Frisians are the "North Frisians" of Schleswig has
been supported by Grein (*Eberts Jahrbuch*, IV, 270) and, following him, by many
scholars, including recently Sedgefield (*Beowulf*, p 258). The difficulties of
this view are very many: one only need be emphasized. We first hear of these
North Frisians of Schleswig in the 12th century, and Saxo Grammaticus tells
us expressly that they were a colony from the greater Frisia (Book XIV, ed.
Holder, p. 465). At what date this colony was founded we do not know. The
latter part of the 9th century has been suggested by Langhans: so has the end
of the 11th century by Lauridsen. However this may be, all the evidence
precludes our supposing this North Friesland, or, as Saxo calls it, Fresia Minor,
to have existed at the date to which we must attribute the origin of the Finn
story. On this point the following should be consulted: Langhans (V.), *Ueber
den Ursprung der Nordfriesen*, Wien, 1879 (most valuable on account of its
citation of documents: the latter part of the book, which consists of an attempt
to rewrite the Finn story by dismissing as corrupt or spurious many of the
data, must not blind us to the value of the earlier portions): Lauridsen, *Om
Nordfrisernes Indvandring i Sønderjylland*, *Historisk Tidsskrift*, 6 R., 4 B. II,
318–67, Kjøbenhavn, 1893: Siebs, *Zur Geschichte der Englisch-Friesischen
Sprache*, 1889, 23–6: Chadwick, *Origin*, 94: Much in *Hoops Reallexikon*, s.v.
Friesen; and Bremer in *Pauls Grdr.* (2), III, 848, where references will be found
to earlier essays on the subject.

[2] The theory that Hnæf is a captain of Healfdene is based upon a rendering
of l. 1064 which is in all probability wrong.

[3] The view that the *Eotenas* are the men of Hnæf and Hengest has been
held by Thorpe (*Beowulf*, pp. 76–7), Ettmüller (*Beowulf*, 1840, p. 108), Bouterwek

of Finn and foes of Hnæf.   This view has been more generally
held, and it is, as I shall try to show, only along these lines that
a satisfactory solution can be found.

The poet continues of the woes of Hildeburh.   "Guiltless,
she lost at the war those whom she loved, child and brother.
They fell as was fated, wounded by the spear, and a sad lady
was she.   Not for naught did the daughter of Hoc [i.e. Hilde-
burh] bewail her fate when morning came, when under the sky
she could behold the murderous bale of her kinsfolk...."
Then the poet turns to the figure of Finn, king of the
Frisians.   His cause for grief is as deep as that of Hildeburh.
For he has lost that body of retainers which to a Germanic
chief, even as to King Arthur, was dearer than a wife[1].   "War
swept away all the retainers of Finn, except some few."
What follows is obscure, but as to the general drift there is
no doubt.   After the death of their king Hnæf, the besieged
Danes are led by Hengest.   Hengest must be Hnæf's retainer,
for he is expressly so called (*þēodnes þegn*) "the king's thegn."
So able is the defence of Hengest, and so heavy the loss among
Finn's men, that Finn has to come to terms.   Peace is made
between Finn and Hengest, and the terms are given fully in
the *Episode*.   Unfortunately, owing to the confusion of pro-
nouns, we soon lose our way amidst the clauses of this treaty,
and it becomes exceedingly difficult to say who are the people
who are alluded to as "they."   This is peculiarly unlucky because here again the critical word *Eotena* occurs, but amid such
a tangle of "thems" and "theys" that it is not easy to tell
from this passage to which side the Eotens belong[2].
But one thing in the treaty is indisputable.   In the midst
of these complicated clauses, it is said of the Danes, the retainers

(*Germania*, I, 389), Holtzmann (*Germania*, VIII, 492), Möller (*Volksepos*, 94–5),
Chadwick (*Origin*, 53), Clarke (*Sidelights*, 184).
[1] "And therefore, said the King...much more I am sorrier for my good
knights' loss, than for the loss of my fair queen.   For queens I might have
enow: but such a fellowship of good knights shall never be together in no
company."   Malory, *Morte Darthur*, Bk. xx, chap. ix.
[2] The argument of Bugge (*P.B.B.* xii, 37) that the Eotens here (l. 1088)
must be the Frisians, is inconclusive: but so is Miss Clarke's argument that
they must be Danes (*Sidelights*, 181), as is shown by Lawrence (*Pub. Mod.
Lang. Assoc. Amer.* xxx, 395).

of Hnæf, that they are not to be taunted with a certain fact: or perhaps it may be that they are not, when speaking amongst themselves, to remind each other of a certain fact. However that may be, what *is* clear is the *fact*, the mention of which is barred. Nothing is to be said of it, even though *"they were following the slayer (bana) of their lord, being without a prince, since they were compelled so to do."* Here, at least, are two lines about the interpretation of which we can be certain: and I shall therefore return to them. We must be careful, however, to remember that the word *bana*, "slayer," conveys no idea of fault or criminality. It is a quite neutral word, although it has frequently been mistranslated "murderer," and has thus helped to encourage the belief that Finn slew Hnæf by treachery. Of course it conveys no such implication: *bana* can be applied to one who slays another in self-defence: it implies neither the one thing nor the other.

Then the poet turns to the funeral of the dead champions, who are burned on one pyre by the now reconciled foes. The bodies of Hnæf and of the son (or sons)[1] of Hildeburh are placed together, uncle and nephew side by side, whilst Hildeburh stands by lamenting.

Then, we are told, the warriors, deprived of their friends, departed to Friesland, to their homes and to their high-city.

Hengest still continued to dwell for the whole of that winter with Finn, and could not return home because of the winter storms. But when spring came and the bosom of the earth became fair, there came also the question of Hengest's departure: but he thought more of vengeance than of his sea-journey: "If he might bring about that hostile meeting which he kept in his mind concerning the child (or children) of the Eotens." Here again the word *Eotena* is used ambiguously, but, I think, this time not without some indication of its meaning. It has indeed been urged that the child or children of the Eotens are Hnæf, and any other Danes who may have fallen with him, and that when it is said that Hengest keeps them in mind, it is meant that he is remembering his fallen comrades with a view to taking

---

[1] I say "son" in what follows, without prejudice to the possibility of more than one son having fallen. It in no wise affects the argument.

vengeance for them.　But this would be a queer way of speaking, as Hengest and his living comrades would on this theory be also themselves children of the Eotens[1].　We should therefore need the term to be further defined: "children of the Eotens *who fell at Finnsburg*."　It seems far more likely, from the way in which the expression is used here, that the children of the Eotens are the people *upon* whom Hengest intends to take vengeance.

Then, we are further told, Hunlafing places in the bosom of Hengest a sword of which the edges were well known amongst the Eotens.　Here again there has been ambiguity, dispute and doubt.　Hunlafing has been even bisected into a chief "Hun," and a sword "Lafing" which "Hun" is supposed to have placed in the bosom of Hengest (or of someone else).　Upon this act of "Hun" many an interpretation has been placed, and many a theory built.　Fortunately it has become possible, by a series of rather extraordinary discoveries, such as we had little reason to hope for at this time of day, to put Hunlafing together again. We now know (and this I think should be regarded as outside the region of controversy) that the warrior who put the sword into Hengest's bosom *was* Hunlafing.　And about Hunlafing we gather, though very little, yet enough to help us.　He is apparently a Dane, the son of Hunlaf, and Hunlaf is the brother of the two champions Guthlaf and Ordlaf[2].　Now Guthlaf and Ordlaf, as we know from the *Fragment*, were in the hall together

---

[1] For example, it might well be said of Achilles, whilst thirsting for vengeance upon the Trojans for the death of Patroclus, that "he could not get the children of the Trojans out of his mind."　But surely it would be unintelligible to say that "he could not get the child of the Achaeans out of his mind," meaning Patroclus, for "child of the Achaeans" is not sufficiently distinctive to denote Patroclus.　Cf. Boer in *Z.f.d.A.* xlvii, 134.

[2] In the *Skjoldunga Saga* [extant in a Latin abstract by Arngrim Jonsson, ed. Olrik, 1894], cap. iv, mention is made of a king of Denmark named Leifus who had six sons, three of whom are named Hunleifus, Oddleifus and Gunnleifus—corresponding exactly to O.E. *Hūnlāf, Ordlāf* and *Gūðlāf*. That Hunlaf was well known in English story is proved by a remarkable passage unearthed by Dr Imelmann from *MS Cotton Vesp. D. IV* (fol. 139 *b*) where Hunlaf is mentioned together with a number of other heroes of Old English story—Wudga, Hama, Hrothulf, Hengest, Horsa (*Hoc testantur gesta rudolphi et hunlapi, Unwini et Widie, horsi et hengisti, Waltef et hame*).　See Chadwick, *Origin*, 52 : R. Huchon, *Revue Germanique*, iii, 626 : Imelmann, in *D.L.Z.* xxx, 999 : April, 1909.　This disposes of the translation "Hun thrust or placed in his bosom Lafing, best of swords," which was adopted by Bugge (*P.B.B.* xii, 33), Holder, ten Brink and Gering.　Hun is mentioned in *Widsith* (l. 33) and in the Icelandic *Thulor*. That Guthlaf, Ordlaf and Hunlaf must be connected together had been noted by Boer (*Z.f.d.A.* xlvii, 139) before this discovery of Chadwick's confirmed him.

with Hengest: it was "Guthlaf, Ordlaf and Hengest himself"
who undertook the defence of one of the doors against the
assailants. Guthlaf and Ordlaf were apparently sons of the
king of Denmark. As Scyldings they would be Hnæf's kinsmen,
and accompanied him to his meeting with Finn. Hunlafing,
then, is a nephew of two champions who were attacked in the
hall, and it is possible, though we cannot prove this, that his
father Hunlaf was himself also in the hall, and was slain in the
struggle[1]. At any rate, when Hunlaf's son places a sword in
the bosom of Hengest, this can only mean one thing. It means
mischief. The placing of the sword, by a prince, in the bosom
of another, is a symbol of war-service. It means that Hengest
has accepted obligations to a Danish lord, a Scylding, a kinsman
of the dead Hnæf, and consequently that he means to break
the troth which he has sworn to Finn.

Further, we are told concerning the sword, that its edges
were well known amongst the Eotens. At first sight this might
seem, and to many has seemed, an ambiguous phrase, for a
sword may be well known amongst either friends or foes. The
old poets loved nothing better than to dwell upon the adorn-
ments of a sword, to say how a man, by reason of a fine sword
which had been given to him, was honoured amongst his associates at table[2]. But if this had been the poet's meaning here,
he would surely have dwelt, not upon the edges of the sword,
but upon its gold-adorned hilt, or its jewelled pommel. When
he says the *edges* of the sword were well known amongst the
Eotens, this seems to convey a hostile meaning. We know that
the ill-faith of the Eotens was the cause of the trouble. The
phrase about the sword seems therefore to mean that Hengest
used this sword in order to take vengeance on the Eotens,
presumably for their treachery.

The *Eotenas*, therefore, far from being the men of Hnæf and
Hengest, must have been their foes.

Then the poet goes on to tell how "Dire sword-bale came
upon the valiant Finn likewise." The Danes fell upon Finn at

[1] The fragment which tells of the fighting in the hall is so imperfect that
there is nothing impossible in the assumption, though it is too hazardous to
make it.
[2] Cf. *Beowulf*, ll. 1900 *etc.*

his own home, reddened the floor of his hall with the life-blood of his men, slew him, plundered his town, and led his wife back to her own people.

Here the *Episode* ends.

SECTION III. MÖLLER'S THEORY

Now our first task is to find what is the relation between the events told in the *Fragment* and the events told in the *Episode* in *Beowulf*. It can, I think, be shown that the events of the *Fragment* precede the events of the *Episode* in *Beowulf*; that is to say that the fight in the hall, of which we are told in the *Fragment*, is the same fight which has taken place before the *Episode* in *Beowulf* begins, the fight which has resulted in the slaughter over which Hildeburh laments, and which necessitates the great funeral described in the first part of the *Episode* (ll. 1108–24).

How necessary it is to place the *Fragment* here, before the beginning of the *Episode*, will be best seen, I think, if we examine the theory which has tried to place it elsewhere.

This is the theory, worked out elaborately and ingeniously by Möller[1], a theory which has had considerable vogue, and many of the assumptions of which have been widely accepted. According to Möller and his followers, the story ran something like this:

> "Finn, king of the Frisians, had carried off Hildeburh, daughter of Hoc (1076), probably with her consent. Her father Hoc seems to have pursued the fugitives, and to have been slain in the fight which ensued on his overtaking them. After the lapse of some twenty years, the brothers Hnæf and Hengest, Hoc's sons, were old enough to undertake the duty of avenging their father's death. They make an inroad into Finn's country."

Up to this, all is Möller's hypothesis, unsupported by any evidence, either in the *Fragment* or the *Episode*. It is based, so far as it has any real foundation, upon a mythical interpretation of Finn, and upon parallels with the Hild-story, the Gudrun-story, and a North Frisian folk-tale[2]. Some of the

---

[1] *Das Altenglische Volksepos*, 46–99.
[2] C. P. Hansen, *Uald' Söld'ring tialen*, Møgeltønder, 1858. See Möller, *Volksepos*, 75 etc.

parallels are striking, but they are not sufficient to justify Möller's reconstruction. The authenticity of large portions of the folk-tale is open to doubt[1]: and these portions are vital to any parallel with the story of *Finnsburg*; whilst we have no right to read into the Finn story details from the Hild or Gudrun stories, unless we can show that they are really versions of the same tale: and this cannot be shown. Möller's suppositions as to the events before the *Episode* in *Beowulf* opens, must therefore be dismissed. Möller's reconstruction then gets into relation with the real story, as narrated in *Beowulf*:

> "A battle takes place in which many warriors, among them Hnæf and a son of Finn (1074, 1079, 1115), are killed. Peace is therefore solemnly concluded, and the slain warriors are burnt (1068–1124).
>
> As the year is too far advanced for Hengest to return home (ll. 1130 ff.), he and those of his men who survive remain for the winter in the Frisian country with Finn. But Hengest's thoughts dwell constantly on the death of his brother Hnæf, and he would gladly welcome any excuse to break the peace which has been sworn by both parties. His ill-concealed desire for revenge is noticed by the Frisians, who anticipate it by themselves taking the initiative and attacking Hengest and his men whilst they are sleeping in the hall. *This is the night attack described in the Fragment.* It would seem that after a brave and desperate resistance Hengest himself falls in this fight[2], but two of his retainers, Guthlaf and Oslaf[2], succeed in cutting their way through their enemies and in escaping to their own land. They return with fresh troops, attack and slay Finn, and carry his queen Hildeburh off with them (1125–1159)[3]."

Now the difficulties of this theory will, I think, be found to be insuperable. Let us look at some of them.

Möller's view rests upon his interpretation of the Eotens as the men of Hnæf[4]. Since the Eotens are the aggressors, he *has* consequently to invent the opening, which makes Hnæf and Hengest the invaders of Finn's country: and he *has* therefore to relegate the *Fragment* (in which Hnæf's men are clearly not the attacking party but the attacked) to a later stage in the story. But we have already seen that this interpretation of the Eotens as the men of Hnæf is not the natural one.

Further, the assumption that Hnæf and Hengest are brothers, though still frequently met with[5], is surely not justifiable.

---

[1] See Müllenhoff in *A.f.d.A.* vi, 86.
[2] So Möller, *Volksepos*, 152.
[3] See *Beowulf*. ed. Wyatt, 1894, p. 145.   [4] *Volksepos*, 71 *etc.*
[5] e.g., Sedgefield, *Beowulf*, 2nd ed., p. 258. So 1st ed., p. 13 (*Hoc* being an obvious misprint).

There is nothing which demands any such relationship, and there is much which definitely excludes it. *After Hnæf's death,* Hengest is described as the thegn of Hnæf: an expression without parallel or explanation, if he was really his brother and successor. Again, we are expressly told in the *Episode* that the Danish retainers make terms with Finn, *the slayer of their lord, being without a prince.* How could this be said, if Hengest was now their lord and prince? These lines are, as we have seen, one of the few clear and indisputable things in the poem. An interpretation which contradicts them flatly, by making Hengest the lord of the Danish retainers, seems self-condemned.

Again, in *Beowulf,* the poet dwells upon the blameless sorrows of Hildeburh. We gather that she wakes up in the morning to find that the kinsfolk whom she loves have, during the night, come to blows. "Innocent, she lost son and brother[1] —a sad lady she." Are such expressions natural, if Hildeburh had eloped with Finn, and her father had in consequence been slain by him some twenty years before? If she has taken that calmly, and continued to live happily with Finn, would her equanimity be so seriously disturbed by the slaughter of a brother in addition?

But these difficulties are nothing compared to the further difficulties which Möller's adherents have to face when they proceed to find a place for the night attack as told in the *Fragment,* in the middle of the *Episode* in *Beowulf,* i.e. between lines 1145 and 1146. In the first place we have no right to postulate that such important events could have been passed over in silence in the summary of the story as given in *Beowulf.* For Möller has to assume that after the reconciliation between Hengest and Finn, Finn broke his pledges, attacked Hengest by night, slew most of the men who were with him, including perhaps Hengest himself; and that the *Beowulf*-poet nevertheless omitted all reference to these events, though they occur in the midst of the story, and are essential to an understanding of it.

But even apart from this initial difficulty, we find that by no process of explaining *can* we make the night attack narrated

---

[1] On the poet's use of plural for singular here, see Osthoff, *I.F.* **xx**, 202–7.

in the *Fragment* fit in at the point where Möller places it. In
the night attack the men are called to arms by a "war-young
king." This "war-young king" cannot be, as Möller supposes,
Hengest, for the simple reason that Hengest, as I have tried to
show above, far from being the brother of Hnæf, and his successor as king, is his servant and thegn. The king can only be
Hnæf. But Hnæf has already been slain before the *Episode*
begins: and this makes it impossible to place the *Fragment* (in
which Hnæf appears) in the middle of the *Episode*. Further,
it is said in the *Fragment* that never did retainers repay a lord
better than did his men repay Hnæf. Now these words would
only be possible if the retainers were fighting for their lord;
that is, either defending him alive or avenging him dead. But
Möller's theory assumes that we are dealing with a period when
the retainers have definitely left the service of their lord Hnæf,
after his death, and have entered the service of his slayer, Finn.
They have thus dissolved all bonds with their former lord: they
have taken Finn's money and become *his* men. If Finn then
turns upon his new retainers and treacherously tries to slay
them, it might be said that the retainers defended their own
lives stoutly: but it would be far-fetched to say that in doing
so they repaid their lord Hnæf. Their lord, according to
Möller's view, is no longer Hnæf, but Finn, who is seeking their
lives.

Against such difficulties as these it is impossible to make
headway, and we must therefore turn to some more possible
view of the situation[1].

Section IV. Bugge's Theory

Let us therefore examine the second theory, which is more
particularly associated with the name of Bugge, though it was
the current theory before his time, and has been generally accepted since.

According to this view, the *Eotenas* are the men of Finn,
and since upon them is placed the blame for the trouble, it

---

[1] I have thought it necessary to give fully the reasons why Möller's view
cannot be accepted, because in whole or in part it is still widely followed in
England. Chadwick (*Origin*, 53) still interprets "Eotens" as "Danes"; and
Sedgefield (*Beowulf* (2), p. 258) gives Möller's view the place of honour.

must be Finn that makes a treacherous attack upon his wife's
brother Hnæf, who is his guest in Finnsburg[1]. This is the fight of
which the *Fragment* gives us the beginning. Hnæf is slain,and then
follow the events as narrated in the *Episode*: the treaty which
Finn makes with Hengest, the leader of the survivors: and the
ultimate vengeance taken upon Finn by these survivors.

Here I think we are getting nearer to facts, nearer to a view
which can command general acceptance: at any rate, in so far
as the fight narrated in the *Fragment* is placed before the beginning of the *Episode* in *Beowulf*. Positive evidence that this
is the right place for the *Fragment* is scanty, yet not altogether
lacking. After all, the fight in the *Fragment* is a night attack,
and the fight which precedes the *Episode* in *Beowulf*, as I have
tried to show, is a night attack[2]. But our reason for putting
the *Fragment* before the commencement of the *Episode* is mainly
negative: it lies in the insuperable difficulties which meet us
when we try to place it anywhere else.

But, it will be objected, there are difficulties also in placing
the *Fragment* before the *Episode*. Perhaps: but I do not think
these difficulties will be found to survive examination.

The first objection to supposing that the *Fragment* narrates
the same fight as precedes the *Episode* is, that the fight in the
Fragment takes place at Finnsburg[3], whilst the fight which
precedes the *Episode* apparently takes place away from Finn's
capital: for after the fighting is over, the dead burned, and the
treaty made, the warriors depart "to see Friesland, their homes,
and their high-town (*hēa-burh*)[4]."

---

[1] The treachery of Finn is emphasized, for example, by Bugge (*P.B.B.*
xii, 36), Koegel (*Geschichte d. deut. Litt.* 164), ten Brink (*Pauls Grdr.* (1), ii,
545), Trautmann (*Finn und Hildebrand*, 59), Lawrence (*Pub. Mod. Lang. Assoc.
Amer.* xxx. 397, 430), Ayres (*J.E.G.Ph.* xvi, 290).

[2]   syþðan morgen cōm
        ðā hēo under swegle gesēon meahte, *etc.*

[3] l. 36. The swords flash *swylce eal Finnsburuh fȳrenu wǣre*, "as if all
Finnsburg were afire." I think we may safely argue from this that the swords
are flashing near Finnsburg. It would be just conceivable that the poet's
mind travels back from the scene of the battle to Finn's distant home: "the
swords made as great a flash as would have been made had Finn's distant
capital been aflame": but this is a weak and forced interpretation, which we
have no right to assume, though it may be conceivable.

[4] *Beowulf*, ll. 1125–7. I doubt whether it is possible to explain the difficulty away by supposing that "the warriors departing to see Friesland, their
homes and their head-town" simply means that Finn's men, "summoned by
Finn in preparation for the encounter with the Danes, return to their respective

But I do not see that this involves us in any difficulty.   It
is surely quite reasonable that Finnsburg—Finn's castle—where
the first fight takes place, is not, and was never meant to be,
the same as Finn's capital, his *hēaburh*, his "own home." After
all, when a king's name is given to a town, the presumption is
rather that the town is *not* his capital, but some new settlement
built in a newly acquired territory. *Ēadwinesburh* was not the
capital of King Eadwine: it was the stronghold which he held
against the Picts on the outskirts of his realm.   Aosta was not
the capital of Augustus, nor Fort William of William III, nor
Harounabad of Haroun al Raschid.   So here: we know that the
chief town of the Frisians was not Finnsburg, but Dorestad:
"Dorostates of the Frisians[1]."   The fight may have taken place
at some outlying castle built by Finn, and named after him
Finnsburg: then he returned, we are told, to his *hēaburh*: and
it is here, *æt his sylfes hām*, "in his own home" (the poet himself
seems to emphasize a distinction) that destruction in the end
comes upon him.   There is surely no difficulty here.

A second discrepancy has often been indicated.   In the
Fragment the fight lasts five days before any one of the defenders falls: in the *Episode* (it is argued) Hildeburh in the
morning finds her brother slain[2].   Even were this so, I do not
know that it need trouble us much.   In a detail like this, which

homes in the country," and that "*hēaburh* is a high sounding epic term that
should not be pressed."   This is the explanation offered by Klaeber (*J.E.G.Ph.*
vi, 193) and endorsed by Lawrence (*Pub. Mod. Lang. Assoc. Amer.* xxx, 401).
But it seems to me taking a liberty with the text to interpret *hēaburh* (singular)
as the "respective homes in the country" to which Finn's warriors resort on
demobilisation.   And the statement of ll. 1125-7, that the warriors departed
from the place of combat to see Friesland, seems to necessitate that such place
of combat was not in Friesland.   Klaeber objects to this (surely obvious)
inference: "If we are to infer [from ll. 1125–7] that Finnsburg lies outside
Friesland proper, we might as well conclude that *Dyflen* (Dublin) is not situated
in Ireland according to the *Battle of Brunanburh* (*gewitan him þā Norðmenn...
Dyflen sēcan and eft Īraland*)."   But how could anyone infer this from the
Brunanburh lines?   What we *are* justified in inferring, is, surely, that the *site
of the battle of Brunanburh* (from which the Northmen departed to visit Ireland
and Dublin) was not identical with Dublin, and did not lie in Ireland.   And
by exact parity of reason, we are justified in arguing that Finnsburg, the site
of the first battle in which Hnæf fell (from which site the warriors depart to
visit Friesland and the *hēaburh*) was not identical with the *hēaburh*, and did not
lie in Friesland.   Accordingly the usual view, that Finnsburg is situated outside
Friesland, seems incontestable.   See Bugge (*P.B.B.* xii, 29–30), Trautmann
(*Finn und Hildebrand*, 60) and Boer (*Z.f.d.Ā.* xlvii, 137).   Cf. Ayres (*J.E.G.Ph.*
xvi, 294).
[1] See below, p. 289.   [2] So Brandl, 984, and Heinzel.

does not go to the heart of the story, there might easily be a discrepancy between two versions[1].

But the whole difficulty merely arises from reading more into the words of the *Episode* than the text will warrant. It is not asserted in the *Episode* that Hildeburh found her kinsfolk dead in the morning, but that in the morning she found "murderous bale amid her kinsfolk." Hildeburh woke up to find a fight in progress: how long it went on, the *Episode* does not say: but that it was prolonged we gather from ll. 1080–5: and there is no reason why the deadly strife which Hildeburh found in the morning might not have lasted five days or more, before it culminated in the death of Hnæf.

Thirdly, the commander in the *Fragment* is called a "war-young king." This, it has been said, is inapplicable to Hnæf, since he is brother of Hildeburh, who is old enough to have a son slain in the combat.

But an uncle may be very young. Beowulf speaks of his uncle Hygelac as young, even though he seems to imply that his own youth is partly past[2]. And no advantage, but the reverse, is gained, even in this point, if, following Möller's hypothesis, and assuming that the fight narrated in the *Fragment* takes place after the treaty with Finn, we make the "war-young king" Hengest. For those who, with Möller, suppose Hengest to be brother of Hnæf, will have to admit the avuncular difficulty in him also.

SECTION V.   SOME DIFFICULTIES IN BUGGE'S THEORY

We may then, I think, accept as certain, that first come the events narrated in the *Fragment*, then those told in the *Episode* in *Beowulf*. But we are not out of our troubles yet. There are difficulties in Bugge's view which have still to be faced.

The cause of the struggle, according to Bugge and his adherents, is a treacherous attack made by Finn upon his brother-in-

---

[1] Or just as the attack on the Danes began at night, we might suppose (as does Trautmann) that it equally culminated in a night assault five days later. There would be obvious advantage in night fighting when the object was to storm a hall: Flugumýrr was burnt by night, and so was the hall of Njal. So, too, was the hall of Rolf Kraki. It would be, then, on the morning after this second night assault, that Hildeburh found her kinsfolk dead.

[2] *Beowulf*, l. 1831: cf. l. 409.

law Hnæf. According to the *Episode*, it is the Eotens who are treacherous; so Eotens must be another name for the Frisians. The word occurs three times in the genitive, *Eotena*; once in the dative, *Eotenum*: as a common noun it means "giant," "monster": earlier in *Beowulf* it is applied to Grendel and to the other misbegotten creatures descended from Cain. But how "giant" can be applied to the Frisians, or to either of the contending parties in the Finnsburg fight, remains inexplicable[1]. *Eotena* must rather be the name of some tribe. But what tribe? The only people of whom we know, possessing a name at all like this, are the people who colonized Kent, whom Bede calls Jutes, but whose name would in Anglian be in the genitive *Ēotna*, but in the dative *Ēotum*, or perhaps occasionally *Ēotnum*, *Ēotenum*[2]. Now a scribe transliterating a poem from an Anglian dialect into West-Saxon should, of course, have altered these forms into the corresponding West-Saxon forms *Ȳtena* and *Ȳtum*. But nothing would have been more likely than that he would have misunderstood the tribal name as a common noun, and retained the Anglian forms (altering *eotum* or *eotnum* into *eotenum*) supposing the word to mean "giants." After all, the common noun *eotenum*, "giants," was quite as like the tribal name *Ēotum*, which the scribe presumably had before him, as was the correct West-Saxon form of that name, *Ȳtum*.

It is difficult therefore to avoid the conclusion that the "Eotens" are Jutes: and this is confirmed by three other pieces of evidence, not convincing in themselves, but helpful as subsidiary arguments[3].

---

[1] Leo (*Beowulf*, 1839, 67), Müllenhoff (*Nordalbingische Studien*, I, 157), Rieger (*Lesebuch*; *Z.f.d.Ph.* III, 398–401), Dederich (*Studien*, 1877, 96–7), Heyne (in his fourth edition) and in recent times Holthausen have interpreted *eoten* as a common noun "giant," "monster," and consequently "foe" in general. But they have failed to produce any adequate justification for interpreting *eoten* as "foe," and Holthausen, the modern advocate of this interpretation, has now abandoned it. Grundtvig (*Beowulfes Beorh*, 1861, pp. 133 etc.) and Möller (*Volksepos*, 97 etc.) also interpret "giant," Möller giving an impossible mythological explanation, which was, at the time, widely followed.

[2] Like *oxnum*, *nefenum* (cf. Sievers, § 277, Anm. 1).

[3] I do not attach much importance to the argument which might be drawn from the statement of Binz (*P.B.B.* XX, 185) that the evidence of proper names shows that in the Hampshire district (which was colonized by Jutes) the legend of *Finnsburg* was particularly remembered. For on the other hand, as Binz points out, similar evidence is markedly lacking for Kent. And why, indeed, should the Jutes have specially commemorated a legend in which their part appears not to have been a very creditable one?

(1) We should gather from *Widsith* that the Jutes were concerned in the *Finnsburg* business. For in that poem generally (though not always) tribes connected in story are grouped together; and the Jutes and Frisians are so coupled:

> Ȳtum [weold] Gefwulf
> Fin Folcwalding Frēsna cynne.

(2) There is another passage in *Beowulf* in which *Eotenas* is possibly used in the sense of "Jutes."

We have seen above[1] that according to a Scandinavian tradition Lotherus was exiled *in Jutiam*: and Heremod, who has been held to be the counterpart of Lotherus

> *mid Eotenum* wearð
> on fēonda geweald forð forlācen.

But the identification of Lotherus and Heremod is too hypothetical to carry the weight of much argument.

(3) Finn comes into many Old English pedigrees, which have doubtless borrowed from one another. But the earliest in which we find him, and the only one in which we find his father Folcwald, is that of the Jutish kings of Kent[2]. Here, too, the name Hengest meets us.

The view that the name "Eoten" in the *Finnsburg* story is a form of the word "Jute" is, then, one which is very difficult to reject. It is one which has in the past been held by many scholars and is, I think, held by all who have recently expressed any opinion on the subject[3]. But this renders very difficult the assumption of Bugge and his followers that the word "Eoten" is synonymous with "Frisian[4]." For Frisians were not Jutes.

---

[1] p. 97, note 2.

[2] See above, p. 200. Zimmer, *Nennius Vindicatus*, 84, assumes that the Kentish pedigree borrowed these names from the Bernician: but there is no evidence for this.

[3] Among those who have so held are Kemble, Thorpe (*Beowulf*, pp. 76–7), Ettmüller (*Beowulf*, 1840, p. 23), Bouterwek (*Germania*, I, 389), Grein (*Eberts Jahrbuch*, IV, 270), Köhler (*Germania*, XIII, 155), Heyne (in first three editions), Holder (*Beowulf*, p. 128), ten Brink (*Pauls Grdr.* (1), II, 548), Heinzel (*A.f.d.A.* x, 228), Stevenson (*Asser*, 1904, p 169), Schücking (*Beowulf*, 1913, p. 321), Klaeber (*J.E.G.Ph* XIV, 545), Lawrence (*Pub. Mod. Lang. Assoc. Amer.* XXX. 3ᶜ3), Moorman (*Essays and Studies*, V, 99), Björkman (*Eigennamen im Beowulf*, 21).

So too, with some hesitation, Chadwick (*Origin*, 52–3): with much more hesitation, Bugge (*P B.B.* XII, 37). Whilst this is passing through the press Holthausen has withdrawn his former interpretation *eotena*, "enemies,' in favour of *Eotena* = *Ēotna*, "Jutes" (*Engl. Stud.* LI, 180).

[4] *P.B.B.* XII, 37.

The tribes were closely related; but the two words were not synonymous. The very lines in *Widsith*, which couple Jutes and Frisians together, as if they were related in story, show that the names were regarded as those of distinct tribes. And this evidence from *Widsith* is very important, because the compiler of that list of names clearly knew the story of Finn and Hnæf.

But this is not the only difficulty in Bugge's interpretation of the Eotens as Frisians. The outbreak of war, we are told, is due to the treachery of the Eotens. This Bugge and his followers interpret as meaning that Finn must have treacherously attacked Hnæf. Yet the poet speaks of "the warriors of Finn when the sudden danger fell upon them": *þā hīe se fǣr begeat*. It is essential to *fǣr* that it signifies a sudden and unexpected attack[1]: and the unexpected attack must have come, not upon the assailants but upon the assailed.

Yet this difficulty, though it has been emphasized by Möller[2] and other opponents of Bugge's view, is not insuperable[3], and I hope to show below that there is no real difficulty. But it leads us to a problem not so easily surmounted. If Finn made a treacherous attack upon Hnæf, and slew him, how did it come that Hengest, and Hnæf's other men, made terms with their murderous host?

In the primitive heathen days it had been a rule that the retainer must not survive his vanquished lord[4]. The ferocity of this rule was subsequently softened, and, in point of fact, we *do* often hear, after some great leader has been slain, of his followers accepting quarter from a chivalrous foe, without being

---

[1] The cognate of O.E. *fǣr* (Mod. Eng. "fear') in other Germanic languages, such as Old Saxon and Old High German, has the meaning of "ambush." In the nine places where it occurs in O.E. verse it has always the meaning of a peril which comes upon one suddenly, and is applied, e.g. to the Day of Judgement (twice) or some unexpected flood (three times). In compounds *fǣr* conveys an idea of suddenness: "*fǣr-dēað*, repentina mors."

[2] *Volksepos*, 69.

[3] It has been surmounted in two ways. (1) By altering *eaferum* to *eaferan* (a very slight change) and then making *fǣr* refer to the *final* attack upon Finn, in which he certainly *was* on the defensive (Lawrence, 397 *etc.*, Ayres, 284, Trautmann, *BB.* ii, Klaeber, *Anglia*, xxviii, 443, Holthausen). (2) By making *hīe* refer to *hæleð Healf-Dena* which follows (Green in *Pub. Mod. Lang. Assoc. Amer.* xxxi, 759-97); but this is forced. See also below, p. 284.

[4] Cf. Tacitus, *Germania*, xiv.

therefore regarded as having acted disgracefully[1]. But, if Finn had invited Hnæf and Hnæf's retainers to be his guests, and had fallen upon them by treachery, the action of the retainers in coming to terms with Finn, in entering his service, and stipulating how much of his pay they shall receive, would be contrary to all standards of conduct as understood in the Heroic Age, and would deprive Hnæf's men of any sympathy the audience might feel for them. But Hnæf's men are not censured: they are in fact treated most sympathetically in the *Episode*, and in the *Fragment*, at an earlier point in the story, they are enthusiastically applauded[2].

It is strange enough in any case that Hnæf's retainers should make terms with the slayer of their lord. But it is not merely strange, it is absolutely unintelligible, if we are to suppose that Finn has not merely slain Hnæf, but has lured him into his power, and then slain him while a guest.

It is to the credit of Bugge that he felt this difficulty: but his attempt to explain it is hardly satisfactory. He fell back upon a parallel between the story of the death of Rolf Kraki and the story of *Finnsburg*. We have already seen that the resemblance is very close between the *Bjarkamál*, which narrates the death of Rolf, and the opening of the *Finnsburg Fragment*. The parallel which Bugge invoked comes from the sequel to the Rolf story[3] which tells how Hiarwarus, the murderer of Rolf Kraki, astonished by the devotion of Rolf's retainers, lamented their death, and said how gladly he would have given quarter to such men, and taken them into his service. Thereupon Wiggo, the one survivor, who had previously vowed to avenge his lord, and had concealed himself with that object, came forward and offered to accept these terms. Accordingly he placed his hand upon the hilt of his new master's drawn sword, as if about to swear fealty to him: but instead of swearing, he ran him through.

"Glorious and ever memorable hero, who valiantly kept his vow," says Saxo[4]. Whether or no we share the exultation of

---

[1] For examples of this see pp. 278–82 below.
[2] *Fragment*, 40–1. [3] See above, p. 30.
[4] Book II (ed. Holder, p. 67).

that excellent if somewhat bloodthirsty ecclesiastic, we must admit that Wiggo's methods were sensible and practical. If, singlehanded, he was to keep his vow, and avenge his lord, he could only hope to do it by some such stratagem.

Bugge tries to explain Hengest's action on similar lines: "He does not hesitate to enter the service of Finn in order thereby to carry out his revenge[1]."

But the circumstances are entirely different. Wiggo was left alone, the only survivor of Rolf's household, to face a whole army. But Hengest is no single survivor: he and his fellows have made so good a defence that Finn cannot overcome them by conflict on the *meðel-stede*. Not only so, but, if we accept the interpretation that almost every critic and editor has put upon the passage (ll. 1184–5), Hengest's position is even stronger. Finn has lost almost all his thegns; the usual interpretation puts him at the mercy of Hengest: at best it is a draw[2]. If, then, Hengest wants vengeance upon Finn, why does he not pursue it? Instead of which, according to Bugge, he enters Finn's service in order that he may get an opportunity for revenge.

And note, that Wiggo did not swear the oath of fealty to the murderer of his master Rolf: he merely put himself in the posture to do so, and then, instead, ran the tyrant through forthwith. But Hengest *does* swear the oath, and *does not* forthwith slay the tyrant. He spends the winter with him, receives a sword from Hunlafing, after which his name does not occur again. Finn is ultimately slain, but the names which are found in that connection are those of Guthlaf and Oslaf [Ordlaf].

So Bugge's explanation comes to this: Hengest is fighting with success against Finn, but he refrains from vengeance: instead, he treacherously enters his service in order that he may take an opportunity of vengeance, which opportunity, however, it is never made clear to us that he takes.

Had Hengest been a man of that kind, he would not have been a hero of Old English heroic song.

[1] *P.B.B.* xii, 34.
[2] For a discussion of the interpretation of the difficult *forþringan*, see Carlton Brown in *M.L.N.* xxxiv, 181–3.

Section VI. Recent Elucidations.

Prof. Ayres' Comments

It is one of the merits of Bugge's view—one of the proofs of its general soundness—that it admits of successive improvements at the hands of succeeding commentators. No one has done more in this way than has Prof. Ayres to clear up the story, particularly the latter part of the *Episode*. Ayres evolves unity out of what had been before "a rapid-fire of events that hit all around a central tragic situation and do not once touch it." Hengest does not, Ayres thinks, enter the service of Finn with any such well-formed plan of revenge as Bugge had attributed to him. Hengest was in a difficult situation. It is his mental conflict, "torn between his oath to Finn and his duty to the dead Hnæf," which gives unity to all that follows. It is a tragedy of Hengest, hesitating, like Shakespeare's Hamlet, over the duty of revenge. Prof. Ayres' statement here is too good to summarize; it must be quoted at length:

"How did he feel during that long, blood-stained winter? He naturally thought about home (*eard gemunde*, 1129), but there was no question of sailing then, no need yet of decision while the storm roared outside. By and by spring came round, as it has a way of doing. How did he feel then? Then, like any other Northerner, he wanted to put to sea:

> fundode wrecca,
> gist of geardum.

That is what he would naturally do. He would speak to Finn and be off; in the spring his business was on the sea. That is all right as to Finn, but as to the dead Hnæf it is very like running away; it is postponing vengeance sadly. Will he prove so unpregnant of his cause as that? No; though he would like to go to sea, he thought *rather* of vengeance, and staid in the hope of managing a successful surprise against Finn and his people:

> hē tō gyrn-wræce
> swīðor þōhte   þonne tō sǣ-lāde,
> gif hē torn-gemōt   þurhtēon mihte,
> þæt hē Eotena bēarn   inne gemunde.

All this says clearly that Hengest was thinking things over, whether he should or should not take vengeance upon Finn; it tells us also very clearly, with characteristic anticipation of the outcome of the story, that in the end desire for vengeance carried the day:

> Swā hē ne-forwyrnde   worold-rǽdenne,

he did not *thus* prove recreant to his duty. But we have not been told the steps by which Hengest arrived at his decision. That seems to be what we should naturally want to know at this point, and that is precisely what we are about to be told. Occasions gross as earth informed against him[1]."

Then Ayres goes on to explain the "egging," through the presentation of a sword by Hunlafing. This feature of the story is now pretty generally so understood; but Ayres has an interpretation of the part played by Guthlaf and Oslaf, which is new and enlightening.

"Hengest's almost blunted purpose was not whetted by Hunlafing alone. The latter's uncles, Guðlaf and Oslaf [Ordlaf] took occasion to mention to Hengest the fierce attack (the one, presumably, in which Hnæf had fallen); cast up to him all the troubles that had befallen them ever since their disastrous sea-journey to Finnsburg; they had plenty of woes to twit him with:

> siððan grimne gripe Gūðlāf and Ōslāf
> æfter sæ-siðe sorge mændon,
> ætwiton wēana dǣl.

The effect of all this on Hengest is cumulative. Where he was before in perfect balance, he is now wrought to action by the words of his followers; he can control himself no longer; the balance is destroyed. The restless spirit (Hengest's in the first instance, but it may be thought of as referring to the entire attacking party, now of one mind) could no longer restrain itself within the breast:

> ne meahte wæfre mōd
> forhabban in hreðre.

Vengeance wins the day[2]."

By this interpretation Ayres has, as he claims, "sharpened some of the features" of the current interpretation of the Finn story. For, as he says, "in some respects the current version was very unsatisfactory; there seemed to be little relation between the presentation of the sword to Hengest and the spectacle of Guðlaf and Oslaf howling their complaints in the face of Finn."

That Ayres' interpretation enhances the coherency of the story is beyond dispute: that it does so at the cost of putting some strain upon the text in one or two places may perhaps be urged[3]. But that in its main lines it is correct seems to me certain: the story of Finnsburg is the tragedy of Hengest—his hesitation and his revenge. If we keep this well in view, many of the difficulties disappear.

---

[1] *J.E G.Ph.* xvi, 291–2. [2] *Ib.* 293–4.

[3] I wish I could feel convinced, with Ayres, that the person whom Guthlaf and Oslaf blame for their woes is Hengest rather than Finn. Such an interpretation renders the story so much more coherent; but if the poet really meant this, he assuredly did not make his meaning quite clear.

Section VII. Problems still outstanding

Many of the difficulties disappear: but the two big ones remain. Firstly, if "Eoten" means "Jute," as it is usually agreed that it does, why should the Frisians be called Jutes, seeing that a Frisian is not a Jute? Secondly, when Hengest and the other thegns of Hnæf enter the service of the slayer of their lord, they are not blamed for so doing, but rather excused, *þā him swā geþearfod wæs*. Such a situation is unusual; but it becomes incredible if that slayer, whose service they enter, had fallen upon and slain their lord by treachery, when his guest.

It seems to me that neither of these difficulties is really inherent in the situation, but rather accidental, and owing to the way Bugge's theory, right enough in its main lines, has been presented both by Bugge and his followers. For it is not necessary to assume that Frisians *are* called *Eotenas* or Jutes. All that we are justified in deducing from the text is that Frisians and *Eotenas* are both under the command of Finn. If we suppose what the text demands, *and no more*, we are at one stroke relieved of both our difficulties. Though "Jute" can hardly have been synonymous with "Frisian," nothing is more probable, as I shall try to show[1], than that a great Frisian king should have had a tribe of Jutes subject to him, or should have had in his pay a band of Jutish mercenaries. Now if the trouble was due to these "Eotens"—and we are told that it was[2]—our second difficulty is also solved. It would be much more natural for Hengest to come to terms with Finn, albeit the *bana* of his lord, if Finn's conduct had not been stained by treachery, and if the blame for the original attack did not rest with him.

And, as I have said, there is nothing in the text which justifies us in assuming that *Eotenas* means "Frisians" and that therefore *Eotena trēowe* refers to Finn's breach of faith. It has indeed been argued that *Eotenas* and Frisians are synonymous,

---

[1] See below, pp. 276, 288–9.
[2] Ne hūru Hildeburh herian þorfte
Eotena trēowe.

because in the terms of peace, whilst it is stipulated that Hengest and his comrades are to have equal control with the *Eotena bearn*, it is further stipulated that Finn is to give Hengest's men gifts equal to those which he gives to the *Frēsena cynn*[1]. Here then *Eotena bearn* and *Frēsena cynn* are certainly parallel, and are both contrasted with Hengest and his troops. But surely this in no wise proves *Eotena bearn* and *Frēsena cynn* synonymous: they may equally well be different sections of Finn's host, just as in *Brunanburh* the soldiers of Athelstan are spoken of first as *Westseaxe*, and then as *Myrce*. Are we to argue that West-Saxons are Mercians? So in the account of Hygelac's fatal expedition[2] the opponents are called Franks, Frisians, *Hūgas*, *Hetware*. A reader ignorant of the story might suppose these all synonymous terms for one tribe. But we know that they are not: the *Hetware* were the people immediately attacked —the Frankish overlord hastened to the rescue, and was apparently helped by the neighbouring Frisians, who although frequently at this date opposed to the Franks, would naturally make common cause against the pirate from overseas[3].

It was quite natural that the earlier students of the *Finnsburg Episode*, thinking of the two opposing forces as two homogeneous tribes, and finding mention of three tribal names, Danes, Eotens and Frisians, should have assumed that the Eotens must be exactly synonymous with *either* Danes *or* Frisians. But it is now recognized that the conditions of the time postulate not so much tribes as groups of tribes[4]. In the *Fragment* we have, on the side of the Danes, *Sigeferth*, prince of the *Secgan*. The *Secgan* are not necessarily Danes, because their lord is fighting on the Danish side. Neither need the *Eotenas* be Frisians, because they are fighting on the Frisian side.

We cannot, then, argue that two tribes are identical, because engaged in fighting a common foe: still less, because they are

---

[1] Ayres, in *J.E.G.Ph.* xvi, 286. So Lawrence in a private communication.
[2] ll. 2910, *etc.*
[3] We can construct the situation from such historical information as we can get from Gregory of Tours and other sources. The author of *Beowulf* may not have been clear as to the exact relation of the different tribes. We cannot tell, from the vague way he speaks, how much he knew.
[4] I have argued this at some length below, but I do not think anyone would deny it. Bugge recognized it to be true (*P.B.B.* xii, 29–30) as does Lawrence (392). See below, pp. 288–9.

mentioned with a certain parallelism[1]. And anyway, it is impossible to find in the use of the expression *Eotena bearn* in
l. 1088 any support for the interpretation which makes *Eotena
trēowe* signify the treachery of Finn himself. For, assuredly,
the proviso that Hengest and his fellows are to have half control
as against the *Eotena bearn* does not mean that they are to have
half control as against Finn himself. For the very next lines
make it clear that they are to enter Finn's service and become
his retainers. That Hengest and his men are to have equal
rights with Finn's Jutish followers (*Eotena bearn*) is reasonable
enough: but they obviously have not equal rights with Finn,
their lord whom they are now to follow. *Eotena bearn* in l. 1088,
then, does *not* include Finn: how *can* it then be used as an
argument that *Eotena trēowe* must refer to *Finn's* faith and his
breach of it?

Finn, then, is the *bana* of Hnæf, but there is nothing in the
text which compels us to assume that he is the slayer of his
guest.

The reader may regard my zeal to clear the character of Finn
as excessive. But it is always worth while to understand a good
old tale. And it is only when we withdraw our unjust asper-
sions upon Finn's good faith that the tale becomes intelligible.

This, I know, has been disputed, and by the scholars whose
opinion I most respect.

The poet tells us that Finn was the *bana* of Hnæf, so, says
Ayres, "it is hard to see how it helps matters[2]" to argue that
Finn was not guilty of treachery. And Lawrence argues in the
same way:

> "How is it possible to shift the blame for the attack from Finn to
> the Eotenas when Finn is called the *bana* of Hnæf? It does not
> matter whether he killed him with his own hands or not; he is clearly
> held responsible; the lines tell us it was regarded as disgraceful for the

---

[1] We can never argue that words are synonymous because they are parallel.
Compare Psalm cxiv; in the first verse the parallel words are synonymous, but
in the second and third not:
"When Israel came out of Egypt and the house of Jacob from among the
strange people" [Israel = house of Jacob: Egypt = strange people].
"Judah was His sanctuary and Israel His dominion." [Judah is only one
of the tribes of Israel.]
"The sea saw that and fled: Jordan was driven back." [The Red Sea and
Jordan are distinct, though parallel, examples.]
[2] *J.E.G.Ph.* xvi, 288.

Danes to have to follow him, and the revenge at the end falls heavily upon him. The insult and hurt to Danish pride would be very little lessened by the assumption that someone else started the quarrel; and for this assumption, too, the lines give no warrant'."

Let us take these objections in turn. I do not see how the fact that Finn is called the *bana* of Hnæf can prove *anything* as to "the blame for the attack." Of course the older editors may have thought so. Kemble translates *bana* "slaughterer," which implies brutality, and perhaps culpability. Bosworth-Toller renders *bana* "murderer," which certainly implies blame for attack. But we know that these are mere mistranslations. Nothing as to "blame for attack" is implied in the term *bana*: "*bana* 'slayer' is a perfectly neutral word, and must not be translated by 'murderer,' or any word connoting criminality. A man who slays another in self-defence, or in righteous execution of the law, is still his 'bane'[2]." Everyone admits this to be true: and yet at the same time *bana* is quoted to prove that Finn is to blame; because, for want of a better word, we half-consciously render *bana* "murderer": and "murderer" *does* imply blame. "Words," says Bacon, "as a Tartar's bow, do shoot back upon the understanding of the wisest."

Lawrence continues: "The lines tell us that it was regarded as disgraceful for the Danes to have to follow him." But surely this is saying too much. That the Frisians are not to taunt the Danes with following the slayer of their lord is only one of two possible interpretations of the ll. 1101-3. And even if we accept this interpretation, it does not follow that the Danes are regarded as having done anything with which they can be *justly* taunted. It is part of the settlement between Gunnar and Njal, that Njal's sons are not to be taunted: if a man repeats the taunts he shall fall unavenged[3]. Surely a man may be touchy about being taunted, without being regarded as having done anything disgraceful. Indeed, in our case, the poet implies that taunts would *not* be just, *þā him swā geþearfod wæs.* But, as I try to show below, no *þearf* could have excused the submission of retainers to a foe who had just slain their lord by deliberate treachery.

[1] *Pub. Mod. Lang. Assoc. Amer.* xxx, 430.
[2] Plummer, *Two Saxon Chronicles Parallel*, ii, 47.
[3] *Njáls Saga*, cap. 45.

"The revenge at the end falls heavily upon Finn." It does;
as so often happens where the feud is temporarily patched up,
it breaks out again, as in the stories of Alboin, Ingeld or Bolli.
But this does not prove that the person upon whom the revenge
ultimately falls heavily had been a guest-slayer. The possibility of even temporary reconciliation rather implies the reverse.

"The insult and hurt to Danish pride would be very little
lessened by the assumption that someone else [than Finn]
started the quarrel; and for this assumption, too, the lines give
no warrant." But they *do*: for they tell us that it was due
to the bad faith of the Eotens. Commentators may argue, if
they will, that "Eotens" means Finn. But the weight of proof
lies on them, and they have not borne it, or seriously attempted
to bear it.

Section VIII. The Weight of Proof: the Eotens

Finn is surely entitled to be held innocent till he can be
proved guilty. And the argument for his guilt comes to this:
the trouble was due to the bad faith of the Eotens: "Eotens"
means "Jutes": "Jutes" means "Frisians": "Frisians" means
"Finn": therefore the trouble was due to the treachery of Finn.

Now I agree that it is probable that *Eotenas* means Jutes;
and, as I have said, there is nothing improbable in a Frisian
king having had a clan of Jutes, or a body of Jutish mercenaries, subject to him. But that the Frisians as a whole should
be called Jutes is, *per se*, exceedingly improbable, and we have
no shadow of evidence for it. Lawrence tries to justify it by
the authority of Siebs:

> "Siebs, perhaps the foremost authority on Frisian conditions, con-
> jectures that...the occupation by the Frisians of Jutish territory after
> the conquest of Britain assisted the confusion between the two names."

But *did* the Frisians occupy Jutish territory? When we ask
what is Siebs' authority for the hypothesis that Frisians occupied
Jutish territory, we find it to be this: that because in *Beowulf*
"Jute" means "Frisian," some such event must have taken
place to account for this nomenclature[1]. So it comes to this:
the Frisians must have been called Jutes, because they occupied

---

[1] *Pauls Grdr.* (2), II, 524.

Jutish territory: the Frisians must have occupied Jutish territory because they are called Jutes.   I do not think we could
have a better example of what Prof. Tupper calls "philological
legend."

Siebs rejects Bede's statement, which places the Jutes in
what is now Jutland: he believes them to have been immediately
adjacent to the Frisians.   For this belief that the Jutes were
immediate neighbours of the Frisians there is, of course, some
support, though not of a very convincing kind: but the belief
that the Frisians occupied the territory of these adjacent Jutes
rests, so far as I know, solely upon this identification of the
Eotenas-Jutes with the Frisians, which it is then in turn used
to prove.

But if by Jutes we understand (following Bede) a people
dwelling north of the Angles, in or near the peninsula of
Jutland, then it is of course true that (at a much later date)
a colony of Frisians *did* occupy territory which is near Jutland,
and which is sometimes included in the name "Jutland."   But,
as I have tried to show above, this "North Frisian" colony
belongs to a period much later than that of the Finn-story: we
have no reason whatever to suppose that the Frisians of the
Finn story are the North Frisians of Sylt and the adjoining
islands and mainland—the *Frisiones qui habitabant Juthlandie*[1].

And when we have assumed, without evidence, that, at the
period with which we are dealing, Frisians had occupied Jutish
territory, we are then further asked to assume that, from this
settlement in Jutish territory, such Frisians came to be called
Jutes.   Now this is an hypothesis *per se* conceivable, but very
improbable.   Throughout the whole Heroic Age, for a thousand
years after the time of Tacitus, Germanic tribes were moving,
and occupying the territory of other people.   During this period,
how many instances can we find in which a tribe took the name
of the people whose territory it occupied?   Even where the
name of the new home is adopted, the old tribal name is *not*
adopted.   For instance, the Bavarians occupied the territory of
the Celtic Boii, but they did not call themselves Boii, but
Bai(haim)varii, "the dwellers in the land of the Boii"—a very

[1] Helmhold.

different thing. In the same way the Jutes who settled in the land of the Cantii did not call themselves *Kente*, but *Cantware*, "dwellers in Cantium." Of course, where the old name of a country survives, it does often *in the long run* come to be applied to its new inhabitants; but this takes many ages. It was not till a good thousand years after the English had conquered the land of the Britons, that Englishmen began to speak and think of themselves as "Britons." In feudal or 18th century days all the subjects of the ruler of Britain, Prussia, Austria, may come to be called British, Prussians, Austrians. But this is no argument for the period with which we are dealing. The assumption, then, that a body of Frisians, simply because they inhabited land which had once been inhabited by Jutes, should have called themselves Jutes, is so contrary to all we know of tribal nomenclature at this date, that one could only accept it if compelled by very definite evidence to do so. And of such evidence there is no scrap[1]. Neither is there a scrap of evidence for the underlying hypothesis that any Frisians *were* settled at this date in Jutish territory.

And as if this were not hypothetical enough, a further hypothesis has then to be built upon it: viz., that this name "Jutes," belonging to such of the Frisians as had settled in Jutish territory, somehow became applicable to Frisians as a whole. Now this might conceivably have happened, but only as a result of certain political events. If the Jutish Frisians had become the governing element in Frisia, it would be conceivable. But after all, we know something about Frisian history, and I do not

---

[1] I know of only one parallel for such assumed adoption of a name: that also concerns the Jutes. The Angles, says Bede, dwelt between the Saxons and Jutes: the Jutes must, then, according to Bede, have dwelt north of the Angles, since the Saxons dwelt south. But the people north of the Angles are now, and have been from early times, Scandinavian in speech, whilst the Jutes who settled Kent obviously were not. The best way of harmonizing known linguistic facts with Bede's statement is, then, to assume that Scandinavians settled in the old continental home of these Jutes and took over their name, whilst introducing the Scandinavian speech.

Now many scholars have regarded this as so forced and unlikely an explanation that they reject it, and refuse to believe that the Jutes who settled Kent can have dwelt north of the Angles, in spite of Bede's statement. If we are asked to reject the "Scandinavian-Jute" theory, as too unlikely on *a priori* grounds, although it is demanded by the express evidence of Bede, it is surely absurd to put forward a precisely similar theory in favour of "Frisian-Jutes" upon no evidence at all.

think we are at liberty to assume any such changes as would have enabled the Frisian people, as a whole, to be called Jutes. How is it that we never get any hint anywhere of this Jutish preponderance and Jutish ascendancy?

The argument that the "treachery of the Jutes" means the treachery of Finn, King of the Frisians, has, then, no support at all.

One further argument there is, for attributing treason to Finn.

It has been urged that in other stories a husband entraps and betrays the brother of his wife. But we are not justified in reading pieces of one story into another, unless we believe the two stories to be really connected. The Signy of the *Vǫlsunga Saga* has been quoted as a parallel to Hildeburh[1]. Signy leaves the home of her father Volsung and her brother Sigmund to wed King Siggeir. Siggeir invites the kin of his wife to visit him, and then slays Volsung and all his sons, save Sigmund. But it is the difference of the story, rather than its likeness, which is striking. No hint is ever made of any possibility of reconciliation between Siggeir and the kin of the men he has slain. The feud admits of no atonement, and is continued to the utterance. Siggeir's very wife helps her brother Sigmund to his revenge.

How different from the attitude of Sigmund and Signy is the willingness of Hengest to come to terms, and the merely passive and elegiac bearing of Hildeburh! These things do not suggest that we ought to read a King Siggeir treachery into the story of Finn.

Again, the fact that Atli entices the brother of his wife into his power, has been urged as a parallel. But surely it is rather unfair to erect this into a kind of standard of conduct for the early Germanic brother-in-law, and to assume as a matter of course that, because Finn is Hnæf's brother-in-law, therefore he must have sought to betray him. The whole atmosphere of the Finn-Hnæf story, with its attempted reconciliation, is as opposed to that of the story of Atli as it is to the story of Siggeir.

[1] Koegel (164), Lawrence (382).

18—2

The only epithet applied to Finn is *ferhð-freca,* "valiant in soul." Though *freca* is not necessarily a good word, and is applied to the dragon as well as to Beowulf, yet it denotes grim, fierce, almost reckless courage. It does not suggest a traitor who invites his foes to his house, and murders them by night.

I interpret the lines, then, as meaning that the trouble arose from the Jutes, and, since the context shows that these Jutes were on Finn's side, and against the Danes, we must hold them to be a body of Jutes in the service of Finn[1].

SECTION IX. ETHICS OF THE BLOOD FEUD

But, as we have seen, it is objected that this interpretation of the situation, absolving Finn from any charge of treachery or aggression, does not "help matters[2]." Or, as Prof. Lawrence puts it, "the hurt to Danish pride [in entering the service of Finn] would be very little lessened by the assumption that some-one else [than Finn] started the quarrel."

These objections seem to me to be contrary to the whole spirit of the old heroic literature.

I quite admit that there is a stage in primitive society when the act of slaying is everything, and the circumstances, or motives, do not count. In the Levitical Law, it is taken for granted that, if a man innocently causes the death of another, as for instance if his axe break, and the axe-head accidentally kill his comrade, then the avenger of blood will seek to slay the homicide, just as much as if he had been guilty of treacherous murder. To meet such cases the Cities of Refuge are established, where the homicide may flee till his case can be investigated; but even though found innocent, the homicide may be at once slain by the avenger, should he step outside the City of Refuge. And this "eye for eye" vengeance yields slowly: it took long to establish legally in our own country the distinction between murder and homicide.

---

[1] Björkman (*Eigennamen im Beowulf,* 23) interprets the *Eotenas* as Jutish subjects of Finn. This suggestion was made quite independently of anything I had written, and confirms me in my belief that it is a reasonable interpretation.

[2] Ayres in *J.E.G.Ph.* XVI, 288.

For "The thought of man" it was held "shall not be tried: as the devil himself knoweth not the thought of man." Nevertheless, even the Germanic *wer-gild* system permits consideration of circumstances: it often happens that no *wer-gild* is to be paid because the slain man has been unjust, or the aggressor[1], or no *wer-gild* will be accepted because the slaying was under circumstances making settlement impossible.

Doubtless in Germanic barbarism there was once a stage similar to that which must have preceded the establishment of the Cities of Refuge in Israel[2]; but that stage had passed before the period with which we are dealing; in the Heroic Age the motive *did* count for a very great deal. Not but what there were still the literal people who insisted upon "an eye for an eye," without looking at circumstances; and these people often had their way; but their view is seldom the one taken by the characters with whom the poet or the saga-man sympathises. These generally hold a more moderate creed. One may almost say that the leading motive in heroic literature is precisely this difference of opinion between the people who hold that under any circumstances it is shameful to come to an agreement with the *bana* of one's lord or friend or kinsman, and the people who are willing *under certain circumstances* to come to such an agreement.

It happens not infrequently that after some battle in which a great chief has been killed, his retainers are offered quarter, and accept it; but I do not remember any instance of their doing this if, instead of an open battle, it is a case of a treacherous attack. The two most famous downfalls of Northern princes afford typical examples: after the battle of Svold, Kolbjorn Stallari accepts quarter from Eric, the chivalrous *bani* of his lord Olaf[3]; but Rolf's men refuse quarter after the treacherous murder of their lord by Hiarwarus[4].

---

[1] e.g. *Njáls Saga*, cap. 144: *Laxdæla Saga*, cap. 51.

[2] Of course a primitive stage can be conceived at which homicide is regarded as worse than murder. Your brother shoots *A* intentionally: he must therefore have had good reasons, and you fraternally support him. But you may feel legitimate annoyance if he aims at a stag, and shooting *A* by mere misadventure, involves you in a blood-feud.

[3] *Heimskringla, Ól. Tryggv.* K. 111; *Saga Olafs Tryggvasonar*, K. 70 (*Fornmanna Sǫgur*, 1835, x.)

[4] Saxo Grammaticus (ed. Holder, p. 67).

That men, after a fair fight, could take quarter from, or give it to, those who had slain their lord or closest kinsman, is shown by abundant references in the sagas and histories. For instance, when Eric, after the fight with the Jomsvikings, offers quarter to his prisoners, that quarter is accepted, even though their leaders, their nearest kin, and their friends have been slain. The first to receive quarter is young Sigurd, whose father Bui has just been killed: yet the writer obviously does not the less sympathize with Sigurd, or with the other Jomsviking survivors, and feels the action to be generous on the part of Eric, and in no wise base on the part of the Jomsvikings[1]. But this is natural, because the Jomsvikings have just been defeated by Eric in fair fight. It would be impossible, if Eric were represented as a traitor, slaying the Jomsvikings by a treacherous attack, whilst they were his guests. Is it to be supposed that Sigurd, under such circumstances, would have taken quarter from the slayer of Bui his father?

In the *Laxdæla Saga*, Olaf the Peacock, in exacting vengeance for the slaying of his son Kjartan, shows no leniency towards the sons of Osvif, on whom the moral responsibility rests. But he accepts compensation in money from Bolli, who had been drawn into the feud against his will. Yet Bolli was the actual slayer of Kjartan, and he had taken the responsibility as such[2]. And Olaf is not held to have lowered himself by accepting a money payment as atonement from the slayer of his son—on the contrary "he was considered to have grown in reputation" from having thus spared Bolli. But after Olaf's death, the feud bursts out again, and revenge in the end falls heavily upon Bolli[3], as it does upon Finn.

On this question a fairly uniform standard of feeling will be found from the sixth century to the thirteenth. That it *does* make all the difference in composing a feud, whether the slaying from which the feud arises was treacherous or not, can be abundantly proved from many documents, from Paul the Deacon, and possibly earlier, to the Icelandic Sagas. Such composition of feuds may or may not be lasting; it may or may

[1] *Heimskringla, Ól. Tryggv.* K. 41.
[2] *lýsti vigi á hendr sér. Laxdæla Saga,* cap. 49.
[3] Cap. 55.

not expose to taunt those who make it; but the questions which
arise are precisely these: Who started the quarrel? Was the
slaying fair or treacherous? Upon the answer depends the
possibility of atonement. There may be some insult and hurt
to a man's pride in accepting atonement, even in cases where
the other side has much to say for itself. But if the slaying
has been fair, composition is felt to be possible, though not
without danger of the feud breaking out afresh.

Prof. Lawrence has suggested that perhaps, in the original
version of the *Finnsburg* story, the Danes were reduced to
greater straits than is represented to be the case in the extant
Beowulf Episode. He thinks that it is "almost incomprehensible" that Hengest should make terms with Finn, if he had
really reduced Finn and his thegns to such a degree of helplessness as the words of the *Episode* state. It seems to me that the
matter depends much more upon the treachery or the honesty
of Finn. If Finn was guilty of treachery and slaughter of his
guests, then it *is* "unintelligible" that Hengest should spare
him: but if Finn was really a respectable character, then the
fact that Hengest was making headway against him is rather
a reason why Hengest should be moderate, than otherwise. To
quote the *Laxdæla Saga* again: though Olaf the Peacock lets
off Bolli, the *bani* of his son Kjartan, with a money payment,
he makes it clear that he is master of the situation, before he
shows this mercy. Paradoxical as it sounds, it was often easier
for a man to show moderation in pursuing a blood feud, just
because he was in a strong position. It is so again in the *Saga
of Thorstein the White*. But the adversary must be one who
deserves to be treated with moderation.

Of course it is quite possible that Prof. Lawrence is right,
and that in some earlier and more correct version the Danes
may have been represented as so outnumbered by the Frisians
that they had no choice except to surrender to Finn, and enter
his service, or else to be destroyed. But, whether this be so
or no, all parallel incidents in the old literature show that their
choice between these evil alternatives will depend upon whether
Finn, the *bana* of their lord, slew that lord by deliberate and
premeditated treachery whilst he was his guest, or whether he

was embroiled with him through the fault of others, under circumstances which were perfectly honourable. If the latter is the case, then Hnæf's men *might* accept quarter. Their position is comparable with that of Illugi at the end of the *Grettis Saga*[1]. Illugi is a prisoner in the hands of the slayers of Grettir, and he charges them with having overcome Grettir, when already on the point of death from a mortifying wound, which they had inflicted on him by sorcery and enchantment. The slayers propose to Illugi terms parallel to those made to the retainers of Hnæf. "I will give thee thy life," says their leader, "if thou wilt swear to us an oath not to take vengeance on any of those who have been in this business."

Now, note the answer of Illugi: "That might have seemed to me a matter to be discussed, if Grettir had been able to defend himself, and if ye had overcome him with valour and courage; but now it is not to be looked for that I will save my life by being such a coward as art thou. In a word, no man shall be more harmful to thee than I, if I live, *for never can I forget how it was that ye have vanquished Grettir*. Much rather, then, do I choose to die."

Now of course it would have been an "insult and hurt" to the pride of Illugi, or of any other decent eleventh century Icelander, to have been compelled to swear an oath not to avenge his brother, even though that brother had been slain in the most chivalrous way possible; and it would doubtless have been a hard matter, even in such a case, for Illugi to have kept his oath, had he sworn it. But the treachery of the opponents puts an oath out of the question, just as it must have done in the case of the followers of King Cynewulf[2] or of Rolf Kraki, and as it must have done in the case of the followers of Hnæf, had the slaying of Hnæf been a premeditated act of treachery on the part of Finn.

In the *Njáls Saga*, Flosi has to take up the feud for the slain Hauskuld. Flosi is a moderate and reasonable man, so the first thing he does is to enquire into the *circumstances* under which Hauskuld was slain. Flosi finds that the circumstances, and the outrageous conduct of the slayers, give him no choice

---

[1] Cap. 85.   [2] *Anglo-Saxon Chronicle*, anno 755.

but to prosecute the feud. So in the end he burns Njal's hall, and in it the child of Kari.

Now to have burned a man's child to death might well seem a deed impossible of atonement. Yet in the end Flosi and Kari are reconciled by a full atonement, *the father of the slain child actually taking the first step*[1]. And all this is possible because Flosi and Kari recognise that each has been trying to play his part with justice and fairness, and that each is dragged into the feud through the fault of others. When Flosi has said of his enemy, "I would that I were altogether such a man as Kari is," we feel that reconciliation is in sight.

Very similar is the reconciliation between Alboin and Thurisind in Longobard story, but with this difference, that here it is Alboin who seeks reconciliation by going to the hall of the man whose son he has slain, thus reversing the parts of Flosi and Kari; and reconciliation is possible—just barely possible.

Again, when Bothvar comes to the hall of Rolf, and slays one of Rolf's retainers, the other retainers naturally claim full vengeance. Rolf insists upon investigating the *circumstances*. When he learns that it was his own man who gave the provocation, he comes to terms with the slayer.

Of course it was a difficult matter, and one involving a sacrifice of their pride, for the retainers of Hnæf to come to any composition with the *bana* of their lord; but it is not unthinkable, if the quarrel was started by Finn's subordinates without his consent, and if Finn himself fought fair. But had the slaying been an act of premeditated treachery on the part of Finn, the atonement would, I submit, have been not only difficult but impossible. If the retainers of Hnæf had had such success as our poem implies, then their action under such circumstances is, as Lawrence says, "almost incomprehensible." If they did it under compulsion, and fear of death, then their action would be contrary to all the ties of Germanic honour, and would entirely deprive them of any sympathy the audience might otherwise have felt for them. Yet it is quite obvious that the retainers of Hnæf are precisely the people with whom the audience is expected to sympathise[2].

---

[1] *Njáls Saga*, cap. 158.   [2] *Fragment*, ll. 40–1.

In any case, the feud was likely enough to break out again, as it did in the case of Alboin and Thurisind, and equally in that of Hrothgar and Ingeld.

Indeed, the different versions of the story of the feud between the house of Hrothgar and the house of Froda are very much to the point.

Much the oldest version—probably in its main lines quite historical—is the story as given in *Beowulf*. Froda has been slain by the Danes in pitched battle. Subsequently Hrothgar, upon whom, as King of the Danes, the responsibility for meeting the feud has devolved, tries to stave it off by wedding his daughter Freawaru to Ingeld, son of Froda. The sympathy of the poet is obviously with the luckless pair, Ingeld and Freawaru, involved as they are in ancient hatreds which are not of their making. For it is foreseen how some old warrior, who cannot forget his loyalty to his former king, will stir up the feud afresh.

But Saxo Grammaticus tells the story differently. Froda (Frotho) is treacherously invited to a banquet, and then slain. By this treachery the whole atmosphere of the story is changed. Ingeld (Ingellus) marries the daughter of his father's slayer, and, for this, the old version reproduced by Saxo showers upon him literally scores of phrases of scorn and contempt. The whole interest of the story now centres not in the recreant Ingeld or his wife of treacherous race, but in the old warrior Starkad, whose spirit and eloquence is such that he can bring Ingeld to a sense of his "vast sin[1]," can burst the bonds of his iniquity, and at last compel him to take vengeance for his father.

In the *Saga of Rolf Kraki* the story of Froda is still further changed. It is a tale not only of treachery but also of slaying of kin. Consequently the idea of any kind of atonement, however temporary, has become impossible; there is no hint of it.

Now the whole atmosphere of the Hengest-story in *Beowulf* is parallel to that of the *Beowulf* version of the Ingeld-story: agreement is possible, though it does not prove to be permanent. There is room for much hesitation in the minds of Hengest and of Ingeld: they remain the heroes of the story. But if Finn had, as is usually supposed, invited Hnæf to his fort and then

---

[1] p. 213 (ed. Holder).

deliberately slain him by treachery, the whole atmosphere would have been different. Hengest could not then be the hero, but the foil: the example of a man whose spirit fails at the crisis, who does the utterly disgraceful thing, and enters the service of his lord's treacherous foe. The hero of the story would be some other character—possibly the young Hunlafing, who, loyal in spite of the treachery and cowardice of his leader Hengest, yet, remaining steadfast of soul, is able in the end to infuse his own courage into the heart of the recreant Hengest, and to inspire all the perjured Danish thegns to their final and triumphant revenge on Finn.

But that is not how the story is presented.

Section X. An Attempt at Reconstruction

The theory, then, which seems to fit in best with what we know of the historic conditions at the time when the story arose, and which fits in best with such details of the story as we have, is this:

Finn, King of Frisia, has a stronghold, Finnsburg, outside the limits of Frisia proper. There several clans and chieftains are assembled[1]: Hnæf, Finn's brother-in-law, prince of the Hocings, the Eotens, and Sigeferth, prince of the Secgan; whether Sigeferth has his retinue with him or no is not clear.

But the treachery of the Eotens causes trouble: they have some old feud with Hnæf and his Danes, and attack them by surprise in their hall. There is no proof that Finn has any share in this treason. It is therefore quite natural that in the *Episode*—although the treachery of the Eotens is censured—Finn is never blamed; and that in the *Fragment*, Finn has apparently no share in the attack on the hall, at any rate during those first five days to which the account in the *Fragment* is limited.

The attack is led by Garulf (*Fragment*, l. 20), presumably the prince of the Eotens: and some friend or kinsman is urging Garulf not to hazard so precious a life in the first attack. And

---

[1] Finn may perhaps be holding a meeting of chieftains. For similar meetings of chieftains, compare *Sǫrla þáttr*, cap 4; *Laxdæla Saga*, cap. 12; *Skáldskaparmál*, cap. 47 (50).

here, too, the situation now becomes clearer: if Garulf is the chief of the attacking people, we can understand one of his kinsmen or friends expostulating thus: but if he is merely one of a number of subordinates despatched by Finn to attack the hall, the position would not be so easily understood.

Garulf, however, does not heed the warning, and falls, "first of all the dwellers in that land." The *Fragment* breaks off, but the fight goes on: we can imagine that matters must have proceeded much as in the great attack upon the hall in the *Nibelungen lied*[1]. One man after another would be drawn in, by the duty of revenge, and Finn's own men would wake to find a battle in progress. "The sudden bale (*fǣr*) came upon them." Finn's son joins in the attack, perhaps in order to avenge some young comrade in arms; and is slain, possibly by Hnæf. Then Finn *has* to intervene, and Hnæf in turn is slain, possibly, though not certainly, by Finn himself. But Hengest, the thegn of Hnæf, puts up so stout a defence, that Finn is unable to take a full vengeance upon all the Danes. He offers them terms. What are Hengest and the thegns to do?

Finn has slain their lord. But they are Finn's guests, and they have slain Finn's son in his own house. Finn himself is, I take it, blameless. *It is here that the tragic tension comes in.* We can understand how, even if Hengest had Finn in his power, he might well have stayed his hand. So peace is made, and all is to be forgotten: solemn oaths are sworn. And Finn keeps his promise honestly. He resumes his position of host, making no distinction between Eotens, Frisians and Danes, who are all, for the time at least, his followers.

I think we have here a rational explanation of the action of Hengest and the other thegns of Hnæf, in following the slayer of their lord.

The situation resembles that which takes place when Alboin seeks hospitality in the hall of the man whose son he has slain, or when Ingeld is reconciled to Hrothgar. Very similar, too,

---

[1] There is assuredly a considerable likeness between the Finn story and the Nibelungen story: this has been noted often enough. It is more open to dispute whether the likeness is so great as to justify us in believing that the Nibelungen story is *copied* from the Finn story, and may therefore safely be used as an indication how gaps in our existing versions of that story may be filled. See Boer in *Z.f.d.A.* xlvii, 125 *etc.*

is the temporary reconciliation often brought about in an Icelandic feud by the feeling that the other side has something to say for itself, and that both have suffered grievously. The death of Finn's son is a set off against the death of Hnæf[1]. But, as in the case of Alboin and of Ingeld, or of many an Icelandic Saga, the passion for revenge is too deep to be laid to rest permanently. This is what makes the figure of Hengest tragic, like the figure of Ingeld: both have plighted their word, but neither can keep it.

The assembly breaks up. Finn and his men go back to Friesland, and Hengest accompanies them: of the other Danish survivors nothing is said for the moment: whatever longings they may have had for revenge, the poet concentrates all for the moment in the figure of Hengest.

Hengest spends the winter with Finn, but he cannot quiet his conscience: and in the end, he accepts the gift of a sword from a young Danish prince Hunlafing, who is planning revenge. The uncles of Hunlafing, Guthlaf and Oslaf [Ordlaf], had been in the hall when it was attacked, and had survived. It is possible that the young prince's father, Hunlaf, was slain then, and that his son is therefore recognised as having the nominal leadership in the operations of vengeance[2]. Hengest, by accepting the sword, promises his services in the work of revenge, and makes a great slaughter of the treacherous Eotens. Perhaps he so far respects his oath that he leaves the simultaneous attack upon Finn to Guthlaf and Oslaf [Ordlaf]. Here we should have an explanation of *swylce*: "in like wise[3]"; and also an explanation of the omission of Hengest's name from the final act, the slaying of Finn himself. Hengest made the Eotens

---

[1] The fact that both sides have suffered about equally facilitates a settlement in the Teutonic feud, just as it does among the Afridis or the Albanians at the present day.

[2] The situation would then be parallel to that in *Laxdæla Saga*, cap. 60–5, where the boy Thorleik, aged fifteen, is nominally in command of the expedition which avenges his father Bolli, but is only able to accomplish his revenge by enlisting the great warrior Thorgils, who is the real leader of the raid.

[3] Bugge (*P.B.B.* xii, 36) interpreted this *swylce* as meaning that sword-bale came upon Finn in like manner as it had previously come upon Hnæf. But this is to make *swylce* in l. 1146 refer back to the death of Hnæf mentioned (72 lines previously) in l. 1074. Möller (*Volksepos*, 67) tries to explain *swylce* by supposing the passage it introduces to be a fragment detached from its context.

feel the sharpness of his sword: and in like wise Guthlaf and Oslaf conducted their part of the campaign. Of course this is only a guess: but it is very much in the manner of the Heroic Age to get out of a difficulty by respecting the letter of an oath whilst breaking its spirit—just as Hogni and Gunnar arrange that the actual slaying of Sigurd shall be done by Guttorm, who had not personally sworn the oath, as they had.

Section XI.   Gefwulf, Prince of the Jutes

Conclusive external evidence in favour of the view just put forward we can hardly hope for: for this reason, amongst others, that the names of the actors in the Finn tragedy are corrupted and obscured in the different versions.   Hnæf and Hengest are too well known to be altered: but most of the other names mentioned in the *Fragment* do not agree with the forms given in other documents.   Sigeferth is the Sæferth of *Widsith*: the Ordlaf (correct) of the *Fragment* is the Oslaf of the *Episode*. The first Guthlaf is confirmed by the Guthlaf of the *Episode*: the other names, the second Guthlaf, Eaha and Guthere, we cannot control from other sources: but they have all, on various grounds, been suspected.

Tribal names are equally varied.   Sigeferth's people, the Secgan, are called Sycgan in *Widsith*.   And he would be a bold man who would deny (what almost all students of the subject hold) that *Eotena, Eotenum* in the *Episode* is yet another scribal error: the copyist had before him the Anglian form, *eotna, eotnum,* and miswrote *eotena, eotenum,* when he should have written the West-Saxon equivalent of the tribal name, Ȳtena, Ȳtum—the name we get in *Widsith*:

> Ȳtum [weold] Gefwulf
> Fin Folcwalding Frēsna cynne.

But in *Widsith* names of heroes and tribes are grouped together (often, but not invariably) according as they are related in story. Consequently Gefwulf is probably (not certainly) a hero of the Finn story.   What part does he play?   If, as I have been trying to show, the Jutes are the aggressors, then, as their chief, Gefwulf would probably be the leader of the attack upon the hall.

This part, in the *Fragment*, is played by Garulf.

Now *Gārulf* is not *Gefwulf*, and I am not going to pretend that it is. But *Gārulf* is very near *Gefwulf*: and (what is important) more so in Old English script than in modern script[1]. It stands to *Gefwulf* in exactly the same relation as *Heregār* to *Heorogār* or *Sigeferð* to *Sæferð* or *Ordlāf* to *Ōslāf*: that is to say the initial letter and the second element are identical. And no serious student, I think, doubts that *Heregār* and *Heorogār*, or *Sigeferð* and *Sæferð*, or *Ordlāf* and *Ōslāf* are merely corruptions of one name. And if it be admitted to be probable that *Gefwulf* is miswritten for *Gārulf*, then the theory that Garulf was prince of the Jutes, and the original assailant of Hnæf, in addition to being the only theory which satisfactorily explains the internal evidence of the *Fragment* and the *Episode*, has also powerful external support.

SECTION XII. CONCLUSION

But, apart from any such confirmation, I think that the theory offers an explanation of the known facts of the case, and that it is the only theory yet put forward which does. It enables us to solve many minor difficulties that hardly otherwise admit of solution. But, above all, it gives a tragic interest to the story by making the actions of the two main characters, Finn and Hengest, intelligible and human: they are both great chiefs, placed by circumstances in a cruel position. Finn is no longer a treacherous host, plotting the murder of his guests, without even having the courage personally to superintend the dirty work: and Hengest is not guilty of the shameful act of entering the service of a king who had slain his lord by treachery when a guest. The tale of *Finnsburg* becomes one of tragic misfortune besetting great heroes—a tale of the same type as the stories of Thurisind or Ingeld, of Sigurd or Theodric.

---

[1] f, r, s, þ, w, p (ꝼꞃꞅþƿp), all letters involving a long down stroke, are constantly confused. For examples, see above, p. 245, and cf. e.g. *Beowulf*, l. 2882 (*fergendra* for *wergendra*); *Crist*, 12 (*cræstga* for *cræftga*); *Phœnix*, 15 (*fnæft* for *fnæst*); Riddles III (IV), 18 (*þyran* for *þuwan*); XL (XLI), 63 (*þyrre* for *þyrse*): XLII (XLIII), 4 (*speoþ* for *spēow*), 11 (*wæs* for *þæs*); LVII (LVIII), 3 (*rope* for *rōfe* or *rōwe*), etc.

FRISIA IN THE HEROIC AGE

It is now generally recognised that loose confederacies of tribes were, at the period with which we are dealing, very common. Lawrence says this expressly: "The actors in this drama are members of two North Sea tribes, or *rather groups of tribes*[1]"; and again[2]: "At the time when the present poem was put into shape, we surely have to assume for the Danes and Frisians, not compact and unified political units, but groups of tribes held somewhat loosely together, and sometimes known by tribal names."

This seems to me a quite accurate view of the political situation in the later Heroic Age. The independent tribes, as they existed at the time of Tacitus, tended to coalesce, and from such coalition the nations of modern Europe are gradually evolved. In the seventh and eighth centuries a great king of Northumbria or Frisia is likely to be king, not of one only, but of many allied tribes. I cannot therefore quite understand why some scholars reject so immediately the idea that the Eotens are not necessarily Frisians, but rather a tribe in alliance with the Frisians. For if, as they admit, we are dealing not with two compact units, but with two groups of tribes, why must we assume, as earlier scholars have done, that *Eotenas* must be synonymous either with Frisians or Danes? That assumption is based upon the belief that we *are* dealing with two compact units. It has no other foundation. I can quite understand Kemble and Ettmüller jumping at the conclusion that the Eotens *must* be identical with the one side or the other. But once we have recognised that confederacies of tribes, rather than individual tribes, are to be expected in the period with which we are dealing, then surely no such assumption should be made.

I think we shall be helped if we try to get some clear idea of the nationalities concerned in the struggle. For to judge by the analogy of other contemporary Germanic stories, there probably is some historic basis for the *Finnsburg* story: and even if the fight is purely fictitious, and if Finn Folcwalding never existed, still the Old English poets would represent the fictitious Frisian king in the light of what they knew of contemporary kings.

Now the Frisians were no insignificant tribe. They were a power, controlling the coasts of what was then called the "Frisian Sea[3]." Commerce was in Frisian hands. Archaeological evidence points to a lively trade between the Frisian districts and the coast of Norway[4]. From about the sixth century, when "Dorostates of the Frisians" is mentioned by the Geographer of Ravenna (or the source from which he drew) in a manner which shows it to have been known even in Italy as a place of peculiar

[1] p. 392.   [2] p 431.
[3] *Nennius Interpretatus*, ed. Mommsen (*Chronica Minora*, iii, 179, in *Mon. Germ. Hist.*)
[4] "De norske oldsager synes at vidne om, at temmelig livlige handelsforbindelser i den ældre jernalder har fundet sted mellem Norge og de sydlige Nordsøkyster." Undset, *Fra Norges ældre Jernalder* in the *Aarbøger for Nordisk Oldkyndighed og Historie*, 1880, 89–184, esp. p. 173. See also Chadwick, *Origin*, 93. I am indebted to Chadwick's note for this reference to Undset.

importance[1], to the ninth century, when it was destroyed by repeated attacks of the Vikings, the Frisian port of Dorestad[2] was one of the greatest trade centres of Northern Europe[3]. By the year 700 the Frisian power had suffered severely from the constant blows dealt to it by the Frankish Mayors of the Palace. Yet evidence seems to show that even at that date the Frisian king ruled all the coast which intervened between the borders of the Franks on the one side and of the Danes on the other[4]. When a zealous missionary demonstrated the powerlessness of the heathen gods by baptizing three converts in the sacred spring of Fosetisland, he was carried before the King of Frisia for judgement[5].

At a later date the "Danes" became the controlling power in the North Sea; but in the centuries before the Viking raids began, the Frisians appear to have had it all their own way.

Finn, son of Folcwald, found his way into some English genealogies[6] just as the Roman Emperor did into others. This also seems to point to the Frisian power having made an impression on the nations around.

We should expect all this to be reflected in the story of the great Frisian king. How then would a seventh or eighth century Englishman regard Finn and his father Folcwalda? Probably as paramount chiefs, holding authority over the tribes of the South and East coast of the North Sea, similar to that which, for example, a Northumbrian king held over the tribes settled along the British coast. Indeed, the whole story of the Northumbrian kings, as given in Bede, deserves comparison: the relation with the subordinate tribes, the alliances, the feuds, the attempted assassinations, the loyalty of the thegns—this is the atmosphere amid which the Finn story grew up in England, and if we want to understand the story we must begin by getting this point of view.

But, if this be a correct estimate of tribal conditions at the time the *Finnsburg* story took form, we no longer need far-fetched explanations to account for Finnsburg not being in Friesland. It is natural that it should not be, just as natural as that the contemporary Eadwinesburg should be outside the ancient limits of Deira. Nor do we need any far-fetched explanations why the Frisians should be called *Eotenas*. That the King of Frisia should have had Jutes under his rule is likely enough. And this is all that the words of the *Episode* demand.

---

[1] *Ravennatis anonymi cosmographia*, ed. Pinder et Parthey, Berolini, 1860, pp. 27, 28 (§ I, 11).

[2] The modern Wijk bij Duurstede, not far from Utrecht, on the Lower Rhine.

[3] An account of the numerous coins found among the ruins of the old town will be found in the *Forschungen zur deutschen Geschichte*, IV (1864), pp. 301–303. They testify to its commercial importance.

[4] So Adam of Bremen, following Alcuin. Concerning "Heiligland" Adam says: "Hanc in vita Sancti Willebrordi Fosetisland appellari discimus, quae sita est in confinio Danorum et Fresonum." Adam of Bremen in Pertz, *Scriptores*, VII, 1846, p. 369.

[5] Alcuin's *Life of Willibrord* in Migne (1851)—Alcuini *Opera*, vol. II, 699–702.

[6] See above, pp. 199–200.

PART IV

APPENDIX

A. A POSTSCRIPT ON MYTHOLOGY IN *BEOWULF*

(1) *Beowulf the Scylding and Beowulf son of Ecgtheow*

IT is now ten years since Prof. Lawrence attacked the mythological theories which, from the time when they were first enunciated by Kemble and elaborated by Müllenhoff, had wielded an authority over *Beowulf* scholars which was only very rarely disputed[1].

Whilst in the main I agree with Prof. Lawrence, I believe that there *is* an element of truth in the theories of Kemble. It would, indeed, be both astonishing and humiliating if we found that a view, accepted for three-quarters of a century by almost every student, had no foundation. What is really remarkable is, not that Kemble should have carried his mythological theory too far, but that, with the limited information at his disposal, he at once saw certain aspects of the truth so clearly.

The mythological theories involve three propositions:

(*a*) That some, or all, of the supernatural stories told of Beowulf the Geat, son of Ecgtheow (especially the Grendel-struggle and the dragon-struggle), were originally told of Beowulf the Dane, son of Scyld, who can be identified with the Beow or Beaw[2] of the genealogies.

---

[1] It had been disputed by Skeat, Earle, Boer, and others, but never with such strong reasons.

[2] I use below the form "Beow," which I believe to be the correct one. "Beaw" is the form in the *Anglo-Saxon Chronicle*. But as the name of Sceldwa, Beaw's father, is there given in a form which is not West-Saxon (*sceld*, not *scield* or *scyld*), it may well be that "Beaw" is also the Anglian dialect form, if it be not indeed a mere error: and this is confirmed by *Beo* (Ethelwerd), *Beowius* (William of Malmesbury), *Boerinus* (for *Beowinus*: Chronicle Roll), perhaps too by *Beowa* (Charter of 931) and *Beowi* (*MS Cott. Tib. B. IV*). For the significance of this last, see pp. 303–4, below, and Björkman in *Engl. Stud.* LII, 171, *Anglia, Beiblatt,* XXX, 23.

(*b*)   That this Beow was an ancient "god of agriculture and fertility."

(*c*)   That therefore we can allegorize Grendel and the dragon into culture-myths connected with the "god Beow."

Now (*c*) would not necessarily follow, even granting (*a*) and (*b*); for though a hero of story be an ancient god, many of his most popular adventures may be later accretion.   However, these two propositions (*a*) and (*b*) would, together, establish a very strong probability that the Grendel-story and the dragon-story were ancient culture-myths, and would entitle to a sympathetic hearing those who had such an interpretation of them to offer.

That Beow is an ancient "god of agriculture and fertility," I believe to be substantially true.   We shall see that a great deal of evidence, unknown to Kemble and Müllenhoff, is now forthcoming to show that there *was* an ancient belief in a corn-spirit Beow: and this Beow, whom we find in the genealogies as son of Scyld or Sceldwa and descendant of Sceaf, is pretty obviously identical with Beowulf, son of Scyld Scefing, in the *Prologue* of *Beowulf.*

So far as the *Prologue* is concerned, there is, then, almost certainly a remote mythological background.   But before we can claim that this background extends to the supernatural adventures attributed to Beowulf, son of Ecgtheow, we must prove our proposition (*a*): that these adventures were once told, not of Beowulf, son of Ecgtheow, but of Beowulf or Beow, son of Scyld.

When it was first suggested, at the very beginning of *Beowulf*-criticism, that Beowulf was identical with the Beow of the genealogies, it had not been realized that there were in the poem *two* persons named Beowulf: and thus an anonymous scholar in the *Monthly Review* of 1816[1], not knowing that Beowulf the slayer of Grendel is (at any rate in the poem as it stands) distinct from Beowulf, son of Scyld, connected both with Beow, son of Scyld, so initiating a theory which, for almost a century, was accepted as ascertained fact.

[1] Vol. LXXXI, p. 517.

Kemble's identification was probably made independently of the work of this early scholar. Unlike him, Kemble, of course, realized that in our poem Beowulf the Dane, son of Scyld, is a person distinct from, is in fact not related to, Beowulf son of Ecgtheow. But he deliberately identified the two: he thought that two distinct traditions concerning the same hero had been amalgamated: in one of these traditions Beowulf may have been represented as son of Scyld, in the other as son of Ecgtheow, precisely as the hero Gunnar or Gunter is in one tradition son of Gifica (Giuki), in another son of Dankrat.

Of course such duplication as Kemble assumed is conceivable. Kemble might have instanced the way in which one and the same hero reappears in the pages of Saxo Grammaticus, with somewhat different parentage or surroundings, as if he were a quite different person. The *Lives of the Two Offas* present another parallel: the adventures of the elder Offa have been transferred to the younger, so that, along with much that is historical or semi-historical, we have much in the *Life of Offa II* that is simply borrowed from the story of Offa I. In the same way it is conceivable that reminiscences of the mythical adventures of the elder Beowulf (Beow) might have been mingled with the history of the acts of the younger Beowulf, king of the Geatas. A guarantee of the intrinsic reasonableness of this theory lies in the fact that recently it has been put forward again by Dr Henry Bradley. But it is not enough that a theory should be conceivable, and be supported by great names. I cannot see that there is any positive evidence for it at all.

The arguments produced by Kemble are not such as to carry conviction at the present day. The fact that Beowulf the Geat, son of Ecgtheow, "is represented throughout as a protecting and redeeming being" does not necessarily mean that we must look for some god or demigod of the old mythology —Frey or Sceaf or Beow—with whom we can identify him. This characteristic is strongly present in many Old English monarchs and magnates of historic, Christian, times: Oswald or Alfred or Byrhtnoth. Indeed, it might with much plausibility be argued that we are to see in this "protecting" character of the hero evidence of Christian rather than of heathen influence[1].

Nor can we argue anything from the absence of any historic record of a king Beowulf of the Geatas; our records are too scanty to admit of argument from silence: and were such argument valid, it would only prove Beowulf fictitious, not mythological—no more necessarily an ancient god than Tom Jones or Mr Pickwick.

There remains the argument of Dr Bradley. He points out that

> "The poem is divided into numbered sections, the length of which was probably determined by the size of the pieces of parchment of which an earlier exemplar consisted. Now the first fifty-two lines, which are concerned with Scyld and his son Beowulf, stand outside this numbering. It may reasonably be inferred that there once existed a written text of the poem that did not include these lines. Their substance, however, is clearly ancient. Many difficulties will be obviated if we may suppose that this passage is the beginning of a different poem, the hero of which was not Beowulf the son of Ecgtheow, but his Danish namesake[2]."

In this Bradley sees support for the view that "there were circulated in England two rival poetic versions of the story of the encounters with supernatural beings: the one referring them to Beowulf the Dane" [of this the *Prologue* to our extant poem would be the only surviving portion, whilst] "the other (represented by the existing poem) attached them to the legend of the son of Ecgtheow."

But surely many objections have to be met. Firstly, as Dr Bradley admits, the mention of Beowulf the Dane is not confined to the *Prologue*; this earlier Beowulf "is mentioned at the beginning of the first numbered section" and consequently Dr Bradley has to suppose that "the opening lines of this section have undergone alteration in order to bring them into connection with the prefixed matter." And why should we assume that the "passus" of *Beowulf* correspond to pieces of

---

[1] It has indeed been so argued by Brandl: "Beowulf...ist nur der Erlöser seines Volkes...und dankt es schliesslich dem Himmel, in einer an den Heiland gemahnenden Weise, dass er die Seinen um den Preis des eigenen Lebens mit Schätzen beglücken konnte." *Pauls Grdr.* (2), II, 1. 1002.

[2] *Encyclopædia Britannica*, 11th edit., III, 760-1.

parchment of various sizes of which an earlier exemplar consisted? These "passus" vary in length from 43 lines to 142, a disproportion by no means extraordinary for the sections of one and the same poem, but very awkward for the pages of one and the same book, however roughly constructed. One of the "passus" is just twice the average length, and 30 lines longer than the one which comes next to it in size. Ought we to assume that an artificer would have made his book clumsy by putting in this one disproportionate page, when, by cutting it in two, he could have got two pages of just about the size he wanted? Besides, the different "passus" do not seem to me to show signs of having been caused by such mechanical reasons as the dimensions of the parchment upon which they were written. On the contrary, the 42 places where sections begin and end almost all come where a reader might reasonably be expected to pause: 16 at the beginning or end of a speech: 18 others at a point where the narrative is resumed after some digression or general remark. Only eight remain, and even with these, there is generally some pause in the narrative at the point indicated. In only two instances does a "passus" end at a flagrantly inappropriate spot; in one of these there is strong reason to suppose that the scribe may have caused the trouble by beginning with a capital where he had no business to have done so[1]. Generally, there seems to be some principle governing the division of chapter from chapter, even though this be not made as a modern would have made it. But, if so, is there anything extraordinary in the first chapter, which deals with events three generations earlier than those of the body of the poem, being allowed to stand outside the numbering, as a kind of prologue?

The idea of a preface or prologue was quite familiar in Old English times. The oldest MSS[2] of Bede's *History* have, at the end of the preface, *Explicit praefatio incipiunt capitula.* So we have in one of the two oldest MSS[3] of the *Pastoral Care* "Ðis is seo forespræc." On the other hand, the prologue or preface might be left without any heading or colophon, and the next

---

[1] l. 2039, where a capital O occurs, but without a section number.
[2] *Moore, Namur, Cotton.*   [3] *Cotton Tiberius B. XI.*

chapter begin as No. I. This is the case in the other MS of the *Pastoral Care*[1]. Is there, then, such difficulty in the dissertation on the glory of the ancient Danish kings being treated as what, in fact, it is: a prologue or preface; and being, as such, simply left outside the numbering?

Still less can we argue for the identification of our hero, the son of Ecgtheow, with Frotho, and through him with Beow, from the supposed resemblances between the dragon fights of Beowulf and Frotho. Such resemblances have been divined by Sievers, but we have seen that it is the dissimilarity, not the resemblance, of the two dragon fights which is really noteworthy[2].

To prove that Beow was the original antagonist of Grendel there remains, then, only the mention in the charter of a *Grendles mere* near a *Bēowan hamm*[3]. Now this was not known to Kemble at the time when he formed his theory that the original slayer of Grendel was not Beowulf, but Beow. And if the arguments upon which Kemble based his theory had been at all substantial, this charter would have afforded really valuable support. But the fact that two names occur near each other in a charter cannot confirm any theory, unless that theory has already a real basis of its own.

(2) *Beow*

Therefore, until some further evidence be discovered, we must regard the belief that the Grendel and the dragon stories were originally myths of Beow, as a theory for which sufficient evidence is not forthcoming.

But note where the theory breaks down. It seems indisputable that Beowulf the Dane, son of Scyld Scefing, is identical with Beo(w) of the genealogies: for Beo(w) is son of Scyld[4] or Sce(a)ldwa[5], who is a Scefing. But here we must stop. There is, as we have seen, no evidence that the Grendel or dragon adventures were transferred from him to their present hero,

---

[1] *Hatton*, 20.   [2] See above, pp. 92–7.   [3] See above, pp. 43–4.
[4] Ethelwerd.   [5] *Chronicle.*

Beowulf the Geat, son of Ecgtheow.   It would, of course, be
quite possible to accept such transference, and *still* to reject
the mythological interpretation of these adventures, just as it
would be possible to believe that Gawain was originally a
sun-hero, whilst rejecting the interpretation as a sun-myth of
any particular adventure which could be proved to have been
once told concerning Gawain.   But I do not think we need even
concede, as Boer[1] and Chadwick[2] do, that adventures have been
transferred from Beowulf the Dane to Beowulf the Geat.   We
have seen that there is no evidence for such transference, however intrinsically likely it may be.   Till evidence *is* forthcoming,
it is useless to build upon Kemble's conjecture that Beowulf
the Scylding sank into Beowulf the Wægmunding[3].

But it is due to Kemble to remember that, while he only
put this forward as a tentative conjecture, what he *was* certain
about was the identity of Beowulf the Scylding with Beow, and
the divinity of these figures.   And here all the evidence seems
to justify him.

> "The divinity of the earlier Beówulf," Kemble wrote, "I hold for
> indisputable....Beo or Beow is...in all probability a god of agriculture
> and fertility....It strengthens this view of the case that he is the
> grandson of Sceáf, *manipulus frumenti*, with whom he is perhaps in
> fact identical[4]."

Whether or no Beow and Sceaf were ever identical, it is
certain that Beow (grain) the descendant of Sceaf (sheaf) suggests a corn-myth, some survival from the ancient worship of
a corn-spirit.

Now *bēow*, 'grain, barley,' corresponds to Old Norse *bygg*,
just as, corresponding to O.E. *trīewe*, we have O.N. *tryggr*, or
corresponding to O.E. *glēaw*, O.N. *glǫggr*.   Corresponding to the
O.E. proper name *Bēow*, we might expect an O.N. name, the
first letters in which would be *Bygg(v)-*.

And pat he comes, like the catastrophe of the Old Comedy.
When Loki strode into the Hall of Ægir, and assailed with
clamour and scandal the assembled gods and goddesses, there
were present, among the major gods, also Byggvir and his wife

---

[1] Boer, *Beowulf*, 135, 143: *Arkiv f. nord. Filologi*, XIX, 29.
[2] *Heroic Age*, 126.   [3] *Postscript to Preface*, p. **ix.**
[4] *Postscript*, pp. xi, xiv

Beyla, the servants of Frey, the god of agriculture and fertility.
Loki reviles the gods, one after the other: at last he exchanges
reproaches with Frey. To see his lord so taunted is more than
Byggvir can endure, and he turns to Loki with the words:

> Know thou, that were my race such as is that of Ingunar-Frey,
> and if I had so goodly a seat, finer than marrow would I grind thee,
> thou crow of ill-omen, and pound thee all to pieces[1].

Byggvir is evidently no great hero: he draws his ideas from
the grinding of the homely hand-mill, with which John Barleycorn has reason to be familiar:

> A miller used him worst of all,
> For he crushed him between two stones[2].

Loki, who has addressed by name all the other gods, his
acquaintances of old, professes not to know who is this insignificant being: but his reference to the hand-mill shows that in
reality he knows quite well:

> What is that little creature that I see, fawning and sneaking and
> snuffling: ever wilt thou be at the ears of Frey, and chattering at the
> quern[3].

Byggvir replies with a dignity which reminds us of the
traditional characteristics of Sir John Barleycorn, or Allan
O'Maut. For:

> Uskie-bae ne'er bure the bell
> Sae bald as Allan bure himsel[4].

---

[1] See *Lokasenna* in *Die Lieder der Edda*, herausg. von Sijmons u. Gering,
I, 134.

> Byggvir kvaþ:
> "[Veiztu] ef [ek] øþle ǽttak sem Ingunar-Freyr,
>   ok svá sǽllekt setr,
> merge smǽra mølþak [þá] meinkrǿko
>   ok lempa alla í liþo."

[2] **Lines** corresponding to these of Burns are found both in the Scotch ballad
recorded by Jamieson, and in the English ballad (Pepys Collection). See
Jamieson, *Popular Ballads and Songs*, 1806, II, 241, 256.

[3]
> Loki kvaþ:
> "Hvat's þat et lítla, es [ek] þat lǫggra sék,
>   ok snapvíst snaper?
> at eyrom Freys mont[u] ǽ vesa
>   ok und kvernom klaka."

[4] Jamieson, II, 239. So Burns: "John Barleycorn was a hero bold," and the
ballad

> John Barleycorn is the wightest man
> That ever throve in land.

Byggvir adopts the same comic-heroic pose:

> Byggvir am I named, and all gods and men call me hasty; proud am I, by reason that all the children of Odin are drinking ale together[1].

But any claims Byggvir may make to be a hero are promptly dismissed by Loki:

> Hold thou silence, Byggvir, for never canst thou share food justly among men: thou didst hide among the straw of the hall: they could not find thee, when men were fighting[2].

Now the taunts of Loki, though we must hope for the credit of Asgard that they are false, are never pointless. And such jibes as Loki addresses to Byggvir *would* be pointless, if applied to one whom we could think of as in any way like our Beowulf. Later, Beyla, wife of Byggvir, speaks, and is silenced with the words "Hold thy peace—wife thou art of Byggvir." Byggvir must have been a recognized figure of the old mythology[3], but one differing from the monster-slaying Beow of Müllenhoff's imagination.

Byggvir is a little creature (*et litla*), and we have seen above[4] that Scandinavian scholars have thought that they have discovered this old god in the Pekko who "promoted the growth of barley" among the Finns in the sixteenth century, and who is still worshipped among the Esthonians on the opposite side of the gulf as a three year old child; the form *Pekko* being derived, it is supposed, from the primitive Norse form **Beggwuz*. This is a corner of a very big subject: the discovery, among the Lapps and Finns, of traces of the heathendom of the most

---

[1]   Byggvir kvaþ:
"Byggver ek heite, en mik bráþan kveþa
        goþ ǫll ok gumar;
því emk hér hrópogr, at drekka Hrópts meger
        aller ǫl saman."

[2]   Loki kvaþ:
"þege þú, Byggver! þú kunner aldrege
        deila meþ mǫnnom mat;
[ok] þik í flets strae finna né mǫtto,
        þás vǫgo verar."

[3] This follows from the allusive way in which he and his wife are introduced —there must be a background to allusions. If the poet were inventing this figure, and had no background of knowledge in his audience to appeal to, he must have been more explicit. Cf. Olsen in Christiania *Videnskapsselskapets Skrifter*, 1914, ii, 2, 107.

[4] p. 87.

ancient Teutonic world, just as Thomsen has taught us to find
in the Finnish language traces of Teutonic words in their most
antique form.

The Lappish field has proved the most successful hunting
ground[1] : among the Finns, apart from the Thunder-god, connection with Norse beliefs is arguable mainly for a group of
gods of fruitfulness[2]. The cult of these, it is suggested, comes
from scattered Scandinavian settlers in Finland, among whom
the Finns dwelt, and from whom they learnt the worship of
the spirits of the seed and of the spring, just as they learnt
more practical lessons.   First and foremost among these stands
Pekko, whom we know to have been especially the god of barley,
and whose connection with Beow or Byggvir (*Beggwuz*) is
therefore a likely hypothesis enough[3].   Much less certain is
the connection of Sämpsä, the spirit of vegetation, with any
Germanic prototype; he may have been a god of the rush-grass[4]
(Germ. *simse*).   Runkoteivas or Rukotivo was certainly the god
of rye, and the temptation to derive his name from Old Norse
(*rugr-tivorr*, "rye-god") is great[5].   But we have not evidence for

---

[1] See Olrik, "Nordisk og Lappisk Gudsdyrkelse," *Danske Studier*, 1905,
pp. 39–57; "Tordenguden og hans dreng," 1905, pp. 129–46; "Tordenguden og
hans dreng i Lappernes myteverden," 1906, pp. 65–9; Krohn, "Lappische
beiträge zur germ. mythologie," *Finnisch-Ugrische Forschungen*, VI, 1906,
pp. 155–80.

[2] See Axel Olrik in *Festgabe f. Vilh. Thomsen*, 1912 (= *Finnisch-Ugrische
Forschungen*, XII, 1, p. 40). Olrik refers therein to his earlier paper on the
subject in *Danske Studier*, 1911, p. 38, and to a forthcoming article in the
Germanisch-Romanische Monatsschrift, which has, I think, never appeared.
See also K. Krohn in *Göttingische gelehrte Anzeigen*, 1912, p. 211. Reviewing
Meyer's *Altgermanische Religionsgeschichte*, Krohn, after referring to the Teutonic
gods of agriculture, continues "Ausser diesen agrikulturellen Gottheiten sind
aus der finnischen Mythologie mit Hülfe der Linguistik mehrere germanische
Naturgötter welche verschiedene Nutzpflanzen vertreten, entdeckt worden:
der Roggengott Runkoteivas oder Rukotivo, der Gerstengott Pekko (nach
Magnus Olsen aus urnord. Beggw-, vgl. Byggwir) und ein Gott des Futtergrases
Sämpsä (vgl. Semse od. Simse, 'die Binse')." See also Krohn, "Germanische
Elemente in der finnischen Volksdichtung," *Z.f.d.A.* LI, 1909, pp. 13–22; and
Karsten, "Einige Zeugnisse zur altnordischen Götterverehrung in Finland,"
Finnisch-Ugrische Forschungen, XII, 307–16.

[3] As proposed by K. Krohn in a publication of the Finnish Academy at
Helsingfors which I have not been able to consult, but as to which see Setälä
in *Finnisch-Ugrische Forschungen*, XIII, 311, 424. Setälä accepts the derivation
from *beqqwu-*, rejecting an alternative derivation of Pekko from a Finnish root.

[4] This is proposed by J. J. Mikkola in a note appended to the article by
K. Krohn, "Sampsa Pellervoinen < Njordr, Freyr?" in *Finnisch-Ugrische
Forschungen*, IV, 231–48. See also Olrik, "Forårsmyten hos Finnerne," in
Danske Studier, 1907, pp. 62–4.

[5] See note by K. Krohn, *Finnisch-Ugrische Forschungen*, VI, 105.

the worship among Germanic peoples of such a rye-god, as we have in the case of the barley-god Byggvir-Beow. These shadowy heathen gods, however, do give each other a certain measure of mutual support.

And, whether or no Pekko be the same as Byggvir, his worship is interesting as showing how the spirit of vegetation may be honoured among primitive folk. His worshippers, the Setukese, although nominally members of the Greek Orthodox Church, speak their own dialect and often hardly understand that of their Russian priests, but keep their old epic and lyric traditions more than almost any other section of the Finnish-Esthonian race. Pekko, who was honoured among the Finns in the sixteenth century for "promoting the growth of barley," survives among the present-day peasantry around Pskoff, not only as a spirit to be worshipped, but as an actual idol, fashioned out of wax in the form of a child, sometimes of a three year old child. He lives in the corn-bin, but on certain occasions is carried out into the fields. Not everyone can afford the amount of wax necessary for a Pekko—in fact there is usually only one in a village: he lodges in turn with different members of his circle of worshippers. He holds two moveable feasts, on moonlight nights—one in spring, the other in autumn. The wax figure is brought into a lighted room draped in a sheet, there is feasting, with dancing hand in hand, and singing round Pekko. Then they go out to decide who shall keep Pekko for the next year—his host is entitled to special blessing and protection. Pekko is carried out into the field, especially to preside over the sowing[1].

I doubt whether, in spite of the high authorities which support it, we can as yet feel at all certain about the identification of Beow and Pekko. But I think we can accept with fair certainty the identification of Beow and Byggvir. And we can at any rate use Pekko as a collateral example of the way in which a grain-spirit is regarded. Now in either case we find no support whatever for the supposition that the activities of

---

[1] See above, p. 87, and M. J. Eisen, "Ueber den Pekokultus bei den Setukesen," *Finnisch-Ugrische Forschungen*, VI, 104–11.

Beow, the spirit of the barley, could, or would, have been typified under the guise of battles such as those which Beowulf the Geat wages against Grendel, Grendel's mother, and the dragon. In Beowulf the Geat we find much that suggests the hero of folk-tale, overlaid with much that belongs to him as the hero of an heroic poem, but nothing suggestive of a corn-myth. On the other hand, so long as we confine ourselves to Beow and his ancestor Sceaf, we *are* in touch with this type of myth, however remotely. The way that Sceaf comes over the sea, as recorded by William of Malmesbury, is characteristic. That "Sheaf" should be, in the language of Müllenhoff, "placed in a boat and committed to the winds and waves in the hope that he will return new-born in the spring" is exactly what we might expect, from the analogy of harvest customs and myths of the coming of spring.

In Sætersdale, in Norway, when the ice broke up in the spring, and was driven ashore, the inhabitants used to welcome it by throwing their hats into the air, and shouting "Welcome, Corn-boat." It was a good omen if the "Corn-boats" were driven high and dry up on the land[1]. The floating of the sheaf on a shield down the Thames at Abingdon[2] reminds us of the Bulgarian custom, in accordance with which the venerated last sheaf of the harvest was floated down the river[3]. But every neighbourhood is not provided with convenient rivers, and in many places the last sheaf is merely drenched with water. This is an essential part of the custom of "crying the neck."

The precise ritual of "crying the neck" or "crying the mare" was confined to the west and south-west of England[4]. But there is no such local limitation about the custom of drenching the

---

[1] See M. Olsen, *Hedenske Kultminder i Norske Stedsnavne*, Christiania *Videnskapsselskapets Skrifter*, II, 2, 1914, pp. 227–8.

[2] See above, p. 84.

[3] Mannhardt, *Mythologische Forschungen*, 332.

[4] In view of the weight laid upon this custom by Olrik as illustrating the story of Sceaf, it is necessary to note that it seems to be confined to parts of England bordering on the "Celtic fringe." See above, pp. 81, *etc.* Olrik and Olsen quote it as Kentish (see *Heltedigtning*, II, 252) but this is certainly wrong. Frazer attributes the custom of "crying the mare" to Hertfordshire and Shropshire (*Spirits of the Corn*, I, 292 = *Golden Bough*, 3rd edit., VII, 292). In this he is following Brand's *Popular Antiquities* (1813, I, 443; 1849, II, 24; also Carew Hazlitt, 1905, I, 157). But Brand's authority is Blount's *Glossographia*, 1674, and Blount says *Herefordshire*.

last sheaf, or its bearers and escort, with water. This has been recorded, among other places, at Hitchin in Hertfordshire[1], in Cambridgeshire[2], Nottinghamshire[3], Pembrokeshire[4], Wigtown-shire[5] as well as in Holstein[6], Westphalia[7], Prussia[8], Galicia[9], Saxon Transsylvania[10], Roumania[11] and perhaps in ancient Phrygia[12].

Now it is true that drenching the last sheaf with water, as a rain charm, is by no means the same thing as floating it down the river, in the expectation that it will come again in the spring. But it shows the same sense of the continued existence of the corn-spirit. That the *seed*, when sown, should be sprinkled with water as a rain charm (as is done in places) seems obvious and natural enough. But when the *last sheaf* of the preceding harvest is thus sprinkled, to ensure plenteous rain upon the crops of next year, we detect the same idea of continuity which we find expressed when Sceaf comes to land from over the sea: the spirit embodied in the sheaf of last year's harvest returning, and bringing the renewed power of vegetation.

The voyage of the Abingdonian sheaf on the Thames was conducted upon a shield, and it may be that the "vessel without a rower" in which "Sheaf" came to land was, in the original version, a shield. There would be precedent for this. The shield was known by the puzzling name of "Ull's ship" in Scaldic poetry, presumably because the god Ull used his shield as a boat. Anyway, Scyld came to be closely connected with Sceaf and Beow. In Ethelwerd he is son of the former and father of the latter: but in the *Chronicle* genealogies five names intervene between Scyld and Sceaf, and the son of Sceaf is Bedwig, or as he is called in one version, Beowi. *Bedwig* and *Beowi* are probably derived from *Beowius*, the Latinized

[1] Brand, *Popular Antiquities*, 1849, II, 24.
[2] Frazer in the *Folk-Lore Journal*, VII, 1889, pp. 50, 51; *Adonis, Attis and Osiris*, I, 237.
[3] Frazer, *Adonis, Attis and Osiris*, I, 238 (*Golden Bough*, 3rd edit.).
[4] Frazer, *Spirits of the Corn and of the Wild*, I, 143–4.
[5] Frazer in the *Folk-Lore Journal*, VII, 1889, pp. 50, 51.
[6] Mannhardt, *Forschungen*, 317.
[7] Frazer, *Spirits of the Corn*, I, 138.
[8] Mannhardt, 323; Fraser, *Adonis*, I, 238.
[9] Mannhardt, 330.   [10] Mannhardt, 24; Frazer, *Adonis*, I, 238.
[11] Frazer, *Adonis*, I, 237.   [12] Frazer, *Spirits of the Corn*, I, 217

form of *Beow*. A badly formed *o* might easily be mistaken for a *d*, and indeed *Beowius* appears in forms much more corrupt. In that case it would appear that while some genealogies made Beow the son of Scyld, others made him son of Sceaf, and that the compiler of the pedigree got over the difficulty in the usual way, by adding the one version to the other[1].

But all this is very hypothetical; and how and when Scyld came to be connected with Sceaf and with Beow we cannot with any certainty say. At any rate we find no trace of such connection in Danish traditions of the primitive King Skjold of the Danes. But we can say, with some certainty, that in Beowulf the Dane, the son of Scyld Scefing, in our poem, we have a figure which is identical with Beow, son of Scyld or of Sceldwa and descendant of Sceaf, in the genealogies, and that this Beow is likely to have been an ancient corn-spirit, parallel to the Scandinavian Byggvir. That amount of mythology probably *does* underlie the *Prologue* to *Beowulf*, though the author would no doubt have been highly scandalized had he suspected that his pattern of a young prince was only a disguised heathen god. But I think that any further attempt to proceed, from this, to mythologize the deeds of Beowulf the Geat, is pure conjecture, and probably quite fruitless conjecture.

I ought not to conclude this note without reference to the admirable discussion of this subject by Prof. Björkman in *Englische Studien*[2]. This, with the elucidation of other proper names in *Beowulf*, was destined to be the last big contribution to knowledge made by that ripe and good scholar, whose premature loss we all deplore; and it shows to the full those qualities of wide knowledge and balanced judgment which we have all learnt to admire in him.

B.   GRENDEL

It may be helpful to examine the places where the name of Grendel occurs in English charters.

---

[1] See Björkman in *Anglia, Beiblatt*, xxx, 1919, p. 23. In a similar way Sceaf appears twice in William of Malmesbury, once as Sceaf and once as Strephius.
[2] Vol. LII, p. 145.

A.D. 708. Grant of land at Abbots Morton, near Alcester, co. Worcester, by Kenred, King of the Mercians, to Evesham (extant in a late copy).

Ǣrest of grindeles pytt on wiðimǣre; of wiðimǣre on þǣt rēade slōh...of ðēre dice on þene blace pōl; of þām pōle ǣfter long pidele in tō þām mersce ; of þām mersce þā ǣft on grindeles pytt[1].

The valley of the Piddle Brook is about a mile wide, with hills rising on each side till they reach a height of a couple of hundred feet above the brook. The directions begin in the valley and run "From Grindel's 'pytt' to the willow-mere; from the willow-mere to the red morass"; then from the morass the directions take us up the hill and along the lea, where they continue among the downs till we again make our descent into the valley, "from the ditch to the black pool, from the pool along the Piddle brook to the marsh, and from the marsh back to Grindel's 'pytt.'" In modern English a "pit" is an artificial hole which is generally dry: but the word is simply Latin *puteus*, "a well," and is used in this sense in the Gospel translations. Here it is a hole, and we may be sure that, with the willow-mere and the red slough on the one side, and the black pool and the marsh on the other, the hole was full of water.

A.D. 739. Grant of land at Creedy, co. Devon, by Æthelheard, King of Wessex, to Bishop Forthhere.

of doddan hrycge on grendeles pyt; of grendeles pytte on ifigbearo (ivy-grove)...[2].

The spot is near the junction of the rivers Exe and Creedy, with Dartmoor in the distance. The neighbourhood bears uncanny names, *Cāines ǣcer, egesan trēow*. If, as has been suggested by Napier and Stevenson, a trace of this pit still survives in the name Pitt farm, the mere must have been in the uplands, about 600 feet above sea level.

---

[1] *MS Cott. Vesp. B. XXIV*, fol. 32 (Evesham Cartulary). See Birch, *Cart. Sax.* I, 176 (No. 120); Kemble, *Cod. Dipl.* III, 376. Kemble prints *þæt æjt* for *þā æft* (MS "þ æft"). For examples of "þ" for *þā*, see *Ælfrics Grammatik*, herausg. Zupitza, 1880; 38, 3; 121, 4; 291, 1.

[2] There are two copies, one of the tenth and one of the eleventh century, among the Crawford Collection in the Bodleian. See Birch, *Cart. Sax.* III, 667 (No. 1331); Napier and Stevenson, *The Crawford Collection* (*Anecdota Oxoniensia*), 1895, pp. 1, 3, 50.

A.D. 931. Grant of land at Ham in Wiltshire by Athelstan to his thane Wulfgar. Quoted above, p. 43. It is in this charter that *on Bēowan hammes hecgan, on Grendles mere*[1] occur.

"Grendel pits or meres" are in most other cases in low-lying marshy country: but this, like (perhaps) the preceding one, is in the uplands—it must have been a lonely mere among the hills, under Inkpen Beacon.

Circa A.D. 957. A list of boundaries near Battersea[2].

Ðis synd ðā landgemǣre tō Batriceseie. Ǣrst at hēgefre; fram hēgefre to gǣtenesheale; fram gǣteneshǣle to gryndeles syllen; fram gryndeles sylle to russemere; fram ryssemere to bǣlgenham....

All this is low-lying land, just south of the Thames. *Hēgefre* is on the river; *Bǣlgenham* is Balham, co. Surrey. "From Grendel's mire to the rushy mere" harmonizes excellently with what we know of the swampy nature of this district in early times.

A.D. 958. Grant of land at Swinford, on the Stour, co. Stafford, by King Eadred to his thane Burhelm[3].

Ondlong bæces wið neopan eostacote; ondlong dīces in grendels-mere; of grendels-mere in stāncōfan; of stāncōfan ondlong dūne on stiran mere....

A.D. 972. Confirmation of lands to Pershore Abbey (Worcester) by King Edgar[4].

of Grindles bece swā þæt gemǣre ligð....

A.D. 972. Extract from an account of the descent of lands belonging to Westminster, quoting a grant of King Edgar[5].

andlang hagan to grendeles gatan æfter kincges mearce innan brægentan....

The property described is near Watling Street, between Edgware, Hendon, and the River Brent. It is a low-lying

---

[1] *MS Cotton Ch. VIII*, 16. See Birch, *Cart. Sax.* II, 363 (No. 677); Kemble, *Cod. Dipl.* II, 172.
[2] A nearly contemporary copy: *Westminster Abbey Charters*, III. See Birch, *Cart. Sax.* III, 189 (No. 994), and W. B. Sanders, *Ord. Surv. Facs.* II, plate III.
[3] A fourteenth to fifteenth century copy preserved at Wells Cathedral (*Registr. Album*, f. 289 *b*). See Birch, *Cart. Sax.* III, 223 (No. 1023).
[4] *MS Cotton Aug. II*, 6. See Birch, *Cart. Sax.* III, 588 (No. 1282).
[5] *Brit. Mus. Stowe Chart.* No. 32. See Birch, *Cart. Sax.* III, 605 (No. 1290)

district almost surrounded by the hills of Hampstead, Highgate, Barnet, Mill Hill, Elstree, Bushey Heath and Harrow. The bottom of the basin thus formed must have been a swamp[1]. What the "gate" may have been it is difficult to say. A foreign scholar has suggested that it may have been a narrow mountain defile or possibly a cave[2]: but this suggestion could never have been made by anyone who knew the country. The "gate" is likely to have been a channel connecting two meres—or it might have been a narrow piece of land between them—one of those *enge ānpaðas* which Grendel and his mother had to tread. Anyway, there is nothing exceptional in this use of "gate" in connection with a water-spirit. Necker, on the Continent, also had his "gates." Thus there is a "Neckersgate Mill" near Brussels, and the name "Neckersgate" used also to be applied to a group of houses near by, surrounded by water[3].

All the other places clearly point to a water-spirit: two meres, two pits, a mire and a beck: for the most part situated in low-lying country which must in Anglo-Saxon times have been swampy. All this harmonizes excellently with the *fenfreoðo* of *Beowulf* (l. 851). Of course it does not in the least follow that these places were named after the Grendel of our poem. It may well be that there was in England a current belief in a creature Grendel, dwelling among the swamps. Von Sydow has compared the Yorkshire belief in Peg Powler, or the Lancashire Jenny Greenteeth. But these aquatic monsters are not exactly parallel; for they abide in the water, and are dangerous only to those who attempt to cross it, or at any rate venture too near the bank[4], whilst Grendel and even his mother are capable of excursions of some distance from their fastness amid the fens.

---

[1] Cf. the *Victoria History*, Middlesex, II, p. 1.

[2] "*Grendeles gate* har väl snarast varit någon naturbildning t. ex. ett trångt bergpass eller kanske en grotta": C. W. von Sydow, in an excellent article on *Grendel i anglosaxiska ortnamn*, in *Nordiska Ortnamn: Hyllningsskrift tillägnad A. Noreen*, Upsala, 1914, pp. 160–4.

[3] Près du *Neckersgat molen*, il y avait jadis, antérieurement aux guerres de religion, des maisons entourées d'eau et appelées *de hoffstede te Neckersgate*: Wauters (A.), *Histoire des Environs de Bruxelles*, 1852, III, 646.

[4] Peg Powler lived in the Tees, and devoured children who played on the banks, especially on Sundays: Peg o' Nell, in the Ribble, demanded a life every seven years. See Henderson (W.), *Notes on the Folk-Lore of the Northern Counties of England*, 1879 (*Folk-Lore Society*), p. 265.

Of course the mere-haunting Grendel *may* have been identified only at a comparatively late date with the spirit who
struggles with the hero in the house, and flees below the earth
in the folk-tale.

At any rate belief in a Grendel, haunting mere and fen, is
clearly demonstrable for England—at any rate for the south
and west of England: for of these place-names two belong to
the London district, one to Wiltshire, one to Devonshire, two
to Worcester and one to Stafford. The place-name *Grendele* in
Yorkshire is too doubtful to be of much help. (*Domesday Book*,
I, 302.) It is the modern village Grindale, four miles N.W. of
Bridlington. From it, probably, is derived the surname *Grindle*,
Grindall (Bardsley).

Abroad, the nearest parallel is to be found in Transsylvania,
where there is a *Grändels môr* among the Saxons of the Senndorf
district, near Bistritz. The Saxons of Transsylvania are supposed to have emigrated from the neighbourhood of the lower
Rhine and the Moselle, and there is a *Grindelbach* in Luxemburg
which may possibly be connected with the marsh demon[1].

Most of the German names in *Grindel-* or *Grendel-* are connected with *grendel*, "a bar," and therefore do not come into
consideration here[2]: but the Transsylvanian "Grendel's marsh[3],"
anyway, reminds us of the English "Grendel's marsh" or "mere"
or "pit." Nevertheless, the local story with which the Transsylvanian swamp is connected—that of a peasant who was
ploughing with six oxen and was swallowed up in the earth—
is such that it requires considerable ingenuity to see any connection between it and the *Beowulf-Grendel*-tale[4].

[1] See Kisch (G.), *Vergleichendes Wörterbuch der siebenbürgischen und moselfränkischluxemburgischen Mundart, nebst siebenbürgischniederrheinischem Ortsund Familiennamen-verzeichnis* (vol. XXXIII, 1 of the *Archiv des Vereins f.
siebenbürg. Landeskunde*, 1905).

[2] See *Grindel* in Förstemann (E.), *Altdeutsches Namenbuch*, Dritte Aufl.,
herausg. Jellinghaus, II, 1913, and in Fischer (H.), *Schwäbisches Wörterbuch*,
III, 1911 (nevertheless Rooth legitimately calls attention to the names recorded
by Fischer in which *Grindel* is connected with *bach*, *teich* and *moos*).

[3] There is an account of this by G. Kisch in the *Festgabe zur Feier der
Einweihung des neuen evang. Gymnasial Bürger- und Elementar-schulgebäudes in
Besztercze (Bistritz) am 7 Oct.* 1911; a document which I have not been able to
procure.

[4] Such a connection is attempted by W. Benary in Herrig's *Archiv*, CXXX, 154.
Alternative suggestions, which would exclude any connection with the Grendel
of *Beowulf*, are made by Klaeber, in *Archiv*, CXXXI, 427.

The Anglo-Saxon place-names may throw some light upon the meaning and etymology of "Grendel[1]." The name has generally been derived from *grindan*, "to grind"; either directly[2], because Grendel grinds the bones of those he devours, or indirectly, in the sense of "tormentor[3]." Others would connect with O.N. *grindill*, "storm," and perhaps with M.E. *gryndel*, "angry[4]." It has recently been proposed to connect the word with *grund*, "bottom": for Grendel lives in the *mere-grund* or *grund-wong* and his mother is the *grund-wyrgin*. Erik Rooth, who proposes this etymology, compares the Icelandic *grandi*, "a sandbank," and the common Low German dialect word *grand*, "coarse sand[5]." This brings us back to the root "to grind," for *grand*, "sand" is simply the product of the grinding of the waves[6]. Indeed the same explanation has been given of the word "ground[7]."

However this may be, the new etymology differs from the old in giving Grendel a name derived, not from his grinding or tormenting others, but from his dwelling at the bottom of the lake or marsh[8]. The name would have a parallel in the Modern English *grindle*, *grundel*, German *grundel*[9], a fish haunting the bottom of the water.

The Old English place-names, associating Grendel as they do with meres and swamps, seem rather to support this.

As to the Devonshire stream *Grendel* (now the Grindle or Greendale Brook), it has been suggested that this name is also

---

[1] A very useful summary of the different etymologies proposed is made by Rooth in *Anglia, Beiblatt*, xxviii (1917), 335–8.

[2] So Skeat, "On the significance of the monster Grendel," *Journal of Philology*, Cambridge, xv (1886), p. 123; Laistner, *Rätsel der Sphinx*, 1889, p. 23; Holthausen, in his edition.

[3] So Weinhold in the *SB. der k. Akad. Wien, Phil.-Hist. Classe*, xxvi, 255.

[4] Cf. Gollancz, *Patience*, 1913, Glossary. For *grindill* as one of the synonyms for "storm," see *Ed la Snorra Sturlusonar*, Hafniae, 1852. ii, 486, 569.

[5] This will be found in several of the vocabularies of Low German dialects published by the *Verein für Niederdeutsche Sprachforschung*.

[6] See *grand* in Falk and Torp, *Etymologisk Ordbog*, Kristiania, 1903–6.

[7] See Feist, *Etymol. Wörterbuch der Gotischen Sprache*, Halle, 1909; *grunduwaddjus*.

[8] With Grendel, thus explained, Rooth would connect the "Earth man" of the fairy-tale "Dat Erdmänneken" (see below, p. 370) and the name *Sandhaug, Sandey*, which clings to the Scandinavian *Grettir-* and *Orm-*stories. We have seen that a *sandhaug* figures also in one of the Scandinavian cognates of the folk-tale (see above, p. 67). These resemblances may be noted, though it would be perilous to draw deductions from them.

[9] *Schweizerisches Idiotikon*, ii, 1885, p. 776.

connected with the root *grand*, "gravel," "sand." But, so far
as I have been able to observe, there is no particular suggestion
of sand or gravel about this modest little brook. If we follow
the River Clyst from the point where the Grindle flows into it,
through two miles of marshy land, to the estuary of the Exe,
we shall there find plenty. But it is clear from the charter of
963 that the name was then, as now, restricted to the small
brook. I cannot tell why the stream should bear the name, or
what, if any, is the connection with the monster Grendel. We
can only note that the name is again found attached to water,
and, near the junction with the Clyst, to marshy ground.

Anyone who will hunt Grendel through the shires, first on
the 6-in. ordnance map, and later on foot, will probably have to
agree with the Three Jovial Huntsmen

This huntin' doesn't pay,
But we'n powler't up an' down a bit, an' had a rattlin' day.

But, if some conclusions, although scanty, can be drawn
from place-names in which the word *grendel* occurs, nothing
can be got from the numerous place-names which have been
thought to contain the name *Bēow*. The clearest of these is
the *on Bēowan hammes hecgan*, which occurs in the Wiltshire
charter of 931. But we can learn nothing definite from it: and
although there are other instances of strong and weak forms
alternating, we cannot even be quite certain that the Bcowa
here is identical with the Beow of the genealogies[1].

The other cases, many of which occur in *Domesday Book*
are worthless. Those which point to a weak form may often
be derived from the weak noun *bēo*, "bee": "The Anglo-Saxons
set great store by their bees, honey and wax being indispensables
to them[2]."

Bēas brōc, Bēas feld (*Bewes feld*) occur in charters: but here
a connection with *bēaw*, "horsefly," is possible: for parallels, one
has only to consider the long list of places enumerated by
Björkman, the names of which are derived from those of beasts,

---

[1] See above. pp. 43, *etc.*; below, p. 311.
[2] Duignan, *Warwickshire Place Names*, p. 22. Duignan suggests the same
etymology for *Beoshelle*, *beos* being "the Norman scribe's idea of the gen. plu."
This, however, is very doubtful.

birds, or insects[1]. And in such a word as *Bēolēah*, even if the
first element be *bēow*, why may it not be the common noun
"barley," and not the name of the hero at all?

No argument can therefore be drawn from such a conjecture
as that of Olrik, that *Bēas brōc* refers to the water into which
the last sheaf (representing Beow) was thrown, in accordance
with the harvest custom, and in the expectation of the return
of the spirit in the coming spring[2].

C. THE STAGES ABOVE WODEN IN THE WEST-SAXON GENEALOGY

The problems to which this pedigree gives rise are very
numerous, and some have been discussed above. There are
four which seem to need further discussion.

(I) A "Sceafa" occurs in *Widsith* as ruling over the
Longobards. Of course we cannot be certain that this hero is
identical with the Sceaf of the genealogy. Now there is no one
in the long list of historic or semi-historic Longobard kings,
ruling after the tribe had left Scandinavia, who bears a name
at all similar. It seems therefore reasonable to suppose that
Sceafa, if he is a genuine Longobard king at all, belongs to the
primitive times when the Longobardi or Winnili dwelt in
"Scadan," before the historic or semi-historic times with which
our extant list deals. And Old English accounts, although
making Sceaf an ancestor of the Saxon kings, are unanimous in
connecting him with Scani or Scandza.

Some scholars[3] have seen a serious difficulty in the weak
form "Sceafa," as compared with "Sceaf." But we have the
exactly parallel cases of *Horsa*[4] compared with *Hors*[5], and
Hrǣdla[6] compared with *Hrǣdel*[7], *Hrēðel*. Parallel, but not
quite so certain, are *Sceldwa*[8] and *Scyld*[9], *Gēata*[10] and *Gēat*[11],
Bēowa[12] and *Bēaw*, *Bēo(w)*[13].

---

[1] *Engl. Stud.* LII, 177.   [2] *Heltedigtning*, II, 255. See above, pp. 81–7.
[3] Binz in *P.B.B.* XX, 148; Chadwick, *Origin*, 282. So Clarke, *Sidelights*,
128. Cf. Heusler in *A.f.d. A.* XXX, 31.
[4] *A.-S. Chronicle.*   [5] *Historia Brittonum.*
[6] "hrædlan" (gen.), *Beowulf*, 454.   [7] "hrædles," *Beowulf*, 1485.
[8] *A.-S. Chronicle.*   [9] *Beowulf*, Ethelwerd.
[10] Geata, Geta, *Historia Brittonum*; Asser; *MS Cott. Tib. A. VI*; *Textus
Roffensis.*
[11] *A.-S. Chronicle.*   [12] Charter of 931.   [13] *A.-S. Chronicle*, Ethelwerd.

I do not think it has ever been doubted that the forms *Hors* and *Horsa*, or *Hrēðel* and *Hrǣdla*, relate to one and the same person. Prof. Chadwick seems to have little or no doubt as to the identity of *Scyld* and *Sceldwa*[1], or *Bēo* and *Bēowa*[2]. Why then should the identity of *Scēaf* and *Scēafa* be denied because one form is strong and the other weak[3]? We cannot demonstrate the identity of the figure in the genealogies with the figure in *Widsith*; but little difficulty is occasioned by the weak form.

(II) Secondly, the absence of the name *Scēaf* from the oldest MS of the *Chronicle* (the *Parker MS, C.C.C.C.* 173) has been made the ground for suggesting that when that MS was written (*c.* 892) Sceaf had not yet been invented (Möller, *Volksepos*, 43; Symons in *Pauls Grdr.* (2), III, 645; Napier, as quoted by Clarke, *Sidelights*, 125). But Sceaf, and the other names which are omitted from the *Parker MS*, are found in the other MSS of the *Chronicle* and the allied pedigrees, which are known to be derived independently from one and the same original. Now, unless the names were older than the *Parker MS*, they could not appear in so many independent transcripts. For, even though these transcripts are individually later, their *agreement* takes us back to a period earlier than that of the *Parker MS* itself[4].

An examination of the different versions of the genealogy, given on pp. 202–3, above, and of the tree showing the connection between them, on p. 315, will, I think, make this clear.

The versions of the pedigree given in the *Parker MS* of the *Chronicle*, in Asser and in *Textus Roffensis I*, all contain the stages *Friþuwald* and *Friþuwulf*. Asser and *Roff. I* are connected by the note about *Gēata*: but *Roff. I* is not derived from that text of Asser which has come down to us, as that

---

[1] *Origin*, 273.   [2] *Origin*, 282.

[3] Some O.H.G. parallels will be found in *Z.f.d.A.* XII, 260. The weak form *Gēata*, Mr Stevenson argues, is due to Asser's attempt to reconcile the form *Gēat* with the Latin *Geta* with which he identifies it (Asser, pp. 160–161). See also Chadwick, *Heroic Age*, 124 footnote. Yet we get *Gēata* in one text of the *Chronicle*, and in other documents.

[4] This is the view taken by Plummer, who does not seem to regard any solution as possible other than that the names are missing from the *Parker MS* by a transcriber's slip (see *Two Saxon Chronicles Parallel*, II, p. xciv).

text has corrupted *Fin* and *Godwulf* into one name and
has substituted *Seth* for *Scēaf* ["Seth, *Saxonice* Sceaf":
Florence of Worcester]. *Roff. I* is free from both these
corruptions.

Ethelwerd is obviously connected with a type of genealogy
giving the stages *Friþuwald* and *Friþuwulf*, but differs from all
the others in giving no stages between *Scyld* and *Scēf*.

None of the other versions contain the names *Friþuwald* and
Friþuwulf. They are closely parallel, but fall into groups
showing special peculiarities.

MSS Tib. A. VI and *Tib. B. I* of the *Chronicle* show only
trifling differences of spelling. The MSS belong respectively
to about the years 1000 and 1050, and are both derived from
an Abingdon original of about 977[1].

MS Cott. Tib. B. IV is derived from a copy of the *Chronicle*
sent North about 892[2].

MS Cott. Tib. B. V and *Textus Roffensis II* are closely
connected, but neither is derived from the other. For *Roff. II*
preserves *Teþwa* and *Hwāla*, who are lost in *Tib. B. V*; *Tib. B. V*
preserves *Iterman*, who is corrupted in *Roff. II*. Both *Tib. B. V*
and *Roff. II* carry the pedigree down to Edgar, mentioning
his three sons *Ēadweard and Ēadmund and Æþelred æðelingas
syndon Ēadgāres suna cyninges*. The original therefore apparently belongs to some date before 970, when Edmund died
(cf. Stevenson's Asser, 158, note).

Common features of *MS Cott. Tib. B. V* and *Roff. II* are
(1) *Eat(a)* for *Geat(a)*, (2) the omission of *d* from *Scealdwa*, and
(3) the expression *se Scēf*, "this Scef." Features (1) and (3)
are copied in the Icelandic pedigrees. *Scealdwa* is given correctly there, but the Icelandic transcriber could easily have got
it from *Scealdwaging* above. The Icelandic was, then, ultimately derived either from *Tib. B. V* or from a version so
closely connected as not to be worth distinguishing.

Accordingly *Cott. Tib. B. V, Textus Roffensis II, Langfeðgatal* and *Flateyjarbók* form one group, pointing to an archetype *c.* 970.

---

[1] Plummer, II, pp. xxix, xxxi, lxxxix.
[2] Plummer, II, p. lxxi. Note *Beowi* for *Bedwig*.

The pedigrees can accordingly be grouped on the system shown on the opposite page[1].

(III) Prof. Chadwick, in his *Origin of the English Nation*, draws wide deductions from the fact that the Danes traced the pedigree of their kings back to Skjold, whilst the West-Saxons included Sceldwa (Scyld) in their royal pedigree:

> "Since the Angli and the Danes claimed descent from the same ancestor, there can be no doubt that the bond was believed to be one of blood [2]."

This belief, Prof. Chadwick thinks, went back to exceedingly early times[3], and he regards it as well-founded:

> "It is true that the Angli of Britain seem never to have included themselves among the Danes, but the reason for this may be that the term *Dene* (*Danir*) had not come into use as a collective term before the invasion of Britain[4]."

Doubtless the fact that the name of a Danish king *Scyld* or *Sceldwa* is found in a pedigree of West-Saxon kings, as drawn up at a period certainly not later than 892, points to a belief, at that date, in some kind of a connection. But we have still to ask: How close was the connection supposed to be? And how old is the belief?

Firstly as to the closeness of the connection. Finn also occurs in the pedigree—possibly the Frisian king: Sceaf occurs, possibly, though not certainly, a Longobard king. Noah and Adam occur; are we therefore to suppose that the compiler of the *Genealogy* believed his kings to be of one blood with the Hebrews? Certainly he did: but only remotely, as common descendants of Noah. And the occurrence of Sceldwa and Sceaf and Finn in the genealogies—granting the identity of these heroes with Skjold of the Danes, Sceafa of the Longobards and Finn of the Frisians, might only prove that the genealogist believed in their common (Germanic) race.

Secondly, how old is the belief? The Anglian genealogies (Northumbrian, Mercian and East Anglian), as reproduced in

---

[1] This table shows the relationship of the genealogies only, not of the whole MSS, of which the genealogies form but a small part. MS-relationships are always liable to fluctuation, as we pass from one part of a MS to another, and for obvious reasons this is peculiarly the case with the *Chronicle* MSS.

[2] *Origin*, 295. [3] *Origin*, 292. [4] *Origin*, 296.

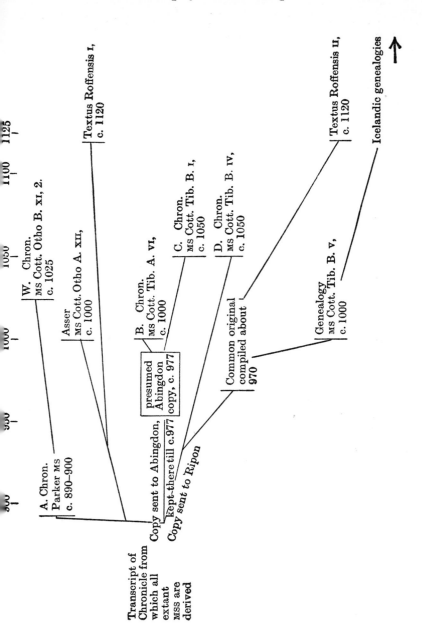

Textus Roffensis I,
c. 1120

W. Chron.
MS Cott. Otho B. XI, 2.
c. 1025

Asser
MS Cott. Otho A. XII,
c. 1000

Textus Roffensis II,
c. 1120

Icelandic genealogies

C. Chron.
MS Cott. Tib. B. I,
c. 1050

D. Chron.
MS Cott. Tib. B. IV,
c. 1050

B. Chron.
MS Cott. Tib. A. VI,
c. 1000

Common original
compiled about
970

Genealogy
MS Cott. Tib. B. v,
c. 1000

presumed
Abingdon
copy, c. 977

A. Chron.
Parker MS
c. 890–900

Copy sent to Abingdon,
Kept-there till c.977
Copy sent to Ripon

Transcript of
Chronicle from
which all
extant
MSS are
derived

the *Historia Brittonum* and in the *Vespasian MS*, form part
of what is doubtless, as is said above, the oldest extant English
historical document. But in this document *there is no mention
of Scyld.* Indeed, it contains no pedigree of the West-Saxon
kings at all. From whatever cause, the West-Saxon genealogy
is not extant from so early a date as are the pedigrees of the
Northumbrian, Mercian, East Anglian and Kentish kings[1]. Still,
this may well be a mere accident, and I am not prepared to
dispute that the pedigree which traces the West-Saxon kings
to Woden dates back, like the other genealogies connecting
Old English kings with Woden, to primitive and heathen times.
Now the West-Saxon pedigree is found in many forms: some
which trace the royal house only to Woden, and some which go
beyond Woden and contain a list of names by which Woden
is connected with Sceaf, and then with Noah and Adam.

(1) The nucleus of the whole pedigree is to be found in the
names between Cynric or Cerdic and Woden. These occur in
every version. The pedigree in this, its simplest form, is found
twice among the entries in the *Chronicle* which deal with the
events of heathen times, under 552 and 597. These names fall
into verse:

> [Cynrīc Cerdicing], Cerdic Elesing,
> Elesa Esling, Esla GiWising,
> GiWis Wīging, Wīg Frēawining,
> Frēawine Friðugāring, Friðugār Bronding,
> Brond Bǽldæging, Bǽldæg Wōdening.

Like the mnemonic lists in *Widsith*, these lines are probably
very old. Their object is clearly to connect the founder of the
West-Saxon royal house with Woden. Note, that not only do
the names alliterate, but the alliteration is perfect. Every line
attains double alliteration in the first half, with one alliterating
word only in the second half. The lines must go back to times
when lists of royal ancestors, both real and imaginary, had to

---

[1] The absence of the West-Saxon pedigree may be due to the document
from which the *Historia Brittonum* and the *Vespasian MS* derive these pedigrees
having been drawn up in the North: Wessex may have been outside the purview
of its compiler; though against this is the fact that it contains the Kentish
pedigree. But another quite possible explanation is, that Cerdic, with his odd
name, was not of the right royal race, but an adventurer, and that it was only
later that a pedigree was made up for his descendants, on the analogy of those
possessed by the more blue-blooded monarchs of Mercia and Northumbria.

be arranged in correct verse; times when such things were recorded by memory rather than by writing. They are pre-literary, and were doubtless chanted by retainers of the West-Saxon kings in heathen days.

(2) An expanded form of this genealogy occurs in *MSS C.C.C.C.* 183 and *Cotton Tib. B. V.* Woden is here furnished with a father Frealaf. We know nothing of any Frealaf as father of the All-Father in heathen days, though Frealaf is found in this capacity in other genealogies written down in the ages after the conversion. Frealaf breaks the correct alliterative system. In both MSS the pedigree is brought down to King Ine (688–726): both MSS are ultimately, no doubt, derived from a list current in the time of that king, that is to say less than a century after the conversion of Wessex.

(3) A further expansion, which Prof. Napier has held on linguistic grounds[1] to have been written down as early as 750, is incorporated in a genealogical and chronological note regarding the West-Saxon kings, which is extant in many MSS[2]. *In its present form* this genealogical note is a recension, under Alfred, of a document coming down to the death of his father Æthelwulf. It traces the pedigree of Æthelwulf to Cerdic, but it keeps this distinct from the rhythmical nucleus, in which it traces Cerdic to Woden, and no further.

(4) Then, in the *Anglo-Saxon Chronicle*, under the year 855, the pedigree is given in its most elaborate form. There the genealogy of Æthelwulf is traced in one unbroken series, not merely through Cerdic to Woden, but from Woden through a long line of Woden's ancestors, including Frealaf, Geat, Sceldwa and Sceaf, to Noah and Adam.

It has been noted above[3] that none of the *Chronicle* pedigrees

---

[1] See *M.L.N.* 1897, XII, 110–11.

[2] It is prefixed to the *Parker MS* of the *Chronicle*, and is found also in the Cambridge MS of the Anglo-Saxon Bede (*Univ. Lib. Kk.* 3. 18) printed in Miller's edition; in *MS Cott. Tib. A. III*, 178 (printed in Thorpe's *Chronicle*): and in *MS Add.* 34652, printed by Napier in *M.L.N.* 1897, XII, 106 *etc.* There are uncollated copies in *MS C.C.C.C.* 383, fol. 107, and according to Liebermann (Herrig's *Archiv*, CIV, 23) in the *Textus Roffensis*, fol. 7 *b.* There is also a fragment, which does not however include the portion under consideration, in *MS Add.* 23211 (*Brit. Mus.*) printed in Sweet's *Oldest English Texts*, p. 179. The statement, sometimes made, that there is a copy in *MS C.C.C.C.* 41, rests on an error of Whelock, who was really referring to the *Parker MS* of the *Chronicle* (*C.C.C.C.* 173).

[3] p. 73.

stop at Sceaf. The *Chronicle*, in the stages above Woden, recognizes as stopping places only Geat (Northumbrian pedigree, anno 547) or Adam (West-Saxon pedigree, anno 855).

(5) The Chronicle of Ethelwerd (*c.* 1000) does, however, stop at Scef[1]. Now it has been argued that Ethelwerd's pedigree is merely abbreviated from the pedigree in the *Anglo-Saxon Chronicle* under 855, and that, in making Scef the final stage, and in what he tells us about that hero, Ethelwerd is merely adapting what he had read in *Beowulf* about Scyld[2]. But this seems hardly possible. Ethelwerd, it is true, borrows most of his facts from the *Chronicle*, from Bede, and other known sources: but there are some passages which show that he had access to a source now lost. Ethelwerd was a member of the West-Saxon royal house, and he wrote his Chronicle for a kinswoman, Matilda, in order, as he says, to explain their common stock and race. They were both descended from Æthelwulf, the chronicler being great-great-grandson of Æthelred, and the lady to whom he dedicates his work being great-great-granddaughter of Alfred. So he writes to tell "who and whence were their kin, so far as memory adduces, and our parents have taught us." Accordingly, though he begins his Chronicle with the Creation, the bulk of it is devoted to the deeds of his or Matilda's ancestors. Is it credible that he would have cut out all the stages in their common pedigree between Scyld and Scef, that he would have sacrificed all the ancestors of Scef, thus severing relations with Noah and Adam, and that he would have attributed to Scef the story which in *Beowulf* is attributed to Scyld, all this simply in order to bring his English pedigree into some harmony with what is told about the Danish pedigree in *Beowulf*—a poem of which we have no evidence that he had ever heard?

To suppose him to have done this, is to make him sacrifice, *without any reason*, just that part of the pedigree in the *Chronicle* under 855 which, from all we know of Ethelwerd, was most likely to have interested him: that which connected his race with Noah and Adam. Further, it is to suppose him to have reproduced just those stages in the pedigree which on critical

---

[1] See above, p. 70, and p. 202.
[2] Brandl in Herrig's *Archiv*, cxxxvii, 12–13.

grounds modern scholars can show to be the oldest, and to have modified or rejected just those which on critical grounds modern scholars can show to be later accretion. When Brandl supposes Ethelwerd to have produced his pedigree by comparing together merely the materials which have come down to us to-day, namely *Beowulf* and the *Chronicle*, he is, in reality, attributing to him the mind and acumen of a modern critic. An Anglo-Saxon alderman could only have detected and rejected the additions by using some material which has *not* come down to us. What more natural than that Ethelwerd, who writes as the historian of the West-Saxon royal family, should have known of a family pedigree which traced the line up to Sceaf and his arrival in the boat, and that he should have (rightly) thought this to be more authoritative than the pedigree in the *Chronicle* under the year 855, which had been expanded from it? Prof. Chadwick, it seems to me, is here quite justified in holding that Ethelwerd had "acquired the genealogy from some unknown source, in a more primitive form than that contained in the *Chronicle*[1]."

But, because the source of Ethelwerd's pedigree is more primitive than that contained in the *Chronicle* under the year 855, it does not follow that it goes back to heathen times. Wessex had been converted more than two centuries earlier.

We are now in a position to make some estimate of the antiquity of Scyld and Sceaf in the West-Saxon pedigree. The nucleus of this pedigree is to be found in the verses connecting Cynric and Cerdic with Woden. (Even as late as Æthelwulf and Alfred this nucleus is often kept distinct from the later, more historic stages connecting Cerdic with living men.) Pedigrees of other royal houses go to Woden, and many stop there; however, in times comparatively early, but yet Christian, we find Woden provided with five ancestors: later, Ethelwerd gives him ten: the *Chronicle* gives him twenty-five. It is evidently a process of accumulation.

Now, if the name of Scyld had occurred in the portion of the pedigree which traces the West-Saxon kings up to Woden,

---

[1] *Origin*, p. 272.

it would possess sufficient authority to form the basis of an argument. But Scyld, like Heremod, Beaw and Sceaf, occurs in the fantastic development of the pedigree, by which Woden is connected up with Adam and Noah. The fact that these heroes occur *above* Woden makes it almost incredible that their position in the pedigree can go back to heathen times. Those who believed in Woden as a god can hardly have believed at the same time that he was a descendant of the Danish king Scyld. This difficulty Prof. Chadwick admits: "It is difficult to believe that in heathen times Woden was credited with five generations of ancestors, as in the *Frealaf-Geat* list." Still less is it credible that he was credited with 25 generations of ancestors, as in the *Frealaf-Geat-Sceldwa-Sceaf-Noe-Adam* list.

The obvious conclusion seems to me to be that the names above Woden were added in Christian times to the original list, which in heathen times only went back to Woden, and *which is still extant in this form*. A Christian, rationalizing Woden as a human magician, would have no difficulty in placing him far down the ages, just as Saxo Grammaticus does[1]. Obviously *Noe-Adam* must be an addition of Christian times, and the same seems to me to apply to all the other names above Woden, which, though ancient and Germanic, are not therefore ancient and Germanic in the capacity of ancestors of Woden.

And even if these extraordinary ancestors of Woden were really believed in in heathen times, they cannot have been regarded as the special property of any one nation. For it was never claimed that the West-Saxon kings had any unique distinction in tracing their ancestry to Woden, such as would give them a special claim upon Woden's forefathers. How then can the ancient belief (if indeed it *were* an ancient belief) that Woden was descended from Scyld, King of Denmark, prove that the Anglo-Saxons regarded *themselves* as specially related to the Danes? For any such relationship derived through Woden must have been shared by all descendants of the All-Father.

Prof. Chadwick avoids this difficulty by supposing that Woden did not originally occur in the pedigree, but is a later

---

[1] So Ethelwerd (*Lib.* i) sees in Woden a *rex multitudinis Barbarorum*, in error deified. It is the usual point of view, and persists down to Carlyle (*Heroes*).

insertion[1]. But how can this be so when, of the two forms in which the West-Saxon pedigree appears, one (and, so far as our evidence goes, much the older one) traces the kings to Woden *and stops there.* The *object* of this pedigree is to connect the West-Saxon kings with Woden. The expanded pedigrees, which carry on the line still further, from Woden to Sceldwa, Sceaf and Adam, though very numerous, are all traceable to one, or at most two, sources. It is surely not the right method to regard Woden as an interpolation (though he occurs in that portion of the pedigree which is common to all versions, some of which we can probably trace back to primitive times), and to regard as the original element Scyld and Sceaf (though they form part of the continuation of the pedigree found only in, at most, two families of MSS which we cannot trace back beyond the ninth century).

Besides, there is the strongest external support for Woden in the very place which he occupies in the West-Saxon pedigree. That pedigree is traced in all its texts up to one Baldæg and his father Woden. Those texts which further give Woden's ancestry make him a descendant of Frealaf—they generally make Woden son of Frealaf, though some texts insert an intermediate Frithuwald.

Now the very ancient Northumbrian pedigree also goes up, by a different route, to "Beldæg," and gives him Woden for a father. In some versions (e.g. the *Historia Brittonum*) the Northumbrian pedigree stops there: in others (e.g. the *Vespasian MS*) Woden has a father Frealaf. How then *can* it be argued, contrary to the unanimous evidence of all the dozen or more MSS of the West-Saxon pedigree, that *Woden*, standing as he does between his proper father and his proper son, is an interpolation? There is no evidence whatsoever to support such an argument, and everything to disprove it.

The fact that Sceaf, Sceldwa and Beaw occur above Woden, that some versions of the pedigree stop at Woden, and that in heathen times presumably all must have stopped when they reached the All-Father, seems to me a fatal argument—not against the antiquity of the legends of Sceaf, Sceldwa, and

[1] *Origin*, p. 293.

Beaw, but against the antiquity of these characters in the capacity (given to them in the *Anglo-Saxon Chronicle*) of ancestors of the West-Saxon kings, and against the vast deduction concerning the origin of the English nation which Prof. Chadwick draws from this supposed antiquity.

(IV) Precisely the same argument—that Sceaf, Sceldwa and Beaw are found *above Woden* in the pedigree of the English kings, and are not likely to have occupied that place in primitive heathen times, is fatal to the attempt to draw from this pedigree any argument that the myths of these heroes were specially and exclusively Anglo-Saxon. The argument of Müllenhoff and other scholars for an ancient, *purely Anglo-Saxon* Beowa-myth[1] falls, therefore, to the ground.

D. EVIDENCE FOR THE DATE OF *BEOWULF*. THE RELATION OF *BEOWULF* TO THE CLASSICAL EPIC

A few years ago there was a tendency to exaggerate the value of grammatical forms in fixing the date of Old English poetry, and attempts were made to arrange Old English poems in a chronological series, according to the exact percentage of "early" to "late" forms in each. There has now been a natural reaction against the assumption that, granting certain forms to be archaic, these would necessarily be found in a percentage diminishing exactly according to the dates of composition of the various poems in which they occur. The reaction has now gone to the other extreme, and grammatical facts are in danger of being regarded as not being "in any way valid or helpful indications of dates[2]."

Schücking[3], in an elaborate recent monograph on the date of *Beowulf*, rejects the grammatical evidence as valueless, and proceeds to date the poem about two centuries later than has usually been held, placing its composition at the court of some christianized Scandinavian monarch in England, about 900 A.D.

---

[1] *Beowulf*, p. 5. For a further examination of this "Beowa-myth" see Appendix A, above.

[2] Cf. Tupper in *Pub. Mod. Lang. Assoc. Amer.* xxvi, 275.

[3] *P.B.B.* xlii, 347–410. A theory as to the date of *Beowulf*, in some respects similar, was put forward by Mone in 1836: *Untersuchungen zur Geschichte der teutschen Heldensage*, p. 132.

But it surely does not follow that, because grammatical data have been misused, therefore no use can be made of them. And, if *Beowulf* was composed about the year 900, from stories current among the Viking settlers, how are we to account for the fact that the proper names in *Beowulf* are given, not in the Scandinavian forms of the Viking age, nor in corruptions of such forms, but in the correct English forms which we should expect, according to English sound laws, if the names had been brought over in the sixth century, and handed down traditionally[1]?

For example, King Hygelac no doubt called himself *Hugilaikaz*. The *Chochilaicus* of Gregory of Tours is a good—if uncouth—shot at reproducing this name. The name became, in Norse, *Hugleikr* and in Danish *Huglek* (*Hugletus* in Saxo): traditional kings so named are recorded, though it is difficult to find that they have anything in common with the King Hygelac in *Beowulf*[2]. Had the name been introduced into England in Viking times, we should expect the Scandinavian form, not *Hygelāc*[3].

Even in the rare cases where the character in *Beowulf* and his Scandinavian equivalent bear names which are not phonologically identical, the difference does not point to any corruption such as might have arisen from borrowing in Viking days[4]. We have only to contrast the way in which the names of Viking chiefs are recorded in the *Anglo-Saxon Chronicle*, to be convinced that the Scandinavian stories recorded in *Beowulf* are due to contact during the age when Britain was being conquered, not during the Viking period three or four centuries later[5].

And the arguments from literary and political history, which Schücking adduces to prove his late date, seem to me to point in exactly the opposite direction, and to confirm the orthodox view which would place *Beowulf* nearer 700 than 900.

---

[1] See above, p. 103; and Brandl in *Pauls Grdr.* (2) II, 1000, where the argument is excellently stated.   [2] See Olrik, *Sakses Oldhistorie*, 1894, 190–91.

[3] See Björkman, *Eigennamen im Beowulf*, 77.

[4] Sarrazin's attempt to prove such corruption is an entire failure. Cf. Brandl in Herrig's *Archiv*, cxxvi, 234; Björkman, *Eigennamen im Beowulf* 58 (*Heaðo-Beardan*).

[5] A few Geatic adventurers may have taken part in the Anglo-Saxon invasion, as has been argued by Moorman (*Essays and Studies*, v). This is likely enough on *a priori* grounds, though many of the etymologies of place-names quoted by Moorman in support of his thesis are open to doubt.

Schücking urges that, however highly we estimate the civilizing effect of Christianity, it was only in the second half of the seventh century that England was thoroughly permeated by the new faith. Can we expect already, at the beginning of the eighth century, a courtly work, showing, as does *Beowulf*, such wonderful examples of tact, modesty, unselfishness and magnanimity? And this at the time when King Ceolwulf was forced by his rebellious subjects to take the cowl. For Schücking[1], following Hodgkin[2], reminds us how, in the eighth century, out of 15 Northumbrian kings, five were dethroned, five murdered; two abdicated, and only three held the crown to their death; and how at the end of the century Charlemagne called the Northumbrian Angles "a perfidious and perverse nation, murderers of their lords."

But surely, at the base of all this argument, lies the same assumption which, as Schücking rightly holds, vitiates so many of the grammatical arguments; the assumption that development must necessarily be in steady and progressive proportion. We may take Penda as a type of the unreclaimed heathen, and Edward the Confessor of the chaste and saintly churchman; but Anglo-Saxon history was by no means a development in steady progression, of diminishing percentages of ruffianism and increasing percentages of saintship.

The knowledge of, and interest in, heathen custom shown in *Beowulf*, such as the vivid accounts of cremation, would lead us to place it as near heathen times as other data will allow. So much must be granted to the argument of Prof. Chadwick[3]. But the Christian tone, so far from leading us to place *Beowulf* late, would *also* lead us to place it near the time of the conversion. For it is precisely in these times just after the conversion, that we get the most striking instances in all Old English history of that "tact, modesty, generosity, and magnanimity" which Schücking rightly regards as characteristic of *Beowulf*.

King Oswin (who was slain in 651) was, Bede tells us, handsome, courteous of speech and bearing, bountiful both to great

---

[1] *P.B.B.* XLII, 366-7.
[2] *History of England to the Norman Conquest*, I, 245.
[3] *Heroic Age*, 52-6. I have tried to show (Appendix F) that these accounts of cremation are not so archaeologically correct as has sometimes been claimed.

and lowly, beloved of all men for his qualities of mind and body, so that noblemen came from all over England to enter his service—yet of all his endowments gentleness and humility were the chief. We cannot read the description without being reminded of the words of the thegns in praise of the dead Beowulf. Indeed, I doubt if Beowulf would have carried gentleness to those around him quite so far as did Oswin. For Oswin had given to Bishop Aidan an exceptionally fine horse—and Aidan gave it to a beggar who asked alms. The king's mild suggestion that a horse of less value would have been good enough for the beggar, and that the bishop needed a good horse for his own use, drew from the saint the stern question "Is that son of a mare dearer to thee than the Son of God?" The king, who had come from hunting, stood warming himself at the fire, thinking over what had passed; then he suddenly ungirt his sword, gave it to his squire, and throwing himself at the feet of the bishop, promised never again to grudge anything he might give in his charities.

Of course such conduct was exceptional in seventh century Northumbria—it convinced Aidan that the king was too good to live long, as indeed proved to be the case. But it shows that the ideals of courtesy and gentleness shown in *Beowulf* were by no means beyond the possibility of attainment—were indeed surpassed by a seventh century king. I do not know if they could be so easily paralleled in later Old English times.

And what is true from the point of view of morals is true equally from that of art and learning. In spite of the misfortunes of Northumbrian kings in the eighth century, the *first third* of that century was "the Golden Age of Anglo-Saxon England[1]." And not unnaturally, for it had been preceded by half a century during which Northumbria had been free both from internal strife and from invasion. The empire won by Oswiu over Picts and Scots in the North had been lost at the battle of Nectansmere: but that battle had been followed by the twenty years reign of the learned Aldfrid, whose scholarship did not prevent him from nobly retrieving the state of the kingdom[2], though he could not recover the lost dominions.

---

[1] Oman, *England before the Norman Conquest,* 319.
[2] Bede, *Hist. Eccles.* IV, 26.

Now, whatever we may think of *Beowulf* as poetry, it is remarkable for its conscious and deliberate art, and for the tone of civilization which pervades it. And this half century was distinguished, above any other period of Old English history, precisely for its art and its civilization. Four and a half centuries later, when the works of great Norman master builders were rising everywhere in the land, the buildings which Bishop Wilfrid had put up during this first period of conversion were still objects of admiration, even for those who had seen the glories of the great Roman basilicas[1].

Nor is there anything surprising in the fact that this "golden age" was not maintained. On the contrary, it is "in accordance with the phenomena of Saxon history in general, in which seasons of brilliant promise are succeeded by long eras of national eclipse. It is from this point of view quite in accordance with natural likelihood that the age of conversion was one of such stimulus to the artistic powers of the people that a level of effort and achievement was reached which subsequent generations were not able to maintain. The carved crosses and the coins certainly degenerate in artistic value as the centuries pass away, and the fine barbaric gold and encrusted work is early in date[2]."

Already in the early part of the eighth century signs of decay are to be observed. At the end of his *Ecclesiastical History*, Bede complains that the times are so full of disturbance that one knows not what to say, or what the end will be. And these fears were justified. A hundred and forty years of turmoil and decay follow, till the civilization of the North and the Midlands was overthrown by the Danes, and York became the uneasy seat of a heathen jarl.

How it should be possible to see in these facts, as contrasted with the Christian and civilized tone of *Beowulf*, any argument for late date, I cannot see. On the contrary, because of its Christian civilization combined with its still vivid, if perhaps not always quite exact, recollection of heathen customs, we should be inclined to put *Beowulf* in the early Christian ages.

---

[1] "Nunc qui Roma veniunt idem allegant, ut qui Haugustaldensem fabricam vident ambitionem Romanam se imaginari jurent." William of Malmesbury, *Gesta Pontificum*, Rolls Series, p. 255.

[2] Baldwin Brown, *The Arts in Early England*, ii, 1903, p. 325.

A further argument put forward for this late date is the old one that the Scandinavian sympathies of *Beowulf* show it to have been composed for a Scandinavian court, the court, Schücking thinks, of one of the princes who ruled over those portions of England which the Danes had settled[1]. Of course Schücking is too sound a scholar to revive at this time of day the old fallacy that the Anglo-Saxons ought to have taken no interest in the deeds of any but Anglo-Saxon heroes. But how, he asks, are we to account for such *enthusiasm* for, such a burning interest in, a people of alien dialect and foreign dynasty, such as the Scyldings of Denmark?

The answer seems to me to be that the enthusiasm of *Beowulf* is not for the Danish nation as such: on the contrary, *Beowulf* depicts a situation which is most humiliating to the Danes. For twelve years they have suffered the depredations of Grendel; Hrothgar and his kin have proved helpless: all the Danes have been unequal to the need. Twice at least this is emphasized in the most uncompromising, and indeed insulting, way[2]. The poet's enthusiasm is not, then, for the Danish race as such, but for the ideal of a great court with its body of retainers. Such retainers are not necessarily native born— rather is it the mark of the great court that it draws men from far and wide to enter the service, whether permanently or temporarily, even as Beowulf came from afar to help the aged Hrothgar in his need.

It is this ideal of personal valour and personal loyalty, rather than of tribal patriotism, which pervades *Beowulf*, and which certainly suits the known facts of the seventh and early eighth centuries. The bitterest strife in England in the seventh century had been between the two quite new states of Northumbria and Mercia, both equally of Anglian race. Both these states had been built up by a combination of smaller units, and not without violating the old local patriotisms of the diverse elements from which they had been formed. At first, at any rate, no such thing as Northumbrian or Mercian patriotism can have existed. Loyalty was personal, to the king. Neither the kingdom nor the *comitatus* was homogeneous. We have seen

[1] p. 407.   [2] *Beowulf*, ll. 201, 601–3.

that Bede mentions it as a peculiar honour to a Northumbrian prince that *from all parts of England* nobles came to enter his service. We must not demand from the seventh or eighth century our ideals of exclusive enthusiasm for the land of one's birth, ideals which make it disreputable for a "mercenary" to sell his sword. The ideal is, on the contrary, loyalty to a prince whose service a warrior *voluntarily* enters. And the Danish court is depicted as a pattern of such loyalty—before the Scyldings began to work evil[1], by the treason of Hrothulf.

Further, the fact that the Danish court at Leire had been a heathen one might be matter for regret, but it would not prevent its being praised by an Englishman about 700. For England was then entirely Christian. In the process of conversion no single Christian had, so far as we know, been martyred. There had been no war of religion. If Penda had fought against Oswald, it had been as the king of Mercia against the king of Northumbria. Penda's allies were Christian, and he showed no antipathy to the new faith[2]. So that at this date there was no reason for men to feel any deep hostility towards a heathendom which had been the faith of their grandfathers, and with which there had never been any embittered conflict.

But in 900 the position was quite different. For more than a generation the country had been engaged in a life-and-death struggle between two warring camps, the "Christian men" and the "heathen men." The "heathen men" were in process of conversion, but were liable to be ever recruited afresh from beyond the sea. It seems highly unlikely that *Beowulf* could have been written at this date, by some English poet, for the court of a converted Scandinavian prince, with a view perhaps, as Schücking suggests, to educating his children in the English speech. In such a case the one thing likely to be avoided by the English poet, with more than two centuries of Christianity behind him, would surely have been the praise of that Scandinavian heathendom, from which his patron had freed himself, and from which his children were to be weaned. The martyrdom of S. Edmund might have seemed a more appropriate theme[3].

---

[1] Cf. *Beowulf*, l. 1018.   [2] Bede, *Eccles. Hist.* III, 21.
[3] See Oman, pp. 460, 591, for the honour done to this saint by converted Danes.

The tolerant attitude towards heathen customs, and the almost antiquarian interest in them, very justly, as it seems to me, emphasized by Schücking[1], is surely far more possible in A.D. 700 than in A.D. 900. For between those dates heathendom had ceased to be an antiquarian curiosity, and had become an imminent peril.

If those are right who hold that *Beowulf* is no purely native growth, but shows influence of the classical epic, then again it is easier to credit such influence about the year 700 than 900. At the earlier date we have scholars like Aldhelm and Bede, both well acquainted with Virgil, yet both interested in vernacular verse. It has been urged, as a *reductio ad absurdum* of the view which would connect *Beowulf* with Virgil, that the relation to the *Odyssey* is more obvious than that to the *Æneid*. Perhaps, however, some remote and indirect connection even between *Beowulf* and the *Odyssey* is not altogether unthinkable, about the year 700. At the end of the seventh century there was a flourishing school of Greek learning in England, under Hadrian and the Greek Archbishop Theodore, both "well read in sacred *and in secular* literature." In 730 their scholars were still alive, and, Bede tells us, could speak Greek and Latin as correctly as their native tongue. Bede himself knew something about the *Iliad* and the *Odyssey*. Not till eight centuries have passed, and we reach Grocyn and Linacre, was it again to be as easy for an Englishman to have a first-hand knowledge of a Greek classic as it was about the year 700. What scholarship had sunk to by the days of Alfred, we know: and we know that all Alfred's patronage did not produce any scholar whom we can think of as in the least degree comparable to Bede.

So that from the point of view of its close touch with heathendom, its tolerance for heathen customs, its Christian magnanimity and gentleness, its conscious art, and its learned tone, all historic and artistic analogy would lead us to place *Beowulf* in the great age—the age of Bede.

This has brought us to another question—more interesting to many than the mere question of date. Are we to suppose

[1] p. 393.

any direct connection between the classical and the Old English epic?

As nations pass through their "Heroic Age," similar social conditions will necessarily be reflected by many similarities in their poetry. In heroic lays like *Finnsburg* or *Hildebrand* or the Norse poems, phrases and situations may occur which remind us of phrases and situations in the *Iliad*, without affording any ground for supposing classical influence direct or indirect.

But there is much more in *Beowulf* than mere accidental coincidence of phrase or situation.

A simple-minded romancer would have made the *Æneid* a biography of Æneas from the cradle to the grave. Not so Virgil. The story begins with mention of Carthage. Æneas then comes on the scene. At a banquet he tells to Dido his earlier adventures. Just so *Beowulf* begins, not with the birth of Beowulf and his boyhood, but with Heorot. Beowulf arrives. At the banquet, in reply to Unferth, he narrates his earlier adventures. The *Beowulf*-poet is not content merely to tell us that there was minstrelsy at the feast, but like Virgil or Homer, he must give an account of what was sung. The epic style leads often to almost verbal similarities. Jupiter consoling Hercules for the loss of the son of his host says:

> stat sua cuique dies, breve et inreparabile tempus
> omnibus est vitae; sed famam extendere factis
> hoc virtutis opus[1].

In the same spirit and almost in the same words does Beowulf console Hrothgar for the loss of his friend:

> Ūre ǣghwylc sceal ende gebīdan
> worolde līfes; wyrce sē þe mōte
> dōmes ǣr dēaþe; þæt biþ drihtguman
> unlifgendum æfter sēlest.

On the other hand, though we are often struck by the likeness in spirit and in plan, it must be allowed that there is no tangible or conclusive proof of borrowing[2]. But the influence may have been none the less effective for being indirect: nor is

---

[1] *Æneid*, x, 467–9.
[2] In the two admirable articles by Klaeber (*Archiv*, cxxvi, 40 *etc.*, 339 *etc.*) every possible parallel is drawn: the result, to my mind, is not complete conviction.

it quite certain that the author, had he known his Virgil, would necessarily have left traces of direct borrowing. For the deep Christian feeling, which has given to *Beowulf* its almost prudish propriety and its edifying tone, is manifested by no direct and dogmatic reference to Christian personages or doctrines.

I sympathize with Prof. Chadwick's feeling that a man who knew Virgil would not have disguised his knowledge, and would probably have lacked both inclination and ability to compose such a poem as *Beowulf*[1]. But does not this feeling rest largely upon the analogy of other races and ages? Is it borne out by such known facts as we can gather about this period? The reticence of *Beowulf* with reference to Christianity does not harmonize with one's preconceived ideas; and Bishop Aldhelm gives us an even greater surprise. Let anyone read, or try to read, Aldhelm's *Epistola ad Acircium, sive liber de septenario et de metris*. Let him then ask himself "Is it possible that this learned pedant can also have been the author of English poems which King Alfred—surely no mean judge—thought best of all he knew?" These poems may of course have been educated and learned in tone. But we have the authority of King Alfred for the fact that Aldhelm used to perform at the cross roads as a common minstrel, and that he could hold his audiences with such success that they resorted to him again and again[2]. Only after he had made himself popular by several performances did he attempt to weave edifying matter into his verse. And the popular, secular poetry of Aldhelm, his *carmen triviale*, remained current among the common people for centuries. Nor was Aldhelm's classical knowledge of late growth, something superimposed upon an earlier love of popular poetry, for he had

---

[1] Chadwick, *Heroic Age*, 74.

[2] "Litteris itaque ad plenum instructus, nativae quoque linguae non negligebat carmina; adeo ut, teste libro Elfredi, de quo superius dixi, nulla umquam aetate par ei fuerit quisquam. Poesim Anglicam posse facere, cantum componere, *eadem apposite vel canere vel dicere*. Denique commemorat Elfredus carmen triviale, quod adhuc vulgo cantitatur, Aldelmum fecisse, aditiens causam qua probet rationabiliter tantum virum his quae videantur frivola instituisse. Populum eo tempore semibarbarum, parum divinis sermonibus intentum, statim, cantatis missis, domos cursitare solitum. Ideo sanctum virum, super pontem qui rura et urbem continuat, abeuntibus se opposuisse obicem, quasi artem cantitandi professum. Eo plusquam semel facto, plebis favorem et concursum emeritum. Hoc commento sensim inter ludicra verbis Scripturarum insertis, cives ad sanitatem reduxisse." William of Malmesbury, *De gestis pontificum Anglorum*, ed. Hamilton, *Rolls Series*, 1870, 336.

studied under Hadrian as a boy[1]. Later we are told that King Ine imported two Greek teachers from Athens for the help of Aldhelm and his school[2]; this may be exaggeration.

Everything seems to show that about 700 an atmosphere existed in England which might easily have led a scholarly Englishman, acquainted with the old lays, to have set to work to compose an epic. Even so venerable a person as Bede, during his last illness, uttered his last teaching not, as we should expect on *a priori* grounds, in Latin hexameters, but in English metre. The evidence for this is conclusive[3]. But, at a later date, Alcuin would surely have condemned the minstrelsy of Aldhelm[4]. Even King Alfred seems to have felt that it needed some apology. It would have rendered Aldhelm liable to severe censure under the Laws of King Edgar[5]; and Dunstan's biographer indignantly denies the charge brought against his hero of having learnt the heathen songs of his forefathers[6].

The evidence is not as plentiful as we might wish, but it rather suggests that the chasm between secular poetry and ecclesiastical learning was more easily bridged in the first generations after the conversion than was the case later.

But, however that may be, it assuredly does not give any grounds for abandoning the old view, based largely upon grammatical and metrical considerations, which would make *Beowulf* a product of the early eighth century, and substituting for it a theory which would make our poem a product of mixed Saxon and Danish society in the early tenth century.

---

[1] "Reverentissimo patri meaeque rudis infantiae venerando praeceptori Adriano." *Epist.* (Aldhelmi *Opera*, ed. Giles, 1844, p. 330).

[2] Faricius, Life, in Giles' edition of Aldhelm, 1844, p. 357.

[3] Letter of Cuthbert to Cuthwine, describing Bede's last illness. "Et in nostra lingua, hoc est anglica, ut erat doctus in nostris carminibus, nonnulla dixit. Nam et tunc Anglico carmine componens, multum compunctus aiebat, *etc.*" The letter is quoted by Simeon of Durham, ed. Arnold, *Rolls Series*, 1882, I, pp. 43–46, and is extant elsewhere, notably in a ninth century MS at St Gall.

[4] "quid Hinieldus cum Christo."

[5] "þæt ǣnig prēost ne bēo ealuscop, ne on ǣnige wīsan glīwige, mid him sylfum oþþe mid ōþrum mannum"—Thorpe, *Ancient Laws and Institutes of England*, 1840, p. 400 (Laws of Edgar, cap. 58).

[6] "avitae gentilitatis vanissima didicisse carmina." This charge is dismissed as "scabiem mendacii." *Vita Sancti Dunstani*, by "B," in *Memorials of Dunstan,* ed. Stubbs, *Rolls Series*, 1874, p. 11. Were these songs heroic or magic?

E. THE "JUTE-QUESTION" REOPENED

The view that the Geatas of *Beowulf* are the Jutes (Iuti, Iutae) of Bede (i.e. the tribe which colonized Kent, the Isle of Wight and Hampshire) has been held by many eminent scholars. It was dealt with only briefly above (pp. 8–9) because I thought the theory was now recognized as being no longer tenable. Lately, however, it has been maintained with conviction and ability by two Danish scholars, Schütte and Kier. It therefore becomes necessary once more to reopen the question, now that the only elaborate discussion of it in the English language favours the "Jute-theory," especially as Axel Olrik gave the support of his great name to the view that "the question is still open[1]" and that "the last word has not been said concerning the nationality of the Geatas[2]."

As in most controversies, a number of rather irrelevant side issues have been introduced[3], so that from mere weariness students are sometimes inclined to leave the problem undecided. Yet the interpretation of the opening chapters of Scandinavian history turns upon it.

Supporters of the "Jute-theory" have seldom approached the subject from the point of view of Old English. Bugge[4] perhaps did so: but the "Jute-theory" has been held chiefly by students of Scandinavian history, literature or geography, like Fahlbeck[5], Steenstrup[6], Gering[7], Olrik[8], Schütte[9] and Kier[10]. But, now that the laws of Old English sound-change have been

---

[1] *The Heroic Legends of Denmark*, New York, 1919, p. 32 (footnote).
[2] *Ibid.* p. 39.
[3] Thus, much space has been devoted to discussing whether "Gotland," in the eleventh century Cotton MS of Alfred's Orosius, signifies Jutland. I believe that it does; but fail to see how it can be argued from this that Alfred believed the Jutes to be "Geatas." Old English had no special symbol for the semi-vowel *J*; so, to signify *Jótland*, Alfred would have written "Geotland" (Sievers, *Gram.* §§ 74, 175). Had he meant "Land of the Geatas" he would have written "Geataland" or "Geatland." Surely "Gotland" is nearer to "Geotland" than to "Geatland." [4] *P.B.B.* xii, 1–10.
[5] See above, p. 8. Fahlbeck has recently revised and re-stated his arguments.
[6] *Danmarks Riges Historie*, i, 79 *etc.*
[7] *Beowulf*, übersetzt von H. Gering, 1906, p. vii.
[8] See above, also *Nordisk Aandsliv*, 10, where Olrik speaks of the Geatas as "Jyderne." His arguments as presented to the Copenhagen *Philologisk-historisk Samfund* are summarized by Schütte, *J.E.G. Ph.* xi, 575–6. Clausen also supports the Jute-theory, *Danske Studier*, 1918, 137–49.
[9] *J.E.G.Ph.* xi, 574–602.
[10] *Beowulf, et Bidrag til Nordens Oldhistorie* af Chr. Kier, København, 1915.

clearly defined, it seldom happens that anyone who approaches the subject primarily as a student of the Anglo-Saxon language holds the view that the Geatas are Jutes.

And this is naturally so: for, from the point of view of language, the question is not disputable. The *Gēatas* phonologically are the *Gautar* (the modern Götar of Southern Sweden). It is admitted that the words are identical[1]. And, equally, it is admitted that the word *Gēatas* cannot be identical with the word *Iuti, Iutae*, used by Bede as the name of the Jutes who colonized Kent[1]. Bede's *Iuti, Iutae*, on the contrary, would correspond to a presumed Old English *$*\bar{I}uti$* or *$*\bar{I}utan$*[2], current in his time in Northumbria. This in later Northumbrian would become *Īote, Īotan* (though the form *Īute, Īutan* might also survive). The dialect forms which we should expect (and which we find in the genitive and dative) corresponding to this would be: Mercian, *Ēote, Ēotan*; Late West-Saxon, *Ȳte, Ȳtan* (through an intermediate Early West-Saxon *$*\bar{I}ete$, *$*\bar{I}etan$*, which is not recorded).

If, then, the word *Gēatas* came to supplant the correct form *Īote, Īotan* (or its Mercian and West-Saxon equivalents *Ēote, Ēotan, Ȳte, Ȳtan*), this can only have been the result of confusion. Such confusion is, on abstract grounds, conceivable: it is always possible that the name of one tribe may come to be attached to another. "Scot" has ceased to mean "Irishman," and has come to mean "North Briton"; and there is no intrinsic impossibility in the word *Gēatas* having been transferred by Englishmen, from the half-forgotten Gautar, to the Jutes, and having driven out the correct name of the latter, *Īote, Īotan*. For example, there might have been an exiled Geatic family among the Jutish invaders, which might have become so prominent as to cause

---

[1] This is admitted by Bugge, *P.B.B.* xii, 6. "*Geátas*...ist sprachlich ein ganz anderer name als altn. *Jótar, Jútar*, bei Beda *Jutae*, und nach Beda im *Chron. Sax.* 449 *Jotum, Jutna*...Die *Geátas*...tragen einen namen der sprachlich mit altn. *Gautar* identisch ist."

[2] From a presumed Prim. Germ. *$*Eutiz$, *$*Eutjaniz$. The word in O.E. seems to have been declined both as an *i*-stem and an *n*-stem, the *n*-stem forms being used more particularly in the gen. plu., just as in the case of the tribal names, *Seaxe, Mierce* (Sievers, § 264). The Latinized forms show the same duplication, the dat. *Euciis* pointing to an *i*-stem, the nom. *Euthio* to an *n*-stem, plu. *$*Eutiones$. For a discussion of the relation of the O.E. name to the Danish *Jyder*, see Björkman in *Anglia, Beiblatt*, xxviii, 274–80: "Zu ae. *Eote, Yte*, dän. *Jyder* 'Jüten'."

the name *Gēatas* to supplant the correct *Īote*, *Ēote*, etc. But, whoever the Geatas may have been, *Beowulf* is their chief early record: indeed, almost all we know of their earliest history is derived from *Beowulf*. In *Beowulf*, therefore, if anywhere, the old names and traditions should be remembered. The word *Gēat* occurs some 50 times in the poem. The poet obviously wishes to use other synonyms, for the sake of variety and alliteration: hence we get *Weder-Gēatas*, *Wederas*, *Sǣ-Gēatas*, *Gūð-Gēatas*. Now, if these Geatas are the Jutes, how comes it that the poet *never* calls them such, never speaks of them under the correct tribal name of *Ēote*, etc., although this was the current name at the time *Beowulf* was written, and indeed for centuries later?

For, demonstrably, the form *Ēote*, etc., *was* recognized as the name of the Jutes till at least the twelfth century. Then it died out of current speech, and only Bede's Latin *Iuti* (and the modern "Jute" derived therefrom) remained as terms used by the historians. The evidence is conclusive:

(*a*) Bede, writing about the time when *Beowulf*, in its present form, is supposed to have been composed, uses *Iuti*, *Iutae*, corresponding to a presumed contemporary Northumbrian *Īuti, *Īutan.

(*b*) In the "Alfredian" translation of Bede, made almost two centuries after Bede's time, we do indeed in one place find "Geata," "Geatum" used to translate "Iutarum," "Iutis," instead of the correctly corresponding Mercian form "Eota," "Eotum." Only two MSS are extant at this point. But since both agree, and since they belong to different types, it is probable that "Geata" here is no mere copyist's error, but is due to the translator himself[1]. But, later, when the translator

---

[1] I regard it as simply an *error* of the translator, possibly because he had before him a text in which Bede's *Iutis* had been corrupted in this place into *Giotis*, as it is in Ethelwerd: *Cantuarii de Giotis traxerunt originem, Vuhtii quoque.* (Bk. I: other names which Ethelwerd draws from Bede in this section are equally corrupt.)

Bede's text runs: (I, 15) *Aduenerant autem de tribus Germaniae populis fortioribus, id est Saxonibus, Anglis, Iutis.* *De Iutarum origine sunt Cantuarii et Victuarii*; in the translation: "Comon hi of þrim folcum ðam strangestan Germanie, þæt [is] of Seaxum and of Angle and of Geatum. Of Geata fruman syndon Cantware and Wihtsætan": (IV, 16) *In proximam Iutorum prouinciam translati...in locum, qui uocatur Ad Lapidem*; "in þa neahmægðe, seo is gecegd Eota lond, in sume stowe seo is nemned Æt Stane" (Stoneham, near Southampton). *MS C.C.C.C. 41* reads "Ytena land": see below.

has to render Bede's "Iutorum," he gives, not "Geata," but the correct Mercian "Eota." There can be no possible doubt here, for five MSS are extant at this point, and all give the correct form—four in the Mercian, "Eota," whilst one gives the West-Saxon equivalent, "Ytena."

Now the *Gēata*-passage in the Bede translation is the chief piece of evidence which those who would explain the Geatas of *Beowulf* as "Jutes" can call: and it does not, in fact, much help them. What they have to prove is that the *Beowulf*-poet could *consistently and invariably* have used *Gēatas* in the place of *Ēote*. To produce an instance in which the two terms are both used by the same translator is very little use, when what has to be proved is that the one term had already, at a much earlier period, entirely ousted the other.

All our other evidence is for the invariable use of the correct form *Īote, Īotan*, etc. in Old English.

(c) The passage from Bede was again translated, and inserted into a copy of the *Anglo-Saxon Chronicle*, which was sent quite early to one of the great abbeys of Northumbria[1]. In this, "Iutis, Iutarum" is represented by the correct Northumbrian equivalent, "Iutum," "Iotum"; "Iutna."

(d) This Northumbrian Chronicle, or a transcript of it, subsequently came South, to Canterbury. There, roughly about the year 1100, it was used to interpolate an Early West-Saxon copy of the Chronicle. Surely at Canterbury, the capital of the old Jutish kingdom, people must have known the correct form of the Jutish name, whether *Gēatas* or *Īote*. We find the forms "Iotum," "Iutum"; "Iutna."

(e) Corresponding to this Northumbrian (and Kentish) form *Īote*, Mercian *Ēote*, the Late West-Saxon form should be *Ȳte*. Now *MS Corpus Christi College, Cambridge*, 41, gives us "the Wessex version of the English Bede" and is written by a scribe who knew the Hampshire district[2]. In this MS the "Eota" of the Mercian original has been transcribed as "Ytena," "Eotum" as "Ytum," showing that the scribe understood the tribal name and its equivalent correctly. This was about the

---

[1] *Two Saxon Chronicles*, ed. Plummer, 1899. *Introduction*, pp. lxx, lxxi.

[2] *The O.E. version of Bede's Ecclesiastical History*, ed. Miller, ii, xv, xvi, 1898.

time of the Norman Conquest, but the name continued to be understood till the early twelfth century at least. For Florence of Worcester records that William Rufus was slain *in Noua Foresta quae lingua Anglorum Ytene nuncupatur*; and in another place he speaks of the same event as happening *in prouincia Jutarum in Noua Foresta*[1], which shows that Florence understood that "Ytene" was *Ȳtena land*, "the province of the Jutes."

It comes, then, to this. The "Jute-hypothesis" postulates not only that, at the time *Beowulf* was composed, *Gēatas* had come to mean "Jutes," but also that it had so completely ousted the correct old name *Īuti, Īote, Ēote, Ȳte*, that none of the latter terms are ever used in the poem as synonyms for Beowulf's people[2]. Yet all the evidence shows that *Īuti* etc. was the recognized name when Bede wrote, and we have evidence at intervals showing that it was so understood till four centuries later. But not only was *Īuti, Īote* never superseded in O.E. times; there is no real evidence that *Gēatas* was ever *generally* used to signify "Jutes." The fact that one translator in one passage (writing probably some two centuries after *Beowulf* was composed) uses "Geata," "Geatum," where he should have used "Eota," "Eotum," does not prove the misnomer to have been general—especially when the same translator subsequently uses the correct form "Eota."

I do not think sufficient importance has been attached to what seems (to me) the vital argument against the "Jute-theory." It is not merely that *Gēatas* is the exact phonological equivalent of *Gautar* (Götar) and cannot be equivalent to Bede's *Īuti*. This difficulty may be got over by the assumption that somehow the *Īuti*, or some of them, had adopted the name *Gēatas*: and we are not in a position to disprove such assumption. But the advocates of the "Jute-theory" have further to assume that, at the date when *Beowulf* was written, the correct name *Īuti* (Northumbrian *Īote*, Mercian *Ēote*, West-Saxon *Ȳte*) must have so passed into disuse that it could not be once used as a

---

[1] Florentii Wigorn. *Chron.*, ed. Thorpe, ii, 45; i, 276.
[2] It cannot be said that this is due to textual corruption in our late copy for the alliteration constantly demands a G-form, not a vowel-form.

synonym for Beowulf's people, by our synonym-hunting poet. And this assumption we *are* in a position to disprove.

The Jute-theory would therefore still be untenable on the ground of the name, even though it were laboriously proved that, from the historical and geographical standpoint, there was more to be said for it than had hitherto been recognized. But even this has not been proved: quite the reverse. As I have tried to show above, historical and geographical considerations, though in themselves not absolutely conclusive, point emphatically to an identification with the Götar, rather than with the Jutes[1].

The relations of Beowulf and the Geatas with the kings of Denmark and of Sweden are the constant topic of the poem. Now the land of the Götar *was* situated between Denmark and Sweden. But if the Geatas be Jutes, their neighbours were the Danes on the east and the Angles on the south; farther away, across the Cattegat lay the Götar, and beyond these the Swedes. If the Geatas be Jutes, why should their immediate neighbours, the Angles, never appear in *Beowulf* as having any dealings with them? And why, above all, should the Götar never be mentioned, whilst the Swedes, far to the north, play so large a part? Even if Swedes and Götar had at this time been under one king, the Götar could not have been thus ignored, seeing that, owing to their position, the brunt of the fighting must have fallen on them[2]. But we know that the Götar were independent. The strictly contemporary evidence of Procopius shows quite conclusively that they were one of the strongest of the Scandinavian kingdoms[3]. How then could warfare be carried on for three generations between Jutes and Swedes without concerning the Götar, whose territory lay in between?

Again, in the "Catalogue of Kings" in *Widsith*, the Swedes are named with their famous king Ongentheow. The Jutes ($\overline{Y}te$) are also mentioned, with *their* king. And their king is

---

[1] See pp. 8, 9 above, §§ 2–7.

[2] Just as, for example, in *Heimskringla: Haraldz saga ins hárfagra*, 13–17, the Götar are constantly mentioned, because the kingdom of Sweden is being attacked from their side.

[3] Procopius tells us that there were in Thule (i.e. the Scandinavian peninsula) thirteen nations, each under its own king: βασιλεῖς τέ εἰσι κατὰ ἔθνος ἔκαστον... ὧν ἔθνος ἐν πολυάνθρωπον οἱ Γαυτοί εἰσι (*Bell. Gott.* ii, 15).

not Hrethel, Hæthcyn, Hygelac or Heardred, but a certain
Gefwulf, whose name does not even alliterate with that of any
known king of the Geatas[1].

Again, in the (certainly very early) *Book on Monsters*,
Hygelac is described as *Huiglaucus qui imperavit Getis.* Now
Getis can mean Götar[2], but can hardly mean Jutes.
The geographical case against the identification of Geatas
and Götar depends upon the assumption that the western sea-
coast of the Götar in ancient times must have coincided with
that of West Gothland (Vestra-Götland) in mediæval and
modern times. Now as this coast consists merely of a small
strip south of the river Götaelv, it is argued that the Götar
could not be the maritime Geatas of *Beowulf*, capable of undertaking a Viking raid to the mouth of the Rhine. But the
assumption that the frontiers of the Götar about A.D. 500 were
the same as they were a thousand years later, is not only improbable on *a priori* grounds, but, as Schück has shown[3], can
be definitely disproved. Adam of Bremen, writing in the
eleventh century, speaks of the river Gothelba (Götaelv) as
running through the midst of the peoples of the Götar. And
the obvious connection between the name of the river and the
name of the people seems to make it certain that Adam is
right, and that the original Götar must have dwelt around the
river Götaelv. But, if so, then they were a maritime folk: for
the river Götaelv is merely the outlet which connects Lake Wener
with the sea, running a course almost parallel with the shore and
nowhere very distant from it[4]. But even when Adam wrote, the

---

[1] On this alliteration-test, which is very important, see above, pp. 10–11.

[2] *Geta* was the recognized Latin synonym for *Gothus*, and is used in this
sense in the sixth century, e.g. by Venantius Fortunatus and Jordanes. And
the Götar are constantly called *Gothi*, e.g. in the formula *rex Sueorum et Gothorum*
(for the date of this formula see Söderqvist in the *Historisk Tidskrift*, 1915: *Ågde
Uppsvearne rätt att taga och vräka konung*); or Saxo, Bk. XIII (ed. Holder, p. 420,
describing how the *Gothi* invited a candidate to be king, and slew the rival
claimant, who was supported by the legally more constitutional suffrages of
the Swedes); or Adam of Bremen (as quoted below).

[3] *Folknamnet Geatas*, p. 5 *etc.*

[4] Speaking of the Götaelv, Adam says "Ille oritur in praedictis alpibus,
perque *medios Gothorum populos* currit in Oceanum, unde et Gothelba dicitur."
Adami Canonici Bremensis, *Gesta Hamm. eccl. pontificum*, Lib. IV, in Migne,
CXLVI, 637. Modern scholars are of the opinion that the borrowing has been
rather the other way. According to Noreen the river Götaelv (Gautelfr) gets
its name as the outflow from Lake Væner. (Cf. O.E. *gēotan, gēat*, "pour.")
Götland (Gautland) is the country around the river, and the Götar (Gautar)

Götar to the north of the river had long been politically subject to Norway[1]: and the *Heimskringla* tells us how this happened.

Harold Fairhair, King of Norway (a contemporary of King Alfred), attacked them: they had staked the river Götaelv against him, but he moored his ships to the stakes[2] and harried *on either shore*: he fought far and wide in the country, had many battles *on either side of the river*, and finally slew the leader of the Götar, Hrani Gauzki (the Götlander). Then he annexed to Norway all the land north of the river and west of Lake Wener. Thenceforward the Götaelv was the boundary between Norway and West Gothland, though the country ultimately became Swedish, as it now is. But it is abundantly clear from the *Heimskringla* that Harold regarded as hostile all the territory north of the Götaelv, and between Lake Wener and the sea[3] (the old Ránriki and the modern Bohuslän).

But, if so, then the objection that the Götar are not a sufficiently maritime people becomes untenable. For precisely to this region belong the earliest records of maritime warfare to be found in the north of Europe, possibly the earliest in Europe. The smooth rocks of Bohuslän are covered with incised pictures of the Bronze age: and the favourite subject of these is ships and naval encounters. About 120 different pictures of ships and sea fights are reproduced by one scholar alone[4]. And at the present day this province of Göteborg and Bohus is the most important centre in Sweden both of fishery and shipping. Indeed, more than one quarter of the total tonnage of the modern Swedish mercantile marine comes from this comparatively tiny strip of coast[5].

get their name from the country. See Noreen, *Våra Ortnamn och deras Ursprungliga Betydelse*, in *Spridda Studier*, II, 91, 139.

[1] The Scholiast, in his commentary on Adam, records the later state of things, when the Götar were confined to the south of the river: "Gothelba fluvius a Nordmannis Gothiam separat."

[2] *Heimskringla*, cap. 17.

[3] "Hann [Haraldr] er úti á herskipum allan vetrinn ok herjar á Ránríki" (cap. 15). "Haraldr konungr fór víða um Gautland herskildi, ok átti þar margar orrostur tveim megin elfarinnar....Síðan lagði Haraldr konungr land alt undir sik fyrir norðan elfína ok fyrir vestan Væni " (cap. 17). *Heimskringla: Haraldz saga ins hárfagra*, udgiv. F. Jónsson, København, 1893–1900.

[4] Baltzer (L.), *Glyphes des rochers du Bohuslän, avec une préface de V. Rydberg*, Gothembourg, 1881. See also Baltzer, *Några af de viktigaste Hällristningarna*, Göteborg, 1911.

[5] Guinchard, *Sweden: Historical and Statistical Handbook*, 1914, II, 549.

It is surely quite absurd to urge that the men of this coast could not have harried the Frisians in the manner in which Hygelac is represented as doing. And surely it is equally absurd to urge that the people of this coast would not have had to fear a return attack from the Frisians, after the downfall of their own kings. The Frisians seem to have been "the chief channel of communication between the North and West of Europe[1]" before the rise of the Scandinavian Vikings, and to have been supreme in the North Sea. The Franks were of course a land power, but the Franks, *when in alliance with the Frisians*, were by no means helpless at sea. Gregory of Tours tells us that they overthrew Hygelac on land, and *then in a sea fight annihilated his fleet*. Now the poet says that the Geatas may expect war when the Franks *and Frisians* hear of Beowulf's fall. The objection that, because they feared the Franks, the Geatas must have been reachable by land, depends upon leaving the "and Frisians" out of consideration.

"Now we may look for a time of war" says the messenger "when the fall of our king is known among the Franks and Frisians": then he gives a brief account of the raid upon the land of the Frisians and concludes: "Ever since then has the favour of the Merovingian king been denied us[2]." What is there in this to indicate whether the raiders came from Jutland, or from the coast of the Götar across the Cattegat, 50 miles further off? The messenger goes on to anticipate hostility from the Swedes[3]. To this, at any rate, the Götar were more exposed than the Jutes. Further, he concludes by anticipating the utter overthrow of the Geatas[4]: and the poet expressly tells us that these forebodings were justified[5]. There must therefore be a reference to some famous national catastrophe. Now the Götar *did* lose their independence, and *were* incorporated into the Swedish kingdom. When did the Jutes suffer any similar downfall at the hands of either Frisians, Franks, or Swedes?

The other geographical and historical arguments urged in favour of the Jutes, when carefully scrutinized, are found either

---

[1] See Chadwick, *Origin*, 93; *Heroic Age*, 51.
[2] ll. 2910–21. See Schütte, 579, 583.
[3] ll. 2922–3007.
[4] ll. 3018–27.
[5] ll. 3029–30.

equally indecisive, or else actually to tell against the "Jute-theory." Schütte[1] thinks that the name "Wederas" (applied in *Beowulf* to the Geatas) is identical with the name *Eudoses* (that of a tribe mentioned by Tacitus, who *may*[2] have dwelt in Jutland). But this is impossible phonologically: *Wederas* is surely a shortened form of *Weder-Gēatas*, "the Storm-Geatas." Indeed, we have, in favour of the Götar-theory, the fact that the very name of the Wederas survives on the Bohuslän coast to this day, in the Wäder Öar and the Wäder Fiord.

Advocates of the "Jute-theory" lay great stress upon the fact that Gregory of Tours and the *Liber Historiae Francorum* call Hygelac a Dane[3]: *Dani cum rege suo Chochilaico.* Now, when Gregory wrote in the sixth century, either the Jutes were entirely distinct from, and independent of, the Danes, or they were not. If they were distinct, how do Gregory's words help the "Jute-theory"? He must be simply using "Dane," like the Anglo-Saxon historians, for "Scandinavian." But if the Jutes were not distinct from the Danes, then we have an argument against the "Jute-theory." For we know from *Beowulf* that the Geatas *were* quite distinct from the Danes[4], and quite independent of them[5].

It is repeatedly urged that the Geatas and Swedes fight *ofer sǣ*[6]. But *sǣ* can mean a great fresh-water lake, like Lake Wener, just as well as the ocean[7]: and as a matter of fact we know that the decisive battle did take place on Lake Wener, *in stagno Waener, á Vænis isi*[8]. Lake Wener is an obvious battle place for Götar and Swedes. They were separated by the great and almost impassable forests of "Tived" and "Kolmård," and the lake was their simplest way of meeting[9]. But it does not equally fit Jutes and Swedes.

It is repeatedly objected that the Götar are remote from the Anglo-Saxons[10]. Possibly: but remoteness did not prevent

---

[1] pp. 575, 581.

[2] The reason for locating the *Eudoses* in Jutland is that the name has, very hazardously, been identified with that of the Jutes, *Eutiones*. Obviously this argument could no longer be used, if the *Eudoses* were the "Wederas."

[3] See e.g. Schütte, 579–80.   [4] *Beowulf*, 1856.   [5] *Beowulf*, 1830 *etc.*

[6] *Beowulf*, 2394. See Schütte, 576–9.

[7] *Sēo ēa þǣr wyrcþ micelne sǣ.* Orosius, ed. Sweet, 12, 24.

[8] See above, p. 7.   [9] As Miss Paues, herself a *Geat*, points out to me.

[10] Kier, 39; Schütte, 582, 591 *etc.*

the Anglo-Saxons from being interested in heroes of the Huns or Goths or Burgundians or Longobards, who were much more[1] distant. And the absence of any direct connection between the history of the Geatas and the historic Anglo-Saxon records, affords a strong presumption that the Geatas *were* a somewhat alien people. If the people of Beowulf, Hygelac, and Hrethel, were the same people as the Jutes who colonized Kent and Hampshire, why do we never, in the Kentish royal genealogies or elsewhere, find any claim to such connection? The Mercians did not so forget their connection with the old Offa of Angel, although a much greater space of time had intervened. The fact that we have no mention among the ancestors of Beowulf and Hygelac of any names which we can connect with the Jutish genealogy affords, therefore, a strong presumption that they belonged to some other tribe.

The strongest historical argument for the "Jute-theory" was that produced by Bugge. The *Ynglinga tal* represents Ottar (who is certainly the Ohthere of *Beowulf*) as having fallen in Vendel, and this Vendel was clearly understood as being the district of that name in North Jutland. The body of this Swedish king was torn asunder by carrion birds, and he was remembered as "the Vendel-crow," a mocking nickname which pretty clearly goes back to primitive times. Other ancient authors attributed this name, not to Ottar, but to his father, who can be identified with the Ongentheow of *Beowulf*. This would seem to indicate that the hereditary foes of Ongentheow and the Swedish kings of his house were, after all, the Jutes of Vendel.

But Knut Stjerna has shown that the Vendel from which "Ottar Vendel-crow" took his name was probably not the Vendel of Jutland at all, but the place of that name north of Uppsala, famous for the splendid grave-finds which show it to have been of peculiar importance during our period[2]. And subsequent research has shown that a huge grave-mound, near this Vendel, is mentioned in a record of the seventeenth century as King

---

[1] See above, pp. 99, 100.
[2] *Vendel och Vendelkråka* in *A.f.n.F.* xxi, 71–80: see *Essays*, trans. Clark Hall, 50–62.

Ottar's mound, and is still popularly known as the mound of Ottar Vendel-crow[1]. But, if so, this story of the Vendel-crow, so far from supporting the "Jute-hypothesis," tells against it: nothing could be more suitable than Vendel, north of Uppsala, as the "last ditch" to which Ongentheow retreated, if we assume his adversaries to have been the Götar: but it would not suit the Jutes so well.

An exploration of the mound has proved beyond reasonable doubt that it *was* raised to cover the ashes of Ottar Vendel-crow, the Ohthere of *Beowulf*[2]. That Ohthere fell in battle against the Geatas there is nothing, in *Beowulf* or elsewhere, to prove. But the fact that his ashes were laid in mound at Vendel in Sweden makes it unlikely that he fell in battle against the Jutes, and is quite incompatible with what we are told in the *Ynglinga saga* of his body having been torn to pieces by carrion fowl on a mound in Vendel in Jutland. It now becomes clear that this story, and the tale of the crow of wood made by the Jutlanders in mockery of Ottar, is a mere invention to account for the name Vendel-crow: the name, as so often, has survived, and a new story has grown up to give a reason for the name.

What "Vendel-crow" originally implied we cannot be quite sure. Apparently "Crow" or "Vendel-crow" is used to this day as a nickname for the inhabitants of Swedish Vendel. Ottar may have been so called because he was buried (possibly because he lived) in Vendel, not, like other members of his race, his son and his father, at Old Uppsala. But however that may be, what is clear is that, as the name passed from the Swedes to those Norwegian and Icelandic writers who have handed it down

---

[1] This grave mound is mentioned as "Kong Ottars Hög" in *Ättartal för Swea och Götha Kununga Hus*, by J. Peringskiöld, Stockholm, 1725, p. 13, and earlier, in 1677, it is mentioned by the same name in some notes of an antiquarian survey. That the name "Vendel-crow" is now attached to it is stated by Dr Almgren. These early references seem conclusive: little weight could, of course, be carried by the modern name alone, since it might easily be of learned origin. The mound was opened in 1914–16, and the contents showed it to belong to about 500 to 550 A.D., which agrees excellently with the date of Ohthere. See two articles in *Fornvännen* for 1917: an account of the opening of the mound by S. Lindqist entitled "Ottarshögen i Vendel" (pp. 127–43) and a discussion of early Swedish history in the light of archaeology, by B. Nerman, "Ynglingasagan i arkeologisk belysning" (esp. pp. 243–6). See also Björkman in *Nordisk Tidskrift*, Stockholm, 1917, p. 169, and *Eigennamen im Beowulf*, 1920, pp. 86–99.

[2] See Appendix F: *Beowulf* and the Archæologists, esp. p. 356, below.

to us, Vendel of Sweden was naturally misunderstood as the
more familiar Vendel of Jutland. Stjerna's conjecture is confirmed. The Swedish king's nickname, far from pointing to
ancient feuds between Jute and Swede, is shown to have nothing
whatsoever to do with Jutland.

It appears, then, that *Gēatas* is phonologically the equivalent
of "Götar," but not the equivalent of "Jutes"; that what we
know of the use of the word "Jutes" (*Īote*, etc.) in Old English
makes it incredible that a poem of the length of *Beowulf* could
be written, concerning their heroes and their wars, without
even mentioning them by their correct name; that in many
respects the geographical and historical evidence fits the Götar,
but does *not* fit the Jutes; that the instances to the contrary,
in which it is claimed that the geographical and historical
evidence fits the Jutes but does not fit the Götar, are all found
on examination to be either inconclusive or actually to favour
the Götar.

F. *BEOWULF* AND THE ARCHÆOLOGISTS

The peat-bogs of Schleswig and Denmark have yielded finds
of the first importance for English archæology. These "moss-
finds" are great collections, chiefly of arms and accoutrements,
obviously deposited with intention. The first of these great
discoveries, that of Thorsbjerg, was made in the heart of ancient
Angel: the site of the next, Nydam, also comes within the area
probably occupied by either Angles or Jutes; and most of the
rest of the "moss-finds" were in the closest neighbourhood of
the old Anglian home. The period of the oldest deposits, as is
shown by the Roman coins found among them, is hardly before
the third century A.D., and some authorities would make it
considerably later.

An account of these discoveries will be found in Engelhardt's
Denmark in the Early Iron Age[1], 1866: a volume which sum-

[1] By the Early Iron Age. Engelhardt meant from 250 to 450 A.D.: but more
recent Danish scholars have placed these deposits in the fifth century, with some
overlapping into the preceding and succeeding centuries (Müller, *Vor Oldtid*,
561; Wimmer, *Die Runenschrift*, 301, etc.). The Swedish archæologists, Knut
Stjerna and O. Almgren, agree with Engelhardt, dating the finds between about
250 and 450 A.D. (Stjerna's *Essays*, trans. Clark Hall, p. 149, and *Introduction*,
xxxii–iii).

marizes the results of Engelhardt's investigations during the preceding seven years. He had published in Copenhagen *Thorsbjerg Mosefund*, 1863; *Nydam Mosefund*, 1865. Engelhardt's work at Nydam was interrupted by the war of 1864: the finds had to be ceded to Germany, and the exploration was continued by German scholars. Engelhardt consoled himself that these "subsequent investigations...do not seem to have been carried on with the necessary care and intelligence," and continued his own researches within the narrowed frontiers of Denmark, publishing two monographs on the mosses of Fünen: *Kragehul Mosefund*, 1867; *Vimose Fundet*, 1869.

These deposits, however, obviously belong to a period much earlier than that in which *Beowulf* was written: indeed most of them certainly belong to a period earlier than that in which the historic events described in *Beowulf* occurred; so that, close as is their relation with Anglian civilization, it is with the civilization of the Angles while still on the continent.

The Archæology of *Beowulf* has been made the subject of special study by Knut Stjerna, in a series of articles which appeared between 1903 and his premature death in 1909. A good service has been done to students of *Beowulf* by Dr Clark Hall in collecting and translating Stjerna's essays[1]. They are a mine of useful information, and the reproductions of articles from Scandinavian grave-finds, with which they are so copiously illustrated, are invaluable. The magnificent antiquities from Vendel, now in the Stockholm museum, are more particularly laid under contribution[2]. Dr Clark Hall added a most useful "Index of things mentioned in *Beowulf*[3]," well illustrated. Here again the illustrations, with few exceptions, are from Scandinavian finds.

---

[1] *Essays on questions connected with the O.E. poem of Beowulf*, trans. and ed. by John R. Clark Hall, (Viking Club), Coventry. (Reviews by Klaeber, *J.E.G.Ph.* XIII, 167–73, weighty; Mawer, *M.L.N.* VIII, 242–3; *Athenæum*, 1913, I, 459–60; *Archiv*, CXXXII, 238–9; Schütte, *A.f.n.F.* XXXIII, 64–96, elaborate.)

[2] An account of these was given at the time by H. Stolpe, who undertook the excavation. See his *Vendelfyndet*, in the *Antiqvarisk Tidskrift för Sverige*, VIII, 1, 1–34, and Hildebrand (H.) in the same, 35–64 (1884). Stolpe did not live to issue the definitive account of his work, *Graffältet vid Vendel, beskrifvet af H. Stolpe och T. J. Arne*, Stockholm, 1912.

[3] Also added as an Appendix to his *Beowulf* translation, 1911.

Two weighty arguments as to the origin of *Beowulf* have been based upon archæology. In the first place it has been urged by Dr Clark Hall that:

"If the poem is read in the light of the evidence which Stjerna has marshalled in the essays as to the profusion of gold, the prevalence of ring-swords, of boar-helmets, of ring-corslets, and ring-money, it becomes clear how strong the distinctively Scandinavian colouring is, and how comparatively little of the *mise-en-scène* must be due to the English author[1]."

Equally, Prof. Klaeber finds in Stjerna's investigations a strong argument for the Scandinavian character of *Beowulf*[2].

Now Stjerna, very rightly and naturally, drew his illustrations of *Beowulf* from those Scandinavian, and especially Swedish, grave-finds which he knew so well: and very valuable those illustrations are. But it does not follow, because the one archæologist who has chosen to devote his knowledge so wholeheartedly to the elucidation of *Beowulf* was a Scandinavian, using Scandinavian material, that therefore *Beowulf* is Scandinavian. This, however, is the inference which Stjerna himself was apt to draw, and which is still being drawn from his work. Stjerna speaks of our poem as a monument raised by the Geatas to the memory of their saga-renowned king[3], though he allows that certain features of the poem, such as the dragon-fight[4], are of Anglo-Saxon origin.

Of course, it must be allowed that accounts such as those of the fighting between Swedes and Geatas, if they are historical (and they obviously are), must have originated from eyewitnesses of the Scandinavian battles: but I doubt if there is anything in *Beowulf* so purely Scandinavian as to compel us to assume that any line of the story, in the poetical form in which we now have it, was *necessarily* composed in Scandinavia. Even if it could be shown that the conditions depicted in *Beowulf* can be better illustrated from the grave-finds of Vendel in Sweden than from English diggings, this would not prove *Beowulf* Scandinavian. Modern scientific archæology is surely based on chronology as well as geography. The English finds date from

---

[1] Clark Hall's *Preface* to Stjerna's *Essays*, p. xx.
[2] *J.E.G.Ph.* xiii, 1914, p. 172.
[3] *Essays*, p. 239: cf. p. 84.   [4] p. 39.

the period before 650 A.D., and the Vendel finds from the period
after. *Beowulf* might well show similarity rather with contemporary art abroad than with the art of earlier generations at
home. For intercourse was more general than is always realized.
It was not merely trade and plunder which spread fashions from
nation to nation. There were the presents of arms which Tacitus
mentions as sent, not only privately, but with public ceremony,
from one tribe to another[1]. Similar presentations are indicated
in *Beowulf*[2]; we find them equally at the court of the Ostro-
gothic Theodoric[3]; Charles the Great sent to Offa of Mercia
unum balteum et unum gladium huniscum[4]; according to the
famous story in the *Heimskringla*, Athelstan sent to Harold
Fairhair of Norway a sword and belt arrayed with gold and
silver; Athelstan gave Harold's son Hakon a sword which was
the best that ever came to Norway[5]. It is not surprising, then,
if we find parallels between English poetry and Scandinavian
grave-finds, both apparently dating from about the year 700 A.D.
But I do not think that there is any *special* resemblance, though,
both in *Beowulf* and in the Vendel graves, there is a profusion
lacking in the case of the simpler Anglo-Saxon tomb-furniture.

Let us examine the five points of special resemblance, alleged
by Dr Clark Hall, on the basis of Stjerna's studies.

"The profusion of gold." Gold is indeed lavishly used in
Beowulf: the golden treasure found in the dragon's lair was so
bulky that it had to be transported by waggon. And, certainly,
gold is found in greater profusion in Swedish than in English
graves: the most casual visitor to the Stockholm museum must
be impressed by the magnificence of the exhibits there. But,
granting gold to have been rarer in England than in Sweden, I
cannot grant Stjerna's contention that therefore an English
poet could not have conceived the idea of a vast gold hoard[6];
or that, even if the poet does deck his warriors with gold somewhat more sumptuously than was actually the case in England,

[1] *Germania*, cap. xv.   [2] ll. 378, 470.
[3] Cassiodorus, *Variae*, v, 1.
[4] Walter, *Corpus juris Germanici antiqui*, 1824, ii, 125.
[5] *Heimskringla, Haraldz saga*, cap. 38–40.
[6] "The idea of a gold hoard undoubtedly points to the earlier version of the
Beowulf poem having originated in Scandinavia. No such 'gold period' ever
existed in Britain." *Essays*, p. 147.

we can draw any argument from it. For, if the dragon in *Beowulf* guards a treasure, so equally does the typical dragon of Old English proverbial lore[1]. Beowulf is spoken of as *gold-wlanc*, but the typical thegn in *Finnsburg* is called *gold-hladen*[2]. The sword found by Beowulf in the hall of Grendel's mother has a golden hilt, but the English proverb had it that "gold is in its place on a man's sword[3]." Heorot is hung with golden tapestry, but gold-inwoven fabric has been unearthed from Saxon graves at Taplow, and elsewhere in England[4]. Gold glitters in other poems quite as lavishly as in *Beowulf*, sometimes more so. Widsith made a hobby of collecting golden *bēagas*. The subject of *Waldere* is a fight for treasure. The byrnie of Waldere[5] is adorned with gold: so is that of Holofernes in *Judith*[6], so is that of the typical warrior in the *Elene*[7]. Are all these poems Scandinavian?

"The prevalence of ring-swords." We know that swords were sometimes fitted with a ring in the hilt[8]. It is not clear whether the object of this ring was to fasten the hilt by a strap to the wrist, for convenience in fighting (as has been the custom with the cavalry sword in modern times) or whether it was used to attach the "peace bands," by which the hilt of the sword was sometimes fixed to the scabbard, when only being worn cere-monially[9]. The word *hring-mæl*, applied three times to the sword in *Beowulf*, has been interpretated as a reference to these "ring-swords," though it is quite conceivable that it may refer only to the damascening of the sword with a ringed pattern[10]. Assuming that the reference in *Beowulf is* to a "ring-sword," Stjerna illustrates the allusion from seven ring-swords, or frag-ments of ring-swords, found in Sweden. But, as Dr Clark Hall himself points out (whilst oddly enough accepting this argument

---

[1] *Cottonian Gnomic Verses*, ll. 26–7.   [2] l. 14.
[3] *Exeter Gnomic Verses*, l. 126.   [4] Baldwin Brown, III, 385, IV, 640.
[5] *B.* l. 19.   [6] l. 339.   [7] l. 991.
[8] Cf. Falk, *Altnordische Waffenkunde*, 28.
[9] I would suggest this as the more likely because, if the ring were inserted for a practical purpose, it is not easy to see why it later survived in the form of a mere knob, which is neither useful nor ornamental. But if it were used to attach the symbolical "peace bands," it may have been retained, in a "fossilized form," with a symbolical meaning.
[10] Most editors indeed do take it in this sense, though recently Schücking has adopted Stjerna's explanation of "ring-sword." In l. 322, Falk (27) takes *hring-iren* to refer to a "ring-adorned sword," though it may well mean a ring-byrnie.

as proof of the Scandinavian colouring of *Beowulf*) four ring-swords at least have been found in England[1]. And these English swords are *real* ring-swords; that is to say, the pommel is furnished with a ring, within which another ring moves (in the oldest type of sword) quite freely. This freedom of movement seems, however, to be gradually restricted, and in one of these English swords the two rings are made in one and the same piece. In the Swedish swords, however, this restriction is carried further, and the two rings are represented by a knob growing out of a circular base. Another sword of this "knob"-type has recently been found in a Frankish tomb[2], and yet another in the Rhineland[3]. It seems to be agreed among archæologists that the English type, as found in Kent, is the original, and that the Swedish and continental "ring-swords" are merely imitations, in which the ring has become conventionalized into a knob[4]. But, if so, how can the mention of a ring-sword in *Beowulf* (if indeed that be the meaning of *hring-mæl*) prove Scandinavian colouring? If it proved anything (which it does not) it would tend to prove the reverse, and to locate *Beowulf* in Kent, where the true ring-swords have been found.

"The prevalence of boar-helmets." It is true that several representations of warriors wearing boar-helmets have been found in Scandinavia. But the only certainly Anglo-Saxon

[1] Actually, I believe, more: for two ring swords were found at Faversham, and are now in the British Museum. For an account of one of them see Roach Smith, *Collectanea Antiqua*, 1868, vol. VI, 139. In this specimen both the fixed ring and the ring which moves within it are complete circles. But in the Gilton sword (*Archæologia*, XXX, 132) and in the sword discovered at Bifrons (*Archæologia Cantiana*, X, 312) one of the rings no longer forms a complete circle, and in the sword discovered at Sarre (*Archæol. Cant.* VI, 172) the rings are fixed together, and one of them has little resemblance to a ring at all.

[2] At Concevreux. It is described by M. Jules Pilloy in *Mémoires de la Société Académique de St Quentin*, 4e Sér. tom. XVI, 1913; see esp. pp. 36–7.

[3] See Lindenschmit, "Germanisches Schwert mit ungewöhnlicher Bildung des Knaufes," in *Die Altertümer unserer heidnischen Vorzeit*, V Bd., V Heft, Taf. 30, p. 165, Mainz, 1905.

[4] Salin has no doubt that the Swedish type from Uppland (his figure 252) is later than even the latest type of English ring-sword (the Sarre pommel, 251) which is itself later than the Faversham (249) or Bifrons (250) pommel. See Salin (B.), *Die Altgermanische Thierornamentik*, Stockholm, 1904, p. 101. The same conclusion is arrived at by Lindenschmit: "Die ursprüngliche Form ist wohl in dem, unter Nr. 249 von Salin abgebildeten Schwertknopf aus Kent zu sehen"; and even more emphatically by Pilloy, who pronounces the Swedish Vendel sword both on account of its "ring" and other characteristics, as "inspirée par un modèle venu de cette contrée [Angleterre]."

helmet yet found in England has a boar-crest[1]; and this is, I believe, the only actual boar-helmet yet found. How then can the boar-helmets of *Beowulf* show Scandinavian rather than Anglo-Saxon origin?

"The prevalence of ring-corslets." It is true that only one trace of a byrnie, and that apparently not of ring-mail, has so far been found in an Anglo-Saxon grave. (We have somewhat more abundant remains from the period prior to the migration to England: a peculiarly fine corslet of ring-mail, with remains of some nine others, was found in the moss at Thorsbjerg[2] in the midst of the ancient Anglian continental home; and other ring-corslets have been found in the neighbourhood of Angel, at Vimose[3] in Fünen.) But, for the period when *Beowulf* must have been composed, the ring-corslet is almost as rare in Scandinavia as in England[4]; the artist, however, seems to be indicating a byrnie upon many of the warriors depicted on the Vendel helm (Grave 14: seventh century). Equally, in England, warriors are represented on the Franks Casket as wearing the byrnie: also the laws of Ine (688–95) make it clear that the byrnie was by no means unknown[5]. Other Old English poems, certainly not Scandinavian, mention the ring-byrnie. How then can the mention of it in *Beowulf* be a proof of Scandinavian origin?

"The prevalence of ring-money." Before minted money became current, rings were used everywhere among the Teutonic peoples. Gold rings, *intertwined* so as to form a chain, have been found throughout Scandinavia, presumably for use as a medium of exchange. The term *locenra bēaga* (gen. plu.) occurs in *Beowulf*, and this is interpreted by Stjerna as "rings *intertwined or locked* together[6]." But *locen* in *Beowulf* need not have the meaning of "intertwined"; it occurs elsewhere in Old English of a single jewel, *sincgim locen*[7]. Further, even if *locen* does mean "inter-

---

[1] The Benty Grange helmet; see below, p. 358.
[2] Depicted by Clark Hall, Stjerna's *Essays*, p. 258.
[3] Clark Hall's *Beowulf*, p. 227.
[4] "Von Skandinavien gibt es aus der Völkerwanderungszeit und Wikinger-epoche keine archäologischen Anhaltspunkte für das Tragen des Panzers, weder aus Funden noch aus Darstellungen," Max Ebert in Hoops' *Reallexikon*, III, 395 (1915–16). But surely this is too sweeping. Fragments of an iron byrnie, made of small rings fastened together, were found in the Vendel grave 12 (seventh century). See *Graffältet vid Vendel, beskrifvet af* H. Stolpe och T. J. Arne, pp. 49, 60, plates xl, xli, xlii.
[5] 54–1. Liebermann, p. 114.   [6] *Essays*, 34–5.   [7] *Elene*, 264.

twined," such intertwined rings are not limited to Scandinavia proper. They have been found in Schleswig[1]. And almost the very phrase in *Beowulf*, *londes ne locenra bēaga*[2], recurs in the *Andreas*. The phrase there may be imitated from *Beowulf*, but, equally, the phrase in *Beowulf* may be imitated from some earlier poem. In fact, it is part of the traditional poetic diction: but its occurrence in the *Andreas* shows that it cannot be used as an argument of Scandinavian origin.

Whilst, therefore, accepting with gratitude the numerous illustrations which Stjerna has drawn from Scandinavian grave-finds, we must be careful not to read a Scandinavian colouring into features of *Beowulf* which are at least as much English as Scandinavian, such as the ring-sword or the boar-helmet or the ring-corslet.

There is, as is noted above, a certain atmosphere of profusion and wealth about some Scandinavian grave-finds, which corresponds much more nearly with the wealthy life depicted in *Beowulf* than does the comparatively meagre tomb-furniture of England. But we must remember that, after the spread of Christianity in the first half of the seventh century, the custom of burying articles with the bodies of the dead naturally ceased, or almost ceased, in England. Scandinavia continued heathen for another four hundred years, and it was during these years that the most magnificent deposits were made. As Stjerna himself points out, "a steadily increasing luxury in the appointment of graves" is to be found in Scandinavia in these centuries before the introduction of Christianity there. When we find in Scandinavia things (complete ships, for example) which we do not find in England, we owe this, partly to the nature of the soil in which they were embedded, but also to the continuance of such burial customs after they had died out in England.

Helm and byrnie were not necessarily unknown, or even very rare in England, simply because it was not the custom to bury them with the dead. On the other hand, the frequent mention of them in *Beowulf* does not imply that they were common: for

---

[1] Engelhardt, *Denmark in the Early Iron Age*, p. 66.   [2] *Andreas*, 303.

Beowulf deals only with the aristocratic adherents of a court, and even in *Beowulf* fine specimens of the helm and byrnie are spoken of as things which a king seeks far and wide to procure for his retainers[1]. We cannot, therefore, argue that there is any discrepancy. However, if we do so argue, it would merely prove, not that *Beowulf* is Scandinavian as opposed to English, but that it is comparatively late in date. Tacitus emphasizes the fact that spear and shield were the Teutonic weapons, that helmet and corslet were hardly known[2]. Pagan graves show that at any rate they were hardly known *as tomb-furniture* in England in the fifth, sixth, and early seventh centuries. The introduction of Christianity, and the intercourse with the South which it involved, certainly led to the growth of pomp and wealth in England, till the early eighth century became "the golden age of Anglo-Saxon England."

It might therefore conceivably be argued that *Beowulf* reflects the comparative abundance of early Christian England, as opposed to the more primitive heathen simplicity; but to argue a Scandinavian origin from the profusion of *Beowulf* admits of an easy *reductio ad absurdum*. For the same arguments would prove a heathen, Scandinavian origin for the *Andreas*, the *Elene*, the *Exodus*, or even for the Franks Casket, despite its Anglo-Saxon inscription and Christian carvings.

However, though the absence of helm and byrnie from Anglo-Saxon graves does not prove that these arms were not used by the living in heathen times, one thing it assuredly *does* prove: that the Anglo-Saxons in heathen times did not sacrifice helm and byrnie recklessly in funeral pomp. And this brings us to the second argument as to the origin of *Beowulf* which has been based on archæology.

Something has been said above of this second contention[3] —that the accuracy of the account of Beowulf's funeral is confirmed in every point by archæological evidence: that it must

---

[1] l. 2869.
[2] "Few have corslets and only one here and there a helmet" (*Germania*, 6). In the *Annals* (ii, 14) Tacitus makes Germanicus roundly deny the use of either by the Germans: *non loricam Germano, non galeam.*
[3] See above, p. 124.

therefore have been composed within living memory of a time when ceremonies of this kind were still actually in use in England: and that therefore we cannot date *Beowulf* later than the third or fourth decade of the seventh century.

To begin with; the pyre in *Beowulf* is represented as hung with helmets, bright byrnies, and shields. Now it is impossible to say exactly how the funeral pyres were equipped in England. But we *do* know how the buried bodies were equipped. And (although inhumation cemeteries are much more common than cremation cemeteries) all the graves that have been opened have so far yielded only one case of a helmet and byrnie being buried with the warrior, and one other very doubtful case of a helmet without the byrnie. Abroad, instances are somewhat more common, but still of great rarity. For such things could ill be spared. Charles the Great forbade the export of byrnies from his dominions. Worn by picked champions fighting in the forefront, they might well decide the issue of a battle. In the mounds where we have reason to think that the great chiefs mentioned in *Beowulf*, Eadgils or Ohthere, lie buried, any trace of weapons was conspicuously absent among the burnt remains. Nevertheless, the belief that his armour would be useful to the champion in the next life, joined perhaps with a feeling that it was unlucky, or unfair on the part of the survivor to deprive the dead of his personal weapons, led in heathen times to the occasional burial of these treasures with the warrior who owned them. The fifth century tomb of Childeric I, when discovered twelve centuries later, was found magnificently furnished—the prince had been buried with treasure and much equipment[1], sword, scramasax[2], axe, spear. But these were his own. Similarly, piety might have demanded that Beowulf should be burnt with his full equipment. But would the pyre have been hung with helmets and byrnies? Whose? Were the thegns asked to sacrifice theirs, and go naked into the next fight in honour of their lord? If so, what archæological authority have we for such a custom in England?

[1] See Chifflet, J. J., *Anastasis Childerici I...sive thesaurus sepulchralis*, Antverpiæ, *Plantin*, 1655.

[2] That *both* sword and scramasax were buried with Childeric is shown by Lindenschmit, *Handbuch*, I, 236–9: see also pp. 68 *etc.*

Then the barrow is built, and the vast treasure of the dragon (which included "many a helmet[1]") placed in it. Now there are instances of articles which have not passed through the fire being placed in or upon or around an urn with the cremated bones[2]. But is there any instance of the thing being done on this scale—of a wholesale burning of helmets and byrnies followed by a burial of huge treasure? If so, one would like to know when, and where. If not, how can it be argued that the account in *Beowulf* is one of which "the accuracy is confirmed in every point by archæological or contemporary literary evidence?" Rather we must say, with Knut Stjerna, that it is "too much of a good thing[3]."

For the antiquities of Anglo-Saxon England, the student should consult the *Victoria County History*. The two splendid volumes of Professor G. Baldwin Brown on *Saxon Art and Industry in the Pagan Period*[4] at length enable the general reader to get a survey of the essential facts, for which up to now he has had to have recourse to innumerable scattered treatises. *The Archæology of the Anglo-Saxon Settlements* by Mr E. Thurlow Leeds will also be found helpful.

Side-lights from the field of Teutonic antiquities in general can be got from Prof. Baldwin Brown's *Arts and Crafts of our Teutonic Forefathers*, 1910, and from Lindenschmit's *Handbuch der deutschen Alterthumskunde, I. Theil: Die Alterthümer der Merovingischen Zeit* (Braunschweig, 1880–89), a book which is still indispensable. Hoops' *Reallexikon der germanischen Altertumskunde*, Strassburg, 1911–19, 4 vols., includes a large number of contributions of the greatest importance to the student of *Beowulf*, both upon archæological and other subjects. By the completion[5] of this most valuable work, amid heart-breaking difficulties, Prof. Hoops has placed all students under a great obligation.

Much help can be got from an examination of the antiquities of Teutonic countries other than England. The following books are useful—for Norway:

[1] l. 2762–3.
[2] Worsaae, *Nordiske Oldsager*, Kjøbenhavn, 1859; see No. 499; Roach Smith, *Collectanea Antiqua*, 1852, II, 164; Montelius, *Antiq. Suéd.* 1873, No. 294 (p. 184).
[3] *Essays*, p. 198. See also above, p. 124. Mr Reginald Smith writes to me: "Unburnt objects with cremated burials in prehistoric times (Bronze, Early and Late Iron Ages) are the exception, and are probably accidental survivals from the funeral pyre. In such an interpretation of *Beowulf* I agree with the late Knut Stjerna, who was an archæologist of much experience."
[4] Forming vols. 3 and 4 of *The Arts in Early England*, 1903–15.
[5] It was, however, necessary to leave over for a supplementary volume some of the contributions most interesting from the point of view of the archæology of *Beowulf*: e.g. spatha, speer, schild.

Gustafson (G.), *Norges Oldtid*, 1906; for Denmark: Müller (S.), *Vor Oldtid,* 1897; for Sweden: Montelius (O.), *Civilization of Sweden in Heathen Times,* 1888, *Kulturgeschichte Schwedens*, 1906; for Schleswig: Mestorf (J.), *Vorgeschichtliche Alterthümer aus Schleswig*; for the Germanic nations in their wanderings on the outskirts of the Roman Empire: Hampel (J.), *Alterthümer des frühen Mittelalters in Ungarn*, 3 Bde, 1905; for Germanic remains in Gaul: Barrière-Flavy (M. C.), *Les Arts industriels des peuples barbares de la Gaule du Vme au VIIIme siècle*, 3 tom. 1901.

Somewhat popular accounts, and now rather out of date, are the two South Kensington handbooks: Worsaae (J. J. A.), *Industrial Arts of Denmark*, 1882, and Hildebrand (H.), *Industrial Arts of Scandinavia*, 1883.

Scandinavian Burial Mounds

The three great "Kings' Mounds" at Old Uppsala were explored between 1847 and 1874: cremated remains from them can be seen in the Stockholm Museum. An account of the tunnelling, and of the complicated structure of the mounds, was given in 1876 by the Swedish State-Antiquary[1]. From these finds Knut Stjerna dated the oldest of the "Kings' Mounds" about 500 A.D.[2], and the others somewhat later. Now, as we are definitely told that Athils (Eadgils) and the two kings who figure in the list of Swedish monarchs as his grandfather and great-grandfather (Egil and Aun) were "laid in mound" at Uppsala[3], and as the chronology agrees, it seems only reasonable to conclude that the three Kings' Mounds were raised over these three kings[4].

That Athils' father Ottar (Ohthere) was not regarded as having been buried at Uppsala is abundantly clear from the account given of his death, and of his nickname Vendel-crow[5]. A mound near Vendel north of Uppsala is known by his name. Such names are often the result of quite modern antiquarian conjecture: but that such is not the case here was proved by the recent discovery that an antiquarian survey (preserved in MS in the Royal Library at Stockholm) dating from 1677, mentions in Vendel "widh Hussby, [en] stor jorde högh, som heeter Otters högen[6]." An exploration of Ottar's mound showed a striking similarity with the Uppsala mounds. The structure was the same, a cairn of stones covered over with earth; the

[1] B. E. Hildebrand, *Grafhögarne vid Gamla Upsala, Kongl. Vitterhets Historie och Antiqvitets Akademiens Månadsblad*, 1875-7, pp. 250-60.
[2] *Fasta fornlämningar i Beovulf*, in *Antiqvarisk Tidskrift för Sverige*, xviii, 48-64.
[3] *Heimskringla: Ynglingasaga*, cap. 25, 26, 29.
[4] See B. Nerman, *Vilka konungar ligga i Uppsala högar?* Uppsala, 1913, and the same scholar's *Ynglingasagan i arkeologisk belysning*, in *Fornvännen* 1917, 226-61.
[5] *Heimskringla: Ynglingasaga*, cap. 27
[6] A discovery made by Otto v. Friesen in 1910: see S. Lindqvist in *Fornvännen*, 1917, 129. Two years earlier (1675) "Utters högen i Wändell" is mentioned in connection with an investigation into witchcraft. See Linderholm, *Vendelshögens konunganamn*, in *Namn och Bygd*, vii, 1919, 36, 40.

cremated remains were similar, there were abundant traces of burnt animals, a comb, half-spherical draughts with two round holes bored in the flat side, above all, there was in neither case any trace of weapons. In Ottar's mound a gold Byzantine coin was found, pierced, having evidently been used as an ornament. It can be dated 477–8; it is much worn, but such coins seldom remained in the North in use for a century after their minting[1]. Ottar's mound obviously, then, belongs to the same period as the Uppsala mounds, and confirms the date attributed by Stjerna to the oldest of those mounds, about 500 A.D.

Weapons

For weapons in general see Lehmann (H.), *Über die Waffen im angel-sächsischen Beowulfliede*, in *Germania*, xxxi, 486–97; Keller (May L.), *The Anglo-Saxon weapon names treated archæologically and etymologically*, Heidelberg, 1906 (*Anglistische Forschungen*, xv: cf. Holthausen, *Anglia, Beiblatt*, xviii, 65–9, Binz, *Litteraturblatt*, xxxi, 98–100); ‡Wagner (R.), *Die Angriffswaffen der Angelsächsischen*, Diss., Königsberg; and especially Falk (H.), *Altnordische Waffenkunde*, in *Videnskapsselskapets Skrifter, Hist.-Filos. Klasse*, 1914, Kristiania.

The Sword. The sword of the Anglo-Saxon pagan period (from the fifth to the seventh century) "is deficient in quality as a blade, and also... in the character of its hilt[2]." In this it contrasts with the sword found in the peat-bogs of Schleswig from an earlier period: "these swords of the Schleswig moss-finds are much better weapons[3]," as well as with the later Viking sword of the ninth or tenth century, which "is a remarkably effective and well-considered implement[4]." It has been suggested that both the earlier Schleswig swords and the later Viking swords (which bear a considerable likeness to each other, as against the inferior Anglo-Saxon sword) are the product of intercourse with Romanized peoples[5], whilst the typical Anglo-Saxon sword "may represent an independent Germanic effort at sword making[6]." However this may be, it is noteworthy that nowhere in *Beowulf* do we have any hint of the skill of any sword-smith who is regarded as contemporary. A good sword is always "an old heir-loom," "an ancient treasure[7]." The sword of Wiglaf, which had belonged to Eanmund, and the sword with which Eofor slays Ongentheow, are

---

[1] For a preliminary account of the discovery, see *Ottarshögen i Vendel*, by S. Lindqvist in *Fornvännen*, 1917, 127–43, and for discussion of the whole subject, B. Nerman, *Ottar Vendelkråka och Ottarshögen i Vendel*, in *Upplands Fornminnesförenings Tidskrift*, vii, 309–34.

[2] Baldwin Brown, iii, 216.   [3] 213.   [4] 218.

[5] So Baldwin Brown, iii, 213; Lorange, *Den Yngre Jernalders Sværd*, Bergen, 1889, passim.

[6] Baldwin Brown, iii, 215.

[7] It is somewhat similar in Norse literature, where swords are constantly indicated as either inherited from of old, or coming from abroad: cf. Falk, 38–41.

described by the phrase *ealdsweord eotenisc*, as if they were weapons of which the secret and origin had been lost—indeed the same phrase is applied to the magic sword which Beowulf finds in the hall of Grendel's mother.

The blade of these ancestral swords was sometimes damascened or adorned with wave-like patterns[1]. The swords of the Schleswig moss-finds are almost all thus adorned with a variegated surface, as often are the later Viking swords; but those of the Anglo-Saxon graves are *not*. Is it fanciful to suggest that the reference to damascening is a tradition coming down from the time of the earlier sword as found in the Nydam moss? A few early swords might have been preserved among the invaders as family heirlooms, too precious to be buried with the owner, as the product of the local weapon-smith was.

See, for a full discussion of the sword in *Beowulf*, Stjerna, *Hjälmar och svärd i Beovulf* (*Studier tillägnade O. Montelius*, Stockholm, pp. 99–120 = *Essays*, transl. Clark Hall, pp. 1–32). The standard treatise on the sword, *Den Yngre Jernalders Sværd*, Bergen, 1889, by A. L. Lorange, deals mainly with a rather later period.

The Helmet. The helmet found at Benty Grange in Derbyshire in 1848 is now in the Sheffield Museum[2]: little remains except the boar-crest, the nose-piece, and the framework of iron ribs radiating from the crown, and fixed to a circle of iron surrounding the brow (perhaps the *frēawrāsn* of *Beowulf*, 1451). Mr Bateman, the discoverer, described the helmet as "coated with narrow plates of horn, running in a diagonal direction from the ribs, so as to form a herring-bone pattern; the ends were secured by strips of horn, radiating in like manner as the iron ribs, to which they were riveted at intervals of about an inch and a half: all the rivets had ornamented heads of silver on the outside, and on the front rib is a small cross of the same metal. Upon the top or crown of the helmet, is an elongated oval brass plate, upon which stands the figure of an animal, carved in iron, now much rusted, but still a very good representation of a pig: it has bronze eyes[3]." Helmets of very similar construction, but without the boar, have been found on the Continent and in Scandinavia (Vendel, Grave 14, late seventh century). The continental helmets often

---

[1] *Beowulf*, 1489, *wǣgsweord*; cf. *Vægir* as a sword-name in the *Thulur*. In ll. 1521, 1564, 2037, *hringmǣl* may refer to the ring in the hilt, and terms like *wunden-* are more likely to refer to the serpentine ornament of the hilt. This must be the case with *wyrm-fāh* (1698) as it is a question of the hilt alone. Stjerna (p. 111=*Essays*, 20) and others take *āter-tānum fāh* (1459) as referring to the damascened pattern (cf. *eggjar...eitrdropom innan fáþar*; *Brot af Sigurðar-kviðu*). It is suggested however by Falk (p. 17) that *tān* here refers to an edge welded-on: the Icelandic *egg-teinn*.

[2] The only certainly Anglo-Saxon helmet as yet discovered: traces of what may have been a similar head-piece were found near Cheltenham: Roach Smith, *Collectanea Antiqua*, II, 1852, 238.

[3] *Coll. Ant.* II, 1852. 239; Bateman, *Ten Years' Diggings*, 30; *Catalogue of the Antiquities preserved in the Museum of Thomas Bateman*, Bakewell, 1855.

stand higher[1] than the Benty Grange or Vendel specimens, being sometimes quite conical (cf. the epithet "war-steep," *heaðo-stēap, Beowulf*). Many of the continental helmets are provided with cheek-protections, and these also appear in the Scandinavian representations of warriors on the Torslunda plates and elsewhere. These side pieces have become detached from the magnificent Vendel helmet, which is often shown in engravings without them[2], but they can be seen in the Stockholm Museum[3]. If it ever possessed them, the Benty Grange helmet has lost these side pieces Such cheek-protections are, however, represented, together with the nose-protection, on the head of one of the warriors depicted on the Franks Casket. In the Vendel helms, the nose-pieces were connected under the eyes with the rim of the helmet, so as to form a mask[3]; the helmet in *Beowulf* is frequently spoken of as the battle-mask[4].

Both helmet and boar-crest were sometimes gold-adorned[5]: the golden boar was a symbol of the god Freyr: some magic protective power is still, in *Beowulf*[6], felt to adhere to these swine-likenesses, as it was in the days of Tacitus[7].

In Scandinavia, the Torslunda plates show the helmet with a boar-crest: the Vendel helmet has representations of warriors whose crests have an animal's head tailing off to a mere rim or roll: this may be the *walu* or *wala* which keeps watch over the head in *Beowulf*[8]. The helmet was bound fast to the head[9]; exactly how, we do not know.

See Lehmann (H.), *Brünne und Helm im ags. Beowulfliede* (Göttingen Diss., Leipzig; cf. Wülker, *Anglia*, VIII, *Anzeiger*, 167–70; Schulz, *Engl. Stud.* IX, 471); Hoops' *Reallexikon*, s.v. *Helm*; Baldwin Brown, III, 194–6; Falk, *Altnord. Waffenkunde*, 155–73; Stjerna, *Hjälmar och svärd*, 1907, as above: but the attempt of Stjerna to arrange the helmets he depicts in a

---

[1] A very good description of these continental "Spangenhelme" is given in the magnificent work of I. W. Gröbbels, *Der Reihengräberfund von Gammertingen*, München, 1905. These helms had long been known from a specimen (place of origin uncertain) in the Hermitage at Petrograd, and another example, that of Vézeronce, supposed to have been lost in the battle between Franks and Burgundians in 524. Seven other examples have been discovered in the last quarter of a century, including those of Baldenheim (for which see Henning (R.), *Der helm von Baldenheim und die verwandten helme des frühen mittelalters*, Strassburg, 1907, cf. Kauffmann, *Z.f.d.Ph.* XL, 464–7) and Gammertingen. They are not purely Germanic, and may have been made in Gaul, or among the Ostrogoths in Ravenna, or further east.

[2] Stjerna, *Essays*, p. 11=*Studier tillägnade Oscar Montelius af Lärjungar*, 1903, p. 104: Clark Hall, *Beowulf*, 1911, p. 228.

[3] See also *Graffället vid Vendel, beskrifvet af* H. Stolpe och T. J. Arne, Stockholm, 1912, pp. 13, 54; Pl. v, xli.

[4] ll. 396, 2049, 2257, 2605; cf. *grīmhelm*, 334.

[5] 2811, 304, 1111 (cf. Falk, 156).

[6] 1453–4 (cf. Falk, 157–9).

[7] *securum etiam inter hostes praestat. Germ.* cap. 45.

[8] 1031 (cf. Falk, 158).

[9] 1630, 2723. Cf. *Exodus*, 174, *grīmhelm gespēon cyning cinberge*, and *Genesis*, 444. (See Falk, 166.)

chronological series is perilous, and depends on a dating of the Benty Grange helmet which is by no means generally accepted.

The Corslet. This in *Beowulf* is made of rings[1], twisted and interlaced by hand[2]. As stated above, the fragments of the only known Anglo-Saxon byrnie were not of this type, but rather intended to have been sewn "upon a doublet of strong cloth[3]." Byrnies were of various lengths, the longer ones reaching to the middle of the thigh (*byrnan side, Beow.* 1291, cf. *loricæ longæ, siðar brynjur*).

See Falk, 179; Baldwin Brown, III. 194.

The Spear. Spear and shield were the essential Germanic weapons in the days of Tacitus, and they are the weapons most commonly found in Old English tombs. The spear-shaft has generally decayed, analysis of fragments surviving show that it was frequently of ash[4]. The butt-end of the spear was frequently furnished with an iron tip, and the distance of this from the spear-head, and the size of the socket, show the spear-shaft to have been six or seven feet long, and three-quarters of an inch to one inch in diameter.

See Falk, 66–90; Baldwin Brown, III, 234–41.

The Shield. Several round shields were preserved on the Gokstad ship, and in the deposits of an earlier period at Thorsbjerg and Nydam. These are formed of boards fastened together, often only a quarter of an inch thick, and not strengthened or braced in any way, bearing out the contemptuous description of the painted German shield which Tacitus puts into the mouth of Germanicus[5]. It was, however, intended that the shield should be light. It was easily pierced, but, by a rapid twist, the foe's sword could be broken or wrenched from his hand. Thus we are told how Gunnar gave his shield a twist, as his adversary thrust his sword through it, and so snapped off his sword at the hilt[6]. The shield was held by a bar, crossing a hole some four inches wide cut in the middle. The hand was protected by a hollow conical boss or umbo, fixed to the wood by its brim, but projecting considerably. In England the wood of the shield has always perished, but a large number of bosses have been preserved. The boss seems to have been called *rond*, a word which is also used for the shield as a whole. In *Beowulf*, 2673, *Gifts of Men*, 65, the meaning "boss" suits *rond* best, also in *rand sceal on scylde, fæst fingra gebeorh* (*Cotton. Gnomic Verses*, 37–8). But the original meaning of *rand* must have been the circular rim round the edge, and this

---

[1] Cf. ll. 1503, 1548, 2260, 2754.
[2] Cf. ll. 322, 551, 1443.
[3] Bateman, *Ten Years' Diggings*, 1861, p. 32.
[4] Cf. *Beowulf*, 330, 1772, 2042.
[5] "ne scuta quidem ferro neruoue firmata, sed...tennis et fucatas colore tabulas," *Annals*, II, 14; cf. *Germania*, 6, "scuta tantum lectissimis coloribus distinguunt."
[6] *Njáls Saga*, cap. **xxx.**

meaning it retains in Icelandic (Falk, 131). The linden wood was sometimes bound with bast, whence *scyld* (*sceal*) *gebunden, lēoht linden bord* (*Exeter Gnomic Verses*, 94–5).

See Falk (126–54); Baldwin Brown, III, 196-204; Pfannkuche (K.), *Der Schild bei den Angelsachsen,* Halle Dissertation, 1908.

The Bow is a weapon of much less importance in *Beowulf* than the spear. Few traces of the bow have survived from Anglo-Saxon England, though many wooden long-bows have been preserved in the moss-finds in a remarkably fine state. They are of yew, some over six feet long, and in at least one instance tipped with horn. The bow entirely of horn was, of course, well known in the East, and in classical antiquity, but I do not think traces of any horn-bow have been discovered in the North. It was a difficult weapon to manage, as the suitors of Penelope found to their cost. Possibly that is why Hæthcyn is represented as killing his brother Herebeald accidentally with a horn-bow: he could not manage the exotic weapon.

See Falk, 91–103; Baldwin Brown, III, 241.

The Hall

It may perhaps be the fact that in the church of Sta. Maria de Naranco, in the north of Spain, we have the hall of a Visigothic king driven north by the Mohammedan invasion. But, even if this surmise[1] be correct, the structure of a stone hall of about 750 A.D. gives us little information as to the wooden halls of early Anglo-Saxon times. Heorot is clearly built of timber, held together by iron clamps[2]. These halls were oblong, and a famous passage in Bede[3] makes it clear that, at any rate at the time of the Conversion, the hall had a door at both ends, and the fire burnt in the middle. (The smoke escaped through a hole in the roof, through which probably most of the light came, for windows were few or none.) The *Finnsburg Fragment* also implies two doors. Further indications can be drawn from references to the halls of Norse chiefs. The Scandinavian hall was divided by rows of wooden pillars into a central nave and side aisles. The pillars in the centre were known as the "high-seat pillars." Rows of seats ran down the length of the hall on each side. The central position, facing the high-seat pillars and the fire, was the most honourable. The place of honour for the chief guest was opposite: and it is quite clear that in *Beowulf* also the guest did not sit next his host[4].

Other points we may note about Heorot, are the tapestry with which its walls are draped[5], and the paved and variegated floor[6]. Unlike so

---

[1] It is the guess of A. Haupt, *Die Älteste Kunst der Germanen,* p. 213.
[2] ll. 773–5, 998.
[3] *Hist. Eccl.* II, 13. The life of man is compared to the transit of a sparrow flying from door to door of the hall where the king sits feasting with his thanes and warriors, with a fire in the midst.
[4] ll. 617–24, 2011–3.   [5] 995.   [6] 725.

many later halls, Heorot has a floor little, if anything, raised above the ground: horses can be brought in[1].

In later times, in Iceland, the arrangement of the hall was changed, and the house consisted of many rooms; but these were formed, not by partitioning the hall, but by building several such halls side by side: the *stufa* or hall proper, the *skáli* or sleeping hall, etc.

See M. Heyne, *Ueber die Lage und Construction der Halle Heorot*, Paderborn, 1864, where the scanty information about Heorot is collected, and supplemented with some information about Anglo-Saxon building. For the Icelandic hall see Valtýr Guðmundsson, *Privatboligen på Island i Sagatiden*, København, 1889. This has been summarized, in a more popular form, in a chapter on *Den islandske Bolig i Fristatstiden*, contributed by Guðmundsson to Rosenberg's *Træk af Livet paa Island i Fristatstiden*, 1894 (pp. 251–74). Here occurs the picture of an Icelandic hall which has been so often reproduced—by Olrik, Holthausen, and in *Beowulf*-translations. But it is a conjectural picture, and we can by no means assume all its details for Heorot. Rhamm's colossal work is only for the initiated, but is useful for consultation on special points (*Ethnographische Beiträge zur Germanisch-slawischen Altertumskunde*, von K. Rhamm, 1905–8. I. *Die Grosshufen der Nordgermanen*; II. *Urzeitliche Bauernhöfe*). For various details see Hoops' *Reallexikon*, s.v. *flett*; Neckel in *P.B.B.* XLI, 1916, 163–70 (*under edoras*); Meiringer in *I.F.*, especially XVIII, 257 (*under eoderas*); Kaufmann in *Z.f.d.Ph.* XXXIX, 282–92.

Ships

In a tumulus near Snape in Suffolk, opened in 1862, there were discovered, with burnt bones and remains thought to be of Anglo-Saxon date, a large number of rivets which, from the positions in which they were found, seemed to give evidence of a boat 48 feet long by over nine feet wide[2]. A boat, similar in dimensions, but better preserved, was unearthed near Bruges in 1899, and the ribs, mast and rudder removed to the Gruuthuuse Museum[3].

Three boats were discovered in the peat-moss at Nydam in Schleswig in 1863, by Engelhardt. The most important is the "Nydam boat," clinker-built (i.e. with overlapping planks), of oak, 77 feet [23·5 m.] long, by some 11 [3·4 m.] broad, with rowlocks for fourteen oars down each side. There was no trace of any mast. Planks and framework had been held together, partly by iron bolts, and partly by ropes of bast. The boat had fallen to pieces, and had to be laboriously put together in the museum at Flensborg. Another boat was quite fragmentary, but a third boat, of fir, was found

[1] 1035 *etc.*

[2] *Proc. Soc. Ant., Sec. Ser.* II, 177–82.

[3] Jonckheere (É.), *L'origine de la Côte de Flandre et le Bateau de Bruges*, Bruges, 1903.

tolerably complete. Then the war of 1864 ended Engelhardt's labours at Nydam. The oak-boat was removed to Kiel, where it now is.

The fir-boat was allowed to decay: many of the pieces of the oak-boat had been rotten and had of necessity been restored in facsimile, and it is much less complete than might be supposed from the numerous reproductions, based upon the fine engraving by Magnus Petersen. The rustic with a spade, there depicted as gazing at the boat, is apt to give a wrong impression that it was dug out intact[1].

Such was, however, actually the case with regard to the ship excavated from the big mound at Gokstad, near Christiania, by Nicolaysen, in 1880. This was fitted both as a rowing and sailing ship; it was 66 feet [20·1 m.] long on the keel, 78 feet [23·8 m.] from fore to aft and nearly 17 feet [5·1 m.] broad, and was clinker-built, out of a much larger number of oaken planks than the Nydam ship. It had rowlocks for sixteen oars down each side, the gunwale was lined with shields, some of them well preserved, which had been originally painted alternately black and yellow. The find owed its extraordinary preservation to the blue clay in which it was embedded. Its discoverer wrote, with pardonable pride: "Certain it is that we shall not disinter any craft which, in respect of model and workmanship, will outrival that of Gokstad[2]."

Yet the prophecy was destined to prove false: for on Aug. 8, 1903, a farmer came into the National Museum at Christiania to tell the curator, Prof. Gustafson, that he had discovered traces of a boat on his farm at Oseberg. Gustafson found that the task was too great to be begun so late in the year: the digging out of the ship, and its removal to Christiania, occupied from just before Midsummer to just before Christmas of 1904. The potter's clay in which the ship was buried had preserved it, if possible, better than the Gokstad ship: but the movement of the soft subsoil had squeezed and broken both ship and contents. The ship was taken out of the earth in nearly two thousand fragments. These were carefully numbered and marked: each piece was treated, bent back into its right shape, and the ship was put together again plank by plank, as when it was first built. With the exception of a piece about half a yard long, five or six little bits let in, and one of the beams, the ship as it stands now consists of the original woodwork. Two-thirds of the rivets are the old ones. Till his death in 1915 Gustafson was occupied in treating and preparing for exhibition first the ship, and then its extraordinarily rich contents: a waggon and sledges beautifully carved, beds, chests, kitchen utensils which had been buried with the princess who had owned them. A full account of the find is only now being published[3].

---

[1] Engelhardt (H. C. C.), *Nydam Mosefund*, Kjöbenhavn, 1865.
[2] Nicolaysen (N.), *Langskibet fra Gokstad*, Kristiania, 1882.
[3] *Osebergfundet. Udgit av den Norske Stat, under redaktion av* A. W. Brøgger, Hj. Falk, H. Schetelig. Bd. I, Kristiania, 1917.

The Oseberg ship is the pleasure boat of a royal lady: clinker-built, of oak, exquisitely carved, intended not for long voyages but for the land-locked waters of the fiord, $70\frac{1}{2}$ feet [21·5 m.] long by some $16\frac{1}{2}$ feet [5 m.] broad. There are holes for fifteen oars down each side, and the ship carried mast and sail.

The upper part of the prow had been destroyed, but sufficient fragments have been found to show that it ended in the head of a snake-like creature, bent round in a coil. This explains the words *hringed-stefna*[1], *hring-naca*[2], *wunden-stefna*[3], used of the ship in *Beowulf*. A similar ringed prow is depicted on an engraved stone from Tjängvide, now in the National Historical Museum at Stockholm. This is supposed to date from about the year 1000[4].

The Gokstad and Oseberg ships, together with the ship of Tune, a much less complete specimen (unearthed in 1867, and found like the others on the shore of the Christiania fiord) owe their preservation to the clay, and the skill of Scandinavian antiquaries. Yet they are but three out of thousands of ship- or boat-burials. Schetelig enumerates 552 known instances from Norway alone. Often traces of the iron rivets are all that remain.

Ships preserved from the Baltic coast of Germany can be seen at Königsberg, Danzig and Stettin; they are smaller and apparently later; the best, that of Brösen, was destroyed.

The seamanship of *Beowulf* is removed by centuries from that of the (? fourth or fifth century) Nydam boat, which not only has no mast or proper keel, but is so built as to be little suited for sailing. In *Beowulf* the sea is a "sail-road," the word "to row" occurs only in the sense of "swim," sailing is assumed as the means by which Beowulf travels between the land of the Geatas and that of the Danes. Though he voyages with but fourteen companions, the ship is big enough to carry back four horses. How the sail may have been arranged is shown in many inscribed stones of the eighth to the tenth centuries: notably those of Stenkyrka[5], Högbro[6], and Tjängvide[7].

The Oseberg and Gokstad ships are no doubt later than the composition of *Beowulf*. But it is when looking at the Oseberg ship, especially if we picture the great prow like the neck of a swan ending in a serpent's coil, that we can best understand the words of *Beowulf*

> flota fāmī-heals fugle gelīcost,
> wunden-stefna,

well rendered by Earle "The foamy-necked floater, most like to a bird—the coily-stemmed."

[1] *Beowulf*, ll. 32, 1131, 1897.   [2] 1862.   [3] 220.
[4] Noreen, *Altschwedische Grammatik*, 1904, p. 499.
[5] All these places are in Gotland. The Stenkyrka stone is reproduced in Stjerna's *Essays*, transl. Clark Hall, fig. 24.
[6] The same, fig. 27.
[7] Reproduced in Montelius, *Sveriges Historia*, p. 283.

See Boehmer (G. H.), *Prehistoric Naval Architecture of the North of Europe, Report of the U.S. National Museum for* 1891 (now rather out of date); Guðmundsson (V.), *Nordboernes Skibe i Vikinge- og Sagatiden,* København, 1900; ‡Schnepper, *Die Namen der Schiffe u. Schiffsteile im Altenglischen* (Kiel Diss.), 1908; Falk (H.), *Altnordisches Seewesen* (*Wörter u. Sachen,* IV, Heidelberg, 1912); Hoops' *Reallexikon,* s.v. *Schiff.*

G.   LEIRE BEFORE ROLF KRAKI

That Leire was the royal town, not merely of Rolf Kraki, but of Rolf's predecessors as well, is stated in the *Skjoldunga Saga,* extant in the Latin abstract of Arngrim Jonsson: *Scioldus in arce Selandiae Hledro sedes posuit, quae et sequentium plurimorum regum regia fuit* (ed. Olrik, Kǿbenhavn, 1894, p. 23 [105]). Similarly we are told in the *Ynglinga Saga,* concerning Gefion, *Hennar fekk Skjǫldr, sonr Óðins; þau bjoggu at Hleiðru* (*Heimskringla,* udgivne ved F. Jónsson, Kǿbenhavn, I, 15 [cap. v]).

Above all, it is clear from the *Annales Lundenses* that, in the twelfth century, Dan, Ro (Hrothgar) and Haldan (Healfdene) were traditionally connected with Leire, and three of the grave mounds there were associated with these three kings. See the extract given above, pp. 204–5, and cf. p. 17.

H.   BEE-WOLF AND BEAR'S SON

The obvious interpretation of the name *Bēowulf* is that suggested by Grimm[1], that it means "wolf, or foe, of the bee." Grimm's suggestion was repeated independently by Skeat[2], and further reasons for the interpretation "bee-foe" have been found by Sweet[3] (who had been anticipated by Simrock[4] in some of his points), by Cosijn[5], Sievers[6], von Grienberger[7], Panzer[8] and Björkman[9].

From the phonological point of view the etymology is a

---

[1] *Deutsche Mythologie,* 3te Ausgabe, 1854, pp. 342, 639.
[2] *Academy,* XI, 1877, p. 163.
[3] *Engl. Stud.* II, 314.
[4] *Beowulf,* p. 177.
[5] *Aanteekeningen op den Beowulf,* 1892, p. 42.
[6] *P.B.B.* XVIII, 413.
[7] *Z.f.ö.G.* LVI, 759.
[8] *Beowulf,* p. 392.
[9] *Engl. Stud.* LII, 191. Among the many who have accepted the explanation "bee-wolf," without giving additional reasons, may be mentioned R. Müller, *Untersuchungen über die Namen des Liber Vitae,* 1901, p. 94.

perfect one, but many of those who were convinced that
"Beowulf" meant "bee-foe" had no satisfactory explanation
of "bee-foe" to offer[1]. Others, like Bugge, whilst admitting
that, so far as the form of the words goes, the etymology is
satisfactory, rejected "bee-foe" because it seemed to them
meaningless[2].

Yet it is very far from meaningless. "Bee-foe" means
"bear." The bear has got a name, or nickname, in many northern
languages from his habit of raiding the hives for honey. The
Finnish name for bear is said to be "honey-hand": he is certainly called "sweet-foot," *sötfot*, in Sweden, and the Old
Slavonic name, "honey-eater," has come to be accepted in
Russian, not merely as a nickname, but as the regular term
for "bear."

And "bear" is an excellent name for a hero of story. The
O.E. *beorn*, "warrior, hero, prince" seems originally to have
meant simply "bear." The bear, says Grimm, "is regarded, in
the belief of the Old Norse, Slavonic, Finnish and Lapp peoples,
as an exalted and holy being, endowed with human understanding and the strength of twelve men. He is called 'forest-
king,' 'gold-foot,' 'sweet-foot,' 'honey-hand,' 'honey-paw,'
'honey-eater,' but also 'the great,' 'the old,' 'the old grand-
sire[3].'" "Bee-hunter" is then a satisfactory explanation of
Bēowulf: while the alternative explanations are none of them
satisfactory.

Many scholars have been led off the track by the assumption
that Beow and Beowulf are to be identified, and that we must
therefore assume that the first element in Beowulf's name is
Bēow—that we must divide not *Bēo-wulf* but *Bēow-ulf*, "a
warrior after the manner of Beow[4]." But there is no ground

[1] Both Grimm and Skeat suggested the woodpecker, which feeds upon bees
and their larvae: Grimm appealing to classical mythology, Skeat instancing the
bird's courage. But nothing seems forthcoming from Teutonic mythology to
favour this interpretation. Cosijn, following Sijmons, *Z.f.d.Ph.* xxiv, 17,
thought bees might have been an omen of victory. But there is no satisfactory
evidence for this. The term *sigewif* applied to the swarming bees in the *Charms*
(Cockayne's *Leechdoms*, I, 384) is insufficient.

[2] *Tidskr. f. Philol. og Pædag.* viii, 289.

[3] *Deutsches Wörterbuch*, 1854, I, 1122.

[4] "Das compositum Beóvulf, wie Gôzolf, Irminolf, Reginolf, und andre
gebildet, zeigt nur einen helden und krieger im geist und sinn oder von der
art des Beówa an. Ihm entspricht altn. Biôlfr." (Müllenhoff, in *Z.f.d.A.* xii,

for any such assumption. It is true that in ll. 18, 53, "Beowulf" is written where we should have expected "Beowa." But, even if two words of similar sound have been confused, this fact affords no reason for supposing that they must necessarily have been in the first instance connected etymologically. And against the "warrior of Beow" interpretation is the fact that the name is recorded in the early Northumbrian *Liber Vitae* under the form "Biuuulf[1]." This name, which is that of an early monk of Durham, is presumably the same as that of the hero of our poem, though it does not, of course, follow that the bearer of it was named with any special reference to the slayer of Grendel. Now *Biuuulf* is correct Northumbrian for "bee-wolf," but the first element in the word cannot stand for *Bēow*[2], unless the

---

284.) But certainly this interpretation is impossible for O.N. *Biólfr:* "warrior of Beowa" would be **Byggulfr*, which we nowhere find. See Björkman in *Engl. Stud.* LII, 191. Müllenhoff at this date, whilst not connecting *Bēowulf* directly with *bēo*, "bee," did so connect *Bēowa*, whom he interpreted as a bee-god or bee-father. But there is no evidence for this, and the *w* of *Bēowa* tells emphatically against it. Müllenhoff subsequently abandoned this explanation.

[1] It is actually written *Biu^wulf*.

[2] *Biu* in *Biuuulf* cannot stand for *Bēo* [older *Beu*] because in Old Northumbrian *iu* and *eo* are rigidly differentiated, as an examination of all the other names in the *Liber Vitae* shows. As Sievers points out, if *Biuuulf* is to be derived from **Beuw (w)ulf*, then it would afford an isolated and inexplicable case of *iu* for *eo[eu]*, unique in the *Liber Vitae*, as in the whole mass of the oldest English texts: "Soll ein zusammenhang mit st. *beuwa-* stattfinden, so muss man auch diesen stamm für einen urspr. s-stamm erklären, und unser *biu-* auf die stammform *biuwi(z)-* nicht auf *beuwa(z)-* zurückführen." (Sievers, *P.B.B.* XVIII, 413.) The word however is a neut. *wa-* stem, whether in O.E. (*bēow*), Old Saxon (*bēo*) or Icelandic (*bygg*): see Sievers, *Ags. Grammatik*, 3te Aufl. § 250; Gallée, *Altsächsische Grammatik*, 2te Aufl. § 305; Noreen, *Altisländische Grammatik*, 3te Aufl. § 356. The word is extant in Old English only in the Glossaries, in the gen. sing., "handful beouaes," *etc.*, and in Old Saxon only in the gen. plu. *beuuo*. It is thought to have been originally a *wu-*stem, which subsequently, as e.g. in O.E., passed into a *wa-*stem. (See Noreen, *A.f.n.F.* I, 166, arguing from the form *begg* in the Dalecarlian dialect.) The presumed Primitive Norse form is *beggwu*, whence the various Scandinavian forms, Icel. *bygg*, Old Swedish and Old Danish *biug(g)*. See Hellquist in *A.f.n.F.* VII, 31; von Unwerth, *A.f.n.F.* XXXIII, 331; Binz, *P.B.B.* XX, 153; von Helten, *P.B.B.* XXX, 245; Kock, *Umlaut u. Brechung im Aschw.* p. 314, in *Lunds Universitets årsskrift*, Bd. XII). The proper name *Byggvir* is a *ja-*stem, but *Bēow* cannot have been so formed, as a *ja-*stem would give the form *Bēowe*. Cosijn (*Aanteekeningen*, 42) was accordingly justified in pointing to the form *Biuuulf* as refuting Kögel's attempt to connect *Bēowulf* with *Bēow* through a form **Bawiwulf* (*A.f.d.A.* XVIII, 56). Kögel replied with a laboured defence (*Z.f.d.A.* XXXVII, 268): he starts by assuming that *Bēow* and *Bēowulf* are etymologically connected, which is the very point which has to be proved: he has to admit that, if his etymology be correct, the *Biuuulf* of the *Liber Vitae* is not the same form as *Bēowulf*, which is the very point Cosijn urged as telling against his etymology: and even so his etymological explanations depend upon stages which cannot be accepted in the present state of our knowledge (see especially Sievers in *P.B.B.* XVIII, 413; Björkman in *Engl. Stud.* LII, 150).

affinities and forms of that word are quite different from all that the evidence has hitherto led us to believe. So much at least seems certain. Besides, we have seen that Byggvir is taunted by Loki precisely with the fact that he *is* no warrior. If we can estimate the characteristics of the O.E. Beow from those of the Scandinavian Byggvir, the name "Warrior after the manner of Beow" would be meaningless, if not absurd. Bugge[1], relying upon the parallel O.N. form *Bjólfr*[2], which is recorded as the name of one of the early settlers in Iceland[3], tried to interpret the word as *Bæjólfr* "the wolf of the farmstead," quoting as parallels *Heimulf, Gardulf*. But *Bjólfr* itself is best interpreted as "Bee-wolf[4]." And admittedly Bugge's explanation does not suit the O.E. *Bēowulf*, and necessitates the assumption that the word in English is a mere meaningless borrowing from the Scandinavian: for *Bēowulf* assuredly does not mean "wolf of the farmstead[5]."

Neither can we take very seriously the explanation of Sarrazin and Ferguson[6] that *Bēowulf* is an abbreviation of *Beadu-wulf*, "wolf of war." Our business is to interpret the name *Bēowulf*, or, if we cannot, to admit that we cannot; not to substitute some quite distinct name for it, and interpret that. Such theories merely show to what straits we may be reduced, if we reject the obvious etymology of the word.

And there are two further considerations, which confirm, almost to a certainty, this obvious interpretation of "Beowulf" as "Bee-wolf" or "Bear." The first is that it agrees excellently with Beowulf's bear-like habit of hugging his adversaries to death—a feature which surely belongs to the original kernel of our story, since it is incompatible with the chivalrous, weapon-

---

[1] *Tidskr. f. Philol og Pædag.* VIII, 289.

[2] First pointed out by Grundtvig in Barfod's *Brage og Idun*, IV, 1841, p. 500, footnote.

[3] "Lodmundr hinn gamli het madr enn annarr. Biólfr fostbrodir hans. þeir foru til Islands af Vors af þvlvnesi" (Voss in Norway). See *Landnámabók*, København, 1900, p. 92.

[4] Noreen, *Altisländische Grammatik*, 3te Aufl. p. 97. See also Noreen in *Festskrift til H. F. Feilberg*, 1911, p. 283. Noreen seems to have no doubt as to the explanation of *Bjólfr* as *Bý-olfr*, "Bee-wolf."

[5] Bugge, has, however, been followed by Gering, *Beowulf*, 1906, p. 100.

[6] Ferguson in the *Athenæum*, June 1892, p. 763: "Beadowulf by a common form of elision (!) would become Beowulf." Sarrazin admits "Freilich ist das eine ungewöhnliche verkürzung" (*Engl. Stud.* XLII, 19). See also Sarrazin in *Anglia*, V. 200; *Beowulf-Studien*, 33, 77; *Engl. Stud.* XVI, 79.

loving trappings in which that story has been dressed[1]. The second is that, as I have tried to show, the evidence is strongly in favour of Bjarki and Beowulf being originally the same figure[2]: and Bjarki is certainly a bear-hero[3]. His name signifies as much, and in the *Saga of Rolf Kraki* we are told at length how the father of Bjarki was a prince who had been turned by enchantment into a bear[4].

If, then, Beowulf is a bear-hero[5], the next step is to enquire whether there is any real likeness between his adventures at Heorot and under the mere, and the adventures of the hero of the widely-spread "Bear's Son" folk-tale. This investigation has, as we have seen above[6], been carried out by Panzer in his monumental work, which marks an epoch in the study of *Beowulf*.

Panzer's arguments in favour of such connection would, I think, have been strengthened if he had either quoted textually a number of the more important and less generally accessible folk-tales, or, since this would have proved cumbersome, if he had at least given abstracts of them. The method which Panzer follows, is to enumerate over two hundred tales, and from them to construct a story which is a compound of them all. This is obviously a method which is liable to abuse, though I do not say that Panzer has abused it. But we must not let a story so constructed usurp in our minds the place of the actual recorded folk-tales. Folk-tales, as Andrew Lang wrote long ago, "consist of but few incidents, grouped together in a kaleidoscopic variety of arrangements." A collection of over two hundred cognate tales offers a wide field for the selection therefrom of a composite story. Further, some geographical discrimination is necessary: these tales are scattered over Europe and Asia, and it is important to keep constantly in mind whether a given type of tale belongs, for example, to Greece or to Scandinavia.

---

[1] This incompatibility comes out very strongly in ll. 2499–2506, where Beowulf praises his sword particularly for the services it has *not* been able to render him.

[2] See above, pp. 60–1.

[3] Olrik, *Heltedigtning*, I, 140: F. Jónsson, *Hrólfs Saga Kraka*, 1904, *Inledning*, XX.

[4] *Hrólfs Saga Kraka*, cap. 17–20.

[5] The trait is wanting in the *Grettis saga*: Grettir son of Asmund was too historical a character for such features to be attributed to him.

[6] See pp. 62–7.

A typical example of the Bear's son tale is *Der Starke Hans* in Grimm[1]. Hans is brought up in a robber's den: but quite apart from any of the theories we are now considering, it has long been recognized that this is a mere toning down of the original incredible story, which makes a bear's den the nursery of the strong youth[2]. Hans overcomes in an empty castle the foe (a mannikin of magic powers) who has already worsted his comrades Fir-twister and Stone-splitter. He pursues this foe to his hole, is let down by his companions in a basket by a rope, slays the foe with his club and rescues a princess. He sends up the princess in the basket; but when his own turn comes to be pulled up his associates intentionally drop the basket when halfway up. But Hans, suspecting treason, has only sent up his club. He escapes by magic help, takes vengeance on the traitors, and weds the princess.

In another story in Grimm[3], the antagonist whom the hero overcomes, but does not in this case slay, is called the Earthman, *Dat Erdmänneken*. This type begins with the disappearance of the princesses, who are to the orthodox number of three; otherwise it does not differ materially from the abstract given above. Grimm records four distinct versions, all from Western Germany.

The versions of this widespread story which are most easily accessible to English readers are likely to prejudice such readers against Panzer's view. The two versions in Campbell's *Popular Tales of the West Highlands*[4], or the version in Kennedy's *Legendary Fictions of the Irish Celts*[5] are not of a kind to remind any unprejudiced reader strongly of *Beowulf*, or of the *Grettir*-story either. Indeed, I believe that from countries so remote as North Italy or Russia parallels can be found which are closer than any so far quoted from the Celtic portions of the British Isles. Possibly more Celtic parallels may be forthcoming in the future: some striking ones at any rate are promised[6].

[1] No. 166. Translated as "Strong Hans." (*Grimm's Household Tales, trans. by M. Hunt, with introduction by A. Lang*, 1884.)

[2] As, for example, by Cosquin, *Contes populaires de Lorraine*, I, 7. A comparison of the different versions in which the "strange theme" is toned down, in a greater or less degree, seems to make this certain.   [3] No. 91.

[4] Edinburgh, 1860, vol. I, No. XVI, "The king of Lochlin's three daughters": vol. III, No. LVIII, "The rider of Grianaig."

[5] London, 1866: p. 43, "The Three Crowns."   [6] Notably by von Sydow.

So, too, the story of the "Great Bird Dan" (*Fugl Dam*[1]), which is accessible to English readers in Dasent's translation[2], is one in which the typical features have been overlaid by a mass of detail.

A much more normal specimen of the "Bear's son" story is found, for example, in a folk-tale from Lombardy—the story of *Giovanni dell' Orso*[3]. Giovanni is brought up in a bear's den, whither his mother has been carried off. At five, he has the growth of a man and the strength of a giant. At sixteen, he is able to remove the stone from the door of the den and escape, with his mother. Going on his adventures with two comrades, he comes to an empty palace. The comrades are defeated: it becomes the turn of Giovanni to be alone. An old man comes in and "grows, grows till his head touched the roof[4]." Giovanni mortally wounds the giant, who however escapes. They all go in search of him, and find a hole in the ground. His comrades let Giovanni down by a rope. He finds a great hall, full of rich clothes and provision of every kind: in a second hall he finds three girls, each one more beautiful than the other: in a third hall he finds the giant himself, drawing up his will[5]. Giovanni kills the giant, rescues the damsels, and, in spite of his comrades deserting the rope, he escapes, pardons them, himself weds the youngest princess and marries his comrades to the elder ones.

I cannot find in this version any mention of the hero smiting the giant below with a magic sword which he finds there, as suggested by Panzer[6]. But even without this, the first part of the story has resemblances to *Beowulf*, and still more to the *Grettir*-story.

There are many Slavonic variants. The South Russian story of the Norka[7] begins with the attack of the Norka upon the King's park. The King offers half his kingdom to anyone who will destroy the beast. The youngest prince of three watches,

[1] Asbjørnsen og Moe, *Norske Folkeeventyr*, Christiania, 1852, No. 3.
[2] *Popular Tales from the Norse* (third edit., Edinburgh, 1888, p. 382).
[3] Visentini, *Fiabe Mantovane*, 1879, No. 32, 157–161.
[4] "fino a che col capo tocca le travi." Cf. Glam in the *Grettis Saga*.
[5] "e qui vede il gigante seduto, che detteva il suo testamento."
[6] p. 153. This is Panzer's version 97.
[7] "A fabulous creature, but zoologically the name Norka (from *nora*, a hole) belongs to the otter," Ralston, *Russian Folk Tales*, p. 73.

after the failure of his two elder brothers, chases and wounds the monster, who in the end pulls up a stone and disappears into the earth. The prince is let down by his brothers, and, with the help of a sword specially given him in the underworld, and a draught of the water of strength, he slays the foe, and wins the princesses. In order to have these for themselves, the elder brothers drop what they suppose to be their youngest brother, as they are drawing him up: but it is only a stone he has cautiously tied to the rope in place of himself. The prince's miraculous return in disguise, his feats, recognition by the youngest princess, the exposure of the traitors, and marriage of the hero, all follow in due course[1].

A closer Russian parallel is that of *Ivashko Medvedko*[2], "John Honey-eater" or "Bear." John grows up, not by years, but by hours: nearly every hour he gains an inch in height. At fifteen, there are complaints of his rough play with other village boys, and John Bear has to go out into the world, after his grandfather has provided him with a weapon, an iron staff of immense weight. He meets a champion who is drinking up a river: "Good morning, John Bear, whither art going?" "I know not whither; I just go, not knowing where to go." "If so, take me with you." The same happens with a second champion whose hobby is to carry mountains on his shoulder, and with a third, who plucks up oaks or pushes them into the ground. They come to a revolving house in a dark forest, which at John's word stands with its back door to the forest and its front door to them: all its doors and windows open of their own accord. Though the yard is full of poultry, the house is empty. Whilst the three companions go hunting, the river-swallower stays in the house to cook dinner: this done, he washes his head, and sits at the window to comb his locks. Suddenly the earth shakes, then stands still: a stone is lifted, and from under it appears Baba Yaga driving in her mortar with a pestle: behind her comes barking a little dog. A short dialogue ensues, and the champion, at her request, gives her food; but the second helping she throws to her dog, and thereupon beats the champion with

[1] Afanasief (A. N.), *Narodnuiya Russkiya Skazki*, Moscow, 1860–63, I, 6. See Ralston, p. 73.   [2] Afanasief, VIII, No. 6.

her pestle till he becomes unconscious; then she cuts a strip of skin from his back, and after eating all the food, vanishes. The victim recovers his senses, ties up his head with a handkerchief, and, when his companions return, apologizes for the ill-success of his cooking: "He had been nearly suffocated by the fumes of the charcoal, and had had his work cut out to get the room clear." Exactly the same happens to the other champions. On the fourth day it is the turn of John Bear, and here again the same formulas are repeated. John does the cooking, washes his head, sits down at the window and begins to comb his curly locks. Baba Yaga appears with the usual phenomena, and the usual dialogue follows, till she begins to belabour the hero with her pestle. But he wrests it from her, beats her almost to death, cuts three strips from her skin, and imprisons her in a closet. When his companions return, they are astonished to find dinner ready. After dinner they have a bath, and the companions try not to show their mutilated backs, but at last have to confess. "Now I see why you all suffered from suffocation," says John Bear. He goes to the closet, takes the three strips cut from his friends, and reinserts them: they heal at once. Then he ties up Baba Yaga by a cord fastened to one foot, and they all shoot at the cord in turn. John Bear hits it, and cuts the string in two; Baba Yaga falls to the earth, but rises, runs to the stone from under which she had appeared, lifts it, and vanishes. Each of the companions tries in turn to lift the stone, but only John can accomplish it, and only he is willing to go down. His comrades let him down by a rope, which however is too short, and John has to eke it out by the three strips previously cut from the back of Baba Yaga. At the bottom he sees a path, follows it, and reaches a palace where are three beautiful maidens, who welcome him, but warn him against their mother, who is Baba Yaga herself: "She is asleep now, but she keeps at her head a sword. Do not touch it, but take two golden apples lying on a silver tray, wake her gently, and offer them to her. As soon as she begins to eat, seize the sword, and cut her head off at one blow." John Bear carries out these instructions, and sends up the maidens, two to be wives to his companions, and the youngest to be his own wife. This leaves the third companion wifeless

and, in indignation, he cuts the rope when the turn comes to
pull John up. The hero falls and is badly hurt. [John has forgotten, in this version, to put his iron club into the basket
instead of himself—indeed he has up to now made no use of his
staff.] In time the hero sees an underground passage, and makes
his way out into the white world. Here he finds the youngest
maiden, who is tending cattle, after refusing to marry the false
companion. John Bear follows her home, slays his former comrades with his staff, and throws their bodies on the field for the
wild beasts to devour. He then takes his sweetheart home to
his people, and weds her.

The abstract given above is from a translation made by one
of my students, Miss M. Steine, who tells me that she had heard
the tale in this form many times from her old nurse "when we
were being sent to sleep, or sitting round her in the evening." I
have given it at this length because I do not know of any accessible translation into any Western language.

Panzer enumerates two hundred and two variants of the
story: and there are others[1]. But there is reason in the criticism
that what is important for us is the form the folk-tale may have
taken in those countries where we must look for the original
home of the *Beowulf*-story[2]. The Mantuan folk-tale may have
been carried down to North Italy from Scandinavia by the
Longobards: who can say? But Panzer's theory must stand or
fall by the parallels which can be drawn between the *Beowulf-
Grettir*-story on the one hand, and the folk-tales as they have
been collected in the countries where this story is native: the
lands, that is to say, adjoining the North Sea.

Now it is precisely here that we do find the most remarkable
resemblances: in Iceland, the Faroes, Norway, Denmark, Jutland, Schleswig, and the Low German lands as far as the Scheldt.

An Icelandic version exists in an unprinted MS at Reykjavik[3] which can be consulted in a German translation[4]. In this

---

[1] For example, "Shepherd Paul," in *The Folk-Tales of the Magyars*, by
W. H. Jones and L. L. Kropf, *Folk-Lore Society*, 1889, p. 244. The latest col-
lection contains its version, 'The Story of Tāling, the Half-boy' in *Persian
Tales, written down for the first time and translated* by D. L. R. and E. O. Lorimer,
London, 1919.   [2] Cf. von Sydow in *A.f.d.A.* xxxv, 126.

[3] Ión Arnason's MSS, No. 536, 4°.

[4] Rittershaus (A.), *Die Neuisländischen Volksmärchen*, Halle, 1902, No. 25.

version a bear, who is really an enchanted prince, carries off a
princess. He resumes his human form and weds the princess,
but must still at times take the bear's form. His child, the
Bear-boy (Bjarndreingur), is to be kept in the house during the
long periods when the enchanted husband is away. But at
twelve years old the Bear-boy is too strong and unmanageable,
bursts out, and slays a bear who turns out to be his father.
His mother's heart is broken, but Bear-boy goes on his adventures, and associates with himself three companions, one of
whom is Stein. They build a house in the wood, which is
attacked by a giant, and, as usual, the companions are unable
to withstand the attacks. Bear-boy does so, ties the giant's
hands behind his back, and fastens him by his beard. But the
giant tears himself free. As in *Beowulf*, Bear-boy and his companions follow the track by the drops of blood, and come to a
hole. Stein is let some way down, the other companions
further, but only Bear-boy dares to go to the bottom. There he
finds a weeping princess, and learns that she, and her two sisters,
have been carried off by three giants, one of whom is his former
assailant. He slays all three, and sends their heads up, together
with the maidens and other treasures. But his companions
desert the rope, and he has to climb up unaided. In the end he
weds the youngest princess.

The story from the Faroe Islands runs thus:

Three brothers lived together and took turns, two to go out
fishing, and one to be at home. For two days, on each of
which one of the two elder brothers was at home, came a giant
(Skeggjatussi) and ate and drank all the food. Then comes the
turn of the despised youngest brother, who is called in one version
Øskudólgur—"the one who sits and rakes in the ashes"—a kind
of male Cinderella. This brother routs the giant, either by catch-
ing his long beard in a cleft tree-trunk, or by branding him in
the nose with a hot iron. In either case the mutilated giant
escapes down a hole: in one version, after the other brothers
come home, they follow him to this hole by the track of his
blood. The two elder brothers leave the task of plunging down
to the youngest one, who finds below a girl (in the second version,
two kidnapped princesses). He finds also a magic sword hanging

on the wall, which he is only able to lift when he has drunk
a magic potion. He then slays the giant, rescues the maiden or
maidens, is betrayed in the usual way by his brothers: in the
one version they deliberately refuse to draw him up: in the
other they cut the rope as they are doing so: but he is discreetly
sending up only a big stone. The hero is helped out, however,
by a giant, "Skræddi Kjálki" or "Snerkti risi," and in the end
marries the princess[1].

In the Norwegian folk-tale the three adventurers are called
respectively the Captain, the Lieutenant and the Soldier. They
search for the three princesses, and watch in a castle, where the
Captain and Lieutenant are in turn worsted by a strange visitor
—who in this version is not identical with the troll below ground
who guards the princesses[2]. When the turn of the Soldier comes,
he seizes the intruder (the man, as he is called).

> "Ah no, Ah no, spare my life," said the man, "and you
> shall know all. East of the castle is a great sandheap, and
> down in it a winch, with which you can lower yourself.
> But if you are afraid, and do not dare to go right down,
> you only need to pull the bell rope which you will find
> there, and up you will come again. But if you dare venture
> so far as to come to the bottom, there stands a flask on a
> shelf over the door: you must drink what is in it: so will
> you become so strong that you can strike the head off the
> troll of the mountain. And by the door there hangs a
> Troll-sword, which also you must take, for no other steel
> will bite on his body."
>
> When he had learnt this, he let the man go. When the
> Captain and the Lieutenant came home, they were not a
> little surprised to find the Soldier alive. "How have you
> escaped a drubbing," said they, "has not the man been

[1] *Færøske Folkesagn og Æventyr*, ed. by Jakob Jakobsen, 1898–1901,
pp. 241–4 (*Samfund til Udgivelse af gammel Nordisk Litteratur*).
[2] This folk-tale is given in a small book, to be found in the Christiania
University Library, and no doubt elsewhere in Norway: *Nor, en Billedbog for
den norske Ungdom* (Tredie Oplag, Christiania, 1865). *Norske Folke Eventyr og
Sagn*, fortalte af P. Chr. Asbjørnsen. A copy of the story, slightly altered,
occurs in the *Udvalgte Eventyr og Sagn for Børn*, of Knutsen, Bentsen and
Johnsson, Christiania, 1877, p. 58 *etc.*

here?" "Oh yes, he is quite a good fellow, he is," said the
Soldier, "I have learnt from him where the princesses are,"
and he told them all. They were glad when they heard that,
and when they had eaten, they went all three to the sandheap.

As usual, the Captain and the Lieutenant do not dare to go
to the bottom: the hero accomplishes the adventure, is (as usual)
betrayed by his comrades, but is saved because he has put a
stone in the basket instead of himself, and in the end is rescued
by the interposition of "Kløverhans."

What is the explanation of the "sandheap" (*sandhaug*) I do
not know. But one cannot forget that Grettir's adventure in
the house, followed by his adventure with the troll under the
earth, is localized at Sandhaugar. This may be a mere accident;
but it is worth noting that in following up the track indicated
by Panzer we come across startling coincidences of this kind.
As stated above, it can hardly be due to any influence of the
Grettis Saga upon the folk-tale[1]. The likeness between the two
is too remote to have suggested a transference of such details
from the one story to the other.

We find the story in its normal form in Jutland[2]. The hero,
a foundling, is named Bjørnøre (Bear-ears). There is no explanation offered of this name, but we know that in other versions of
the story, where the hero is half bear and half man, his bear
nature is shown by his bear's ears. "Bear-ears" comes with his
companions to an empty house, worsts the foe (the old man,
den gamle) who has put his companions to shame, and fixes him
by his beard in a cloven tree. The foe escapes nevertheless; they
follow him to his hole: the companions are afraid, but "Bear-
ears" is let down, finds the enemy on his bed, and slays him.
The rest of the story follows the usual pattern. "Bear-ears"
rescues and sends up the princesses, his comrades detach the
rope, which however is hauling up only the hero's iron club. He
escapes miraculously from his confinement below, and returns to
marry the youngest princess. In another Danish version, from
the South of Zealand[3], the hero, "Strong Hans" (nothing is said

---

[1] pp. 66–7.
[2] Berntsen (K.), *Folke-Æventyr*, 1873, No. 12, pp. 109–115.
[3] Grundtvig (Sv.), *Gamle Danske Minder*, 1854, No. 34, p. 33: from Næstved.

about his bear-origin), comes with his companions to a magnificent but empty castle. The old witch worsts his comrades and imprisons them under the trap-door: but Hans beats her, and rescues them, though the witch herself escapes. Hans is let down, rescues the princesses, is betrayed by his comrades (who, thinking to drop him in drawing him up, only drop his iron club), and finally weds the third princess.

A little further South we have three versions of the same tale recorded for Schleswig-Holstein[1]. The hero wins his victory below by means of "a great iron sword" (*en grotes ysernes Schwäert*) which he can only wield after drinking of the magic potion.

From Hanover comes the story of Peter Bär[2], which shows all the familiar features: from the same district came some of Grimm's variants. Others were from the Rhine provinces: but the fullest version of all comes from the Scheldt, just over the Flemish border. The hero, Jean l'Ourson, is recovered as a child from a bear's den, is despised in his youth[3], but gives early proof of his strength. He defends an empty castle *un superbe château*, when his companion has failed, strikes off an arm[4] of his assailant *Petit-Père-Bidoux*, chases him to his hole, *un puits vaste et profond*. He is let down by his companion, but finding the rope too short, plunges, and arrives battered at the bottom. There he perceives *une lumière qui brillait au bout d'une longue galerie*[5]. At the end of the gallery he sees his former assailant, attended by *une vieille femme à cheveux blancs, qui semblait âgée de plus de cent ans*, who is salving his wounded arm. The hero quenches the light (which is a magic one) smites his foe on the head and kills him, and then rekindles the lamp[6]. His companion above seeks to rob him of the two princesses he has won, by detaching the rope. Nevertheless, he escapes, weds the good princess, and punishes his faithless companion by making him wed the bad one.

The white-haired old woman is not spoken of as the mother

---

[1] *Hans mit de ysern Stang'*, Müllenhoff, *Sagen, Märchen u. Lieder*...1845. No. XVI, p. 437.
[2] Colshorn (C. and Th.), *Märchen u. Sagen*, Hannover, 1854, No. V, pp. 18–30.
[3] Cf. *Beowulf*, ll. 2183–8.
[4] Cf. *Beowulf*, ll. 815 *etc.*
[5] Cf. *Beowulf*, ll. 1516–17; cf. *Grettis Saga*, LXVI.
[6] Cf. *Grettis Saga*, LXVI, *hann kveikti ljós*; cf. *Beowulf*, 1570.

of the foe she is nursing, and it may be doubted whether she is in any way parallel to Grendel's mother. The hero does not fight her: indeed it is she who, in the end, enables him to escape. Still the parallels between Jean l'Ourson and Beowulf are striking enough. Nine distinct features recur, in the same order, in the *Beowulf*-story and in this folk-tale. It needs a more robust faith than I possess to attribute this solely to chance.

Unfortunately, this French-Flemish tale is found in a somewhat sophisticated collection. Its recorder, as Sainte-Beuve points out in his letter introductory to the series[1], uses literary touches which diminish the value of his folk-tales to the student of origins. Any contamination from the *Beowulf*-story or the *Grettir*-story is surely improbable enough in this case: nevertheless, one would have liked the tale taken down verbatim from the lips of some simple-minded narrator as it used to be told at Condé on the Scheldt.

But if we take together the different versions enumerated above, the result is, I think, convincing. Here are eight versions of one folk-tale taken as representatives from a much larger number current in the countries in touch with the North Sea: from Iceland, the Faroes, Norway, Jutland, Zealand, Schleswig, Hanover, and the Scheldt. The champion is a bear-hero (as Beowulf almost certainly is, and as Bjarki quite certainly is); he is called, in Iceland, *Bjarndreingur*, in Jutland, *Bjørnøre*, in Hanover, *Peter Bär*, on the Scheldt *Jean l'Ourson*. Like Beowulf, he is despised in his youth (Faroe, Scheldt). In all versions he resists his adversary in an empty house or castle, after his comrades have failed. In most versions of the folk-tale this is the third attack, as it is in the case of Grettir at Sandhaugar and of Bjarki: in *Beowulf*, on the contrary, we gather that Heorot has been raided many times. The adversary, though vanquished, escapes; in one version after the loss of an arm (Scheldt): they follow his track to the hole into which he has vanished, sometimes, as in *Beowulf*, marking traces of his blood (Iceland, Faroe, Schleswig). The hero always ventures down alone, and gets into

---

[1] *Contes du roi Cambrinus*, par C. Deulin, Paris, 1874 (I. *L'intrépide Gayant*). The story is associated with Gayant, the traditional hero of Douai.

an underworld of magic, which has left traces of its mysteriousness in *Beowulf*. In one tale (Scheldt) the hero sees a magic lamp burning below, just as he sees the fire in *Beowulf* or the *Grettis Saga*. He overcomes either his original foe, or new ones, often by the use of a magic sword (Faroe, Norway, Schleswig); this sword hangs by the door (Norway) or on the wall (Faroe) as in *Beowulf*. After slaying his foe, the hero rekindles the magic lamp, in the Scheldt fairy tale, just as he kindles a light in the *Grettis Saga*, and as the light flashes up in *Beowulf* after the hero has smitten Grendel's mother. The hero is in each case deserted by his companions: a feature which, while it is marked in the *Grettis Saga*, can obviously be allowed to survive in *Beowulf* only in a much softened form. The chosen retainers whom Beowulf has taken with him on his journey could not be represented as unfaithful, because the poet is reserving the episode of the faithless retainers for the death of Beowulf. To have twice represented the escort as cowardly would have made the poem a satire upon the *comitatus*, and would have assured it a hostile reception in every hall from Canterbury to Edinburgh. But there is no doubt as to the faithlessness of the comrade Stein in the *Grettis Saga*. And in Zealand, one of the faithless companions is called *Stenhuggeren* (the Stone-hewer), in Schleswig *Steenklöwer*, in Hanover *Steinspieler*, whilst in Iceland he has the same name, *Stein*, which he has in the *Grettis Saga*.

The fact that the departure home of the Danes in *Beowulf* is due to the same cause as that which accounts for the betrayal of his trust by Stein, shows that in the original *Beowulf*-story also this feature must have occurred, however much it may have become worn down in the existing epic.

I think enough has been said to show that there is a real likeness between a large number of recorded folk-tales and the *Beowulf-Grettir* story. The parallel is not merely with an artificial, theoretical composite put together by Panzer. But it becomes equally clear that *Beowulf* cannot be spoken of as a version of these folk-tales. At most it is a version of a portion of them. The omission of the princesses in *Beowulf* and the *Grettis Saga* is fundamental. With the princesses much else falls away. There is no longer any motive for the betrayal of trust by the watchers. The disguise of the hero and his vengeance are now no longer necessary to the tale.

It might be argued that there was something about the three princesses which made them unsatisfactory as subjects of story. It has been thought that in the oldest version the hero married all three: an awkward episode where a *scop* had to compose a poem for an audience certainly monogamous and most probably Christian. The rather tragic and sombre atmosphere of the stories of Beowulf and Grettir fits in better with a version from which the princesses, and the living happily ever afterwards, have been dropped. On the other hand, it might be argued that the folk-tale is composite, and that the source from which the *Beowulf-Grettir*-story drew was a simpler tale to which the princesses had not yet been added.

And there are additions as well as subtractions. Alike in *Beowulf* and in the *Grettis Saga*, the fight in the house and the fight below are associated with struggles with monsters of different sex. The association of "The Devil and his Dam" has only few and remote parallels in the "Bear's-son" folk-tale.

But Panzer has, I think, proved that the struggle of Beowulf in the hall, and his plunging down into the deep, is simply an epic glorification of a folk-tale motive.

I. THE DATE OF THE DEATH OF HYGELAC.

Gregory of Tours mentions the defeat of Chochilaicus (Hygelac) as an event of the reign of Theudoric. Now Theudoric succeeded his father Chlodoweg, who died 27 Nov. 511. Theudoric died in 534. This, then, gives the extreme limits of time; but as Gregory mentions the event among the first occurrences of the reign, the period 512–520 has generally been suggested, or in round numbers about 515 or 516.

Nevertheless, we cannot attach much importance to the mere order followed by Gregory[1]. He may well have had no means of dating the event exactly. Of much more importance than the order, is the fact he records, that Theudoric did not

[1] Cf. Schmidt, *Geschichte der deutschen Stämme*, II, 495, 499, *note* 4.

defeat Chochilaicus in person, but sent his son Theudobert to repel the invaders.

Now Theudobert was born before the death of his grandfather Chlodoweg. For Gregory tells us that Chlodoweg left, not only four sons, but a grandson Theudobert, *elegantem atque utilem*[1]: *utilem* cannot mean that, at the time of the death of Chlodoweg, Theudobert was of age to conduct affairs of state, for Chlodoweg was only 45 at death[2]. The Merovingians were a precocious race; but if we are to allow Theudobert to have been at least fifteen before being placed in charge of a very important expedition, and Chlodoweg to have been at least forty before becoming a grandfather, the defeat of Hygelac cannot be put before 521; and probability would favour a date five or ten years later.

There is confirmation for this. When Theudobert died, in 548, he left one son only, quite a child and still under tutelage[3]; probably therefore not more than twelve or thirteen at most. We know the circumstances of the child's birth. Theudobert had been betrothed by his father Theudoric to a Longobardic princess, Wisigardis[4]. In the meantime he fell in love with the lady Deoteria[5], and married her[6]. The Franks were shocked at this fickleness (*valde scandalizabantur*), and Theudobert had ultimately to put away Deoteria[7], although they had this young son (*parvulum filium*), who, as we have seen, could hardly have been born before 535, and possibly was born years later. Theudobert then married the Longobardic princess, in the seventh year after their betrothal. So it cannot have been much before 530 that Theudobert's father was first arranging the Longobardic match. A king is not likely to have waited to find a wife for a son, upon whom his dynasty was to depend, till fifteen years after that son was of age to win a memorable victory[8].

---

[1] III, 1. [2] II, 43.

[3] Παῖς...νέος ἦν κομιδῇ, καὶ ἔτι ὑπὸ παιδοκόμῳ τιθηνούμενος, Agathias, I, 4: *parvulus*, Gregory, IV, 6.

[4] Gregory, III, 20. [5] III, 22. [6] III, 23. [7] III, 27.

[8] Many recent historians have expressed doubts as to the conventional date, 515, for Hygelac's death. J. P. Jacobsen, in the Danish translation of Gregory (1911) suggested 525–30: following him Severinsen (*Danske Studier*, 1919, 96) suggested c. 526, as did Fredborg, *Det första årtalet i Sveriges historia*. L. Schmidt (*Geschichte der deutschen Stämme*, II, 500, note, 1918) suggested c. 528.

*   *   *   *   *   *   *

So far I had written in 1921. Since then, these reasons have been disputed by Klaeber[1] and by Nerman[2]. Both are scholars with whom I find myself so often in agreement, and to whom I owe so much, that it seems necessary to re-examine the problem rather fully, especially as Hygelac's death is the one fixed point from which early Scandinavian history has to be dated, forward or backward.

Klaeber, following Cook[3], emphasizes the early maturity of Merovingian days. But this, as we shall see later, is the very reason which makes the date 516 difficult.

Both Klaeber and Nerman seem to think that Gregory's authority tells so heavily in favour of 516 that we must not desert it on mere grounds of probability. But is this really so?

Gregory, in Chapter 2 of Book III of his *History*, deals with an event of 516, the enthronement of Quintianus as Bishop of Clermont. Hygelac's raid, which is narrated in Chapter 3, was, we are told, subsequent to this (*his ita gestis*). But this only gives us a *terminus a quo*. Then in the next chapter (4) Gregory tells how Herminafrid, king of Thuringia, murdered his brothers, first Berthachar and then Baderich. Now in the standard critical edition of Gregory's *History* (ed. Arndt and Krusch, 1884, in the *Monumenta*), the date 516 is placed in the margin against the death of Baderich. But, so far as I can gather, this dating goes back ultimately to the dates given by Gloël[4]; and the date (516) which Gloël gives for the death of Baderich largely depends upon the place of that event in Gregory's narrative next to the expedition of Hygelac, which Gloël dates 515.

So the argument goes in a circle, the death of Baderich dated from that of Hygelac, and then the death of Hygelac from that of Baderich.

Of course, if there were any independent evidence that this Thuringian affair happened in 516, then it *could* be argued that Hygelac's raid, since Gregory places it between two events of

[1] *Anglia*, L (N.F. XXXVIII), 242–4.
[2] *Det svenska rikets uppkomst*, 1925, pp. 85–87.
[3] *J.E.G.Ph.* XXII, 424–7.
[4] *Zur Geschichte der alten Thüringer*, von Ad. Gloël, in *Forschungen zur deutschen Geschichte*, 1864. See especially p. 214.

516, is also to be dated in that year. But I know of no such evidence, and, even if we had it, the argument would be a very doubtful one, for Gregory was writing nearly sixty years later (c. 575) and may well have had no means of dating Hygelac's raid exactly. He had to put it somewhere, and such chronological inferences, derived merely from Gregory's order, are perilous[1].

But, as a matter of fact, the whole tale of these Thuringian murders has been suspected by historians, for what seem very weighty reasons[2]. What Fortunatus tells us about the kinsfolk of St Radegund seems very difficult to harmonize with this story of domestic murder. And, granting it to be really true that Berthachar and Baderich *were* murdered by their brother Herminafrid, this must have taken place some considerable time after 516. For Berthachar, the first to be murdered according to Gregory, was the father of Radegund, and all the evidence[3] points to her not having been born till about 521. Berthachar had also a son, who was born, it would seem, later still[4], apparently not very much before 530. So, if these murders *did* take place, there seems no reason why we need necessarily date them much before the great Thuringian war of c. 531, which put a stop to the career of Herminafrid.

---

[1] See Ludwig Schmidt, *Geschichte der deutschen Stämme*, ii, 495, 499, note 4. On the uncertainty of Gregory's chronology of the reign of Chlodoweg, see Levison in the *Bonner Jahrbücher*, ciii, 42–67 (1898), *Zur Geschichte des Frankenkönigs Chlodowech*.

[2] See Schmidt, *as above*.

[3] The account given by Fortunatus (*Vita Sanctae Radegundis*, cap. 2) makes it clear that she was not of marriageable age when she fell into the hands of the Franks, which was not before 531. A considerable period of education at Athies intervened before she married Lothar I. In 531 she must have been "a very young girl," "a child of ten." (See notes to Gregory of Tours, *History of the Franks*, translated by O. M. Dalton, i, 67, 102.)

[4] Apparently St Radegund withdrew to the cloister about 550. (For evidence, see Wilhelm Meyer, *Der Gelegenheitsdichter Venantius Fortunatus*, in the *Abhandlungen der königl. Gesellschaft der Wissenschaften zu Göttingen*, N.F., iv, 5, Berlin, 1901.) This withdrawal was caused by the murder of her brother, who was, Fortunatus tells us, *juvenis tenera lanugine barbae* (Fortunatus, *de excidio Thoringiae*, l. 133), therefore born hardly more than twenty years before—if indeed quite as much—and so presumably born about 530. This is confirmed by the fact that this brother had been intending to visit his cousin Hamalafred at the Byzantine court, but was dissuaded by his sister. Hamalafred was carried off to Byzantium with Witigis and other Gothic captives in 540: we must allow some time for him to rise in the Byzantine service, for news of this to reach Gaul, for his cousin to contemplate a visit to him, and subsequently to be murdered. All this tends to put the murder of Radegund's brother towards 550 and therefore his birth towards 530. (See Ad. Gloël in *Forschungen zur deutschen Geschichte*, 1864, p. 212.)

Therefore all that we seem able to gather from the position of Hygelac's raid between chapters 2 and 4 of Gregory's *History* is, that it would be most suitably dated between 516 and some date preceding 531.

It has been argued[1] that Gregory placed Hygelac's raid where it comes in his *History*, because he had information that it occurred not long before the great Thuringian war of 531, and, by a misunderstanding, put it before his account of these obscure Thuringian murders. But this attempt to read into Gregory's arrangement of events an argument approximating Hygelac's raid to 531 seems just as forced as the more usual custom of approximating it to 516. Gregory merely places it between two events, and we cannot decide, from Gregory's words, its nearness to either.

Then Gregory goes on in the next chapter (5) to deal with Burgundian affairs, from 516, leading up to the horrible story of how Sigismund, king of Burgundy, caused his own son to be strangled. This was in 522. The fact that this chapter comes later in Gregory's *History* than Hygelac's raid, affords an argument that Hygelac's raid was before or in 522, but it certainly affords no argument that it was before or in 516. For although Gregory has to mention the accession of Sigismund in 516 before he goes on to speak of his murder of his son, the relevant date of this chapter is 522.

Yet all these chronological arguments, derived from the order in which Gregory places Hygelac's raid amid the events of the reign of Theudoric (511–534), are perilous; so that it is best to leave the date of the raid vague until we have seen if we can date it more accurately from the circumstances of the battle itself.

We have seen that Theudoric sent his son Theudobert to repel this (certainly very dangerous) raid: what is the earliest date when we can suppose him to have been in charge of a very important expedition? Historians who have no axe to grind, one way or another, place Theudobert's birth not before 510[2].

---

[1] Fredborg, *Det första årtalet i Sveriges historia (Umeå högre allmänna läroverks årsredogörelse*, 1916–17).

[2] Cf. Gregory of Tours, *History of the Franks*, transl. by O. M. Dalton, I, 50.

If so, then, making all possible allowances for Merovingian pre-
cocity, we can hardly put the battle before 522.

And this is confirmed by the facts about Theudobert's marriage, quoted above. Here we have to reckon back from the
age of his son, Theudobald. When St Gall, Bishop of Clermont,
died in 551[1] Theudobald was so young that in electing a successor the bishops felt free to ignore their king (*rex vero parvulus
est*, Gregory of Tours, IV, 6). Agathias also emphasizes his
extreme youth when his father died in 548[2]. A boy who in 551
was *parvulus*, as *parvulus* went in Merovingian days, cannot have
been born before, say, 538. Now, as we have seen, it was at
most (and this is stretching the case) in the seventh year before
the birth of this boy that Theudobert's father Theudoric was
looking for a wife for him. This, then, can hardly have been
before 531; nor can it be later than 534, since Theudoric died
in the latter year. (Theudobert, however, had a will of his own,
and it was not till after his father's death, in the seventh year
of their betrothal, that he accepted the long-suffering Longobardic bride whom his father had provided for him[3].) A king
did not, in Merovingian days, wait till his only son was becoming
middle-aged before seeking for a bride for him; fifteen years is
a long space to allow between Theudobert's appearance as a
victorious general and as a potential bridegroom.

Further, on the death of Theudobert's father in 534, his
uncles, Childebert and Lothar I, tried to deprive him of his
kingdom: he was established as king by the support of his
leudes[4]. This attempt at deprivation again suggests youth.

On the other hand we have seen that Gregory tells us that
when Chlodoweg died at the end of 511 he left, not only four
sons, but this grandson Theudobert, whom Gregory speaks of
as *elegantem atque utilem*. Klaeber[5] argues that Gregory would
not have characterized a small child in this way. This would be
a strong argument if we were dealing with a strictly contem-

[1] This is the date given in Dalton (II, 516). Arndt and Krusch in their margin
give the date 554; but it is safer to take the figure least favourable to the argument put forward.
[2] See above, p. 382, note 3.
[3] Gregory, III, 20, 22, 27.
[4] Gregory, III, 23.
[5] Klaeber in *Anglia*, L (N.F. XXXVIII), 243.

porary account. But Gregory, writing two generations later, naturally gives his description and character of the prince in the place where he first has occasion to mention him; it is surely putting an impossible strain on the words of such a historian as Gregory, to suppose that he would not have used the word *utilis* of the prince, unless at this date he had actually proved himself to be *utilis*.

Nerman adheres to the early date (516), arguing that Gregory may have been mistaken in thinking that Theudobert was in command of the Franks: the infant Theudobert may have happened to be in that part of the land when the raid took place, and so in later days may wrongly have been supposed to have commanded the defenders. And of course, if we had substantial evidence to date Hygelac's raid in 516, we might be driven to explanations like this to account for Gregory's assertion that a prince, apparently at that date not more than six or seven, was sent by his father to repel the invaders. But we need no such explanations. All the evidence points to Hygelac's raid having been after 516 and probably after 520, although perhaps before 522 and certainly before 531.

PART V

RECENT WORK ON *BEOWULF* TO 1930

CHAPTER I

TWO NEW ATTEMPTS AT SYNTHESIS.
BY KLAEBER AND LAWRENCE

Klaeber's edition of *Beowulf* (1922: new issue, with additions, 1928) is the most important edition published since Kemble's of 1833. It is impossible to praise too highly the range and the accuracy of its scholarship. It has an excellent glossary, and notes which, thanks to Klaeber's knowledge of O.E. syntax, never fail to throw light on the problems discussed. Further, it is furnished with an Introduction, which, while it deals with the problems which are the subject of this present book, also contains full studies of the structure, tone, metre, style and language of the poem, and of its relation to other O.E. poems, thus exploring fields which this book leaves unattempted.

Klaeber's edition has now been followed by a monograph by Prof. W. W. Lawrence, *Beowulf and Epic Tradition*. This covers much the same ground as my own monograph, in about half the number of words. Lawrence states that whilst my book is addressed primarily to the scholar and the student, his volume "makes its appeal to those who wish to gain a sound knowledge of *Beowulf* so far as it may be done without an understanding of Anglo-Saxon, and to those who are just beginning a reading of the poem in that language." His book is certainly not as argumentative as mine, and it may be true that "it is concerned with the fruits of research, rather than with the processes by which those fruits have been ripened and gathered." But since the publication twenty years ago of his paper on "Some disputed points in *Beowulf* criticism," Lawrence has been one of the leaders in that process of research, and the fruits gathered in his book have been much more largely of his own planting than his modesty permits him to make clear. And, as will appear below, further most important additions to our knowledge are made in this, his latest publication.

When the first edition of my own monograph came out in 1921, I was half inclined to agree with a reviewer that "it seems presumptuous in any man, who has little or no new evidence, to attempt the solution of a mass of problems, on which a large number of able investigators have been unable to reach agreement[1]."

It is my peculiar good fortune to have been followed in my presumptuous sin by two such fellow-sinners as Klaeber and Lawrence. And indeed, though very little new evidence *is* forthcoming, the attempt, however arduous, had to be made.

For the study of *Beowulf* is one of those fields where the evidence is already known, and no student can expect to add more than a small proportion of new material. Meanwhile, many acute brains are seeking to arrive at new results: and, if novelty be our aim, a very large number of new permutations can be got, even from a small body of evidence, each new combination producing a new theory, inconsistent with the earlier ones.

One of the most distinguished of our English scholars has recently written:

> "So many theories let loose in the air produce a feeling that everything is uncertain, but that in the meanwhile all theories are interesting. *This frame of mind, which hardly even seeks to form decisions or convictions, is indeed disastrous[2].*"

Bishop Gore was speaking of the greatest issues in life and faith. But the same rule applies even to the smallest matters of scholarship. There is a tendency nowadays to be satisfied with the formula, "Professor A thinks this, Dr B that"; we are too modest to decide between them, or to form a view of our own. In Gore's words, this is disastrous.

In every subject which we study, we shall do well to repeat to ourselves the warning of Conscience in *Piers Plowman*, not to be like the lady who read "*Omnia probate*" at the bottom of a

---

[1] J. R. Hulbert in *Modern Philology*, xx, 436 (1923).
[2] Gore, *Jesus of Nazareth*, pp. 252–3.

page, but failed to go on and read "*quod bonum est tenete*" on the back of the leaf, because there was no cunning clerk to turn the leaf for her[1]. If we do not take this warning, we shall, in the end, make our subject ridiculous, and people will abandon it in favour of studies where men can make decisions—Physiology for example, or Chemistry. For the man who "thinking he drinks H_2O, drinks H_2SO_4" soon ceases even to find his mistaken theory interesting.

So it is time to try and reach a decision with regard to the controversial problems of *Beowulf*.

For although, about 1890, a number of efforts were made to get a comprehensive view of these problems, little was done in the following thirty years by way of a general survey. In 1883 Rönning had published his study, *Beovulfs-Kvadet*—a study which, in a remarkable way, anticipates the results to which scholars, after nearly half a century, are now returning. Then, in 1888-9, had appeared the three monographs of ten Brink, Sarrazin and (posthumously) Müllenhoff. These had been followed by the "Introduction" which Earle prefixed to his translation of *Beowulf* in 1892.

The theories expressed in these five books differed fundamentally, and no prospect of agreement seemed to be in sight. Rönning's work, in many ways the best balanced of all five, was handicapped partly by its appearing in Danish, and partly by the fact that the views which it put forward were at the moment unpopular.

During the thirty years following (1892–1921) there had been comparatively few and brief attempts at synthesis (honourable mention must be made of Brandl's fine sketch in *Pauls Grundriss*). Yet during all this time there had appeared a constant stream of publications on the subject of *Beowulf* or on allied subjects. And the study had been revolutionized in many ways, of which at least five need special mention.

(1) W. P. Ker in his *Epic and Romance* (1896) had done a good deal to shatter the belief that (in the words he was fond of quoting) "all epic poetry is written by A, B, and an Interpolator."

[1] I had written this before noticing that, in his new edition of 1928, Prof. Klaeber prefixes to his additional notes the words *Omnia autem probate, quod bonum est tenete.*

(2) Ker's work had more influence after its importance had been emphasized by Andreas Heusler in his *Lied und Epos* (1905). Heusler followed this up by a number of invaluable contributions to the study of Germanic heroic legend.

(3) Olrik published in 1903 and 1910 his studies of early Danish history as reflected in Denmark's ancient heroic poetry.

(4) In 1910 Friedrich Panzer brought a vast knowledge of folk-tale to bear upon *Beowulf*, thus reinforcing the view that Beowulf's adventures with Grendel and Grendel's mother belonged rather to folk-lore than to mythology.

(5) In a number of essays, Knut Stjerna placed his large archæological experience at the service of *Beowulf* students, and this led to further studies by other Swedish historians and archæologists, notably Birger Nerman and Sune Lindqvist.

Contemporary with these definite contributions, there had been that slow shifting of standpoint which comes with the years. The views as to the amalgamation of epics from earlier lays, which had seemed axiomatic to Lachmann and his pupil Müllenhoff, and the mythological and allegorical assumptions which Müllenhoff had inherited from Kemble, had ceased to be generally believed.

It has therefore become necessary to hew a way through the jungle. Now, whilst the monographs of 1883–92 leave one with a bewildered wondering where truth is to be found amid all this difference, I find an agreement between the views of Klaeber, Lawrence and myself which is almost embarrassing. A hostile critic might liken our voices to the docile harmonious utterance of a stage crowd: "where they do agree on the stage, their unanimity is wonderful."

And indeed it must be granted to such a potential critic that we are not absolutely independent of each other. What Klaeber published in 1922 he had written in 1918, and therefore without any knowledge of my book, which was not then out; but I, on my part, had learnt a good deal from various monographs which he had printed; whilst (as I said in my preface) my debt to Lawrence, who read the proofs of my book and discussed all its details with me, is a heavy one. Still, none of us would, I hope, accept any view on trust from the other. We have all tried to use independent judgment, and on some subjects, of which *Finnsburg* is the most important, we differ. But these differences are episodic, hardly affecting the main argument.

Of course, every decade has its atmosphere and its prepossessions, and perhaps, after all, our judgments are not as independent as we believe them to be. Anyway, I think it is worth while to go over the ground, and show how close the agreement is between the three of us.

As to the origin of the poem, Klaeber holds that, whilst the subject matter is Scandinavian, "the Christian elements are almost without exception so deeply ingrained in the very fabric of the poem that they cannot be explained away as the work of a reviser or later interpolator[1]." "That the poem was composed in the Anglian parts of England is one of the few facts bearing upon its genesis that can be regarded as fairly established[2]." Klaeber would assign the poem to "the first half of the eighth century, perhaps not far from the middle of it[3]."

Similarly Lawrence rejects the view that the Christian elements can possibly be due to revision of an older epic written before the change of faith[4]. "That *Beowulf* was originally composed in the Anglian territory of England is hardly open to question[5]." The widest limits of date Lawrence holds to be from 650 to 750[6] and probably between 675 and 725: he thus suggests a date a quarter of a century earlier than Klaeber.

My agreement on all these points has been stated above[7]. If there be any difference, it is that Klaeber and Lawrence speak rather more definitely than I do myself. For instance, I doubt whether we can define the date more exactly than by vaguely saying "the Age of Bede"; this covers equally the period favoured by Klaeber and that favoured by Lawrence. Both Lawrence and Klaeber would, I think, agree that the difference is not worth fighting about. We simply cannot date *Beowulf* to a quarter of a century.

The only real point at issue is that Klaeber would attach a rather stronger meaning than Lawrence does, or than I do, to

---

[1] Klaeber, p. l.   [2] *Ibid.* p. cxxi.   [3] *Ibid.* p. cxvi.
[4] Lawrence, p. 236.   [5] *Ibid.* p. 262.   [6] *Ibid.* p. 263.
[7] See above, pp. 121 *etc.*, 105, 329.

the formula that the subject matter is Scandinavian. But here again it is well to realize how narrow are the limits of the difference: it is simply a question of whether, at some very early date, these stories travelled across the North Sea from Scandinavia to England direct, or by way of continental Angel.

The downfall of the kingdom of the Geatas is prophesied in *Beowulf*—pretty clearly a prophecy after the event. But if the Royal House of the Geatas was destroyed, and the remnant of the *comitatus* scattered, there would have been many exiles of Geatic stock in the middle and end of the sixth century. Some of them may easily have wandered south to continental Angel, and there told stories and sung lays about the great days of the Geatic kingdom. There would be time for these stories to have been brought across by the latest groups of Anglian immigrants to Northern England. It was just in this second half of the sixth century that the Anglian settlements north of the Humber were rising into eminence under the first leaders who claimed the name of king: Ida and his sons in Bernicia, Ælle in Deira. In the warlike days of the sixth century we may pretty safely assert that when Ida and Ælle claimed to rank, not as mere earls, but as kings, this meant that they had collected a sufficient *comitatus* —*duguð* and *geoguð, scop* and *þyle*—to justify the assumption of the royal title: and this might well mean recruits from the old continental home. And so, quite naturally and easily, these stories may have been brought from Scandinavia to continental Angel, and from Angel to England, as Lawrence thinks. It is all in accordance with the known fact that "the Germanic nations had a reciprocal free trade in subjects for epic poems." Every extant fragment of the Old English epic testifies to the vigour of this free trade—*Widsith* above all—and no further explanation seems needed.

It is conceivable that there may have been specially close relations—due perhaps to intermarriage—between some English and some Scandinavian court. Klaeber assumes this; but I do not think that any such assumption is necessary to account for the facts.

But however this may have been, the old idea that *Beowulf* is a poem brought from Scandinavia and merely translated into

Anglo-Saxon speech is as conclusively rejected by Klaeber as by Lawrence. "If nothing else, the style and tone of *Beowulf* would disprove it, since they are utterly unlike anything to be expected in Scandinavian poetry[1]." That is the essential thing: whether the lays from which the Christian English poet drew his subject matter had been brought to England by Anglian settlers in the later sixth century (as Lawrence and I incline to believe) or were due to some slightly later intercourse with Scandinavia (as Klaeber believes), is surely impossible to decide dogmatically, and really immaterial. "That *Beowulf* was written by an Anglian poet of the age of Bede, working upon earlier lays current in England" is a formula as definite as we need ask for.

Now as to the contents of the poem: both Klaeber and Lawrence hold the "folk-tale" view[2], naturally without committing themselves to the details so minutely worked out by Panzer. This means, of course, rejecting the mythological interpretations which originated with Kemble and were elaborated by Müllenhoff; and it means also rejecting the assumed connection between Beaw (Beowulf the Scylding) and Beowulf the Geat: "Neither the Grendel- nor the dragon-fight is to be shifted back from the Geat hero to the Dane or the Anglo-Saxon progenitor[3]."

Klaeber is convinced that there is a connection between the Beowulf story and the story of Bothvar Bjarki; and in this case, as also in the case of the parallels with the story of Grettir, he thinks it safest "to attribute the undeniable parallelism to the use of the same or similar Scandinavian sources, both in the Old English and in the Old Norse accounts[4]." Prof. Lawrence has been arguing this for the past twenty years: he has now added to the obligations under which he has placed us, by producing new and, I think, very important evidence, of which much more must be said below[5].

That *Beowulf* has a historic background no one since the time of Earle has denied, but Klaeber and Lawrence feel (and more

---

[1] Klaeber, p. cxix; cf. Lawrence, p. 257, and see above, pp. 98–104.

[2] "The deeds of Beowulf are of the folk-tale order, adjusted in the epic to the level of Germanic hero-life." Klaeber, p. xxvi. Cf. Lawrence, pp. 246–7, and the whole of his Chapter VI. See also above, pp. 41 *etc.*, 369 *etc.*

[3] Klaeber, p. xxxv. Cf. Lawrence, p. 147. See also above, pp. 43, 92–7, 291–6.

[4] Klaeber, p. xix. Cf. Lawrence, chapter VI, *passim.* See above, pp. 50–2, 59–61.   [5] See pp. 451, 455 *etc.*

strongly than I ventured to express) doubts whether Beowulf himself be not a fictitious character[1], inserted into this genuinely historic background. The historic background has been the cause of many controversies: Klaeber and Lawrence agree in identifying the Geatas with the Gautar[2], Heorot with Leire[3], and hold that it is Froda who slays Healfdene, not the reverse[4]. Into the associations of Ohthere with Vendel, Lawrence does not enter; but Klaeber agrees in identifying Vendel with the Swedish, and not the Jutish country of that name[5]. Of late years this view has been confirmed by the historical and archæological work of Nerman and Lindqvist, of which also more will have to be said below[6].

Such agreement in books published simultaneously and independently does, I think, indicate that certain broad features are emerging from the fog of controversy. After all allowances have been made, and remembering how many things thirty years ago were generally accepted which are now generally denied, I think this agreement affords some support against the rather depressing view put forward by my critic in *Modern Philology*[7], that there is "almost no evidence" upon which to reach a positive conclusion as to many of these problems.

I do not for a moment suggest that even Prof. Klaeber's fine contribution to *Beowulf* studies has settled such problems. It *has* shown that, *if we can agree upon the method to be used*, a good many problems may be settled. As to this method, Prof. Klaeber (though he believes, as we all do, that a number of ancient lays must have preceded our extant epic) does not believe in the possibility of disengaging earlier lays from *Beowulf* by means of internal evidence alone. Here and there external evidence may help us: the sapphics and hexameters of Saxo compared with the speech of the *eald æscwiga* or the slaying of

---

[1] Klaeber, p. xxvii; cf. Lawrence, p. 101. See also above, p. 13: Deutschbein in 1913 was, I believe, actually the first to suggest this.

[2] Klaeber, p. xlvi; cf. Lawrence, p. 40. See also above, pp. 8–10, 333–44.

[3] Klaeber, p. xxxvii; cf. Lawrence, p. 32. See also above, pp. 16–20.

[4] Klaeber, p. xxxvi; cf. Lawrence, p. 80. See also above, p. 21, and below, p. 430, note.

[5] Klaeber, p. xliii. See also above, pp. 343–5.

[6] pp. 411–8. [7] xx, 436.

Beowulf's dragon seem to Klaeber to show connection[1]. But Klaeber holds that in *Beowulf* "no serious differences of language, diction or meter can be adduced in favor of multiple author-ship." The only differences discoverable are such that "it would be hazardous, in fact presumptuous, to assign any decisive weight to such insecure and fragmentary criteria. Contrariwise, it is entirely pertinent to emphasize the general homogeneity of the poem in matters of form, as well as substance and atmo-sphere" (cvii).

So Lawrence speaks of "the *Beowulf* poet," "who composed the epic essentially as we have it[2]."

Of course, on these points, there is not absolute agreement among modern students: Prof. Boer continued to the last to believe that, though Müllenhoff and ten Brink might have applied their methods wrongly, it was still possible to divide up our extant epic of *Beowulf* into the different lays and interpola-tions out of which it was compounded[3]. But there is now a general agreement with a view such as that of Lawrence or Klaeber, which would make *Beowulf* the work of one man, a Christian, working for a Christian Anglian court, probably in the eighth century or perhaps at the very end of the seventh. This too is the view of Liebermann and Cook, whose attempts at placing the poet more exactly, in time and space, will be men-tioned below[4]. And if an eminent *Beowulf* scholar like Schücking would make our poet later than the eighth century (for reasons which have been considered above[5] and which will also have to be briefly re-considered[6]) it is only reasonable to remember that an equally eminent *Beowulf* scholar like Chadwick would make our poet earlier than the eighth century. May we allow Chad-wick and Schücking to pair, and having thus got rid of our ex-tremists, decide the matter by the solid block of votes in the centre? Schücking says sternly, "No": he thinks it unreasonable that I, having refused on pp. 122–6 to be convinced by Chad-wick's arguments, should then later pick up these arguments

---

[1] Klaeber, pp. xxxv, xxi–xxii. But in the case of the dragon-slaying I am more sceptical about the connection than Klaeber is. See above, pp. 92–7.

[2] Lawrence, p. 17.

[3] Boer states his case in *English Studies*, v, 105–18 (1923). I have attempted a reply in *English Studies*, xi, 81–100 (1929). See also below, pp. 424 *etc.*

[4] pp. 486 *etc.*   [5] pp. 322 *etc.*   [6] pp. 486 *etc.*

again and use them on p. 324 as material against him[1]. And perhaps he is right here: but I am not sure. Chadwick's arguments, though not of force to prove the poem as old as he would make it, *do* seem to me to prove that it cannot be as late as Schücking thinks. On the other hand, Schücking's arguments, whilst they do not convince me that the poem is as late as A.D. 900, *do* very emphatically convince me that it is not a poem dating back to heathen times, with a mere Christian veneer. "The resoun of thynges is in the myddes."

But the difference between the point of view of Schücking and that of Cook, Liebermann, Klaeber, Lawrence and myself, though real, is one which it is important not to exaggerate. The essential thing is the agreement. We agree that *Beowulf* reflects the civilization of an age when the old heroic ideas and the new Christian ideas were both strong: it is a matter of less importance whether we connect *Beowulf* in our minds with those Christian fighting men whom we know dimly from the pages of Bede, or with the figure of Alfred, more vivid because it is revealed to us in the very words of that fighting saint himself.

Prof. Schücking allows me to quote some words which he used in a recent lecture in London:

> "It is a fact that the thorough amalgamation of ideas of Christian origin with those of indigenous growth shows itself at an early period already more conspicuously in England than anywhere else. Where in all the world is there anything like the old English epic of *Beowulf*, which endeavours to draw a hero whose figure embodies the new Christian ideal of sobriety and moderation, without robbing him of the old heroic qualities? It is most astonishing—no matter whether you date the *Beowulf* with Professor Chambers at about 730 or almost two hundred years later—that at so early a time a complete blending of two so different 'Weltanschauungen' should have been attempted. But the other Anglo-Saxon poems offer many—if less perfect—parallels. That in this case however literature to a certain extent mirrors the conditions of real life seems to be proved by history, e.g. by a character like King Alfred, who, for all his emulation of Charles the Great, shows in his private life a restraint quite foreign to his great Frankish model[2]."

---

[1] *P.B.B.* XLVII, 301: "Im zweiten teil aber sucht Chambers nach gründen gegen meine hypothese, und da erweckt er nun die von ihm selbst früher erschlagenen Chadwickschen argumente halbwegs wieder zu leben, um sie gegen mich ins feld zu führen. Aber ich kann nichts besseres tun, als gegen sie wiederum Chambers eigene waffe anzuwenden."

[2] This lecture has not yet been published, but a similar argument will be found in Schücking's Presidential Address to the Modern Humanities Research Association, 1929. The ideal in *Beowulf* is "eine Mischung aus germanisch-heroischen mit stoisch-christlichen Ideen."

But, although most of us now think in terms of a *"Beowulf* poet" (as did Earle and Rönning), not (as did Müllenhoff) in terms of four distinct authors followed by Interpolator A and Interpolator B, nevertheless, interpolation is possible enough. Since most of us think that nearly three centuries of transmission intervene between the *"Beowulf* poet" and the book as it lies before us in *MS Cotton Vitellius A XV*, and since most of us think that the poem has been altered to the speech in which we now find it from an original Anglian dialect, is it intrinsically likely that there have been no additions to, or omissions from, the original text? Lawrence's warning is very much to the point, that, whilst we speak of a *Beowulf* poet, we must remember that "additions and alterations may have been made in his work, in the course of later copyings, and transference to another dialect[1]."

That the original *Beowulf* poem had undergone interpolation has been the opinion of two of the most far-sighted scholars England and Germany have ever produced—Henry Bradley and Eduard Sievers.

Ten years ago Henry Bradley outlined, in a private letter to me, his view of how these interpolations in *Beowulf* might have arisen, and added a very necessary warning that an appearance of uniformity may be deceptive:

> "The intrinsic likelihood of later interpolations remains. I doubt whether it is quite true that *every* Christian passage contains archaisms that conclusively refer it to the early eighth century. And how do we know that some archaisms (syntactical if not morphological) may not have long survived in minstrel tradition and in the imitative epic dialect, so that the writer or interpolator of a heroic poem would fall into them naturally, though the same man would never think of using them in a poem of a different kind? *The Battle of Maldon* seems rather to point to something of this sort."

Five years ago, Eduard Sievers expressed his view that the original Northumbrian *Beowulf* had undergone a Kentish recension[2].

---

[1] p. 17. Compare, in the same sense, Ekwall in *Anglia, Beiblatt,* xxxiii, 183.

[2] Speaking of *Andreas*, Sievers says: "Seine Verlegung nach Kent aber wird gerade bei den nahen Beziehungen des Andreas zum Beowulf vielleicht nicht mehr ganz so wunderlich aussehen wie sie im ersten Augenblick erscheinen mag, wenn es mir (wie ich hoffe, in absehbarer Zeit!) noch gelingt, den Nachweis zu führen, welche wichtige Rolle gerade Kent in der Entwicklung unseres Beowulftextes gespielt hat, nachdem das alte Grundgedicht seine nordhumbrische Heimat verlassen hatte." *Zu Cynewulf* in *Neusprachliche Studien, Festgabe Karl Luick...dargebracht,* Marburg, 1925, p. 81 (*Die Neueren Sprachen,* 6 Beiheft).

That Sievers may soon give us the full result of his *Beowulf* studies must be the earnest wish of every lover of the English language and literature, throughout the world.

Meantime, we may be grateful for the "Note concerning the genesis of *Beowulf*" with which Klaeber concludes his new edition of 1928. Klaeber's view in some respects resembles that of Earle, who believed the poem to be the work of a cleric, and to have been written with special didactic purpose for the benefit of a king's son—as the "institution of a prince." But Earle, with his characteristic admixture of recklessness, carried his dislike of the theory of separate lays so far that he put himself out of court by denying that *Beowulf* was even dependent for its subject matter upon earlier historic lays.

Scholarship seems now, after fifty years, to be settling down to the view put forward by Rönning in the first elaborate monograph ever published on the *Beowulf* problem. Rönning took up a middle place between Müllenhoff's belief that the original traditional lays could be separated out, and such a disbelief in any traditional background as later led Earle to suppose the realm of Hygelac to be entirely the invention of an English author. Rönning's view was that the poems upon which the story is based arose among the Geatas in Southern Sweden, wandered to Northern England either direct or by way of the ancient Anglian home, and in England, perhaps in the eighth century, were worked up into an epic, probably by a Northumbrian poet. And with this view, neglected as it was in 1883, most people in 1931 would concur.

If much that has been written about *Beowulf* in this past half-century has had to be abandoned, much solid knowledge has been gained. *Beowulf* study has not been entirely a wandering in the wilderness, even if the achievement of proven fact is not proportionate to the labour expended.

CHAPTER II

THE HISTORICAL ELEMENTS

SECTION I. THE GĒATAS ONCE AGAIN

THE question is still being debated whether the wars which
figure so largely in the later part of *Beowulf* were waged between
Swedes and Gauts (*Gautar*, the *Götar* of what is now Southern
Sweden) or between Swedes and Jutes.

It was, as we all know, the paper by Pontus Fahlbeck in
favour of the Jute-theory which "first raised the question from
the region of guesswork to that of scholarly discussion[1]."
Nearly thirty years after this publication, Fahlbeck reinforced
his case by a further paper of the same title, read before the
Swedish Academy. This was published in 1924.

I do not mean again to reopen the "Jute question" at length,
after having discussed it twice above[2]. Yet Fahlbeck's re-
appearance in the arena cannot be passed over quite in silence.

Fahlbeck now lays greatest stress upon the phrases like *ofer
sǣ*, which occur so often in the account of the wars of Swedes
and Geatas: "What I must maintain," he says, "is, that the
words *ofer sǣ, ofer sǣ sīde, ofer wīd wæter, ofer heafo*, can have
only one meaning, 'over the sea,' and that sea must be either
the West Sea or the East Sea"—or, to use English terminology,
either the Cattegat or the Baltic.

Fahlbeck's argument is that the Geatas must have been
separated from the Swedes by "sea," in the limited sense which
that word bears in Modern English, of the open salt water.
Therefore, he argues, they must be Jutes, not Gautar.

But it is only in Modern English that the meaning of the
word "sea" has become limited in this way. In Old English (as
to this day in German) the word can mean either a fresh-water
lake or the salt sea. It has been objected that the same word

---

[1] Nerman, *Det svenska rikets uppkomst*, 1925, p. 109.
[2] pp. 6–10 and 333–45.

would not be used in the same poem in both senses and that, in certain places in *Beowulf*, *sǣ* certainly means the open sea. But, in fact, the word can be used in both senses in one sentence. Take the description of the Nile in Alfred's *Orosius*: it rises not far from the Red Sea (*þǣre Rēadan Sǣs*), sinks in the sand, rises from the sand and makes a great lake (*ond þǣr wyrcð micelne sǣ*); from this lake (*of þǣm sǣ*) it flows on, again becomes a great lake (*wyrð to miclum sǣ*), passes near its original source not far from the Red Sea (*þone Rēadan Sǣ*) and flows out into the Mediterranean (*ūt on þone Wendelsǣ*). In one paragraph, then, *sǣ* is three times used for a fresh-water lake, three times for the salt sea. It may be that the inland sense is the more primitive of the two: for the oldest examples of the word (in Gothic) invariably have an inland meaning[1].

We have less information about *heafo*. It occurs in the *Corpus* gloss[2] as a synonym of Latin *salum*, "sea"; elsewhere it is found in English only in this passage in *Beowulf*, and is conjecturally restored in another *Beowulf* passage. But, however rare in English, the word is common Germanic; and in Low German it signifies a sheet of inland water, as in *das Frische Haff*.

Sǣ and *heafo*, then, are the very words which would naturally be used of a great inland lake like Wener. And Lake Wener would naturally come into the fighting, if Swedes and Western Gautar attacked each other.

But Fahlbeck has a further objection that, in that case, the fighting would be not entirely "over the sea" but partly at least by land. Yet surely this *is* precisely the impression which the account of the fighting recorded in *Beowulf* actually does give, to any unprejudiced reader. That is how it struck Brandl: "It suits the geographical position of the Gautar that Beowulf's people fight the Swedes, sometimes after crossing the water (2380, 2394, 2473) and sometimes by land (2477, 2925, *etc.*)[3]."

It is indisputable that we are dealing with two great sea powers. The Geatas, whether they be Jutes or Gautar, are able to make a Viking expedition as far as Friesland; the Swedes had

---

[1] *Saiws* is used to translate the Greek λίμνη in Luke v, 1, 2, and viii, 22, 23, 33: *saiws* is also used in the Naples Gothic charter to signify "a marsh."

[2] Sweet, *Oldest English Texts*, 1885, *salum*, haeb, p. 95 (1778).

[3] *Pauls Grundriss*, second edition, II. 1, 997.

been famous for their ships from the time of Tacitus[1]. How is it
that, even when the opposing forces reach each other by water,
the actual fighting always takes place on land, so that we never
hear of fighting from ships? Is it reasonable to suppose that
Jutes and Swedes, two peoples altogether cut off from each other
by the sea, could for generations have made a practice of harrying
each other's country by sea-raids, and yet never have had a
sea-fight? This is the state of things depicted in *Beowulf*, between the Geatas and the Swedes. Yet surely it is an axiom
that there is no more risky business than a landing over the sea
in an enemy's country, when that enemy has a fleet in being
equal or superior to one's own. Between Jutes and Swedes there
must have been a fight for the command of the sea, and *then*
the victorious party would invade the land of the vanquished.
Why then does fighting by sea not come into the story?

Surely the answer is that we have an example of that Scandinavian manner of fighting which the Northman Ohthere explained to King Alfred: "There are very large fresh-water lakes,"
we read in the *Orosius*, "and the Cwenas carry their ships overland to the lakes, and thence they harry the Northmen: they
have very small ships and very light ones." I have always
regarded the *synn ond sacu Swēona ond Gēata ofer wīd wæter* as
fighting of this kind, and so I suppose has every other editor of
Beowulf.

And so, if the raiding takes place between Gautar and Swedes,
everything is as it should be. Both sides, no doubt, had plenty of
sea-going ships; but these salt-water vessels would be much too
heavy to be used in raids made through a line of great lakes,
rivers and portages. Canoes would be used drawing little water
and capable of being carried considerable distances. Neither
party would, probably, keep up permanent fleets on scattered
waterways, unconnected as yet by canals. The light canoes,
carried across and launched first on one piece of water and then
on another, were not fighting ships. That is why the two forces
always meet, as fighting men, on land (or ice), for all that they
are harrying each other *ofer wīd wæter*.

It may be said that all this is not very conclusive, because

---

[1] *Germania*, xliv.

the account in *Beowulf*, as we have it, was composed in a strange
land some two hundred years after the events; what right have
we to ask that it should reflect exactly the facts of the actual
fighting? And I admit that arguments and deductions of the
kind which have just been drawn are not quite conclusive. For
that reason it is important to keep always clearly in mind that
the interpretation of *Gēatas* as *Gautar* is not based upon this, or
any number of similar geographical and historical considerations,
but upon the simple fact that the word *Gēatas* is the O.E. form
of the O.N. *Gautar*, and is quite distinct from Jutes, which in
O.E. is *Ēote*, *Ȳte*.

In the text of *Beowulf* as we have it, Hygelac's people are
always called *Gēatas*, never *Ēote* or *Ȳte*, and the alliteration upon
G proves that the text which lies before us in this respect represents the original. It is the supporters of the Jute-theory who
ask us to ignore these obvious facts, on the ground that the
account of the fighting *ofer sǣ* suits Jutes better than Gautar.
We look into it, and we find that the exact reverse is the case:
it suits Gautar better than Jutes. Possibly the argument from
the words *ofer sǣ* is not conclusive on either side: the point is
that, for what it *is* worth, it does not support the Jute-theory,
but tells against it.

The same lakes which formed an avenue of attack by light
boats in summer would, when frozen in winter, offer a broad road
into the enemy's country. We are told that Beowulf with his
army supported Eadgils against Onela, king of Sweden, *ofer sǣ
sīde*, took vengeance upon Onela, and slew him in "chill journeys
fraught with woe," *cealdum cearsīðum*. This need not *necessarily*
mean that Beowulf attacked in winter over the frozen lake, for
ceald in Old English can be used metaphorically, as we say
"bitter" or "sharp." But when we turn to the Scandinavian
sources we have a record of this very battle in which Onela (Áli)
was slain: it is said to have been fought on Lake Wener, then
frozen over, *á ísi vats þess er Væni heitir*[1], *á Vænis ísi, in stagno
Waener, glacie jam obducto*[2]. These are late sources, it may be
replied. But in the *Kálfsvísa*, which dates apparently from the

---

[1] Snorri, *Edda*, ed. Jónsson, p. 108.
[2] See above, p. 7.

Viking time and is certainly a record of early tradition, the same battle is spoken of as taking place "when they rode to the ice[1]."

So the historical and geographical argument, called in to support the Jute-theory, is found, here again and even more conclusively, to count, if it counts at all, against it. For a battle fought on the ice of Lake Wener exactly suits Swedes and Western Gautar.

For an understanding of the early history of Scandinavia it is essential to decide this question; to the best of our power we *must* settle it before going further. Yet a scholar has recently spoken of the discussion as "futile[2]," and it is easy to understand the irritation which led him to use the term, and subsequently himself to make a (quite necessary) contribution[3] to the "futile" discussion.

Now that Fahlbeck, who began the debate in 1883, has made his reply, it is surely time for the discussion to be closed. In opening it, Fahlbeck did not deny that *Gēatas* is the Old English word corresponding to *Gautar*. Now if we are going to interpret a tribal name as something quite different from its obvious linguistic meaning, overwhelming geographical and historical reasons should be found for doing so. But they have not been found. On the contrary, the very reasons in virtue of which we are asked to set aside the obvious interpretation of *Gēatas* as *Gautar* can be shown, on examination, to favour Gautar rather than Jutes. All that the partizans of the Jute-theory seem now to be doing is to claim a verdict of "not proven" on certain obscure and irrelevant side-issues. Thus a very able young Swedish historian, Curt Weibull, has recently revived the controversy[4]. Some of his points may be quite sound: but they do not touch the real question. I am, and always have been, ready to admit that Schück went too far in claiming Halland as part of the Geatic kingdom. But although that may concern the student of early Scandinavian history, trying to make out the exact boundaries of the different kingdoms, it does not concern

---

[1] See above, as before, and also Nerman, *Det svenska rikets uppkomst*, 1925, p. 102.

[2] Kemp Malone, *M.L.R.* xx, 11 (1925).

[3] *Acta Philologica Scandinavica*, iv, 84–90 (1929).

[4] *Om det svenska och det danska rikets uppkomst, Historisk Tidskrift för Skåneland*, vii, 301–60. See especially footnote to p. 312.

the student of *Beowulf*, because Schück's case that the Geatas
are the Gautar is not weakened, even if he be wrong about
Halland[1]. Inferences such as Schück drew[2] from the *Heimskringla* or Adam of Bremen are, it has been urged, very uncertain evidence as to what the coastline of the Vestgötar really
was as early as the sixth century A.D.[3] Of course they are: but
this only tells the more against those who, on admittedly ambiguous and uncertain grounds, seek to ignore the obvious
meaning of two tribal names. The difficulties which the defenders of the Jute-theory have to explain away are (*a*) how the
word *Gēatas*, which means *Gautar*, comes in *Beowulf* to be
applied to a different people, viz. the Jutes; and (*b*)—a much
more serious difficulty—how, if Hygelac's people were Jutes, a
poem as long as *Beowulf* could be written in Anglo-Saxon England about them without ever mentioning them by their correct
name of Jutes (*Ēote*, *Ȳte*). Weibull refuses to go into these linguistic difficulties. But they are crucial[4]. It will not do to base
our argument upon the assumption that when *Beowulf* says one
thing it means another. A treatment of the subject which claims
serious attention must face this linguistic problem.

In his recent book[5] Prof. E. Wadstein *does* face the difficulty:
and in this way. Let it be supposed, he says, that the subject
matter of *Beowulf* reached England through the Frisians, and
that the English poet adopted the name of the Jutes in the form
in which he heard it from the Frisians. This form, Wadstein
argues, would be "Iatar" (the name is not recorded in Frisian)
and this would be represented in English spelling by "Geatas."

This theory is put forward with such learning and conviction
that it is held by many to have placed the Jute-theory on its legs
again, so far at least as to demand a new examination of the
subject[6].

---

[1] See the arguments in Nerman, *Det svenska rikets uppkomst*, 1925, pp. 43, 51.
[2] See above, p. 339.
[3] As is urged by Ekwall in *Anglia, Beiblatt*, XXXIII, 180 (1922).
[4] See above, pp. 333–8.
[5] *Norden och Västeuropa i gammal tid*, Stockholm, 1925, pp. 18 ff., 161 ff.
[6] "Falls Wadsteins Ausführungen das richtige treffen, sind es nicht die
Gautar (Götar) sondern die Jüten von denen im Beowulf die Rede ist. Die
ganze Frage erheischt eine erneute Prüfung." Uhlenbeck in *Acta Philologica
Scandinavica*, III, 174. Wadstein's arguments are met by Kemp Malone, *Acta
Phil.* IV, 84–90.

Yet the theory seems to undermine its own foundations. For, *if* the Geatas are Jutes, why should knowledge of their deeds reach England by way of the Frisians? The Jutes, according to Bede, were the first of the Germanic tribes to make a settlement in England; and for generations the Angles, their next neighbours on the Continent, were crossing over and settling in England. There was intimacy and intermarriage between the Jutish court of Kent and the Anglian court of Northumbria. Why should Englishmen in England have to hear, through the Frisians, of the deeds of their Jutish kinsmen who had remained on the Continent[1]? Again, how is the theory that the subject matter of *Beowulf* reached the English through the Frisians compatible with the fact that we find no further traces of this supposed Frisian origin in other proper names in *Beowulf*? Again, how is it compatible with the fact that the story is emphatically not influenced by any Frisian standpoint? Frisians are mentioned not infrequently in *Beowulf*[2], but always as a foreign or hostile nation, and incidents concerning them are invariably told from the non-Frisian point of view.

And, even if the English *had* learnt of the deeds of their kinsmen remaining on the Continent through the Frisians, why should they therefore have attempted to express in English the Frisian pronunciation of the name of one of the tribes of which they themselves were composed? They would assuredly, in repeating the story, have repeated the familiar name in its English form, according to the dialect, Anglian, Saxon, or Kentish, which they spoke; and none of these dialects would have given them the form "Geatas[3]."

Finally, it has been shown by Prof. Kemp Malone that it is exceedingly improbable that the Frisian form of the name Jute *was* "Iatar"—the one form which is necessary to support the argument[4].

How is an improbable theory rendered more plausible by

---

[1] Wadstein would no doubt reply to this that he rejects the whole of Bede's account of the Jutes and Angles as unhistorical. See *The Origin of the English*, by E. Wadstein, Uppsala, 1927.

[2] 1069–1159, 1207, 2912–15.

[3] This is very excellently urged by Wessén, *De nordiska folkstammarna*, 1927, p. 56.

[4] See his important discussion of this in detail, *Acta Phil.* IV, 85–7.

being made to depend upon another theory, itself improbable, through a series of deductions, each also highly improbable? Yet it is thus, if at all, that the identification of Geatas as Jutes has now to be defended. The controversy seems to be drifting away from reality altogether.

Yet it cannot be denied that in the past there has been unreality in the arguments, not only on one, but on both sides, because the Icelandic authorities actually *do* represent, not the Gautar, but the Jutes of Vendel in North Jutland as the foes of one of the very Swedish kings whom *Beowulf* mentions. This can only be accounted for if we suppose a confusion between two places of the same name, "Vendel." So it has been open to the Jute-theorists to retort that their opponents, by assuming such a "name shift," are doing the very thing which they are refusing to permit the Jute-theorists to do. But, fortunately, recent archæological investigation has settled this particular problem, and with it, let us hope, concluded for ever this memorable controversy. To this archæological investigation we must now turn.

SECTION II. RECENT ARCHÆOLOGICAL DISCOVERY: THE BURIAL MOUND OF OTTAR VENDEL-CROW, COMPARED WITH THE KINGS' MOUNDS AT UPPSALA[1]

The only valid historical argument in favour of the Jute-theory was that brought forward by Bugge. In the *Ynglinga tal*, and in its prose paraphrase and expansion, the *Ynglinga saga*, the early Swedish kings are enumerated. Three of them, Athils, his father Ottar, and Ottar's father Egil, are clearly identical with Eadgils, his father Ohthere, and (despite the difference of name here) Ohthere's father Ongentheow[2]. Now, in *Beowulf*, we hear of raids which Ohthere made upon the Geatas. But the district which Ottar raids in the *Ynglinga saga* is not Gautland, but Vendel in the north of Jutland. He was

---

[1] I was able to give a very hasty account of these discoveries in my first edition (see above, pp. 343–5), but so much work has been done since, and the discoveries are of such importance, that it seemed better to restate them at length.

[2] See note 2 to p. 411 below.

slain, and his body exposed, we are told, upon a mound in Vendel, to be torn to pieces by carrion birds. Then the victors made a crow of wood, and sent it to Sweden, telling the Swedes that their king was worth no more than that. So Ottar was called *Vendel-kråka*, "the Vendel-crow." But other early documents attributed this name (without any explanatory story), not to Ottar, but to his father Egil, who is to be identified with the Ongentheow who, according to *Beowulf*, was slain by the Geatas.

This certainly seems to depict not the Gautar, but the Jutes of Vendel as the hereditary foes of Ohthere and his father Ongentheow. Until this difficulty has been accounted for, the question of the nationality of the Geatas of *Beowulf* cannot be regarded as finally settled.

The late Dr Knut Stjerna published three papers dealing with the Swedes and Geatas. He was a strong advocate of the view that the Geatas are the Gautar (Götar). He tried to connect with the stories given in *Beowulf* the three great mounds which stand at Old Uppsala. He re-examined the discoveries which had been made when these mounds had been explored, and came to the conclusion that the mounds formed a series, the one nearest to the church being the oldest. He dated this mound about the year A.D. 500 or a little before[1]. He did not identify any one of these mounds with any individual king, though he is known to have believed that Athils-Eadgils was probably buried under one of them[2].

Stjerna further called attention to a mound near the Swedish Vendel (a place some twenty-two miles north of Uppsala). This mound in size was comparable with the largest of the royal mounds at Old Uppsala. Stjerna tried to show that the word "Vendel-crow" had been given to the Swedish kings because of their connection, not with the Jutish district of Vendel, but with the Swedish place of the same name. He supposed that they had had a stronghold there, and that it was there that Ongentheow had taken refuge when he retreated before the victorious Geatas. But Stjerna thought that, by a natural confusion, the Norwegian authors connected Vendel with Vendel in Jutland,

---

[1] *Essays on Beowulf*, translated by Clark Hall, Coventry, 1912, p. 234.
[2] Nerman, *Vilka konungar ligga i Uppsala högar?*, p. 14.

which was more familiar to them. This, he conjectured, had given rise to the story that Ottar died in the Jutish Vendel.

Such a theory of name-shifting is open to the gravest suspicion, unless backed by documentary evidence. Now one piece of such evidence in support of Stjerna's theory was, that there *is* a grave mound, called by the name of Ottar (*Ottarshögen*), and that this is not in the Jutish, but in the Swedish Vendel. Stjerna did not think it necessary to mention this. He probably believed the name to be a mere piece of recent antiquarian conjecture. In modern times, prominent mounds have so often been christened with ancient names by romantic antiquaries, that it is well to be cautious.

Stjerna's premature death in 1909 interrupted these studies. But in the following year a discovery was made which gave a new importance to his conjecture.

It was found that for much more than two centuries the mound at the Swedish Vendel had been commonly called by Ottar's name. For in the latter half of the seventeenth century an official survey of antiquities was carried out throughout Sweden. It was in 1677 that a meeting of the leading parishioners was held at Vendel, and they reported, among other things, that "many earthen barrows are to be found here, but especially by Hussby there is a great earthen barrow, which is called *Otters högen*." The records of this survey were deposited in the Royal Library at Stockholm, and there this entry was found[1]. Later, this was confirmed by the discovery of an allusion, in 1675, to "Utters högen i Wändell[2]." The mound is mentioned in connection with the practice of sorcery, and in a way which shows the name to have been current. But if the name was in popular use as early as 1675, it cannot reasonably be attributed to the modern romantic archæologist. Whoever the Ottar may have been, after whom the mound was named, the name presumably comes down from ancient times.

The conjecture of Knut Stjerna, that Ottar Vendel-crow got his name not from the Danish but from the Swedish Vendel,

---

[1] Otto v. Friesen, *När Sverige blev till* (*Upsala Nya Tidnings Julnummer*, 1910).
[2] See E. Linderholm, *Vendelshögens konunganamn i socknens 1600-talstradition*, in *Namn och Bygd*, VII, 36–40 (1919).

received therefore documentary support. But not support of a conclusive kind, since it was by no means *proved* that the Ottar after whom the mound was named was the Ottar king of Sweden to whom *Beowulf* and the *Ynglinga tal* refer. The nickname "Vendel-crow" would have put the identification with the king of the *Ynglinga tal* beyond doubt. But this nickname was not so authentically connected with the mound as was the name Ottar. And there have been many Ottars.

Meanwhile, in 1913, Prof. Birger Nerman published his short but most important pamphlet on the question, "What kings lie buried under the mounds at Uppsala?" Tradition, as he pointed out, had regarded the three great mounds as "Kings' mounds." But what kings?

Apart from *Beowulf*, our knowledge of the early Swedish kings is entirely derived from the *Ynglinga tal*, which, if we neglect the three names of gods with which it begins, covers twenty-seven generations, ending with Ragnvald, who was living when the *Ynglinga tal* was composed in his honour, say about 870. The surviving fragments of the *Ynglinga tal* have come down to us because they are embodied in the *Ynglinga saga* of Snorri, which forms the first section of the *Heimskringla*. Snorri's prose gives us some further information. How much this is paraphrased from the portions of the *Ynglinga tal* which he does *not* quote, it is difficult to decide.

Now Nerman's point was that three of the Swedish kings, as enumerated by Snorri in the *Ynglinga saga*, are mentioned by him as having been laid in mound in Uppsala[1]. One of these is Athils, the Eadgils of *Beowulf*. Athils' father Ottar is out of the reckoning, for according to the *Ynglinga saga* he was devoured by carrion fowls in Vendel in Jutland: and even if this be an error, and if "Ottar's mound" in the Swedish Vendel was raised over him, that is equally inconsistent with burial at Uppsala. Ottar's father Egil (the Ongentheow[2] of *Beowulf*) is also said to

---

[1] See also Nerman, *Det svenska rikets uppkomst*, 1925, p. 139.

[2] Despite the difference of name, there would seem to be a shadowy personality which we can claim as identical. Egil and Ongentheow occupy the same place in the genealogy, that of father of Ohthere-Ottar. Ongentheow was slain by the Geatic warrior Eofor (Boar). Of Egil it is recorded in the *Ynglinga tal* that his blood reddened *farra trióno*. Now *farra* can be interpreted either as "bull" (O.E. *fearr*) or as "boar" (O.E. *fearh*). But *trjóna*, "snout," is decisive

have been laid in mound in Uppsala, and *his* father, Aun the ancient, likewise.

No other Swedish kings are mentioned as having been buried in Uppsala[1].

It is to be noted that this mention of burial at Uppsala is found only in the prose of Snorri. The very much older *Ynglinga tal* does not, in its extant fragments, mention this *burial*, although in the case of both Aun and Athils *death* at Uppsala is mentioned, and that might be held to involve burial there. Anyway, it is noteworthy that Snorri should mention three, and three only, of these Swedish kings as buried at Uppsala, and that there should be the three great "kings' mounds" there.

Now, as Nerman pointed out, we can date these kings fairly accurately from *Beowulf*, and from the one firm chronological fact which *Beowulf* gives us, Hygelac's death. Hygelac is succeeded by his young son, Heardred, who grows up, befriended by Beowulf. Ohthere dies, apparently leaving his sons Eadgils and Eanmund too young to take the throne. Anyway, Ohthere's brother Onela becomes king, and Eadgils and Eanmund revolt against him, and take refuge with Heardred. Onela follows his nephews, and slays Heardred, but Beowulf and Eadgils escape. So Ohthere's death must have fallen probably a little later than Hygelac's, say somewhere about[2] the year 525. Ohthere can hardly have been very aged at the time of his death; his brother comes to the throne presumably because Ohthere's sons are too

in favour of "boar," although Snorri understood "bull." (See *Ynglinga tal, text, översättning och kommentar* av Ad. Noreen, 1925; *Akademiens Handlingar,* XXVIII, 2, pp. 202–3, 236.) It can hardly be mere accident that the father of Ohthere in one version is slain by a warrior named "Boar," and in the other by a boar. The problem of the different names remains unsolved. The difficulties in the way of supposing the one or the other a nickname, or Egil (*Agilaʀ) a shortened form of the longer name, are discussed by Björkman (*Eigennamen im Beowulf*, pp. 91–9). For a suggestion of *Ongenþēow* as a title, see Malone, *Literary History of Hamlet*, I, 117 etc.

[1] The three gods with whom the list begins may be left out of the reckoning. Of them, Frey is said to have been buried in Uppsala. The Danish king Halfdan is also said by Snorri to have conquered Sweden and to have been buried in Uppsala. But this lacks any kind of confirmation. It is not, of course, in the *Ynglinga tal*.

[2] Nerman originally suggested 530–40 (*Uppsala högar*, p. 11). Subsequently he suggested 525 (*Det svenska rikets uppkomst*, 1925, p. 137). I think Nerman reckons Hygelac's death at least four or five years too early: but he allows more time than I should between Hygelac's death and that of Ohthere: so that I agree with the year 525 as being the likeliest approximation we can get to the death of Ohthere.

young to succeed[1]. The father of Ohthere, Ongentheow (Egil), *was* however old when he was slain: *Beowulf* is very explicit about that.

So something much less than a full generation should be allowed between his death and that of his son Ohthere. On the other hand, Ongentheow was killed in the campaign with which Hygelac's reign begins—so he presumably died some considerable time before 520. We may put his death, then, in the opening years of the century, say about 510.

The father and predecessor of Ongentheow is not mentioned in *Beowulf*, but the *Ynglinga tal* records him as Aun. He is the stock example of a very aged man, so that when a man dies of old age it is known as "Aun's sickness." His death may be placed therefore much less than a full generation before that of his son, Ongentheow (Egil): say at the end of the fifth century, or at the latest about the year 500.

We have been reckoning backwards from the death of Ohthere, c. 525. If now we reckon forwards, allowing for the fact that his son Athils was apparently only a boy when Ohthere died, that after returning from his exile he had a long and prosperous reign, and died, as the *Ynglinga tal* tells us, *dægsæll*, "full of days," we can hardly date his death before 570, the date Nerman gives. It might possibly be dated even later; if we allow threescore years and ten for a man who was *dægsæll*, and make Eadgils fifteen at his father's death in 525, we need not kill him till the year of grace 580. (This date, as we shall see, would suit Nerman's calculations even better than 570. But it is characteristic of the caution Nerman shows in working out these dates that he never presses a date the least bit in favour of his own argument.)

Taking then the three Swedish kings whom Snorri records to have been buried at Uppsala, the youngest, Athils, seems to have died 570–580. The next in age, Athils' grandfather, Ongentheow

---

[1] This seems clear from *Beow.* 2381: "They had revolted against Onela," and from the fact that, according to *Ynglinga tal*, their father Ohthere (Ottar) had been king. If either of them had been of age to succeed to the throne on Ohthere's death, Onela might nevertheless have driven them out: but in that case they could hardly have been regarded as revolting against him. Eadgils was clearly able enough: youth must have been the disability. That Ohthere was the elder, Onela the younger brother, seems clear (see Malone in *Philological Quarterly*, VIII, 406).

(Egil), seems to have died quite early in the century, say about 510, and his father (Aun) say at the end of the fifth century, or at latest about 500.

Nerman then proceeded to compare these dates with the dates which antiquaries had given to the three mounds. Stjerna, as we have seen, had dated the oldest mound, that nearest the church, at the end of the fifth century, or about 500. This fits in exactly with the date of the death of Aun.

Montelius had dated the latest mound about 600, and this agrees as well as can reasonably be expected with the date we have attributed to Athils' death, 570–580.

The mound between has never been properly explored, and the actual burial—presumably a cremation one—has not been examined, but the preliminary investigation seemed to show that the mound, in structure as in position, was intermediate between the other two mounds, but had much greater similarity to the earlier one. This fits in with the date of Ongentheow (Egil), not long after 500, say perhaps 510.

Anyone who studies carefully Stjerna's arguments for the dating of the oldest mound about 500, must see how approximate and provisional all this dating of necessity is. But the point to emphasize is that these dates were given to the mounds by archæologists on purely archæological grounds, and with no idea whatever of making them fit in with these particular kings, or with the dates which, working upon *Beowulf*, we should attribute to these kings.

Nerman concluded his study in 1913 by pointing out that this provisional dating of the Uppsala mounds made an investigation of Ottar's mound in Vendel desirable. Outwardly, that mound closely resembled the Uppsala mounds. If its contents showed it to belong to the same period as the Uppsala finds, the identification of four of the most noteworthy early monuments in Sweden would be confirmed.

The State Antiquary, Bernhard Salin, was particularly interested in this kind of collation of literary with archæological evidence, to which he himself had made an important contribution. He began the excavation of Ottar's mound in 1914. Other duties however intervened, and responsibility for the work fell upon Sune Lindqvist. The war delayed matters, but Lindqvist finished his task in 1916, and published an account of the discoveries in *Fornvännen*[1] in 1917.

A briefer account of the discoveries, with a running comment explaining their importance, was published in the same year by Nerman[2]. Then in 1925, in his epoch-making book on "The Foundation of the Swedish Kingdom" (*Det svenska rikets uppkomst*), Nerman gave a full explanation of all that the new discoveries meant. The year before, a paper on this subject from him had been read to the Viking Society in London, and this has now been published[3]. Readers will find it a useful summary. But it is much to be wished that a complete English translation of Nerman's remarkable book were forthcoming. Meantime I have to thank Prof. Nerman for permission to translate the relevant pages from his pamphlet *Ottar Vendel-kråka.*

"Ottar's mound is about 8 metres in height, and 40 in diameter, as compared with the Third Mound at Uppsala[4], which is 10½ metres high and 60 metres in diameter. In its structure it proved to be closely related to the Uppsala mounds: it consisted of sand covered by a layer of earth a metre thick, and had a cairn of stones at the bottom approximately in the centre. As in the case of the Uppsala mounds, this cairn had been heaped over burnt remains. For at Vendel, as at Uppsala, the dead king had been cremated at the place of burial: at Vendel a hole had been dug in the ground, the burnt remains had been swept into a heap and the hole filled with them: in the middle of the hole had been placed a handsome little wooden bucket, adorned with broad horizontal bands of gilded bronze, and filled to the brim with burnt bones, which had been cleaned: the other burnt remains, for which there was no room in the hole, had been collected round it, and the cairn raised over them. In the First Uppsala mound the arrangement had been just the same, only with the difference that the vessel containing the bones was of pottery. In the Third Uppsala mound there was neither a hole, nor a vessel for the burnt remains.

"It is interesting to compare the stone cairn at Vendel with the Uppsala cairns. At Uppsala the cairns formed a series, diminishing in

---

[1] *Ottarshögen i Vendel*, pp. 127–43.
[2] *Ottar Vendelkråka och Ottarshögen i Vendel*, Uppsala.
[3] *Saga Book of the Viking Society*, x, 1928, 113–31.
[4] [The mounds have long been known to Scandinavian archæologists as Odin's, Frey's and Thor's mounds. But in translating I have avoided this modern nomenclature, as it confuses the reader who is trying to remember them by the names of the kings in the *Ynglinga tal*. I number them in their order from the church (site of the temple), which is also their chronological order.]

size and elaboration. The cairn in the First Uppsala mound had a diameter of about fifteen metres, and was surrounded at the bottom by a carefully constructed stone wall, 1·2 metres high. The cairn in the Second Uppsala mound (which has only been cursorily examined) has a diameter of 10 metres: there was no stone wall. Finally, the cairn in the Third Uppsala mound, where again there was no stone wall, had a diameter of only 1·05 metres. The cairn in Ottar's mound had a diameter of about 7 metres, and there was no stone wall there either. So in the size of its cairn Ottar's mound is intermediate between the Second Uppsala mound [the mound of Egil-Ongentheow] and the Third [the mound of Athils-Eadgils], which agrees with the date of his death, between that of Egil and Athils.

The finds in Ottar's mound show a close resemblance to those in the mounds at Old Uppsala. It is noteworthy that in Ottar's mound, just as in the mounds at Uppsala, there is no indication of weapons. Just as in the Uppsala mounds, the finds in Ottar's mound were comparatively insignificant.

Amongst the burnt remains in Ottar's mound were found: some small and obscure fragments of gold and silver; a belt-plate of iron; a strap-buckle of the same material and other belt-fittings of bronze; fragments of a glass vessel; a number of more or less complete half-spherical bone draughtsmen, provided with two holes on the under side, and a great number of fragments of such draughtsmen; fragments of a bone comb with its case, and of a little bone spoon. Besides the burnt human bones there were also found those of different animals.

But a surprisingly lucky discovery was also made in Ottar's mound. Among the burnt remains, close to the side of the bucket, was discovered a gold solidus of the Eastern Empire struck under the Emperor Basiliscus, who reigned A.D. 476–477. A hole is pierced in the coin, showing that it was used as a pendant. It is very worn.

The finds in the mound allow of its being accurately dated.

The belt-fitting in Ottar's mound was similar to one found in the First Uppsala mound, but similar ones have been found much earlier than c. 500. Draughtsmen of the same form as those in Ottar's mound were also found in the First Uppsala mound—but they are also found much later. Prof. Almgren has however pointed out to me, that whilst the earlier draughtsmen if pierced with holes have usually two, so far as is known hitherto draughtsmen after about 650 have never more than one. This connects Ottar's mound with the First Uppsala mound, but gives no definite dating.

The bone comb belongs to a type which is found in the Fifth and Sixth Centuries, but which undergoes certain changes in the latter part of the Sixth Century. It can therefore not be later than the second half of that century, and belongs rather to the time before 550 than after.

The gold coin is so much worn that a long time must have passed between the date when it was struck and when it was buried, so that we may date the burial some way on in the Sixth Century. On the other hand, solidi found in the North can generally be assumed not to have been in circulation for more than 75 to 100 years before being buried.

Finally, wooden buckets similar to the one found are known from Norway and Denmark. Docent Lindqvist tells me, that they can to some extent be classified in a series, and that the type of bucket found in Ottar's mound agrees, broadly, with the period indicated by the other finds.

The discoveries in Ottar's mound show, then, that it cannot be earlier than the Sixth Century, and hardly belongs to the very beginning of that century: on the other hand it cannot be later than the Sixth Century and belongs rather to the time before 550 than after.

The size of the cairn in Ottar's mound is intermediate between the Second and the Third Uppsala mounds. So far as one can judge from this feature, it seems to indicate a date nearly contemporary with the Second mound, but a little later. And the Second mound has been shown[1] to belong to a time not long before 516.

So it appears from the enquiry, that Ottar's mound was raised in the first half of the Sixth Century, but not at the very beginning—that is to say, just at the time when the historic Ottar Vendel-crow must have died, 525–530.

So, the tradition maintained in Vendel in Uppland is proved correct: Ottar Vendel-crow was buried in the mound which bears his name today—the tradition has maintained itself for nearly 1400 years. It is an excellent example of the tenacity and trustworthiness of a local tradition of a certain type. At the same time it confirms in the strongest way my conjecture that Aun, Egil [Ongentheow] and Athils [Eadgils] were laid in mound in Old Uppsala.

On the other hand the tradition preserved by the *Ynglinga tal* and by Snorri has made a mistake regarding the Vendel with which Ottar is connected. Norwegian and Icelandic tradition, better acquainted with Jutland than with the more remote Uppland, has substituted Vendel in Jutland for Vendel in Uppland.

And so the discrepancy between *Beowulf* and the *Ynglinga saga* is explained: *Beowulf*, the older source, which mentions Ottar [Ohthere] in connection with the wars between Swedes and Gautar (Götar), is right, as against the later *Ynglinga saga,* which makes him fight the Danes. But when Norwegian and Icelandic tradition represented the Vendel with which Ottar's name and burial were connected as Vendel in Jutland, it followed that some reason had to be found for Ottar's assumed presence there. The most obvious supposition was, that Ottar had made a raid upon Vendel and fallen there. The story of Ottar's raid, then, simply arises from a misunderstanding of the name Vendel: there is no reason to suppose, as I once believed, that it has its origin in traditions of battles between Swedes and Gautar, and of a Gautish invasion of Uppland, in which Ottar falls in Vendel. Our oldest source, *Beowulf,* knows nothing of any such story: *Beowulf* has nothing to say about the death of Ottar [Ohthere]. The whole story about Ottar in the *Ynglinga saga,* which is intrinsically open to suspicion, is thus shown to be fictitious. How its details arose it is impossible to decide. So much only is clear, that behind the story Snorri tells, of the body of Ottar being placed on a mound in Vendel in Jutland, lies the story that Ottar was laid in mound in Vendel in Uppland.

Snorri's story of the origin of the name 'Vendel-crow' can no longer be defended. It is merely an attempt to explain a nickname which had become unintelligible. But how is the nickname itself to be explained?

Schück[2] thought the name 'Vendel-crow' a title of honour. The crow, as a carrion bird, was, like the raven and the vulture, associated

---

[1] [Egil is the second of the three Swedish kings said by Snorri to have been buried in Uppsala. Accepting the identification of Egil with Ongentheow, which can hardly be denied, his mound must have been raised some time before Hygelac's death, which Nerman here places in 516. See above.]

[2] *Studier i Ynglingatal*, p. 126.

with battle. So the name 'Vendel-crow' ought to mark its bearer as 'a bird preying on the carrion of the foes of Vendel.'

But meantime Oskar Lundberg, in an article published shortly after the opening of Ottar's mound, seems to have found the right explanation[1].

Lundberg mentions that even today, when men from Vendel... come in the winter with their carts of charcoal through Dannemora, it may happen that a small boy will stand near the waggon, but out of range of the driver's whip, and make a long nose with the rhyme

> Vendels kråka
> får jag åka.

'Crows' is a nickname for the men of Vendel, just as those of Österby are called *sjuror*, 'magpies,' and those of Morkarla 'ravens'....

Lundberg shows that the name 'crows' for inhabitants of Uppland was known already soon after 1630: it is mentioned by I. H. Rhezelius as a nickname of the people of Malsta and Estuna in Eastern Uppland. Lundberg finds it therefore very probable that the nickname 'crows' for inhabitants of Vendel is very old. The name 'Vendel-crow,' according to him, is a rather derisive indication that Ottar was a 'Vendel-dweller.'...Ottar's grandfather, father and son were buried in Uppsala: Ottar broke the tradition: and so the name was imposed upon him by a local patriotism which favoured burial near the Uppsala sanctuary."

The archæologists have, then, finally disposed of the only serious historical argument which has ever been brought forward in favour of identifying the Geatas with the Jutes. Stjerna's reasoning alone was not convincing, and did not, for example, convince Axel Olrik, always one of the most determined supporters of the "Jute-theory." "I think," Olrik wrote at the very end of his life[2], "that the last word has not been said concerning the nationality of the Geatas." Nerman and Lindqvist can surely claim to have settled for ever that most obstinate of all "philological legends," the identification of the Geatas with the Jutes.

But they have done more. The stories given in *Beowulf* of the struggle between Swedes and Geatas, with the prophecies of the complete subjugation of the Geatas by the Swedes, mark the beginnings of Sweden as we know it, which dates from this uniting into one nation of the Swedes and Geatas. The chronology which, with the help of *Beowulf*, has been demonstrated, shows Sweden to be one of the oldest of European states. Indeed, if we date Sweden back to the powerful state which Tacitus

---

[1] *Ottar Vendelkråka* in *Stockholms-Tidningen*, August 6, 1916.
[2] *Heroic Legends of Denmark*, p. 39.

mentions, it must rank as the oldest of all European kingdoms; but modern Sweden begins with the beginning of the incorporation of the Geatas into the Swedish realm in the sixth century. And simultaneously, under Hrothgar and his house, the mighty kings of Denmark, that realm also rises to eminence. And the Old English epic is the primary authority for these two events, with which begins the history of the nations of modern Europe[1].

SECTION III. BEOWULF AND EARLY DANISH HISTORY

Olrik's interrupted work on methods of legend study. Knut Liestøl

Whilst archæological discoveries have helped to clear up the relation of *Beowulf* to early Swedish history, the bearings of our poem on early Danish history have been made plain by a systematic study of conflicting legends. Here the services of that great Dane, Axel Olrik, have been not less eminent than those of Stjerna, Nerman and Lindqvist with regard to the early history of Sweden. And, far beyond the range of the immediate subject under consideration, Olrik has outlined general principles which must be followed in the investigation of legend[2].

Even when some accident has led Olrik wrong, his method is often vindicated. For although the new discovery as to the meaning of "Vendel-crow" has disproved the view, which Olrik shared, that the Geatas are the Jutes, nevertheless nothing could show more neatly than this discovery does how sound are the principles which Olrik lays down at the beginning of his great work, where he demonstrates how a tradition is lost save for some nickname or epithet, and how then a new story is invented to account for the misunderstood name or words.

---

[1] On this see Nerman, *Det svenska rikets uppkomst*, 1925, p. 267.

[2] Olrik was planning, at the end of his life, a book on *Method of Legend Research*; his notes on this subject were published posthumously: *Nogle grundsætninger for sagnforskning, efter forfatterens død udgivet af Dansk Folkemindesamling* ved Hans Ellekilde, København, 1921. We also have accessible, both in Danish and (as to Part I) English, *Danmarks Heltedigtning*, with the general principles outlined in the opening pages, and the constant application of such principles to specific problems throughout the book. Then there is Olrik's *Episke Love i Folkedigtningen*, in *Danske Studier*, 1908, pp. 69–89, *Folkedigtningens Episke Love* was printed in the *Nordisk Tidsskrift*, 1908, and reprinted in *Folkelige Afhandlinger*, 1919. A German version appeared in Z.f.d.A. LI, 1–12 (1909). With this should be compared *Episke Grundlove*, by Moltke Moe, *Edda*, II, 1–16 (1914).

Of course, here, as everywhere, caution is needed. It is going too far to speak of epic *laws*—they are, as Heusler has said, rather tendencies than laws[1]. Nor can we always use them as a criterion of historic fact and epic fiction—for historic fact will often conform to the rules of fiction. Thus Olrik emphasizes the love of the folk-tale for the number three[2]. Liestøl shows how prominent this number is in the story of Knut Skraddar, coming eleven times in less than fourteen octavo pages. Yet a study of documents shows again and again that these suspicious threes correspond to actual fact. "Some of the things which have been written about the 'Epic law of three' remind us not a little of the arguments which, with many and good reasons, have shown that Napoleon and Gladstone were sun-myths[3]."

In the study of legend, as in textual criticism, we have to find out *what kind of change* is likely to have taken place and what is not, and to reconstruct accordingly. No method is infallible, and sometimes I have ventured to differ from Olrik's conclusions[4]. But Olrik was a very skilful critic, and one whose methods will always repay study.

Yet he had been only a few months dead when one of his censors was beginning to talk about "his great torso *Danmarks Heltedigtning*" as a building which was falling to pieces like a house of cards, because its foundations were not as strong as they had been thought to be[5].

Fortunately we need not waste much time over *this* attack. Olrik had asserted (and the fact is hardly open to doubt) that the hero *Scyld*, *Skjold*, is not a historic personage, but an eponymous creation, a supposed progenitor invented to explain the name

---

[1] See Liestøl, *Islendske Ættesaga*, 1929, p. 101 (=*Origin of the Icelandic Family Sagas*, p. 105). An example which occurs to me is "the law of initial and terminal stress" emphasized by Schütte and Olrik. I admit that in drawing up any epic list there is a tendency that the first should be the one of greatest general importance, the last one of greatest special interest. But this seems to me a *tendency* rather than a conscious law, as I ventured to argue long ago (*Widsith*, p. 256). For Olrik's reply see *Nogle Grundsætninger for Sagnforskning*, pp. 76, 77. The reader must judge.

[2] *Nogle Grundsætninger for Sagnforskning*, p. 75.

[3] Liestøl, *Islendske Ættesaga*, p. 75 (=*Origin of the Icelandic Family Sagas*, p. 76).

[4] e.g. above, p. 61, below, p. 430, note 1.

[5] J. Neuhaus, *Om Skjold* in *A.f.N.F.* xxxv, 166 (1919).

Scyldingas, Skjoldungar[1]. Yet such eponymous traditions may
be quite ancient, and matters of serious interest to the student of
national legend. It is for having treated the *Scyld*-tradition thus
seriously that Olrik is criticized.

Neuhaus asserts that the true form of the name in Old
English is *Sceldwa*: that therefore the correspondingly correct
form should be a Scandinavian *Skjolde*, and that therefore the
O.E. *Scyld* and the O.N. *Skjold* are late and valueless inventions.

But, as I have tried to show above, a large number of these
early heroes have names both in the weak and strong form[2]: for
example, *Hors* and *Horsa* are both excellently authenticated.
And, whilst the weak form *Sceldwa* is authenticated by the
pedigree as given in the *Anglo-Saxon Chronicle* drawn up about
892, the form *Scyld* is guaranteed by the even more ancient
pedigree given by Ethelwerd. For it is certain that Ethelwerd
"acquired the genealogy from some unknown source in a more
primitive form than that contained in the *Anglo-Saxon Chronicle*[3]." And the form *Scyld* is further confirmed by *Beowulf*,
which almost all scholars would regard as an earlier authority
than the *Chronicle*[4]. Olrik is therefore absolutely right: for
Sceldwa would not invalidate *Scyld*, and *Scyld* is in fact the
better authenticated form. In any case the matter is a detail,
which leaves the main structure of Olrik's great book untouched:
what tumbles down like a house of cards is the critic's attack
upon him. *Scyld* or *Skjold* is not a historic king, but a legendary
figure of ancient Danish tradition, and Olrik's attempts to investigate the tradition are in no degree invalidated by the
existence of an O.E. form *Sceldwa*.

Here then we may leave Mr Neuhaus, and his meditations
upon *Scyld*, with nothing more than an expression of mild
wonder how such an attack upon a great scholar came to be
published in so distinguished a periodical as the *Arkiv*.

When we pass from the legendary Scyld to the stories of

---

[1] *Heroic Legends*, p. 440; see above, pp. 77–8.

[2] See above, pp. 311, 312, where half a dozen examples are given; so too
Latin has *Cato* but also *Catus*: *Rufo* and *Rufus*: Modern English *Black* (*blæc*) but
also *Blake* (*blaca*).

[3] See p. 319 above, and Chadwick, *Origin of the English Nation*, p. 272.

[4] It occurs also in place names, *Scyldes treow*, *Scildes well*; although we cannot
tell if the *Scyld* here mentioned is the hero of story.

Hrothgar and his house, we reach for Denmark that debatable ground between history and legend which we have just been considering for Sweden; and, as before, we find *Beowulf* our primary authority.

In this connection the work of Knut Liestøl in a parallel field is noteworthy. Liestøl has examined the oral traditions which were current among the peasantry of nineteenth-century Norway concerning the events of the preceding two or three centuries. These traditions are, of course, peculiarly valuable in the analogies they offer to the Icelandic sagas; but the analogy is also applicable, albeit not so directly, to *Beowulf*. Liestøl's comparisons give us something of a touchstone by which we can separate fictitious elements from historic fact; further, by his work, just as by the researches of Swedish archæologists, our belief is confirmed in the broad general accuracy with which historical events were handed down by word of mouth from generation to generation in Scandinavia[1] (and, in a somewhat similar way, in Anglo-Saxon England).

An investigator of northern legend who starts with a considerable belief in his material can now point to recent discovery and observation of fact in justification of his method.

And there are few fields in which discovery and observation of fact are more necessary, or the words of Francis Bacon more applicable, when he warns us against that "too great reverence of the mind and understanding of man" which has led scholars to neglect observation and to "tumble up and down in their own reason."

Olrik's reconstruction of early Danish history, of the stories of Hrothgar, Hrethric and Hrothulf, and the feud with Froda and Ingeld, was based upon the widest and most sympathetic study of the data, and therefore Olrik was able to see things which Müllenhoff had not been able to see, because Olrik did not

---

[1] This was shown in a very striking way in three lectures on "Modern Saga and the reliability of Oral Tradition" delivered by Liestøl in University College, London, in March, 1926. See also his *Upphavet til den Islendske Ættesaga*, Oslo (Aschehoug), 1929.

allow theories and the "higher criticism" of *Beowulf* to stand in the way of his observation of facts.

Müllenhoff, for example, had regarded the crucial passages in which Hrethric is referred to (ll. 1189, *etc.*, 1836, *etc.*) as the work of his "Interpolator A." And so he dismissed Hrethric into the limbo of things "suspicious[1]." Yet the curious thing is that Müllenhoff knew that this name also existed in Scandinavian tradition[2]. But he allowed his theories of interpolation to prevent him from following up a clue which might have revealed to him, as it did later reveal to Olrik, a whole field of forgotten Danish history.

In the past ten years there have been two studies of this period of Scylding history—one by Boer and one by Wessén— in which conclusions fundamentally different from those of Olrik are maintained: and it appears to me in both cases that Olrik is quite demonstrably right in the points which come under dispute. Boer, like Müllenhoff before him, seems to be prevented from giving its true value to all the evidence, because of his preconceived theories of criticism and interpretation. Wessén's reconstruction of early Danish history is dominated by a theory of wholesale "name-shift": and a theory of that kind must always be examined with the utmost caution. Thirty years ago, it was a mark of up-to-date Homeric scholarship to believe that the Argos where Agamemnon held sway was not the Peloponnesian Argos of history, but an obscure place of that name in Thessaly[3]. Where is that theory now?

It was in the year after this name-shift theory had been propounded for the Homeric Argos, that Rudolf Koegel produced *his* theory of name-shift[4], by which he interpreted the Heathobeardan of *Beowulf* as having been, in historic fact, not the hereditary foes of the Danes but the Danes themselves; and the

---

[1] *Beowulf*, p. 26.   [2] p. 40.

[3] The Argos-theory seems to have been first put forward by Busolt in the second edition of his *Griechische Geschichte*, 1893 (I, 223), and was propounded in the same year by Beloch in his *Griechische Geschichte* (I, 157). It was adopted by Cauer (*Grundfrage der Homercritik*, 1895, p. 153) and introduced to English readers by Bury in his *History of Greece*, 1900. It was ejected from Bury's edition of 1913.

[4] *Geschichte der deutschen Litteratur*, I, 1, p. 157.

people called Danes in *Beowulf*, Hrothgar's subjects, as having been, in historic fact, not the Danes, but the Danes' hereditary enemies. I did not mention this "name-shift" of Koegel in the earlier issue of this book, because I thought it was no longer taken seriously; but now that it is showing such vigorous life in the hands of Wessén, it must be considered below[1].

Prof. Boer and his reconstruction of the Scylding feud

The chief exponent, during the past generation, of the critical methods of which Müllenhoff and ten Brink were the earlier protagonists has been that great Dutch scholar whose loss we all deplore, Prof. Boer. His recent views on *Beowulf* were given in two articles in periodicals in 1922 and 1923, the one dealing particularly with the Scylding feud[2], the other with the *Beowulf* problem generally[3]. It is easiest to consider them both together, because what is at issue in each case, as Boer clearly saw, is a question of method.

Boer's essential thesis is that

> "*Beowulf* is a literary production, with a history about which it is imperative to acquire a clear notion, *previous* to any attempt at comparing contents and subject matter with remote collateral sources[4]."

Consequently, if we are considering (for example) the two Grendel fights, we must first concentrate on the internal evidence:

> "The relation between the two Grendel fights should first be ascertained from internal evidence; *not till then* is there room for the question whether the older form of the narrative, *as revealed to us by criticism*, is traceable in a folk-tale[5]."

Now there may be cases where the method advocated by Prof. Boer is the right one; cases where internal criticism can show results so convincing that we are justified in dealing with them before passing on to any other considerations whatsoever. Sievers' demonstration that two different poems had been combined in the Anglo-Saxon *Genesis* was so overwhelming that (even if it had not been confirmed by subsequent discovery) it was bound to form the starting point of all later discussion. So

---

[1] pp. 434–45.
[2] *Studier over Skjoldungedigtningen* in the *Aarbøger for Nordisk Oldkyndighed og Historie*, III, 12, pp. 133–266 (1922).
[3] *English Studies* (Amsterdam), V, 105–18.
[4] *Ibid.* p. 106. The italics here and in the next quotation are mine.
[5] *Ibid.* p. 107.

with the old play of *Sir Thomas More*; the first fact to grasp is that the manuscript is extant in six different hands. Yet the *Beowulf* problem is surely different.

But Prof. Boer held that we can, and should, acquire a clear notion of the origin and history of the poem *previous* to comparing remote collateral sources. It seems to me, on the other hand, that we ought to try to get light from the collateral sources, whether more or less remote, before we finally formulate our notion of the origin and history of *Beowulf*. Just as Richard Hooker argued that we must investigate "all the sources of light and truth with which man finds himself encompassed," so I believe that we must investigate, simultaneously, all the sources from which information about *Beowulf* can possibly be gathered. Only when we have brought to bear every possible means of knowledge, from literary and linguistic criticism, folk-lore, archæology, and history, whether cultural, political or religious, ought we to form our conclusions. This conviction must be my excuse if, in the previous edition of this book, I have, as Prof. Boer complained, passed over his criticism of *Beowulf*, whilst repeatedly quoting him on minor points. I may perhaps repeat what I have said elsewhere in testimony of the respect which all students feel for Boer's work both on *Beowulf* and on the *Grettis saga*: work which has earned him a permanent place in the history of the study of those two great pieces of literature:

> "If many of us, rightly or wrongly, attach greater weight to Boer's elucidation of what he calls 'minor points' than to his 'criticism of the poem,' this is because the so-called 'minor points' are such as an acute brain and deep scholarship *can* elucidate: whilst the 'criticism of the poem' seems to us an attempt to penetrate by conjecture into a stage of literary history which even the acutest brain and the deepest scholarship cannot fathom[1]."

There is something magnificent in the way in which Prof. Boer has never been willing to admit defeat. He has remained

> "Still nursing the unconquerable hope,"

believing that it is possible to pluck out the heart of the mystery of our poem by internal evidence: the mind of the critic compelling the poem to give up its secret.

Yet it seems to me that it was this confidence in what the

---

[1] *English Studies* (Amsterdam), XI, 100.

critic can learn from purely internal evidence which hid from Boer things which Olrik, with his less embarrassed gaze, could see quite clearly.

Beowulf tells us how, in the Danish royal hall, by the side of King Hrothgar sits Hrothulf, his mighty nephew; and twice in *Beowulf* and once in *Widsith* it is quite clearly implied that the friendship of uncle and nephew will not remain unbroken. Hrothulf in the end will clearly make a bid for the throne at the expense of his young cousins Hrethric and Hrothmund. Wealhtheow fears it, and tries "to shame Hrothulf into righteousness[1]":

> "I know," she says, "that my gracious Hrothulf will support the young princes in honour, if thou, King of the Scyldings, shouldst leave the world sooner than he. I ween that he will requite our children, if he remembers all that we two have done for his pleasure and honour, being yet a child[2]."

Even if we had no more than this to go on, yet this, together with some knowledge of the history of times when the law of primogeniture was not binding[3], would make it fairly clear that Hrothulf will put aside—and probably slay—his cousin, Hrethric[4].

The *Bjarkamál* and later Scandinavian sources tell us quite definitely that Hrothulf (*Hrolfr, Roluo*) *did* slay a king named Hrethric (*Hrærekr, Røricus*). There is no doubt as to the correspondence of the names, and that being so, surely the Scandinavian evidence puts the fate of Hrethric beyond doubt.

Then we hear of Heoroweard. He is the son of Heorogar, the elder brother[5], who had reigned[6] before Hrothgar. Yet Heoroweard has not come to the throne: presumably because at the time of his father's death he was only a lad. All we are told of Heoroweard is that Hrothgar gives to Beowulf—for Hygelac— the war-gear which Heoroweard's father, Heorogar, had once possessed. It certainly looks as if Heoroweard had been, in Olrik's words, "slighted[7]."

---

[1] Kemp Malone, "Hrethric," *Pub. Mod. Lang. Assoc. Amer.* XLII, 270.

[2] *Beowulf*, pp. 1180–7.

[3] Compare Charles Kingsley in *Hereward the Wake*, chapter IX, on the tragedies of the house of Baldwin of Flanders and "many another royal house."

[4] Hrethric is mentioned first, and is therefore presumably older than his brother Hrothmund.

[5] l. 468.

[6] l. 2158.

[7] Olrik, *Heroic Legends of Denmark*, p. 27.

Heoroweard might reasonably be expected to make *his* bid for the throne. And in the *Bjarkamál* we are definitely told that Hrothulf, after having slain King Hrethric (*Hrærekr, Røricus*), was himself slain by Heoroweard (*Hjǫrvarðr, Hiarwarus*), who seized the throne from him.

This is the way in which, following the hints of various earlier scholars, Olrik reconstructed the story. And it is really not theory at all: it is a putting together of two different traditions, the English and the Scandinavian. They interlock, dovetail into one another, and make a connected whole which, though it leaves details obscure, seems in its main outlines established beyond doubt. The Scandinavian stories help us to understand the hints in *Beowulf*: *Beowulf* shows the real bearing upon each other of the *disjecta membra* of Scandinavian tradition.

But Boer does not read the story so. He puts an interpretation upon two passages in *Beowulf* which, if it be correct, cannot be harmonized with the Scandinavian account at all. For, as he interprets these passages, Hrethric is slain by the Heathobeardan at the tragic wedding of Freawaru and Ingeld; Heoroweard is argued to have been dead at an earlier stage still; so neither of them can have played any part in the domestic feud: Hrothulf cannot have killed Hrethric, nor Heoroweard have killed Hrothulf. That being so, the Scandinavian account of these matters, Boer holds, must be altogether rejected; there only remains what *Beowulf* tells us of the feud between Hrothgar and Hrothulf: so, according to Boer, we must suppose that, in a struggle at Heorot, Hrothgar and Hrothulf fall as each other's opponents.

Everything turns upon the correctness of Boer's interpretation of two passages. If that interpretation were inevitable, then we might perhaps be driven to dismiss all the Scandinavian versions as worthless: but only an *inevitable* interpretation would justify such a desperate treatment of our Scandinavian evidence.

The young Danish warrior who is slain at the wedding of Freawaru and Ingeld is spoken of as *þāra banena byre nāthwylces*, "the son of one or other of the slaughtering Danes." Boer's argument is that we *must* suppose this son of some anonymous Dane to be the son of Hrothgar. But this interpretation, though it seemed self-evident to Boer, is not a necessary one; and it does not seem to me to be even a reasonable one, since it does not agree with the forebodings of Wealhtheow: for it is clearly from Hrothulf, not from the Heathobeardan, that she anticipates danger for her sons. Anyway, it is assuredly not necessary.

Boer argues in the second place that Heoroweard must have been dead when Beowulf visits Heorot; that, in fact, he must have predeceased his father Heorogar; for he did not receive his father's arms, and if he had been alive he would have been his father's natural heir. Of course he is his father's natural heir: but a natural heir does not always get all that he expects. And we are told that Heorogar would not (*ne wolde*) leave this heir-loom to his son, although he loved him well (*þeah he him hold wǣre*). If Heoroweard had been already dead, there would have been no occasion for such comment; at most it might have been said that it was not granted to the father to leave his arms to his much loved son. But to say that the father "*would* not, *though* he loved his son*" implies clearly that the son was alive, and therefore *might* have received the legacy, *though* he did not.

Heoroweard did not inherit his father's arms; equally he did not inherit his father's throne—presumably because he was too young at the time. Hrothgar was himself young then[1], and the nephew of a man who is himself young is likely to be a mere lad. Therefore Heorogar, *though he loves his son*, leaves the armour to his brother, Hrothgar, upon whom the task of defending the realm will fall, rather than to a son who is too young to use the weapons. All that is natural. But when Beowulf visits Heorot, many years later, Hrothgar is too old to fight[2]. Heoroweard *now* might perhaps hope to receive his father's arms. But, if Hrothgar gives the ancestral royal battle weeds to "the valiant Heoro-weard[3]," will not that be interpreted to mean that Hrothgar's nephew, rather than his young son, is the man marked out to defend the realm after his day? So Hrothgar gives the arms to Beowulf to give to Hygelac. Beowulf does so. And then Beo-wulf's conduct is pointedly contrasted with that of the kinsman

---

[1] *Beowulf*, 1. 466.   [2] ll. 1885–7.
[3] *hwatum Heorowearde*, l. 2161.

who "weaves cunning snares for the other with secret craft."
What can this allusion mean, if there be not some reference to
Heoroweard and *his* relation to *his* kinsfolk?

The poem of *Beowulf* is separated by more than a century,
and in all probability by some two centuries, from the events it
narrates. If Heoroweard had died before his father Heorogar,
who himself dies whilst his brother Hrothgar is young, how
would he come to be remembered at all? A boy must have done
or suffered something, if his memory is to live in heroic song
throughout the centuries. Boer's explanation is that the *name*
was remembered: and then, after many centuries, a *deed*—the
slaying of Hrothulf—was in Scandinavian tradition wrongly
attached to the name[1].

But is this the way things actually work out?

It is necessary to go into this, because Boer's standing as a
philologist and a student of legend entitles whatever he writes to
respectful examination. He makes a study of the field covered
by Olrik, and assures us that Olrik's book, despite the intuition
and scholarship of its writer, "from the point of view of criticism
suffers from essential defects, and therefore its results are in
great part very doubtful." Such an indictment must be taken
seriously.

It is an invidious thing to judge between two eminent
scholars, both of whom have passed away. But Boer has insisted upon such comparison, by attacking Olrik's method.
Surely, then, the verdict must be that Olrik's method is the right
one. Olrik compares all the accounts, and things are found to fall
into their place. There is a minimum of mere theorizing: rather
the seeing eye of the critic (his intuition, as Boer rightly calls it)
marshals each bit of evidence in its right place, till we wonder
that we could not see it all for ourselves. Against this, Boer
erects his method of internal criticism, of an interpretation of
certain passages in *Beowulf* which seems to him convincing; then
he dismisses the Scandinavian evidence because it does not
agree with this interpretation. But *Beowulf* is a difficult and
ambiguous poem. The interpretation which seems to Boer cer-

---

[1] "Hans navn var bevaret og kunde altså bruges...den mand, der bar
dette navn, passede altså netop til at indtage Hroars plads i en fortælling om en
familiestrid." Boer, *Aarbøger*, as above, p. 208.

tainly right will seem to others doubtful. To me, as I have said, it seems, on internal evidence *alone*, certainly wrong. How can we reject the whole of the Scandinavian tradition because it does not harmonize with an interpretation in itself so highly problematical?

Heathobeardan and Heruli

Readers of Olrik's great book will remember how he elucidates the feud between the Danes and the Heathobeardan. First come the wars of the Heathobard king, Froda, against the Danes, who were flourishing under Healfdene "the high," "the old," and his son Hrothgar, the founder of Heorot. Froda is slain by the Danes[1]. To compose the feud, Hrothgar gives his daughter Freawaru in marriage to Froda's son, Ingeld. But the peace is not to last. So much we learn from *Beowulf*. *Widsith* tells us how Hrothgar and his nephew Hrothulf repulsed Ingeld's attack and hewed down the Heathobeardan at Heorot. From the ancient *Bjarkamál*, preserved by Saxo Grammaticus, we learn how Agnar, son of Ingeld, was slain by Bothvar Bjarki, Bjarki being a champion in the service of the Danish king Rolf Kraki [Hrothulf].

These events, then, cover three generations[2], and they can be dated.

---

[1] See Olrik, *Heroic Legends of Denmark*, pp. 304–10. Olrik thinks that *Beowulf* implies that Healfdene slew Froda. But all that we can gather from *Beowulf* is that Froda fell in battle against the Danes: *Beowulf* does not tell us whether Healfdene slew him, or whether he was slain by the descendants and successors of Healfdene, taking vengeance for their predecessor. Saxo's Danish account makes Healfdene slay Froda, but the Old Norse accounts make Froda slay Healfdene, and this fits in best with the (admittedly inconclusive) data of *Beowulf*. In *Beowulf* Hrothgar is very old, and Hrothulf, the grandson of Healfdene, already a champion of renown. Nevertheless, Ingeld is a youth who has not yet taken vengeance for Froda. Chronologically, this is quite reasonable, if the slaying of Froda was an act of Hrothgar's manhood (perhaps with his young nephew Hrothulf helping); it would be less reasonable if the slaying were an act of an earlier generation, of Hrothulf's grandfather Healfdene. The *Quern Song* is often quoted as supporting this view: but it is only by altering the text that any such interpretation can be arrived at. For an interpretation of the text as it stands, see Kemp Malone, *Literary History of Hamlet*, I, 196; *A.f.N.F.* XLII, 234 etc.; *Acta Phil. Scand.* IV, 270.

[2] Yet there are chronological difficulties. It is not clear how Ingeld can have had a son old enough to be slain in combat by Bjarki, especially as the fight is thought of as at the beginning of Bjarki's career as a warrior—the combat from which he gets his nickname of Bothvar-Bjarki, "Battle-Bjarki." See Herrmann, *Erläuterungen zu Saxo Grammaticus*, 1922, II, 169. For a full discussion of the whole problem of Ingeld and Agnar, by Prof. Kemp Malone, see *Modern Philology*, XXVII, 257–76.

For Ingeld's attack on Heorot takes place not very long after Beowulf's visit. So does Hygelac's attack on Friesland. We may date both about 520. On this basis we may roughly place Hrothgar's reign in the first quarter of the sixth century, Hrothulf's in the second quarter[1].

Now it is just during the glorious reign of Hrothgar and his nephew Hrothulf that we first find the name of the Danes mentioned by Latin and Greek writers; and, as in *Beowulf, we hear of them as conquerors.* Jordanes, writing about the year 550, tells us that the Danes drove the Heruli from their homes—the tallest of all the people of "Scandia," taller even than the tall Swedes[2]. There is little doubt that Jordanes got his information from the lost *History* of Cassiodorus, which was finished before 533. Before that date, then, the Danes had expelled the Heruli from whatever part of "Scandia" this somewhat mysterious people had once occupied.

Can we get much further back in Danish history than Hrothgar and the early sixth century? Well, the Heruli at any rate had been known to writers within the Roman Empire for two centuries and a half. Some time before 512 they had a powerful kingdom near the Danube in the modern Hungary or the more modern Czecho-Slovakia. But since the latter half of the third century they had been raiding, sometimes East, sometimes West, and serving as mercenaries in the Roman armies.

Scholars have been tempted to connect the driving out of the Heruli by the Danes from their home in the North with the appearance of the Heruli on the borders of the Roman Empire. In that case this first act in the recorded history of the Danes must have taken place about 250, and can have no connection with Hrothgar's struggles with the Heathobeardan mentioned in *Beowulf,* for these must have happened two centuries and a half later.

[1] All very approximate; but confirmed by Scandinavian traditions which make Athils (Eadgils) contemporary with Rolf (Hrothulf). Heusler (*Archiv,* cxxiv, 9–14) makes Healfdene die A.D. 495, Hrothgar A.D. 520. But I place Hygelac's death, the date upon which all turns, at least five years later than Heusler does, and consequently date Hrothgar's reign 500–525.

[2] *Suetidi, cogniti in hac gente reliquis corpore eminentiores; quamvis et Dani, ex ipsorum stirpe progressi, Herulos propriis sedibus expulerunt, qui inter omnes Scandiae nationes nomen sibi ob nimia proceritate affectant praecipuum. Getica,* ed. Mommsen, p. 59.

Now the Danes, when we hear of them at the beginning of the sixth century, whether under Hrothgar in *Beowulf*, or by casual mention in Latin or Byzantine historians, are a mighty race. Yet, among the numerous tribes which Tacitus and Ptolemy[1] had recorded centuries earlier, the Danes are not to be found. Hence, it has been supposed that the Danes were originally a small people who had grown to greatness by absorbing other tribes. Who the Danes originally were, we do not know. Jordanes, as we have seen, speaks of the Suetidi, and then says that the Danes were *ex ipsorum stirpe progressi*. This has been taken to mean that the Danes started from Sweden (that is, the original Sweden around the Mälar district), and emigrated to the land known later as Denmark. Jordanes' words need not bear that interpretation, but, on the other hand, from what Tacitus tells us of the Swedes, we may well believe they had a navy capable of such an expedition. Since we are told that the Danes drove out the Heruli, it has been supposed that these Heruli were the original inhabitants of Denmark. But if the Danes were a mere raiding offshoot of the Swedes, it has been further argued that they were relatively few, and that whilst they drove out many of the Heruli, they also absorbed many. The bulk, then, of the Danes of history, it has been supposed, may have been of Herulian blood.

All this has been persuasively urged. But we must never forget that it is conjecture built on conjecture. Besides, ten years ago Olrik pointed out that the idea of the Danes as immigrants from Sweden, who had driven out the original inhabitants of Denmark, rested upon a misinterpretation of Jordanes' expression, which "does not contain a piece of historic or geographic, but only ethnographic information[2]." And an examination of the other places where Jordanes uses the word *stirps* confirms this: apparently all that Jordanes really says is that the Danes came of the same stock as the Swedes—not necessarily that they were immigrants from Sweden[3], but that they were, like the Swedes, Scandinavians.

[1] Some have supposed that "Daukiones" in Ptolemy is a corruption of the Danish name. But such a supposition is very perilous.

[2] *Heroic Legends of Denmark*, p. 34.

[3] See also on this a review by Zachrisson, *Studia Neophilologica*, I, 87–8. And it is even disputed whether *Suetidi* in Jordanes *does* mean the Swedes at all. See Kemp Malone, *Literary History of Hamlet*, I, 11.

Those however who would make Jordanes' words mean more than this, have found some support in ancient legend, and some support in archæology. We have really so little information that we cannot dogmatize. We can only note that Olrik is sure that the written sources give us no basis "indicating the home of the Danes to have been anywhere but where we find it in historic times," that is to say, in Denmark. Meantime Swedish historians not less weighty believe the Danes to have been conquerors from Sweden, an aristocracy who absorbed the originally Herulian majority[1]. Into such a Dano-Swedish discussion it were indecent for an Englishman to intrude, especially as it is a side issue, and the English student of *Beowulf* is not concerned with the historic Denmark till about the year 500. To what extent one tribe may have driven out or absorbed another tribe, closely akin in blood and speech, from or in the present Denmark, in the third and fourth centuries of our era, who can say? Only archæology can throw any new light upon the problem, if even that can; and both sides claim the support of archæology for their contentions. At any rate, Denmark in the third and fourth centuries of our era lies outside the ken of the *Beowulf* scholar. He has troubles enough of his own.

But there is, of course, a quite different interpretation which can be put upon Jordanes' words. The Heruli whom we hear of in Europe from the third to the fifth century need not have been forcibly expelled from their old home; for they may have been volunteer adventurers whom the love of wandering and plunder had drawn from their ancient seats. It may well have been much later, say about 500, a few decades before Cassiodorus and Jordanes wrote, that the expulsion of the Heruli, of which Jordanes speaks, took place. This would be quite reasonable: the voluntary emigration of fighting men to the borders of the Roman Empire would have weakened the Heruli, and the last stay-at-homes may not have been driven out by the increasing power of the Danes till somewhere about 500. In support of that,

---

[1] The subject is very fully and carefully worked out by B. Nerman in *Fornvännen*, 1922, pp. 129–40, *Härstamma danerna ifrån Svealand?* See also H. Schück, *Svenska folkets historia*, I, 1, p. 107.

we have a line of Sidonius who, writing soon after 475, can still describe a Herulian as

"imos Oceani colens recessus."

If we interpret Jordanes' words in that way, they would represent the Danes in conflict with the Heruli about the same time that *Beowulf* represents them in conflict with the Heathobeardan. Naturally, therefore, Müllenhoff and others have identified the Heruli with the Heathobeardan of *Beowulf*. But the identification is not inevitable, for, as *Beowulf* reminds us[1], the Danes in their rise to power had come into conflict with many tribes (*monegum mǣgþum*). Olrik rejected the identification altogether; but again the question is not a vital one.

Wessén on the Peoples of "Beowulf"

But a recent publication of Prof. Wessén[2] has revived the old controversy in a way which does demand the attention of students of *Beowulf*. For Wessén's position is revolutionary, and strikes at the root, not only of Olrik's results, but of his methods. Wessén accepts, as if it were ascertained fact, the inference that the Danes started from Sweden, made a military expedition to Denmark, and absorbed the Heruli whom they found there. *But he places all this, not c. 250, but c. 500–550.* Now, so long as we place these rather hypothetical events in the third century, they need not disturb the equanimity either of the *Beowulf* student, or of the reader of Olrik's great book. But it is another matter when they are put in the sixth century, because they will not harmonize with the known data of that century. For *Beowulf* represents Hrothgar as ruling a great Danish kingdom from his capital at Heorot at a period shortly before Hygelac's expedition. Hygelac's expedition was about 520. And Hrothgar is at the end of a long[3] and glorious reign. He must have begun to rule the Danes *before* the date at which Wessén makes the Danes arrive in Denmark. Further, according to *Beowulf*, Hroth-

---

[1] See above, p. 24.

[2] *De Nordiska Folkstammarna i Beowulf*, Stockholm, 1927 (*Kungl. Vitterhets Historie och Antikvitets Akademiens Handlingar*, 36, 2).

[3] Hrothgar is represented as aged: yet he was young when he began to reign (*Beowulf*, 1. 466).

gar has had predecessors upon his Danish throne—some generations of them have been building up the Danish realm.

And this picture is confirmed by the Scandinavian stories.

Wessén is accordingly compelled to fall back on the theory of a "name-shift." His theory assumes that the people called "Danes" in *Beowulf*, the Scyldings, with their kings Hrothgar and Hrothulf, are really not Danes, but the indigenous Heruli, the foes of the Danes: that *Beowulf* and all the Old Norse and Danish records have made a mistake. Further, the theory assumes that the Heathobeardan are not the hereditary enemies of the Danes, but the Danes themselves: that *Beowulf* has simply turned things into the reverse of what they really were.

This summary, of course, does no justice to the ingenuity, plausibility and persuasiveness of Prof. Wessén's arguments, or the learning with which he marshals his material. Wessén has already earned himself a distinguished name by his researches into Northern history and tradition. His restatement of early Danish history has been accepted, alike in Germany, America and England, if not with conviction, at any rate without marked dissent, or rather perhaps with that languid neutrality which Bishop Gore deplores in another field: the feeling that "everything is uncertain, but that in the meantime all theories are interesting."

Yet it seems to me to be only another example of what Prof. Frederick Tupper has christened "philological legend," the glamour of the learned and elaborate argument, based upon—just nothing. "The Danes conquered and absorbed the Heruli." The absorbent power of Danes is the thing that seems to have burnt itself into the consciousness of scholars; also the smallness of their numbers[1], so that they were outnumbered by those whom they absorbed. If we put this in the third century, it lies beyond our ken: we can neither affirm it nor deny it. And so, because we cannot deny it, it becomes a fixed dogma. Then Wessén

---

[1] "En relativt fåtalig krigarstam," Wessén, p. 28; "En jämförelsevis fåtalig krigareskara," Nerman, *Fornvännen*, 1922, p. 140; "Ett jämförelsevis fåtaligt krigarfölje," Schück, *Svenska folkets historia*, 1914, I, 1, p. 107; "Die zurückbliebenden Herulen verschmelzen mit den herrschenden Dänen, *die wahrscheinlich nur eine Minorität* gebildet haben, und nehmen deren Namen an," Nerman, *Die Herkunft...der Germanen*, 1924, Stockholm (*Kungl. Vitterhets Historie och Antikvitets Akademiens Handlingar*, 34, 5).

intrudes it into the sixth century, where, however, it will not harmonize with the known data. But our dogma has by now become far too firm to be shaken. So Wessén asks us to reject the known data instead. That the Danes were few in number, but absorbent, and above all absorbent of Heruli, is the one fixed doctrine to which everything else must at all costs conform.

And yet there is no evidence for any such thing. All we know is that, at some date certainly before 552, probably before 533, possibly much before, the Danes *had driven the Heruli from their seats*, and that the Heruli are, in fact, found wandering in many places in Europe.

Obviously, the Danes could not have expelled the Heruli unless they had at one time been neighbours; and, since it is likely that the Danes occupied the territory of the people they expelled, the Heruli are likely to have dwelt in some part of what later became Denmark. But Wessén assumes that the Heruli occupied almost all of Denmark—Scani, the Danish islands and the greater part of Jutland, *and that they remained there*, and that therefore the Scylding kings, Hrothgar and Hrothulf, must have been, as a matter of history, Herulian. Not till about the year 500, he assumes, did the real Danes first come from Sweden to Denmark, as invaders. During the next fifty years (500–550) these real Danes (wrongly called in *Beowulf* "Heathobeardan") made themselves masters of the whole kingdom formerly ruled by the Scylding dynasty of Hrothgar and Hrothulf (really Heruli, albeit mistakenly called Danes in *Beowulf* and everywhere else). But the Danish conquerors were, he believes, a small minority. (This follows, I suppose, from their being thought of as rovers who had come in a fleet from the Mälar district of Sweden; and this in its turn rests, as we have seen, upon a more than doubtful interpretation of Jordanes. But it is essential to Wessén's argument that the Danes must have been much outnumbered by the Heruli whom they had overcome.) Furthermore, Wessén assures us, the Heruli had a higher culture which, together with their preponderance in numbers, enabled them to impose their traditions about the glories of the Scylding race, and of the reigns of Hrothgar and Hrothulf, upon their Danish conquerors. Yet these were the masters, and after them the people and the kingdom took the name of Danes, whilst the name of the Heruli disappears from history, from popular tradition, and from heroic poetry.

Now why should the Heruli have had a higher culture than the Danes? The Heruli had the reputation of being the most savage of the Germanic tribes known to Procopius—and he had reason to know a good deal about them. The Heruli had been wont, he tells us, to offer human sacrifices, to kill off their sick and aged, to compel their widows to commit suicide: their morals were as filthy as their manners. And this barbarism extended to material things: at a time when the Germanic warrior was coming to rejoice in helm and byrnie, the Heruli went into battle naked, save for a loin cloth. Yet, in the islands which Wessén would people with these barbarians, there is evidence for a high culture: in Fünen the moss-finds of Kragehul and Vimose, and in Zealand the finds of the Himlingöje period. The material civilization shown by these finds seemed to Olrik inconsistent with the belief that the savage Heruli could have been dwelling there at the date to which the finds belong[1]. Whether we accept Olrik's argument or not, it should surely warn us against assuming that the Heruli possessed a *higher* culture than their neighbours, the Danes.

Now it is proverbially difficult to prove a negative, especially in a period and a place so obscure as the Denmark of the early sixth century. But it so happens that we have means of refuting this assumption of a Herulian nation in the early sixth century in the present Denmark, superior in numbers and culture to their Danish neighbours: for we happen to have independent evidence showing that at the beginning of the sixth century, when Hrothgar must have been reigning, there *was* no Herulian nation left in Denmark. Scattered as the Heruli had been, their main body at this date formed, as we have seen, a considerable kingdom by the Danube[2]. There they were crushed, and their king

---

[1] *Heroic Legends of Denmark,* pp. 31–41.

[2] It is generally held that there was another Herulian kingdom in the Netherlands, but this is not so well authenticated. A letter was addressed by Theodoric the Great to the king of the Heruli; Theodoric's object was to gain support against Chlodoweg the Frank, and it was probably also with this aim that Theodoric gave the king of the Heruli gifts of weapons and adopted him as his son (much as Hrothgar does Beowulf). Now, geographically, such an alliance

slain, by the Longobards. One Herulian remnant took refuge
within the Roman Empire; another set out to find a home in the
far north. The almost contemporary Byzantine historian, Procopius, gives us a full account of their journey. Leaving the
Danube they traversed all the Slavonic tribes, then a great
desert, then the Warni, then passed the tribes of the Danes, re-
ceiving no hurt from them. Then they took shipping and crossed
over to Thule [i.e. the Scandinavian peninsula], where they
settled by the side of a very mighty tribe—the Gautoi [the
Gautar, the *Gēatas* of *Beowulf*]. All this happened about 512
[that is to say, when Hrothgar was ruling in Heorot].

So, the Byzantine historian gives us the same geography
which *Beowulf* does: Danes on one side, Gautar on the other,
and a sea voyage in between. The mention of "tribes of the
Danes" seems to point to the Danes as a numerous confederation
—compare the East Danes, West Danes, North Danes and
South Danes of *Beowulf*.

And so the theory that the Danes had arrived in South
Jutland ten or a dozen years before, a relatively small band of
warriors coming in a pirate fleet from the Mälar district of
Sweden, and that except for this settlement all modern Denmark

against Chlodoweg best suits the Netherlandish Heruli, if such a kingdom existed:
yet many have believed that it is the king of the Danubian Heruli who is addressed. Theodoric's letter was written soon before 507; the Herulian kingdom
on the Danube was destroyed by the Longobards some years before 512. Wessén's
objection that, if the letter had been addressed to the Danubian monarch,
Theodoric would have avenged the death of his adopted son by a war against the
Longobards is hardly valid. Theodoric's object was to form an anti-Frankish
coalition: it failed, and from 507, for some years, Theodoric was consequently
involved in critical wars against the Franks and Burgundians. Theodoric was a
practical man, and might, I suspect, have said that if his Herulian "son," instead
of helping his "father" against the Franks with his Herulian light-armed mercenaries, chose to get involved in a quarrel of his own with the Longobards, that
was *his* business.
    The fullest summary of our information about the Heruli is still that of
Zeuss (*Die Deutschen*, 1837, pp. 476–84). English readers will get a good idea of
their activities from Hodgkin, *Italy and her Invaders*, especially III, 206, 354 *etc.*;
v, 103–16. For the West Heruli see Pallmann, *Geschichte der Völkerwanderung*,
II, 1864, 67–76. Seelmann, *Das Norddeutsche Herulerreich, Jahrb. d. Vereins f.
Niederd. Sprachforschung*, 1886, 53–8, argues (very doubtfully) for a Herulian
kingdom in Thuringia. See also Schmidt, *Geschichte der deutschen Stämme*, 1905,
I, 268 *etc.*, 312 *etc.*, 333–49; Chadwick, *Origin of the English Nation*, 1907, especially p. 139; Bremer in Pauls *Grdr.* (2), III, 833–6; Much in Hoops *Reallexikon*,
II, 517–9; G. Schütte, *Vor Folkegruppe; Gottjod*, II (English translation in the
press). Quite recently, in answer to the conjectures of O. v. Friesen (*Uppsala
årsskrift*, 1924) Schmidt has summarized the evidence once more, *Die Heruler*,
in *P.B.B.* LI, 103–7 (1927).

was still in the hands of the original Herulian inhabitants, can
no more be harmonized with the contemporary account of Procopius than it can with the account of *Beowulf*. And here Procopius is likely to be accurate. He had played with the idea of
visiting "Thule" himself, so was likely to have noted the
itinerary carefully. And the route remained open. The Heruli
within the Roman Empire, whom Procopius knew, kept up some
kind of communication with their kinsmen who had settled in
Scandinavia near the Gautar: we hear of a later embassy, and of
an emissary who died *in the land of the Danes* on the way from
the Scandinavian Heruli to their southern kinsfolk. How can
this fit with the theory that there was a great Herulian people,
more numerous and civilized than the Danes, situated in the
present Denmark, on the very route which the Herulian envoys
must travel on their way between that section of their nation
which had settled in the Roman Empire and that section which
had settled by the side of the Gautar, in the modern Sweden?

The "name-shift," and its place in the study of legend

Of course, there *is* such a thing as name-shift in legend.
Many instances can be quoted in which one place has undoubtedly
been mistaken for another of the same name: we have seen how
Ottar's connection with Vendel in Sweden came to be forgotten,
and shifted to a connection with Vendel in Jutland. Or a hero
may change his nationality: one version makes Offa a king in
England, another king of Denmark.

Nevertheless, of all theories which interfere with our appreciation of the facts, the name-shift theory is one of the most
insidious. Theories which run directly counter to the evidence
do at least give us warning by their very violence: it is as if a
player should claim victory at chess by sweeping the pieces from
the board. But the danger of the 'name-shift' theory is greater:
it amounts to rearranging the pieces on the board, and then
proceeding with the game—and the danger is that this process
appears to be less violent than the other, whereas really it is *not*.

The game cannot be played under these conditions, as Earl
Ulf had the courage to inform King Canute, even at the cost of
his life.

Where there are a number of quite contradictory versions of a tale, and where the assumption of a name-shift in the later and more corrupt versions brings order out of chaos, the possibility of such name-shift must be carefully considered. But we must never base an argument on the assumption that all our authorities mean the reverse of what they say. Obviously, where the documents differ, we must weigh one against another: the first thing is to find out on what they agree. To quote Olrik again:

> "The principle by which we must unswervingly abide is that we must first of all be sure of what is common to all traditions[1]."

It sounds too obvious to need stating. But Wessén's theory asks us to believe that the English, the Danish, and the Old Norse accounts all made the same mistake in thinking that Hrothgar and Hrothulf ruled over the Danes, when they really ruled over the Heruli, a tribe warring on the Danes; and that a parallel mistake had earlier been made by the Latin and Greek historians who were actually living whilst Hrothgar and Hrothulf were reigning. (For the historian of the Byzantine Empire knows only of Danes in Denmark, and nothing of Heruli; and the historian of the Goths asserts that the Danes had driven the Heruli out; which is not consistent with the supposition that they were there all the time, in preponderating numbers, and enjoying a higher civilization.)

If we treat our authorities like that, are we not sawing off the very branch on which we sit, and in fact making all serious study impossible? For this "new orientation"—whatever the learning with which it is put forward—compels us to dismiss the evidence of all our documents and to substitute conjectures (themselves of the most perilous kind) built upon the legend that the Danes were really Heruli upon whom a small conquering caste had imposed the Danish name—a legend which my researches so far have not enabled me to trace back further than the early years of the twentieth century.

Against the attitude which holds "that everything is uncertain, but that in the meanwhile all theories are interesting," I would submit that there *is* such a thing as the study of legend, and that such study is based upon the belief that, though legend

---

[1] *Heroic Legends of Denmark*, p. 381.

changes, *everything* is not uncertain—that there *are* some stable elements; if there were not, we should have nothing solid to work on. We have got to discriminate.

In Olrik's words:

> "The only possible way to arrive at a clear conception is to plunge down into the multitude of traditions and the chaos of contradictions, in order to evolve from them the law of change that determines the growth of legends; that is, to find which elements change, and which remain[1]."

Undoubtedly tradition does, in the course of ages, undergo very great alterations; and when a historian like Saxo, after the lapse of six or eight centuries, tries to weave scattered traditions into one consistent whole, the strangest results will ensue: Ermanaric the Goth and Offa the Angle appear as Danish kings; so do Ingeld and Froda. But this does not mean that we can assume any change we like, taking place in any way we like, at any time we like. Still less does it mean that we can, without ground, dismiss as error statements upon which all our extant authorities *do* agree.

For, as a story branches off among many different tribes possessing a kindred speech and a kindred taste for heroic lays, that story will take different forms in different lands. One poet, who knows the story well, may compose a lay in which many things are stated only in an allusive way: his audience also know the story, and he has no need to be more explicit. In later days, or in another land, his lay may be repeated by heart. The background of knowledge may be no longer there; yet the lay may be popular, and people may be interested in its allusions, although they misunderstand them, and in order to account for them a new turn may be given to the old story[2]. But, amid all these many varying and divergent versions, that which is common to all is not lightly to be set aside.

And even when we have two divergent accounts, there are principles to guide us. Quarrels and battles arose out of the political clash of the different nations of the time of the Migrations. But in that rapidly changing age these political relations

---

[1] *Heroic Legends of Denmark*, p. 1.
[2] Cf. Olrik, *Danmarks Heltedigtning*, I, 18.

shifted, lost their meaning, and were forgotten: the human interest remained.

The story of Offa illustrates one of the "laws of change which determine the growth of legends." In *Widsith* the young English prince Offa defends his kingdom—the continental Angel—at the river Eider against the attack of *another tribe* from the South. Some eight centuries after that historic event, the story was still remembered in the midland shires of England. But continental Angel and its surroundings had by this time been forgotten. Consequently Offa is thought of as an English prince, living in England: his foes are thought of as domestic usurpers. At the same period the story was remembered in Denmark: but the frontier which Offa defended against the foes of those primitive English had in the meantime become the southern frontier of Denmark. This is reflected in the story, and Offa is represented as a Danish prince, defending his right against Saxon aggressors.

But the story of the young prince remains essentially the same, so far as the individual hero goes. The politics change.

Now one of the principles pointed out in Olrik's great book is precisely this: the earlier accounts represent the struggles of the time of the Migrations as being what they actually were— struggles between *peoples*. In later versions this political aspect is dimmed: the story is one of struggles between *individuals*, the nations are forgotten and confused.

It is precisely on this ground that Olrik finds *Beowulf* and *Widsith* trustworthy:

> "As a ground for our belief in the trustworthiness of the accounts given in *Beowulf* and *Widsith*, we must place first and foremost the character of these accounts. The political events are depicted with all the variety of real life: the story has not yet been re-arranged for the special glorification of a few favourite heroic figures. *Nations* are depicted as struggling, whereas a freer poetic version would have given us individual heroes[1]."

Thus the feud between Danes and Heathobeardan is represented as a national business: Ingeld is powerless: the hatreds nursed by his tribe carry him away despite himself:

> "þȳ ic Heaðobearna   hyldo ne telge
> dryht-sibbe dæl   Denum unfæcne
> frēond-scipe fæstne."

[1] *Danmarks Heltedigtning*, I, 18.

Now Wessén says very much the same thing as Olrik: "National contests are altered in later legend to family quarrels, struggles between peoples into struggles between individual chiefs or heroes[1]." Accordingly, and quite rightly, Wessén rejects the much later Scandinavian version which makes the struggle of Froda and Healfdene into a private quarrel between two rival brothers of the same royal family. He accepts the historical, political character of the events as depicted in *Beowulf*.

But, if we accept the historical character of the story, as we get it in *Beowulf*, we have no right at the same time to assume that kind of unhistorical confusion as to the nationality of the hero which we sometimes find, after the lapse of very many centuries, in a version of a story where all question of nationality has ceased to interest those who tell the story, and where they are concerned with the individual hero only.

The parallels which Wessén gives for shifting of nationality in legend do not seem to me to justify his treatment of *Beowulf*. On the contrary, they seem to mark it as unjustifiable. According to *Beowulf*, Eadgils is put on the throne of Sweden by the help of the Geatas: much later, Scandinavian tradition, as Wessén points out, makes Eadgils triumph by the help of the Danes[2]. But this offers no parallel—for it is precisely in a point where *Beowulf* and Scandinavian tradition *agree*—that Hrothgar and Hrothulf are Danish kings—that Wessén proposes to put their *joint evidence* aside. The Finn-Episode in *Beowulf* seems to represent Hengest as the foe of the Jutes: yet far from being the foe of the Jutes, he was in reality, argues Wessén, the historic Hengest, the leader of the Jutes who conquered Kent[3]. But this is very doubtful. True, many scholars are in favour of the identity of the two Hengests—Chadwick for example. But Chadwick is equally convinced that the Finn-Episode in *Beowulf*, far from representing Hengest as the foe of the Jutes, represents him as a member of that tribe[4]. And even if such a shifting in tradition had taken place, it would afford no parallel to Wessén's

[1] *De Nordiska Folkstammarna*, p. 28.
[2] *Ibid.* p. 32.   [3] *Ibid.* p. 33.
[4] *Origin of the English Nation*, 1907, p. 53; 1924, p. 49.

theory. For it is found in the Episode in *Beowulf* only, not in the *Finnsburg Fragment*. Not only may one individual version of a story play tricks with the nationality of one individual hero, but, for the matter of that, one individual himself may change sides. Among the first things we hear about the historic Hengest is that he was an exile[1]: and an exile, or refugee, a Coriolanus or a Robert Bruce, may lead men of a nation against which earlier he has fought. A parallel to Wessén's assumptions regarding the Danes would be, if we had two versions of the Finn story in England, and a considerable number in Friesland, and all these versions agreed *quite consistently* in reversing the nationality of the Frisians and all their champions, during a period of quarrel lasting through more than a generation.

Beowulf, according to the commonly accepted date, was composed 150 to 200 years after the events it narrates, and such a space of time, Wessén claims, is sufficient for such modifications. But the very instances quoted[2] to prove this, disprove it. The story of Ermanaric's death, as given by Jordanes nearly two hundred years after, may, or may not, contain a large admixture of fiction. We simply cannot tell how far the details of the story are historic: what is clear is, that the relationship of the Goths to the Huns, and of Ermanaric to both, is retained correctly. Jordanes narrates this as the contemporary Ammianus Marcellinus had recorded it. In both accounts, Ermanaric, the warlike and triumphant ruler of the mighty Gothic kingdom, is attacked by the Huns; in both accounts he fails to make headway against them, and worries over the situation, but meets his death before the final and crushing blow of the Huns has fallen. Again, the story of the death of Alboin, as told by Paul the Deacon, *may* contain legendary elements: but it certainly represents Alboin's nationality correctly.

It is the great merit of Olrik's study that, under his hands, chaos vanishes[3]: everything falls into its place. The almost contemporary notices of Latin or Greek historians, as to the extent of the Danish tribes, and their driving out of their foes; the pæan

---

[1] Nennius. On all this, cf. Kemp Malone, *The Literary History of Hamlet*, I, 20 *etc.*

[2] Wessén, *De Nordiska Folkstammarna*, p. 81; cf. p. 31.

[3] See *Heroic Legends of Denmark*, p. 8.

in *Beowulf* on the glory and victories of the Danes and their wide
domain; the glory of the great chiefs, Hrothgar and Hrothulf,
as depicted in *Beowulf* and *Widsith*; the glory of Rolf Kraki as
told in the Scandinavian tales—all these give us a consistent
picture.

Instead, we are invited to believe that all our authorities
agree to give a mistaken account of the facts.

And all this assumption of mistake only leads to further confusion: we have finally to postulate, not merely error, but
deliberate misrepresentation. For *Beowulf* and *Widsith* represent
Hrothgar and Hrothulf as victorious in their struggles against
Froda and his house. But, according to this newest theory,
Hrothgar and his dynasty, the defeated Heruli, ought to have
been represented as declining, not triumphing. Yes, says
Wessén, and so they really were, but *Beowulf* gives us a pre-
judiced and partizan account [1], "uppenbart partisk."

So Wessén's theory cannot be reconciled with history, for
history knows nothing of any Herulian realm in Denmark between 500 and 550. In order to reconcile it with the tradition of
Beowulf, a theory of name-shift has to be called in; although a
name-shift, on such an extensive scale, so soon after the events,
and in *all* our sources, is contrary to everything we know as to
the trustworthiness of Germanic legend. And, then, after all, in
place of Olrik's consistent scheme, we get a story which can only
be explained as a deliberate perversion of the truth.

If *Beowulf* be really as historically inaccurate as Wessén's
theory compels him to assume, then how can there be any
purpose in trying to base upon it the kind of historical investigation which he is making? *Beowulf* would still remain as valuable
as ever for literary and grammatical study, and we should in
that case be wise to confine ourselves to such study.

Further Elucidation of Scylding History.
Kemp Malone and Herrmann

But, as I have tried to show above, the archæological work
of recent years, and the studies of Knut Liestøl in the development of legend, enable us to start with a belief in the value of

---

[1] *De Nordiska Folkstammarna*, p. 29.

our legendary material. And even where legend becomes most confused, as in the Scandinavian versions of latest date, a re-sifting of the evidence may enable us to sort out a few more grains of fact from among the confusion.

During the last eight years, Prof. Kemp Malone has made many attempts to elucidate the story of the kings mentioned in *Beowulf*, by a comparison of all the numerous (and often highly inconsistent) Scandinavian accounts. Prof. Malone's attempts show the combination of an independent mind with a determination to benefit by what Olrik has to teach us.

Malone's first contribution to the study of the stories alluded to in *Beowulf* bore the rather surprising title of *The Literary History of Hamlet*[1].

His thesis is that *Hamlet, Amlóþi,* can be analysed *Aml + óþi,* and that, since the tradition passed through Ireland, we are justified in reading this as *Anle óþe. Anle* he identifies with the *Onela* of *Beowulf,* Hamlet is "the wild Onela." It is a pleasing, if daring, hypothesis which would identify Hamlet with the hero who in *Beowulf* is spoken of as "the best of sea-kings who dealt out treasure in Sweden—the famous prince." But, if Malone's thesis were disproved, though the relevance of the title he has given to his book would of course vanish, the book would continue to have value. It deals (amongst others) with nearly all the heroes mentioned in *Beowulf*—Swedish, Geatic and Danish.

The book is full of bold speculation: but in order to indulge in this speculation Malone builds a very solid platform based on wide reading and sober scholarship, which no student of *Beowulf* can afford to ignore. It is left for the second volume, when it appears, to carry us from Saxo to Shakespeare. But this first part is for Beowulfians rather than Shakespeareans, and, this being so, its title has sometimes led to the book being overlooked by those to whom it would have been most useful. Editors of periodicals, misled by the title, have sent the book for review to the Shakespearean scholars, who admit to being out of their depth: one of the best of them can only say, "Dr Malone writes with vigour and assurance, and prefers a bold conjecture to the dullness of security."

[1] Part I, *Anglistische Forschungen,* 59, Heidelberg, 1923.

It is therefore fortunate that Malone has picked out many of the most important problems and dealt with them more fully in distinct studies published in periodicals[1]. One such study is on *The Daughter of Healfdene*—the lady whose name is missing in the *Beowulf* MS, but whom he identifies with Yrsa, the mother of Rolf Kraki and wife of Athils (Eadgils). A second (perhaps the most important) of these studies is that devoted to Hrethric.

If we return to the prophetic address of Wealhtheow to Hrothgar in *Beowulf*, it will be remembered that she speaks of the support she vainly hopes her sons will receive from the "gracious" Hrothulf, "if thou, Lord of the Scyldings, shouldst leave the world sooner than he." It is a not unnatural assumption from these words that it will be only after the death of Hrothgar that conflict will arise between Hrothulf and Hrethric: and this was the inference which Olrik drew[2]. Yet it is not a necessary inference. The tragic irony of Wealhtheow's speech would even be increased if Hrothgar "leaves the world," not in the course of nature, but with the sword of the "gracious" Hrothulf in his body. And the two other references distinctly hint at trouble between Hrothgar himself and Hrothulf. Further, in the later Icelandic documents, despite their almost inextricable confusion, "Hróarr [= Hrothgar] is almost uniformly made a victim of a close kinsman[3]."

Further, the Scandinavian sources duplicate Hrethric; he comes twice into the genealogy: once as "Hrethric the hoarder of rings," *Hrærekr Hnauggvanbaugi*, and once as "Hrethric the thrower away of rings," *Hrærekr Slaungvanbaugi*.

From a careful study of the many and complicated documents, Malone reconstructs the story thus:

"We may conclude that Hrothulf overthrew and killed his uncle, Hrothgar, and usurped the throne; that Hrothgar's son Hrethric, aided by the Geats, defeated Hrothulf, forced him into exile, and took possession of the Danish kingdom; finally, that Hrothulf later returned to the attack with a fleet, overthrew and killed Hrethric, and ascended the Danish throne for the second time[4]."

---

[1] See Bibliography, pp. 546–50, belo.
[2] *Heroic Legends of Denmark*, p. 59.
[3] Malone in *Pub. Mod. Lang. Assoc. Amer.* XLII, 285.
[4] *Ibid.* p. 295.

Such a story would account for the later development:

> "Since Hrethric both succeeded Hrothulf on the throne and was succeeded by him, he might be looked upon as Hrothulf's successor or his predecessor. In this way two Hrethrics might come into being, as history became tradition and tradition became a genealogical table. And in fact Saxo knows two Hrethrics, who come before and after Hrothulf respectively.... The order of succession being what it was— Hrothulf, Hrethric, Hrothulf—one might expect that two Hrothulfs, rather than two Hrethrics, would develop. But in truth such a development could not take place, because Hrothulf held the stage. A character cannot be bisected in the full glare of publicity; a decent obscurity is essential if the operation is to be successful. Indeed, it is just this obscurity that accomplishes the bisection. Hrethric was bathed in a Hrothulfian light at two spots: the beginning and the end of his reign. But the region between was left in darkness. What wonder, then, that each spot became a person?
>
> The traditional (as against the historical) order of succession, then, came to be: Hrethric, Hrothulf, Hrethric[1]."

Hrethric must have had powerful backing if he was able, even temporarily, to drive out the mighty Hrothulf; and this lends further meaning to the passage in which Beowulf promises help to his Danish friends in time of trouble, and adds a courteous invitation to Hrethric to visit the court of the Geatas[2]. Anyway, the *Bjarkamál* represents the Geatas as amongst the enemies of Hrothulf in his last fight against Heoroweard:

> "Ergo duces ubi sunt Gothorum militiæque
> Hiarthvari? Veniant et vires sanguine pensent."

This interpretation of the action of Beowulf and the Geatas is exactly in accordance with what *Beowulf* tells us of their policies as against Sweden: the pretenders Eadgils and Eanmund are supported; even after the death of one and the defeat of the other, Beowulf perseveres, and "in later days" helps the exiled Eadgils to the throne of Sweden. It would be an exactly parallel story which would make him help Hrethric against Hrothulf, and, after the fall of Hrethric, help Hrethric's cousin Heoroweard to destory the Danish king. This interpretation would enable us to attribute a meaning to a passage in *Beowulf* which is otherwise unintelligible[3]. And it would be a natural thing.

---

[1] Malone in *Pub. Mod. Lang. Assoc. Amer.* XLII, 297–8.

[2] 1822–39. On this cf. Malone, p. 272: Malone's interpretation here certainly seems right, as against that of Olrik. So Malone, p. 294; "It is clear that Hrethric will have Geatish support," and here Olrik seems almost in agreement, *Heroic Legends*, p. 55.

[3] ll. 3003–7.

The power of the Geatas, after the complete destruction of their fighting force in Hygelac's expedition, would be precarious, between the two rising kingdoms of Sweden and Denmark. Yet both those kingdoms were rent by family feuds, and the Geatas might well have sought to maintain themselves by taking advantage of this, and helping to the thrones of those kingdoms any pretenders who were favourable to themselves.

But this at once brings us up against further difficulties. For it is by no means certain that Beowulf is a historical character at all[1]. Yet even if he be an imaginary king, this does not prevent historic achievements of the Geatas being attributed to him. There is the further question how far this interpretation of Beowulf's invitation to Hrethric—an interpretation which makes him a friend of Hrethric and consequently a foe of Hrothulf—is compatible with a belief in his identity with Bothvar Bjarki, the faithful follower of Rolf Kraki. Certainly *Beowulf* avoids any suggestion which would subordinate its hero to Hrothulf. Yet I still believe—as against Olrik and other scholars—that there *is* some connection between the two figures of Beowulf and Bjarki[2], and so does Prof. Malone. Malone's method of harmonizing a contradiction which would make the same figure fight on different sides in different versions of the same story, is one of the most interesting arguments in his useful book[3]. But it is all too complicated to be even summarized here.

Any attempt to reconstruct the history of the Scylding kings must have the great book of Axel Olrik as its groundwork and point of departure. When, in 1921, Paul Hermann completed his invaluable commentary upon Saxo Grammaticus[4], after twenty-three years labour, he declared that what was best in it was due to Olrik's life-work. Hermann's book proves that his reverence is not of that superstitious kind which deprives a critic of his own freedom of judgment; but, as he says, "Everyone who writes about Saxo today must be Olrik's disciple." And so, with

---

[1] See above, pp. 13, 396, and Deutschbein, *Beowulf der Gautenkönig*, 1913.
[2] See above, pp. 61, 369, 395.
[3] *Literary History of Hamlet*, I, 90 etc.
[4] *Erläuterungen zu den ersten neun Büchern des Saxo Grammaticus* (II. *Die Heldensagen des Saxo.*) Leipzig, 1922.

a Danish scholar's estimate of Olrik's work, I will conclude this section:

"It is Axel Olrik's achievement to have given us in *Danmarks Heltedigtning* the first comprehensive picture of our Scylding age. For many years he worked at the subject, and gained an intimacy with it and an intuition which few indeed have surpassed. That Olrik could make slips, especially when he was dealing with matters apart from literature or legend or folk-lore, need not surprise us. It will not diminish the veneration with which Danish scholars will ever remember him, for he has given us a new insight into the period where the student of legend meets the student of history: those centuries, in which our nation comes into being, but of which we have such obscure historical information. Here he made a reconstruction, laboriously, from scattered details in saga and poem, and it can be asserted that as yet no Danish scholar has modified in any crucial point the picture which he drew[1]."

[1] V. La Cour, *Skjoldungefejden*, in *Danske Studier*, 1926, p. 147.

CHAPTER III

THE NON-HISTORICAL ELEMENTS

THE GRENDEL STORY AND ITS ANALOGUES: TALES OF THE
WATERFALL TROLLS, COMPARED WITH "THE BEAR'S SON"
OR "THE HAND AND THE CHILD"

A NEW discovery of great importance for the study of
Beowulf is published by Lawrence in his *Beowulf and Epic
Tradition*, and this discovery is of all the more interest because
it puts the finishing touch upon work which he has been doing
for twenty years.

In 1909 Lawrence[1] attacked the old mythological interpretation which allegorized Beowulf's fight with Grendel and
Grendel's mother into the struggle of a god against the hostile
powers of nature. Next year came Panzer's book, "a landmark
in the investigation of *Beowulf*" which "struck boldly into an
almost unexplored field," and suggested an alternative to the
mythological interpretation by identifying the story with the
"Bear's Son" folk-tale. Panzer's monumental work for the first
time forcibly directed attention to the folk-tale element in
Beowulf: yet this point of view, although it had been neglected
in the past, had not been entirely ignored. In 1884 Earle had
declared his belief that "The *Beowulf* itself is a tale of old folk-
lore, which, in spite of repeated editing, has never quite lost the
old crust of its outline." In 1889 Laistner[2] had drawn attention
to the likeness between *Beowulf* and two distinct types of folk-
tale: (1) the "Bear's Son" tale, and (2) the "Hand and the Child"
tale. But Laistner's work made little impression upon a generation of *Beowulf* scholars who were searching in Beowulf for a god
or culture-hero, and in Grendel and his mother for a nature-myth.
Panzer, working independently of Laistner's suggestion, con-
centrated in the main on examining one particular type of story

---

[1] "Some Disputed Questions in Beowulf Criticism," in the *Pub. Mod. Lang.
Assoc. Amer.* XXIV, 220–73.
[2] *Das Rätsel der Sphinx*, II, 26 *etc.*

—the "Bear's Son" tale—and emphasizing its relation to *Beowulf*. Whether or no the reader agrees with Panzer's interpretation in its details, he can hardly rise from a reading of his book without being convinced that the story of Beowulf's adventure with Grendel and his mother is a story of a type akin to those folk-tales which the research of the nineteenth century has collected. This does not of course mean that, at the time when these stories were attributed to Beowulf, they belonged solely to "the folk," as against the nobler classes.

Three years after the appearance of Panzer's book, Lawrence followed up his earlier article by a discussion of the "Haunted Mere in Beowulf[1]," dealing with the well-known parallel between the story of Beowulf's struggle with the monsters and the similar adventure of Grettir the Strong at Sandhaugar, as found in the *Grettis saga*. Lawrence produced strong evidence that the story told of Grettir could not be derived from *Beowulf*, but must be an independent version, ultimately derived from the same original, but in some respects more primitive. This had often been accepted as probable on *a priori* grounds, but the question had never been fully argued. Lawrence maintained that the setting of Grettir's adventure in *a cave behind a waterfall* must have been a feature of the original tale which had come down to the author of *Beowulf* and had been used by him: for the Anglo-Saxon poem contains words and phrases which look like a half-understood, outworn version of such a waterfall-setting as we find in the Icelandic saga[2]. Yet these details are much too blurred and confused to have been able to suggest such a setting to any imitator: the phrases in *Beowulf* could not reasonably be held to be the original of the story of the cave behind the waterfall in the *Grettis saga*: in fact, he argued, without the *Grettis saga* we should not be able to understand *Beowulf* correctly. And it is quite natural that the original scenery should be retained in the *Grettis saga*, because there the story had not wandered away from lands where big waterfalls are common, and was told in a language which has words for such things. The Anglo-Saxon epic, although chronologically so much earlier,

[1] *Pub. Mod. Lang. Assoc. Amer.* **xxvii**, 208–45 (1912).
[2] See above, pp. 52–3.

would naturally lose this "waterfall" feature, because it was composed in a land where waterfalls are comparatively few and meagre—not at all able to shelter monsters in caves behind them.

The importance of Lawrence's demonstration lay in the fact that, if the story as given in *Beowulf* and the story as given in the *Grettis saga* be both independently derived from one original, then, by a comparison of them both together, we ought to be able to form some idea of what that original was like.

But in such reconstructions our task is very greatly eased if we can have more than two props to sustain our reconstructed original. Critics had found a third analogue in the *Story of Orm Storolfsson*; but, as I tried to show above[1], the parallel is too remote to carry much weight. One of the many services which Prof. Boer has conferred upon the study of *Beowulf* and of the *Grettis saga* has been the demonstration that the story of Orm has been directly influenced by the *Grettis saga*; it therefore lacks that independence which alone could give it value.

The story told of Orm undoubtedly belongs to the same general type as that which is told of Beowulf in Denmark or of Grettir at Sandhaugar. The hero has in turn to fight two monsters, mother and son. Orm's fights also take place in a cave. He resembles Beowulf (in contradistinction to Grettir) in that, despite his great strength, he is almost defeated: save for supernatural aid he would have been overcome. But these are all commonplaces—features of a large class of stories. The resemblance between the *Orm*-story and *Beowulf* seems to me too vague to help us very much. But at the same time I must admit that most scholars have not been of this opinion, and have attached considerable importance to it[2].

Another analogue which has just been pointed out bears a remote resemblance to the *Beowulf-Grettir* story. This occurs in the recently published *Flores Saga Konungs ok Sona hans*, and

---

[1] pp. 53–4.

[2] Klaeber says that "a genetic relation of some kind must clearly be admitted." (*Beowulf*, xiv.) For a contrary view see Boer, *English Studies*, v, 109 (1923), and my own discussion in *English Studies*, xi, 82–4 (1929).

its importance has been emphasized by Miss Schlauch[1]. Here, as in the *Orm*-story, the struggle is not actually in a waterfall-cave, but in a cave overlooking the water. But here there is only one enemy, a dragon. The scenery is like that of *Beowulf*: wood and water, high cliff and narrow path. The companion pulls up the rope and deliberately leaves the hero in the lurch, as in the "Bear's Son" tale. This deliberate treachery is, however, as we shall see, not a feature of the *Beowulf-Grettir*-story, or of any of its closest analogues. In all these stories the watchers believe the hero dead: the effect of the episode is merely to emphasize the hero's success by adding the element of surprise; there is no idea that the hero is exposed to the deliberate treachery of his friends[2]. The analogue from the *Flores saga* is, like the *Orm*-story, interesting. But the connection with the *Beowulf-Grettir* story, if there be any, is remote.

But there are three other "waterfall-cave" adventures, each of which seems to have a connection with the *Beowulf-Grettir* story.

First and most important of these is the one of which Lawrence has now for the first time pointed out the value: it is an episode found in the *Saga of Samson the Fair*.

As long ago as 1882 Child, in his *English and Scottish Popular Ballads*[3], mentioned the likeness to *Beowulf* of this episode in the *Saga*. Child only noted it incidentally in his discussion of the various versions of *Lady Isabel and the Elf-Knight*. But the *Saga of Samson the Fair* was not easy of access, it was to be found only in an early eighteenth-century edition[4]; it is probably for this reason that the clue was not followed up.

Twenty years later Finnur Jónsson[5] had occasion to discuss the *Samsons saga*. He noted in passing the remarkable likeness between the episode in *Samson* and in the *Grettis saga*. It is clear

---

[1] I am indebted to Miss Schlauch for kindly communicating its substance to me. (It has now been published in *M.L.N.* xlv, 20–1 (1930).)

[2] I once thought that the action of Stein in deserting the rope might point back to a prototype of the *Beowulf-Grettir* story in which the companions are deliberately treacherous. For arguments against this, see von Sydow, *Beowulf och Bjarke*, p. 27. I now see that von Sydow is right here. In none of the "waterfall-cave" stories does the episode of the *treacherous* companions occur.

[3] i. 50.

[4] *Nordiska Kämpa Dater* (edited by E. J. Björner), Stockholm, 1737.

[5] *Den oldnorske og oldislandske Litteraturs Historie*, iii, 112–3.

that he detected this quite independently of Child. He added that *Samson the Fair* was one of the sagas which most called for a reprint: and an edition was printed at Reykjavik in 1905. This is *not* a reprint of the eighteenth-century text, but a distinct version, showing minor variations.

Then F. R. Schröder, in 1917, in his edition of *Hálfdanar Saga Eysteinssonar*, made in a footnote a collection of all the instances of monsters in caves under waterfalls[1]. He included under these Grendel and his mother; whether independently or as a result of Lawrence's essay, he did not say. I am indebted to Schröder for his useful list.

Still the clue was not followed up. But now that Lawrence has given a summary of the story in his *Beowulf and Epic Tradition*[2], with an extract from the Reykjavik edition of the saga, its importance can no longer be overlooked.

The story, as given by Björner, is briefly as follows:

King Artus of England has, by his wife Silvia of Hungary, a son, Samson the Fair, who is fostered by Earl Salmon and Salmon's wife Olympia. Valintina, a daughter of the Irish king Garlant, is a hostage at the court of Artus. Samson and Valintina fall in love, but, since Valintina is under his care, Artus will not consent to his son's suit for her hand: so he sends Valintina home again, and tells Samson that he must woo her in her father's house.

Valintina's father happens to have great domains in "Brettland[3]," whither he goes, accompanied by Valintina. But Valintina is entrapped by Kvintalin. Kvintalin is the son of the miller Galinn, and of a giantess who lives under the "foss" of his mill[4]; he is a great thief, dwells out in the forests, and by his wonderful music is able to lure women into his power[5]. (Here

---

[1] Independently, Knut Liestøl has given a list in *The American Scandinavian Review*, xviii, 370–3 (1930). This list contains some new examples from modern Icelandic tradition.

[2] A fuller discussion is given by Lawrence in the *Klaeber Miscellany*. See also my article in *English Studies*, xi, 95–100 (1929). The editor of *English Studies* permits me to reproduce some passages from that article in this book.

[3] "Scotland" in the Reykjavik text.

[4] "Einginn maþur vissi moþerni hans, enn þaþ otluþu flestir, aþ Galinn mundi eiga hann viþ Gyþiu, er la undir mylnu fossinum." (Ed. Björner, p. 7.)

[5] "Hann var þiofur ok la uti i skogum, ok kunni morg kindug brogþ, ok margar listir hafþi hann numit. Hann var mikill meistari a horpuslatt, ok þar meþ villti hann margar hæverskar konur i skoginn til sin."

comes in the likeness to the story of *Lady Isabel and the Elf-Knight*.) But, unlike Grendel, Kvintalin does not devour his victims—he does not even, like the Elfin Knight, slay them[1]. Valintina is saved by the fact that Olympia, after her husband's death, has settled in Brettland: Olympia intervenes when Valintina's danger is greatest, and Kvintalin is only able to seize some clothes and jewels which Valintina has cast off in her haste, following the magic music. Garlant, after search, thinking his daughter lost, returns to Ireland, and meantime Olympia continues to protect Valintina.

Samson is equipped by Artus for a viking raid, and in due time pays a friendly visit to Garlant in Ireland, and learns that Valintina has been lost. He goes to the rescue to Brettland, and is advised to seek for counsel from Galinn the miller.

Samson finds Galinn, and tells him that he is seeking Valintina. Galinn says that he thinks the wild beasts have devoured her, but promises to give what help he can. Samson produces a purse and ten marks of gold, and Galinn promises, "If I am in this search with thee, then she cannot be in this forest, if we find her not."

> "And whilst they were speaking, Samson stood on the brink of the foss. And they pledged their hands; and at that moment, before Samson was aware, both his feet were seized and he was thrown down into the foss. There was come a troll-woman, and he had no power against her, but when he grappled with her they struggled, and came down to the bottom, and he saw that she was trying to drag him to the bottom. He managed to draw the knife which Valintina the king's daughter had given him, and plunged it into the troll-woman's breast, and slit her belly so that the entrails fell out, and the river was like blood to look upon. Samson was almost suffocated, but now he got loose, and he found that there was a cave. He crept up into it, and was now so weary that he had to lie there a long time before he was able to move. When he recovered his strength, he wrung out his clothes and explored the cave, and thought he would never come to the end of it. Then he found a second cave opening out of the first, and there he saw much gear, and many treasures of gold and silver. There was a couch exceedingly fair, with curtain and lovely coverlets. There was a stay, and gold knobs at the ends, and much bed gear. Then he saw the kirtle

---

[1] Grendel has no accomplishments; but it is quite in order that the dweller in a waterfall-cave should be skilled in music like Kvintalin (see Lawrence, *Beowulf and Epic Tradition*, p. 186). He may also, like Kvintalin, be amorous rather than carnivorous, as was the eight-handed giant-troll Starkath Aludreng, the grandfather of the hero Starkath. This troll lived under the Alu "foss." He carried off a princess for his wife, and was slain by Thor for so doing. See *Saga Gautreks Konungs,* and *Hervarar Saga* in *Fornaldar Sögur,* 1829, I, 412 and III, 14.

and mantle of Valintina the king's daughter, and her diadem, girdle and brooch. He took of these whatsoever seemed good to him, and went to the end of the cave[1]."

Samson gets out of the cave by the other end, not returning to the waterfall. Finally he goes back to King Garlant in Ireland, tells him of his adventures, and shows him the jewels. They agree that Valintina must be dead.

But meantime the "stealer of women" Kvintalin has been making enquiries about Samson from his father Galinn the miller. Galinn tells him:

"'I think that thy mother must have slain him, for the foss was all stained with blood when they had struggled a little time in it: and now we will go and find her, and she must take counsel with us.'
Then they went into the cave, and only grasped the air. Then they thought it clear that Samson must have killed her[2]."

Now it is indisputable that Child was right in seeing in the *Samson* episode a parallel to *Beowulf*, and Jónsson was right in seeing in it (independently) a parallel to the Sandhaugar episode in the *Grettis saga*. Yet, though it has resemblances to both, it can hardly be derived from either.

For the striking feature of the episode in the *Samsons saga* is the cave behind the foss, as it is also in the *Grettis saga*. Yet there is no clear indication in the poem of *Beowulf*, as we now have it, that the cave lies *just behind* a waterfall.

It is equally unlikely that the episode in the *Samsons saga* can be derived from the Sandhaugar episode in the *Grettis saga*. For it contains features which are found in *Beowulf* but are conspicuously absent from the *Grettis saga*. In *Beowulf* the female monster normally remains at home, the male ranges abroad for his prey. In the *Grettis saga* the parts are reversed. But in the *Samsons saga* the parts are allotted as in *Beowulf*: the male

[1] Ed. Björner, p. 11.
[2] This occurs only in the Reykjavik version. I cannot find it in Björner. But the emphasis placed in Björner's version, at an earlier point, upon the staining of the water with blood, shows that this detail was intended to follow, although it is absent from the text as Björner publishes it.

The passage from the Reykjavik edition I give as Prof. Lawrence has supplied it to me:

"Gallýn tjáir honum [i.e. Kvintalin] af viðræðu sinni við Samson, 'og ætla eg að móðir þin hafi drepið hann því fossinn varð allur blóði drifinn er þau höfðu áttst við stundar korn í fossinum, en nú skulum við fara og finna hana og mun hún leggja á ráð með okkur.' Fara þeir þá í hellirinn en grípa í tómt, þykjast þeir vita að Samson muni hafa drepið hana" (pp. 18–19).

Kvintalin wanders in the forest seeking to lure his victims from
the dwellings of men; his mother lives under the foss. Kvintalin
visits her cave, and carries thither trophies which he has seized.
Again, both in *Beowulf* and in the *Samsons saga* the she-hag
grapples with the hero in the water and drags him to the bottom:
the hag has such a grip on him that for the moment he is helpless; there is nothing of this in Grettir's adventure. Grettir dives
under the waterfall and enters the cave before he meets his foe.

The natural inference seems to be that the story in the
Samsons saga is not derived from *Beowulf*, nor yet from the
Sandhaugar episode in the *Grettis saga*, but gives us a third independent version of the story of which *Beowulf* and the *Grettis
saga* preserve other, independent, versions.

For, if three versions of one story come down independently,
each naturally makes its own individual variations. This leaves
features in which any two of the three agree against the third—
which is exactly what we find here.

The two other stories of monsters dwelling under waterfalls
which offer parallels to the *Beowulf-Grettir-Samson* story are
those of Gull-Thorir and Skeggi. Long ago Olrik, in *Dania*[1],
called attention to the likeness between the story of Beowulf's
dragon and that of the dragons dwelling behind the waterfall in
the *Gull-Thoris saga*. These dragons were originally vikings—
Val and his sons: but to save their treasure they had gone behind
the waterfall, where they lived in the form of flying dragons,
lying on their gold, with helmet on head and swords beneath
their shoulders. (There is an obvious resemblance to Fafnir,
who guarded the gold derived originally from the dwarf Andvari,
who had lived in the form of a pike in a foss[2]. And Val also had
captured the gold which, as a dragon, he later guarded in the
waterfall-cave, from a *jǫtunn* who originally dwelt there.) In
spite of the dragon-form of Val, the story reminds us of the tales
of Grendel's mother and of Grettir's adventure in the foss, rather
than of Beowulf's dragon.

---

[1] I. 237 (1891).

[2] Miss E. C. Batho calls my attention to the fact that when Andvari is robbed
of his gold he goes into a hole in the rock to utter his curse. Is this an outworn
reminiscence of a cave under the waterfall, where the gold had been originally
hidden?

Gull-Thorir is a historical character: he was one of the early settlers of Iceland[1]. The saga tells how he first sought wealth by attempting to rob the grave-mound of Agnar. Agnar appears to him, reproaches him for his impiety (as well he may, being his uncle), and suggests the winning of the gold from the three dragons, Val and his two sons. Gull-Thorir and his companions accordingly sail north to the Arctic, where a river flows through a ravine to the sea. They uproot a tree and shove its branches over the edge: then, by means of a rope, Thorir and three companions reach the cave behind the fall. They are in straits, because the light they are carrying is blown out. But Thorir calls upon Agnar, and a supernatural ray of light is sent. This charms the dragons to sleep, and at the same time reveals the gold on which they rest, and the hilts of the swords under their shoulders. Thorir and his companions seize the swords and stab the dragons: but the dragons fly out, the largest one seizing in his mouth one of Thorir's companions. Two of Thorir's friends are watching the rope outside: they conclude that the adventurers are dead: one of the watchers is killed and the other disabled by the poisonous blood from the dragons' wounds. Therefore (as invariably happens in these stories) Thorir has to climb up from the foss unaided[2].

Very similar is the story of Gullbra (Goldbrow)—she is a witch who has chosen to be buried in a cave under a waterfall. From this lair she destroys men and cattle, and makes her old farmstead uninhabitable. Skeggi, whose herdsmen have been slain, attacks Goldbrow in her cave (there is no preliminary resistance in the house). Skeggi, like Beowulf and Orm and Gull-Thorir, but unlike Grettir, is almost overcome. He puts up a prayer, and is saved by a ray of light which shines into the cave and turns the witch to stone. As always, the watchers assume the hero to be dead, and he has to get out as best he can[3].

There is always a female monster dwelling in the cave, except in the tale of Gull-Thorir, where the dragons have ousted the

---

[1] He went out apparently before 920. His saga in its present form is supposed to date from about 1300.

[2] See below, pp. 498–502.

[3] A summary of the story of Gullbra is given by Panzer (pp. 342–3). It is given in full below, pp. 494–8.

original giant, about whose household we accordingly remain in ignorance[1].

In the *Bærings saga* also we hear of a giantess who dwells in a cave under a waterfall, and who has a monstrous son—he can on occasion take upon him the form of a dragon[2]. In the *Ọrvar Odds Saga* we have the same thing—the giantess dwelling under a foss, the mother of a monstrous son[3]. But the parallel with Grettir and Samson does not go beyond this: the hero does not fight the giantess or penetrate into her cave.

A number of parallels, somewhat less exciting, have been collected by Knut Liestøl from modern Icelandic tradition:

> "On a farm in northern Iceland it is related that on two successive Christmas Eves a female troll killed a shepherd. On the third Christmas Eve the new shepherd, Ketill, was carried away by the troll into a cavern underneath a great waterfall. On a farm called Foss (Waterfall), in Fljótum, lived two brothers. Near by was a river and a fall, and the brothers were in the habit of fishing under the fall. But in the waterfall dwelt a female troll who would not hear of their fishing there. One night she came and seized one of the brothers and dragged him down to the gorge by the waterfall and drowned him there. The surviving brother fled from the farm, which stands deserted to this day. In Thjorsardal a similar monster frequented a waterfall and lived off the fish she caught there. One day a boy threw stones into the waterfall. The next night the troll came and tried to seize the boy while he lay sleeping. After a long struggle she was forced to let go of him, but he was desperately ill for an entire month[4]."

Then there is the fact, to which Liestøl also calls attention, that according to *Landnámabók* the pagan priest Thorstein Raudnef used to make sacrifices to a waterfall: all pointing to the primitive belief in something supernatural in the *foss*.

Everything then seems to show that the story told of Grettir of a struggle with supernatural beings dwelling in a cave beneath a waterfall is indigenous to Scandinavia. But the story told of Beowulf is, indisputably, the same as that told in the Sandhaugar episode concerning Grettir. All this supports the view put for-

---

[1] The female monster in *Grettir* clearly dwells in the cave: for she seeks to drag Grettir to it, and the bones of her victims are found in it.

[2] *Fornsögur Suðrlanda*, ed. Cederschiöld, Lund, 1884, p. 108.

[3] Rafn, *Fornaldar Sögur Nordrlanda*, 1829, II, 241.

[4] *Beowulf and Epic Tradition* in *The American Scandinavian Review*, XVIII, June, 1930, p. 372.

ward by Vigfússon when he first noticed the *Beowulf-Grettir* parallel:

> "The old legend shot forth from its ancient Scandinavian home into two branches, one to England, where it was turned into an epic, and one to Iceland, where it was domesticated and embodied in a popular saga tacked to the name of an outlaw and hero[1] [say, now, four outlaws or heroes: Grettir, Samson, Gull-Thorir and Skeggi]."

There has been a tendency recently to suppose that the Sandhaugar episode in the *Grettis saga* is derived from *Beowulf*[2]: and sometimes those who take this view speak as if we who think differently were making an assumption without grounds.

The question is fundamental for any study of the main plot of *Beowulf*, and it becomes necessary to enter, at length, into an examination of the difficulties which beset those who assume the Sandhaugar episode to have been composed under the influence of a story derived from *Beowulf* as we now have it. To go through these will involve not a little repetition and recapitulation. But it is worth while. All discussion of the relation of the Grendel story in *Beowulf* to this or that group of folk-tales is in the air, till we have decided what is its relation to the tale or tales most nearly related to it.

Now there is certainly nothing intrinsically impossible in the idea of a story, derived from our extant epic of *Beowulf*, having found its way to Scandinavia, and having circulated there till the tale of Grendel and his mother became incorporated as an episode in the *Grettis saga*.

But that theory compels those who adopt it to postulate a quite extraordinary number of coincidences, none of them perhaps impossible when taken separately, but which, as a series, can hardly be assumed without utterly violating probability.

(i) There is Lawrence's argument that a waterfall is implicit in the story as told in *Beowulf*.

If we suppose the Sandhaugar episode in the *Grettis saga* and

---

[1] *Sturlunga Saga, Prolegomena*, xlix; so in *Corpus Poeticum Boreale*, II, 502: "The story in Gretti we take to be an echo not of the present diluted epic, but of the lays from which the epic was later made up."

[2] Boer argues in this sense very strongly in *English Studies*, v, 105 (1923). The view has also been supported by Olrik (*Heroic Legends*, p. 405), von Sydow (*Beowulf och Bjarke*, pp. 26–31) contrary to his earlier view, and Heinz Dehmer (*Primitives Erzählungsgut in den Íslendinga-Sögur*, p. 65 etc., 1927). Heusler in *A.f.d.A.* XLIII, 53 (1924) expresses his agreement with von Sydow.

the Grendel story in *Beowulf* to be independently derived from one original, this is quite natural. The tale of the ogress in the cave under the waterfall remains, "crystal-clear," in a waterfall country: but it becomes blurred in a land where the vast water-fall scenery postulated by the story does not exist, and in a language which had not the exact words to describe it. The English poet had probably never seen a really mighty waterfall, such as the Trollhättan Falls in the land of the Geatas[1]. When the tale travelled to those parts of this island which the English had settled, especially if it came by way of the old home in Schleswig, the lair of the solitary monsters was naturally placed in fens. Grendel is a *þyrs*, and the natural home of a *þyrs*, the Cottonian *Gnomic Verses* tell us, is in the fens:

> "þyrs sceal on fenne gewunian
> āna innan lande."

In a similar way, when the Goths were dwelling among the flat and often swampy districts of what is now Western Russia, they regarded the offspring of witches and evil spirits as a race "which was of old amid the fens[2]." In England the word *Grendel* is connected with meres and pits and mires, for the most part situated in low-lying country, which must in Anglo-Saxon times have been swampy[3]. Naturally then, in *Beowulf*, Grendel and his mother dwell in the fens, and this idea is repeated till the water-fall-idea is obscured[4]. Equally frequent is the mention of moors[5], though that word is ambiguous: the Old English *mōr* includes ravines, precipices and mountain tops.

But, amidst all this fenny country, we have a *fyrgen-strēam*; *fyrgen* indisputably means "mountain," but we must not think of a "mountain stream," filling the hills with music; *fyrgen-strēam* implies large volume—the word may be applied to the currents and mountainous waves of the ocean. This vast torrent comes down (*niþer gewīteð*) beneath the mists of the heights (*næssa genipu*), amid precipices swept by the wind (*windige*

---

[1] Such as the Trollhättan Falls *were*. They must not be judged from the present industrialized remnant.

[2] "quae fuit primum inter paludes." Jordanes, *Getica*, ed. Mommsen, XXIV, 122.

[3] See above, pp. 304–11.

[4] 104, 1295; fen-freoðo, 851; fen-gelād, 1359; fen-hlið, 820; fen-hop, 764.

[5] 103, 162, 710, 1348, 1405.

næssas); a precipice rises out of the water (*holm-clif*). There is a pool, the depth of which no one knows; trees overhang it:

"wudu wyrtum fæst   wæter oferhelmað."

Spray rises to the sky, as the waters from above meet the waters below:

"þonon ȳðgeblond   ūp āstīgeð
won to wolcnum."

Now, those who would derive the story in the *Grettis saga* from *Beowulf* have "the choice of two things—and neither of them is good."

They may deny that the waterfall *is* implicit in *Beowulf*; they may say that the *Beowulf* poet merely threw together absent-mindedly all sorts of picturesque and romantic phrases, and that it is mere accident that, when we turn back to *Beowulf* from reading the *Grettis saga* or the other Scandinavian analogues, we seem to see that the "foss," the essential feature of the story in the Scandinavian versions, must have been in the source which lay before the *Beowulf* poet. Yet it is difficult to accept such a view, when we see how neatly, in Klaeber's words, the story in the *Grettis saga* "serves to make clear the Beowulfian representation of the Grendel abode." And in the *Gull-Thoris saga*, with its other remarkable parallels to *Beowulf*, we have the trees, and the drenching spray from the waterfall, and the promontory jutting into the pool below. When we find exactly these things recurring in *Beowulf*—the water falling, the spray rising—it is difficult to believe that there was no idea of a waterfall in the sources from which the *Beowulf* poet presumably got these phrases[1].

But, on the other hand, those who derive the story in the *Grettis saga* from *Beowulf* may go to the opposite extreme. They may say that the Sandhaugar episode in *Grettir* comes from *Beowulf*, and that the "foss" was suggested by the description in

---

[1] A casual reader might get the impression that these words refer to the tossing sea. But the many words like *sǣ*, *nicor*, which *might* refer to the sea, *can* equally refer to an inland water. The constant allusions to Grendel and his mother haunting moor and fen, are conclusive; still more so the fact that there is never any unambiguous phrase of the kind that must have been used if the poet had thought of his monsters as haunting the deep sea. Klaeber says, "That Grendel lives in the sea cannot be conceded" (p. 176). It seems to me that any interpretation which rejects Klaeber's verdict is in the air.

Beowulf. But in that case it has to be explained why it was so long before critics were able to see that the waterfall-setting, explicit in the *Grettis saga*, was nevertheless implicit in *Beowulf*. To many of us this now seems clear—but only with the *Grettis saga* before us, and even then only after reading Lawrence's excellent demonstration: I remember W. P. Ker saying, "Strange, that none of us ever noticed that before." The waterfall-setting in *Beowulf* is almost obliterated, visible only when searched for, like the original writing of some palimpsests. It is one of those things which, however obvious after they are pointed out, are not noticed till they *are* pointed out; in fact, even now, some scholars deny that the waterfall-setting is to be found in *Beowulf* at all[1]. To me, it seems equally difficult on the one hand to deny that there are traces of a waterfall-setting in *Beowulf*, or on the other to assert that the confused scenery of *Beowulf* can be the origin of the vivid account in the *Grettis saga*.

(ii) In any case it is certain that in *Beowulf* there is no suggestion that the cave is just behind the waterfall. Beowulf plunges to the bottom, and in course of time finds himself in a cave free from the water. Nothing is said of his rising after his dive—the cave appears to be at the bottom of the mere: it is sheer un-reason. Of course such un-reason *does* occur elsewhere in *Beowulf*. But when we confront the *Beowulf* account with the Sandhaugar episode, the episode reveals itself as eminently reasonable. The hero, in order to get *under* the waterfall, *has* to dive to the bottom. "Can it be done?" I remember asking W. P. Ker. "Yes," said Ker, "I have done it." (All depends, of course, upon the volume of the waterfall.)

So here again we have the same phenomenon. What is confused in *Beowulf* is found to be clear in the Sandhaugar episode, and what is fantastic and unreasonable in *Beowulf* is found to be rational in the Sandhaugar episode. The *disjecta membra* turn into something reasonable, in the light of the *Grettis saga*. Chance again?

(iii) In *Beowulf* the hero plunges into the water, swims a long distance, and reaches the cavern, free from water, where he slays Grendel's mother and strikes off Grendel's head. From this

[1] von Sydow, *Beowulf och Bjarke*, p. 31.

cavern the blood somehow flows into the mere, and makes its way across, to the spot where the watchers are. This spot is far distant from the cavern, which it has taken Beowulf *hwīl dæges* to reach—we may render this phrase either "a large part of the day" or "the space of a day," as we will. Of course, again, unreason like this is possible in *Beowulf*, though one wonders how so far-fetched an idea ever occurred to anybody. But when we turn to the Sandhaugar episode, we find that the mutilated body of the giant falls into the stream: the blood and fragments of the body are, inevitably, carried down stream to the watcher below. What in *Beowulf* is absurd, is seen in the Sandhaugar episode to be logical, consistent, and indeed inevitable.

Of course it would be wrong to argue that, given a number of variants of the same story, the most rational version is to be supposed the original one. For, obviously, a later man may retell a story, cutting out what he finds irrational, and substituting a setting as "crystal-clear," to use Lawrence's phrase, as that which we find in the Sandhaugar episode, with the waterfall, the cave behind, and the blood carried down the stream.

But the point is that all these things, the torrent rushing down, the cave and the blood-stained water, *do actually occur in the* Beowulf *story, but that they read there like a confused, half-forgotten and quite unreal version of the setting which comes out so clear in the Sandhaugar episode.*

(iv) It has already been pointed out how the *Samsons saga* provides an awkward problem to those who deny the independent survival of a Scandinavian type of the Grendel story in Scandinavian lands. Such critics must assume that the episode in the *Samsons saga* is also derived from *Beowulf*. It cannot come from the Sandhaugar episode in the *Grettis saga*, for it preserves Beowulfian features which the *Grettis saga* has lost. But how, on the other hand, can we account for the features obscured in *Beowulf* but clear in *Grettir*, which come out equally clearly in the *Samsons saga*? It may be replied that these details were subsequently imported into the *Samsons saga* from the *Grettis saga*. But why? If the story which the *Samsons saga* has in common with *Beowulf* closely resembled the Sandhaugar episode in the *Grettis saga*, then we could understand an author or reviser of the *Samsons saga* who knew the *Grettis saga* being struck by the resemblance, and proceeding to touch up one story from the other. But, in fact, the things in which the *Samsons saga* resembles *Beowulf* (the roving plundering male; his mother haunting the water, grappling with the hero in the water and dragging him down) *do not occur* in the *Grettis saga* at all. What, then, should have set the saga-man upon making his composite by adding, from the *Grettis saga*, the idea of the cave behind the foss, and the rapids stained by the blood of the disembowelled monster whose body they are carrying down?[1] Is it not special pleading to ask us to believe that the saga-man, with the whole field of stories to choose from, just happened to combine the two things that would mislead Prof. Lawrence by giving him the phenomenon his theory demands?

For the phenomena *do* suggest the independent derivation of the three stories attributed to Beowulf, Grettir and Samson; because it is obvious, as I have pointed out above, that, if the Beowulf, Grettir and Samson episodes are independently derived from a common source, each version will lose or obscure something, so that there will be points upon which any two will always agree against the third.

(v) There is one important feature, however, which the story in *Beowulf* possesses, which is found neither in the *Grettis saga* nor in the *Samsons saga*. Grendel's mother has the hero down, and it is twice emphasized that, but for supernatural aid, Beowulf would have been lost. This supernatural help *does* occur, however, in the two other "waterfall-cave" stories, the *Gull-Thoris saga* and the story of *Gullbra*. (Of course it is a common feature, it is found also in the *Orm* story.) It is worth noting how the motive is treated. Gull-Thorir calls upon the spirit of Agnar to help him: in response a ray of light is sent. This ray shines into the cave, and when it reaches the monsters (in this case

---

[1] The episode of the staining of the water with the monster's blood, and the watchers' belief that the hero is dead, comes also in the *Thorsteinssaga Vikingssonar*, cap. 23 (*Fornaldar Sögur*, ii, 1829). The likeness of this to *Beowulf* was noticed by C. N. Gould in *Modern Philology*, vii, 214, though he wisely refused to dogmatize. It looks as if there was some connection between the text of the *Thorsteinssaga* and the text of *Samson* as printed by Björner. Samson rips open his foe *tigulknifi, er Valentina Kongs dottir hafthi gefit honum*: compare *Thorsteinn tekr þá týgilknifinn, sem Sindri gaf honum*, in the corresponding passage (*Fornaldar Sögur*, ii, 452).

dragons) it renders them powerless. By the light of the ray Gull-Thorir and his companions see the magic swords—they draw them and stab the dragons with them. But so venomous is the blood of the wounded dragons that, when it falls upon one of the victors, it destroys him.

In the story of Gullbra the supernatural help is less elaborate. The hero, faced with defeat, implores help, and a ray of light is sent which, without further ado, destroys the monster.

Turning back to *Beowulf*, Grendel's mother overthrows Beowulf, and has him down. She draws her knife to slay him. He would have been destroyed, but for his coat of mail, and the judgment of God. The Lord decides rightly: Beowulf stands up. Then he sees a huge sword among the gear, draws it, and strikes off the monster's head. A glare like sunlight is in the cave:

> "Līxte se lēoma   lēoht inne stōd
> efne swā of hefene   hādre scīneð
> rodores candel."

Beowulf then turns by the wall, sees the body of Grendel, and cuts off his head. Beowulf tells the tale again, on his return to the palace of Hrothgar, emphasizing how he was almost slain, and saved only by the interposition of God, who allowed him to see the mighty old sword hanging on the wall, with which he slew Grendel's mother.

In *Beowulf* it is not clear by what instrumentality the divine interposition worked. If a giantess, knife in hand, is kneeling on your chest, it will afford you small comfort to see a sword hanging on the wall. Is it not intrinsically likely that the original story told how help was sent to the hero in the form of a ray like sunlight? This at the same time dazzles the monster and shows the hero the sword, so that he can spring up and seize it. A detail like this would naturally be obscured in the Old English epic, which never tells a tale in a strictly chronological way, but with a certain backward and forward movement: *ABAB*, as the formula puts it. Indeed it is quite possible that the story, as the author of *Beowulf* here meant to depict it, actually *was* that God intervened by sending a ray of light. Beowulf, we are told, would have been slain had not God decided the issue rightly. Beowulf stood up, saw the wondrous sword, seized it, and struck off his foe's head. The light was gleaming: it was shining within the cave as brightly as the sun in heaven[1]. This is certainly not more disjointed than, for instance, the story of the fugitive robbing the dragon's hoard[2].

Here again, then, we seem to have just the same phenomenon. The Scandinavian waterfall-monster story tells us of the ray of light revealing the magic sword to the hero in distress. In *Beowulf* we have the hero in distress, the magic sword, and the ray of light, but only when we compare the Scandinavian waterfall story do we seem to see the connection of these *disjecta membra*. Chance again?

(vi) Of course the magic sword found in the monster's domain is a commonplace of story; we can base no very elaborate argument upon so trite a feature. In the *Gull-Thoris saga* the hero brings back with him the sword "Hornhilt," *Hornhjalti*. In *Beowulf* only the "golden hilt" of the sword can be brought back to Hrothgar, because so poisonous is the blood of his adversary that the blade of the sword melts like ice. In the *Grettis saga* the weapon found below is used, not by the hero against the monster, but by the monster against the hero:

> "When Grettir came to him, the giant leaped up and seized a halberd (*fleinn*) and hewed at the new-comer: for with that halberd he could both cut and stab. It had a handle of wood: men at that time called a weapon made in such a way a *hepti-sax* (hafted cutlass). Grettir smote against it with his short sword and struck the handle so that he cut it asunder."

So, despite the difference in the situation, we have again the same episode of the wonderful sword with an exceptional haft.

The word *hæft-mēce* (*Beowulf*, l. 1457) occurs nowhere else in Anglo-Saxon, nor is *hepti-sax* found elsewhere in Icelandic. But the *hæft-mēce* in *Beowulf* does not belong to the troll, nor is it found in the cave; on the contrary it is the sword which Unferth

---

[1] A modern reader is likely to be misled by taking *līxte se lēoma, lēoht inne stōd*, as the preterite tense, and as necessarily subsequent to the event which precedes, *bānhringas brǣc*. But we have only to compare the other examples of these phrases in *Beowulf* to see that this is not so: l. 311, *līxte se lēoma*: it had been shining all the time; ll. 726–7, *him of ēagum stōd lēoht unfæger* (as Grendel steps down the hall): we need not suppose that Grendel's eyes were any milder when he was forcing his way in.

Of course, if this interpretation be correct, it destroys the suggested parallel with stories where the hero kindles a light *after* slaying the monster. (See p. 380 above.)

[2] Especially ll. 2280–9. Cf. Klaeber's *Introduction*, pp. lvii–lix.

lends Beowulf for his adventure, and which Beowulf has to throw away, because it proves useless for the task. When Unferth gives it to Beowulf we are told

"wæs þæm hæft-mēce Hrunting nama"

"The hilted sword was named Hrunting." This casual use of the word *hæft-mēce* would not have attracted attention or called for any remark, were it not for its counterpart the *hepti-sax* in the *Grettis saga*. For in *Beowulf*, the bare word *hæft-mēce* is unobtrusive, and is used in another context.

This corresponds once again with what we have so often found already: that features which come out emphatic and "crystal-clear" in one or other of the Scandinavian versions are in *Beowulf* obscure and unobtrusive: so much so that we only perceive their real import when we compare *Beowulf* with the Scandinavian versions.

(vii) Further, the theory which would make these Scandinavian tales derive from the English epic has an *a priori* unlikelihood. Here is a story which, although we first find it in an English epic, is there put before us in a definitely Scandinavian setting: an achievement of a Scandinavian hero at the court of a Scandinavian king. And this story, told in Old English times as a definitely Scandinavian one, is found surviving in Scandinavian lands, and in Scandinavian lands only, in the tales of Grettir and Samson. For, although the rending off or the cutting off of the arm of a supernatural foe is to be found, I will not say "from China to Peru," but certainly from Japan[1] to California[2], nevertheless nothing quite close to the story of Beowulf and Grendel's mother has as yet been found anywhere in the world save in these two Scandinavian sagas, especially that of Grettir.

Of course it is quite conceivable that a Scandinavian story, after being brought to England, might have died out in its own home, and might then have been reintroduced into Scandinavia from England. Such things do happen. But it is illegitimate to assume them, without heavy evidence. What about the other

---

[1] York Powell, "Beowulf and Watanabe-no-Tsema," *Furnivall Miscellany*, 1901, pp. 395–6.
[2] Curtin, *Hero Tales of Ireland*, p. 558. See also below, p. 490.

stories which were current in England in the eighth century and
which we find surviving in Scandinavia in the thirteenth? Is it
going to be argued that the tales of Hrothgar and Hrothulf, of
Eadgils and Onela, were also reintroduced into Scandinavia from
England?

(viii) But, if not, then we are further entitled to point out
that *Beowulf* is a mixture, often a rather intricate mixture, of a
story of monster-quelling with courtly, "heroic," epic elements.
Yet in the *Grettis saga* and in *Samson* it is only the monster-
quelling element that recurs, with no trace of the courtly
setting at Hrothgar's hall. If the composers of these sagas got
their story ultimately from *Beowulf*, someone had managed to
separate the one element from the other in a very skilful way.
This reducing of *Beowulf* back again to the form of simple story,
without its aristocratic setting, is a thing which a skilled student,
with the apparatus of modern research to hand, could do. But
I have tried elsewhere[1] to show the difficulties which would have
beset the Icelandic saga-man who tried to do it. The argument
is too long and complicated to repeat here at length. But it
seems to me to present yet another very real difficulty to
those who suppose the *Grettir* episode to be derived from
Beowulf[2].

(ix) The account in *Beowulf* tells, quite explicitly, how the
hero was seized in the water by Grendel's mother, and carried to
her cave. Now, nine years before the parallel between *Beowulf*
and the *Grettis saga* had been observed, Müllenhoff[3] had argued
that the original version was one which represented the hero as
free penetrating the cave, seeing the monster, and attacking her.
And Müllenhoff makes out a strong case here; it is a "palpable

---

[1] *English Studies*, XI, 91–2 (1929).

[2] Since I wrote these lines a somewhat parallel distinction between Beowulf
and Grettir has been emphasized by Hübener: the Grettir story is more immediately in touch with the world of primitive beliefs than is the Beowulf story:
"Gewiss, Grendel ist noch für den Dichter soweit Wirklichkeit, dass er ihn als
Dämon erkennt und in christlicher Wendung dem Geschlechte Kains zuordnet.
Aber der Hauptgegenstand der Dichtung ist nicht, wie in der Grettirsage er es
ganz deutlich ist, das Dämonische selbst und seine furchtbaren Wirkungen und
das erschütternd Grosse des Mutes und der Kraft, die der heroische Austreiber
zu beweisen hat, sondern dieser ganze überlieferte Stoff wird nur genommen, um
daran ritterliche Lebensart und Form zu entfalten." *England und die Gesittungsgrundlage der europäischen Frühgeschichte*, 1930, p. 104.

[3] *Z.f.d.A.* XIV, 210 (1869).

hit." (We may admit this without following Müllenhoff when, on the strength of a few such "palpable hits," he proceeds to divide the whole of *Beowulf* up, line by line, into its component parts. But it would be bigotry to deny that Müllenhoff *did* put his finger upon certain real inconsistencies in our extant poem[1].) Now the Sandhaugar episode does actually give the story in the form which Müllenhoff, quite independently and without any knowledge of the bearing of the Sandhaugar episode upon *Beowulf*, had nevertheless perceived to be the original version. How did the Icelandic writer get it? Unless he possessed critical powers equal to those of Müllenhoff, he certainly could not have got his account out of the *Beowulf* story as we now have it.

(x) Few of us, nowadays, have much hope of arriving at the primitive lays which lie behind our extant poem of *Beowulf*. We realize that the number of variants of lays and episodes and allusions must have been vast in days when every chief had his official *scop* performing every evening, to say nothing of the minstrels at the cross roads and the bridges, and amateurs who would take a hand after a feast when there was *blisse intinga gedēmed*. We can see how an elaborate poem like *Beowulf* may easily reflect inconsistent stories, without our being able to share the hopes of Müllenhoff or ten Brink or Boer that we can dissect our epic into its component lays. The analogy of the epic of William Morris, "The Story of Sigurd the Volsung," shows us how a poem may be emphatically the work of one man, bearing the mark of his individuality, and may yet reflect in its inconsistencies the inconsistent lays which lie behind it. This is the way in which I have always accounted to myself for the inconsistency in the story of the grappling of Beowulf with Grendel's mother. That there *is* an inconsistency seems to me undeniable. I said so sixteen years ago: "Here the discrepancy is a more real one than usual. The monster has seized Beowulf at the bottom of the [mere], and carried him to her hall, powerless to use his weapons. Yet ll. 1518–22 give the impression that

[1] This was very excellently pointed out by Earle nearly forty years ago; whilst dissenting from Müllenhoff's theories, Earle admitted that "Zeal for theory has wonderfully sharpened the keen eye of observation. The study of the 'Beowulf' has been over and over again greatly indebted to the shrewd remarks of Müllenhoff." (Earle, *Deeds of Beowulf*, 1892, p. xliii.)

Beowulf enters the hall, able to fight, and there, by the light of the fire, sees Grendel's mother for the first time." The version which makes Beowulf enter the hall and attack is found in the *Grettis saga*, agreeing even to the detail of the fire, by the light of which the hero sees the monster. The version which makes the monster grapple with Beowulf as he enters the water from above, so that he is dragged to the bottom, powerless for the moment to use his weapons, has now, within the last few months, been rediscovered in the *Samsons saga*. What is blurred in *Beowulf* comes out clear in the other versions: two inconsistent accounts have been combined in the Old English, but each left its descendants in its original Scandinavian home. In the course of time these are found in two Scandinavian versions of what is indisputably the same story as the *Beowulf* story, each Scandinavian version reflecting one of the variants which the story, as told in *Beowulf*, compels us to assume. Is this again to be dismissed as accident?

Now, against all these arguments, what is there to set on the other side?

It is urged, by those who believe the Sandhaugar episode to be derived from *Beowulf*, that the words *hæft-mēce* and *hepti-sax* point to a connection of a kind which could not have survived through many centuries of oral tradition. "Oral tradition cannot, for more than a limited time, retain a subsidiary motive which has no signification for the main story[1]."

The argument is, that this word *might* have survived through the comparatively short period of oral tradition intervening between *Beowulf* and the *Grettis saga*, but that such an insignificant feature would not have survived the long period of oral

---

[1] von Sydow, *Beowulf och Bjarke*, p. 29. Boer also argues that *hepti-sax* shows a literary connection and can be directly traced back to O.E. *hæft-mēce* (*English Studies*, v, 108). Sarrazin in 1905 argued from *hæft-mēce* and *hepti-sax* the exact reverse—namely, that *Beowulf* was derived from the Scandinavian: "Nicht selten kommen gerade in diesem abschnitt ungewöhnliche wörter und wendungen vor, welche auffallend mit aldnordischen übereinstimmen, zb. v. 1458 *hæftmēce*, vgl. altnord. *hepti-sax*....Für diese partie des Beowulfliedes wird also jedenfalls ziemlich genau wiedergabe der urdänischen überlieferung wahrscheinlich." ("Neue Beowulf-Studien," in *Englische Studien*, xxxv, 22.) It is curious that the argument, at one time used to prove *Beowulf* derived from the Scandinavian, should at another time be used to prove the exact reverse.

tradition intervening between an assumed remote common original and its late descendants, *Beowulf* and the *Grettis saga*. The answer is that the word may have been weighty in the original story and may only have become trivial and unimportant in *Beowulf*. So that the argument becomes double-edged; in fact, on examination, it tells for the theory of the common original, rather than against it. For it is difficult to see why the mention of the *hæft-mēce* should have survived from *Beowulf*, where it is so very casual, and so have reached the *Grettis saga*, where indeed it has significance. For we have seen that in the *Grettis saga* the peculiarity of the "hafted-cutlass" (*hepti-sax*) *is* stressed, but in *Beowulf* the bare word *hæft-mēce* is used of the sword which Unferth lends to Beowulf, and used in a way which would not call for any remark were it not for the *hepti-sax* of the *Grettis saga*; and we have seen that this corresponds to what we have so often found before: that features which come out emphatic and "crystal-clear" in the *Grettis saga* are in *Beowulf* obscure or unobtrusive: so much so that we only perceive their true import after we have read the *Grettis saga*.

Presumably, in the original story, as it existed before our *Beowulf* was composed, an important part was played by the sword with a wonderful hilt which the hero met with in the cave. In *Beowulf* ten lines are devoted to describing the presentation of the hilt to Hrothgar, twelve lines to describing the hilt itself. The sword is characterized by its hilt: it is called first *fetel-hilt*, then *wreoþen-hilt*. The hilt is of gold (*gylden hilt*), or it may be that *Gylden-hilt* is the name of the sword: and it has been thought that we have an echo of this in the sword *Gullin hjalti*, which appears in the corresponding passage in the *Saga of Rolf Kraki*, as the name of the sword by which the monster is struck.

When we turn to the prose of the *Grettis saga*, we find that much is made of the "hafted cutlass" (*hepti-sax*) which Grettir encounters in the hands of the giant in the cave. Further, that this was an important part of the story, as the compiler of the *Saga* knew it, is also indicated by the important part the *hepti-sax* is made to play in the verses, late as these doubtless are. Just as Beowulf brings back to Hrothgar the rune-inscribed hilt which is all that is left of the sword, so Grettir leaves with Stein a stave of wood upon which is inscribed in runes an account of the separation of the haft of the "hafted cutlass" from its blade:

"Harþeggjat létk hoggvet
heptesax af skapte."

If the *Grettis saga* were derived from *Beowulf*, we might have expected the sword which the hero meets below in the cave to go by the name *fetill-hjalti*, or *gullin-hjalti*, corresponding to *fetel-hilt*, *gylden-hilt*, the names given to it in *Beowulf*.

In the original story—say of the sixth century—the sword was probably described in a number of words compounded with the element *haft* or *hilt*: one of these *haft*-compounds survives in the *Grettis saga*, whilst in *Beowulf* it also survives, but has got into a different context[1].

There is nothing unprecedented in this "haft"-motive having survived in oral tradition through many centuries. In a similar way the "gallows"-motive runs through the *Hamþismál* in the *Elder Edda*, and is found surviving in the sixteenth-century Low German Lay of *King Ermanaric's Death*: it has passed through ages of oral tradition quite comparable to the length of time we have to postulate if we suppose the "haft"-motive to have passed by oral tradition from a sixth-century original to the composer of the *Grettis saga*.

We can point to other features which these two lays concerning the onslaught on Ermanaric have preserved from the original to which they must both ultimately owe their origin, though more than six centuries of oral tradition must lie between the latest extant version and the earliest version we can divine[2]. Again, a very close parallel to the two compound words *hæft-mēce*, *hepti-sax*, is afforded by the survival of the word *fīfel-dōr*, "the monster gate," in Old English poetry; the correct form, preserving the name of the river Eider (*ēgor-dōr*), is recorded in continental story. Here, again, an oral tradition lasting over many centuries can alone account for the facts.

---

[1] There would be no impossibility in the original story having mentioned runes upon the hilt: for inscriptions are found on swords of the fifth and sixth centuries.

[2] Heusler (*Lied und Epos*, p. 4) suggests eight centuries (from an eighth-century original, from which come on the one hand the *Hamþismál* as it survives in the *Codex Regius*, and on the other the ballad of *King Ermanaric's Death* as it was printed in the sixteenth century).

It may be objected that it is in the nature of a sword to have a hilt or haft, and that there is no reason why such a trite and commonplace feature should persist in the story through many centuries. Equally it is in the nature of a tyrant to keep and use a gallows; yet we find the gallows stressed in the Ermanaric story, alike in the *Elder Edda* and in the sixteenth-century lay, and stressed in the same way; and it is this which makes the "gallows"-motive such a valuable parallel.

Three swords in Northern story have names derived from their hilt: (1) "Hornhilt, adorned with gold[1]," in the story of Gull-Thorir and his cave-fight, (2) Golden-hilt (*gylden-hilt*), in Beowulf's cave-adventure (if indeed that be a name at all), and (3) Golden-hilt (*Gullin-hjalti*), in the corresponding place in the *Saga of Rolf Kraki*. So important a part does this sword play in the *Saga of Rolf Kraki* that the hero who wields *Gullin-hjalti* is supposed to be named after it, *Hjalti*: "Thou shalt be called Hilt," says Rolf to him, "after the sword Goldenhilt," and under that name he has a place in Northern tradition[2]. Among the 176 names of swords famous in Northern story which Falk[3] has collected, these are the only names derived from the hilt. Then we have the *hepti-sax* episode in the *Grettis saga*, and the word *hæft-mēce* in *Beowulf*.

Now I can imagine a scholar dismissing all this as accidental coincidence, and perhaps he would be right. But *if* we are to argue from it at all, our argument must surely be that in the original story an important part was played by a sword with a wondrous haft or hilt. In some versions this is obscured; in *Beowulf* the word *hæft-mēce* has ceased to have any signification for the main story. In the *Grettis saga* it remains significant. But to argue that the word in *Beowulf*, because of its insignificance, must be the original of the name in the *Grettis saga*, is surely a *non-sequitur*[4].

It seems to me that the evidence that all these stories are

---

[1] *Gull-Thoris saga*, cap. 4; "sverð þat sem Hornhjalti hét, þat var mjǫk gulli buit," *Hálfdanar saga Eysteinssonar*, cap. 26.

[2] For a hero developed from the name of a weapon, compare the giants *Hildr* and *Grimr*, who grow out of the name of the helmet *Hildegrim* (*Thidreks saga*, 17). For the name Hjalti, see Olrik, *Heroic Legends*, p. 252 etc.

[3] *Altnordische Waffenkunde*, pp. 47–64.

[4] See also *English Studies*, XI, 92–4.

independent versions of one original quite clearly stands. If so, a comparison of them should reveal something like the original story. If we neglect elements which are peculiar to one version only, we get a tale like this:

(1) A creature with superhuman powers ravages a place, and carries off human beings. In *Beowulf* the victims are the retainers from the King's hall; in *Grettir* and *Skeggi* they are the inhabitants of Icelandic homesteads; in *Samson* it is the Princess Valintina. In the first three stories the victims are taken by force; the Princess Valintina is enticed by music into the forest. The ravager himself wanders abroad, but he has a mother who lives in a cave. This feature is preserved in *Beowulf* and *Samson*; in *Grettir* the sexes are reversed; in *Skeggi* there is only one ravager, a female. Only in *Gull-Thorir* are the dragons quiescent till attacked for their gold (compare the dragon in *Beowulf*). But these dragons are only the later inhabitants of the cave: they won it and its treasure from its original owner, who was a *jǫtunn*, just as Grendel is an *eoten*[1].

(2) This cave is behind a waterfall, in all the four Scandinavian versions. In *Beowulf* it is "under the torrent," near a pool where "the torrent comes down," and the "mingled waters rise up towards the clouds," and "the torrent pours away below the level of the ground[2]"; but the exact position of the cave relative to the falling torrent is not defined.

(3) A champion comes from a far distance, purposely to the rescue (*Beowulf, Grettir, Samson*). This seems to be an original feature of the story, for in *Grettir* it persists, although quite inappropriate; since Grettir is haunted by "Glam's eyes" and fears the dark, though he fears nothing else, he should be the last man to seek out these dwellers in darkness. In *Gull-Thorir* also the champion comes from a distance. In *Skeggi* alone the champion is a neighbour.

(4) In *Beowulf* and *Grettir* the champion awaits the attack of the ravisher within the house, lying down[3], wrestles with him and defeats him. But he is not completely successful: the enemy gets away with the loss of an arm, and the conqueror has not the satisfaction of showing the corpse. (This detail does not occur in *Samson, Skeggi* or *Gull-Thorir*.)

(5) The hero plunges into the water (*Beowulf, Grettir*); in *Samson* he is plunged, involuntarily. In *Skeggi* and *Gull-Thorir* a rope is used by which the hero gets to the cave behind, without swimming *under* the foss. In *Grettir* a rope is provided for the hero to get back, but he prefers to dive and swim to the cave.

(6) In *Beowulf* the hero is seized by his foe in the water, yet he later enters the cave, apparently free, and renews the attack. In *Samson* the struggle takes place in the water; in the other three versions the battle does not begin till the hero has entered the cave.

(7) In all versions save *Grettir* and *Samson* the hero is so overmatched that without supernatural help he would have been destroyed.

---

[1] But the Icelandic *jǫtunn* is descended from Thor, not from Cain. *Hálfdanar saga Eysteinssonar*, xxvi (ed. Schröder, 1917).

[2] *flóð under foldan*, i.e. the earth and rocks rise above the water. Lawrence compares *bāt under beorge*. I assume that l. 2128 refers to the cave.

[3] On this see Hübener, *England und die Gesittungsgrundlage der europäischen Frühgeschichte*, cap. 3.

In *Beowulf* the enemy has got him down, but through God's help he sees a magic sword upon the wall; he rises up, smites off his foe's head; a gleam of light like the sun is shining in the cave. In *Gull-Thorir* the ray of light is sent in response to an appeal for help; it bemuses the foe and shows the hero where the swords can be found. In *Skeggi* the light is sent in response to a prayer, and itself destroys the foe.

(8) In *Beowulf*, *Grettir* and *Gull-Thorir* the sword which the hero meets below is characterized by its *haft* or *hilt*.

(9) In every case the hero is thought to be slain. The reasons vary: in *Beowulf*, *Grettir* and *Samson* the water is seen to be blood-stained; in *Gull-Thorir* the watchers see a dragon flying with one of the adventurers in his mouth; in *Skeggi* there seem to have been two variant versions, giving different reasons why the watchers desert their post. But in every case the watcher or watchers believe the hero dead: in *Gull-Thorir* they are put out of action by the dragons; in the other versions they[1] depart voluntarily.

(10) There is always gold in the cave, but apparently a curse is upon it. Here the stories branch into two distinct types. *Beowulf*, the Sandhaugar episode of *Grettir* and *Samson* are all tales with a happy ending so far as the cave adventure is concerned; that adventure may, as in the case of *Grettir*, have been fitted into a tragic life-story, but there is nothing to connect the adventure itself with any misfortunes which may befall the hero. In these tales emphasis is always laid upon the hero taking something which links the cave adventure with earlier episodes in the tale—Grendel's head, or the bones of the trolls' victims, or the jewels of the princess. On the other hand, in *Skeggi* and *Gull-Thorir*, the hero carries off a vast gold hoard; but the gold is uncanny, if not actually accursed, and the hero takes it back to the tomb with him. Like the dragon hoard in the latter part of *Beowulf*, the gold is only rescued from the cavern into which it had been taken by an earlier owner, to return to the grave with the hero who rescues it. It remains

"eldum swā unnyt   swā hit ǣror wæs[2]."

(11) But anyway, the hero is not dead *yet*; and his adventure ends with the surprise of the watchers at his unexpected return.

All this seems to confirm the opinion expressed above[3], that it is going too far to speak of *Beowulf* as a version of the "Bear's Son" folk tale. We have now compared *Beowulf* with four analogues, two of which, *Grettir* and *Samson*, are really very close. There are obvious points of resemblance between *Beowulf-Grettir* and the "Bear's Son" tale: a fight in a house followed by a fight underground; the wonderful sword; companions or spectators who leave the hero below. The essential difference remains—the Bear's son rescues princesses in the underworld, and it is *because* they wish to rob him of his princesses that his companions leave him in the lurch. There is nothing of this in *Beowulf*.

[1] In *Beowulf*, of course, only some of them.
[2] *Beowulf*, l. 3168.
[3] pp. 67-8.

Not only is there nothing of this in *Beowulf*, there is nothing of it in any of the other four parallel adventures, in the stories of Grettir, Samson, Gull-Thorir or Skeggi. It is true that in the story of Samson a princess is introduced. She has been spirited from her father's care; the hero comes to the rescue. But here the essential difference comes in between these stories and the "Bear's Son" tale. The hero does *not* find the princess in the cave below. And he has *not* companions who desert him and leave him below *in order to rob him of his princess.*

Despite a general resemblance, the adventure of the hero in the water cave is not the same thing as the "Bear's Son" story. Nevertheless, there *is* a general resemblance. How are we to account for some of the more specific resemblances between certain Icelandic and Norwegian versions of the "Bear's Son" story and the Sandhaugar episode in the *Grettis saga*—such resemblances as the recurrence in both stories of the name Stein for the companion who watches the rope? It may perhaps be, as von Sydow suggests, that an Icelandic version of the "Bear's Son" story has influenced the Sandhaugar episode in the *Grettis saga*[1].

For forty years scholars have also from time to time been comparing the *Beowulf* story with another type of tale—one of the many versions of "The Hand and the Child." In the last year or two this has become the fashionable theory once more. And here again there is, undoubtedly, a general resemblance. There is a struggle in a house which results in the tearing off of a monster's arm, and this is often followed by a pursuit, in the course of which a second encounter takes place. Yet the essential feature of the story is not to be found in *Beowulf* or in any of the variants most nearly allied to *Beowulf*. The essential thing in "The Hand and the Child" is that young children have, in turn, been stolen from a room, year after year, no one knows how. The hero watches, he seizes the arm which comes through a window or chimney to steal the child, and wrenches the arm off. Pursuit is given, and all the children are recovered. Now there is surely a fundamental difference between the story of a monster who,

[1] *Beowulf och Bjarke*, p. 28.

like Grendel, destroys those who remain overnight in the haunted dwelling, and the story of the furtive arm which steals away one child after another, till the hero comes and restores all the children to their parents.

Nevertheless the resemblances in detail have proved sufficient to strike a large number of scholars. The first, I think, to notice the likeness was Laistner[1] in 1889; then Stopford Brooke[2] in 1892, then A. S. Cook[3] in 1899. All three noticed this likeness independently of each other—each compared *Beowulf* with a different, albeit closely related, variant of the "Hand and the Child" story. Then Kittredge[4] in 1903 made an elaborate study of this type of story, noting the likeness to *Beowulf*, but not theorizing further. Brandl[5] noted it again in 1908, and gave a summary of the same version which Laistner had mentioned. The summary is sufficiently striking for a most competent critic[6] to think that the story ought to have been given among the illustrative documents in this book—and I am accordingly giving it in this new edition.

Quite recently (1927) the field has been re-examined by Heinz Dehmer[7]. His essay on Beowulf's Fight with Grendel in the light of the modern study of folk-lore emphasizes again the likeness between *Beowulf* and the "Hand and the Child" story. Dehmer's work is important and should attract attention: it is independent of the work of Kittredge, of which Dehmer does not seem to have been aware. Indeed Kittredge's study has been generally neglected by *Beowulf* students—including myself[8]— to

---

[1] *Das Rätsel der Sphinx*, II, 25. Laistner compares the Icelandic version in Árnason, II, 472, translated by Poestion (34): "Die wesentliche Ähnlichkeit mit dem Grendelabenteuer bedarf keiner Erläuterung."

[2] *History of Early English Literature*, I, 120; Stopford Brooke compares the version in Curtin's *Myths and Folk Lore of Ireland*, p. 270. "I wonder," Stopford Brooke adds, "if the Grendel tale may not be a Celtic story, which in very ancient times became Teutonic."

[3] Herrig's *Archiv*, CIII, 154–6. Cook compares the version in Kennedy's *Legendary Fictions of the Irish Celts*.

[4] Kittredge was making a study of this whole group of stories (*Arthur and Gorlagon* in *Harvard Studies and Notes in Philology and Literature*, VIII, 227 etc.).

[5] *Pauls Grundriss* (2), II, 1, p. 993. Brandl compares the same version as Laistner.

[6] Mr Bruce Dickins (*Times Literary Supplement*, January 12, 1922, p. 26).

[7] *Die Grendelkämpfe Beowulfs im Lichte moderner Märchenforschung* in *Germanisch-Romanische Monatsschrift*, XVI, 202–18 (1928).

[8] *Mea maxima culpa*. I have to thank the editor of *Harvard Studies* for calling my attention to my omission.

our great loss. Kittredge's essay would have supplied Dehmer with additional analogues, and, together with Lawrence's recent book (published about the same time as Dehmer's article), will call, I think, for considerable modification of his arguments. The best examples of the "Hand and the Child" story at present known are Celtic: even when the story is found in an Icelandic folk-tale it is thought to be of Celtic origin. Dehmer's study therefore naturally goes hand in hand with the more elaborate but up to now unpublished researches of von Sydow.

There seem to me to be serious difficulties, but it must remain to be seen how far they can be met when Dehmer and von Sydow state their case more fully. Some of these difficulties I may tentatively suggest.

It is claimed by Dehmer that the story of the daemonic arm, stretched out to grasp some human being, but seized by the hero, and, after a struggle, torn from the shoulder, is a specifically Celtic-Irish form of the Haunted House story[1], and that the essential feature of Beowulf's fight with Grendel is this seizing and tearing off of the arm[2].

The answer to Dehmer, as it seems to me, has been already given by Kittredge[3]:

> "*The Hand and the Child* belongs, obviously enough, to the type of which the adventure of Béowulf with Grendel is the most famous representative. The similarities are striking; but, before one infers historical or literary connection between the Celtic tale and the Anglo-Saxon epic, there are several phenomena to be reckoned with. The child-stealing motive is no part of the *Béowulf*, nor of a Japanese legend which resembles *Béowulf* in the most striking way, nor of an episode in the *Perceval* which should also be compared.... Finally, the loss of the hand and the stealing of the child occur, *in combination*, in a North American Indian tale from California and in the Welsh *mabinogi* of *Pwyll*.... We must put behind us the temptation to genealogize. One fact is clear: the defence of a hall or a hut against the demon that haunts it is a simple theme, to which the theory of 'independent origins' must apply if it ever applies to anything. That the defence should result in the demon's losing his arm seems a not unnatural development: at all events, this feature is found in Ireland, in Wales, in England, in Japan, and in California[4]. The other main

---

[1] p. 208.　　　　　　　　　　　　[2] p. 212.

[3] *Arthur and Gorlagon*, pp. 227–31.

[4] We may compare also the cutting off of the ghoul's leg in Swynnerton, *Indian Nights' Entertainment*, pp. 358–359. The house-haunting goblin in *Jataka*, II, 155 (Cowell, II, 12), is subdued in a more recondite manner. So is the hand that rises from the sea and steals men in the *Peregrinaggio di tre Giovani, Figliuoli del Re di Serendippo*, ed. Gassner, *Erlanger Beiträge*, x, 23–4, 28 ff.; cf.

element in our story—the kidnapping of the children—is too common-place to make any trouble. All manner of uncanny beings are charged with carrying off infants, and everybody knows that the moment of birth, is like the moment of death, is a mysterious time and full of strange peril from the darker powers. The genesis of *The Hand and the Child,* then, is not hard to conjecture. It is an easy combination of two *motifs,* (1) the Defence of the Hall and (2) the Child-stealing Monster, to which...other familiar bits of folk-lore (the Skilful Companions, for instance, and the One-eyed Giant) have associated themselves. The whole, in a highly elaborated form, has become a part of the Finn cycle, and is used to explain how Finn procured his famous dog Bran."

After all, the vast demon arm is found all over the world—as Kittredge pointed out in his note, it had been seen in England within living memory. As to the cutting or rending off of the arm —there are the instances Kittredge quotes: the arm is found in the *Mabinogion*[1] ("after the tumult, behold a claw came through the window into the house and it seized the colt by the mane: then Teirnyon drew his sword and struck off the arm at the elbow"); but it is also found, as York Powell had pointed out, in Japanese legend. A deserted temple near Kiyoto was haunted by a demon. As Watanabe-no-Tsuna approached it, a hand came out of the door and seized him. He slashed off the demon arm and kept it as a trophy; but (and here the resemblance is striking) the demon, in female disguise, rescued the griesly arm[2]. And in the Indian version from California of "The Arm and the Child," the defenders of the child hew off the arm which the ogress has thrust into the house; but she rescues it and runs off with it[3]. And to these examples (quoted by Kittredge) many others might easily be added. In Sicilian story the youngest of three princes has to guard the garden—"at midnight he saw a gigantic arm stretched over the wall, plucking the fruit. He drew his sword, and hewed off the arm[4]." In Russia, the witch puts her arm through the window of a cottage to sprinkle the inmates

the parallels cited by Huth, *Zt. f. vergl. Litteraturgesch.*, N.F., III, 313–14. Cf. also the Demon Hand in Miss Burne, *Shropshire Folk-Lore*, p. 113. In a Greek *märchen* (Hahn, *Griech. u. alban. Märchen*, II, 50) a Hand robs the king's apple-tree; the prince shoots into a cloud and draws blood (cf. Cosquin, *Contes pop. de Lorraine*, I, 12). (Kittredge's note.)

[1] *Pwyll Prince of Dyved* (transl. by Lady Charlotte Guest, Everyman Library, p. 28).

[2] *An English Miscellany presented to Dr Furnivall*, 1901, pp. 395–6. See also Mitford, *Tales of Old Japan.*

[3] This Californian tale is quoted by Curtin in a note to his *Hero Tales of Ireland*, Boston, 1894, p. 557.

[4] Gonzenbach, *Sicilianische Märchen*, Leipzig, 1870, II, 50.

with Death, and the Cossack hews it off[1]. A similar story comes in a ballad from Lithuania: the Plague demon (in the form of a woman) puts her arm through the window to slay her victims—the hero cuts it off[2]. In a medieval Indian story a hero undertakes to watch in the chamber of a princess, all of whose husbands have been slain, night after night. A monster thrusts his arm into the room—the hero hews it off. The arm is kept as a trophy, in a way that really does remind us of *Beowulf*. The similarity of this story to *Beowulf* has quite recently been pointed out by Krappe[3].

Naturally a motive so widespread and so obvious is brought into connection with innumerable stories; and of course it would be possible to take a number of Celtic stories in which a monstrous arm is hewn or torn off, and, by selecting one detail here and another there, to form a Celtic composite which would show a likeness to the *Beowulf* story. But what would that prove? Or, if we limit ourselves to versions of the "Hand and the Child" story, we shall find these versions reminding us of *Beowulf* in various ways—at one time there are adventures in the water, at another a female monster is found which may be held to resemble Grendel's mother. But these likenesses in detail cannot conceal the essential difference between *Beowulf* (which is a story of the purging of a hall from monsters that make it uninhabitable) and "The Hand and the Child" (which is a story of the recovery of kidnapped children).

I do not think that any of these "Hand and the Child" stories show anything like such closeness to *Beowulf* as does that "Bear's Son" story which is quoted by Panzer from a French-Flemish source, and of which an abstract is given above (*Jean l'Ourson*)[4]. To this it has been answered[5] that this version owes its likeness to *Beowulf* to the fact that it is a composite. It has added to the ordinary features of the "Bear's Son" tale two others which are not usually found there, namely that the

[1] Ralston, *Russian Folk Tales*, p. 269.
[2] Wojcicki, K. W., *Polnische Volkssagen und Märchen* (translated by F. H. Lewestam), Berlin, 1839, pp. 61–2.
[3] *Eine mittelalterlich-indische Parallele zum Beowulf*, by A. H. Krappe, in the *Germanisch-Romanische Monatsschrift*, xv, 54–8 (1927).
[4] pp. 378–9.
[5] von Sydow, *Beowulf och Bjarke*, pp. 34–5.

monster is routed with the loss of his *arm*, and that he has a
female as companion in his den. These resemblances to *Beowulf*
are found, one invariably, the other sometimes, in versions of
"The Hand and the Child"—for example in the Icelandic version
quoted below[1]. *Jean l'Ourson*, then, it would seem, attains its
likeness to *Beowulf* by a cunning combination of the "Bear's
Son" story and of features drawn from "The Hand and the
Child" story—the two folk-tales most nearly akin to *Beowulf*.

I am not prepared to dispute that this may well be so: and
it brings us up against a problem which to me appears insoluble.
Folk-tales "consist of but few incidents, grouped together in a
kaleidoscopic variety of arrangements." These shifting com-
binations seem to place us at the mercy of chance.

A warning against hasty deductions is afforded by the
eleventh-century Indian tale in the *Ocean of Story*[2], mentioned
above. Here comes the incident of the hero defending a chamber
and hewing off the monster's arm; subsequently the hero has a
second struggle in which he takes his foe by the hair—again like
Beowulf—though he relents before actually striking off the head.
And between these two adventures is an adventure in the sea,
which reminds us both of the "Bear's Son" story and also of
Beowulf's adventures in the mere and in the ocean. Of course
there are differences. The Indian hero wins and leaves behind
a wife with each adventure, and the story ends with his collecting
them all and setting up housekeeping. But what Krappe's
article had not prepared me for was this. It will be remembered
how Beowulf's ocean adventure terminates with the moralization

"wyrd oft nereþ
unfǣgne eorl   þonne his ellen dēah."

The ocean adventure of the Indian hero leads to exactly the
same moral:

"For even destiny takes the part of men of distinguished valour."

This *can* only be an accident. Yet if there had been some
eleventh-century Celtic document showing equal resemblance,

---

[1] pp. 491–3.
[2] The Ocean of Story, being C. H. Tawney's translation of Somadeva's
Kathā Sarit Sāgara, edited by N. M. Penzer, II, 54–80, *Story of Vidūshaka*.

what theories of influence, this way and that, would have been built upon it. Surely this should be a warning of the tricks which the long arm of coincidence can play. What limit is there to the similarities which similar situations can call forth?

Some limit there must be. When in a version of the "Hand and the Child" the monster who is slain on the ocean colours it with his blood, this reminds us of *Beowulf* or *Grettir*. But the thought is an obvious one. It is a different matter when, in *Beowulf* and *Grettir*, not only is the water stained with the blood of the monster, but also this is observed by the watcher or watchers on the shore, and *interpreted by him or them to signify the hero's death*. Yet even this is a commonplace of story. It is found also in one of the late romantic, invented sagas[1]. And it would be perilous to dogmatize as to how it got there.

But, although the arm of coincidence is as long, and almost as disconcerting, as the arm which the ogre puts through the window, nevertheless no one ventures to suggest that the resemblances between *Beowulf* and the Sandhaugar episode in the *Grettis saga* are a matter of mere coincidence. Every responsible critic is agreed that they cannot be accounted for as stock ideas coming together accidentally in the same order. So, if the arguments put forward above are sound, and prove that the Sandhaugar episode is not derived from *Beowulf*, then it must be an independent version of the same tale. And, granted the existence of this original, then, though the likenesses are not so striking, it would be natural to suppose that the *Samsons saga* and the other tales of waterfall-trolls are connected with it.

To this tale both the "Bear's Son" story and the "Hand and the Child" story show certain resemblances. I do not see that we can say more than that, in the present state of our knowledge. We may, then, stress the "folk-tale" element in *Beowulf*, and see analogies between our poem and this or that among the mass of "Kinder- und Hausmärchen." But this does not mean that the main story of Beowulf's adventures is trivial or childish, nor yet that it belongs to the folk, as opposed to the aristocracy.

---

[1] *Thorsteins saga Vikingssonar*, cap. 23.

Many things, of which traces survive in folk-tale, may have been in earlier days part of the common creed of all classes, or may even have been aristocratic.

Many critics have felt that the story of Beowulf is inferior in human interest to the great stories of the migration period—the tales for instance of Theodoric or of Guthhere. Others have invented a mythology which, by erecting Beowulf into an ancient god, and his adversaries into the personified powers of nature, gives, they feel, dignity to the story. But indeed it does not need any such adventitious dignity. This has been very forcibly argued by Hübener in his recent study of the figure of the exorcizing champion, struggling, like Grettir, with the powers of darkness[1].

[1] "Dietrich von Bern, Günther von Burgund, Giselher, Wittich, Heime und Wieland, alle diese festländischen Sagenhelden haben ihre Spuren auch auf der Insel hinterlassen.—Dass im Beowulf nicht nur ein Stoff vom Rande dieser Sagenwelt überliefert ist, wie man häufig liest, dass wir im Gegenteil durch ihn in das Herz der hinter ihr stehenden geschichtlichen Wirklichkeit geführt werden, möchte ich jetzt näher zu zeigen versuchen." *England und die Gesittungsgrundlage der europäischen Frühgeschichte,* von Gustav Hübener, 1930, pp. 71-2.

CHAPTER IV

THEORIES AS TO THE ORIGIN AND DATE
OF THE POEM

LIEBERMANN; COOK; SCHÜCKING

THERE is a tendency for the dating of *Beowulf* "about 700 A.D." to become a dogma; whereas it is, in truth, only an inference drawn from a large number of data; which data seem, to the majority of present-day students, to agree in pointing in that direction. Still, in these days, when facts of literary history, certified by strong documentary evidence, are constantly being challenged, it is important that we should not go to the other extreme, and treat as a certified fact what is, after all, only an inference.

It is therefore well that we should be reminded that so eminent a *Beowulf* scholar as Schücking does not share the current view. Prof. Schücking has been a leading *Beowulf* "specialist" since the publication of his syntactical studies a quarter of a century ago; to him the veteran Heyne handed over the duties of editorship, which he had carried through so many editions, and Schücking addressed himself to the struggle against the growing monster of "*Beowulf* literature," much in the spirit in which Beowulf came to the help of the veteran Hrothgar. Since then Schücking has carried on the struggle through another five editions. Yet he is no narrow specialist, and his authority over the whole field of English literature lends special weight to his attempt to locate *Beowulf* in time and place within that field.

Schücking's defence[1] (against Liebermann and myself) of his view that *Beowulf* is a poem composed c. 900 at the court of some Christianized Scandinavian monarch in England is therefore of special value. I cannot go into it here in detail. In his criticism of the arguments commonly alleged for the conventional dating

[1] *P.B.B.* XLVII, 293–311 (1923).

c. 700, Schücking is often in the right. Yet it seems to me that
enough reasons are left to compel us, with every reservation and
caution, to adhere to the conventional dating. One example
may suffice.

Liebermann points to the passage where the Frankish king
is called "The Merovingian": now the *fainéant* rule of the
Merovingians continued till 750, when Childeric was deposed.
That a poet about 700 or 730 should refer to the Frankish king
as "the Merovingian," *and expect his audience to understand his
allusion,* is therefore quite in order. Is it equally natural about
900? Five generations of stirring history had passed since the
last inglorious Merovingian faded away. Of course, the *Beowulf*
poet *may* have indulged in a piece of conscious archaism, and
chanced his audience understanding it. But is this likely?

Now to this Schücking makes two answers. Firstly, that the
word Merovingian in this passage is not altogether above suspicion. Yet it is there, in the manuscript, written with more than
usual clearness. I can see no objection to it whatsoever, except
that its presence is one of many arguments against a late date for
Beowulf[1]. Secondly (and this is the vital objection), Schücking
says:

> "I cannot see why this particular name Merovingian should have
> been less intelligible about 900 than the other names of heroes, and,
> above all, of peoples, in *Beowulf.*"

Exactly, that is the crux. *Beowulf* is full of the names of heroes,
nations, and even of families and clans, supposed to be flourishing
in Scandinavia in the days of Hygelac, that is, the early sixth
century: the *Scylfingas, Helmingas, Wǣgmundingas*; and the
poet seems to expect his audience to know all about them. How
are we to account for these allusions, so matter of fact, and, in
the rare cases where we can check them (e.g. *Hetware*) so
accurate? Surely they point to the poem having been written
at a time when the lore brought across from the Continent by
the Angles and Saxons was still vivid in the mind of the poet and
his hearers. And together with this we have the fact, which to
most of us seems very significant, that, where the phonology of
the name enables us to judge (e.g. *Hygelāc*), we find that it must

---

[1] The note by Prof. Klaeber in his new edition of *Beowulf* (1928), pp. 434–5,
seems to me to put the matter beyond any doubt.

have been introduced into England at a very early date—not
brought over by the later Scandinavian invaders of the ninth
century [1].

Hence it is not surprising that some scholars have been convinced, as Chadwick is, that *Beowulf* cannot be later than the
seventh century. Dr Routh, in his *God, Man and Epic Poetry*,
approaching the problem from another point of view, is sure that
"the man who put his soul into *Beowulf* was not, as Klaeber
argues, a Christian in thought and spirit [2]." Yet many of us feel
the exact reverse. One of the wisest things that have ever been
said about *Beowulf* seems to me the sentence of Brandl, "We
cannot remove from *Beowulf* those elements which are not
heathen, without rewriting the whole poem [3]." And it is just
because he feels the Christian spirit of *Beowulf* so very strongly,
that Schücking believes that there must lie behind it more
generations of Christianity than are compatible with the early
date usually attributed to the poem. Yet experience shows that
newly converted heathen often take their Christianity quite as
seriously as later generations do.

To one set of critics the Christianity of *Beowulf* is all on the
surface: "the real vitality of the epic lies in its paganism."
Other critics (I think the majority) would say quite the opposite.
But the quarrel can be settled by the verdict of Prof. Malone:
"In fact, there is vitality enough on both sides [4]." It is just this
which seems to me to point to the Age of Bede rather than the
Age of Alfred. Bede shows us examples of Christianity as complete in their gentleness, humility and charity as any we shall
find in English history. Yet the old pagan heroic ideals were
certainly still alive. The stories of the minstrelsy of Cædmon and
of Aldhelm show us men quite consciously trying to harmonize
the new and the old. The songs of Aldhelm were still remembered
and loved in the days of Alfred, but circumstances had changed.
Bands of ravaging heathen were in conflict with a Christianity
already centuries old.

---

[1] Schücking admits this, though he attaches, as it seems to me, strangely
little importance to it.

[2] II, 79.

[3] *Wer die unheidnischen Elemente aus dem Beowulfepos vollständig entfernen
will, muss es umdichten.* Brandl in *Pauls Grdr.* (2), II, 1, 1003.

[4] *Speculum*, III, 613.

How excellently the Age of Bede would suit the data of *Beowulf* has been demonstrated by the two veteran Anglo-Saxon scholars whom we have recently lost, Cook and Liebermann. Cook in his paper "The Possible Begetter of the Old English *Beowulf* and *Widsith*[1]" suggested the court of King Aldfrith of Northumbria (d. 705) as the place where *Beowulf* originated. In the nature of things proof is impossible, but no one can read Cook's pamphlet without feeling how very well it all fits in. Aldfrith had many qualifications to be a patron of many kinds of literature, as Cook shows. He had studied in Ireland:

> "Bede, in his prose life of Cuthbert (chap. 24), is not very explicit with regard to Aldfrith's place of sojourn, but says he 'was then living as an exile in the Irish islands, in order to gratify his love for literature'; and a little later remarks that 'he had been devoting himself for not a few years ('non paucis antea temporibus') to reading in the regions of the Irish, having endured voluntary exile for his love of wisdom.' These 'regions' and 'islands' of the Irish are rather vague, and might be interpreted to cover Iona for at least part of the time, since Bede always considers that island as belonging to Ireland."

Aldfrith was himself a poet (in the Irish tongue) and a friend of Aldhelm, whom King Alfred later thought the best of all English poets, and of Adamnan. Both dedicated books to him.

Cook's suggestion was quite independent of that of Liebermann[2], who a little earlier had suggested the court of Aldfrith's wife Cuthburg, later Abbess of Wimborne, as the place of origin of *Beowulf*. Here again proof is of course out of the question, but it all seems possible enough.

Beowulf is a poem which stands, like Hervor at the tomb of Angantyr, "between the worlds": it seems natural to place it in the first generations after the Conversion.

---

[1] *Transactions of the Connecticut Academy of Arts and Sciences*, xxv, 281–346 (1922).

[2] Ort und Zeit der Beowulfdichtung, *Nachrichten der königl. Gesellschaft der Wissenschaften zu Göttingen: Phil.-Hist. Kl.* pp. 255–76.

CHAPTER V

ADDITIONAL ANALOGUES TO THE BEOWULF STORY

(i) Two versions of "The Hand and the Child"

KITTREDGE has collected the following Celtic tales in which the story of "The Hand and the Child" plays an important part:

(a) A group in which the story is combined with that of the "Skilful Companions"—the widely-spread motive of the brother specialists who co-operate to recover the stolen children—a theme which has been studied by Theodor Benfey (*Kleinere Schriften*, II, iii, 94–156, *Das Märchen von den "Menschen mit den wunderbaren Eigenschaften," seine Quelle und seine Verbreitung*).

(1) *Feunn MacCüail and the Bent Grey Lad* (a quite different story, to which, however, the story of "The Hand and the Child" is added): D. MacInnes, *Folk and Hero Tales*, 1890, pp. 32–67, in *Waifs and Strays of Celtic Tradition*, Argyllshire, II.

(2) *How Finn kept his children for the big young hero of the ship and how Bran was found:* J. MacDougall, *Folk and Hero Tales*, 1891, pp. 1–16, in *Waifs and Strays*, Argyllshire, III.

(3) *How Fionn found Bran:* J. G. Campbell, *The Fians*, 1891, pp. 204–10, in *Waifs and Strays*, Argyllshire, IV.

(4) *The Queen with the Speckled Dagger:* P. Kennedy, *Legendary Fictions of the Irish Celts*, 1866, pp. 227 etc.

(5) *Fin MacCool, the three giants, and the small men:* Jeremiah Curtin, *Hero Tales of Ireland*, Boston, 1894, pp. 438–62.

(6) *Fin MacCumhail; the seven brothers and the king of France:* J. Curtin, *Myths and Folk Lore of Ireland*, pp. 270–80.

(b) A group in which the child is rescued by a man who has been transformed into a wolf.

(1) *Morraha*, in W. Larminie, *West Irish Folk-Tales and Romances*, 1893, pp. 10–30.

(2) A version recorded by D. O'Foharta in the *Zeitschrift für Celtische Philologie*, I (1897), pp. 477–91.

(3) A version recorded by the Rev. John G. Campbell, of Tiree, in the *Scottish Celtic Review*, I, 61–77.

Two versions of "The Hand and the Child" are known from Iceland. One of these is given in Ritterhaus' *Die Neuisländische Volksmärchen*, Halle, 1902, pp. 44–5. The other is the one known through Jón Árnason's *Íslenzkar Þjóðsögur* and through Poestion's translation: its resemblance to *Beowulf* had already been noticed. Ritterhaus supplies two additional variants of this version, pp. 177–80, 181. All these Icelandic tales are of the "Skilful Companions" type. I give below the version of Jón Árnason, and, as a specimen of the other type, in which the rescuer is a werewolf, an extract from the version recorded by J. G. Campbell of Tiree.

(a) Icelandic Version

From *Íslenzkar þjóðsǫgur og Æfintýri, safnað hefir* Jón Árnason. Leipzig, 1864, vol. II, pp. 472–3.

Uxu nú bræðurnir upp hjá foreldrum sínum, þángað til þeir voru upp komnir. Þá sǫgðust þeir vilja fara burtu úr kotinu og reyna til að framast á ǫðrum stǫðum. Foreldrar þeirra leyfðu þeim það. Lǫgðu þeir nú á stað, og segir ekki af ferðum þeirra, fyrr en þeir koma til kóngsins. Þeir biðja kónginn veturvistar, en segjast vilja fá hana annaðhvort allir, eða einginn. Kóngur sagði, að þeir skyldu fá að vera hjá sèr um veturinn, ef þeir vilji vaka yfir og gæta dætra sinna á jólanóttina. Þeir játa því, og verða nú allir hjá kóngi. En svo stóð á, að kóngur hafði átt fimm dætur. En tvær seinustu jólanæturnar hǫfðu tvær þeirra horfið, sín hvora nótt, úr meyaskemmunni, og var þó vakað yfir þeim. Einginn vissi hvernig þær hefðu horfið, og hvergi fundust þær, þrátt fyrir allar leitir og rannsóknir, sem kóngur hafði látið gjǫra. Þegar bræðurnir vissu, hvernig ástatt var, lètu þeir konúng láta smíða nýa meyaskemmu einstaka sèr, og mjǫg rammgjǫrva. Nú komu jólin. Fóru þá kóngsdæturnar þrjár, sem eptir voru, í skemmuna, og bræðurnir allir fimm. Ætluðu þeir nú að vaka á jólanóttina yfir kóngsdætrunum. En þeir sofnuðu allir, nema hann Velvakandi. Ljós var í skemmuni, og hún harðlæst. Fyrri part nætur sèr Velvakandi, að skugga ber á einn skemmugluggann, og því næst seilist inn hǫnd ógnarlega stór og hrikaleg og yfir rúm einnar kóngsdótturinnar. Þá vekur Velvakandi bræður sína í snatri, og þrífur Velhaldandi í loppuna, sem inn seildist, svo sá gat ekki dregið hana að sèr, sem átti, þó hann streittist við. Kom þá Velhǫggvandi og hjó af hendina við gluggann. Hljóp þá sá frá, sem úti var, og eltu bræðurnir hann. Gat Velsporrekjandi rakið fǫrin. Komu þeir loks að afarbrǫttum hǫmrum, sem einginn komst upp, nema Velbergklifrandi. Hann klifraði upp hamarinn og kastaði festi niður til bræðranna. Dró hann þá svo upp alla. Voru þeir þá staddir við hellismunna stóran. Þeir geingu inn í hann. Þar sáu þeir skessu; hún var grátandi. Þeir spurðu, hvað að henni geingi. Hún var treg til að segja þeim það, en þó gjǫrði hún það á endanum. Sagði hún, að

karlinn sinn hefði í nótt mist aðra hǫndina og því lægi svo illa á
sèr. Þeir báðu hana, að huggast, og bera sig vel; því þeir gætu
læknað karlinn. "En það má einginn horfa á okkur," segja
þeir, "á meðan við erum að lækna, og erum við svo varkárir
með leyndardóm okkar að við bindum alla, sem nærri eru, svo
einginn geti komið að okkur á meðan á lækníngunni stendur;
því þar liggur mikið við." Buðu þeir nú skessunni að lækna karl
hennar undir eins, ef hún leyfði þeim að binda sig. Ekki var
henni um það, en lèt þó til leiðast á endanum. Bundu þeir
skessuna nú rammlega, og geingu svo inn í hellinn til karlsins.
Var hann hið ferlegasta trǫll, og hǫfðu þeir eingar sveiflur á því,
nema drápu hann undir eins. Að því búnu forú þeir til skessun-
nar, og drápu hana.

Translation

[The five brothers receive their names from an old woman, who has
asked and received a drink from them.]

The brothers lived with their parents till they were grown up.
Then they said that they would leave the cottage to push their
fortunes elsewhere: and their parents gave consent. They went
away, and nothing is told of their journey till they came to the
king. They asked the king to be allowed to stay over the winter,
but they said that they wished to stay either all, or none. The
king said that they might stay with him over the winter, if they
would watch over his daughters on Yule-night. They agreed to
that, and so were all with the king.

And so it was, that the king had had five daughters. For two
years past one had disappeared each Yule-night, out of the
Maiden-Bower, although there had been a guard. No one knew
how they had vanished, and nowhere could they be found, for all
the searchings that the king had caused to be made. As soon as
the brothers knew how matters stood, they caused the king to
build a new Maiden-Bower, standing alone, and very strong.
Now Yule came. The three princesses who were left went into
the Bower, and all five brothers: they meant to keep watch over
the princesses, but they all slept except Wideawake. There was
a light in the Bower, and it was fast locked. Early in the night,
Wideawake saw a shadow on the window, and then a terribly

gigantic hand stretched in over the bed of one of the princesses.
Then Wideawake roused his brothers quickly, and Holdfast
seized the paw which was stretched in, so that its owner could
not withdraw it, though he strove hard. Then came Strong-in-
the-Blow, and struck off the hand on the window-ledge. Then
the creature outside sprang away, and the brothers chased him.
Sharp-tracker followed the footsteps. At last they came to some
steep rocks, which no one could climb, except Good-Climber: he
climbed up the rocks and cast a rope down to his brothers, and
so drew them all up. They found themselves by a great mouth
of a cave, and went in. There they saw a troll who was weeping.
They asked what troubled her. She did not wish to tell them,
but in the end she said that her man had lost one hand in the
night, and therefore it was so ill with her. They told her to be
comforted, for they would cure the man. "But no one must look
at us," said they, "whilst we are curing him; and we are so
cautious about our mysteries that we bind all who are near, so
that no one can come about us whilst we are doing the medicine:
for a lot depends upon that." So they offered the troll to cure
her man at once, if she would let them bind her. She had no
fancy for that, but in the end she let them. They bound her fast
and so went into the cave to the man. He was a monstrous troll,
and the brothers did not beat about the bush, but killed him on
the spot. After that they went to the she-troll and killed her.

(b) *Translation of a West Highland Tale*

[Recorded by the Rev. J. G. Campbell of Tiree in the *Scottish Celtic
Review*, 1885, vol. I, p. 76. The Werewolf speaks:]

...When the time came when [the captain's wife] was to be
delivered, they got midwives. She had a male child. When they
had arranged about the woman and child, the midwives slept.
I was lying below the bed; a big hand came in at the roof of the
house; and when I saw the hand coming I sprang and caught
the hand; and the hand took me up to the roof of the house; and
I took the hand from the shoulder off him, and I took it below
the bed; and he put in the other hand, and took the child away.
I ran out after him, and followed him to the shore. There was

snow on the ground, and I followed him by his blood. I saw an island over opposite to me, and I swam to the island. I went into the cave that he had; and he was asleep in the upper part of the cave, and the child under his arm, and the other two children he had taken with him playing on the floor of the cave. I sprang at his throat, and tore his throat for him. He had a little skiff in the island; and I got the two children and the babe put into the skiff and hurried home.

(ii) GULLBRA AND SKEGGI

[From *Íslenzkar þjóðsǫgur og Æfintýri, safnað hefir* Jón Árnason. Leipzig, 1862, vol. I, pp. 148–50.]

...Kallaði hún þá húskarla sína til sín, og skipaði þeim að flytja sig að gljúfri nokkru og renna sèr þar niður. Kvaðst hún liggja vilja þar, er aldrei sæi sól, og aldrei heyrðist klukknahljóð. En svo er háttað gljúfrinu, að það er foss í gili nokkru móti norðri og hellir inn undir. Gljúfrið er afardjúpt og svo iðan undir fossinum. Gullbrá gekk í hellinn og lagðist á gullið. Þegar hún var orðin apturgánga í fossinum, eyddi hún bæ á Gullbrárhjalla; hèldust þar á hjallanum eða í hlíðinni hvorki menn nè skepnur lifandi, er rǫkkva tók; og hefir sauðamonnum jafnan þókt þar reymt síðan; en ǫll apturgánga fór þar af, eptir að kirkja var reist í Hvammi. Þar heitir nú Gullbrárgil og Gullbrárfoss, er Gullbrá lèt færa sig í....

Þess er getið í Kristnisǫgu og víðar, að þá er Þángbrandur prestur fór um Vestfirði, þá kom hann að Hvammi; var máli hans þar illa tekið; húsfreyja kom eigi út, og var inni að blóti; en Skeggi son hennar gjǫrði gabb að þeim Þángbrandi á meðan.

Það er sagt að Skeggi þessi hafi búið leingi í Hvammi og eflt mjǫg heiðinn átrúnað; var hann fjǫlkunnugur sjálfur og ram-heiðinn eins og móðir hans. Þó hafði hann eigi fjǫlkynngi svo mikla að hann gæti haft við apturgaungu Gullbrár. Drap hún opt fyrir honum smalamenn og fè, er það kom á Gullbrárhjalla. Fèll Skeggja þetta illa, því heldur sem honum lèk jafnan hugur á að ná kistu Gullbrár úr fossinum. Sagði hann, eins og satt var, hún væri betur geymd hjá sèr, en hjá henni, dauðum draugnum. Lagði hann á stað einn góðan veðurdag og bjó sig út til að gánga í Gullbrárfoss. Lǫng var leið innar eptir dalnum og var farið að skyggja, er hann kom að fossinum. Húskarlar tveir voru með, og skyldu þeir festum halda. Seig Skeggi í fossinn, og leið ekki á laungu, áður festarmenn heyrðu dýnki mikla, skurk og óhljóð; var svo að heyra, sem harður aðgángur væri undir fossinum. Urðu þeir þá hræddir mjög, og lá við, þeir mundu frá hverfa; en í því gjörði Skeggi þeim bending að draga upp festarnar. Þeir gjörðu það, en í því kista Gullbrár var komin upp á gljúfurbrúnina, varð þeim litið við; sýndist þeim þá allur dalurinn alt neðan frá Hvammi vera í einu báli, lagði logann milli beggja fjallanna. Urðu þeir þá svo hræddir, að þeir stukku frá festunum og kistan hlúnkaði niður aptur í fossinn. Þegar þeir voru komnir niður af hjallanum, sáu þeir eingin venjubrigði, en staðnæmdust þó eigi fyrri en heima. Skeggi kom laungu síðar þjakaður mjög; var hann blár og blóðugur. Ketil mikinn bar hann á handlegg sèr, fullan af gulli; hafði hann fylt hann úr kistu Gullbrár, og lesið sig svo á handvaði upp úr gljúfrinu. Hafði aðgángur þeirra Gullbrár og Skeggja orðið harður og lángur, og ekki hafði Skeggi getað eytt apturgaungu Gullbrár, því aldrei varð Gullbrá verri en eptir þetta; drap hún hvern smalamann af öðrum fyrir Skeggja, og fór svo að lokum, að einginn fèkkst til fjárgæzlu, því þeir voru allir drepnir.

Af Skeggja er það að segja, að hann varð aldrei samur eptir að hann gekk í fossinn, fèkk honum það svo mikils og smalamanna drápið, að hann lagðist í rekkju. En þegar svo var komið, að einginn fèkkst til fjárgæzlu, reis Skeggi úr rekkju einn dag, og gekk til kinda sinna. Leið svo dagurinn og nóttin með, að Skeggi kom eigi heim, en seint næsta dag kom hann heim nær dauða en lífi, því einginn þorði að vitja hans. Bar hann þá kistu Gullbráar á bakinu. Sagði hann, að eigi mundi mein verða framar að apturgaungu hennar, en sjálfur mundi hann lika á eptir fara. Lagðist hann þá aptur, og stóð ekki upp framar. Mælti hann svo fyrir, aður en hann lètzt, að gulli því, sem í katlinum var, skyldi verja til að kaupa fyrir kirkjuvið svo kirkja yrði reist í Hvammi. Sagðist hann í fyrra sinn, er hann gekk í fossinn og tókst á við Gullbrá, hafa heitið a Þór, vin sinn, en hann hafi brugðizt sèr, en in seinna sinn hafi hann, enn þá nauðulegar á vegi staddur, unnið það heit, að leggja fè til kirkjubyggíngar í Hvammi, ef hann frelsaðist úr klóm Gullbrár; við

það kom ljós mikið í glyrnur hennar, svo hann vissi eigi fyrr en
hún var orðin að steini þar niðri i gljúfrinu, og sèzt draugurinn
enn í dag í Gullbrárfossi. Ekki vildi Skeggi að heldur taka trú,
eða láta grafa sig að kirkju í Hvammi, heldur sagði hann svo
fyrir, að hann yrði heygður þar norður í túninu. Var það gjǫrt,
og kista Gullbrár látin undir hǫfuð honum. Er þar nú steinn
mikill, og heitir hann Skeggjasteinn.

Translation of "Gullbra and Skeggi"

Then she called her house-carls to her, and bade them carry
her to a ravine and sink her there. For she said she wished to
rest in a place where the sun could not be seen, nor the sound of
church bells heard. Now in this ravine there is a waterfall in a
chasm, looking to the north, and a cave in the rock behind the
waterfall. The ravine is exceeding deep, and beneath the waterfall is a whirlpool. Gullbra went into the cave, and lay down
upon her gold. After she began to haunt the waterfall, she laid
waste the farmstead at Gullbrarhjalli: there, and on all that
mountain side, neither men or live stock were safe, after dusk.
Shepherds have always looked upon the place, since then, as
haunted: but after a church was built at Hvamm all these
hauntings ceased. The place where Gullbra caused herself to be
put into the river is now called Gullbra's Gill, and Gullbra's
Foss....

It is told in the *Kristnisaga*, and elsewhere, that when the
priest Thangbrand visited the Western Firths, he came to
Hvamm. But there his gospel was ill received: the mistress of
the house would not have it, but remained indoors sacrificing;
and meantime Skeggi her son mocked Thangbrand and those
with him.

This Skeggi is said long to have dwelt at Hvamm, and
mightily to have supported the heathen faith; he was himself a
wizard, and a rank heathen, like his mother. Yet he had no
magic so great that he could resist the hauntings of Gullbra.
That displeased him greatly, and all the more because it was
ever in his mind to get Gullbra's chest of gold from behind the
waterfall. He said (and that was true enough) that the chest
would be better with him than with a dead witch like her. So

one day, when the weather was fine, he essayed to prepare himself to go to Gullbra's Foss. It was a long way up the valley, and it was beginning to get dark when he came to the foss. There were two house-carls with him, and they were to hold the rope. Skeggi went down into the foss, and it was not long before the men by the rope heard a great noise, tumult and din: it sounded as if there was a hard struggle going on under the foss. They were much afraid, and were on the point of running away when Skeggi gave them the sign to pull up the rope. They did so, but at the moment when Gullbra's chest came level with the brink of the ravine, they looked, and it seemed to them as if all the dale, all the way up from Hvamm, was in one blaze, reaching from one mountain side to the other. They were so terrified that they ran from the rope, and the chest fell down with a noise back into the foss. As soon as they were come down from the mountain side they could see nothing out of the common: but still they did not stop till they got home.

Skeggi came much later, utterly exhausted—black and blue and bloodstained. He bore on his arm a great kettle full of gold; he had filled it from Gullbra's chest, and had pulled himself up out of the ravine. Hard and long had been his struggle with Gullbra, but he had not put a stop to Gullbra's hauntings, for she had never been worse than she was after that. She killed first one and then another of Skeggi's shepherds; and the end of it was that no one would undertake to look after his flocks, for they all got killed.

Now of Skeggi it must be said that he was never the same man after he went into the foss; that and the death of his shepherds so shook him that he took to his bed. But when it reached the point that no one would look after his flocks, Skeggi rose up one day, and went to his cattle. The day passed, and the night followed, and Skeggi did not come home; but late next day he came home more dead than alive—no one had dared to search for him. He carried Gullbra's chest on his back. He said that there would be no further trouble from her hauntings, but that he himself was likely to follow her—then he took to his bed, and never rose up again. But before he died he gave orders that the gold in the kettle should be laid out in buying timber so that a

church could be built at Hvamm. He said that the first time he
went into the foss and struggled with Gullbra, he had called
upon Thor, his friend, but Thor had failed him. But the second
time, in yet greater straits, he had vowed to lay out the money
in building a church at Hvamm, if he escaped from the clutches
of Gullbra. With that a great gleam of light shone into her eyes,
and before he knew anything she was turned into stone down
there in the ravine. And the Semblance can still be seen to-day
in Gullbra's Foss.

None the less, Skeggi would not become a Christian, or be
buried in the churchyard at Hvamm; but he gave orders that he
should be buried on the northern side of the meadow round his
house. So it was done, and Gullbra's chest was placed under his
head. There is now a great stone there, and it is called Skeggi's
stone.

(iii) Gull-Thorir

[From the *þorskfirðinga saga*, or *Gull-þóris saga*. *Íslendinga sǫgur,*
Reykjavik, 1897, vol. xvii, pp. 10–13.]

Eftir þat vitkuðust þeir ok vakna; fóru heim síðan. Þeir
sǫgðu Úlfi, hvat fyrir þá hafði borit ok báðu hann vísa sér til
hellis Vals. Úlfr latti þá þeirar ferðar ok bauð þeim fé til at þeir
færi eigi, ok segir engan aftr hafa komit, þann er farit hafði, enn
kvað ilt þykkja, at þeir menn týndist, er Sigmundr vin hans
hafði sent honum. Enn Þórir vill fara fyrir hvern mun, ok litlu
síðar ráðast þeir félagar til ferðar ok fara norðr fyrir Finnmǫrk
þar til er þeir koma norðr fyrir Blesaberg; svá hét fjallit þat er
hellir Vals var í, enn þat er norðr við Dumbshaf; þar fellr á mikil
í gljúfrunum fram af bergi og alt út í sjá. Þórir kendi þá, at þeir
váru þar komnir er honum var til vísat. Þeir fóru á bergit ok
hǫfðu þann umbúnað, er Agnarr hafði kent þeim; hjuggu upp
tré mikit ok færðu limarnar fram af berginu ok báru grjót á
rótina; síðan tóku þeir kaðal ok festu við limarnar. Þá bauð
Þórir fǫrunautum sínum að fara ok hafa fé þat er fengi; enn engi
þeira bar traust til at ná hellinum, þótt engi væri ǫnnur hætta
enn sú, ok báðu þeir hann frá hverfa. Þórir segir: "Eigi mun
nú þat verða; er þat líkast, at ek hætta á ok hafa ek fé skuldlaust
slíkt er fæst." Þeir létust eigi mundu til fjár kalla ok sǫgðu hann

ærit til vinna, ef hann næði. Þeir fundu at Þórir var allr maðr annarr enn hann hafði verit. Þórir fór af klæðum sínum ok gerði sik léttbúinn; hann fór í kyrtilinn Agnarsnaut ok tók glófana, beltit ok knífinn ok línu mjóva, er Agnarr fekk honum; hann hafði snærisspjót, er faðir hans gaf honum; gekk hann svá fram á tréit; þá skaut hann spjótinu yfir ána, ok festi þat öðrum megin árinnar í viðinum; eftir þat fór hann í festina ok lét línuna draga sik af berginu undir forsinn; ok er Ketilbjǫrn sá þat, lézt hann fara vilja með Þóri, ok kvað eitt skyldu yfir þá ganga; ferr hann þá ofan með strenginum. Þórhallr Kinnarson kveðst ok fara vilja, enn Þrándr langi kvað Sigmund þat eigi spyrja skulu, at hann þyrði eigi at fylgja þeim, er hann hafði þó heitit sinni liðveizlu. Þórir var nú kominn í hellinn, ok dró þá til sín hvern er ofan kom. Bergsnǫs nǫkkur gekk fram við sjóinn alt fyrir fossinn ok fóru þeir Bjǫrn Beruson ok Hyrningr þar á fram ok þaðan upp undir forsinn; þeir hǫfðu þar tjald hjá snǫsinni, því at eigi mátti nær vera forsinum fyrir skjálfta ok vatnfalli ok regni. Þeir Þórir tendruðu ljós í hellinum ok gengu þar til er vindi laust í móti þeim ok sloknuðu þá login. Þá hét Þórir á Agnar til liðs, ok þegar kom elding mikil frá hellis-dyrunum, ok gengu þá um stund við þat ljós, þar til er þeir heyrðu blástr til drekanna. Enn jafnskjótt sem eldingin kom yfir drekana, þá sofna þeir allir; enn þá skorti eigi ljós, er lýsti af drekunum ok gulli því, er þeir lágu á. Þeir sáu hvar sverð váru ok kómu upp hjá þeim meðalkaflarnir; þeir Þórir þrifu þá skjótt til sverðanna, ok síðan hlupu þeir yfir drekana ok lǫgðu undir bægsl þeim ok svá til hjartans. Þórir fekk tekit hjálminn af hinum mesta drekanum, ok í þessarri svipan þrífr hinn mesti drekinn Þránd lang ok fló með hann út ór hellinum ok þegar hverr at öðrum ok hraut eldr af munni þeim með miklu eitri. Nú sá þeir er úti váru, at glæddi ór forsinum; þeir hlupu ór tjaldinu, enn drekarnir flugu upp ór forsinum, ok sá þeir Bjǫrn, at einn drekinn hafði mann í munni sér; þóttust þeir þá vita, at allir mundu þeir látnir, er í hellinn hǫfðu farit. Hinn mesti drekinn flaug lengst, sá er mann-inn hafði í munni, ok er þeir flugu upp yfir bergsnǫsina, hljóp hann Bjǫrn þá upp á bergit ok lagði málaspjóti á drekanum. Enn er hann hrepti áverkann, þá hljóp ór sárinu mikit blóð í andlit honum ok fekk hann af því skjótan bana, enn blóðit ok

eitrit kom á fót Hyrningi, ok sló þar í æði-verk, svá at hann
mátti trautt standast. Nú er at segja frá Þóri ok hans félǫgum,
at þeir afla sér mikils fjár í hellinum, svá at þat var margra
manna fullfengi í gulli ok mǫrgum dýrgripum; er svá sagt, at
þeir hafi á þriðja dag verit í Valshelli; þar fann Þórir sverðit
Hornhjalta, er Valr hafði borit. Síðan las Þórir sik fyrstr upp ok
dró upp fé ok þá félaga sína.

TRANSLATION OF EXTRACT FROM THE GULL-ÞÓRIS SAGA

After that they recovered their senses, awoke, and went
home. They told Ulf what had happened, and asked him to guide
them to the cave of Val. Ulf spoke against the journey, and
offered them money not to go, telling them that no one had
returned who had essayed it; and he said that it would be
reckoned an evil thing that those men should be lost, whom
Sigmund his friend had sent to him. But Thorir would in any
wise go; and a little later he and his fellows undertook their
journey, and went north, coasting Finnmark till they came
north over against Blesaberg: for so was the mountain called in
which was the cave of Val. And it is by the Arctic Sea; and there
a mighty river flows through a chasm from the mountain out into
the sea. Then Thorir saw that they had come to the place to
which he had been directed. They went to the mountain and
did as Agnar had told them: they uprooted a great tree and
pushed its branches over the ravine and heaped rocks around its
root; then they took a rope and fastened it to the branches.
Then Thorir bade his companions to go, and each have the
wealth that he took. But none of them dared to venture to the
cave, though that had been the only danger, and they begged
Thorir to turn back. Thorir said, "That cannot now be: it looks
as if I should make the venture and have the wealth encumbered
with few other claimants." They said they would make no
claim on the money, and said he would have enough, if he got it.
They found that Thorir was quite another man from what he
had been. Thorir took off all his spare clothing: he had the kirtle,
gloves, belt and knife, and the slender line which Agnar had
given him; he had the javelin with a thong, which his father had
given him. He went along the tree and hurled his javelin over

the river, and it stuck fast in the wood on the other side. After
that he let himself down by the rope, and let the line pull him
from the cliff, under the foss.

And when Ketilbjorn saw that, he said that he would go with
Thorir and share his luck; then he let himself down with the rope.
Thorhall Kinnarson too said he would go, and Thrand the Tall
said that Sigmund should never learn that he did not dare to
follow those to whom he had promised backing. Thorir had now
reached the cave, and he drew each of the others to him, as they
came from above. A promontory jutted into the lake in front
of the foss; Bjorn Beruson and Hyrning went onto it, and so up
below the foss; they had a tent there on the promontory, for no
one could go near the foss by reason of the spray.

Thorir and his companions kindled a light in the cave, and
went till a wind blew against them and quenched the light.
Then Thorir called on Agnar for help, and at once there came a
great ray of light from the door of the cave, and they went for
a while with the light till they heard the hissing of the dragons.
But as soon as the ray of light reached the dragons they all
slept; and the light did not fail till it lighted up the dragons and
the gold they were lying on. Then they saw where there were
swords with the hilts projecting: then quickly Thorir and his
companions grasped the swords, leapt upon the dragons, and
stabbed them to the heart under the shoulders. Thorir managed
to take the helm from the largest dragon: at the same moment
that dragon seized Thrand the Tall and flew with him out of the
cave; and then each after the other, and fire sprang from their
mouths with much poison. Now those who were outside saw a
glow from the foss; they leapt from the tent, and the dragons
flew up from the foss, and Bjorn saw that one of the dragons had
a man in his mouth; they thought then for certain that all the
men who had gone into the cave must have been killed. The
greatest dragon flew furthest, the one who had the man in his
mouth; and when they flew up over the promontory, Bjorn
rushed up onto the precipice and stabbed that dragon with his
inlaid spear. But when the dragon received the wound, there
rushed from it so much blood into Bjorn's face that he was
killed forthwith; and the blood and poison fell on the foot of

Hyrning, and gave him furious pain, so that he could scarcely stand.

Now it must be told of Thorir and his fellows that they got much wealth in the cave, so that there was booty enough for many men in gold and various treasures; and it is said, that they remained in Val's cave till the third day: there Thorir found the sword Hornhjalti, which Val had borne. Afterwards Thorir hauled himself up first, and then drew up the wealth and his fellows.

(iv) SAMSON

[From the *Samson Fagres saga*, p. 11, in *Nordiska Kämpa Dater*, ed. E. J. Björner, Stockholm, 1737.]

Enn a methann their voru thetta at tala, stoth Samson a brunni vith fossinn, oc toku their nu hondum samann, oc i thvi finnur Samson ei fyrri til, enn tækit var um hans bætha fœtur, oc var honum kipt ofann i fossinn. Er thar kominn ein Trollkona, oc hefur hann ecki afl vith hana, enn thegar hann kemur hondum vith, sviptast thau, oc koma nithur a grunn, oc skilur hann, at hun muni ætla at fœra hann vith grunnit. Oc bryst hann um, oc getur nath tigulknifi, er Valintina Kongs dottir hafthi gefit honum, oc setur hann fyrir hennar briost, oc ristir a henni allann kvithinn, sva at hlaupa innifinn, verthur a inn sem bloth at sia. Er Samson nu buit vith at kafna, verthur hann nu laus oc kafar undir ithuna, finnur hann thar muni hellir nockur, oc skrithur upp undir bergit, er hann nu sva mattdreiginn, at hann verthur nu leingi thar at liggia, athur enn hann mætti sig hræra. Enn er hann rettist vith, vindur hann klæthi sin, enn sithann kannar hann hellirinn, oc ætlar hann at hann muni alldrei komast fyrir hans enda. Oc nu finnur hann einn afhellir, sier hann thar mikinn varning oc marga gotha gripi af gulli oc silfri. Sæng var thar agiæta væn, meth fortialldi oc agiætum blæum. Stag var thar oc knappar af gulli a endunum, thar voru oc abreid morg klæthi. Thar ser hann kyrtil oc mottul Valintinu Kongs dottir, thar sier hann oc hennar diasn, mittisband oc tigulsilgio. Hann tekur her af slikt sem honum syndist, oc geingur sithann hellirinn a enda. Finnur hann nu eina steinhurth, var hun hnigginn aptur enn ecki læst, oc geck hann thar ut, vissi hann tha

ecki hvort hann skylldi fara (snua). Oc a hinum fiortha deigi
thathann fann hann fyrir ser breidar gotur, geck hann tha i
bygthir manna, var honum tha visat til sva at hann fann Finn-
laug Jarl. Jarl fagnathi honum vel, oc spurthi hvorsu honum
hefthi farist, hann sagthi honum af hit liosasta, oc syndi honum
gripina, oc thotti theim likast at hun mundi dauth vera. Litlu
sithar siglir Samson til Irlands, oc fann Garlant Kongs, oc sagthi
honum af sinum ferthum oc synir honum gripina, oc vertha
their a thath sættir, at hun muni dauth vera.

[A translation of this will be found above, pp. 456–7. A
somewhat different text of this passage, from the Reykjavik
edition, with translation, is given in Lawrence's *Beowulf and
Epic Tradition*, pp. 189, 318.]

PART VI

RECENT WORK ON *BEOWULF*
TO 1958

BY

C. L. WRENN

PART VI

RECENT WORK ON *BEOWULF* TO 1958

INTRODUCTION

THE aim of this supplement is to bring together as briefly as possible all the more significant facts, theories and ideas concerned with *Beowulf* which have become known during the quarter of a century which has elapsed since the publication of "Recent Work on *Beowulf* to 1930," which formed the concluding Part V of the second edition of 1932: and at the same time to add a supplement to the bibliography to bring this especially useful feature of the book also as far as possible up to date. In both the survey of recent work and in the supplementary bibliography, however, I have sought to limit myself to those aspects of *Beowulf* and of the stories of Offa and Finn which the late R. W. Chambers chose to treat of, rather than to attempt anything like a survey of the whole field. A purely literary appreciation of the poem, for example, would be out of place in this book. Nor will merely textual criticism, unless it has some wider historical or generally interpretative significance, be dealt with here otherwise than in the bibliography—again following Chambers's practice. For similar reasons the problem of the *Finnsburg Fragment* and its relations with the Finn Episode in *Beowulf* will only be mentioned with brief indications of recent study rather than re-examined. I think it best merely to repeat Chambers's words in the Preface to the second edition: "The fact that I leave that section unaltered does not mean that I am satisfied with it, but that I do not see my way at present to any satisfactory solutions." All the important work on the Finnsburg question has, nevertheless, been included in the bibliography: and I have in fact here gone beyond the limits indicated above, so as to make the supplementary bibliography fairly complete generally, except for literary criticism and "background books."

CHAPTER I

By far the greatest single event in *Beowulf* studies in the period under review was the excavating of the East Anglian king's ship-cenotaph with its treasures almost intact in the summer of 1939. Indeed this may well seem the most important happening since the Icelander Jón Grímur Thorkelin made his transcripts of the *Beowulf* MS. and from them published the first edition of the poem. For by the recognition of the significance of the Sutton Hoo finds has come about the illumination in a truly revolutionary manner of the whole background of the poem—historical, archæological and folkloristic—as well as to some extent the means towards the reassessment of the problem of its genesis. By study of the actual parallels from the Sutton Hoo treasures from the third quarter of the seventh century has been established a historical basis in reality for that loving connoisseurship of material art which used to astonish the critics of this "Dark Age" poem. The swords and helmets, the royal standards, the precious drinking-bowls of *Beowulf* and its harp, have become suddenly vitally related to actual history. The seemingly ambivalent relationships of pagan Germanic and Christian elements in *Beowulf* have become natural and intelligible through their material parallels at Sutton Hoo. The so puzzling and basic position of the Swedes and the Geats of southern Sweden in the poem has become convincingly historical. *Beowulf* is seen, as a result of the Sutton Hoo finds and the immense stimulus to Anglo-Saxon archæological studies they have provided, to be the product of a civilization of the highest then known cultivation, centuries in advance of the rest of Western Europe. The funeral departure of Scyld Scefing (ll. 26 ff.), the hoard of ancient treasures in the dragon's mound with its *maððumsigla fealo* (ll. 2756 ff.), and the account of Beowulf's own funeral rites, all these now may be seen to contain memories of factual traditions not far from living recollection when the poem was composed. It is true that nothing like a full assimilation of the knowledge derived from Sutton Hoo has yet taken place among *Beowulf* scholars: but the way to the new understanding of the poem which its discovery has made ready has clearly been opened in the years since the war of 1939–45 with its inevitable delays.

All works referred to in conveniently abbreviated forms in what follows will be found fully set out in the supplement to the bibliography.

Mr C. W. Phillips, in his vivid article on the Sutton Hoo discoveries which forms chapter VII of Mr Bruce-Mitford's collection of papers on recent archaeological excavations in Britain (1956), has narrated the first facts of this, the greatest Germanic archæological event of the century. On 14 August 1939 there was a coroner's inquest on the whole collection of these treasures, to determine whether they were "treasure trove" and therefore the property of the Crown, or should belong to the finders. In the village hall of Sutton, near to the place of the discovery, a jury of Suffolk men had to determine whether the treasures had been deliberately hidden with a view to later refinding—in which case they were "treasure trove", or had been publicly buried without intention to recover—which would make them the property of the finders. The late Mrs Pretty, owner of the land on which the finds were made, was legally declared the finder. It was decided after full hearing of evidence that the treasures were buried in public with intent of finality—and hence were not "treasure trove", and thus they found their way through the great generosity of Mrs Pretty to their present most satisfactory home in the British Museum: a gift conjecturally valued at some half a million pounds. There can be little doubt that the Crown would have acted as did their owner, had the verdict of the coroner's inquest gone in favour of a royal claim. What is especially interesting for the student of *Beowulf* is that this verdict was directly influenced by the account of the ship-funeral of Scyld Scefing which so remarkably parallels the Sutton Hoo Cenotaph and was clearly a very public affair: and the matter was clinched by a reference to the dragon's hoard in *Beowulf* which again in several respects parallels the East Anglian royal burial-goods. And finally, the disposal of the dragon's hoard (once of course royal property) was explained from *Beowulf,* ll. 3156 ff. Here the absence of any intention to recover in those who had first placed the treasures in the mound as well as in those who took them from the supernatural guardianship of the dragon, became patent:

> Forleton eorla gestreon eorðan healdan,
> gold on greote, þær hit nu gen lifað,
> eldum swa unnyt swa hit æror wæs.   (ll. 3166–8)

Though this public citation of *Beowulf* and its parallels with Sutton Hoo in a court of law might be thought to have drawn the first attention to the light which the one might throw upon the other, it was not till 1948 that an outstanding scholar took especial pains to emphasize the fundamental importance of the new finds for the study of the poem. In his brief article "Sutton Hoo and *Beowulf,*" which appeared in its English version in 1948 (*Antiquity,* XXIII), Professor Sune Lindqvist of Uppsala sketched the kind of evidence which, as he wrote, pointed to the conclusion that "it is obvious that the *rapprochement* that was at once made between the Sutton Hoo burial and the substance of *Beowulf* was fully warranted and rich with possibilities. Everything seems to show that these two documents complement one another admirably. Both become the clearer by the comparison [1]."

Professor Lindqvist showed that, given the date for the Sutton Hoo ship-cenotaph determined on the evidence of the Merovingian gold coins which had fallen from the royal purse as *c.* A.D. 670, the ceremonial public funeral in heathen style implied must have been given to a Christian king. The Church, he thinks, did not strongly discourage rich grave-furnishings: and the two silver spoons with the words *Saulos* and *Paulos* cut on them in Greek majuscules could only be explained as baptismal gifts to symbolize the conversion to Christianity of St Paul described in the Acts of the Apostles, whereby Saul became Paul after the miracle on the road to Damascus. Only a Christian king would

---

[1] *Op. cit.* p. 140. The original Swedish article is in *Fornvännen* for 1948: "Sutton Hoo och *Beowulf.*"

have had such mementos among his family heirlooms—even
though the cruciform designs on the silver bowls, which also
suggest specifically a Christian king, may be paralleled in non-
Christian environments. All now generally agree with the decision of the coroner's inquest that the burial of the funeral
treasures was a public affair. But at such a date an East Anglian
king would almost certainly be Christian, as the silver spoons
imply. Professor Lindqvist suggests that the traces of the corpse
have disappeared entirely, as against an earlier idea that the king
was Æthelhere who, having been drowned at the battle of
Winwæd in 655, had his burial rites without the body. But it
would seem far more probable that a Christian king must have
had in this case a private burial with the proper rites of the
Church, and that the public pagan affair was a concession to a
still strong Germanic family sentiment for the ancient traditions.
A Christian king, whose nobler subjects had only recently been
converted from paganism, received the traditional Germanic
pagan funeral and grave-furnishings, with a ship-cenotaph of the
kind made familiar to archæologists by the Swedish boat-burials
of Uppland.

Professor Lindqvist then points out that some of the ornaments—on the sword and its belt, for instance, seem of distinctively Swedish workmanship; and that the helmet and shield
(heavily reconstructed from their *disjecta membra* by the experts)
are definitely like Swedish work of the early sixth century though·
of far finer and richer quality. While it is generally known that
the large silver dish which bears the hall-mark of the Byzantine
Emperor Anastasius who died in A.D. 518 must have been already
some 150 years old when buried at Sutton Hoo, the added fact
that the helmet and shield too were both foreign and already
nearly as old at inhumation brings the natural suggestion that
these were all something like ancestral heirlooms buried with the
royal warrior along with his newer and more personal treasures
and symbols. Here—to the frequent references to weapons and
armour as ancestral heirlooms in *Beowulf*—I would add especially
for comparison with the Sutton Hoo finds the emphasis in
Beowulf on the fact that parallel treasures in the dragon's hoard
were "drinking-vessels of men of ancient days lacking those who

should polish them and bereft of their trappings," and "many a helmet, old and rust-covered":

> Geseah ða sigehreðig, þa he bi sesse geong,
> magoþegn modig, maððumsigla fealo,
> gold glitinian, grunde getenge,
> wundur on wealle, geond þæs wyrmes denn,
> ealdes uhtflogan, *orcas stondan,*
> *fyrnmanna fatu feormendlease,*
> *hyrstum behrorene*: þær wæs *helm monig*
> *eald ond omig*, earmbeaga fela
> searwum gesæled.   (ll. 2756–64)

It seems then that Beowulf too, like the Sutton Hoo king, was to have been accompanied to another life by ancestral treasures already ancient. Like Sutton Hoo too is the employment of pagan Germanic apparatus in an essentially Christian environment.

At this point Professor Lindqvist begins deliberately to speculate on whether the Sutton Hoo finds might hold the key to the fact that the chief characters and scenes of *Beowulf*—an English poem addressed to an English audience—are Scandinavian. It seems clear that the royal warrior of Sutton Hoo was of the East Anglian family of the *Wuffingas*, as Mr Bruce-Mitford and others have shown[1]: and this is perhaps to be connected with the traces of the figure of a wolf on fragments of the royal staff which survive. For the wolf would be the natural symbol of the Wuffingas or "people of the wolf": and we know from Bede that the East Anglian kings were (W)uffingas. Whether one may link these Wuffingas with the *Wylfingas* of *Beowulf* 471 (the *Wilfingas* of 461) and the *Wulfingas* of *Widsith* 29, it is not yet possible to say[2]. But Professor Lindqvist takes up Mr Bruce-Mitford's suggestion which would connect the *Wehha* of the East Anglian royal genealogy of the ninth-century MS. Cotton Vespasian B 6 with Wihstan (Weohstan), father of Wiglaf, Beowulf's one loyal helper in his last fight. Now the *Wægmundingas*, Wiglaf's tribe, seem to have been originally Swedish: and if this kind of approach proved sound, we should have another and a very important link between the Sutton Hoo

---

[1] "The Sutton Hoo Ship-burial," *Proc. Suffolk Institute of Archæology,* vol. xxv, pt. i, 1949.

[2] On the Wulfingas cf. Kemp Malone's ed. of *Widsith*, pp. 199 ff.

ship-burial and *Beowulf.* One might then possibly regard the poem as having been originally composed as a compliment to a king of the house of the Wuffingas or one related to it by marriage. Like the original Swedish founder of the East Anglian royal family of the Wuffingas, Beowulf had come from Sweden, where the Geatas had their home: and this fact would make his story especially appealing to an aristocracy whose ancestors had come from Sweden. Professor Nerman's argument showing that the royal warrior of the Sutton Hoo cenotaph was a Swedish leader who died in England[1] is rejected because of the English quality of much of the goldsmiths' and gem-craftsmen's work of his treasures, and because such a chief in the third quarter of the seventh century must have been a pagan. The silver spoons, as already remarked, confirm the Christianity of the Sutton Hoo king, it seems clear, despite the arguments of Professor Nerman that the whole nature of the ship-cenotaph requires that he was a pagan. But since Beowulf himself had, as we know from the poem, no surviving family, what more natural than that Wiglaf, the ideally loyal chief member of Beowulf's comitatus, should be the ancestral link remembered in the poem among his East Anglian descendants and their circle?

Professor Lindqvist finds the explanation of the evident confusion in the account of Beowulf's burial between memories of an inhumation such as that of Sutton Hoo and an earlier lay in which Beowulf had been cremated in the older Germanic fashion, in the idea that phenomena like the ship-cenotaph were still remembered as a living or very recent tradition by the poet: "The Christian skald imagined that lavish burials after the fashion of the one still remembered in his own day, at Sutton Hoo, and notions then current such as leaving the grave-goods unburnt in the ground, were the rule in more ancient times too[2]." Wiglaf was, in some sense, a hero of the poem second only to Beowulf himself. If we link him with the Wehha of the royal East Anglian genealogy, he would be a Swede of the royal house of Uppsala from the country from which the Wuffingas had first

---

[1] Birger Nerman, "Sutton Hoo: en svensk Kunga- eller hövdinggrav?" *Fornvännen,* h. 2–3, 1948.
[2] *Op. cit.* p. 139.

come to rule in England. Such speculations as those of Mr Bruce-Mitford and Professor Lindqvist may well lead to the shedding of new light on the date of the composition of *Beowulf* by the Sutton Hoo finds.

In view of the necessity of assuming a Christian king for Sutton Hoo and that this king must have been given his public pagan funeral as nearly as may be to the date of the Merovingian coins found among his grave-goods, Professor Lindqvist is probably right in preferring to regard Æthelwald, Æthelhere's brother, a much more certain Christian who died in the year 663–4, as the royal warrior concerned. This highly probable hypothesis for the time of the Sutton Hoo ship-cenotaph would bring the date of composition of *Beowulf* to something like *c.* 700, which is still frequently accepted.

But the usual assumption of a Northumbrian origin for the poem, based as it is on the fact that Northumbria of the age of Bede was, till the discovery of Sutton Hoo, the only known cultural environment in which so civilized a composition could have developed, now becomes far less compelling. For the astonishingly high standard of material art displayed in the Suffolk treasures—especially the beauty and craftsmanship of the work of goldsmiths and gem-cutters—makes it equally easy to believe in an East Anglian culture which might have produced *Beowulf*: and, as far as the language of the poem is concerned, it could as well have been originally Mercian as Northumbrian.

If my reading of ll. 3156–8 is correct, Beowulf, it may be worth noticing, was given his funeral barrow on just such a headland as has given us the name Sutton Hoo:

> Geworhton ða Wedera leode
> *hleo on hoe*, se wæs heah ond brad,
> wegliðendum wide gesyne[1].

I take the expression *hleo on hoe* to mean "a sheltered place on a headland"; and the *Hoo* of Sutton Hoo is the modern development of O.E. *hoh*, of which *hoe* is the dative singular. At the beginning of the eighth century there would still have been very old men alive who could remember the public event (as affirmed

---

[1] See *Beowulf*, ed. Wrenn, 2nd ed. and supplement.

by the coroner's inquest of 14 August 1939) of the inhumation
of the treasures of the East Anglian king. Whether we accept the
tradition of Nennius that Wehha, Wuffa's father, was the founder
of the royal house[1], or the implication of Bede's narrative that
it was Wuffa himself who did this, it would be a legitimate
inference that there is a real link between *Beowulf* and East
Anglia. Now Rædwald of East Anglia, who died about the year
617, had, as is well known, the title of *Bretwalda* which signified
a very considerable general importance in the England of the
early seventh century: and the Sutton Hoo finds make it
abundantly clear that in the third quarter of this century there
were still men in East Anglia of an outstandingly high cultural
development. Though we have no clear knowledge of culture in
East Anglia at later relevant historical times, there seems no
definite bar to a theory that there was a possible Anglian cultural
environment at the appropriate date comparable to that of
Bede's Northumbria which has hitherto made that country the
most widely accepted place of origin for *Beowulf*.

Nothing is clearly known of the many types within "Mercian"
that must once have existed, nor how far any of them differed
from the East Anglian dialect (of which we know nothing before
the late tenth-century Suffolk charters). *Beowulf*, so far as the
linguistic evidence goes, could have been as well Mercian in its
archetype as Northumbrian: and the reasons for preferring a
Northumbrian origin have been rather "kulturgeschichtlich"
than linguistic. Nor are we in a position definitely to deny the
possibility of an East Anglian origin for the poem, since we cannot
distinguish that kingdom's dialect, in the absence of documents,
from that of other Mercian areas.

Miss Dorothy Whitelock, however, has, in an important little
book, very persuasively though very tentatively suggested the
realm of King Offa of Mercia as the original home of the poem's
composition, at a date near the close of the eighth century[2].
Even so late a date would be less than 150 years after the Sutton
Hoo inhumation. Offa's vast imperium included the whole of
East Anglia in the later part of his reign: and one might therefore

[1] Quoted by Sir Frank Stenton in his *Anglo-Saxon England* (Oxford, 1943),
p. 50.

[2] *The Audience of* Beowulf (Oxford, 1951), pp. 63–4.

look for some East Anglian family connexion of his which would serve to explain the genesis of *Beowulf* as in part a kind of compliment to Offa himself, as well as to the ancient East Anglian royal house of the Wuffingas. The original language of the poem could have been that literary Mercian *koiné* which seems to have been in use in the midlands and south of England at the height of the eighth-century Mercian hegemony[1]. On the other hand, as suggested above, the memories of the Sutton Hoo ship-cenotaph which seem to lie behind the funeral ceremonies described in *Beowulf* would seem to point to an earlier date.

In his latest supplement to his great edition of *Beowulf*, Klaeber decided to restore the much-disputed MS. reading of l. 1382 as *wundini golde*: "it may, after all, be advisable to give *wundini* (instead of *wundnum*) as an archaic instrumental form a place in the text[2]." This form would, of course, then remain the strongest evidence for an early date. Mr Ritchie Girvan, in his valuable lectures on *Beowulf* delivered at University College, London in 1935[3], has strongly argued for an even earlier date near the close of the seventh century: and Professor Dobbie, though putting *wundnum golde* in his text, seems to prefer the "orthodox" date *circa* 700.

While pointing out then the interesting and attractive possibilities of the Sutton Hoo finds throwing light on the date and origin of *Beowulf*, it is still probably wiser to conclude with Professor Dobbie's cautious statement: "The problems of the date and place of writing of *Beowulf* are, therefore, still unsettled, in spite of the erudition which has been brought to bear upon them during the last half-century[4]."

The variety, continuity and assimilative creativeness of Anglo-Saxon culture with its progressive adaptations of pagan elements into Christian contexts, have often been observed. Equally are such features illustrated by the Sutton Hoo finds and by *Beowulf*. The *Beowulf* poet, describing the passing of King Scyld in a manner so strongly reminiscent of the Sutton Hoo

[1] For a valuable though hypothetical discussion of "the Mercian literary dialect" of the eighth century, cf. Dr R. Vleeskruyer's ed. of *The Life of St Chad* (Amsterdam, 1953), pp. 39 ff.
[2] Second Supplement to 3rd edition (1951), p. 467.
[3] *Beowulf and the Seventh Century* (London, 1935).
[4] In his edition of *Beowulf and Judith*, Introduction, p. lvii.

ship-cenotaph, emphasizes the variety and heterogeneity of the
royal treasures:

> Aledon þa leofne þeoden,
> beaga bryttan, on bearm scipes,
> mærne be mæste. *Þær wæs madma fela,*
> *of feorwegum, frætwa gelæded.*   (ll. 34–7)

At Sutton Hoo were found a shield and helmet already old when
buried, of Swedish workmanship, which had undergone some
necessary repairs. Frankish were the gold coins fallen from the
king's purse of exquisite gold and inlaid frame; and Frankish too
were probably some of the settings of the precious stones in gold
ornaments. Byzantine were probably the silver baptismal spoons,
and certainly the large silver dish with the stamp of the Emperor
Anastasius I. Celtic culture had left its mark on the bronze
hanging-bowls; and some of the animal and bird figure-work on
the large gold buckle, itself native English craft, remind us of
the Irish-Latin illuminated figures on such MSS. as the Gospels
at St Gallen in Switzerland. Again, the silver spoons certainly,
and the cruciform designs on silver bowls probably, are Christian.
Yet there are strong pagan elements—apart from the fact that
the whole idea of such a ship-cenotaph is heathen—in the figure
of the stag on the frame of the standard (reminding us of the
name Heorot), and in the "Wodanistic" symbolic sword-dance
apparently figured on the helmet. And yet the bulk of the best
of the goldsmiths' and gem-cutters' work seems clearly to be
native English in origin: and even the seemingly Byzantine
baptismal spoons may be English copying of Greek craftsmanship
in view of the fact that the Greek *l* in *Saulos* is turned the wrong
way round in a way not likely from a native Byzantine worker.

The sheer joy in exquisite fashioning of gold and silver and
the inlaying of precious stones suggested by the buckle and
clasps and epaulets which is communicated as one looks at the
Sutton Hoo treasures so admirably displayed on black velvet in
the British Museum, is paralleled by that loving connoisseurship
of treasure so often illustrated in *Beowulf*. It will be worth while
now to examine more narrowly some of the passages in the poem
which find parallels or explanations in the Sutton Hoo finds, by
way of illustrating the foregoing remarks.

In her article on "Significant Objects at Sutton Hoo" in the Chadwick Memorial Volume of 1950 (pp. 109 ff.), Mrs Martin-Clarke argued convincingly that the iron framework and decorations supporting a figure of a stag were probably a royal standard: and this view has been widely accepted. It has been shown by Professor Karl Hauck in his important paper entitled "Herrschaftszeichen eines Wodanistischen Königtums[1]" that both this Sutton Hoo standard and the helmet and shield designs are in origin *signa sacra* or ritually significant pagan elements in the cult of Woden, who was the especial god of the East Anglian royal house of the Wuffingas or Wulfingas. But at the same time these features of pagan warfare could be specifically Christian symbols—the "Vexilla Regis," the "Shield of Faith" and the "Helmet of Salvation." Thus the cult of Woden—so powerful in ancient Sweden whence the Geatas had come—is linked with Christian transitional art. For instance, too, the royal stag surmounting the standard-holder, which suggests the name Heorot of Hrothgar's hall, could at the same time symbolize the thirsting stag of Psalm 42 and the cult of an ancestral Woden. There could be similarly complex double symbolism in the name Heorot. The royal standard, bringing victory and guarding treasure, is an outstanding feature both of the Sutton Hoo ship-cenotaph and of *Beowulf*. No doubt, like the royal purse whose gold and gem-enchased frame remains, the standard has lost all trace of its gold-embroidered self.

The funeral treasures of King Scyld were waved over by the royal standard in *Beowulf* as at Sutton Hoo:

> Þa gyt hie him asetton *segen gyldenne*
> *heah ofer heafod.* (ll. 47–8)

And again, among the noble treasures with which Hrothgar rewarded Beowulf for his victory over Grendel was the same kind of gold-embroidered standard:

> Forgeaf þa Beowulfe brand Healfdenes
> *segen gyldenne sigores to leane,*
> *hroden hildecumbor,* helm ond byrnan. (ll. 1020–2)

---

[1] Festgabe Anton Ernstberger, *Jahrbuch Nr. 14 für fränkische Landesforschung herausgegeben vom Institut für fränkische Landesforschung an der Universität Erlangen* (1954), pp. 9 ff.

Yet a third time the royal gold-embroidered standard is found in *Beowulf* waving over the treasures buried in the dragon-guarded mound:

> Swylce he siomian geseah *segn eallgylden*
> *heah ofer horde*, hondwundra mæst,
> gelocen leoðocræftum. (ll. 2767–9)

Always the standard seems to be associated with royalty and with the protection of treasure. In *Beowulf* always it is *gylden*, suggesting a gold embroidery which must also have formed the Sutton Hoo standard and its king's purse. In *Beowulf* we are reminded too of that magnificent *opus anglicanum* for which the Anglo-Saxons were later famed, in the description of Hrothgar's hall:

> Goldfag scinon
> web æfter wagum, wundorsiona fela
> secga gehwylcum þara þe on swylc starað. (ll. 994–6)

Of the nature of the helmets in *Beowulf* much has come to light from Sutton Hoo. Five times in the poem the boar is mentioned or implied as a *protective* symbol on the warrior's helmet, just as there are boars over the cheek-guards protecting the eyes on the Sutton Hoo helmet and that in grave 14 at Vendel in Sweden. Compare ll. 303 ff., 1285 ff., 1111–12, 1448 ff., and 1326 ff. Professor Hatto, in his valuable paper "Snake-swords and Boar-helm in *Beowulf*," has shown the true significance of these boar-crests and other similar figures as protective[1]: and with this knowledge it becomes possible at last to interpret rightly ll. 302–5:

> Eoforlic scionon
> ofer hleorbergan: gehroden golde,
> fah ond fyrheard, ferhwearde heold
> guþmod grimmon.

The hitherto puzzling term *walu* in l. 1031 also becomes much clearer after the examination of the reconstructed Sutton Hoo helmet. For this shows traces of that kind of silver wire-work described by Miss Vera Evison in her article on "Early Anglo-Saxon Inlaid Metalwork[2]" (though she expressly excludes the Sutton Hoo helmet as being Swedish): and from the reconstruction we can clearly see that this *wirum bewunden walu* was a

---

[1] *English Studies*, xxxviii, 4 (1957), especially pp. 12 ff.
[2] *The Antiquaries Journal*, xxxv (1955), pp. 20 ff.

tubular hollow ridge of metal extending from the top of the head to the nose, adorned with a delicate decoration of silver wire embroidery.

Professor Hauck has shown the importance of the cult of Woden which ancient Sweden shared with the earlier Anglo-Saxon England: and he has plausibly suggested a connexion between the wolf as Woden's symbol and the royal East Anglian Wuffingas (Wulfingas) who may have been indirectly commemorated in *Beowulf*[1]. He also seeks to bring out the special ritual significance in the ancient Germanic religion of Woden of the sword-dance figured on the Sutton Hoo helmet with Woden himself, with the traditional one eye, as dancer. When this is borne in mind, the traditional phrases of *Beowulf* such as *sweorda gelac* (1040) and *æt ecga gelacum* (1168) are clearly seen to have a cultural inheritance, to be more than mere warlike metaphors, and the depth of poetic meaning is enhanced[2]. Nevertheless, Karl Hauck's valuable emphasis on the Wodanistic inherited substratum in *Beowulf*, as in the Sutton Hoo finds, should not be accepted without some reservations. For instance: while it seems probable that the five-rayed sun-decoration on the Sutton Hoo shield once symbolized the protective power of Woden's shield, one may yet hesitate to accept any ultimate connexion between the phrase *beorht beacen Godes* of *Beowulf*, l. 570, and the shield of the pagan Germanic god[3]. It is also to be remembered that the Sutton Hoo helmet and shield, which seem to have been heirlooms of the East Anglian originally Swedish Wuffingas, were already old when buried, and that these *signa sacra*, like the standard in all probability, were of the early sixth rather than of the mid-seventh century. It is true that these adorned symbols of war could be given a Christian as well as their original pagan connotations through a half-conscious memory of a still significantly attractive Germanic tradition having been, as it were, ingrafted in the new civilization. But certainly the pagan elements in *Beowulf* should never be thought of as conscious or deliberate—whatever may be the case with Sutton Hoo.

For the background to the whole of this matter of the parallels

---

[1] *Op. cit.* p. 51 and footnotes.   [2] Cf. Hauck, *op. cit.* pp. 45 ff.
[3] Hauck, *op. cit.* p. 38 and footnote.

between Sutton Hoo and *Beowulf*, the three volumes edited by
Dr P. E. Schramm on *Herrschaftszeichen und Staatssymbolik*
which form a continuous study by various contributors of the
whole subject from the third to the sixteenth century are invaluable; and from their excellent index many references to
Beowulf can be found[1]. But they treat especially of Sutton Hoo
and *Beowulf* in chapter 6 on "Die eiserne 'Standarte' und das
steinerne 'Szepter.'"

The accustomed collocation of the sound of the harp and the
poetry of the scop is mentioned near the beginning of *Beowulf*:

> þær wæs hearpan sweg,
> swutol sang scopes.   (ll. 89–90)

And the function of the O.E. harp in the recitation of poetry has
been discussed by Professor Pope in his outstanding work *The
Rhythm of Beowulf*[2]. But until the finding of the little harp, later
reconstructed from hundreds of pieces, at Sutton Hoo, no clear
idea of this *hearpan sweg* or *hearpan wynn* could be had[3]. The
account of the scop's recitations on this occasion has often
reminded scholars of Bede's story of the making of the first
poetry of Cædmon: and it is of especial interest that the date of
the inhumation of the Sutton Hoo harp, *c.* 665 as suggested above,
seems to correspond almost exactly with that of Cædmon's first
Hymn as indicated by Bede in the familiar passage in Lib. iv,
Cap. 24, of his *Historia ecclesiastica*. The Sutton Hoo public
funeral inhumation must have taken place at just about the
same time as the poet Cædmon was fearfully watching the
approach of the harp in the convivium or *gebeorscipe*. Though
the tentative reconstruction of this surprisingly small harp from
Sutton Hoo may not entirely satisfy anyone, it certainly goes a
long way to enabling one to form some definite impression of
what kind of an instrument it was that the *Beowulf* scop used
to mark the rhythm of his lays. It has six strings, is made of
maple wood with willow pegs for the strings, and is some 16 in.
tall. Through the kindness of Mr Bruce-Mitford, who had a tape-
recording made, it has been possible for some few of us to hear

---

[1] In *Schriften der Monumenta Germaniae historica*, 13, Stuttgart, 1954, 1955
and 1956.
[2] Pp. 88 ff.   [3] Cf. ll. 2458, 3023, 2107 and 2262.

the reconstructed harp (its sounding-board had to be added) in action accompanying a recitation of Cædmon's *Hymn* by Dr Bessinger of Toronto University, in accordance with the now well-known methods devised by Professor Pope and set forth in his *The Rhythm of Beowulf*. To me the result, though of course based so far as the harp-music was concerned on conjecture not very clearly founded, was convincing as a demonstration of the probable Anglo-Saxon manner of combining harp and voice in recitation, somewhat after the style of the Dalmatian or Serbian ballads as accompanied by the *gusle*[1].

The difficulty with the Sutton Hoo harp is its unexpected smallness. We wonder how so small an instrument could have served as accompaniment and rhythm-keeper to the recitation of exciting verse in a noble hall such as the Heorot of *Beowulf*. Professor Francis Magoun, Jnr., in a note appended to his admirable and exhaustive "Chronological Bibliography of the Sutton Hoo Ship-burial" in *Speculum* for 1954, suggests (it is not certain how seriously) that the little instrument of maple wood might have been a sort of "after-dinner harp": and possibly one should try to imagine Cædmon's companions in their *gebeorscipe* passing round just such an instrument as they took it in turns to *cantare*, or as the O.E. version puts it, *be hearpan singan*. I have sometimes thought that the smallness of the harp might be regarded as an indication that it was merely a symbolic model, which at the same time would be effective practically in a small room when the king himself would use it. It may have been buried with him as symbolizing his proficiency in the art of poetry as a fitting accompaniment to a Germanic king who possessed all the heroic virtues—which included those of the scop. However, in view especially of the fact that the reconstruction of the Sutton Hoo harp, done with the expert aid of the famous musical instrument firm of Dolmetsch, was made from hundreds of little pieces which could not supply a complete instrument, any statement about this, the oldest Germanic harp yet known, must remain almost entirely speculative.

---

[1] For an account of the Sutton Hoo harp see R. L. S. Bruce-Mitford's writings listed in the Bibliography, and particularly his *Archaeological News Letter*, I, 1948.

The Sutton Hoo discoveries, then, have furnished new evidence bearing on the date and genesis of *Beowulf*, clearing away obstacles to the early dating of the poem and affording a possible explanation of why so much Scandinavian subject-matter should appear in an English poem. They have further clarified the blend of Christian and pagan elements in a yet homogeneous work. They have shown that the highly aesthetic approach to treasures in gold and gems and craftsmanship, which appears in *Beowulf* at first sight to be anachronistic, is paralleled at Sutton Hoo: that that joy in such treasures and the power to appreciate them which seemed a sophistication in *Beowulf* shared by its poet with his audience, had already been demonstrated by the craftsmen of East Anglian Rendlesham in the ship-burial of Sutton Hoo. Much light too has been thrown by comparison of the Sutton Hoo objects on the nature of some of the weapons and armour mentioned in *Beowulf*, as well as on the type of harp which must have accompanied its recitation.

CHAPTER II

THE MANUSCRIPT AND THE INTERPRETATION
OF THE TEXT

THE great event in the primary study of the text of *Beowulf* since the second edition of the *Introduction* was the publication of Professor Kemp Malone's *The Thorkelin Transcripts of Beowulf in Facsimile*, in 1951. Not only does this complete set of reproduced photostats of both the transcripts of 1786–7 for the first time make available outside of Copenhagen these indispensable documents, but the editor's very thorough introductory study of the scribal practises and likely errors of each makes it possible to get nearer to understanding the damaged portions of the Cottonian MS. than ever before. The possibility of a new epoch in *Beowulf* textual criticism is thus opened up.

Zupitza's *Autotypes* of the Cotton MS., published in 1882 and the basis of most subsequent editing, had cited Thorkelin's transcripts only when he thought them relevant: their appearance at full length will certainly affect the study of the text profoundly. But Zupitza had also set on foot the generally accepted view that, as he says, "All that is distinct in the facsimile in Fol. 179 has been freshened up by a later hand in the MS." For the first time this really hypothetical view of this damaged leaf was challenged by Sedgefield[1], with the result that more efforts began to be made by editors and commentators to examine the MS. for themselves instead of relying on Zupitza.

In 1938 the application of the newest techniques of scientific photography by Professor A. H. Smith to the so often illegible last folio of *Beowulf* in his study of "The Photography of Manuscripts[2]" resulted in several new and convincing clarifications which resolved some textual problems. Then in 1942 Professor J. C. Pope made outstanding contributions to the reading of this

---

[1] Cf. Zupitza's *Autotypes*, p. 102, with the Preface to Sedgefield's third edition of 1935.

[2] See *London Mediæval Studies*, vol. I, pt. 2, pp. 179 ff. The illustrative photographs are on pp. 199 ff. and plates III to VI.

same last portion by the use of Professor Smith's photographs[1]. Especially important for the interpretation of the subject-matter of the poem is his reading of *Geatisc meowle* in 3150 for Zupitza's *seo* (or *sio*) *geomeowle*. This is accepted into the text by Holthausen (eighth edition of 1948) and by Professor Dobbie as well as by myself, and Klaeber's "Second Supplement" approves.

In his *Studies in the History of Old English Literature*, published in 1953, Mr Kenneth Sisam, who had already done so much for the study of the whole MS., produced a long paper on "The Compilation of the *Beowulf* Manuscript," which gives an important and attractive hypothesis of the matter[2], ending with the suggestion that, "if a cataloguer of those days had to describe it briefly, he might well have called it 'Liber de diversis monstris, anglice.'"

Less directly relevant, but touching on the real foundations of textual study, are Mr Sisam's papers in the same volume on "The Authority of Old English Poetical Manuscripts," and "Dialect Origins of the Earlier Old English Verse[3]." The one pleads for a more courageous judiciary among editors, and the other seriously calls in question the common assumption of the Anglian origins of most Old English poetry merely on the basis of apparently dialectal forms in the late MSS.

The publication in 1957 of Mr N. R. Ker's amazingly accurate and thorough *Catalogue of Manuscripts containing Anglo-Saxon*, in which of course the *Beowulf* MS. is succinctly described in the light of the latest knowledge and provided with a bibliography, is the latest important happening for the student of the MS. as well as for those of related poems and other Old English documents.

In effect six complete editions of *Beowulf* have appeared in this period, all of which in some measure have added to our understanding of the poem. In 1935 Sedgefield's third revised edition, though intended primarily for university students, paid

---

[1] See *The Rhythm of Beowulf*, pp. 232–3. By a printer's lapse apparently he omits in his version l. 3154: *Wælfylla worn, werudes egesan.*

[2] Pp. 65 ff. Cf. his article on the same theme reproduced in this volume from *M.L.R.* XI, 335 ff.

[3] Pp. 29 ff. (reprinted from *R.E.S.* XXII, 257 ff. of 1946); and pp. 119 ff.

special attention to the text, based on a new first-hand examination of the MS., though his many emendations often seem too bold. The next year saw a third and fully revised edition of Klaeber's supremely authoritative and complete version, in which all that was known or conjectured about every aspect of the poem was included. Until the publication of the Variorum edition which Professor Kemp Malone is editing, this must remain the fullest and most accurate presentation of *Beowulf*. In 1941, and again in 1950, Klaeber reprinted his edition, adding respectively a "First" and a "Second Supplement" so as to bring each part of the work up to date. But he could take little note of the Sutton Hoo discoveries. Dr Else von Schaubert's thorough revision of the famous Heyne-Schücking edition of 1940, revised in 1958–9, is the most significant presentation of *Beowulf* since Klaeber: and much of its study of the text—especially on syntactical and semantic matters—is original and important.

The veteran Anglist Ferdinand Holthausen's eighth edition was published in 1948 as far as the mere printing of the text was concerned: but the commentary and other apparatus for this are still in preparation by Professor Matthes of Erlangen since Holthausen's death. This version of the text is, however, important for a number of new and interesting readings and emendations.

In 1953 Professor E. van Kirk Dobbie produced *Beowulf* in the series *The Anglo-Saxon Poetic Records*. Though the plan of the series precluded more than a brief introduction and mainly textual notes and bibliography, his work on the text itself makes valuable contributions to our knowledge and includes reference to everything of significance that had gone before. My own edition, also of 1953 (so that Professor Dobbie and I could not see each other's work till too late for reference), was the first to make some use of the Sutton Hoo ship-burial, attempts a somewhat literary presentation of the poem in its *Introduction*, aims at a very conservative text, and brings forward some few new readings and interpretations. But it is limited by the fact that it was intended especially for university students, as was Sedgefield's. A second edition adds a brief "Supplement" (1958), following the example of Klaeber.

A facsimile of the *Beowulf* MS. is to be included under the editorship of Professor A. H. Smith among the forthcoming volumes of *Early English Manuscripts in Facsimile,* in which the Thorkelin Transcripts have already appeared as noticed above. I think there can be no doubt that the greatest event for the textual historian of *Beowulf* in the period under review has been the publication of the photostats of the Thorkelin transcripts: but the textual study of the poem has also made considerable advances. Since, however, Chambers's *Introduction to Beowulf* did not aim at dealing with textual matters except in their wider implications, I shall not enter into further details, but refer those interested to the bibliography to Part VI. This, following Chambers's practice, includes all the significant work on the text I have encountered. An important event in 1958, it is hoped, will be the publication by the Early English Text Society of a new edition of Zupitza's *Autotypes,* but with entirely new photographs which should in some respects surpass anything now available.

All editions of *Beowulf* save that of Professor Dobbie include the Finnsburg *Fragment*—his version having been included in his *Anglo-Saxon Minor Poems* which forms vol. VI of *The Anglo-Saxon Poetic Records,* published in 1942. Professor Dobbie's *Beowulf and Judith,* vol. IV of the same series but published in 1953, includes a discussion of the Finn Episode of *Beowulf* which takes briefly into account all the work done on the problem of the relationship of the Episode to the *Fragment*: and his notes often throw further light on the interpretation of the Finn *Fragment.*

This chapter must not close without some reference to the two volumes of the late Johannes Hoops of 1932, which together make up well-nigh a complete edition of the poem: his *Kommentar zum Beowulf* and the slim but extremely important *Beowulfstudien.* These have been the foundation for much of the interpretative scholarship on *Beowulf* in the last quarter of a century, and embody much that is new, both in textual criticism, semantics and wider related matters. The *Kommentar* deals with all the principal divisions and passages of the poem; and the *Beowulfstudien*—besides handling some difficult words and phrases— treats of the Sigemund, Finn, Offa and Heathobard episodes.

CHAPTER III

GENESIS, DATE AND STRUCTURE OF *BEOWULF*

THE problem of the genesis of *Beowulf* has continued to attract interest among scholars throughout our period, though it can scarcely be said that any firm conclusions have been established. Even more have questions of structure—often hardly separable from those of origins—received attention: and here the results seem to have far more satisfying value. Less energy has been spent on the date of composition, though, as indicated in the first chapter of this Supplement, new material has come from the Sutton Hoo discoveries which may affect our views both on the date and the place of composition of *Beowulf*. An increasing amount of attention has been given to the primarily literary qualities of the poem.

(i) THE GENESIS OF "BEOWULF"

A new small piece of evidence for the Anglian origin of the poem has been noted by Professor Dorothy Whitelock in her *The Audience of Beowulf* (pp. 47–8). She shows that the Leyden MS. of the *Liber Monstrorum* was copied about A.D. 900 from an English exemplar; and that therefore its forms *Higlacus* and *Hyglacus* for the name of the King of the Geatas are probably the traditional English type. But, as is generally agreed, *Hyglac* would be the normal Anglian form for *Hygelac*: and the metre seems to require this Anglian type in l. 1530b, which I would read as *mæg Hyglaces*[1]. Wilhelm Levison cites an example of the name as *Higlacum* from two early eleventh-century MSS. in his *England and the Continent in the Eighth Century* (Oxford, 1946)[2]. These MSS. seem to be of Northern origin.

The general effect of recent work has been to widen the scope of hypothesis concerning the genesis of *Beowulf*. At the same time views based originally on the hypothetical suggestions of

---

[1] Cf. *Beowulf*, ed. Wrenn, p. 48 on the form, and p. 17 on the metre.
[2] Incipit epistola...ad *Higlacum* Lectorem et Presbiterum (p. 297).

books in themselves good, which had tended imperceptibly to become almost established dogmas, have been reconsidered and made less secure. The placing, for instance, of *Beowulf* in Northumbria of the age of Bede with a date *c.* 700 has been called in question. The general trend of thought is implied in Professor James Hulbert's article "The Genesis of *Beowulf*: a Caveat" of 1951[1], which demands caution and rethinking in again examining the whole matter. In the same year Professor Dorothy Whitelock's *The Audience of Beowulf* argued that we should not accept Bede's Northumbria merely because that seemed to be the only place which could furnish the proper cultural context for the composition of so highly sophisticated and civilized a poem. We might suppose any other part of England throughout the eighth century, she thinks, to have produced *Beowulf* if we could recover enough historical evidence. While she would concur in the usual rejection of Professor Schücking's hypothesis that *Beowulf* was written for the sons of a king of a Danish area at the turn of the ninth to tenth centuries because on internal evidence the poem must be pre-Viking in view of its attitude to the Danes, she would regard any date and place prior to *c.* 835 as possible[2]. In view of the importance of Offa in the poem, she would not reject Earle's old idea of the court of Offa of Mercia as the place of origin, since late in the eighth century is not too late, and a Mercian home is quite as possible as a Northumbrian. She emphasizes effectively evidence that *Beowulf* was made for a Christian audience who, though lay, had enough specifically Christian education to appreciate and understand Biblical allusions and even Patristic expressions—an audience therefore removed some distance in time from the conversion of their country to Christianity. In the first chapter of this supplement reasons for thinking that the Sutton Hoo ship-burial might still have been within the living memory of aged people at the time of the composition of *Beowulf* were given: but Professor Whitelock does not find these convincing. She would, however, I imagine, not rule out the possibility of connecting the poem with the East Anglian royal

---

[1] *Pub. Mod. Lang. Assoc. Amer.* LXVI.
[2] See "Wann entstand der *Beowulf?*", *P.B.B.* XLII of 1917: and cf. pp. 322 ff. of the present work.

family—whether directly or indirectly—referred to there. It may be added that Dr R. Vleeskruyer's hypothesis of an important Mercian literary culture and dialect throughout the eighth century[1] would strengthen a Mercian genesis for *Beowulf*.

Professor Francis Magoun, Jnr., in an important paper in *Speculum* for 1953[2], initiates a new investigation of oral tradition with its mnemonic formulae as an important factor in the growth of *Beowulf*. Two years earlier Dr L. J. Peters of Tulane University, New Orleans, had tried to show that much of the apparent echoing of *Beowulf* by the poet of *Andreas* was in fact the repetition of originally oral formulae shared by all Old English heroic poetry, especially in its earlier stages. But the amount of "oral-formulaic formulae" in the poem would not easily serve for a criterion as to date and place of origin[3].

The attempt to reconstruct the development of *Beowulf* long ago suggested by Müllenhoff's famous *Liedertheorie* was taken up in a large way by Walter Berendsohn in his elaborate work *Zur Vorgeschichte des Beowulf* (Copenhagen, 1935). He constructs a scheme dividing the work into its original elements and heroic lays, additions of extraneous material which came in later, and the final composite result. And though his work is very speculative and depends considerably on the usual assumption of *c.* 700 as the date of the making of *Beowulf*, he has supplied much valuable material on the relationships of the poem with Scandinavian heroic tales such as those of Hrolf Kraki and Bothvar Bjarki. But the difficulty in all such attempts to make a pre-history of the poem, as we have it, is that they must of necessity be hypothetical, and yet their hypotheses cannot easily be provided with tests or verifications.

Little beyond speculation, indeed, has come to the fore on the origins of *Beowulf*. The reconsiderations suggested by Professor Whitelock leave us with anywhere in England for the place of composition: nor has new light come on just how the poem grew up. But the inclination towards Mercia rather than

---

[1] See *The Life of St Chad, an Old English Homily* (Amsterdam, 1953). The section entitled "The Mercian Literary Dialect" is on pp. 39–62.

[2] "Oral-formulaic Character of Anglo-Saxon Narrative Poetry" (pp. 446 ff.).

[3] See L. J. Peters, "The Relationship of the Old English *Andreas* to *Beowulf*," *Pub. Mod. Lang. Assoc. Amer.* LXVI (1951).

Northumbria has been somewhat strengthened. A West Mercian origin finds some support in links between some forms of the MS. and the Vespasian Psalter Gloss[1]: while considerations discussed in the first chapter of this supplement might seem to make an East Anglian origin possible—especially in view of the seaboard of East Anglia as against the absence of a coast for West Mercia. If a later date is now thought by some to be feasible despite the cultural and historical considerations which formerly made Northumbria of the age of Bede the favourite, both East and West Mercia were part of King Offa's imperium. But it cannot be said that the "orthodox" view, though it has been seriously called in question, has been displaced.

One of the most interesting speculations—in view of the as yet little explored importance of Irish cultural influences in Old English poetry—is the suggestion by Professor James Carney of the Dublin Institute for Advanced Studies of an Irish origin for much of the *Beowulf* story, in his *Studies in Irish Literature and History* (Dublin, 1955). For the effect of his speculations might be to place the composition of *Beowulf* in some community such as that of Iona of the early eighth century, which contained English-Irish bilingual elements[2].

(ii) THE DATE OF "BEOWULF"

A good deal has already been said in the chapter on "Sutton Hoo and *Beowulf*" on the problem of the date of composition. The general effect of the Sutton Hoo finds might be thought to strengthen the position of those who favour a date not later than the early eighth century. On the other hand, Professor Schücking has never changed his view that the poem was made for a Danish court in England *c.* 900: and the weight of his cultural studies of the poem makes it seem unwise to dismiss this finally, though he has found no acceptance, I think, in England. Professor Whitelock discusses the question of the date of *Beowulf* at some length in her *The Audience of Beowulf*[3], as noticed above,

---

[1] Cf. *Beowulf*, ed. Wrenn, pp. 37 ff.
[2] See especially his chapter on "The Irish Elements in *Beowulf*" (pp. 77 ff.). "The picture of the author is completed by the evidence in favour of his having known a tale (*Táin bó Fraích*) in the written Irish vernacular, and it is almost a necessary conclusion that he was bilingual in Irish and Anglo-Saxon" (p. 86).
[3] Especially pp. 22 ff.

emphasizing the possibility of a date as late as the close of the eighth century. She stresses too the importance of the fact that Offa of Mercia is so highly praised in *Beowulf* as well as in the related and probably originally Mercian poem *Widsith*. Like her, Professor Tolkien, in his most influential British Academy lecture "*Beowulf*, the Monsters and the Critics," emphasizes that *Beowulf* was made for a Christian audience whose Christian knowledge was well established; and he also implies that the poet was able to assume in them familiarity with earlier Old English Christian poetry[1]. If say fifty years is allowed for the Cædmonian kind of poetry to have become established, *Beowulf* could not well be dated before the end of the first quarter of the eighth century. On the other hand, if we accept it as true that *Beowulf* influenced the Cynewulf type of poetry, usually placed in the late eighth or early ninth centuries, composition in the reign of Offa the Mercian (who died in 796) would still not be excluded.

The phrase *wundini golde* of l. 1382, noticed in the first chapter of this supplement, is thought by some to be a barrier against a date later than *c.* 750: but its authenticity has been doubted by some very competent scholars such as Mr Sisam, though hesitatingly accepted by Klaeber in his latest supplement to his edition. The promise of the attempt to link the date of composition with evidence from dialect, like that to settle the place of origin on linguistic grounds, has been considerably decreased by the arguments brought forward by Mr Sisam in his "Dialect Origins of the Earlier Old English Verse[2]."

One champion of an early date, however, has had considerable influence: namely Professor Ritchie Girvan in his *Beowulf and the Seventh Century*. These lectures, delivered at University College, London, in 1935, treat of *Beowulf* from the point of view of its language, background, and its content of folk-tale and history: and point vigorously to a date at the end of the seventh century and no later. It would appear from his discussion of the genesis of *Beowulf* sixteen years later in his "The Mediæval Poet and his Public[3]" that he has not changed his mind.

The importance of making proper use of historical method in

[1] See *Proc. of the Brit. Academy*, XXII (1936).
[2] *Studies in the History of Old English Literature*, pp. 119 ff.
[3] In *English Studies Today*, ed. C. L. Wrenn and G. Bullough (Oxford, 1951).

approaching the problem has been well brought out by Professor Whitelock in her paper "Anglo-Saxon Poetry and the Historian" of 1949[1]: while Mr Sisam has shown how unsafe it would be to base any arguments on Anglo-Saxon royal genealogies in his British Academy lecture of 1953[2].

(iii) The Structure of "Beowulf"

Discussion of the structure of the poem has been more fruitful, but has tended to deal rather in literary criticism (which has no place in the present work) than with matters simply of construction. All seem to have accepted the unity of the work, save only Mr T. M. Gang, who will be mentioned later. The general tone of most of the writing is fairly indicated by the opening of Mr J. N. L. O'Loughlin's paper of 1952 entitled "*Beowulf*—its Unity and Purpose[3]": "The object of the following discussion is to demonstrate that, on a level very significant to the author and his audience, but not so significant to the modern reader, *Beowulf* is a homogeneous unity, and, as a corollary to this, that this unity is implicit in the purpose of the poem."

The defence of the structure of *Beowulf* as a great Christian heroic poem was brilliantly taken up in 1936 by Professor J. R. R. Tolkien in his Israel Gollancz British Academy lecture (with appendix) already mentioned. The following quotations (pp. 29–33) indicate Professor Tolkien's point of view:

> "It [*Beowulf*] is essentially a balance, an opposition between ends and beginnings. In its simplest terms it is a contrasted description of two moments in a great life, rising and setting; an elaboration of the ancient and intensely moving contrast between youth and age, first achievement and final death. It is divided in consequence into two opposed portions, different in matter, manner, and length: *A* from 1 to 2199 (including an exordium of 52 lines; *B* from 2200 to 3182 (the end)....This simple and *static* structure, solid and strong, is in each part much diversified, and capable of enduring this treatment.... But the only serious weakness, or apparent weakness, is the long recapitulation: the report of Beowulf to Hygelac....Judgement of the theme goes astray through considering it as the narrative handling of a plot: and it seems to halt and stumble....We have none the less in *Beowulf* a method and structure that within the limits of the verse-kind approaches rather to sculpture or painting. It is a composition not a

---

[1] *Trans. of the Royal Historical Soc.* Fourth Ser., xxx, xxxi.
[2] "Anglo-Saxon Royal Genealogies," in *Proc. Brit. Acad.* xxxix.
[3] *Med. Æv.* xxi, 1 ff.

tune....No terms borrowed from Greek or Latin literature exactly fit: there is no reason why they should. Though if we must have a term, we should choose rather 'elegy'. It is an heroic-elegiac poem: and in a sense all its first 3136 lines are the prelude to a dirge:

> Him ða gegiredan Geata leode
> ad on eorðan unwaclicne:

one of the most moving ever written."

Professor Tolkien would reject emphatically the common view that the monsters of the poem are peripheral, regarding them rather as essential, and in some sense symbolical of the forces of darkness. He does, however, express doubts as to the genuineness of the three passages often suspected of being later additions: ll. 168–9, 181–8, and 1740–60.

In a very lively paper in 1952, Mr T. M. Gang proposed[1] "Approaches to *Beowulf*" which seek to rebut Professor Tolkien's view of the Grendel and his mother part of the poem as forming a structural unity with the dragon-fight. Especially would he deny the symbolic and universal significance of the dragon as a power of evil which has been implied. In effect Mr Gang finds the approach to the discussion of the monsters as essential to the concept and structure of *Beowulf* too subjective and based in part on a modern literary attitude. He decides that

> "If these criticisms are just, then Professor Tolkien's account of the structure of the poem loses some of its force, since it is based on the view that the two parts of the poem are basically akin, representing two aspects of the same struggle. It could, on the other hand, be argued that the poet must have realized that there was no real *connexion* between them, only a certain similarity, and that the long recapitulation of the poem is his not altogether successful means of linking the two." (*Loc. cit.* p. 8.)

The idea of the dragon, it is pointed out, is merely that of the usual Germanic monster who dwells in a barrow and guards treasure: and the tragic motive is provided by the fact that the treasure has a curse upon it which its rifling brings on Beowulf himself. Whereas Grendel, descendant of the race of Cain, may symbolize evil from the devil, the dragon is merely provoked to deeds of slaughter and plunder by the frustration of his guardianship of the treasure.

---

[1] *R.E.S.* New Ser. III, 1 ff.

Professor Tolkien's view has since been very widely taken for granted, and his interpretation of the poem is commonly thought, as Chambers said of it, "the finest appreciation that has yet been written of our finest Old English poem[1]." But there has, as Mr Gang says, been very little discussion in print of the structure from this point of view; and his strictures may well suggest further examination.

Professor Tolkien's view of the structure of *Beowulf* is whole-heartedly accepted by Professor Adrien Bonjour in his important study *The Digressions in Beowulf,* published in 1950 though written some six years earlier. His aim is to apply an "artistic criterion" to the problem of the relationship of the episodes and digressions to the structure of the poem. He seeks to demonstrate that, if *Beowulf* is considered primarily as an artistic conception, it will be found that every episode and digression has its deliberate place of artistic relevance to the structure. He examines each and shows that it contributes something of artistic value to the whole. "The results of this inquiry now allow us to draw the important conclusion that each digression brings its distinct contribution to the organic structure and the artistic value of the poem. In other words, we have found that all of them, though in different degrees, are artistically justified." By means of such devices as emphasis by parallel happenings, contrasts, tragic "ironic" anticipation, the poet uses the digressions of Sigemund, the fight at Finnsburg and the account of the feud between Danes and Heathobards to heighten the tension, to suggest an atmosphere of impending tragedy, or to increase the depth of poetic meaning by breadth of perspective[2]. Professor Bonjour's work has not yet received as much attention as it deserves, and its main thesis should be further explored, though many may disagree with some of its detailed arguments.

On the style and tone of *Beowulf* considered especially on the basis of Professor Tolkien's view of the poem, Joan Blomfield (now Mrs Turville-Petre) has followed somewhat similar lines of thought in her short paper of 1938 on "The Style and Structure

[1] See his Review of Professor Tolkien's lecture in *M.L.R.* xxxiii, 272–3 (1938).

[2] See *The Digressions in Beowulf* published for the Society for the Study of Mediæval Languages and Literature by Basil Blackwell: Oxford, 1950.

of Beowulf[1]." In this she seeks to illustrate and clarify the nature of the structure of *Beowulf* by an examination of certain features of its style. In my edition of the poem I have somewhat elaborated on the structure of *Beowulf* on the basis of the work of Professors Tolkien and Bonjour[2].

The matter of the episodes of Finn and of Offa I shall deal with in the next chapter.

A valuable contribution to the general interpretation of the poem, largely along lines suggested by Professor Tolkien's lecture, is made by Professor Herbert Wright in an essay whose title sufficiently indicates its tenour: "Good and Evil: Light and Darkness: Joy and Sorrow in *Beowulf*" (*R.E.S.* New Ser. VIII of 1958). Here, incidentally, Mr Gang's strictures on the dragon's place in the structure of *Beowulf* are answered. Mr K. Sisam has just provided a remarkably realistic approach to the dragon-fight by a detailed examination of the text, in which he seeks to view the combat exactly as an Anglo-Saxon audience would have done. This close scrutiny of "Beowulf's Fight with the Dragon" (*R.E.S.* New Ser. VIII of 1958), as a careful effort to return to realism in the criticism of *Beowulf*, may well prove to mark an important development. The structure of the poem considered as primarily an exposition of its hero, generally in sympathy with the Tolkinian attitude, has just been considered (1958) in an essay entitled "The Trials of the Epic Hero in *Beowulf*" (*Pub. Mod. Lang. Assoc. Amer.* LXXIII) by Professor Peter Fisher. Here again the structural relevance of the dragon-fight is emphasized, along with parallels between it and Beowulf's two earlier fights.

[1] In *R.E.S.* XIV, 396 ff.
[2] See *Beowulf*, ed. Wrenn, pp. 70 ff.

CHAPTER IV

HISTORICAL AND LEGENDARY MATTERS

THE period under review has produced almost infinite variety of speculations on the historical matter in the poem as well as on its legends and folklore elements; and it has become increasingly difficult to draw a line between history and legend. Some few more solid results have, however, been achieved. Especially have the discoveries at Sutton Hoo, as indicated in the first chapter of this supplement, shed new and often clear light on the historical background of the poem, on the nature of some of its weapons, and on what one might call its cultural milieu. The discovery, noticed in the last chapter, that the *Liber Monstrorum*, a primary document for Hygelac, was probably of English Anglian origin, throws light on the English interest in the Geats; and the appearance in its Leyden MS. of the proper Anglian form of Hygelac as HIGLAC(US) and HYGLAC(US) emphasizes the authenticity of an English historical tradition of Hygelac himself.

Professor Ritchie Girvan has provided a possible historical background for the poem at the close of the seventh century in his *Beowulf and the Seventh Century* of 1935[1], while on the other hand Professor Dorothy Whitelock's *The Audience of Beowulf*[2] offers well-documented arguments tentatively supporting the late eighth-century empire of King Offa of Mercia as providing the appropriate historical and cultural milieu for the composition of the poem. Professor Girvan, by means of an amusing comparison with the story of King Richard I of England in medieval romance, has suggested that, after all, Beowulf himself need not necessarily be dismissed as a historical person solely on the ground of his preternatural deeds. As he says, if the miraculous adventures of King Richard—far more fantastic than those of Beowulf—were to be considered along this line of strict historical discipline, "the inference should surely be that there was no Richard, that he is a figure foisted into the Plantagenet dynasty[3]."

---

[1] See lectures II and III.   [2] See especially pp. 57 ff.   [3] *Op. cit.* p. 76.

Far more important, the Sutton Hoo finds have gone a long way towards explaining how an Anglo-Saxon poet and his audience should have had so marked and profound an interest in the apparently almost entirely Scandinavian subject-matter of *Beowulf*. On the whole, I think it may be fairly said that recent work on the history and legends in *Beowulf* has tended to strengthen the impression of the "Englishness" of it all, and to enlarge the scope of its possibilities in actual history.

In his Israel Gollancz British Academy Lecture of 1940 on the fight at Finnsburg, Professor Girvan sought to revive the old idea that the *Eotan* or *Eote* (the nominative form does not appear in *Beowulf*) should properly be identified with the followers of Hnæf[1]: and from this it would, I think, follow that they were of the historical Jutes afterwards led to Britain by the historical Hengest. Now this hypothesis does, as Professor Dobbie notices, enable one to identify the Hengest of the Finn episode of *Beowulf* and the Finnsburg *Fragment* with the Hengest of history. Unfortunately I have discussed this view not unsympathetically in my edition of *Beowulf* unwittingly at the same time that it was being rejected emphatically and without space for argument by Professor Dobbie[2].

(i) DOCUMENTS

Since this book was written, a new edition of Saxo Grammaticus' *Gesta Danorum* of the highest quality has been appearing from Copenhagen: the Latin text edited by J. Olrik and H. Ræder was published in 1931, and the Index Verborum edited by Professor Franz Blatt came out in parts (1937, 1948, 1957). An Introduction is promised from Professor Blatt shortly. This now clearly becomes the most authoritative and reliable text of this necessary companion to *Beowulf* studies[3]: but it did not seem desirable to revise the extracts from Saxo in Part II as the changes would not have affected the substance.

---

[1] *Proc. of the Brit. Academy*, XXVI, 352–3.
[2] Cf. his *Beowulf and Judith*, pp. xlix–l with my ed. of *Beowulf*, pp. 51–3.
[3] Saxonis Gesta Danorum...recognoverunt et ediderunt J. Olrik & H. Ræder: Tomus I textum continens, Hauniæ: apud Librarios Levin & Munksgaard, MCMXXXI. Tomus II indicem verborum conficiendum curavit Franz Blatt, 1937, 1957.

It is, however, worth while to add to the material on the Offa-saga the following extract from the *Annales Ryenses*, a Danish Latin chronicle of the end of the thirteenth century dealing with *Uffo* (*Offa*), quoted by Klaeber in the third edition of his *Beowulf* (p. 262):

"UFFO STARKE. Iste, a septimo ætatis anno, usque ad trigesimum, noluit loqui: quousque in loco qui adhuc Kunengikamp dicitur, super *Eydoram*, cum filio regis Teutonicorum et meliore pugile totius Teutoniæ solus certans, ambos occidit."

This is one more Danish reference to the youthful dumbness of Offa and a great single combat near the river Eider by which he saved his country: and there can be little doubt that these versions are derived from importations from Britain—the result of the close intercourse between English and Danish religious houses in the eleventh and twelfth centuries[1]. Clearly the English original of this story must lie behind the account in *Widsith* of Offa's triumph *bi Fifeldore*. This extract again reminds us of the folk-tradition so widespread of Offa's dumbness or sluggishness in youth as contrasted with his growth in an instant into a mighty hero who alone saved his people. This is the story which the English poet applied by way of heightening the glory of his hero in ll. 2183 ff.

(ii) OFFA AND HIS QUEEN

To the historian, as well as to the student of *Beowulf* as a poem, the episode of Offa and his queen beginning at l. 1931 b is of very special interest. If we omit the tenuously hypothetical connexion of the Hengest of the Finn episode with English history and the occurrence of the name Finn in genealogies[2], the Continental Anglian Offa of the fourth century is the one certain link of the poem with English history, since this Offa was the ancestor of the famous King Offa of Mercia (757–96) and he alone of Beowulf personages is mentioned in the ninth-century Mercian royal genealogy. There must have been good reason for bringing into the poem the story of the Angle queen whose savageness before her marriage to Offa contrasts so markedly with the excellence of Hygelac's queen Hygd. Still more com-

[1] Cf. Professor Whitelock's *The Audience of Beowulf*, pp. 61–2.
[2] See pp. 199–200.

pelling must have been the motive which caused the poet to
hurry on so quickly to the extolling of the virtues of her husband
Offa. The audience must have been familiar with both the tale
of the froward young Angle queen and with her husband as a
great hero. But they must have been especially interested in this
ancestor of the Mercian royal line if *Beowulf* was composed at
any time during the eighth century, or indeed a little earlier.
As Professor Whitelock has remarked, the high praise given to
this Offa in *Beowulf* is most striking:

> Forðam Offa wæs
> geofum ond guðum, garcene man,
> wide geweorðod, wisdome heold
> eðel sinne.   (ll. 1957–60)

The same kind of praise of Offa appears in the probably Mercian
Widsith (ll. 35 ff.). Any scop of Mercia or within the Mercian
imperium would himself feel, and would assume in his hearers,
a particular interest in this ancestor of four centuries earlier of
the greatest royal house of the time. If the old idea of Earle
of *Beowulf* made at the court of Offa of Mercia late in the eighth
century so attractively brought again to modern notice by Professor Whitelock is to be rejected because of linguistic difficulties
in accepting so late a date, it would still be likely that a poet of
Mercia or of any Anglian territory connected by family ties with
Mercian royalties would find his audience interested and gratified
by the outstanding place given to the ancient Offa in *Beowulf*.

The least satisfying of Professor Bonjour's efforts in his *The
Digressions in Beowulf* to justify the digressive material in the
poem is his presentation of the matter of Offa the Angle and his
queen. Its awkward and abrupt appearance in *Beowulf* has continued to puzzle or disconcert scholars. Five reasons for the
inclusion in this manner of the Offa episode have been proposed.
First—and this is most widely agreed—to make a contrast
between the behaviour of the violent young Angle queen and the
altogether admirable Hygd, thereby heightening her value.
Secondly, as mentioned above, because the poet and his hearers
were particularly interested in Offa as being the glorious ancestor
of some royalty of their own time. Thirdly, to draw or imply a
contrast between the career of Heremod and that of Offa's wife.

For the one passed from young virtue and promise to later
wickedness and disaster, while the other grew from a terrifying
youthful savage to an ideal consort to a king: and this kind of
parallel in reverse would naturally add to the lustre of Offa's
queen and at the same time emphasize the badness of Heremod
who is himself particularly in contrast with Beowulf. This is the
explanation by which Professor Bonjour seeks to present the
episode of Offa as contributing artistically to the poem as an
organic unity[1]. Fourthly, there may be, as Professor Bonjour
argues in his section entitled "Beowulf's inglorious youth," the
intention to heighten Beowulf's heroic stature by emphasizing
his early period of sluggishness and ineffectual unimportance:

> Hean wæs lange,
> swa hyne Geata bearn godne ne tealdon,
> ne hyne on medobence micles wyrðne
> drihten Wedera gedon wolde;
> swyðe wendon þæt he sleac wære,
> æðeling unfrom. (ll. 2183–8)

This would suggest to an audience familiar with the folk-
tradition of Offa a laudatory comparison which would do honour
to both. Fifthly, as has been noticed earlier, there is the possibility that King Offa of Mercia was—directly or indirectly—
the poet's inspiration here.

Yet none of these proposals entirely mitigates the apparent
awkwardness of this sudden and unprepared introduction of
Offa's froward queen at ll. 1931b ff.; and many will think that
this has been done without even mentioning her name, as will
appear below. Of the many textual adjustments which have been
suggested to get over this difficulty, I think that the least happy
is the invention by Grein of a lady incredibly named *Modþryðo*.
This device was incorporated into his text by Klaeber in his
third edition: and his well-merited prestige has led to its adoption
without query by a number of scholars. Professor Bonjour heads
his section dealing with this episode "The Story of Modthrytho,
the Wife of Offa"; and Joan Blomfield, in her excellent paper on
the "Style and Structure of *Beowulf*" noticed earlier, mentions
this ugly phantom Modthrytho as a character in the poem.
The ms. reading is *mod þryðo wæg*: and I have little doubt that

---

[1] *Op. cit.* pp. 54–5.

Mr K. Sisam is right in regarding the two forms *mod* and *þryðo* as elements of one compound abstract noun *modþryðo* meaning "violence of character" or "pride of spirit": for she who *modþryðo wæg*, "showed violence of character," is nameless in the MS. because, as Mr Sisam proposes, some passage has been lost in the copying. No doubt the queen's name was of that fairly common type consisting of a compound ending in *-þryð*, such as *Æðelþryð* (St Etheldreda). The scribe, as Mr Sisam suggests, watching the alliteration, allowed his eye to go lower down the folio from a half-line ending in the queen's name which ended in *-þryð* to 1931 b. Thus some lines were lost between the present 1931 a and 1931 b which contained an introduction of the account of Offa's queen *-þryð*[1]. The fact that *Drida* appears in the *Vitæ duorum Offarum* may, however, be thought to justify Professor Schücking (whose text Chambers here followed) in reading *Mod þryðe ne wæg* "she (Hygd) did not manifest the pride of Thryth." Professors von Schaubert and Dobbie retain the MS. reading with *Thryth* as the queen (or *thrytho*) by taking *mod þryðo wæg* as "Thryth(o) showed pride." But neither of these interpretations avoids the real difficulty of the sudden transition of subject, though Sedgefield could be right in believing that the poet and his audience would not have felt this abruptness because they possessed the necessary knowledge.

Although Earle's hypothesis of Offa of Mercia as the poet's patron may be rightly generally rejected, there is one small piece of evidence in favour of his idea that the *Beowulf* poet was in some way referring to the Mercian queen, whose name was in fact *Cyneþryð*. For, if Professor Bruce Dickins's note of 1936 is right[2], the real queen of Mercia may have "shown pride" in fact. She is the only known example of an Anglo-Saxon queen who issued her own coins with her image and superscription on them: *Cyneðryð Regina*. Recent discussions of this crucial passage will be found in Professor Dobbie's *Beowulf and Judith* (pp. 214–16), and in my

[1] Sir William Craigie had as long ago as 1923 suggested that owing to the misplacing of a leaf the text had become muddled (in *Philologica*, II). This was followed up in 1946 in Mr Sisam's "Notes on O.E. Poetry" (*R.E.S.* XXI, 266–7) with the solution here accepted.

[2] See "Queen Cynethryth of Mercia" in *Proc. of the Leeds Philosoph. Soc.* vol. IV, pt. I.

edition of *Beowulf* (pp. 215 and 275 in the Glossary under *modþryðo*). As a parallel to the phrase *modþryðo wæg* Mr Sisam (*loc. cit.*) cites *hygeþryðe wæg* "showed insolence of character" from *Genesis* 2238 b, and compares for the type of noun the use of *modþracu* in *Beowulf*, l. 385. A valuable discussion of the whole episode is Dr S. Stefanović's paper 'Zur Offa-Thryðo-episode im *Beowulf*" of 1934[1].

(iii) The Fight at Finnsburg

Both the study of the problems of the harmonizing of the account in the Finn episode of *Beowulf* and in the Finn *Fragment*, and those of their historical value if any, have received plenty of attention of late years, as will be seen from the bibliography to this supplement. But, on the whole, the views of Chambers and Lawrence, as set forth in detail in this book, have held the field substantially, despite so much new speculation. I doubt indeed if Chambers would—even at this date—wish much to modify his refusal (quoted at the opening of the supplement) to attempt anything further in his second edition on this subject. A few of the more significant speculations, however, must be briefly noticed.

In 1940 Professor Ritchie Girvan gave his British Academy Lecture on *Finnsburuh*, providing some new and exciting ideas and reviving some old ones[2]. He believes that there was some telescoping of the two fights: first, the initial attack by Finn's men upon Hnæf and his followers, and secondly the later slaying of Finn and his men by the followers of Hengest. In this way he is able to explain the presence of the same two warriors Oslaf (the Ordlaf of the *Fragment*) and Guþlaf both at the slaying of Hnæf with which the *Fragment* deals, and at the final annihilation of Finn and his men described at the close of the Finn episode. For he supposes that Hengest, who had taken over the leadership of the Healfdene on the death of Hnæf, took no part in the killing of Finn because he and his followers had themselves been slain by Finn before that time as a penalty for the breaking of the pact of peace implied in Hengest's acceptance of the sword narrated at ll. 1142–5. He believes that the "Danish" chiefs Oslaf

---

[1] *Engl. Stud.* LXIX, 15–31.
[2] See *Proc. of the Brit. Academy*, XXVI, 327–60.

(Ordlaf) and Guþlaf had not been among the original followers of Hnæf, but had come to Finnsburg after the killing of Hengest for the set purpose of exacting vengeance for this deed by devising the fight which brought about the slaughter of Finn and all his men. This hypothesis, exonerating Hengest completely from any share in the killing of Finn, entirely gets rid of the so much talked-of "tragic dilemma" of Hengest and his inward conflict between the duty of vengeance for his slain leader Hnæf and that of good faith in observing the terms of the treaty by which he had undertaken to become a member of Finn's comitatus as described in ll. 1085–94. At the same time, of course, it would take away those elements which have made Hengest a "tragic hero"—at least to the modern reader of the poem. But, on the other hand, this assumption removes the difficulty of supposing that the poet of *Beowulf* had presented with special sympathy to an audience manifestly admiringly interested in the Danes a man of the "Half-Danes" who had been guilty of the deliberate slaying of the lord (Finn) whom he had sworn to serve—though Hengest would still be something of an oath-breaker by his acceptance of the sword mentioned above. Professor Girvan too, as noticed in the introduction to this chapter, lends his support to the older view that the Healfdene of l. 1069, whose leader Hengest became on the death of Hnæf, were themselves *Eotan* (or *Eote* or "Eotens")—Jutes. Now this identification makes it again possible to believe that Hengest in *Beowulf* was in fact the Hengest of history who conquered Kent. To this it may be added, as mentioned at the opening of the chapter, that I attempted to show[1] that the Hengest of *Beowulf*, like the king of Old and early Middle English tradition, was both an exile and a mercenary. For the *wrecca* of l. 1137 may be Hengest; and the Healfdene may have been a band of Jutes in the service of the Danes in whose feud with the Frisians they took part, even though Finn's men were also Jutes in his service as ruler of the Frisians. There may have been two Jutish groups —the one in Danish service called Healfdene at l. 1069 and Dene at l. 1090, and the other under Finn who ruled the Frisians. Though the attempt to identify the Hengest of history with that

[1] See my ed. of *Beowulf*, pp. 52–3.

of *Beowulf* has of late found little favour, his presence in the poem addressed to an English audience would seem more natural than the supposition that he was merely the poet's fiction. It is worth noticing, perhaps, that so careful and exact a historian as Sir Frank Stenton seems to imply a link between the Hengest of Old English poetry and the historical tradition in this comment: "Their later history [of Hengest and Horsa] was a matter of tradition, not record, and there are indications that, in part at least, it had been handed down in alliterative verse[1]." It is not really difficult to believe that two distinct groups of Jutes could find themselves engaged in a blood-feud because of the quarrel of their respective lords. There is indeed an historical parallel in the deadly fight in which kinsmen were on opposite sides between King Cynewulf of Wessex and his enemy Cyneheard described in the *Anglo-Saxon Chronicle* for the year 755[2].

Professor Kemp Malone has continued to agree with the view that Hengest had no share in the slaying of Finn described in the final lines of the Finn episode, as he had done as early as 1923 in his *The Literary History of Hamlet* (pp. 20–3), though his interpretation of ll. 1142–5 is quite different[3]. But he regards Healfdene as the survival of an older and original name for the Danish royal house of the *Scyldingas* (after Hrothgar's father Healfdene): cf. 1090 and 1158.

The speculations of Professors Girvan and Malone have been very ably challenged in favour of the by now orthodox and traditional account of the whole matter of Finnsburg given by Chambers in this book, by Professor A. G. Brodeur in his *The Climax of the Finn Episode* published by the University of California Press, Berkeley, in 1943. The editions of Dobbie and Klaeber substantially accept the Chambers view, with comparatively minor modifications; and Professor Brodeur's recent articles notably strengthen this, the now generally accepted position[4].

---

[1] *Anglo-Saxon England* (Oxford, 1943), p. 16.
[2] Cf. my paper "A Saga of the Anglo-Saxons" in *History*, New Ser., xxv (1940), 208 ff.
[3] See *J.E.G. Ph.* xxv (1926), 158–9, and *E.L.H.* x (1943), 283–4.
[4] Cf. A. G. Brodeur's *Design and Motive in the Finn Episode* (Berkeley, California, 1943, and "The Structure and the Unity of *Beowulf*" in *Pub. Mod. Lang. Assoc. Amer.* LXVIII (1953). Particularly full are Dobbie's notes on the Finn episode in his ed. of *Beowulf and Judith*, especially pp. 178–83.

Of the very many speculations on all aspects of the Finnsburg question, which cannot be discussed here, those of Professor
Kemp Malone, who has been prolific in his investigations of both
historical and legendary problems, have been the most stimulating and influential. They will be found in his papers listed in
the bibliography. But one more possibly very valuable surmise
must be added in passing.

Professor John Beaty in 1934 added a note on the Finnsburg
Fragment to his important article on "The Echo-word in Beo-
wulf[1]." Since, as he thinks, the chief obstacle to complete
harmony between the *Fragment* and the Finn episode is the
appearance in the *Fragment* of two distinct *Guþlafs*—the one at
l. 16 being the same Guþlaf (Dane or Half-Dane) who with Oslaf
promoted the slaying of Finn in *Beowulf*, l. 1148, and the other
at l. 33 of the *Fragment* who must be a Frisian and the father of
the *Garulf* who is killed at l. 31. Professor Beaty gets rid of this
difficulty entirely by supposing that this *Garulf Guðlafes sunu*
was in fact the son of Finn whose death in the earlier battle is
mentioned in *Beowulf*, ll. 1072–5. This *Garulf* is described in
terms which suggest a king's heir:

ealra ærest eorðbuendra,

as befits the son of King Finn and his queen Hildeburg. The
word *Guðlaf*, it is stated, is "not a proper noun. It is a common
noun which means 'war-survivor,' and is an echo (word) of the
Guðlaf, proper noun, in l. 16." He adds: "*Guðlafes* (l. 33) is,
moreover, a mere 'kenning' for King Finn." After citing some
evidence that such a compound noun as *Guðlaf* is quite ordinary,
he concludes that: "all that is known of the Finn episode and the
Finn Fragment points to the necessity of *Garulf* being the son
of Finn."

(iv) FOLKLORE

Much has been done by way of speculative parallels and
analogues to folkloristic elements in *Beowulf*. Parallels have been
sought as far away as ceremonies of exorcism in India and the

---

[1] "The Echo-word in *Beowulf*, with a Note on the *Finnsburg Fragment*",
in *Pub. Mod. Lang. Assoc. Amer.* XLIX, 372–3.

legends of Mexico[1]. But there has also been a serious defence of the place of the dragon as a symbolic element in the conception and structure of the poem, emphasizing Professor Tolkien's well-known views, by Professor Bonjour. This he has done in a well-argued paper entitled "Monsters Crouching and Critics Rampant, or the *Beowulf* Dragon Debated[2]." A good deal of matter on the attitude of the Anglo-Saxons to dragons and other monsters is in Professor Whitelock's *The Audience of Beowulf*, especially pp. 72 ff., where the evidence of place-names is indicated.

Professor James Carney, in his recent book *Studies in Irish Literature and History* already referred to in discussing the genesis of *Beowulf* in chapter III, has challenged the views on the relationship of Celtic folk-tales to the poem put forward in this book. In the section from his considerable chapter on *Beowulf* entitled "The Folk-tale Element[3]," Professor Carney strongly upholds those critics who, against Chambers, had maintained that there was a clear influence from *Beowulf* to the *Grettissaga* in the matter of the Grendel story. He then argues that the Irish parallels he cites are older than *Beowulf* and that there was influence of some written folk-tale upon the poem. Following Dr Charles Donahue[4] (though from a different standpoint in some respects) he points out that the confusion between *Cain* and *Ham* (*Cam*) which lies behind the errors originally made by the scribe of the *Beowulf* MS. in the two references to Cain as the ancestor of monsters (ll. 107 and 1261) must have been directly due to the same confusion in Irish ecclesiastical documents. Further, that there is a direct link between the monsters listed in *Beowulf*, ll. 111–14 as Cain's descendants and a similar list in MSS. going back to the eleventh century of a much older Irish text, the *Sex Aetates Mundi*. This argument from parallels in folk-material links up of course with Professor Carney's view that the poet of *Beowulf* at the close of the seventh century, being bilingual in Irish and

---

[1] Cf. Gustav Hübener's "*Beowulf*, ein indischer Messerexorzismus und die Sachsen," in *Festschrift für Deutschbein* (Leipzig, 1936) (English version in *R.E.S.* XII), and Mr R. Colgrave's "A Mexican Version of the 'Bear's Son' Folk Tale," in *J. of Amer. Folklore*, LXIV (1951).

[2] See *Pub. Mod. Lang. Assoc. Amer.* LXIX, 305 ff. (1935).

[3] See *op. cit.* pp. 89 ff.

[4] Cf. *J. of Celtic Studies*, I, 167–75.

English, had before him as a source of much of his story the contemporary Irish *Táin Bó Fraich*[1].

Professor Carney has set in motion new lines of thought which may prove fruitful: but his views have not yet received much attention or thorough examination from those qualified to assess them. Meanwhile I doubt whether Chambers would have modified much the view of the relationships of *Beowulf*, *Grettissaga* and Celtic parallels set forth in this book. Yet Professor Carney's work does indicate in a very timely way that there is further evidence to be examined, and that the whole set of problems relating to the Celtic cultural influences on Anglo-Saxon art and literature—which must include *Beowulf*—is in need of serious investigation by scholars familiar with both languages and civilizations.

For Additional Notes to this Supplement see p. 552.

---

[1] See Carney, *op. cit.* pp. 17 ff.

ADDITIONAL NOTES

p. 4. Antoine Thomas, in the *Archivum Latinitatis Medii Ævi*, 1924 (1925), pp. 232–45, gives an account of a third manuscript of the *Liber Monstrorum*, at Leyden (*Is. Vossi cod. lat. oc. No.* 60). Thomas dates the handwriting of this manuscript c. 900. The name of Hygelac is here given correctly: *De Hyglaco*. Thomas assigns the composition of the treatise to England, and dates it c. 700.

p. 9. The king, after his election by the Swedes, had to make a progress through the provinces (the *Eriksgata*) and be received at each Thing. See *Loi de Vestrogothie (Westgöta-Lagen) traduite et annotée par L. Beauchet*, Paris, 1894, pp. 200–2; p. 434; R. Kjellén, *Om Eriksgatan*, Upsala, 1889, p. 7; C. J. Schlyter, *Juridiska Afhandlingar*, Upsala, 1836, pp. 20–1; Montelius in vol. I of *Sveriges historia*, 1877, p. 462.

The right of confirming the king is thus recorded in the Law-book of the Vestergötar. "The Swedes have the right to elect and also to reject the king.... A Thing of all the Götar must be called before him. When the king comes to the Thing, he must swear that he will be faithful to all the Götar, and that he will not break the righteous laws of our land (*sik allum götum trolekan sværia at han skal eigh ræt lagh a landi vorn bryta*). After that the law-man is first to declare him king...."

This could be more than a mere formality, apparently. We read that "the tenth king was Rangvaldr who was proud and haughty...and as he was wanting in respect to all the Vestergötar, he fell by a shameful death."

p. 17. For the reasons for attributing the mounds at Leire to the Stone or Bronze Ages, see Olrik, *Heltedigtning*, I, 191 (*Heroic Legends*, p. 328) and the authorities there quoted.

p. 19. The connection of the name Roskilde with Hrothgar remains disputed. That the element *Ros* in other place names signifies "Horse" is urged by J. B. Løffler (*Les Pierres Tumulaires de la Cathédrale de Roskilde*, 1885, p. xiii). In the later Middle Ages Roskilde was often interpreted as "Spring of Roses." A fifteenth-century bishop of Roskilde is addressed *Tu nomen clarum tractas de fonte rosarum* (Langebek, *Scriptores*, VIII, 473). The fourteenth-century town seal shows three roses swimming in a fountain (see Henry Petersen, *Hvor laa Kongsgaarden i Roskilde*, in *Historisk Tidsskrift*, Kjøbenhavn ((Sjette Række), 1890, II, 353–4). On the other hand, the connection with Hrothgar is not impossible. Roskilde, like the *Roe* of Saxo, must then be referred to the form *Hroí(r)*, which we must regard as a shortened form of *Hróðgeirr* or *Hróarr* (=*Hroðgar*). Some, however, regard *Hroí(r)* as a distinct name, derived from *Hróðvér*. But see Björkman, *Eigennamen im Beowulf*, 1920, p. 74.

p. 34. Six of the drawings are certainly from the pen of Matthew Paris, and his authorship of the *Vitæ* is being maintained afresh by Prof. Grüner and others. See J. Schick, *Die Urquelle der Offa-Konstanze-Sage*, in *Britannica (Max Förster zum sechzigsten Geburtstage)*, 1929, p. 41. For the six drawings, see M. R. James, *The Drawings of Matthew Paris*, in *The Fourteenth Volume of the Walpole Society*, 1925–6, pp. 21–3.

p. 47. Of course the long winter nights give the uncanny visitor scope for his activities: and Boer is right in pointing out that, in certain allied stories, it is at Yule that the ghost-demon appears. But Boer agrees (*English Studies*, Amsterdam, v, 106) that we cannot build on this any theory of a divine helper such as Kemble and Müllenhoff imagined.

p. 94. *ēalond* probably does not mean "island." Boer (*English Studies*, v, 113) disputes this. But the use of *ēalond*, *īȝlond* to signify simply land near (but not necessarily quite surrounded by) water is well authenticated in Old English. It survives in names of peninsulas, "Portland Island," "Hayling Island"; as late as the sixteenth century Norway could be called an "island." The word *ēalond* would suit excellently the great tract of land almost surrounded by the sea, by the Götaelf and by Lake Wener, where we may imagine the palace of Beowulf as standing.

p. 101. Dr H. V. Routh objects to my argument that the scenery around Leire does not show that remarkable likeness to the Grendel-lake which Sarrazin claimed for it:

> "Sarrazin has argued that Grendel's lair was really to be found in Roskilde fiord, whereat Prof. Chambers objects that though there may have been fewer cultivated fields and more beech trees, 'the scenery may have been less tame, but can hardly have been less peaceful.' The scenery can well have been immeasurably less peaceful. The professor forgets the effect of uncleared forest growth. Even now Canadian forests present in places an indescribably weird and disquieting appearance, with their tangle of undergrowth and fallen trees, and these jungles can be found in quite civilized districts, not far from established townships." (*God, Man and Epic Poetry*, II, 19.)

But the grave-mounds, going back to the Stone Age, show that the country round Leire had already been inhabited for thousands of years in Hrothgar's day. The comparison with uncleared Canadian forest, even in places where townships are now being pushed up near to that uncleared forest, is not quite to the point. The district round Leire may well have been much more thickly inhabited in the sixth century, when Leire was the centre of a great kingdom, than it is to-day, when Leire is an insignificant village. Dr Routh goes on (following the description in *Beowulf* itself) to speak of Grendel's lair as surrounded by "wolf-cliffs," "bleak crags," "caverns." Does he seriously argue that cliffs, crags and caverns were to be found in this district about A.D. 500? If not, what is the use of trying to defend Sarrazin's argument that the description in *Beowulf* shows a local knowledge such as argues a Scandinavian poet who knew the locality?

p. 177. Mr Bruce Dickins suggests that *trog* should be rendered trencher "in which sense the word is still preserved in the strongly Scandinavian dialect of Shetland." Anyway the *trog* is part of the regular equipment of a witch wife bent on destroying heroes. See *Heimskringla, Saga of Harold Hardrada*, cap. 83; *Laxdæla Saga*, cap. 48.

p. 201. Another copy of this roll is in the library of Canterbury University College, Christchurch, New Zealand. An edition and translation of it has been published by Prof. Arnold Wall, *Handbook to the Maude Roll*, Whitcombe and Tombs, Ltd., 1919. I am indebted to Prof. Wall for drawing my attention to this copy.

p. 252. "The warrior who put the sword into Hengest's bosom *was* Hunlafing." But Prof. Malone has urged that the poet of *Beowulf* "never uses a patronymic except in connexion with the true name," and that therefore we must, with Olrik, interpret Hunlafing as the name of a sword, not as an (otherwise unknown) son of Hunlaf. See his article in *M.L.N.* xliii, 300–4.

p. 306. *Grendles mere.* Mr G. M. Young writes:

"*Grendles mere* in the Ham Landbook may safely be added to the number of marshy sites. The region in which it lies is known to geologists as the Vale of Ham, and the mere itself can be placed exactly, in a valley bottom, now streamless but still spongy after rain. The northern boundary of Ham running down this valley makes a small right-angled turn a little to the east of Lower Spray Copse. At this point, ⅛ inch to the right of the *y* in *Spray* (1 inch Ordnance Map), a kink in the hedge and the colour of the ground indicate the site of a filled-up pond. Two tracks, coming from the east and the north (the latter is called Olddyke Lane) and converging at the site, suggest that the mere continued in use in mediæval times as a watering place for cattle. It is known that this district is much drier now than in early times: under wetter conditions the valley must have been boggy, with a rivulet running down it after rain and forming small pools—*wudu mere* and *grendles mere.*"

pp. 309–10. Ekwall (*English River-Names*, 1928, p. 186) derives the Grindle or Greendale Brook from *grēne* "green" and *dæl* "valley." He agrees that the name is not likely to be derived from *grand*, "gravel," sand, "while I must take leave to differ from Chambers in his statement that 'there is no particular suggestion of sand or gravel about this modest little brook.'" Which shows that even personal inspection of details does not always produce unanimity. See also Zachrisson in *Miscellany offered to Otto Jespersen*, p. 42.

p. 333, footnote 3. Ekwall (*Anglia, Beiblatt*, xxxiii, 181) argues that *Gotland* is a quite satisfactory way for Alfred in Orosius to have rendered the word *Jōtland*, as he heard it from the Norseman Ohthere. "He could hardly," writes Ekwall, "use the spelling *Geotland*, for that would be read with a diphthong *ēo*." Ekwall's point is that the spelling *ʒeo* in Old English was not merely a scribal way of expressing *jō*, but, often at least, did signify a real diphthongization.

My point is that when Ohthere spoke of Yule he would say *jól*: but Alfred would write *ʒeol*; and by exactly the same process I should expect that Alfred would render Ohthere's *Jotland* by *Geotland*, writing (and probably pronouncing) a diphthong. For, as Englishmen who have to struggle with the impurity of their vowels know, it is very difficult to pronounce a pure vowel in a place where we habitually diphthongize it. It is of course possible that Alfred had a better ear than I have given him credit for, and in that case would have written, as Ekwall and Björkman argue, *Gotland.*

If so, there remains no difficulty whatsoever in the interpretation of Gotland as Jutland; I did not wish to shirk what could reasonably be held to be a difficulty; but, if there is none, so much the better for my argument.

p. 363. "the ship as it now stands consists of the original woodwork." This is no longer true, as it has now proved possible, from the fragments discovered, to reconstruct the prow.

Part VI, chapter I. Dr J. B. Bessinger, whose recorded recitation of Cædmon's *Hymn* is referred to in connexion with the reconstructed Sutton Hoo harp, now at the University of Toronto, is publishing in *Speculum* for 1958 a Supplement to Professor Magoun's invaluable "Chronological Bibliography to the Sutton Hoo Ship-burial" (*Speculum* for 1954). He has also published in the *University of Toronto Quarterly* (January 1958) an important paper too late for discussion here entitled "*Beowulf* and the Harp at Sutton Hoo," which attempts an examination of the musical art of the poem as related to the art-styles of the Sutton Hoo find.

Some new light may soon be thrown on Hrothgar's palace of Heorot as a result of the excavation of the palace and some administrative buildings of the seat of King Edwin of Northumbria at Old Yeavering in Northumberland. So far only general press notices have appeared of this discovery in 1956, but Mr B. Hope-Taylor, who took a leading part in the discoveries, may soon publish an authoritative account. Though probably only traces and measurements of the buildings (which seem to have been of three periods in the seventh century) may be established, these show a highly developed Anglo-Saxon art of planning and building at a date perhaps a little earlier than that of *Beowulf*.

Part VI, chapter II. An interesting new approach to the general problem of the text of *Beowulf* is made by Dr John Nist in his paper "Textual Elements in the *Beowulf* Manuscript" in the *Papers of the Michigan Academy of Science, Arts and Letters* for 1957. For this is a first attempt to apply some of the new techniques of current linguistic science to *Beowulf*.

Part VI, chapter III. Though nothing can certainly be concluded as to the relations (if any) between the Latin epic and *Beowulf* despite a good deal of discussion, there is a useful and somewhat full examination of this whole question in Dr T. B. Haber's book *A Comparative Study of the Beowulf and the Aeneid* (Princeton, 1931).

Supplementary Bibliography. A new monthly, *Abstracts of English Studies*, to include summary notices of all matters in periodicals, with index, is issued by Colorado University (Boulder, Colorado) from January 1958.

BIBLIOGRAPHY OF *BEOWULF* AND *FINNSBURG*

I remember it was with extreme difficulty that I could bring my master to understand the meaning of the word *opinion*, or how a point could be disputable; because reason taught us to affirm or deny only where we are certain; and beyond our knowledge we cannot do either. So that controversies, wranglings, disputes, and positiveness in false or dubious propositions are evils unknown among the *Houyhnhnms*....He would laugh that a creature pretending to reason should value itself upon the knowledge of other people's conjectures, and in things, where that knowledge, if it were certain, could be of no use....

I have often since reflected what destruction such a doctrine would make in the libraries of Europe.

Gulliver's Travels.

The following items are (except in special cases) not included in this bibliography:

(*a*) Articles dealing with single passages in *Beowulf*, or two passages only, in cases where they have already been recorded under the appropriate passage in the footnotes to the text, or in the glossary, of my revision of Wyatt's edition.

(*b*) Articles dealing with the emendation or interpretation of single passages, in cases where such emendations have been withdrawn by their author himself.

(*c*) Purely popular paraphrases or summaries.

(*d*) Purely personal protests (e.g., *P.B.B.* xxi, 436), however well founded, in which no point of scholarship is any longer involved.

Books dealing with other subjects, but illustrating *Beowulf*, present a difficulty. Such books may have a value for *Beowulf* students, even though the author may never refer to our poem, and have occasionally been included in previous bibliographies. But, unless *Beowulf* is closely concerned, these books are not usually mentioned below: such enumeration, if carried out consistently, would clog a bibliography already all too bulky. Thus, Siecke's *Drachenkämpfe* does not seem to come within the scope of this bibliography, because the author is not concerned with Beowulf's dragon.

Obviously every general discussion of Old English metre must concern itself largely with *Beowulf*: for such treatises the student is referred to the section *Metrik* of Brandl's Bibliography (*Pauls Grdr.*); and, for Old English heroic legend in general, to the Bibliography of my edition of *Widsith*.

Many scholars, e.g. Heinzel, have put into their reviews of the books of others, much original work which might well have formed the material for independent articles. Such reviews are noted as "weighty," but it must not be supposed that the reviews not so marked are negligible; unless of some value to scholarship, reviews are not usually mentioned below.

The title of any book, article or review which I have not seen and verified is denoted by the sign ‡.

SUMMARY

§ 1. Periodicals.
§ 2. Bibliographies.
§ 3. The MS and its transcripts.
§ 4. Editions.
§ 5. Concordances, *etc.*
§ 6. Translations (including early summaries).
§ 7. Textual criticism and interpretation.
§ 8. Questions of literary history, date and authorship. *Beowulf* in the light of history, archæology[1], heroic legend, mythology and folk-lore.
§ 9. Style and Grammar.
§ 10. Metre.

§ 1. PERIODICALS

The periodicals most frequently quoted are:

A.f.d.A. = Anzeiger für deutsches Alterthum. Berlin, 1876 *etc.*

A.f.n.F. = Arkiv för nordisk Filologi. Christiania, Lund, 1883 *etc.* *Quoted according to the original numbering.*

Anglia. Halle, 1878 *etc.*

Archiv = Herrigs Archiv für das Studium der neueren Sprachen und Litteraturen. Elberfeld, Braunschweig, 1846 *etc.* *Quoted according to the original numbering.*

D.L.Z. = Deutsche Literatur-Zeitung. Berlin, 1880 *etc.*

Engl. Stud. = Englische Studien. Heilbronn, Leipzig, 1877 *etc.*

Germania. Wien, 1856–92.

I.F. = Indogermanische Forschungen. Strassburg, 1892 *etc.*

J.(E.)G.Ph. = Journal of (English and) Germanic Philology. Bloomington, Urbana, 1897 *etc.*

Lit. Cbl. = Literarisches Centralblatt. Leipzig, 1851 *etc.*

Literaturblatt für germanische und romanische Philologie. Heilbronn, Leipzig, 1880 *etc.*

M.L.N. = Modern Language Notes. Baltimore, 1886 *etc.* *Quoted by the page, not the column.*

M.L.R. = The Modern Language Review. Cambridge, 1906 *etc.*

Mod. Phil. = Modern Philology. Chicago, 1903 *etc.*

Morsbachs Studien zur englischen Philologie. Halle, 1897 *etc.*

P.B.B. = Beiträge zur Geschichte der deutschen Sprache u. Litteratur. Halle, 1874 *etc.*

Pub. Mod. Lang. Assoc. Amer. = Publications of the Modern Language Association of America. Baltimore, 1889 *etc.*

Z.f.d.A. = Zeitschrift für deutsches Alterthum. Leipzig, Berlin, 1841 *etc.*

Z.f.d.Ph. = Zachers Zeitschrift für deutsche Philologie. Halle, 1869 *etc.*

Z.f.ö.G. = Zeitschrift für die österreichischen Gymnasien. Wien, 1850 *etc.*

The titles of other periodicals are given with sufficient fulness for easy identification.

---

[1] Archæological works bearing less directly upon *Beowulf* are enumerated in *Appendix F*; that enumeration is not repeated here.

§ 2. BIBLIOGRAPHIES

Bibliographies have been published from time to time as a supplement to *Anglia*; also in the *Jahresbericht über...german. Philologie*; by Garnett in his *Translation*, 1882 *etc.*; and will be found in

Wülker's *Grundriss* (with very useful abstracts), 1885, pp. 245 *etc.*

Clark Hall's *Translation*, 1901, 1911.

Holthausen's *Beowulf*, 1906, 1909, 1913, 1919.

Brandl's *Englische Literatur*, in *Pauls Grdr.*(2), п, 1015–24 (full, but not so reliable as Holthausen's).

Sedgefield's *Beowulf*, 1910, 1913 (carefully selected).

An excellent critical bibliography of *Beowulf*-translations up to 1903 is that of Tinker: see under § 6, *Translations*.

§ 3. THE MS AND ITS TRANSCRIPTS

Beowulf fills ff. 129 (132)*a* to 198 (201)*b* of the British Museum MS *Cotton Vitellius A. XV.*

Beowulf is written in two hands, the first of which goes to l. 1939. This hand was identified by Prof. Sedgefield (*Beowulf, Introduction*, p. xiv, footnote) with that of the piece immediately preceding *Beowulf* in the MS, and by Mr Kenneth Sisam, in 1916, with that of all three immediately preceding pieces: the *Christopher* fragment, the *Wonders of the East*, and the *Letter of Alexander on the Wonders of India*. The pieces preceding these, however (the *Soliloquies of S. Augustine*, the *Gospel of Nicodemus, Salomon and Saturn*), are certainly not in the same hand, and their connection with the *Beowulf*-MS is simply due to the bookbinder.

From l. 1939 to the end, *Beowulf* is written in a second hand, thicker and less elegant than the first. This second hand seems to be clearly identical with that in which the poem of *Judith*, immediately following *Beowulf*, is written. This was pointed out by Sievers in 1872 (*Z.f.d.A.* xv, 457), and has never, I think, been disputed (cf. Sisam, p. 337; Förster, p. 31). Nevertheless the two poems have probably not always formed one book. For the last page of *Beowulf* was apparently once the last page of the volume, to judge from its battered condition, whilst *Judith* is imperfect at the beginning. And there are trifling differences, e.g. in the frequency of the use of contractions, and the form of the capital H.

This identity of the scribe of the second portion of *Beowulf* and the *Judith* scribe, together with the identity (pointed out by Mr Sisam) of the scribe of the first portion of *Beowulf* and the scribe of the three preceding works, is important. A detailed comparison of these texts will throw light upon the characteristics of the scribes.

That the three preceding works are in the same hand as that of the first *Beowulf* scribe was again announced, independently of Mr Sisam, by Prof. Max Förster, in 1919. Sievers had already in 1871 arrived at the same result (see Förster, p. 35, note) but had not published it.

It seems to me in the highest degree improbable that the *Beowulf*-MS has lost its ending, as Prof. Förster thinks (pp. 82, 88). Surely nothing could be better than the conclusion of the poem as it stands in the MS: that the casual loss of a number of leaves could have resulted in so satisfactory a conclusion is, I think, not conceivable. Moreover, the scribe has crammed as much material as possible into the last leaf of *Beowulf*, making his lines abnormally long, and using contractions in a way he does not use them elsewhere. The only reason for this must be to avoid running over into a new leaf or quire: there could be no motive for this crowded page if the poem had ever run on beyond it.

There is pretty general agreement that the date of the *Beowulf*-MS is about the year 1000, and that it is somewhat more likely to be before that date than after.

The *Beowulf*-MS was injured in the great Cottonian fire of 1731, and the edges of the parchment have since chipped away owing to the damage then sustained. Valuable assistance can therefore be derived from the two transcripts now preserved in the Royal Library of Copenhagen, made in 1787, when the MS was much less damaged.

A. Poema anglosaxonicum de rebus gestis Danorum...fecit exscribi Londini A.D. MDCCLXXXVII Grimus Johannis Thorkelin.

B. Poema anglosaxonicum de Danorum rebus gestis...exscripsit Grimus Johannis Thorkelin. Londini MDCCLXXXVII.

The first description of the *Beowulf*-MS is in 1705 by H. WANLEY (*Librorum Septentrionalium...Catalogus*, pp. 218–19, Oxoniæ, forming vol. II of Hickes' *Thesaurus*). Two short extracts from the MS are given by Wanley. He describes the poem as telling of the wars *quæ Beowulfus quidam Danus, ex regio Scyldingorum stirpe ortus, gessit contra Sueciæ regulos*. The text was printed by THORKELIN in 1815, and the MS was collated by CONYBEARE, who in his *Illustrations* (1826) issued 19 pages of corrections of Thorkelin. These corrections were further corrected by J. M. KEMBLE in 1837 (Letter to M. Francisque Michel, in Michel's *Bibliothèque Anglo-Saxonne*, pp. 20, 51–8). Meantime Kemble's text had been issued in 1833, based upon his examination of the MS. The MS was also seen by THORPE (in 1830: Thorpe's text was not published till 1855) and by GRUNDTVIG (pub. 1861). A further collation was that of E. KÖLBING in 1876 (Zur Beóvulf-handschrift, *Archiv*, LVI, 91–118). Kölbing's collation proves the superiority of Kemble's text to Grundtvig's. Line for line transcripts of the MS were those of Holder, Wülker and Zupitza:

1881 HOLDER, A. Beowulf. Bd. I. Abdruck der Handschrift. Freiburg u. Tübingen. (‡1881, from collation made in 1875.) Reviews: Kölbing, *Engl. Stud.* VII, 488; Kluge, *Literaturblatt*, 1883, 178; Wülker, *Lit. Cbl.* 1882, 1035–6.

      1882. 2 Aufl.

      1895. 3 Aufl. Reviews: Dieter, *Anglia, Beiblatt*, VI, 260–1; Brandl, *Z.f.d.A.* XL, 90.

1881 WÜLKER, R. P. Beowulf: Text nach der handschrift, in Grein's *Bibliothek*, I, 18–148.

1882 ZUPITZA, J. Beowulf. Autotypes of the unique Cotton MS. Vitellius A XV; with a transliteration and notes. *Early English Text Society*, London. Reviews: Trautmann, *Anglia*, VII, *Anzeiger*, 41; Kölbing, *Engl. Stud.* VII, 482 etc.; Varnhagen, *A.f.d.A.* X, 304; Sievers, *Lit. Cbl.* 1884, 124.

Further discussion of the MS by

1890 DAVIDSON, C. Differences between the scribes of Beowulf. *M.L.N.* V,
43–4; McCLUMPHA, C., criticizes the above, *M.L.N.* V, 123; reply by
DAVIDSON, *M.L.N.* V, 189–90.

1910 LAMB, EVELYN H. "Beowulf": Hemming of Worcester. *Notes and
Queries*, Ser. XI, vol. I, p. 26. (Worthless. An assertion, unsupported
by any evidence, that *both* the hands of the Beowulf MS are those of
Hemming of Worcester, who flourished c. 1096.)

1916 SISAM, K. The Beowulf Manuscript. *M.L.R.* XI, 335–7. (Very important.
Gives results of a scrutiny of the other treatises in *MS Vitellius A. XV*
(see above) and shows, among other things, that the Beowulf MS,
before reaching the hands of Sir Robert Cotton, was (in 1563) in those of
Lawrence Nowell, the Elizabethan Anglo-Saxon scholar.)

1919 FÖRSTER, MAX. Die Beowulf-Handschrift, Leipzig, *Berichte der Sächs.
Akad. der Wissenschaften*, Bd. 71. (An excellent and detailed discussion of the problems of the MS, quite independent of that of
Mr Sisam, whose results it confirms.) Review: Schröder, *A.f.d.A.* XL,
85–6.

1920 RYPINS, S. I. The Beowulf Codex. *Mod. Phil.* XVII, 541–8 (promising
further treatment of the problems of the MS).

The MS of Finnsburg has been lost. See above, p. 245.

§ 4. EDITIONS OF BEOWULF AND FINNSBURG

1705 HICKES, G. Linguarum Vett. Septentrionalium Thesaurus. Oxoniæ.
(Vol. I, 192–3, text of Finnsburg Fragment.)

1814 CONYBEARE, J. J. The Battle of Finsborough, in Brydges' *British
Bibliographer*, vol. IV, pp. 261–7; No. XV (Text, Latin translation, and
free verse paraphrase in English: some brief notes).

1815 THORKELIN, G. J. De Danorum rebus gestis secul. III et IV. Poëma
Danicum dialecto Anglo-Saxonica. (Copenhagen, with Lat. transl.)
Reviews: See § 7, *Textual Criticism*, 1815, Grundtvig; also *Dansk
Litteratur-Tidende*, 1815, 401–32, 437–46, 461–2 (defending Thorkelin
against Grundtvig); *Iduna*, VII, 1817, 133–59; *Monthly Review*, LXXXI,
1816, 516–23; ‡*Jenaische Literatur-Zeitung*, 1816, *Ergänzungsblätter*,
353–65 (summary in Wülker's *Grundriss*, p. 252); Outzen in *Kieler
Blätter*, 1816, see § 8, below.

1817 RASK, R. K. Angelsaksisk sproglære. Stockholm (pp. 163–6 contain
Beowulf, ll. 53–114, with commentary).

1820 Text of Finnsburg, given by GRUNDTVIG in *Bjowulfs Drape*, pp. xl–xlv.

1826 Text of Finnsburg, and of large portions of Beowulf, given in CONYBEARE'S
Illustrations. See § 5, *Translations*.

1833 KEMBLE, J. M. Beowulf, the Travellers Song, and the Battle of Finnesburh, edited with a glossary...and an historical preface. London.
1835. Second edit.

1847 SCHALDEMOSE, F. Beo-wulf og Scopes Widsið...med Oversættelse.
Kjøbenhavn. (Follows Kemble's text of 1835: Text and transl. of
Finnsburg also given, pp. 161–4.) 1851, Reprinted.

1849 KLIPSTEIN, L. F. Analecta Anglo-Saxonica. New York. (Selections
from Beowulf, II, 227–61: Text of Finnsburg, 426–7.)

1850 ETTMÜLLER, L. Engla and Seaxna scopas and bōceras. Quedlinburg
u. Leipzig. (Text of large portions of Beowulf, with Finnsburg,
pp. 95–131.)

1855 THORPE, B. The A.S. poems of Beowulf, the scop or gleeman's tale, and
Finnesburg, with a literal translation...Oxford. ‡1875, Reprinted.

1857 GREIN, C. W. M. Bibliothek der angelsächsischen Poesie, I. Göttingen
(pp. 255–343, Beóvulf, Ueberfall in Finnsburg).
1861–4. Bd. III, IV. Sprachschatz.

1861 RIEGER, M. Alt- u. angelsächsisches Lesebuch. Giessen. (Der Kampf zu
Finnsburg, pp. 61–3: aus dem Beovulf, 63–82.)

1861 GRUNDTVIG, N. F. S. Beowulfes Beorh eller Bjovulfs-Drapen. Kiöbenhavn, London. (The Finnsburg Fragment is inserted in the text of
Beowulf, after l. 1106.)

1863 HEYNE, M. Beovulf, mit ausführlichem Glossar. Paderborn. (Anhang:
Der Ueberfall in Finnsburg.) Reviews: Grein, *Lit. Cbl.* 1864, 137–8;
Holtzmann, *Germania*, VIII, 506–7.
1868. ‡2 Aufl. Review: Rieger, *Z.f.d.Ph.* II, 371–4.
1873. 3 Aufl. Review: Sievers, *Lit. Cbl.* 1873, 662–3, brief but
severe.
1879. 4 Aufl. [in this, Kölbing's collation of 1876 was utilized; see
p. 82]. Reviews: Brenner, *Engl. Stud.* IV, 135–9; Gering,
Z.f.d.Ph. XII, 122–5.

1867 GREIN, C. W. M. Beovulf, nebst den Fragmenten Finnsburg u. Valdere.
Cassel u. Göttingen.

1875 ETTMÜLLER, L. Carmen de Beóvulfi, Gautarum regis, rebus praeclare gestis
atque interitu, quale fuerit antequam in manus interpolatoris, monachi
Vestsaxonici, inciderat. (Zürich. University Programme. The additions
of the "interpolator" being omitted, the edition contains 2896 lines
only.) Reviews: Schönbach, *A.f.d.A.* III, 36–46; ‡Suchier, *Jenaer
Literatur-Zeitung*, XLVII, 1876, 732.

1876 ARNOLD, T. Beowulf, with a translation, notes and appendix. London.
Reviews (unfavourable): Sweet, *Academy*, X, 1876, 588; Wülker, *Lit.
Cbl.* 1877, 665–6, and *Anglia*, I, 177–86.

1879 WÜLKER, R. P. Kleinere angelsächsische Dichtungen. Halle, Leipzig.
(Finnsburg, pp. 6–7.)

1883 MÖLLER, H. Das altenglische Volksepos in der ursprünglichen stro-
phischen Form. I. Abhandlungen. II. Texte. Kiel. (Containing only
those parts of the Finn-story and of Beowulf which Möller regarded
as "genuine," in strophic form.) Reviews: Heinzel, *A.f.d.A.* X, 215–33
(important); Schönbach, *Z.f.ö.G.* XXXV, 37–46.

1883 WÜLKER, R. P. Das Beowulfslied, nebst den kleineren epischen...stücken.
Kassel. (In the second edit. of Grein's *Bibliothek der ags. Poesie.*)
Review: Kölbing, *Engl. Stud.* VII, 482 etc.

1883 HARRISON, J. A. and SHARP, R. Beowulf. Boston, U.S.A. (‡1883, on
the basis of Heyne's edition; with Finnsburg.) Reviews: York Powell,
Academy, XXVI, 1884, 220–1; reply by Harrison, 308–9; by York
Powell, 327; Kölbing, *Engl. Stud.* VII, 482; Bright, *Literaturblatt*, 1884,
221–3.
1892. Third edit.
1894. Fourth edit. Reviews: Wülker, *Anglia, Beiblatt*, V, 65–7;
Glöde, *Engl. Stud.* XX, 417–18.

1884 HOLDER, A. Beowulf, II. Berichtigter Text u. Wörterbuch. Freiburg
u. Tübingen. Reviews: York Powell, *Academy*, XXVI, 1884, 220–1;
Wülker, *Lit. Cbl.* 1885, 1008–9; Krüger, *Literaturblatt*, 1884, 468–70.
1899. 2 Aufl. [with suggestions of Kluge and Cosijn]. Reviews:
Trautmann, *Anglia, Beiblatt*, X, 257; Wülfing, *Engl. Stud.* XXIX,
278–9; Holthausen, *Literaturblatt*, 1900, 60–2 (important corrections).

1888 HEYNE, M. and SOCIN, A. [Fifth edit. of Heyne's text.] Paderborn u.
Münster. Reviews: Koeppel, *Engl. Stud.* XIII, 466–72; Heinzel, *A.f.d.A.*
XV, 189–94; Sievers, *Z.f.d.Ph.* XXI, 354–65 (very important corrections);
Schröer, *Literaturblatt*, 1889, 170–1.

1898. 6 Aufl. Reviews: Trautmann, *Anglia, Beiblatt*, x, 257; Holthausen, *Anglia, Beiblatt*, x, 265; Sarrazin, *Engl. Stud.* xxviii, 408–10; Jantzen, *Archiv*, ciii, 175–6.

1903. 7 Aufl. Reviews: Holthausen, *Anglia, Beiblatt*, xviii, 193–4; Klaeber, the same, 289–91; Kruisinga, *Engl. Stud.* xxxv, 401–2; v. Grienberger, *Z.f.ö.G.* lvi, 744–61 (very full); E. Kock, *A.f.n.F.* xxii, 215 (brief).

1894 WYATT, A. J Beowulf, edited with textual footnotes, index of proper names, and glossary. (Text of Finnsburg.) Cambridge. Reviews: Bradley, *Academy*, xlvi, 1894, 69–70; Wülker, *Anglia, Beiblatt*, v, 65–7; Brenner, *Engl. Stud.* xx, 296; Zupitza, *Archiv*, xciv, 326–9.

1898. Second edit. Reviews: Trautmann, *Anglia, Beiblatt*, x, 257; Sarrazin, *Engl. Stud.* xxviii, 407–8.

1902 KLUGE, F. Angelsächsisches Lesebuch. 3 Aufl. Halle. (xxx. Der Überfall von Finnsburuh, pp. 127–8.)

1903 TRAUTMANN, M. Finn u. Hildebrand. *Bonner Beiträge*, vii. (Text, translation and comment on the Episode and Fragment.) Reviews: Binz, *Z.f.d.Ph.* xxxvii, 529–36; Jantzen, *Die Neueren Sprachen*, xi, 543–8; *Neue philol. Rundschau*, 1903, 619–21 (signed -tz- ? Jantzen). Some additional notes by Trautmann, "Nachträgliches zu Finn u. Hildebrand" appeared in *Bonner Beiträge*, xvii, 122.

1904 TRAUTMANN, M. Das Beowulflied...das Finn-Bruchstück u. die Waldhere-Bruchstücke. Bearbeiteter Text u. deutsche Übersetzung. *Bonner Beiträge*, xvi. Reviews: Klaeber, *M.L.N.* xx, 83–7 (weighty); Eckhardt, *Engl. Stud.* xxxvii, 401–3; Schücking, *Archiv*, cxv, 417–21; Barnouw, *Museum*, xiv, 96–8; *Neue philologische Rundschau* (? by Jantzen), 1905, 549–50.

1905–6 HOLTHAUSEN, F. Beowulf nebst dem Finnsburg-Bruchstück. I. Texte. II. Einleitung, Glossar u. Anmerkungen. Heidelberg. Reviews: Lawrence, *J.E.G.Ph.* vii, 125–9; Klaeber, *M.L.N.* xxiv, 94–5; Schücking, *Engl. Stud.* xxxix, 94–111 (weighty); Deutschbein, *Archiv*, cxxi, 162–4; v. Grienberger, *Z.f.ö.G.* 1908, cix, 333–46 (giving an elaborate list of etymological parallels); Barnouw, *Museum*, xiv, 169–70; Wülker, *D.L.Z.* 1906, 285–6; ‡Jantzen, *Neue philologische Rundschau*, 1907, 18.

1908–9. 2 Aufl., nebst den kleineren Denkmälern der Heldensage, Finnsburg, Waldere, Deor, Widsith, Hildebrand. Reviews: Eichler, *Anglia, Beiblatt*, xxi, 129–33; xxii, 161–5; Schücking, *Engl. Stud.* xlii, 108–11; Brandl, *Archiv*, cxxi, 473. cxxiv, 210; Binz, *Literaturblatt*, xxxii, 1911, 53–5: see also Koeppel, *Anglia, Beiblatt*, xxiii, 297.

1912–13. 3 Aufl.

1914–19. 4 Aufl. Reviews: Binz, *Literaturblatt*, xli, 1920, 316–17; Fischer, *Engl. Stud.* liv, 404–6.

1908 SCHÜCKING, L. L. Beowulf [8th edit. of Heyne's text]. Paderborn. Reviews: Lawrence, *M.L.N.* xxv, 155–7; Klaeber, *Engl. Stud.* xxxix, 425–33 (weighty); Imelmann, *D.L.Z.* 1909, 995 (contains important original contributions); v. Grienberger, *Z.f.ö.G.* lx, 1089; Boer, *Museum*, xvi, 139 (brief).

1910. 9 Aufl. Reviews: Sedgefield, *Engl. Stud.* xliii, 267–9; F. Wild, *Z.f.ö.G.* lxiv, 153–5.

1913. 10 Aufl. Reviews: Klaeber, *Anglia, Beiblatt*, xxiv, 289–91; *Engl. Stud.* xlix, 424; ‡Degenhart, *Blätter f. gymnasialschulwesen*, li, 130; E. A. Kock, *A.f.n F.* xxxii, 222–3; Holthausen, *Z.f.d.Ph.* xlviii, 127–31 (weighty).

1918. 11, 12 Aufl. Reviews: Björkman, *Anglia, Beiblatt*, xxx, 121–2, 180; Fischer, *Engl. Stud.* liii, 338–9.

1910 SEDGEFIELD, W. J. Beowulf, edited with Introduction, Bibliography, Notes, Glossary and Appendices. Manchester. Reviews: Thomas, *M.L.R.* VI, 266–8; Lawrence, *J.E.G.Ph.* X, 633–40; Wild, *Anglia, Beiblatt*, XXIII, 253–60; Klaeber, *Engl. Stud.* XLIV, 119–26; Brandl, *Archiv*, CXXVI, 279.

1913. Second edit. Reviews: *M.L.R.* IX, 429; Lawrence, *J.E.G.Ph.* XIV, 609–13; Klaeber, *Anglia, Beiblatt*, XXV, 166–8.

1912 Text of the Finn episode given in MEYER, W., Beiträge zur Geschichte der Eroberung Englands durch die Angelsachsen.

1914 CHAMBERS, R. W. Beowulf with the Finnsburg Fragment, ed. by A. J. WYATT. New edition, revised. Cambridge. Reviews: Jones, *M.L.R.* XI, 230–1; Lawrence, *J.E.G.Ph.* XIV, 609–13; Bright, *M.L.N.* XXXI, 188–9; Schücking, *Engl. Stud.* LV, 88–100.

1915 DICKINS, B. Runic and Heroic Poems (Text of Finnsburg with Notes). Cambridge. Review: Mawer, *M.L.R.* XII, 82–4.

1917 MACKIE, W. L. The Fight at Finnsburg (Introduction, Text and Notes). *J.E.G.Ph.* XVI, 250–73.

1919 SCHÜCKING, L. L. Kleines angelsächsisches Dichterbuch. [Includes Finnsburg Fragment, Finnsburg Episode and "Beowulf's Return" (ll. 1888–2199).] Reviews: Binz, *Literaturblatt*, XLI, 1920, pp. 315–16; Imelmann, *D.L.Z.* XL, 1919, 423–5; Fischer, *Engl. Stud.* LIV, 1920, 302–3.

1920 Text of Finnsburg Fragment and Episode. with commentary, in IMELMANN's "Forschungen zur altenglischen Poesie."

An edition of Beowulf by Prof. F. KLAEBER is in the press.

§ 5. CONCORDANCES, ETC.

1896 HOLDER, A. Beowulf, vol. II *b*, Wortschatz. Freiburg. Review: Brandl, *A.f.d.A.* XXIII, 107.

1911 COOK, A. S. Concordance to Beowulf. Halle. Reviews: Klaeber, *J.E.G.Ph.* XI, 277–9; Garnett, *Amer. Jnl. Philol.* XXXIII, 86–7.

§ 6. TRANSLATIONS (INCLUDING EARLY SUMMARIES)

1881 WÜLKER, R. P. Besprechung der Beowulfübersetzungen, *Anglia*, IV, *Anzeiger*, 69–80.

1886 GUMMERE, F. B. The translation of Beowulf, and the relations of ancient and modern English verse, *Amer. Jour. of Phil.* VII, 46–78. (A weighty argument for translation into "the original metre.")

1891 GARNETT, J. M. The translation of A.S. poetry, *Pub. Mod. Lang. Assoc. Amer.* VI, 95–105. (Agreeing in the main with Gummere.)

1897 FRYE, P. H. The translation of Beowulf, *M.L.N.* XII, 79–82. (Advocating blank verse.)

1898 FULTON, E. On translating A.S. poetry, *Pub. Mod. Lang. Assoc. Amer.* XIII, 286–96. (Recommending an irregular four-accent line.)

1903 GARNETT, J. M. Recent translations of O.E. poetry, *Pub. Mod. Lang. Assoc. Amer.* XVIII, 445–58.

1903 TINKER, C. B. The translations of Beowulf. A critical bibliography. *Yale Studies in English.* New York. Reviews: Klaeber, *J.E.G.Ph.* V, 116–8; Binz, *Anglia, Beiblatt*, XVI, 291–2.

1909 CHILD, G. C. "Gummere's Oldest English Epic," *M.L.N.* XXIV, 253–4. (A criticism advocating prose translation.)

1910 GUMMERE, F. B. Translation of Old English Verse, *M.L.N.* XXV, 61–3. (Advocating alliterative verse.) Reply by CHILD, *M.L.N.* XXV, 157–8. See also reviews of Gummere, under year 1909, below.

1918 LEONARD, W. E. Beowulf and the Niebelungen couplet, *Univ. of Wisconsin Studies in Language and Literature*, II, 99–152.

1805 TURNER, SHARON. History of the manners...poetry...and language of the Anglo-Saxons. London. (From p. 398 to p. 408 is a summary, with translations, of Beowulf, Prol.–VIII. Turner was misled as to the subject of the poem, because a leaf had been misplaced in the MS, so that the account of the fighting between Grendel and Beowulf (ll. 740–82) occurred immediately after l. 91. The struggle between Beowulf and an (unnamed) adversary being thus made to follow the account of Hrothgar's court at Heorot, Turner was led to suppose that the poem narrated the attempt of Beowulf to avenge *on Hrothgar* the feud for a homicide he had committed. "The transition," Turner not unreasonably complains, "is rather violent." The correct placing of the shifted leaf is due to Thorkelin.)

1815 THORKELIN, G. J. [Latin version in his edition, q.v.] The reviewers gave summaries of the poem, with translations of portions of it: English in the *Monthly Review*, LXXXI, 1816, 516–23 (less inaccurate than Turner's summary); Danish in the *Dansk Litteratur-Tidende*, 1815, 401–32, 437–46, and by Grundtvig in the *Nyeste Skilderie* (see below, § 7); Swedish in *Iduna*, VII, 1817, 133–59.

1819 GRUNDTVIG, N. F. S. Stykker af Skjoldung-Kvadet eller Bjovulfs Minde, *Dannevirke*, IV, 234–62.

1820 GRUNDTVIG, N. F. S. Bjowulfs Drape, Kjøbenhavn. (Free rhymed translation of Beowulf: Finnsburg rendered into short lines, unrhymed: Introduction and most important critical notes.) Review: J. Grimm in *Gött. Anzeigen*, 1823 = *Kleinere Schriften*, IV, 178–86. For second edit., see 1865.

1820 TURNER, SHARON. History of the Anglo-Saxons...third edit. London. (Vol. III, pp. 325–48, contains a summary, with translations, of the earlier part of the poem, much less inaccurate than that of 1805.)

1826 CONYBEARE, J. J. Illustrations of Anglo-Saxon poetry. London. (Pp. 35–136 contain a summary of Beowulf, with blank verse transl. and the corresponding text in A.S. and Latin; pp. 175–82, Finnsburg, text with transl. into Latin and into English verse.)

1832 GRUNDTVIG, N. F. S. Nordens mythologi. Anden Udgave. Kiöbenhavn. (Pp. 571–94 give a summary of the Beowulf-stories. This was, of course, wanting in the first edit. of 1808.)

1837 KEMBLE, J. M. Translation...with...glossary, preface and notes. London. (The "postscript to the preface" in which Kemble supplemented and corrected the "Historical Preface" to his edition of 1833, is the basis of the mythological explanations of Beowulf as an Anglian god, Beowa.)

1839 LEO, H. [Summary with translation of extracts.] See § 8, below.

1840 ETTMÜLLER, L. Beowulf, stabreimend übersetzt, mit Einleitung und Anmerkungen (Finnsburg, pp. 36–8). Zürich.

1845 LONGFELLOW, H. W. The Poets and Poetry of Europe. Philadelphia. (Pp. 8–10 contain transl. of extracts from Beowulf.)

1847 SCHALDEMOSE, F. [Danish transl. of Beowulf and Finnsburg, in his edit., q.v.]

1849 WACKERBARTH, A. D. Beowulf, translated into English verse. London. (Imitation of Scott's metre.)

1855 THORPE, B. [In his edit., q.v.]

1857 UHLAND, L. [Prose transl. of Finnsburg.] *Germania*, II, 354–5.

562   *Bibliography*

1857 GREIN, C. W. M. Dichtungen der Angelsachsen, stabreimend übersetzt. Göttingen. (Vol. I, pp. 222–308, Beowulf, trans. into alliterative verse.)
     1883. 2 Aufl. [Incorporating Grein's manuscript corrections, seen through the press by Wülker.] Cassel. Review: Krüger, *Engl. Stud.* VIII, 139–42.

1859 SIMROCK, K. Beowulf übersetzt u. erläutert. Stuttgart u. Augsburg. (Alliterative verse: Finnsburg Fragment inserted after l. 1124.)

1859 SANDRAS, G. S. De carminibus anglo-saxonicis Caedmoni adjudicatis. Paris. (Pp. 8–10 contain extract from Beowulf and Latin transl.)

1861 HAIGH, D. H. (Prose transl. of Finnsburg.) In *Anglo-Saxon Sagas*, pp. 32–3, q.v.

1863 HEYNE, M. Beowulf übersetzt. Paderborn. (Blank verse.) Review: Holtzmann, *Germania*, VIII, 506–7.
     1897–8. 2 Aufl. Paderborn. Reviews: Holthausen, *Archiv*, CIII, 373–6; Wülker, *Anglia, Beiblatt*, IX, 1; Jantzen, *Engl. Stud.* XXV, 271–3; Löhner, *Z.f.ö.G.* XLIX, 563.
     1915. 3 Aufl. Paderborn.

1865 GRUNDTVIG, N. F. S. Bjovulfs-Drapen. Anden Udgave.

1872 VON WOLZOGEN, H. Beovulf aus dem ags. Leipzig. (Verse.)

1876 ARNOLD, T. [In his edit., q.v.]

1877 BOTKINE, L. Beowulf traduite en français. Havre. (Prose: some omissions.) Review: Körner, *Engl. Stud.* II, 248–51.

1881 ZINSSER, G. Der Kampf Beowulfs mit Grendel [vv. 1–836] als Probe einer metrischen Uebersetzung. Saarbrücken. Reviews: *Archiv*, LXVIII, 446; Krüger, *Engl. Stud.* VII, 370–2.

1881 LUMSDEN, H. W. Beowulf...transl. into modern rhymes. London. (Some omissions.) Reviews: *Athenæum*, April 1881, p. 587; Garnett, *Amer. Jour. of Phil.* II, 355–61; Wülker, *Anglia*, IV, *Anzeiger*, 69–80.
     1883. ‡Second edit. Review: York Powell, *Academy*, XXVI, 1884, pp. 220–1.

1882 SCHUHMANN, G. Beowulf, antichissimo poema epico de' popoli germanici. *Giornale Napoletano di filosofia e lettere.* Anno IV, vol. 7, 25–36, 175–190. (A summary only.)

1882 GARNETT, J. M. Beowulf and the Fight at Finnsburg, translated. Boston, U.S.A. Reviews: *Nation* (New York), No. 919, 1883; Harrison, *Amer. Jour. of Phil.* IV, 84–6, reply by Garnett, 243–6; Schipper, *Anglia*, VI, *Anzeiger*, 120–4; Krüger, *Engl. Stud.* VIII, 133–8, and (second edit.) IX, 151; Bright, *Literaturblatt*, 1883, 386–7.
     1885. Second edit., revised.
     1900. Fourth edit.

1883 GRION, GIUSTO. Beovulf, poema epico anglosassone del VII secolo, tradotto e illustrato. In the *Atti della reale Accademia Lucchese*, XXII. (First Italian translation.) Review: Krüger, *Engl. Stud.* IX, 64–77.

1889 ‡WICKBERG, R. Beowulf, en fornengelsk hjältedikt översatt. Westervik.
     1914. ‡Second edit. Upsala. Review: Kock, *A.f.n.F.* XXXII, 223–4.

1892 HALL, JOHN LESSLIE. Beowulf translated. (Verse, with notes.) Boston, U.S.A. Reviews: *M.L.N.* VII, 128, 1892 (brief mention); Miller, *Viking Club Year Book*, I, 91–2; Holthausen, *Anglia, Beiblatt*, IV, 33–6; Glöde, *Engl. Stud.* XIX, 257–60.
     1893. ‡Student's edit.

1892 (1891) EARLE, JOHN. The deeds of Beowulf. Oxford. (Prose translation, somewhat spoilt by its artificial and sometimes grotesque vocabulary; very valuable introduction, with summary of the controversy to date,

Translations 563

and notes.) Reviews: *Athenæum*, 1 Oct. 1892; Koeppel, *Engl. Stud.* XVIII, 93–5 (fair, though rather severe).

1893 HOFFMANN, P. Beówulf...aus dem angelsächsischen übertragen. Züllichau. (In the measure of the Nibelungenlied; incl. Finnsburg.) Reviews (mostly unfavourable): Shipley, *M.L.N.* IX, 121–3, 1894; Wülker, *Anglia, Beiblatt*, V, 67; Wülker, *Lit. Cbl.* 1894, p. 1930; Glöde, *Engl. Stud.* XIX, 412–5; ‡Detter, *Öster. Literaturblatt*, V, 9; ‡Marold, *Deut. Literaturblatt*, XXIII, 332.
    1900. ‡Second edit. Hannover.

1895 MORRIS, W. and WYATT, A. J. The Tale of Beowulf. Kelmscott Press, Hammersmith. (Verse: archaic vocabulary.)
    1898. New edit. Review: Hulme, *M.L.N.* XV, 22–6, 1900.

1896 SIMONS, L. Beówulf...vertaald in stafrijm en met inleiding en aanteekeningen. Gent (*Koninklijke vlaamsche Academie*). Reviews: Glöde, *Engl. Stud.* XXV, 270–1; Uhlenbeck, *Museum* (Groningen), V, 217–8.

1898 STEINECK, H. Altenglische Dichtungen (Beowulf, Elene, u.a.) in wortgetreuer Übersetzung. Leipzig. (Prose, line for line.) Reviews: Binz, *Anglia, Beiblatt*, IX, 220–2; Holthausen, *Archiv*, CIII, 376–8 (both very unfavourable).

1901 HALL, J. R. CLARK. Beowulf and the fight at Finnsburg. A translation into modern English prose. London. Reviews: *Athenæum*, 1901, July, p. 56; *Academy*, LX, 1901, 342; Stedman, *Viking Club Year Book*, III, 72–4; Tinker, *J.E.G.Ph.* IV, 379–81; Holthausen, *Anglia, Beiblatt*, XIII. 225–8; Dibelius, *Archiv*, CIX, 403–4; Vietor, *Die neueren Sprachen*, XI, 439; Wülker, *Lit. Cbl.* 1902, 30–1 ("sehr zu empfehlen").
    1911 (q.v.). New edit., with considerable additions.

1902 TINKER, C. B. Beowulf translated out of the Old English. New York. (Prose.) Reviews: Klaeber, *J.E.G.Ph.* V, 91–3; Holthausen, *Anglia, Beiblatt*, XIV, 7.

1903 ‡BJÖRKMAN, E. Swedish transl. (prose) of Beowulf, Part II (in Schück's *Världslitteraturen*, with introd. by Schück).

1903–4 TRAUTMANN, M., in his editions, q.v.

1904 CHILD, C. G. Beowulf and the Finnesburh Fragment translated. London and Boston. Reviews: Grattan, *M.L.R.* III, 303–4 ("a good prose translation which steers an even course between pseudo-archaisms and modern colloquialisms"); Miller, *Viking Club Year Book*, I, 91–2; Klaeber, *Anglia, Beiblatt*, XVI, 225–7; Brandl, *Archiv*, CXXI, 473.

1904 ‡HANSEN, A. Transl. into Danish of Beowulf, ll. 491–924, *Danske Tidsskrift*.

1905 VOGT, P. Beowulf...übersetzt. Halle. (Text rearranged according to theories of interpolation: Finnsburg Fragment translated, following Möller's text.) Reviews: Binz, *Anglia, Beiblatt*, XXI, 289–91; Eichler, *Z.f.ö.G.* LVII, 908–10; Klaeber, *Archiv*, CXVII, 408–10; Jantzen, *Lit. Cbl.* 1906, 257–8.

1906 GERING, H. Beowulf nebst dem Finnsburg-Bruchstück übersetzt. Heidelberg. (Verse.) Reviews: Lawrence, *J.E.G.Ph.* VII, 129–33 ("thoroughly scholarly"); Jantzen, *Lit. Cbl.* 1907, 64–5; Ries, *A.f.d.A.* XXXIII, 143–7; Binz, *Literaturblatt*, XXXI, 397–8 ("Fliessend und ungezwungen, sinngetreu..."); ‡Zehme, *Monatsschrift*, XIV, 597–600; v. Grienberger, *Z.f.ö.G.* 1908, LIX, 423–8.
    1914. 2 Aufl.

1907 HUYSHE, W. Beowulf...translated into...prose ("Appendix: The Fight at Finn's burgh"). London. ("Translation," to quote Clark Hall, "apparently such as might have been compiled from previous translations by a person ignorant of Ags. Some original mistakes.") Reviews: *Athenæum*, 1907, II, 96 ("Mr Huyshe displays sad ignorance of Old

36—2

English...but an assiduous study of the work of his predecessors has preserved him from misrepresenting seriously the general sense of the text"); *Notes and Queries*, Ser. x, vol. viii, 58; Garnett, *Amer. Jnl. Philol.* xxix, 344–6; Klaeber, *Anglia, Beiblatt*, xix, 257.

1909 GUMMERE, F. B. The oldest English Epic. Beowulf, Finnsburg, Waldere, Deor and the German Hildebrand, translated in the original metres. New York. Reviews: *Athenæum*, 1909, ii, 151; Trautmann, *Anglia, Beiblatt*, xxxiii, 353–60 (metrical debate); Sedgefield, *Engl. Stud.* xli, 402–3 (discussing possibility of reproducing in Mod. Eng. the Old Eng. alliterative verse-rhythm); Derocquigny, *Revue Germanique*, vi, 356–7; see also above, p. 390.

1910 HANSEN, ADOLF. Bjovulf, oversat af A. Hansen, og efter hans død gået efter og fuldført samt forsynet med en inledning og en oversættelse af brudstykket om kampen i Finsborg, af Viggo Julius von Holstein Rathlou; udgivet ved Oskar Hansen. København og Kristiania. An account of this translation, by v. Holstein Rathlou, in *Tilskueren*, June, 1910, pp. 557–62; Review: Olrik, *Danske Studier*, 1910, 112–13.

1911 CLARK HALL, J. R. Beowulf and the Finnsburg Fragment. A translation into Modern English Prose. London. Reviews: Mawer, *M.L.R.* vi, 542 ("probably the best working translation that we have, enriched by a valuable introduction and excellent appendices"); *Academy*, 1911, i, 225–6; Björkman, *Engl. Stud.* xliv, 127–8; *Archiv*, cxxvi, 492–3; Binz, *Literaturblatt*, xxxii, 232.

1912 PIERQUIN, H. Le poème Anglo-Saxon de Beowulf. (An extraordinary piece of work; the version mainly follows Kemble's text, which is reproduced, but with many misprints: Kemble's *Saxons in England* is translated by way of introduction. The Finnsburg Fragment is included.) Reviews: *Academy*, 1912, ii, 509–10 (seems to regard Pierquin as author of *Les Saxons en Angleterre*); Sedgefield, *M.L.R.* viii, 550–2; Klaeber, *Anglia, Beiblatt*, xxiv, 138–9; Imelmann, *D.L.Z.* xxxiv (1913), 1062–3 (very unfavourable); ‡Luick, *Mitt. d. inst. f. österr. gesch.-forsch.* xxxvi, 401; ‡Barat, *Moyen Âge*, xxvi (sec. ser. xvii), 298–302.

1913 KIRTLAN, E. J. The Story of Beowulf. London. (A fair specimen of the less scholarly translations; nicely got up and not exceedingly incorrect.) Reviews: *Athenæum*, 1914, ii, 71; Klaeber, *Anglia, Beiblatt*, xxvii, 129–31.

1914 CLARK HALL, J. R. Beowulf: a metrical translation. Cambridge. (Not so successful as the same writer's prose translation.) Reviews: Sedgefield, *M.L.R.* x, 387–9 (discussing the principles of metrical translation); Klaeber, *Anglia, Beiblatt*, xxvi, 170–2.

1915 OLIVERO, F. Traduzioni dalla Poesia Anglo-sassone. Bari. (Pp. 73–119, extracts from Beowulf.) Review: *M.L.R.* xi, 509.

1916 ‡BENEDETTI, A. La canzone di Beowulf, poema epico anglo-sassone dei vi secolo. Versione italiana, con introduzione e note. Palermo.

1918 LEONARD, W. E. [Specimen, Passus ix, of forthcoming transl., in the measure of the Nibelungenlied.] In *Univ. of Wisconsin Studies*, ii, 149–52; see above.

A translation of Beowulf into the Norwegian "landsmaal," by H. RYTTER, will appear shortly.

Popular paraphrases of Beowulf are not included in the above list. An account will be found in Tinker's *Translations* of those of E. H. Jones (in Cox's *Popular Romances*, 1871); J. Gibb, 1881–4; Wägner-MacDowall, 1883 *etc.*; Miss Z. A. Ragozin, 1898, 1900; A. J. Church, 1898; Miss C L. Thomson, 1899, 1904. Mention may also be made of those of ‡F. A. Turner, 1894; H. E. Marshall, 1908; T. Cartwright, 1908; Prof. J. H. Cox, 1910. An illustrated summary of the *Beowulf* story was issued by Mr W. T. Stead in his penny "Books for the Bairns." The versions of Miss Thomson and Prof. Cox are both good. The paraphrase in the *Canadian Monthly*, II, 83 (1872), attributed in several bibliographies to Earle, is assuredly not the work of that scholar: it is an inaccurate version based upon Jones. An account will be found in Tinker of the German paraphrase of Therese Dahn, 1883 *etc.*; mention may also be made of those of J. Arnheim, 1871; ‡ F. Bässler, sec. edit. 1875 (praised highly by Klaeber in *J.E.G.Ph.* V, 118).

§ 7. TEXTUAL CRITICISM AND INTERPRETATION

1815 GRUNDTVIG, N. F. S. Et Par Ord om det nys udkomne angelsaxiske Digt. *Nyeste Skilderie af Kjøbenhavn*, No. 60 *etc.*, cols. 945, 998, 1009, 1025, 1045; Nok et Par Ord om Bjovulfs Drape, 1106, 1121, 1139 (comment upon Thorkelin's text and translation).

1815 THORKELIN, G. J. Reply to Grundtvig in *Nyeste Skilderie*, cols. 1057, 1073. (There were further articles in the same magazine, but they were purely personal.)

1820 GRUNDTVIG, N. F. S. Emendations to Thorkelin's text, added to *Bjowulfs Drape*, 267–312.

1826 CONYBEARE, J. J. Illustrations of Anglo-Saxon poetry. London. (Beowulf and "Finnsborough," pp. 30–182.)

1859 BOUTERWEK, K. W. Zur Kritik des Beowulfliedes, *Z.f.d.A.* XI, 59–113.

1859 DIETRICH, F. Rettungen, *Z.f.d.A.* XI, 409–20.

1863 HOLTZMANN, A. Zu Beowulf, *Germania*, VIII, 489–97. (Incl. Finnsburg.)

1865 GREIN, C. W. M. Zur Textkritik der angelsächsischen Dichter: Finnsburg, *Germania*, X, 422.

1868–9 BUGGE, SOPHUS. Spredte iagttagelser vedkommende de oldengelske digte om Beówulf og Waldere; *Tidskrift for Philologi og Pædagogik*, VIII, 40–78 and 287–307 (incl. Finnsburg, 304–5). Important.

1871 RIEGER, M. Zum Beowulf, *Z.f.d.Ph.* III, 381–416.

1873 BUGGE, S. Zum Beowulf, *Z.f.d.Ph.* IV, 192–224.

1880 KÖLBING, E. Kleine Beiträge (Beowulf, 168, 169), *Engl. Stud.* III, 92 *etc.*

1882 KLUGE, F. Sprachhistorische Miscellen (Beowulf, 63, 1027, 1235, 1267), *P.B.B.* VIII, 532–5.

1882 COSIJN, P. J. Zum Beowulf, *P.B.B.* VIII, 568–74.

1883 SIEVERS, E. Zum Beowulf, *P.B.B.* IX, 135–44, 370.

1883 KLUGE, F. Zum Beowulf, *P.B.B.* IX, 187–92.

1883 KRÜGER, TH. Zum Beowulf, *P.B.B.* IX, 571–8.

1889 MILLER, T. The position of Grendel's arm in Heorot, *Anglia*, XII, 396–400.

1890 JOSEPH, E. Zwei Versversetzungen im Beowulf, *Z.f.d.Ph.* XXII, 385–97.

1891 SCHRÖER, A. Zur texterklärung des Beowulf, *Anglia*, XIII, 333–48.

1891–2 COSIJN, P. J. Aanteekeningen op den Beowulf. Leiden. (Important.) Reviews: Lübke, *A.f.d.A.* XIX, 341–2; Holthausen, *Literaturblatt*, 1895, p. 82.

1892 SIEVERS, E. Zur texterklärung des Beowulf, *Anglia*, XIV, 133–46.

1895 BRIGHT, J. W. Notes on the Beowulf (ll. 30, 306, 386–7, 623, 737), *M.L.N.* X, 43–4.

1899 TRAUTMANN, M. Berichtigungen, Vermutungen und Erklärungen zum Beowulf (ll. 1–1215). *Bonner Beiträge zur Anglistik*, II, 121–92. Reviews: Binz, *Anglia, Beiblatt*, XIV, 358–60; Holthausen, *Literaturblatt*, 1900, 62–4 (important). See Sievers, *P.B.B.* XXVII, 572; XXVIII, 271.

1901 KLAEBER, F. A few Beowulf notes (ll. 459, 847 *etc.*, 1206, 3024 *etc.*, 3171); *M.L.N.* XVI, 14–18.

1902 KLAEBER, F. Zum Beowulf (497–8; 1745–7), *Archiv*, CVIII, 368–70.

1902 KLAEBER, F. Beowulf's character, *M.L.N.* XVII, 162.

1903 KRACKOW, O. Zu Beowulf, 1225, 2222, *Archiv*, CXI, 171–2.

1904 BRYANT, F. E. Beowulf, 62, *M.L.N.* XIX, 121–2.

1904 ABBOTT, W. C. Hrothulf, *M.L.N.* XIX, 122–5. (Abbott suggests that Hrothulf is the name—missing in whole or part from l. 62—of the husband of the daughter of Healfdene. This suggestion is quite untenable, for many reasons: Hrothulf (Rolf Kraki) is a Dane, and the missing husband is a Swede: but the article led to a long controversy between Bryant and Klaeber; see *M.L.N.* XX, 9–11; XXI, 143, 255; XXII, 96, 160. Klaeber is undoubtedly right.)

1904 KRAPP, G. B. Miscellaneous Notes: *Scūrheard*; *M.L.N.* XIX, 234.

1904 SIEVERS, E. Zum Beowulf, *P.B.B.* XXIX, 305–31. (Criticism of Trautmann's emendations.)

1904 KOCK, E. A. Interpretations and Emendations of Early English Texts: III (Beowulf), *Anglia*, XXVII, 218–37.

1904 SIEVERS, E. Zum Beowulf (l. 5, Criticism of Kock), *P.B.B.* XXIX, 560–76. Reply by Kock, *Anglia*, XXVIII (1905), 140–2.

1905 TRAUTMANN, M. Auch zum Beowulf: ein gruss an herren Eduard Sievers, *Bonner Beiträge zur Anglistik*, XVII, 143–74. (Reply to Sievers' criticism of Trautmann's conjectural emendations.) Review: Klaeber, *M.L.N.* XXII, 252.

1905 SWIGGETT, G. L. Notes on the Finnsburg fragment, *M.L.N.* XX, 169–71.

1905 KLAEBER, F. Notizen zur texterklärung des Beowulf, *Anglia*, XXVIII, 439–47 (incl. Finnsburg); Zum Beowulf, the same, 448–56.

1905 KLAEBER, F. Bemerkungen zum Beowulf, *Archiv*, CXV, 178–82. (Incl. Finnsburg.)

1905 HOLTHAUSEN, F. Beiträge zur Erklärung des altengl. epos. I, Zum Beowulf; II, Zum Finnsburg-fragment; *Z.f.d.Ph.* XXXVII, 113–25.

1905–6 KLAEBER, F. Studies in the Textual Interpretation of "Beowulf," *Mod. Phil.* III, 235–66, 445–65 (Most important).

1906 CHILD, C. G. Beowulf, 30, 53, 132 (i.e. 1323), 2957, *M.L.N.* XXI, 175–7, 198–200.

1906 HORN, W. Textkritische Bemerkungen (Beowulf, 69 *etc.*), *Anglia*, XXIX, 130–1.

1906 KLAEBER, F. Notizen zum Beowulf, *Anglia*, XXIX, 378–82.

1907 KLAEBER, F. Minor Notes on the Beowulf, *J.E.G.Ph.* VI, 190–6.

1908 TINKER, C. B. Notes on Beowulf, *M.L.N.* XXIII, 239–40.

1908 KLAEBER, F. Zum Beowulf, *Engl. Stud.* XXXIX, 463–7.

1909 KLAEBER, F. Textual Notes on Beowulf, *J.E.G.Ph.* VIII, 254–9.

1910 VON GRIENBERGER, T. Bemerkungen zum Beowulf, *P.B.B.* XXXVI, 77–101. (Incl. Finnsburg.)

1910 SIEVERS, E. Gegenbemerkungen zum Beowulf, *P.B.B.* XXXVI, 397–434. (Incl. Finnsburg.)

1910 SEDGEFIELD, W. J. Notes on "Beowulf," *M.L.R.* V, 286–8.

1910 TRAUTMANN, M. Beiträge zu einem künftigen "Sprachschatz der altenglischen Dichter," *Anglia*, XXXIII, 276–9 *(gedræg)*.

1911 BLACKBURN, F. A. Note on Beowulf, 1591–1617, *Mod. Phil.* IX, 555–66. (Argues that a loose leaf has been misplaced and the order of events thus disturbed.)

1911 KLAEBER, F. Zur Texterklärung des Beowulf, vv. 767, 1129, *Anglia, Beiblatt*, XXII, 372–4.

1912 HART, J. M. Beowulf, 168–9, *M.L.N.* XXVII, 198.

1912–14 GREIN, C. W. M. Sprachschatz der angelsächsischen dichter. Unter mitwirkung von F. Holthausen neu herausgegeben von J. J. Köhler. Heidelberg. Reviews: Trautmann, *Anglia, Beiblatt*, XXIV, 36–43; Schücking, *Engl. Stud.* XLIX, 113–5.

1015 CHAMBERS, R. W. The "Shifted leaf" in Beowulf, *M.L.R.* X, 37–41. (Points out that the alleged "confused order of events" is that also followed in the Grettis saga.)

1916 GREEN, A. The opening of the episode of Finn in Beowulf, *Pub. Mod. Lang. Assoc. Amer.* XXXI, 759–97.

1916 BRIGHT, J. W. Anglo-Saxon *umbor* and *seld-guma*, *M.L.N.* XXXI, 82–4; Beowulf, 489–90, *M.L.N.* XXXI, 217–23.

1917 GREEN, A. An episode in Ongenþeow's fall, *M.L.R.* XII, 340–3.

1917 HOLLANDER, L. M. Beowulf, 33, *M.L.N.* XXXII, 246–7. (Suggests the reading *itig.*)

1917 HOLTHAUSEN, F. Zu altenglischen Denkmälern—Beowulf, 1140, *Engl. Stud.* LI, 180.

1918 HUBBARD, F. G. Beowulf, 1598, 1996, 2026: uses of the impersonal verb *geweorþan*, *J.E.G.Ph.* XVII, 119.

1918 KOCK, E. A. Interpretations and emendations of early English Texts: IV, Beowulf, *Anglia*, XLII, 99–124 (Important.)

1918 ‡KOCK, E. A. Jubilee Jaunts and Jottings, in the *Lunds univ. årsskrift*, N. F. avd. 1, bd. 14, nr. 26 (*Festskrift vid...250-årsjubileum*). Reviews: Holthausen, *Anglia, Beiblatt*, XXX, 1–5; Klaeber, *J.E.G.Ph.* XIX, 409–13.

1919 MOORE, SAMUEL. Beowulf Notes (Textual), *J.E.G.Ph.* XVIII, 205–16.

1919 KLAEBER, F. Concerning the functions of O.E. *geweorðan*, *J.E.G.Ph.* XVIII, 250–71. (Cf. paper of Prof. Hubbard above, by which this was suggested.)

1919 KLAEBER, F. Textual notes on "Beowulf," *M.L.N.* XXXIV, 129–34.

1919 BROWN, CARLETON. Beowulf, 1080–1106, *M.L.N.* XXXIV, 181–3.

1919 BRETT, CYRIL. Notes on passages of Old and Middle English, *M.L.R.* XIV, 1–9.

1919–20 KOCK, E. A. Interpretations and emendations of Early English Texts: V (Incl. Beowulf, 2030, 2419–24); VI (Incl. Beowulf 24, 154–6, 189–90, 1992–3, 489–90, 581–3, 1745–7, 1820–1, 1931–2, 2164); VII (Incl. Beowulf, 1230, 1404, 1553–6); *Anglia*, XLIII, 303–4; XLIV, 98 *etc.*, 245 *etc.*

1920 BRYAN W. F. Beowulf Notes (303–6, 532–4, 867–71), *J.E.G.Ph.* XIX, 84–5.

§ 8. QUESTIONS OF LITERARY HISTORY, DATE AND AUTHORSHIP: BEOWULF IN THE LIGHT OF HISTORY, ARCHÆOLOGY, HEROIC LEGEND, MYTHOLOGY AND FOLKLORE

See also preceding sections.

No attempt is made here to deal with Old English heroic legend in general: nor to enumerate the references to *Beowulf* in histories of literature. Probably the earliest allusion to our poem by a great writer is in Scott's *Essay on Romance* (1824):

"The Saxons had, no doubt, Romances,...and Mr Turner...has given us the abridgement of one entitled Caedmon, in which the hero, whose adventures are told much after the manner of the ancient Norse Sagas, encounters, defeats and finally slays an evil being called Grendel...."

1816 OUTZEN, N. Das ags. Gedicht Beowulf, *Kieler Blätter*, III, 307–27. (See above, p. 4, note.)

1816 (Review of Thorkelin in) *Monthly Review*, LXXXI, 516–23. (Beowulf identified with Beaw Sceldwaing of the West Saxon genealogy; see above, p. 292.)

1817 GRUNDTVIG, N. F. S. *Danne-Virke*, II, 207–89. (Identifies Chochilaicus; see above, p. 4, note.)

1826 GRIMM, W. Einleitung über die Elfen, *Kleinere Schriften*, I, 405, esp. p. 467 (extract relating to Grendel's hatred of song). From ‡*Irische Elfenmärchen.*

1829 GRIMM, W. Die deutsche Heldensage. Göttingen. (Pp. 13–17. Extracts from Beowulf, with translation, relating to Weland, Sigemund, Hama and Eormenric.)

1836 KEMBLE, J. M. Über die Stammtafel der Westsachsen. München. Review: J. Grimm, *Göttingische gelehrte Anziegen*, 1836, 649–57, = *Kleinere Schriften*, V, 240.

1836 MONE, F. J. Zur Kritik des Gedichts von Beowulf (in Untersuchungen zur Geschichte der teutschen Heldensage). Quedlinburg u. Leipzig. (Pp. 129–36.)

1839 LEO, H. Bëówulf...nach seinem inhalte, und nach seinen historischen und mythologischen beziehungen betrachtet. Halle.

1841 DISRAELI, I. Amenities of Literature. London. (Beowulf; the Hero-Life. Vol. I, pp. 80–92.)

1841 GRUNDTVIG, N. F. S. Bjovulfs Drape, *Brage og Idun*, IV, 481–538. (Discusses the story, with criticism of previous scholars, and especially of Kemble.)

1843–9 GRIMM, W. Einleitung zur Vorlesung über Gudrun [with an abstract of Beowulf]; see *Kleinere Schriften*, IV, 557–60.

1844 MÜLLENHOFF, K. Die deutschen Völker an Nord- und Ostsee in ältester Zeit, *Nordalbingische Studien*, I, 111 etc.

1845 A brief discussion of Beowulf in *Edinburgh Review*, LXXXII, 309–11.

1845 HAUPT, M. Zum Beowulf, *Z.f.d.A.* V, 10. (Drawing attention to the reference to Hygelac in the *liber de monstris*; see above, p. 4.)

1848 MÜLLENHOFF, K. Die austrasische Dietrichssage, *Z.f.d.A.* VI, 435 etc.

1849 MÜLLENHOFF, K. Sceáf u. seine Nachkommen, *Z.f.d.A.* VII, 410–19; Der Mythus von Beóvulf, *Z.f.d.A.* VII, 419–41.

1849 GRIMM, J. Ueber das Verbrennen der Leichen, *Abhandl. d. Berl. Akad.*, 1849, 191 etc. = *Kleinere Schriften*, II, 211–313 (esp. 261–4).

1849 BACHLECHNER, J. Die Merovinge im Beowulf, *Z.f.d A.* VII, 524–6.

1851 ZAPPERT, G. Virgil's Fortleben im Mittelalter, *Denkschriften der k. Akad. Wien, Phil.-Hist. Classe*, Bd. II, Abth. 2, pp. 17–70. (Gives numerous parallels between Virgil and "Beowulf," somewhat indiscriminately.)

1852 BRYNJULFSSON, G. Oldengelsk og Oldnordisk, *Antikuarisk Tidsskrift*, Kjøbenhavn, 1852–4, pp. 81–143. (An important paper which has been unduly overlooked. Brynjulfsson notes the parallel between Beowulf and Bjarki (see above, p. 61) and in other respects anticipates later scholars, e.g., in noting the close relationship between Angles and Danes (p. 143) and less fortunately (pp. 129–31) in identifying the Geatas with the Jutes.)

1856 BACHLECHNER, J. Eomaer und Heming (Hamlac), *Germania*, I, 297–303 and 455–61.

1856 BOUTERWEK, K. W. Das Beowulflied: Eine Vorlesung; *Germania*, I, 385–418.

1857 UHLAND, L. Sigemund und Sigeferd, *Germania*, II, 344–63 = *Schriften*, VIII, 479 etc. (Incl. Finnsburg.)

1858 WEINHOLD, K. Die Riesen des germanischen Mythus, *Sitzungberichte der K. Akad., Wien, Phil.-Hist. Classe,* XXVI, 225–306. (Grendel and his mother, p. 255.)

1859 RIEGER, M. Ingaevonen, Istaevonen, Herminonen, *Z.f.d.A.* XI, 177–205.

1859 MÜLLENHOFF, K. Zur Kritik des angelsächsischen Volksepos, 2, Widsith, *Z.f.d.A.* XI, 275–94.

1860 MÜLLENHOFF, K. Zeugnisse u. Excurse zur deutschen Heldensage, *Z.f.d.A.* XII, 253–386. (*This portion* of vol. XII was published in 1860.)

1861 HAIGH, D. H. The Anglo-Saxon Sagas. London. (An uncritical attempt to identify the proper names in Beowulf and Finnsburg with sites in England.)

1862 GREIN, C. W. M. Die historischen Verhältnisse des Beowulfliedes, *Eberts Jahrbuch für roman. u. engl. Litt.* IV, 260–85. (Incl. Finnsburg.)

1864 ‡SCHULTZE, M. Ueber das Beowulfslied. *Programm der städtischen Real-schule zu Elbing.* (Not seen, but contents, including the mythical interpretations current at the period, noted in *Archiv,* XXXVII, 232.)

1864 HEYNE, M. Ueber die Lage und Construction der Halle Heorot. Pader-born.

1868 KÖHLER, A. Germanische Alterthümer im Beóvulf, *Germania,* XIII, 129–58.

1869 MÜLLENHOFF, K. Die innere Geschichte des Beovulfs, *Z.f.d.A.* XIV, 193–244. (Reprinted in *Beovulf,* 1889. See above, p. 113 *etc.*)

1870 KÖHLER, A. Die Einleitung des Beovulfliedes. Die beiden Episoden von Heremod, *Z.f.d.Ph.* II, 305–21.

1875 SCHRØDER, L. Om Bjovulfs Drapen. København. (See above, p. 30.)

1876 BOTKINE, L. Beowulf. Analyse historique et géographique. Havre. (Material subsequently incorporated in translation, q.v. § 6.) Review: Körner, *Engl. Stud.* I, 495–6.

1877 SKEAT, W. W. The name "Beowulf," *Academy,* XI (Jan.–June), p. 163. (Suggests Beowulf = "woodpecker"; see above, pp. 365–6, *note.*)

1877 TEN BRINK, B. Geschichte der englischen Litteratur. (Beowulf, Finns-burg, pp. 29–40.)

1877 DEDERICH, H. Historische u. geographische Studien zum ags. Beóvulfliede. Köln. (Incl. Finnsburg.) Reviews: Körner, *Engl. Stud.* I, 481–95; Müllenhoff, *A.f.d.A.* III, 172–82; ‡Suchier, *Jenaer Literatur-Zeitung,* XLVII, 732, 1876.

1877 HORNBURG, J. Die Composition des Beowulf. *Programm des K. Lyceums in Metz.* Full summary by F. Hummel in *Archiv,* LXII, 231–3. See also under 1884.

1877 SCHULTZE, M. Alt-heidnisches in der angelsächsischen Poesie, speciell im Beowulfsliede. Berlin.

1877 SUCHIER, H. Ueber die Sage von Offa u. þryðo, *P.B.B.* IV, 500–21.

1878 MÜLLER, N. Die Mythen im Beówulf, in ihrem Verhältniss zur ger-manischen Mythologie betrachtet. Dissertation, Heidelberg. Leipzig.

1879 LAISTNER, L. Nebelsagen. Stuttgart. (See above, p. 46, note.)

1879 SWEET, H. Old English etymologies: I, *Beóhata, Engl. Stud.* II, 312–14. (See above, p. 365.)

1880 GERING, H. Der Beówulf u. die isländische Grettissaga, *Anglia,* III, 74–87. (Important. Gering announced Vigfússon's discovery to a wider circle of readers, with translation of the Sandhaugar episode, and useful comment. The discovery was further announced to American readers by GARNETT in the *American Journal of Philology,* I, 492 (1880), though its importance was there rather understated. See above, p. 54.)

1881 SMITH, C. SPRAGUE. Beówulf Gretti, *New Englander*, XL (N. S. IV), 49–67. (Translation of corresponding passages in Grettis saga and Beowulf.)

1882 MARCH, F. A. The World of Beowulf, *Proceedings of Amer. Phil. Assoc.* pp. xxi–xxiii.

1883 RÖNNING, F. Beovulfs-kvadet; en literær-historisk undersøgelse. København. Review: Heinzel, *A.f.d.A.* x, 233–9. (Rönning criticises Müllenhoff's theories of separate lays. His book and Heinzel's review are both important.)

1883 MERBOT, R. Aesthetische Studien zur Ags. Poesie. Breslau. Reviews: Koch, *Anglia*, VI, *Anzeiger*, 100–3; Kluge, *Engl. Stud.* VIII, 480–2.

1884 EARLE, J. Anglo-Saxon Literature (The dawn of European Literature). London. (Pp. 120–39 deal with Beowulf. Earle holds Beowulf to be "a genuine growth of that junction in time...when the heathen tales still kept their traditional interest, and yet the spirit of Christianity had taken full possession of the Saxon mind.")

1884 FAHLBECK, P. Beowulfs-kvädet såsom källa för nordisk fornhistoria, *Antikvar. tidskr. för Sverige*, VIII, 1–87. Review: *Academy*, XXIX, 1886, p. 12. (See above, pp. 8, 333.)

1884 HARRISON, J. A. Old Teutonic life in Beowulf, *Overland Monthly*, Sec. Ser. vol. IV, 14–24; 152–61.

1884 HERTZ, W. Beowulf, das älteste germanische Epos, *Nord und Süd*, XXIX, 229–53.

1884 HORNBURG, J. Die komposition des Beovulf, *Archiv*, LXXII, 333–404. (Rejects Müllenhoff's "Liedertheorie.")

1884 KRÜGER, TH. Zum Beowulfliede. Bromberg. Reviewed favourably by Kölbing, *Engl. Stud.* IX, 150; severely by Kluge, *Literaturblatt*, 1884, 428–9. (A useful summary, which had the misfortune to be superseded next year by the publication of Wülker's *Grundriss*.)

1884 KRÜGER, TH. Über Ursprung u. Entwickelung des Beowulfliedes, *Archiv*, LXXI, 129–52.

1884–5 EARLE, J. Beowulf, in *The Times*, London (Aug. 25, 1884, p. 6 (not signed); Oct. 29, 1885, p. 3; Sept. 30. 1885, p. 3. "The Beowulf itself is a tale of old folk-lore which, in spite of repeated editing, has never quite lost the old crust of its outline....This discovery, if established, must have the effect of quite excluding the application of the Wolffian hypothesis to our poem.")

1885 WÜLKER, R. Grundriss zur geschichte der angelsächsischen Litteratur. Leipzig. 6. Die angelsächsische Heldendichtung, Beowulf, Finnsburg, 244–315. (An important and useful summary.)

1885 LEHMANN, H. Brünne und Helm im angelsächsischen Beowulfliede. Dissertation, Göttingen. Leipzig. Reviews: Wülker, *Anglia*, VIII, *Anzeiger*, 167–70; Schulz, *Engl. Stud.* IX, 471.

1886 SKEAT, W. W. On the signification of the monster Grendel...with a discussion of ll. 2076–2100. Read before the Cambridge Philological Society. *Journal of Philology*, XV, 120–31. (Not *American Jour. of Phil.*, as frequently quoted.)

1886 SARRAZIN, G. Die Beowulfsage in Dänemark, *Anglia*, IX, 195–9; Beowa und Böthvar, *Anglia*, IX, 200–4; Beowulf und Kynewulf, *Anglia*, IX, 515–50; Der Schauplatz des ersten Beowulfliedes und die Heimat des Dichters, *P.B.B.* XI, 159–83 (see above, p. 101).

1886 SIEVERS, E. Die Heimat des Beowulfdichters, *P.B.B.* XI, 354–62.

1886 SARRAZIN, G. Altnordisches im Beowulfliede, *P.B.B.* XI, 528–41. (See above, p. 102.)

1886 SIEVERS, E. Altnordisches im Beowulf? *P.B.B.* XII, 168–200.

1886 SCHILLING, H. Notes on the Finnsaga, *M.L.N.* I, 89–92; 116–17.

1886 LEHMANN, H. Über die Waffen im angelsächsischen Beowulfliede, *Germania*, XXXI, 486–97.

1887 SCHILLING, H. The Finnsburg-fragment and the Finn-episode, *M.L.N.* II, 146–50.

1887 MORLEY, H. Beowulf and the Fight at Finnsburg, in *English Writers*, vol. I, 276–354. London.

1887 BUGGE, S. Studien über das Beowulfepos, *P.B.B.* XII, 1–112, 360–75. Important. (Das Finnsburgfragment, pp. 20–8.)

1887 ‡SCHNEIDER, F. Der Kampf mit Grendels Mutter. *Program des Friedrichs Real-Gymnasiums.* Berlin.

1888 TEN BRINK, B. Beowulf. Untersuchungen. (*Quellen u. Forschungen*, LXII.) (Important. See above, p. 113.) Strassburg. Reviews: Wülker, *Anglia*, XI, 319–21 and *Lit. Cbl.* 1889, 251; Möller, *Engl. Stud.* XIII, 247–315 (weighty, containing some good remarks on the Jutes-Geatas); Koeppel, *Z.f.d.Ph.* XXIII, 113–22; Heinzel, *A.f.d.A.* XV, 153–82 (weighty); Liebermann, *Deut. Zeitschr. f. Geschichtswissenschaft*, II, 1889, 197–9; Kraus, *D.L.Z.* XII, 1891, 1605–7, 1846: reply by ten Brink ("Beowulfkritik und *ABAB*"), *D.L.Z.* 1892, 109–12.

1888 SARRAZIN, G. Beowulf-Studien. Berlin. Reviews: Koeppel, *Engl. Stud.* XIII, 472–80; Sarrazin, Entgegnung, *Engl. Stud.* XIV, 421 etc., reply by Koeppel, XIV, 427; Sievers, *Z.f.d.Ph.* XXI, 366; Dieter, *Archiv*, LXXXIII, 352–3; Heinzel, *A.f.d.A.* XV, 182–9; Wülker, *Lit. Cbl.* 1889, 315–16; Wülker, *Anglia*, XI, 536–41. Holthausen, *Literaturblatt*, 1890, 14–16; Liebermann, *Deut. Zeitschr. f. Geschichtswissenschaft*, VI, 1891, 138; Kraus, *D.L.Z.* XII, 1891, pp. 1822–3. (All these reviews express dissent from Sarrazin's main conclusions, though many of them show appreciation of details in his work. See above, p. 101.)

1888 KITTREDGE, G. L. Zu Beowulf, 107 *etc.*, *P.B.B.* XIII, 210 (Cain's kin).

1889 MÜLLENHOFF, K. Beovulf (pp. 110–65 = *Z.f.d.A.* XIV, 193–244). Berlin. See above, pp. 46–7, 113–15. Reviews: Schirmer, *Anglia*, XII, 465–7; Sarrazin, *Engl. Stud.* XVI, 71–85 (important); Wülker, *Lit. Cbl.* 1890, 58–9; Heinzel, *A.f.d.A.* XVI, 264–75 (important); Koeppel, *Z.f.d.Ph.* XXIII, 110–13; Holthausen, *Literaturblatt*, 1890, 370–3; Liebermann, *Deut. Zeitschr. f. Geschichtswissenschaft*, VI, 1891, 135–7; Kraus, *D.L.Z.* XII, 1891, pp. 1820–2; Logeman, *Le Moyen Âge*, III, 266–7 ("personne ne conteste plus…que le poème se composait originairement de plusieurs parties"). Müllenhoff's book, like that of ten Brink, is based on assumptions generally held at the time, but now not so widely accepted; yet it remains important.

1889 LAISTNER, L. Das Rätsel der Sphinx. Berlin. (See above, p. 67.)

1889 LÜNING, O. Die Natur…in der altgermanischen und mittelhochdeutschen Epik. Zürich. Reviews: Weinhold, *Z.f.d.Ph.* XXII, 246–7; Golther, *D.L.Z.* 1889, 710–2; Ballerstedt, *A.f.d.A.* XVI, 71–4; Fränkel, *Literaturblatt*, 1890, 439–44.

1890 ‡DESKAU, H. Zum studium des Beowulf. Berichte des freien deutschen Hochstiftes, 1890. Frankfurt.

1890 ‡KLÖPPER, C. Heorot-Hall in the Anglo-Saxon poem of Beowulf. Festschrift für K. E. Krause. Rostock.

1891 JELLINEK, M. H. and KRAUS, C. Die Widersprüche im Beowulf, *Z.f.d.A.* XXXV, 265–81.

1891 BUGGE, S. and OLRIK, A. Røveren ved Gråsten og Beowulf, *Dania*, I, 233–45.

1891 JELLINEK, M. H. Zum Finnsburgfragment, *P.B.B.* XV, 428–31.

1892 EARLE, J. The Introduction to his Translation (q.v.) gave a summary of the controversy, with "a constructive essay."

1892 BROOKE, STOPFORD A. History of Early English Literature (Beowulf, pp. 17–131). London. Reviews: McClumpha, *M.L.N.* VIII, 27–9, 1892 (attacks in a letter of unnecessary violence); Wülker, *Anglia, Beiblatt,* IV, 170–6, 225–33; Glöde, *Engl. Stud.* XXII, 264–70.

1892 GUMMERE, F. B. Germanic Origins. A study in primitive culture. New York.

1892 FERGUSON, R. The Anglo-Saxon name Beowulf, *Athenæum,* June, 1892, p. 763. See above, p. 368.

1892 HAACK, O. Zeugnisse zur altenglischen Heldensage. Kiel.

1892 ‡KRAUS, K. Hrodulf. (P. Moneta, zum 40 jähr. Dienstjub.) Wien. (p. 4 *etc.*)

1892 OLRIK, A. Er Uffesagnet indvandret fra England? *A.f.n.F.* VIII (N.F. IV), 368–75.

1892 SARRAZIN, G. Die Abfassungszeit des Beowulfliedes, *Anglia,* XIV, 399–415.

1892 SIEVERS, E. Sceaf in den nordischen Genealogien, *P.B.B.* XVI, 361–3.

1892 KÖGEL, R. Beowulf, *Z.f.d.A.* XXXVII, 268–76. (Etymology of the name.) Discussed by Sievers, *P.B.B.* XVIII, 413. See above, p. 367, footnote.

1893 WARD, H. L. D. Catalogue of Romances in the British Museum; Beowulf: vol. II, pp. 1–15, 741–3.

1893 TEN BRINK, B. Altenglische Literatur, *Pauls Grdr.*(1), II, I, 510–50. (Finnsburg, 545–50.)

1894 MCNARY, S. J. Beowulf and Arthur as English Ideals, *Poet-Lore,* VI, 529–36.

1894 ‡DETTER, F. Über die Heaðobarden im Beowulf, *Verhandl. d. Wiener Philologenversammlung,* Mai, 1893. Leipzig. p. 404 *etc.* (Argues that the story is not historical, but mythical—*Ragnarǫk.*)

1895 SIEVERS, E. Beowulf und Saxo, *Berichte der kgl. sächs. Gesellschaft der Wissenschaften,* XLVII, 175–93. (Important, see above, pp. 90–7.)

1895 BINZ, G. Zeugnisse zur germanischen sage in England, *P.B.B.* XX, 141–223. (A most useful collection, though the significance of many of the names collected is open to dispute.)

1895 KLUGE, F. Zeugnisse zur germanischen sage in England, *Engl. Stud.* XXI, 446–8.

1895–6 KLUGE, F. Der Beowulf u. die Hrolfs Saga Kraka, *Engl. Stud.* XXII, 144–5.

1896 SARRAZIN, G. Neue Beowulf-studien, *Engl. Stud.* XXIII, 221–67.

1897 KER, W. P. Epic and Romance. London. (Beowulf, pp. 182–202. Important. See above, p. 116.) Reviews: Fischer, *Anglia, Beiblatt,* X, 133–5; Brandl, *Archiv,* C, 198–200. New edit. 1908.

1897 BLACKBURN, F. A. The Christian coloring in the Beowulf, *Pub. Mod. Lang. Assoc. Amer.* XII, 205–25. (See above, p. 125.)

1897 SARRAZIN, G. Die Hirschhalle, *Anglia,* XIX, 368–92; Der Balder-kultus in Lethra, *ibid.* 392–7; Rolf Krake und sein Vetter im Beowulfliede, *Engl. Stud.* XXIV, 144–5. (Important. See above, p. 31.)

1897 HENNING, R. Sceaf und die westsächsische Stammtafel, *Z.f.d.A.* XLI, 156–69.

1898 ARNOLD, T. Notes on Beowulf. London. Reviews: Hulme, *M.L.N.* XV, 22–6, 1900; Sarrazin, *Engl. Stud.* XXVIII, 410–18; Garnett, *Amer. Jour. of Phil.* XX, 443.

1898 NIEDNER, F. Die Dioskuren im Beowulf, *Z.f.d.A.* XLII, 229–58.

1899 COOK, A. S. An Irish Parallel to the Beowulf Story, *Archiv,* CIII, 154–6.

1899 AXON, W. E. A. A reference to the evil eye in Beowulf, *Trans. of the Royal Soc. of Literature,* London. (Very slight.)

1899 ‡Furst, Clyde. "Beowulf" in "A Group of Old Authors." Philadelphia. (Popular.) Review: Child, *M.L.N.* xv, 31–2.

1900 Förster, Max. Bêowulf-Materialien, zum Gebrauch bei Vorlesungen. Braunschweig. Reviews: Holthausen, *Anglia, Beiblatt,* xi, 289; Behagel, *Literaturblatt,* 1902, 67 (very brief). 1908. 2 Aufl. 1912. 3 Aufl. Review: Wild, *Anglia, Beiblatt,* xxiv, 166–7.

1901 Powell, F. York. Beowulf and Watanabe-No-Tsema, *Furnivall Miscellany,* pp. 395–6. Oxford. (A parallel from Japanese legend.)

1901 Lehmann, E. Fandens Oldemor, *Dania,* viii, 179–94. Repeated ("Teuffels Grossmutter"), *Archiv f. Religionswiss.* viii, 411–30. (See above, p. 49, note, and p. 381.)

1901 ‡Otto, E. Typische Motive in dem weltlichen Epos der Angelsachsen. Berlin. Reviews: Binz, *Engl. Stud.* xxxii, 401–5; Spies, *Archiv,* cxv, 222.

1901 Uhlenbeck, C. C. Het Béowulf-epos als geschiedbron, *Tijdschrift voor nederlandsche taal- en letterkunde,* xx (N. R. xii), 169–96.

1902 Gerould, G. H. Offa and Labhraidh Maen, *M.L.N.* xvii, 201–3. (An Irish parallel of the story of the dumb young prince.)

1902 Gough, A. B. The Constance-Saga. Berlin. (The "Thrytho saga," pp. 53–83.) Reviews: Eckhardt, *Engl. Stud.* xxxii, 110–3; Weyrauch, *Archiv,* cxi, 453.

1902 Boer, R. C. Die Béowulfsage. i. Mythische reconstructionen; ii. Historische untersuchung der überlieferung; *A.f.n.F.* xix (N. F. xv), 19–88.

1902 Brandl, A. Ueber den gegenwärtigen Stand der Beowulf-Forschung, *Archiv,* cviii, 152–5.

1903 Anderson, L. F. The Anglo-Saxon Scop. (*Univ. of Toronto Studies, Phil. Ser.* 1.) Review: Heusler, *A.f.d.A.* xxxi, 113–5.

1903 Olrik, A. Danmarks Heltedigtning: i, Rolf Krake og den ældre Skjold-ungrække. Kobenhavn. (Most important.) Reviews: Heusler, *A.f.d.A.* xxx, 26–36; Golther, *Literaturblatt,* xxviii, 1907, pp. 8–9; Ranisch, *A.f.d.A.* xxi, 276–80. Revised translation 1919 (q.v.).

1903 ‡Boer, R. C. Eene episode uit den Beowulf, *Handelingen van het 3 nederl. phil. congres.,* p. 84 *etc.*

1903 A Summary of the *Lives of the Offas,* with reproductions of a number of the drawings in *MS Cotton Nero D. I,* in *The Ancestor,* v, 99–137.

1903 Hart, J. M. Allotria [on the forms *Bēanstān,* l. 524 and *Þrȳðo,* l. 1931], *M.L.N.* xviii, 117.

1903 Stjerna, K. Hjälmar och svärd i Beovulf, *Studier tillägnade O. Montelius,* 99–120. Stockholm. See above, pp. 346 *etc.*

1903–4 Boer, R. C. Finnsage und Nibelungen-sage, *Z.f.d.A.* xlvii, 125–60.

1904 Rickert, E. The O.E. Offa-saga, *Mod. Phil.* ii, 29–76 and 321–76. (Important. See above, pp. 34 *etc.*)

1904 Hagen, S. N. Classical names and stories in Beowulf, *M.L.N.* xix, 65–74 and 156–65. (Very fantastic).

1904 Stjerna, K. Vendel och Vendelkråka, *A.f.n.F.* xxi (N. F. xvii), 71–80. (Most important: see above, pp. 343–5.)

1904 ‡Vetter, F. Beowulf und das altdeutsche Heldenzeitalter in England, *Deutschland,* iii, 558–71.

1905 Moorman, F. W. The interpretation of nature in English poetry from Beowulf to Shakespeare. Strassburg. *Quellen u. Forschungen,* 95.

1905 ROUTH, J. E. Two studies on the Ballad Theory of the Beowulf: I. The Origin of the Grendel legend; II. Irrelevant Episodes and Parentheses as features of Anglo-Saxon Poetic Style. Baltimore. Reviews: Eckhardt, *Engl. Stud.* XXXVII, 404–5; Heusler, *A.f.d.A.* XXXI, 115–16; Schücking, *D.L.Z.* 1905, pp. 1908–10.

1905 HEUSLER, A. Lied und Epos in germanischer Sagendichtung. Dortmund. (See above, p. 116.) Reviews: Kauffmann, *Z.f.d.Ph.* XXXVIII, 546–8; Seemüller, *A.f.d.A.* XXXIV, 129–35; Meyer, *Archiv*, CXV, 403–4; Helm, *Literaturblatt*, XXVIII, 237–8.

1905 SCHÜCKING, L. L. Beowulfs Rückkehr. (*Morsbachs Studien*, XXI.) Halle. (Important: see above, pp. 118–20.) Review: Brandl, *Archiv*, CXV, 421–3 (dissenting).

1905 SCHÜCK, H. Studier i Ynglingatal, I–III. Uppsala.

1905 HANSCOM, E. D. The Feeling for Nature in Old English Poetry, *J.E.G.Ph.* V, 439–63.

1905 SARRAZIN, G. Neue Beowulf Studien, *Engl. Stud.* XXXV, 19–27.

1905 STJERNA, K. Skölds hädanfärd, *Studier tillägnade H. Schück*, 110–34. Stockholm.

1905 ‡STJERNA, K. Svear och Götar under folkvandringstiden, *Svenska Förnminnesforeningens Tidskr.* XII, 339–60. (Transl. by Clark Hall in *Essays*. See under 1912.)

1905–6 RIEGER, M. Zum Kampf in Finnsburg, *Z.f d.A.* XLVIII, 9–12.

1905–6 HEUSLER, A. Zur Skiöldungendichtung, *Z.f.d.A.* XLVIII, 57–87.

1905–6 NECKEL, J. Studien über Fróði, *Z.f.d.A.* XLVIII, 163–86.

1905–7 STJERNA, K. Arkeologiska anteckningar till Beovulf, *Kungl. vitterhets akademiens månadsblad* for 1903–5 (1907), pp. 436–51.

1906 EMERSON, O. F. Legends of Cain, especially in Old and Middle English (see particularly § VI, "Cain's Descendants"), *Pub. Mod. Lang. Assoc. Amer.* XXI, 831–929. (Important.)

1906 SKEMP, A. R. Transformation of scriptural story, motive, and conception in Anglo-Saxon poetry, *Mod. Phil.* IV, 423–70.

1906 DUFF, J. W. Homer and Beowulf: a literary parallel, *Saga-Book of the Viking Club*. London.

1906 MORSBACH, L. Zur datierung des Beowulf-epos, *Nachrichten der kgl. Ges. d. Wiss. zu Göttingen, Phil.-Hist. Klasse*, pp. 252–77. (Important. See above, pp. 107–12.)

1906 PFÄNDLER, W. Die Vergnügungen der Angelsachsen, *Anglia*, XXIX, 417–526.

1906 GARLANDA, F. Béowulf. Origini, bibliografia, metrica...significato storico, etico, sociologico. Roma. (Slight.)

1906 STJERNA, K. Drakskatten i Beovulf, *Fornvännen*, I, 119–44.

1907 CHADWICK, H. M. Origin of the English Nation. Cambridge. (Important.) Reviews: Andrews, *M.L.N.* XXIII, 261–2; Chambers, *M.L.R.* IV, 262–6; Schütte, *A.f.n.F.* XXV (N. F. XXI), 310–32 (an elaborate discussion of early Germanic ethnology and geography); Huchon, *Revue Germanique*, III, 625–31.

1907 CHADWICK, H. M. "Early National Poetry," in *Cambridge History of English Literature*, vol. I, 19–23, 421–3. Important. See above, pp. 122–6.

1907 HART, WALTER MORRIS. Ballad and Epic. Boston: Harvard *Studies and Notes in Philology and Literature*. (Important: see above, p. 116.) Review: *Archiv*, CXIX, 468.

1907 OLRIK, A. Nordisk Aandsliv i Vikingetid og tidlig Middelalder. København og Kristiania. (Translated into German by W. Ranisch, 1908, as "Nordisches Geistesleben.")

1907 SCHÜCK, H. Folknamnet Geatas i den fornengelska dikten Beowulf. Uppsala. (Important. See above, pp. 8–10, 333 *etc*.) Reviews: Mawer, *M.L.R.* IV, 273; Freeburg, *J.E.G.Ph.* XI, 279–83.

1907 COOK, A. S. Various notes, *M.L.N.* XXI, 146–7. (Further classical parallels to Beowulf, 1408 ff., in succession to a parallel from Seneca quoted in *M.L.N.* XVII, 209–10.)

1907 SARRAZIN, G. Zur Chronologie u. Verfasserfrage Ags. Dichtungen, *Engl. Stud.* XXXVIII, 145 *etc.*, esp. 170–95 (Das Beowulflied und die ältere Genesis).

1907 BRANDL, A. Entstehungsgeschichte des Beowulfepos. A five-line summary of this lecture is given in the *Sitzungsberichte d. k. preuss. Akad. Phil.-Hist. Classe*, p. 615.

1907 HOLTHAUSEN, F. Zur altenglischen literatur—Zur datierung des Beowulf, *Anglia, Beiblatt*, XVIII, 77.

1907 ‡GRÜNER, H. Mathei Parisiensis vitae duorum Offarum, in ihrer manuskript- und textgeschichte. Dissertation, Munich. Kaiserslautern.

1908 BRANDL, A. Geschichte der alteng. Literatur. (Offprint from *Pauls Grdr.*(2): Beowulf, pp. 988–1024; Finnsburg, pp. 983–6; an exceedingly useful and discriminating summary.)

1908 SCHÜCKING, L. L. Das Angelsächsische Totenklagelied, *Engl. Stud.* XXXIX, 1–13.

1908 WEYHE, H. König Ongentheow's Fall, *Engl. Stud.* XXXIX, 14–39.

1908 NECKEL, G. Beiträge zur Eddaforschung; Anhang: Die altgermanische heldenklage (pp. 495–6: cf. p. 376). Dortmund.

1908 KLAEBER, F. Zum Finnsburg Kampfe, *Engl. Stud.* XXXIX, 307–8.

1908 BJÖRKMAN, E. Über den Namen der Jüten, *Engl. Stud.* XXXIX, 356–61.

1908 LEVANDER, L. Sagotraditioner om Sveakonungen Adils, *Antikvarisk Tidskrift för Sverige*, XVIII, 3.

1908 STJERNA, K. Fasta fornlämningar i Beovulf, *Antikvarisk Tidskrift för Sverige*, XVIII, 4.

1908 GRAU, G. Quellen u. Verwandtschaften der älteren germanischen Darstellungen des jüngsten Gerichtes. Halle. (See esp. pp. 145–56.) Review: Guntermann, *Z.f.d.Ph.* XLI, 401–415.

1909 SCHÜCK, H. Studier i Beowulfsagan. Uppsala. Review: Freeburg, *J.E.G.Ph.* XI, 488–97 (a very useful summary).

1909 LAWRENCE, W. W. Some disputed questions in Beowulf-criticism, *Pub. Mod. Lang. Assoc. Amer.* XXIV, 220–73. (Very important.) Review: Brandl, *Archiv*, CXXIII, 473.

1909 EHRISMANN, G. Religionsgeschichtliche Beiträge zum germanischen Frühchristentum, *P.B.B.* XXXV, 209–39.

1909 BUGGE, S. Die Heimat der Altnordischen Lieder von den Welsungen u. den Nibelungen, II, *P.B.B.* XXXV, 240–71.

1909 DEUTSCHBEIN, M. Die Sagenhistorischen u. literarischen Grundlagen des Beowulfepos, *Germanisch-Romanische Monatsschrift*, I, 103–19.

1910 OLRIK, A. Danmarks Heltedigtning: II, Starkad den gamle og den yngre Skjoldungrække. København. (Most important.) Reviews: Heusler, *A.f.d.A.* XXXV, 169–83 (important); Ussing, *Danske Studier*, 1910, 193–203; Boer, *Museum*, XIX, 1912, 171–4.

1910 PANZER, F. Studien zur germanischen Sagengeschichte. I. Beowulf. München. (Most important: see above, pp. 62–8; 365–81. Valuable criticisms and modifications are supplied by the reviews, more particularly perhaps that of von Sydow (*A.f.d.A.* XXXV, 123–31), but also in the elaborate discussions of Heusler (*Engl. Stud.* XLII, 289–98), Binz (*Anglia, Beiblatt*, XXIV, 321–37), Brandl (*Archiv*, CXXVI, 231–5), Kahle

(*Z.f.d.Ph.* XLIII, 383–94) and the briefer ones of Lawrence (*M.L.N.* XXVII, 57–60) Sedgefield (*M.L.R.* VI, 128–31) and Golther (*Neue Jahrbücher f. das klassische Altertum*, XXV, 610–13).)

1910 BRADLEY, H. Beowulf, in *Encyclopædia Britannica*, III, pp. 758–61. (Important. See above, pp. 121, 127–8.)

1910 SCHÜCK, H. Sveriges förkristna konungalängd. Uppsala.

1910 CLARK HALL, J. R. A note on Beowulf, 1142–5, *M.L.N.* XXV, 113–14. (*Hūnlāfing.*)

1910 SARRAZIN, G. Neue Beowulf-studien, *Engl. Stud.* XLII, 1–37.

1910 KLAEBER, F. Die ältere Genesis und der Beowulf, *Engl. Stud.* XLII, 321–38.

1910 HEUSLER, A. Zeitrechnung im Beowulf-epos, *Archiv*, CXXIV, 9–14.

1910 NECKEL, G. Etwas von germanischer Sagenforschung, *Germ.-Rom. Monatsschrift*, II, 1–14.

1910 SMITHSON, G. A. The Old English Christian Epic...in comparison with the Beowulf. Berkeley. *Univ. of California Pub. in Mod. Phil.* (See particularly pp. 363–8, 376–90.)

1911 CLARKE, M. G. Sidelights on Teutonic History. Cambridge. Reviews: Mawer, *M.L.N.* VII, 126–7; Chambers, *Engl. Stud.* XLVIII, 166–8; Fehr, *Anglia, Beiblatt*, XXVI, 19–20; Imelmann, *D.L.Z.* XXXIV, 1913, 1062 *etc.*

1911–19 HEUSLER, A. A series of articles in Hoops' *Reallexikon*: Beowulf, Dichtung, Ermenrich, Gautensagen, Heldensage, Hengest, Heremod, Offa, Skjǫldungar, Ynglingar, *etc.* Strassburg. (Important.)

1911 NECKEL, G. Ragnacharius von Cambrai, *Festschrift zur Jahrhundertfeier der Universität zu Breslau = Mitt. d. Schlesischen Gesellschaft für Volkskunde*, XIII–XIV, 121–54. (A historical parallel between the treatment of Ragnachar by Chlodowech and that of Hrethric by Hrothulf.)

1911 SCHÖNFELD, M. Wörterbuch der altgermanischen Personen- und Völkernamen. Heidelberg. See also Schütte, Noter til Schönfelds Navnesamling, in *A.f.n.F.* XXXIII, 22–49.

1911 KLAEBER, F. Aeneis und Beowulf, *Archiv*, CXXVI, 40–8, 339–59. (Important: see above, p. 330.)

1911 LIEBERMANN, F. Grendel als Personenname, *Archiv*, CXXVI, 180.

1911–12 KLAEBER, F. Die Christlichen Elemente im Beowulf, *Anglia*, XXXV, 111–36, 249–70, 453–82; XXXVI, 169–99. (Most important: demonstrates the fundamentally Christian character of the poem.)

1912 CHADWICK, H. MUNRO. The Heroic Age. Cambridge. (Important: see above, p. 122.) Reviews: Mawer, *M.L.R.* VIII, 207–9; Chambers, *Engl. Stud.* XLVIII, 162–6.

1912 STJERNA, K. Essays on questions connected with the O.E. poem of Beowulf, transl. and ed. by John R. Clark Hall, (Viking Club), Coventry. (Important: see above, pp. 346 *etc.*) Reviews: Klaeber, *J.E.G.Ph.* XIII, 167–73, weighty; Mawer, *M.L.N.* VIII, 242–3; *Athenæum*, 1913, I, 459–60; Brandl, *Archiv*, CXXXII, 238–9; Schütte, *A.f.n.F.* XXXIII, 64–96, elaborate; Olrik, *Nord. Tidskr. f. Filol.* IV, 2. 127; Mogk, *Historische Vierteljahrsschrift*, XVIII, 196–7.

1912 CHAMBERS, R. W. Widsith: a study in Old English heroic legend. Cambridge. Reviews: Mawer, *M.L.R.* VIII, 118–21; Lawrence, *M.L.N.* XXVIII, 53–5; Fehr, *Anglia, Beiblatt*, XXVI, 289–95; Jordan, *Engl. Stud.* XLV, 300–2; Berendsohn, *Literaturblatt*, XXXV (1914), 384–6.

1912 BOER, R. C. Die Altenglische Heldendichtung. I. Béowulf. Halle. (Important.) Reviews: ‡Jantzen, *Z. f. französischen u. englischen Unterricht*, XIII, 546–7; Berendsohn, *Literaturblatt*, XXXV, 152–4; Dyboski, *Allgemeines Literaturblatt*, XXII, 1913, 497–9; Imelmann, *D.L.Z.* XXXIV, 1913, 1062–6 (weighty criticisms); Barnouw, *Museum*, XXI, 53–8.

1912 VON DER LEYEN, F. Die deutschen Heldensagen (Beowulf, pp. 107–23, 345–7). München.

1912 MEYER, W. Beiträge zur Geschichte der Eroberung Englands. Dissertation, Halle. (Finn story.)

1912 LAWRENCE, W. W. The haunted mere in Beowulf. *Pub. Mod. Lang. Assoc. Amer.* XXVII, 208–45. (Important. See above, pp. 52–3.)

1912 SCHÜTTE, G. The Geats of Beowulf, *J.E.G.Ph.* XI, 574–602. (See above, pp. 8, 333 etc.)

1912 STEFANOVIČ, S. Ein beitrag zur angelsächsischen Offa-sage, *Anglia*, XXXV, 483–525.

1912 MUCH, R. Orendel, *Wörter u. Sachen*, IV, 170–3. (Deriving *Vendsyssel*, Vandal, and the *Wendle* of Beowulf from *wandil*—"a bough, wand.")

1912 CHAMBERS, R. W. Six thirteenth century drawings illustrating the story of Offa and of Thryth (Drida) from *MS Cotton Nero D. I.* London, *privately printed.*

1913 ‡FAHLBECK, P. Beowulfskvädet som källa för nordisk fornhistoria. (Stockholm, *N. F. K. Vitterhets Historie och Antikvitets Akademiens Handlingar*, 13, 3.) Review: Klaeber, *Engl. Stud.* XLVIII, 435–7.

1913 NERMAN, B. Studier över Svärges hedna litteratur. Uppsala.

1913 NERMAN, B. Vilka konungar ligga i Uppsala högar? Uppsala.

1913 LAWRENCE, W. W. The Breca episode in Beowulf (Anniversary papers to G. L. Kittredge). Boston.

1913 SARRAZIN, G. Von Kädmon bis Kynewulf. Berlin. Reviews: Dudley, *J.E.G.Ph.* XV, 313–17; Berendsohn, *Literaturblatt*, XXXV (1914), 386–8: Funke, *Anglia, Beiblatt*, XXXI, 121–33.

1913 THOMAS, P. G. Beowulf and Daniel A, *M.L.R.* VIII, 537–9. (Parallels between the two poems.)

1913 BELDEN, H. M. Onela the Scylfing and Ali the Bold, *M.L.N.* XXVIII, 149–53.

1913 STEDMAN, D. Some points of resemblance between Beowulf and the Grettla (or Grettis Saga). From the *Saga Book of the Viking Club*, London. (It should have been held unnecessary to prove the relationship yet once again.)

1913 VON SYDOW, C. W. Irisches in Beowulf[1]. (*Verhandlungen der 52 Versammlung deutscher Philologen in Marburg*, pp. 177–80.)

1913 BERENDSOHN, W. A. Drei Schichten dichterischer Gestaltung im Beowulfepos, *Münchener Museum*, II, i, pp. 1–33.

1913 DEUTSCHBEIN, M. Beowulf der Gautenkönig, *Festschrift für Lorenz Morsbach*, Halle, pp. 291–7, *Morsbachs Studien*, L. (Very important. Expresses very well, and with full working out of details, the doubts which some of us had already felt as to the historic character of the reign of Beowulf over the Geatas.)

[1] Most students nowadays will probably agree with v. Sydow's contention that the struggle of Beowulf, first above ground and then below, is a folk-story, one and indivisible, and that therefore there is no reason for attributing the two sections to different authors, as do Boer, Müllenhoff and ten Brink. But that the folk-tale is exclusively Celtic remains to be proved; v. Sydow's contention that Celtic influence is shown in *Beowulf* by the inhospitable shamelessness of Unferth (compare that of Kai) is surely fanciful. Also the statement that the likeness of Bjarki and Beowulf is confined to the freeing of the Danish palace from a dangerous monster by a stranger from abroad, and that "das sonstige Beiwerk völlig verschieden ist" surely cannot be maintained. As argued above (pp. 54–61) there are other distinct points of resemblance.

v. Sydow's statement no doubt suffers from the brevity with which it is reported, and his forthcoming volume of *Beowulf studien* will be awaited with interest.

578   Bibliography

1913 BENARY, W. Zum Beowulf-Grendelsage, *Archiv*, CXXX, 154–5. (Grändels-
      môr in Siebenbürgen: see above, p. 308.)
1913 KLAEBER, F. Das Grändelsmôr—eine Frage, *Archiv*, CXXXI, 427.
1913 BRATE, E. Betydelsen av ortnamnet Skälv [cf. Scilfingas], *Namn och
      Bygd*, I, 102–8.
1914 MÜLLER, J. Das Kulturbild des Beowulfepos. Halle. *Morsbachs Studien*,
      LIII. Reviews: Klaeber, *Anglia, Beiblatt*, XXVII, 241–4; Brunner,
      Archiv, CXXXVIII, 242–3.
1914 MOORMAN, F. W. English place-names and Teutonic Sagas, in *Essays and
      Studies by members of the English Association*, vol. V, pp. 75–103.
      (Argues that "Gilling" and other place-names in Yorkshire, point to
      an early colony of Scandinavian "Gautar," who may have been instru-
      mental in introducing Scandinavian traditions into England.)
1914 OLSON, O. L. Beowulf and the Feast of Bricriu, *Mod. Phil.* XI, 407–27.
      (Emphasises the slight character of the parallels noted by Deutschbein.)
1914 VON SYDOW, C. W. Grendel i anglosaxiska ortnamn, in*Nordiska Ortnamn,
      hyllningsskrift tillägnad Adolf Noreen*, Uppsala, pp. 160–4 = *Namn och
      Bygd*, II. (Important.)
1915 KIER, CHR. Beowulf, et Bidrag til Nordens Oldhistorie. København.
      (An elaborate and painstaking study of the historic problems of Beowulf,
      vitiated throughout by quite unjustifiable assumptions. See above,
      p. 333 etc.) Review: Björkmann, *Anglia, Beiblatt*, XXVII, 244–6.
1915 BRADLEY, H. The Numbered Sections in Old English Poetical MSS, *Proc.
      Brit. Acad.* vol. VII.
1915 LAWRENCE, W. W. Beowulf and the tragedy of Finnsburg, *Pub. Mod.
      Lang. Assoc. Amer.* XXX, 372–431. (Important. An excellent survey
      of the Finnsburg problems.)
1915 VAN SWERINGEN, G. F. The main...types of men in the Germanic Hero-
      Sagas, *J.E.G.Ph.* XIV, 212–25.
1915–19 LINDROTH, H. Är Skåne de gamles Scadinavia? *Namn och Bygd*, III,
      1915, 10–28. Lindroth denied that the two words are the same, and
      was answered by A. Kock (*A.f.n F.* XXXIV, 1917, 71 etc.), A. Noreen
      (in ‡*Studier tillegn. E. Tegnér*, 1918) and E. Björkman ("Scedeland,
      Scedenig," *Namn och Bygd*, VI, 1918, 162–8). Lindroth replied ("Äro
      Scadinavia och Skåne samma ord," *A.f.n.F.* XXXV, 1918, 29 etc., and
      "Skandinavien och Skåne," *Namn och Bygd*, VI, 1918, 104–12) and
      was answered by Kock ("Vidare om Skåne och Scadinavia," *A.f.n.F.*
      XXXVI, 74–85). Björkman's discussion is the one of chief importance
      to students of Beowulf.
1915 KLAEBER, F. Observations on the Finn episode, *J.E.G.Ph.* XIV, 544–9
1915 ANSCOMBE, A. Beowulf in High-Dutch saga, *Notes and Queries*, Aug. 21,
      1915, pp. 133–4.
1915 BERENDSOHN, WALTER A. Die Gelage am Dänenhof zu Ehren Beowulfs,
      Münchener Museum, III, i, 31–55.
1915–16 PIZZO, E. Zur frage der ästhetischen einheit des Beowulf, *Anglia*,
      XXXIX, 1–15. (Sees in Beowulf the uniform expression of the early
      Anglo-Saxon Christian ideal.)
1916 OLSON, O. L. The relation of the Hrólfs Saga Kraka and the Bjarkarímur
      to Beowulf. Chicago. (Olson emphasises that the monster slain by
      Bjarki in the *Saga* does not attack the hall, but the cattle outside, and
      is therefore a different kind of monster from Grendel (p. 30). But he
      does not disprove the general equation of Beowulf and Bjarki: many
      of the most striking points of resemblance, such as the support given
      to Eadgils(Athils) against Onela (Ali),lie outside the scope of his study.
      Review: Hollander, *J.E.G.Ph.* XVI, 147–9.

1916 NECKEL, G. Adel und gefolgschaft, *P.B.B.* XLI, 385–436 (esp. pp. 410 ff. for social conditions in Beowulf).

1917 FLOM, G. T. Alliteration and Variation in Old Germanic name giving, *M.L.N.* XXXII, 7–17.

1917 MEAD, G. W. Wiðerȝyld of Beowulf, 2051, *M.L.N.* XXXII, 435–6. (Suggests, very reasonably, that Wiðerȝyld is the father of the young Heathobard warrior who is stirred to revenge.)

1917 AYRES, H. M. The tragedy of Hengest in Beowulf, *J.E.G.Ph.* XVI, 282–95. (See above, pp. 266–7.)

1917 AURNER, N. S. An analysis of the interpretations of the Finnsburg documents. (*Univ. of Iowa Monographs: Humanistic Studies,* I, 6.)

1917 BJÖRKMAN, E. Zu ae. *Eote, Yte,* usw., dän. *Jyder,* "Jüten," *Anglia, Beiblatt,* XXVIII, 275–80. (See above, p. 334.)

1917 ROOTH, E. G. T. Der name Grendel in der Beowulfsage, *Anglia, Beiblatt,* XXVIII, 335–40. (Etymologies. Grendel is the "sandman," a maneating monster of the sea-bottom. With this, compare Panzer's interpretation of Grendel as the "earthman." See above, p. 309.)

1917 SCHÜCKING, L. L. Wann entstand der Beowulf? Glossen, Zweifel und Fragen, *P.B.B.* XLII, 347–410. (Important. See above, pp. 322–32.)

1917 FOG, REGINALD. Trolden "Grendel" i Bjovulf: en hypothese, *Danske Studier,* 1917, 134–40. (Grendel is here interpreted as an infectious disease, prevalent among those who sleep in an ill-ventilated hall in a state of intoxication, but to which Beowulf, whose health has been confirmed by a recent sea-voyage, is not liable. This view is not as new as its author believes it to be, and a letter from von Holstein Rathlau is added, pointing this out. It might further have been pointed out that as early as 1879 Grendel was explained as the malaria. Cf. the theories of Laistner, Kögel and Golther, and see above, p. 46.)

1917 NEUHAUS, J. Sillende = vetus patria = Angel, *Nordisk Tidsskrift för Filologi,* IV. Række, Bd. V, 125–6; Helges Prinsesse Svåvå = Eider = den svebiske Flod hos Ptolemæos, VI, 29–32; Halfdan = Frode = Hadbardernes Konge, hvis Rige forenes med det danske, VI, 78–80; Vestgermanske Navne i dansk Historie og Sprog, 141–4. The inherent difficulty of the subject is enhanced by the obscurity of the writer's style: but much of the argument (e.g. that Halfdan and Frode are identical) is obviously based upon quite reckless conjectures. The question is complicated by political feeling: many of Neuhaus' arguments are repeated in his pamphlet, *Die Frage von Nordschleswig im Lichte der neuesten vorgeschichtlichen Untersuchungen,* Jena, 1919. His theories were vigorously refuted by G. SCHÜTTE. "Urjyske 'Vestgermaner,'" *Nordisk Tidsskrift för Filologi,* IV. Række, Bd, VII, 129 *etc.*

1917 ‡FREDBORG. Det första årtalet i Sveriges historia. Umeå.

1917 NERMAN, B. Ynglingasagan i arkeologisk belysning, *Fornvännen,* 1917, 226–61.

1917 NERMAN, B. Ottar Vendelkråka och Ottarshögen i Vendel, *Upplands Fornminnesförenings Tidskrift,* VII, 309–34.

1917 BJÖRKMAN, E. Bēowulf och Sveriges Historia, *Nordisk Tidskrift,* 1917, 161–79.

1917–18 ‡VON SYDOW, C. W. Draken som skattevaktare, *Danmarks folkeminder,* XVII, 103 *etc.*

1918 HACKENBERG, E. Die Stammtafeln der angelsächsischen Königreiche, Dissertation, Berlin. (A useful collection.) Reviews: Fischer, *Anglia, Beiblatt,* XXXI, 73–4; Ekwall, *Engl. Stud.* LIV, 307–10; Liebermann, *D.L.Z.* 1 March, 1919.

1918 LAWRENCE, W. W. The dragon and his lair in Beowulf, *Pub. Mod. Lang Assoc. Amer.* XXXIII, 547–83.

580 Bibliography

1918 BELDEN, H. M. Beowulf 62, once more, *M.L.N.* XXXIII, 123.

1918 BELDEN, H. M. Scyld Scefing and Huck Finn, *M.L.N.* XXXIII, 315.

1918 KLAEBER, F. Concerning the relation between Exodus and Beowulf, *M.L.N.* XXXIII, 218–24.

1918 BJÖRKMAN, E. Bēow, Bēaw, und Bēowulf, *Engl. Stud.* LII, 145–93. (Very important. See above, p. 304.)

1918 BRANDL, A. Die Urstammtafel der Westsachsen und das Beowulf-Epos, *Archiv*, CXXXVII, 6–24. (See above, p. 200, note.)

1918 BRANDL, A. Die urstammtafel der englischen könige, *Sitzungsberichte d. k. preuss. Akad., Phil.-Hist. Classe*, p. 5. (Five line summary only published).

1918 ‡BJÖRKMAN, E. Bēowulf-forskning och mytologi, *Finsk Tidskrift*, 151 etc. (Cf. *Anglia, Beiblatt*, XXX, 207.)

1918 BJÖRKMAN, E. Sköldungaättens mytiska stamfäder, *Nordisk Tidskrift*, 163 etc.

1918 v. UNWERTH, W. Eine schwed. Heldensage als deutsches Volksepos, *A.f.n.F.* XXXV, 113–37. (An attempt to connect the story of Hygelac and Hæthcyn with the M.H.G. *Herbort ûz Tenelant*.)

1918 NEUHAUS, J. Om Skjold, *A.f.n.F.* XXXV, 166–72. (A dogmatic assertion of errors in Olrik's arguments in the *Heltedigtning*.)

1918 CLAUSEN, H. V. Kong Hugleik, *Danske Studier*, 137–49. (Conjectures based upon the assumption Geatas = Jutes.)

1918 ‡LUND University "Festskrift" contains NORLIND, Skattsägner; VON SYDOW, Sigurds strid med Fåvne.

1919 OLRIK, A. The heroic legends of Denmark translated...and revised in collaboration with the author by Lee M. Hollander. New York. (Very important.) Review: Flom, *J.E.G.Ph.* XIX, 284–90.

1919 BJÖRKMAN, E. Bedwig in den westsächsischen genealogien, *Anglia, Beiblatt*, XXX, 23.

1919 BJÖRKMAN, E. Zu einigen Namen im Bēowulf: *Breca, Brondingas, Wealhþēo(w)*; *Anglia, Beiblatt*, XXX, 170–80.

1919 MOGK, E. Altgermanische Spukgeschichten: Zugleich ein Beitrag zur Erklärung der Grendelepisode im Beowulf, *Neue Jahrbücher für das klass. altertum...und deutsche literatur*, XXXIV, 103–17. (Mogk here abandons his older allegorical interpretation of Grendel as the destroying power of the sea, and sees in the Grendel-story a Germanic ghost-tale, poetically adorned.)

1919 BJÖRKMAN, E. Skialf och Skilfing [edited by E. Ekwall, with a note on Björkman's work], *Namn och Bygd*, VII, 163–81.

1919 LINDERHOLM, E. Vendelshögens konunganamn i socknens 1600-tals-tradition, *Namn och Bygd*, VII, 36–40.

1919 FOG, R. Bjarkemaals "Hjalte," *Danske Studier*, 1919, 29–35. (With a letter from A. Olrik.)

1919 SEVERINSEN, P. Kong Hugleiks Dødsaar, *Danske Studier*, 1919, 96.

1920 IMELMANN, R. Forschungen zur altenglischen Poesie. (IX. Hengest u. Finn; X. Enge ānpaðas, uncūð gelād; XII. Þrȳðo; XIII. Hǣþenra hyht.) Berlin. (A weighty statement of some original views.)

1920 BJÖRKMAN, E. Studien über die Eigennamen im Beowulf. Halle. *Morsbachs Studien*, LVIII. (An extremely valuable and discriminating digest. See above, p. 304.)

1920 BARTO, P. S. The *Schwanritter-Sceaf* Myth in *Perceval le Gallois, J.E.G.Ph.* XIX, 190–200.

1920 HUBBARD, F. G. The plundering of the Hoard. *Univ. Wisconsin Stud.* 11.

1920 SCHÜCKING, L. L. Wiðergyld (Beowulf, 2051), *Engl. Stud.* LIII, 468–70.
(Schücking, like Mead, but independently, interprets Withergyld as
the name of the warrior whose son is being stirred to revenge.)

1920 BJÖRKMAN, E. Hæðcyn und Hákon, *Engl. Stud.* LIV, 24–34.

1920 HOOPS, J. Das Verhüllen des Haupts bei Toten, ein angelsächsisch-
nordischer Brauch (Zu Beowulf, 446, *hafalan hȳdan*), *Engl. Stud.* LIV,
19–23.

1920 NOREEN, A. Yngve, Inge, Inglinge [Ingwine], *Namn och Bygd*, VIII, 1–8.

1920 LA COUR, V. Lejrestudier, *Danske Studier*, 1920, 49–67. (Weighty.
Emphasizing the importance of the site of Leire in the sixth century.)
A discussion on the date and origin of Beowulf, by LIEBERMANN, is
about to appear (*Gött. Gelehrt. Gesellschaft*).

§ 9. STYLE AND GRAMMAR

Titles already given in previous sections are not repeated here. General
treatises on O.E. style and grammar are recorded here only if they have a
special and exceptional bearing upon *Beowulf*.

1873 LICHTENHELD, A. Das schwache adjectiv im ags., *Z.f.d.A.* XVI, 325–93.
(Important. See above, pp. 105–7.)

1875 HEINZEL, R. Über den Stil der altgermanischen Poesie. Strassburg.
(*Quellen u. Forschungen*, X.) (Important and suggestive: led to further
studies on the style of Beowulf, such as those of Hoffmann and Bode.)
Review: Zimmer, *A.f.d.A.* II, 294–300.

1877 ‡ARNDT, O. Über die altgerm. epische Sprache. Paderborn.

1877 SCHÖNBACH, A. [A discussion of words peculiar to sections of Beowulf,
added to a review of Ettmüller's Beowulf], *A.f.d.A.* III, 36–46. See
also Möller, *Volksepos*, 60 *etc.*

1879 NADER, E. Zur Syntax des Béowulf. *Progr. der Staats-Ober-Realschule*,
in Brünn. Review: Bernhardt, *Literaturblatt*, 1880, 439–40 (unfavourable: reply by Nader and answer by Bernhardt, 1881, 119–20).

1881 ‡GUMMERE, F. B. The Anglo-Saxon metaphor. Dissertation, Freiburg.

1882 SCHEMANN, K. Die Synonyma im Béowulfsliede, mit Rücksicht auf
Composition u. Poetik des Gedichtes. Hagen. Dissertation, Münster.
(Examines the use of noun-synonyms in the different sections of the
poem as divided by Müllenhoff, and finds no support for Müllenhoff's
theories.) Review: Kluge, *Literaturblatt*, 1883, 62–3.

1882 ‡NADER, E. Der Genitiv im Béowulf. Brünn. Review: Klinghardt,
Engl. Stud. VI, 288.

1882 SCHULZ, F. Die Sprachformen des Hildebrand-Liedes im Beovolf.
Königsberg.

1883 NADER, E. Dativ u. Instrumental im Béowulf. Wien. Review:
Klinghardt, *Engl. Stud.* VII, 368–70.

1883 HARRISON, J. A. List of irregular (strong) verbs in Béowulf, *Amer. Jour.
of Phil.* IV, 462–77.

1883 HOFFMANN, A. Der bildliche Ausdruck im Béowulf u. in der Edda, *Engl.
Stud.* VI, 163–216.

1886 BODE, W. Die Kenningar in der angelsächsischen Dichtung. Darmstadt
and Leipzig. Reviews: Gummere, *M.L.N.* II, 17–19 (important—
praises Bode highly); Kluge, *Engl. Stud.* X, 117, Brandl, *D.L.Z.* 1887,
897–8; Bischoff, *Archiv*, LXXIX, 115–6; Meyer, *A.f.d.A.* XIII, 136.

1886 ‡KÖHLER, K. Der syntaktische gebrauch des Infinitivs und Particips im
Beowulf. Dissertation, Münster.

1886 BANNING, A. Die epischen Formeln im Bêowulf. I. Die verbalen
synonyma. Dissertation, Marburg.

1887 TOLMAN, A. H. The style of Anglo-Saxon poetry, *Trans. Mod. Lang. Assoc. Amer.* III, 17–47.

1888–9 NADER, E. Tempus und modus im Beowulf, *Anglia*, x, 542–63; XI, 444–99.

1889 KAIL, J. Über die Parallelstellen in der Ags. Poesie, *Anglia*, XII, 21–40. (A *reductio ad absurdum* of the theories of Sarrazin. Important.)

1891 DAVIDSON, C. The Phonology of the Stressed Vowels in Béowulf, *Pub. Mod. Lang. Assoc. Amer.* VI, 106–33. Review: Karsten, *Engl. Stud.* XVII, 417–20.

1892 SONNEFELD, G. Stilistisches und Wortschatz im Beówulf. Dissertation, Strassburg. Würzburg.

1893 TODT, A. Die Wortstellung im Beowulf, *Anglia*, XVI, 226–60.

1898 KISTENMACHER, R. Die wörtlichen Wiederholungen im Bêowulf. Dissertation, Greifswald. Reviews: Mead, *J.(E.)G.Ph.* II, 546–7; Kaluza, *Engl. Stud.* XXVII, 121–2 (short but valuable).

1902 BARNOUW, A. J. Textkritische Untersuchungen nach dem gebrauch des bestimmten Artikels und des schwachen Adjektivs in der altenglischen Poesie. Leiden. (Important, see above, p. 107.) Reviews: Kock, *Engl. Stud.* XXXII, 228–9; Binz, *Z.f.d.Ph.* XXXVI, 269–74; Schücking, *Göttingische gelehrte Anzeigen*, 1905, 730–40.

1902 HEUSLER, A. Der dialog in der altgermanischen erzählenden Dichtung. *Z.f.d.A.* XLVI, 189–284.

1903 SHIPLEY, G. The genitive case in Anglo-Saxon Poetry. Baltimore. Reviews: Kock, *Engl. Stud.* XXV, 92–5; Mourek, *A.f.d.A.* XXX, 172–4.

1903 KRACKOW, O. Die Nominalcomposita als Kunstmittel im altenglischen Epos. Dissertation, Berlin. Review: Björkman, *Archiv*, CXVII, 189–90.

1904 SCHÜCKING, L. L. Die Grundzüge der Satzverknüpfung im Beowulf. Pt. I. (*Morsbachs Studien*, XV.) Halle. (Important.) Reviews: Eckhardt, *Engl. Stud.* XXXVII, 396–7; Pogatscher, *D.L.Z.* 1905, 922–3; Behagel, *Literaturblatt*, XXVIII, 100–2; Grossmann, *Archiv*, CXVIII, 176–9.

1904 HÄUSCHKEL, B. Die Technik der Erzählung im Beowulfliede. Dissertation, Breslau.

1905 KRAPP, G. P. The parenthetic exclamation in Old English poetry, *M.L.N.* XX, 33–7.

1905 SCHEINERT, M. Die Adjektiva im Beowulfepos als Darstellungsmittel, *P.B.B.* XXX, 345–430.

1906 THOMAS, P. G. Notes on the language of Beowulf, *M.L.R.* I, 202–7. (A short summary of the dialectal forms.)

1906 BARNOUW, A. J. Nochmals zum ags. Gebrauch des Artikels, *Archiv*, CXVII, 366–7.

1907 RIES, J. Die Wortstellung im Beowulf. Halle. (An important and exhaustive study by an acknowledged specialist.) Reviews: Binz, *Anglia*, *Beiblatt*, XXII, 65–78 (important); Borst, *Engl. Stud.* XLII, 93–101; Delbrück, *A.f.d.A.* XXXI, 65–76 (important); Reis, *Literaturblatt*, XXVIII, 328–30; *Lit. Cbl.* 1907, p. 1474; Huchon, *Revue germanique*, III, 634–8.

1908 KRAUEL, H. Der Haken- und Langzeilenstil im Beowulf. Dissertation, Göttingen.

1908 LORS, A. Aktionsarten des Verbums im Beowulf. Dissertation, Würzburg.

1908 ‡MOUREK, E. Zur Syntax des konjunktivs im Beowulf, *Prager deutsche stud.* VIII.

1909–10 RANKIN, J. W. A study of the Kennings in Ags. poetry, *J.E.G.Ph.* VIII, 357–422; IX, 49–84. (Latin parallels; very important.)

1909 SHEARIN, H. G. The expression of purpose in Old English poetry, *Anglia*, XXXII, 235–52.

1909 ‡RIGGERT, G. Der syntaktische Gebrauch des Infinitivs in der altenglischen Poesie. Dissertation, Kiel.

1910 RICHTER, C. Chronologische Studien zur angelsächsischen Literatur auf grund sprachl.-metrischer Kriterien. Halle. (*Morsbachs Studien*, XXXIII.) Reviews: Binz, *Anglia, Beiblatt*, XXII, 78–80; Imelmann, *D.L.Z.* 1910, 2986–7; Hecht, *Archiv*, CXXX, 430–2.

1910 WAGNER, R. Die Syntax des Superlativs...im Beowulf. Berlin. (*Palaestra*, XCI.) Reviews: Schatz, *D.L.Z.* 1910, 2848–9; Kock, *A.f.n.F.* XXVIII, 347–9.

1910 SCHUCHARDT, R. Die negation im Beowulf. Berlin. (*Berliner Beiträge zur germ. u. roman. Philol.* XXXVIII.)

1912 BRIGHT, J. W. An Idiom of the Comparative in Anglo-Saxon, *M.L.N.* XXVII, 181–3. (Bearing particularly upon Beowulf, 69, 70.)

1912 EXNER, P. Typische Adverbialbestimmungen in frühenglischer Poesie. Dissertation, Berlin.

1912 GRIMM, P. Beiträge zum Pluralgebrauch in der altenglischen Poesie. Dissertation, Halle.

1913 PAETZEL, W. Die Variationen in der altgermanischen Alliterationspoesie. Berlin. See pp. 73–84 for Beowulf and Finnsburg. (*Palaestra*, XLVIII.) Pt I. had appeared in 1905 as a Berlin dissertation.

§ 10. METRE

For bibliography of O.E. metre in general, see *Pauls Grdr.*(2), II, 1022–4.

1870 SCHUBERT, H. De Anglosaxonum arte metrica. Dissertatio inauguralis, Berolini.

1884 SIEVERS, E. Zur rhythmik des germanischen alliterationsverses: I. Vorbemerkungen. Die metrik des Beowulf: II. Sprachliche Ergebnisse, *P.B.B.* X, 209–314 and 451–545. (Most important.)

1894 KALUZA, M. Studien zum altgermanischen alliterationsvers. I. Kritik der bisherigen theorien. II. Die Metrik des Beowulfliedes. (Important.) Reviews: Martin, *Engl. Stud.* XX, 293–6; Heusler, *A.f.d.A.* XXI, 313–17; Saran, *Z.f.d.Ph.* XXVII, 539–43.

1905 TRAUTMANN, M. Die neuste Beowulfausgabe und die altenglische verslehre, *Bonner Beiträge zur Anglistik*, XVII, 175–91. (A discussion of O.E. metre in view of Holthausen's edition.) Review: Klaeber, *M.L.N.* XXII, 252.

1908 MORGAN, B. Q. Zur lehre von der alliteration in der westgermanischen dichtung: I. Die tonverhältnisse der hebungen im Beowulf: II. Die gekreuzte alliteration; *P.B.B.* XXXIII, 95–181.

1908 BOHLEN, A. Zusammengehörige Wortgruppen, getrennt durch Cäsur oder Versschluss, in der angelsächsischen Epik. Dissertation, Berlin. Reviews: Dittes, *Anglia, Beiblatt*, XX, 199–202; Kroder, *Engl. Stud.* XL, 90.

1912 TRAUTMANN, M. Zum altenglischen Versbau, *Engl. Stud.* XLIV, 303–42.

1913 SEIFFERT, F. Die Behandlung der Wörter mit auslautenden ursprünglich silbischen Liquiden oder Nasalen und mit Kontraktionsvokalen in der Genesis A und im Beowulf. Dissertation, Halle. (Concludes the dialect of the two poems to be distinct, but finds no evidence on these grounds which is the earlier.)

1914 FIJN VAN DRAAT, P. The cursus in O.E. poetry, *Anglia*, XXXVIII, 377–404.

1918 LEONARD, W. E. Beowulf and the Niebelungen couplet, in *Univ. of Wisconsin Studies in Language and Literature*, II, 98–152. (Important. Pp. 123–46 advocating the "four-accent theory.")

1920 ‡NEUNER, E. Ueber ein- und dreihebige Halbverse in der altenglischen alliterierenden Poesie. Berlin. Review: Bright, *M.L.N.* XXXVI, 59–63.

ADDITIONS TO THE BIBLIOGRAPHY TO 1930

§ 1. PERIODICALS

Periodicals which have begun to appear since the first edition of this book was printed, and which will need to be frequently quoted, are:

R.E.S. = The Review of English Studies. London, 1925 *etc.*

Speculum = Speculum, a journal of mediæval studies. Cambridge, Mass., 1926 *etc.*

Acta Phil. Scand. = Acta Philologica Scandinavica, Tidsskrift for nordisk Sprogforskning. København, 1926 *etc.*

§ 2. BIBLIOGRAPHIES

Bibliography of English Language and Literature, edited for the Modern Humanities Research Association by A. C. Paues (D. Everett, E. Seaton and M. S. Serjeantson). First issued in 1921, for the year 1920.

The Year's Work in English Studies, edited for the English Association by Sir Sidney Lee (F. S. Boas and C. H. Herford). Vol. I, 1921, for the year 1919–20. (This gives a summary and criticism of work published during the year: I quote it when it adds anything to the discussion relevant to *Beowulf*.)

§ 3. THE MS AND ITS TRANSCRIPTS

1919 FÖRSTER, MAX. Die Beowulf-Handschrift. Leipzig. Reviews: (add to those already given) Keller, *Anglia, Beiblatt*, XXXIV, 1–5; Hecht, *D.L.Z.* XLII, 146-9; Preuzler, *Lit. Cbl.* LXXIII, 95; Binz, *Literaturblatt*, XLI, 97; van Langenhove, *Leuvensche Bijdragen*, XIII, 230–2; Kern, *English Studies* (Amsterdam), III, 91–2.

1921 RYPINS, S. I. A contribution to the study of the Beowulf codex, *Pub. Mod. Lang. Assoc. Amer.* XXXVI, 167-85. (Suggests that the first of the two *Beowulf* scribes is the more accurate.) Reviews and Comments (all doubting the correctness of Rypins' views): Hulbert, *Pub. Mod. Lang. Assoc. Amer.* XLIII, 1196–9; Ekwall, *Anglia, Beiblatt*, XXXVIII, 50; Hoops, *Engl. Stud.* LXI, 439.

1924 RYPINS, S. I. Three Old English Prose Tracts in *MS Cotton Vitellius A. XV. Early English Text Society.* London and Oxford. (The problems of the MS are discussed in the Introduction, pp. vii–xxix. For further important discussion and criticism of Rypins' view, see E. V. Gordon, *Year's Work*, V, 66–72.) Reviews: Magoun, *M.L.N.* XLII, 67–70; Ekwall, *Anglia, Beiblatt*, XXXVIII, 48–52; Hoops, *Engl. Stud.* LXI, 435–40.

1925 CRAIGIE, SIR W. A. Interpolations and omissions in Anglo-Saxon Poetic Texts. *Philologica*, II, 5–19. (Suggests that the archetype of the *Beowulf* MS was written on leaves containing a trifle over 31 lines, and that this accounts for difficulties at ll. 31, 62, 139, 389, 403 *etc.*, and above all for the Thryth-episode, ll. 1931–1962. This is contested by Klaeber in *Anglia*, L, 236–8; Klaeber does not think the evidence sufficient.)

1928 HOOPS, JOHANNES. Die Foliierung der Beowulf-Handschrift. *Engl. Stud.* LXIII, 1–11. (Hoops suggests that the old eighteenth-century numbering of the folios is the one which should be followed—as indeed it is by most editors—except for the portion affected by the leaf, formerly misplaced and numbered 131, which has now been restored to its correct position after the folio numbered 146. For this section Hoops suggests that the pages should be numbered as they now stand, the old erroneous numbers being placed within brackets. This is probably the best way of meeting the difficulty.)

1928 HULBERT, J. R. The Accuracy of the B-scribe of Beowulf. *Pub. Mod. Lang. Assoc. Amer.* XLIII, 1196–9. Review: Daunt, *Year's Work*, IX, 71.

1929 KELLER, WOLFGANG. Zur Worttrennung in den angelsächsischen Handschriften. *Britannica, Max Förster zum sechzigsten Geburtstage*, 89–105.

1929 PROKOSCH, E. Two types of scribal error in the Beowulf MS. *Studies in English Philology, a Miscellany in Honor of Frederick Klaeber*, ed. by Kemp Malone and Martin B. Ruud, 196–207.

§ 4. EDITIONS OF BEOWULF AND FINNSBURG

1918 SCHÜCKING, L. L. Beowulf. 11, 12 Aufl. Paderborn. Reviews: (add to those already given) van Langenhove, *Leuvensche Bijdragen*, XIII, 234–5.

1920 CHAMBERS, R. W. Beowulf with the Finnsburg Fragment, ed. by A. J. WYATT, revised. Second edit. Cambridge. Review: Jiriczek, *Die Neueren Sprachen*, XXIX, 67–9.

1922 KLAEBER, F. Beowulf with the Fight at Finnsburg, edited with Introduction, Bibliography, Notes, Glossary and Appendices. Boston. (See above, pp. 389–97.) Reviews: *Times Lit. Sup.* Feb. 8, 1923, 95; Wardale, *Year's Work*, IV, 39–43; Lawrence, *J.E.G.Ph.* XXIII, 294–300 (weighty); Larsen, *Philol. Quart.* II, 156–8; Menner, *Literary Review*, Jan. 20, 1923, 394; Holthausen, *Anglia, Beiblatt*, XXXIV, 353–7; Flasdieck, *Engl. Stud.* LVIII, 119–24 (contains a valuable discussion on the date of *Beowulf*); Hecht, *A.f.d.A.* XLIII, 46–51; Kock, *A.f.n.F.* XXXIX, 185–9. (Most of these reviews are important.)

        1928. Re-issue, with supplement. Review: Kemp Malone, *J.E.G.Ph.* XXVIII, 416–17.

1929 HOLTHAUSEN, F. Beowulf nebst den kleineren Denkmälern der Heldensage. I. 6 Aufl. II. 5 Aufl. (Text and notes revised; supplement bringing bibliography to 1928.) Reviews: Kemp Malone, *Speculum*, V, 327–8, and also *J.E.G.Ph.* XXIX, 611–3.

1929 SCHÜCKING, L. L. Beowulf. 13 Aufl. Paderborn. (No modifications since 1918. A new revision is promised.)

    Extracts will be found in Wyatt's *Anglo-Saxon Reader*, 1919, 1922; Sedgefield's *Anglo-Saxon Verse Book*, 1922 (reviews: Crawford, *M.L.R.* XIX, 104–8; Klaeber, *J.E.G.Ph.* XXIII, 122–3; Flasdieck, *Anglia, Beiblatt*, XXXV, 165–6); Wyatt's *Threshold of Anglo-Saxon*, 1926; Turk's *Anglo-Saxon Reader*, 1927; Craigie's *Specimens of Anglo-Saxon Poetry*, iii *Germanic Legend*, 1931.

§ 6. TRANSLATIONS

    Translations of small portions of *Beowulf* are of interest during the very early period, before Kemble's translation of 1837 made knowledge of *Beowulf* general. To the early translations of portions of *Beowulf*, mentioned on p. 515 above, the following should be added:

1818 HENDERSON, E. Iceland, or the Journal of a Residence between 1814 and 1815. (In vol. II, pp. 329–330, there is a reference to "the poem which has lately been published by Etatsraad Thorkelin." Three quotations, with English translation, two of some length, follow.) See also the second edition, 1819, p. 517.

1828 TAYLOR, W. Historical Survey of German Poetry, 3 vols. London. (Vol. I, pp. 78–90.) (Taylor attempts a summary of the whole poem, remarking that the notice of Sharon Turner is imperfect: Turner had not carried his summary beyond l. 1698. But Taylor's attempt is not fortunate, and he often goes wrong where Turner, in his edition of 1820, had got the sense right.)

1835 WRIGHT, THOMAS. On Anglo-Saxon Poetry. *Fraser's Magazine*, XII, 76–92. (Gives a good summary of the poem, and some extracts, with renderings into English. These include the whole of Unferth's speech against Beowulf, and Beowulf's reply. The translations are more accurate than anything which had yet appeared in English. The author mentions Kemble's translation as about to appear. The article is anonymous, but was reprinted in Wright's *Essays on England in the Middle Ages*, 1846.)

1838 LONGFELLOW, H. W. Anglo-Saxon Literature. *The North American Review*, XLVII, 91–134. (Published anonymously. Such accuracy as this account of *Beowulf* possesses seems to be due to Conybeare. Kemble's "strong and faithful" translation was known to the writer only after his first sheets had gone to press, in time for him to add a note at the end. Longfellow gives a translation of Passus III (ll. 189–257). This translation was later included (with others) in Longfellow's *Poets and Poetry of Europe*, 1845, and the whole article is included in his *Collected Prose* (Driftwood).)

After the publication of Kemble's translation, interest in *Beowulf* becomes common, and it is unnecessary to mention the various translations of extracts. Mention should however have been made of

1914 WEBSTER, A. BLYTH. Translation from Old English: a note and an experiment. *Essays and Studies by members of the English Association*, V, 153–71. (Gives translation of ll. 4–52.)

1919 THOMAS, W. Bēowulf et les premiers fragments épiques anglo-saxons. Étude critique et traduction. Paris.

1921 RYTTER, HENRIK. Beowulf og Striden um Finnsborg. Frå angelsaksisk. Oslo. (Translated into landsmaal: in alliterative verse.)

1921 SCOTT-MONCRIEFF, C. K. Widsith, Beowulf, Finnsburg, Waldere, Deor. Done into common English after the old manner. With an Introduction by Viscount Northcliffe. Review: Klaeber, *Anglia, Beiblatt*, XXXIV, 321–3.

1922 SPAETH, J. DUNCAN. Old English Poetry. Translations into alliterative verse with Introductions and Notes. Princeton. (Includes translation of most of *Beowulf*.) Review: McKillop, *J.E.G.Ph.* XXIV, 279–81.

1923 LEONARD, W. E. Beowulf: a new verse translation. New York and London. (With the Fight at Finnsburg. Metre based on that of the *Nibelungen Lied*.) Reviews: Croll, *Literary Review*, July 7, 1923, 811; Lewisohn, (*New York*) *Nation*, CXVI, 660; Klaeber, *Anglia, Beiblatt*, XXXIV, 321–2; *Archiv*, CXLVII, 300.

1923 GORDON, R. K. The Song of Beowulf. Rendered into English Prose. London and New York.

1925 (1752) "GOTHIQUE." *The Oxford Magazine*, March 12. A translation of the opening and closing passages of *Beowulf* into heroic couplets, with the inscription "Coppie of verses sent me by my worthie Friend, that ingenious Gentleman Mr Beach of Glostershire. His studdies have lately lain much in our Gothique poetry. 1752." (That an eighteenth-century antiquary should have translated portions of *MS Cotton Vitellius A. XV* with such accuracy and understanding is not more unlikely than many suggestions regarding *Beowulf* which have been seriously put forward during the past ten years in learned periodicals of high repute, and which have then been not less seriously refuted in other not less learned academic publications. However, on subjecting the verses to critical analysis, I found in them a vigour of style and a real poetic force which I was inclined rather to associate with the present Merton Professor of English Language and Literature than with Mr Beach. Prof. Wyld's *Experiments in translating Beowulf* confirms my suspicions. See below.)

1925 STRONG, SIR ARCHIBALD. Beowulf, translated into Modern English rhyming verse, with Introduction and Notes. With a Foreword on "Beowulf

and the Heroic Age" by R. W. Chambers. London. Reviews: S. J.
Crawford, *M.L.R.* xxii, 325–7; Blackman, *R.E.S.* iii, 115–16; E. V.
Gordon, *Year's Work*, vi, 72–4; Ruud, *M.L.N.* xliii, 55; Klaeber,
Anglia, Beiblatt, xxxvii, 257–60; Pompen, *English Studies* (Amsterdam),
ix, 115–17.

1926 CRAWFORD, D. H. Beowulf, translated into English verse, with an In-
troduction, Notes and Appendices. London and New York. Reviews:
S. J. Crawford, *M.L.R.* xxii, 325–7; Blackman, *R.E.S.* iii, 237–9;
Daunt, *Year's Work*, vii, 60; Kemp Malone, *M.L.N.* xlii, 202–3;
MacLean, *Anglia, Beiblatt,* xxxviii, 312–14.

1929 BRANDL, ALOIS. Der Saalkampf im Finns Burg. *Britannica, Max Förster
zum sechzigsten Geburtstage,* 23–5. (A translation of the "Fragment"
into alliterative verse.)

1929 WYLD, H. C. Experiments in translating Beowulf. *Studies in English
Philology, a Miscellany in Honor of Frederick Klaeber,* ed. by Kemp
Malone and Martin B. Ruud, 217–31. (Translations of selected passages
into various metres and styles: in the manner of Pope, Longfellow's
Hiawatha, Tennyson, and into hexameters.)

1929 GERING. Beowulf nebst dem Finnsburg-Bruchstück, übersetzt und erläutert. 2te Auflage. Heidelberg.

§ 7. TEXTUAL CRITICISM AND INTERPRETATION

See also § 9, Vocabulary.

1915 CLASSEN, E. O.E. *Nicras* (*Beowulf,* ll. 422, 575, 845, 1427). *M.L.R.* x,
85–6.

1921 BUSH, J. D. A Note on Beowulf, 1600–5. *M.L.N.* xxxvi, 251.

1921 SEDGEFIELD, W. J. Miscellaneous Notes: The Fight at Finnsburg (ll. 35,
40). *M.L.R.* xvi, 59.

1921–2 KOCK, E. A. Interpretations and Emendations of Early English Texts:
VIII. *Anglia,* xlv, 105–31. (Discusses, among other things, twenty-
eight cruces in *Beowulf,* including *ealu-scerwen.*) IX, X. *Anglia,* xlvi,
63–96; 173–90. (Fifty-eight more passages.)

1922 KLAEBER, F. Zum Bedeutungsinhalt gewisser altenglischer Wörter und
ihrer Verwendung. *Anglia,* xlvi, 232–8.

1922 LIEBERMANN, F. Zu Beowulf, v, 770. *Archiv,* cxliii, 247–8. (Interpretation of *ealu-scerwen*; parallels from Anglo-Saxon Law.)

1922 THOMAS, P. G. Miscellaneous Notes: Beowulf, 1604–5, 2085–91. *M.L.R.*
xvii, 63–4.

1923 HOLTHAUSEN, F. Zum Beowulf. *Anglia, Beiblatt,* xxxiv, 89–90. (*ealu-
scerwen.*)

1923 PATZIG, H. Zum Beowulf-Text. *Anglia,* xlvii, 97–104.

1923 SEDGEFIELD, W. J. Miscellaneous Notes. *M.L.R.* xviii, 471. (*Beowulf,*
ll. 223–4: *sund liden eoletes æt ende.*)

1924 SCHLUTTER, O. B. Weitere Beiträge zur altenglischen Wortforschung.
Anglia, xlviii, 375–7. (Discusses *hitt, Beowulf,* 2650. See also E. V.
Gordon, *Year's Work*, v, 76–7.)

1924 SEWELL, W. A. P. A reading in Beowulf. *Times Lit. Sup.* Sept. 11, 1924,
556. (*egsode Eorlas, Eorlas* being interpreted as the Heruli.)

1925 DUNSTAN, A. C. Beowulf, ll. 223–4. *M.L.R.* xx, 317–18. (*sund liden
eoletes æt ende.* See also E. V. Gordon, *Year's Work*, vi, 78.)

1926 CRAWFORD, S. J. "Ealu-scerwen." *M.L.R.* xxi, 302–3. (See also Daunt,
Year's Work, vii, 70.)

1926 EMERSON, O. F. The punctuation of *Beowulf* and literary interpretation. *Mod. Phil.* XXIII, 393–405. (See also Daunt, *Year's Work*, VII, 60–2.)

1926 KLAEBER, F. Beowulfiana. *Anglia*, L, 107–22, 195–224. (Textual notes on 108 problems. See also § 8, below.)

1926 MACKIE, W. S. Notes on O.E. poetry: Beowulf, ll. 223–4. *M.L.R.* XXI, 301. (*sund liden eoletes æt ende.*)

1926 MALONE, KEMP. A note on Beowulf, 1231. *M.L.N.* XLI, 466–7. (See also Daunt, *Year's Work*, VII, 62.)

1927 ADDY, S. O. The "stapol" in Beowulf. *Notes and Queries*, CLII, 363–5. (See also Daunt, *Year's Work*, VIII, 84.)

1927 THOMAS, P. G. Further notes on Beowulf. *M.L.R.* XXII, 70–3. (358–9, 804, 939, 970–2, 1231, 1537, 1798, 1880, 2394, 2691–2. See also Daunt, *Year's Work*, VIII, 83–4.)

1927 WILLIAMS, R. A. Beowulf, ll. 1086–8. *M.L.R.* XXII, 310–13. (See also Daunt, *Year's Work*, VIII, 82–3.)

1928 CRAWFORD, S. J. Beowulf, ll. 168–9. *M.L.R.* XXIII, 336. (Illustrated by a passage from Gregory's *Dialogues*.)

1928 MALONE, KEMP. The kenning in Beowulf, 2220. *J.E.G.Ph.* XXVII, 318–24. (*bu folc beorna*. See also Daunt, *Year's Work*, IX, 70.)

1929 HOLTHAUSEN, F. Zu Beowulf, 489 f. und 3114 f. *Anglia, Beiblatt*, XL, 90–1.

1929 HOOPS, JOHANNES. War Beowulf König von Dänemark? *Britannica, Max Förster zum sechzigsten Geburtstage*, 26–30. (Suggests the emendation *scildwigan* for *scildingas* in l. 3005.)

1929 HOOPS, JOHANNES. Altenglisch *geap, horngeap, sægeap*. *Engl. Stud.* LXIV, 201–11.

1929 KLAEBER, F. Altenglische wortkundliche Randglossen. *Anglia, Beiblatt*, XL, 21–32.

1929 MALONE, KEMP. Notes on Beowulf. *Anglia*, LIII, 335–6. (ll. 51, 106, 1026, 1142. Defending the reading *selerædenne*, on the analogy of *scyppen*, *sc[e]otenum, woroldrædenne.*)

1929 MALONE, KEMP. A note on Beowulf, 2034. *M.L.R.* XXIV, 322–3.

1929 MOORE, SAMUEL. Notes on Beowulf. *Studies in English Philology, a Miscellany in Honor of Frederick Klaeber*, ed. by Kemp Malone and Martin B. Ruud, 208–12. (ll. 1104–6, 2032–40, 2306–9, 3117–19.)

1929 SCHÜCKING, L. L. Noch einmal: "enge ānpaðas, uncūð gelād." *Studies in English Philology, a Miscellany in Honor of Frederick Klaeber*, ed. by Kemp Malone and Martin B. Ruud, 213–16.

1929 SCHÜCKING, L. L. *Sōna* im Beowulf. *Britannica, Max Förster zum sechzigsten Geburtstage*, 85–8.

1930 ASHDOWN, MARGARET. Beowulf, l. 1543. *M.L.R.* XXV, 78. (*oferwearp*.)

1930 BRYAN, W. F. *Ærgōd* in Beowulf, and other Old English compounds in *Ær*. *Mod. Phil.* XXVIII, 157–61.

1930 MALONE, KEMP. A note on Beowulf, l. 1376. *M.L.R.* XXV, 191. (Defending the reading *felasinnigne*.)

1930 MALONE, KEMP. Three notes on Beowulf (ll. 303–6, 646–51, 1053–57). *J.E.G.Ph.* XXIX, 233–6.

1930 MALONE, KEMP. Notes on Beowulf, *Anglia*, LIV, 1–7, 97–8. (3005: a reply to Hoops, defending the text; 3058–60; 3066–75; 2542–4.)

1931 HENEL, H. *Stānboga* im Beowulf. *Anglia*, LV, 273–81.

1931 IMELMANN, R. Beowulf, 489. *Engl. Stud.* LXV, 190–6. (Suggests reading *onsæl me to.*)

§ 8. LITERARY HISTORY, DATE AND AUTHORSHIP: BEOWULF IN
THE LIGHT OF HISTORY, ARCHÆOLOGY, HEROIC LEGEND,
MYTHOLOGY AND FOLKLORE
See also preceding sections.

As before, no attempt is made to enumerate allusions to *Beowulf*, still less to
the isolated episodes of *Beowulf*. But there are two which, on account of their
early date, should perhaps have been mentioned on p. 521 above. Weber, in his
essay *On the Teutonic Romances*, in *Illustrations of Northern Antiquities*, Edinburgh, 1814, p. 7, footnote, writes:

"A long Anglo-Saxon poem on the expedition of Regner Lodbrog is
preserved in the Museum, the publication of which would be a very desirable object. Prof. Thorkelin had prepared a manuscript and translation
for the press, and from his learning and zeal everything could be expected.
But it is much to be feared, that, together with the other invaluable stores
of his library, it was consumed during the bombardment of Copenhagen."

George Borrow, in *Tales of the Wild and Wonderful* (1825), gives a very free
verse paraphrase of Saxo's version of the Offa story (*The Story of Uffon* in *The
Lord of the Maelstrom*).

1909–12 GRÖNBECH, V. Vor Folkeæt i Oldtiden. København. Review: Ekwall,
Anglia, Beiblatt, XXXI, 1–9, where reference will be found to the other
reviews.

1913 SEIFFERT, F. Die Behandlung der Wörter mit auslautenden ursprünglich
silbischen Liquiden oder Nasalen und mit Kontraktionsvokalen in der
Genesis A und im Beowulf. Dissertation. Halle.

1918 MONTELIUS, O. Ynglingaätten. *Nordisk Tidskrift.*

1919 EBERT, M. Die Bootfahrt ins Jenseits. *Praehistorische Zeitschrift*, XII,
179–96. (Important, though having no special reference to Scyld's
voyage.)

1920 ARON, A. W. Traces of Matriarchy in Germanic Hero-Lore. *University of
Wisconsin Studies*, IX. (pp. 46–51 deal with *Beowulf*.)

1920 AURNER, N. S. Hengest, a study in Early English hero legend. *University
of Iowa Studies*, II, 1. Reviews: Liebermann, *Anglia, Beiblatt*, XXXV, 65–7;
Heusler, *A.f.d.A.* XLII, 180–1; Klaeber, *Archiv*, CXLIV, 278.

1920 BJÖRKMAN, E. Studien über die Eigennamen im Beowulf. Reviews:
Neckel, *Archiv*, CXLVIII, 156; Preusler, *Lit. Cbl.* LXXIII, 75; Binz,
Literaturblatt, XLII, 173–4.

1920 HOLTHAUSEN, F. Ein lappisches Bärensohn-Märchen. *Anglia, Beiblatt*,
XXXI, 66–7.

1920 HUBBARD, F. G. The plundering of the Hoard. Review: Graves, *The So.
Atlantic Quarterly*, XX, 371.

1920 IMELMANN, R. Forschungen zur altenglischen Poesie. Berlin. Reviews:
Holthausen (*Studien zur altenglischen Dichtung*), *Anglia*, XLVI, 55–60;
Heusler, *A.f.d.A.* XLI, 27–35 (esp. *Beowulf*, ll. 1409, 1931 etc.).

1920 LIEBERMANN, F. Ort und Zeit der Beowulfdichtung. *Nachrichten der
königl. Gesellschaft der Wissenschaften zu Göttingen, Phil.-Hist. Kl.*
255–76. Reviews: Ekwall, *Anglia, Beiblatt*, XXXIII, 67–9; Brandl,
Archiv, CXLI, 307.

1920 NECKEL, G. Die Ueberlieferungen vom Gotte Balder dargestellt und ver-
gleichend untersucht. Dortmund. (Herebeald, Hæðcyn, Heremōd.)
Review: Krappe, *Litteris*, II, 170–3.

1920 NECKEL, G. Sigmunds Drachenkampf. *Edda*, XIII, 112–40, 204–29.

1920 SCHÜTTE, G. Vidsid og Slægtssagnene om Hengest og Angantyr. *A.f.n.F.*
XXXVI, 1–32.

1921 CHAMBERS, R. W. Beowulf. An Introduction to the study of the poem, with a discussion of the stories of Offa and Finn. Cambridge. Reviews: Mawer, *M.L.R.* XVIII, 96–8; Wardale, *Year's Work*, II, 33–5; Gosse, *Sunday Times*, Sept. 18, 1921; A. J. Robertson, *Year Book of the Viking Society*, 1921, 78–81; *Notes and Queries*, Sept. 24, 1921, 259; *Observer*, Sept. 25, 1921; *Times Lit. Sup.* Jan. 12, 1922, 26; Patch, *M.L.N.* XXXVII, 418–27; Tupper, *J.E.G.Ph.* XXI, 680–4; Hulbert, *Mod. Phil.* XX, 436–7; Mennen, Literary Review, Jan. 20, 1923, 394; Fehr, *Anglia, Beiblatt*, XXXIII, 121–6; Ekwall, *Anglia, Beiblatt*, XXXIII, 177–85; Jiriczek, *Die Neueren Sprachen*, XXXI, 412–16; Boer, *English Studies* (Amsterdam), V, 105–18; Ricci, *Nuovi Studi Medievali*, 1923.

1921 EMERSON, O. F. Grendel's motive in attacking Heorot. *M.L.R.* XVI, 113–19. (Christian element.) Review: Brandl, *Archiv*, CXLV, 156.

1921 GAIDOS, HENRI. Cûchulainn, Béowulf et Hercule. *Cinquantenaire de l'école pratique des hautes études*: fasc. 230 de la *Bibliothèque*. Paris. (Gaidos points out once again the parallel between the *Feast of Bricriu* and *Beowulf*. This parallel seems to him so striking that he is surprised that it has not been noticed before. It had, of course, been noted by Deutschbein, *Germanisch-Romanische Monatsschrift*, I, 103–19 (1909). That Gaidos should independently be struck by the resemblance is noteworthy, and goes to prove the similarity. But this resemblance is very limited, as has been shown by Olson, *Mod. Phil.* XI, 407–27 (1914). Many a folk-tale gives parallels as close, or closer.)

1921 HÜBENER, G. Das Problem des Flexionsschwundes im Angelsächsischen. *P.B.B.* XLV, 85–102. (Bearing upon the date of *Beowulf*.)

1921 LA COUR, V. Lejrestudier. Mindesmærkerne. *Danske Studier*, 147–66. (Topography of Leire, especially as depicted in Ole Worm's *Monumenta Danica*, 1643.)

1921 LINDQVIST, S. Ynglingaättens gravskick. *Fornvännen*, 83–194. (pp. 119–36 deal with the burial customs of *Beowulf*.) Die Begräbnissarten des Ynglingageschlechtes. *Fornvännen*, 261–75. (A summary of the above.)

1921 OLRIK, A. Nogle Grundsaetninger for sagnforskning; efter forfatterens død udg. af dansk folkemindesamling ved Hans Ellekilde. København. (See above, pp. 419 etc.) Review: Golther, *Literaturblatt*, XLIII, 237–9.

1921 PFOHL, E. Zur Beowulf-Chronologie. MS Dissertation. Rostock. Summary, Rostock, 1922.

1921 SCHREINER, K. Die Sage von Hengest und Horsa. *Eberings German. Stud.* 12. Review: Klaeber, *Archiv*, CXLIV, 276–8.

1922 BOER, R. C. Studier over Skjoldungedigtningen. *Aarbger for Nordisk Oldkyndighed og Historie*, III, 12, 133–266. (See above, pp. 424–30.)

1922 COOK, A. S. The possible begetter of the O.E. Beowulf and Widsith. *Transactions of the Connecticut Academy of Arts and Sciences*, XXV, 281–346. (A valuable summary of our knowledge of conditions in the Northumbria of Bede's day.) Reviews: *Times Lit. Sup.* May 4, 1922, 294; McKillop, *J.E.G.Ph.* XXIII, 305–7; *Literary Review*, 1922, 744; Ekwall, *Anglia, Beiblatt*, XXXIV, 37–9; Flasdieck, *Engl. Stud.* LVIII, 124–6; Liebermann, *Archiv*, CXLIII, 281–2; Mansion, *Musée Belge*, XXVII, 55–6. (See above, p. 489.)

1922 HERRMANN, P. Erläuterungen zu den ersten neun Büchern der Dänischen Geschichte des Saxo Grammaticus. Zweiter Teil. Die Heldensagen des Saxo. Leipzig. (See especially pp. 65–78, Humblus, Lotherus, Skioldus; 124–200, Frotho to Rolvo Krage; 296–309, Vermundus and Uffo; 412–67, Starkatherus, Ingellus; 243–5, Roricus. A series of detailed studies, invaluable for the student, not only of Saxo, but of *Beowulf* also.)

1922 KLAEBER, F. Der Held Beowulf in deutscher Sagenüberlieferung? *Anglia*, XLVI, 193–201.

1922 KNUDSEN, G. Udlejre. *Danske Studier*, 176-7. (Arguing that this is not to be identified with the historic Leire.)

1922 MACKIE, W. S. The Fight at Finnsburg, ll. 35, 40. *M.L.R.* XVII, 288. (Reply to Sedgefield.)

1922 MATTER, H. Englische Gründungssagen. *Anglistische Forschungen*, 58. (Discusses the identity of the two Hengests, p. 183.) Review: Holthausen, *Anglia, Beiblatt*, XXXV, 41.

1922 MEYER, W. Wealhþeow. *Anglia, Beiblatt*, XXXIII, 94–101.

1922 PATZIG, H. Zur Episode von Þrýð im Beowulf. *Anglia*, XLVI, 282–5.

1922 SCHRÖDER, E. Die Leichenfeier für Attila. *Z.f.d.A.* LIX, 240–4. (For comment on this see Naumann, *Zeugnisse der antiken und frühmittelalterlichen Autoren*, in *Germanisch-Romanische Monatsschrift*, XV, 270.)

1923 BRATE. Fitela. Pippings *Studier i nordisk filologi*, XIV, 2.

1923 COHN, M. Ist die Wortstellung ein brauchbares Kriterium für die Chronologie angelsächsischer Denkmäler? *Engl. Stud.* LVII, 321–9. (A reply to Hübener.)

1923 COOK, A. S. Theodebert of Austrasia. *J.E.G.Ph.* XXII, 424–7. (Argues for the usual dating of Hygelac's fall, c. 516. See above, pp. 381–7.)

1923 HAGEN, S. N. Yrsa og Rolv Krake. *Danske Studier*, 180–2. (Etymologies and interpretations of the names.)

1923 HEUSLER, A. Die altgermanische Dichtung. Walzel's *Handbuch der Literaturwissenschaft*. Berlin. Review: Mogk, *Anglia, Beiblatt*, XXXVII, 1–4.

1923 LABORDE, E. D. Grendel's Glove and his immunity from weapons. *M.L.R.* XVIII, 202–4.

1923 LINDQVIST, S. Hednatemplet i Uppsala. *Fornvännen*. (See esp. pp. 110–12: comparison of the architecture of Heorot with that of Scandinavian wooden churches.)

1923 MALONE, KEMP. The Literary History of Hamlet. I. The Early Tradition. Heidelberg. *Anglistische Forschungen*, LIX. (Detailed arguments as to the development of the legends of Onela and Hrothulf and their contemporaries. See above, pp. 445–9.) Reviews: Briggs, *J.E.G.Ph.* XXIV, 413–24 (a valuable summary); Andrews, *Philol. Quart.* III, 318–20 (cf. Malone, *Philol. Quart.* IV, 158–60); *Lit. Cbl.* LXXIV, 485.

1923 SCHÜCKING, L. L. Die Beowulfdatierung: Eine Replik. *P.B.B.* XLVII, 293–311. (See above, pp. 397–8; 486–8.)

1923 VON SYDOW, C. W. Beowulfskalden och nordisk tradition. *Yearbook of the New Society of Letters at Lund*, 77–91. Reviews: Hecht, *Anglia, Beiblatt*, XXXV, 218–19; Liebermann, *Archiv*, CXLVIII, 95.

1923 VON SYDOW, C. W. Beowulf och Bjarke. Helsingfors. *Studier i Nordisk Filologi*, XIV, 3. (Argues that the Grendel story is of Irish origin, and the *Grettir* episode derived, ultimately, from *Beowulf*; emphasizes the importance of a study of oral tradition.) Reviews: Kemp Malone, *J.E.G.Ph.* XXIII, 458–60; Holthausen, *Anglia, Beiblatt*, XXXIV, 357–8; Hecht, Zu Holthausens Bericht über v. Sydow, Beowulf och Bjarke, *Anglia, Beiblatt*, XXXV, 218–19; Heusler, *A.f.d.A.* XLIII, 52–4; Liljegren, *Neophilologus*, X, 73–4.

1924 ANSCOMBE, A. Hama in Beowulf. *Notes and Queries*, CXLVI, 112–13.

1924 COOK, A. S. The Old English *Andreas* and Bishop Acca of Hexham. *Transactions of the Connecticut Academy of Arts and Sciences*, XXVI, 245–332. (*Andreas* and *Beowulf*.)

1924 COOK, A. S. Beowulf, 1422. *M.L.N.* XXXIX, 77–82. (Suggests that *flōd blōde wēol* is derived from Aldhelm's *fluenta cruenta*.)

1924 FAHLBECK, P. Beowulfskvädet som källa för nordisk fornhistoria. *N. F. Kungl. Vitterhets Historie och Antikvitets Akademiens Handlingar*,

XXXIII, 2. (See above, pp. 401–8. This paper was read and privately circulated in 1913, but first published in 1924.)

1924 LA COUR, V. Lejrestudier: Navnet. *Danske Studier*, 13–22. (Instances of the name and its etymology. Cf. A. F. Schmidt, *Lejrskov* in *Danske Studier*, 1926, 77–81.)

1924 MALONE, KEMP. King Aun in the Rök Inscription. *M.L.N.* XXXIX, 223–6.

1924 VON SYDOW, C. W. Hur mytforskningen tolkat Beowulfdikten. *Folkminnen och Folktankar*, XI, 97–134.

1924 VON SYDOW, C. W. Scyld Scefing. *Namn och Bygd*, XII, 63–95.

1924 WESSÉN, E. Studier til Sveriges hedna mytologi och fornhistoria. *Uppsala Universitets Årsskrift*. Review: Uhlenbeck, *Acta Philologica Scandinavica*, III, 172–5.

1924 WILLIAMS, R. A. The Finn Episode in Beowulf. An Essay in Interpretation. Cambridge. Reviews: Sedgefield, *M.L.R.* XX, 338–9; Blackman, *R.E.S.* I, 228–31; E. V. Gordon, *Year's Work*, V, 72–4; *Notes and Queries*, CXLIX, 89; Kemp Malone, *J.E.G.Ph.* XXV, 114–17; Klaeber, *Anglia, Beiblatt*, XXXVII, 5–9; Hecht, *A.f.d.A.* XLIV, 121–5; Kindervater, *Lit. Cbl.* LXXVI, 1744; Flasdieck, *Literaturblatt*, XLVII, 155–64; Schreuder, *Neophilologus*, XI, 294–7.

1925 CHAMBERS, R. W. Beowulf and the Heroic Age. (Foreword to Sir Archibald Strong's translation, q.v.)

1925 COOK, A. S. Aldhelm and the source of Beowulf, l. 2523; Beowulf, ll. 159–63. *M.L.N.* XL, 137–42, 352–4. (*deorc dēapscua...mistige mōras: montes caliginosos...umbram mortis.*)

1925 COOK, A. S. Cynewulf's part in our Beowulf. *Transactions of the Connecticut Academy of Arts and Sciences*, XXVII, 385–406. Reviews: S. J. Crawford, *M.L.R.* XXII, 94–6; Hübener, *Engl. Stud.* LXI, 290–2.

1925 LAMB, E. M. Hemming: Beowulf Queries. *Notes and Queries*, CXLIX, 243–4.

1925 LINDQVIST, S. Vendelhjälmarnas ursprung; De koniska hjälmarna hos de utomnordiska folken under folkvandringstiden. *Fornvännen*, 181–207, 227–40.

1925 MALONE, KEMP. *Widsith* and the *Hervararsaga*. *Pub. Mod. Lang. Assoc. Amer.* XL, 769–813.

1925 MALONE, KEMP. King Alfred's Geatas. *M.L.R.* XX, 1–11. (Argues that the overthrow of the Geatic kingdom led to a Geatic immigration into Jutland, and that this accounts for Alfred's terminology.) Review: E. V. Gordon, *Year's Work*, VI, 77–8.

1925 MUCH, R. Widsith: Beiträge zu einem Commentar. *Z.f.d.A.* LXII, 113–50. (See esp. on Breca and Hōc.)

1925 NERMAN, B. Det svenska rikets uppkomst. Stockholm. (See above, p. 415.) Most important.

1925. PETERSEN, C. Germanische Heldendichtung in Schleswig-Holstein. *Literar. Jahrbuch f. Schleswig-Holstein*. (Offa, Finnsburg, Beowulf, Ingeld.)

1925 POGATSCHER, A. Altenglisch Grendel. *Neusprachliche Studien, Festgabe Karl Luick dargebracht* (*Die Neueren Sprachen, Beiheft* 6, p. 151). (**grandila*, connected with *gram*, wrathful.)

1925 PONS, E. Le Thème et le Sentiment de la Nature dans la Poésie anglosaxonne. *Publications de l'Université de Strasbourg*. London. Reviews: Carleton Brown, *M.L.R.* XXI, 343–4; Batho, *R.E.S.* II, 496–7; E. V. Gordon, *Year's Work*, VI, 70–2; Kemp Malone, *M.L.N.* XLIII, 406–8; Klaeber, *Anglia, Beiblatt*, XXXVIII, 129–32; Brandl, *Archiv*, CLI, 297; Legouis, *Revue Anglo-Américaine*, III, 138–40; Vendryès, *Revue Celtique*, XLII, 205–7; Mossé, *Langues Modernes*, XXIII, 568–71.

1925 THOMAS, A. Un manuscrit inutilisé du "Liber Monstrorum." *Archivum Latinitatis medii aevi* (*Bulletin Du Cange*), I, 232–45.

1925 TRNKA, B. Dņešni stav badání o Beowulfovi (Present State of the Beowulf Problem). *Časopis pro moderni filologii*, XII, 35–48, 124–36, 247–54.

1925 WADSTEIN, E. Beowulf, Etymologie und Sinn des Namens. *Germanica, Eduard Sievers zum 75 Geburtstage*, 323–6. (Suggests connection with Low German *bui(e)* "storm": "Beowulf"=Wind- or Storm-Wolf.)

1925 WADSTEIN, E. Norden och Västeuropa i gammal tid. Stockholm. *Populärt vetenskapliga föreläsningar vid Göteborgs Högskola*, Ny följd, XXII. See above, pp. 406–8. Review: Uhlenbeck, *Acta Philologica Scandinavica*, II, 287.

1925 YNGLINGATAL. Text, översättning och kommentar av Adolf Noreen. Stockholm. *Kungl. Vitterhets Historie och Antikvitets Akademiens Handlingar*, XXVIII, 2. Review: Neckel, *Litteris*, III, 181–2.

1926 COOK, A. S. The Beowulfian maðelode. *J.E.G.Ph.* XXV, 1–6. (Argues for an influence, by Homer, upon the author of *Beowulf*.) Review, of this and the three following articles: Daunt, *Year's Work*, VII, 54–7.

1926 COOK, A. S. Beowulfian and Odyssean voyages. *Transactions of the Connecticut Academy of Arts and Sciences*, XXVIII, 1–20. Review: Hübener, *Engl. Stud.* LXI, 290–2.

1926 COOK, A. S. Hellenic and Beowulfian shields and spears. *M.L.N.* XLI, 360–3.

1926 COOK, A. S. Greek parallels to certain features of the *Beowulf. Philol. Quart.* V, 226–34. (Condensed from a paper written early in 1891, and not hitherto published.)

1926 DEHMER, H. Primitives Erzählungsgut in den Islendinga Sögur. Leipzig. (Examples, among other things, of Waterfall-Trolls.) Review: Reuschel, *Literaturblatt*, LI, 180–2.

1926 HÜBENER, G. Beowulf und die Psychologie der Standesentwicklung. *Germanisch-Romanische Monatsschrift*, XIV, 352–71. Review: Daunt, *Year's Work*, VII, 57–60.

1926 KISSACK, R. A. The Sea in Anglo-Saxon and Middle English poetry. *Washington University Studies.*

1926 KLAEBER, F. Beowulfiana. *Anglia*, L, 107–22, 195–244. (Textual notes: Finnsburg; the Þryð-Offa episode; a note on the two Dragon Fights; the date of Hygelac's death.) Review: Daunt, *Year's Work*, VII, 50–1.

1926 LA COUR, V. Skjoldungefejden. *Danske Studier*, 147–56. (A reply to Boer's *Studier over Skjoldungedigtningen*. See p. 450, above.)

1926 MALONE, KEMP. Danes and Half-Danes. *A.f.n.F.* XLII (N.F. XXXVIII), 234–40. (An argument that *Healfdene* is an older poetic name for the Scyldings.) Review: Daunt, *Year's Work*, VII, 51–2.

1926 MALONE, KEMP. The Finn Episode in Beowulf. *J.E.G.Ph.* XXV, 157–72. Review: Daunt, *Year's Work*, VII, 52–4.

1926 SCHÜTTE, G. Vor Folkegruppe: Gottjod. Kjøbenhavn. (An English translation will shortly be issued from the Cambridge University Press.) Review: Schönfeld, *Acta Philologica Scandinavica*, III, 86–9.

1926 STRÖMHOLM, D. Försök över Beowulfdikten och Ynglingasagan. *Edda*, XXV, 233–49. (A statement of the historical deductions which can be made from these two documents. The writer accounts for English interest by supposing a Geatic settlement in England.) Review: Daunt, *Year's Work*, VII, 62–3.

1926 TRENEER, A. The Sea in English Literature, from Beowulf to Donne. Liverpool. Review: Daunt, *Year's Work*, VII, 65–6.

1927 CORNELIUS, R. D. Palus inamabilis. *Speculum*, II, 321–5. (Hell and the fens.)

1927 KLAEBER, F. Attila's and Beowulf's Funeral. *Pub. Mod. Lang. Assoc. Amer.* XLII, 255–67.

1927 KRAPPE, A. H. Eine mittelalterlich-indische Parallele zum Beowulf. *Germanisch-Romanische Monatsschrift*, xv, 54–8. (Important, see above, pp. 483–4.)

1927 LEICHER, R. Die Totenklage in der deutschen Epik von der ältesten Zeit bis zur Nibelungen-Klage. *Germanistische Abhandlungen*, LVIII. Breslau.

1927 MAGOUN, F. P. The Burning of Heorot. *M.L.N.* XLII, 173–4.

1927 MALONE, KEMP. Hrethric. *Pub. Mod. Lang. Assoc. Amer.* XLII, 268–313. (A very thorough and complete discussion of all the evidence relating to Hrethric. "Anglicists in the past have neglected most of the Scandinavian accounts, particularly that version included in *Sögubrot*, and this neglect has prevented them from coming to a full understanding of the English version.")

1927 RATTRAY, R. F. Beowulf. *Times Lit. Sup.* 1927, p. 12. (Mythological interpretation of Beowulf and Grendel.)

1927 ROUTH, H. V. God, Man and Epic Poetry. A study in comparative Literature. Cambridge. Reviews: Herford, *M.L.R.* XXIII, 255–9; Magoun, *Speculum*, III, 124–7.

1927 SCHLAUCH, M. Chaucer's Constance and Accused Queens. New York. (pp. 64 etc. *Vitae Offarum.*)

1927 SCHRÖER, M. M. A. Grundzüge und Haupttypen der englischen Literaturgeschichte. *Sammlung Göschen*. 3 Aufl. (pp. 40–54, Heldensage, Beowulf.)

1927 SCHÜTTE, G. Daner og Heruler. *Danske Studier*, 65–74. (Arguing against Wessén's reconstruction of Danish history as depicted in *Beowulf*. See pp. 434–45 above.)

1927 VOGT, W. H. Stilgeschichte der eddischen Wissensdichtung: I. Der Kultredner. Breslau. (O.E. *þyle.*) Review: Kemp Malone, *M.L.N.* XLIV, 129–30.

1927 WESSÉN, E. Nordiska namnstudier. *Uppsala Universitets Årsskrift.* Review: Zachrisson, *Studia Neophilologica*, I, 85–7.

1927 WESSÉN, E. De nordiska folkstammarna i Beowulf. *Kungl. Vitterhets Historie och Antikvitets Akademiens Handlingar*, XXXVI, 2 (3. F. 3, 2). (See above, pp. 434–45.) Reviews: Daunt, *Year's Work*, VIII, 79–80; Kemp Malone, *Speculum*, V, 134–5; Holthausen, *Anglia, Beiblatt*, XXXIX, 303–6; Zachrisson, *Studia Neophilologica*, I, 87–8.

1927 WILLIAMS, R. A. Zur Erwiderung an Fr. Klaeber. *Anglia, Beiblatt*, XXXVIII, 61–3. (Cf. also Williams on the Finnsburg Episode, *M.L.R.* XXII, 310–3.)

1928 BRANDL, A. Hercules und Beowulf. *Sitzungsberichte der preussischen Akademie der Wissenschaften*, XIV, 161–7. Review: Daunt, *Year's Work*, IX, 67–8.

1928 COOK, A. S. Beowulf 1039 (*heahcyning*) and the Greek ἀρχι-. *Speculum*, III, 75–80.

1928 CRAWFORD, S. J. Grendel's descent from Cain. *M.L.R.* XXIII, 207–8.

1928 DEHMER, H. Die Grendelkämpfe Beowulfs im Lichte moderner Märchenforschung. *Germanisch-Romanische Monatsschrift*, XVI, 202–18.

1928 FÖRSTER, MAX. Beowulf-Materialien. 5 verbesserte Aufl. *Germanische Bibliothek*. Heidelberg.

1928 HÜBENER, G. Beowulf und nordische Dämonenaustreibung. *Engl. Stud.* LXII, 293–327. Review: Daunt, *Year's Work*, IX, 68–70.

1928 KRETSCHMER, P. Scandinavia. *Glotta*, XVII, 148–51. (Accuracy and priority of different forms: cf. *Scedenig, Scedeland*, in *Beowulf*.)

1928 LAWRENCE, W. W. Beowulf and Epic Tradition. Cambridge, Mass. (Important: see above, pp. 389–97; 451 etc.) Reviews: Chambers, *M.L.R.*

XXIV, 334–7; Blackman, *R.E.S.* v, 333–5; Daunt, *Year's Work*, IX, 66–7; Larsen, *M.L.N.* XLIV, 189–90; Kemp Malone, *Speculum*, III, 612–5; Jiriczek, *Anglia, Beiblatt*, XL, 193–202.

1928 MALONE, KEMP. "Hunlafing." *M.L.N.* XLIII, 300–4. (Argues powerfully that the word is not a patronymic, but the name of a sword. See above, p. 506.) Review: Daunt, *Year's Work*, IX, 70.

1928 MALONE, KEMP. King Alfred's "Götland." *M.L.R.* XXIII, 336–9.

1928 PHILLPOTTS, B. S. Wyrd and Providence in Anglo-Saxon Thought. (Section IV: *Beowulf*.) *Essays and Studies by members of the English Association*, XIII, 7–27. Review: Daunt, *Year's Work*, IX, 64–6.

1928 SCHNEIDER, H. Germanische Heldensage. Bd. I. *Pauls Grundriss*, 10. 1. Review: Dunstan, *M.L.R.* XXIV, 370.

1928 VOGT, W. H. Der Frühgermanische Kultredner. *Acta Philologica Scandinavica*, II, 250–63. (O.E. *þyle*.)

1929 BRANDL, A. Beowulf und die Merowinger. *Sitzungsberichte der preussischen Akademie der Wissenschaften, Phil.-Hist. Klasse*, XI. (This also appeared in the Klaeber Miscellany.)

1929 CHAMBERS, R. W. Beowulf and Waterfall-Trolls. *Times Lit. Sup.* p. 383. Reply by Miss K. M. Buck, p. 403.

1929 CHAMBERS, R. W. Beowulf's Fight with Grendel, and its Scandinavian Parallels. *English Studies* (Amsterdam), XI, 81–100.

1929 MALONE, KEMP. The identity of the Geatas. *Acta Philologica Scandinavica*, IV, 84–90. (A reply to Wadstein's *Norden och Västeuropa*.)

1929 MALONE, KEMP. Note on *Grottasǫngr*. *Acta Philologica Scandinavica*, IV, 270. (Interpretation of *Halfdana*: bearing upon the *Healfdene* of *Beowulf*.)

1929 MALONE, KEMP. On Beowulf 2928 and 2932. *Philol. Quart.* VIII, 406–7. (Arguing, I think conclusively, that Ohthere is the elder brother, and reigned before Onela.)

1929 MALONE, KEMP and RUUD, M. B. Studies in English Philology, a Miscellany in Honor of Frederick Klaeber. Minneapolis. Contains (pp. 120–95):

    BRYAN, W. F. Epithetic compound folk-names in *Beowulf*.

    MALONE, KEMP. The daughter of Healfdene.

    VAN HAMEL, A. G. Hengest and his namesake.

    LAWRENCE, W. W. *Beowulf* and the *Saga of Samson the Fair*.

    BRANDL, A. *Beowulf* und die Merowinger.

    HULBERT, J. R. A note on the psychology of the *Beowulf*-poet.

See also §§ 3, 6, 7, 9, 10.

1929 PHILIPPSON, E. A. Germanisches Heidentum bei den Angelsachsen. Leipzig. (*Kölner Anglistische Arbeiten*, 4.) Grendel, pp. 83–5; Scēaf, Scyld und Scēfing; Bēow, pp. 93–100.

1929 RICCI, A. The Chronology of Anglo-Saxon Poetry. *R.E.S.* v, 257–66. (A discriminating study.)

1929 SCHICK, J. Die Urquelle der Offa-Konstanze-Sage. *Britannica, Max Förster zum sechzigsten Geburtstage*, 31–56.

1929 SCHÜCKING, L. L. Das Königsideal im Beowulf, *Bulletin of the Modern Humanities Research Association*, III, 143–54. (*Presidential Address*.)

1929 WARDALE, E. E. The Nationality of Ecgtheow. *M.L.R.* XXIV, 322.

1929 WARD, H. G. The name Hygelac. *Notes and Queries*, CLVI, 263.

1930 BRANDL, A. Einige Tatsachen betreffend Scyld Scefing, *Miscellany offered to Otto Jespersen*, 31–7. (Brandl reinforces and expands the arguments he had put forward in *Archiv*, CXXXVII, 6–24; CXLIII, 289–90.)

1930 CAWLEY, F. STANTON. Ivarr-Unferþ. *Pub. Mod. Lang. Assoc. Amer.* XLV, 335–6. (Disputing Kemp Malone's identification.)

1930 Hübener, Gustav. England und die Gesittungsgrundlage der europäischen Frühgeschichte. Frankfurt am Main. (Especially chapter III— Der heroische Exorzismus der nordischen Rasse.)

1930 Liestøl, Knut. Beowulf and Epic Tradition, *The American Scandinavian Review*, XVIII, 370–3. (Additional waterfall-troll stories.)

1930 Lotspeich, H. G. Beowulf, 1363, *hrinde bearwas. J.E.G.Ph.* XXIX, 367–9. (Suggests that in this phrase we have a fragmentary survival of the connection of troll-slaying with winter.)

1930 Malone, Kemp. Ifarr and Inwær. *Pub. Mod. Lang. Assoc. Amer.* XLV, 626–8. (A reply to Cawley, to which is appended Cawley's replication to Malone.)

1930 Malone, Kemp. Ingeld. *Mod. Phil.* XXVII, 257–76.

1930 Schlauch, M. Another Analogue of Beowulf. *M.L.N.* XLV, 20–1. (From the *Flores Saga Konungs*. See above, p. 454.)

1930 Steadman, J. M. The Ingeld-episode in Beowulf: History or Prophecy? *M.L.N.* XLV, 522–5. (Emphasizes the rarity of the historic present in Old English: the episode must therefore relate to future time.)

1930 Work, J. A. Odyssean influence on the Beowulf. *Philological Quarterly*, IX, 399–402. (Euryalus and Unferth.)

1930 Zachrisson, R. E. Grendel in Beowulf and in local names, *Miscellany offered to Otto Jespersen*, 39–44.

1931 Malone, Kemp. Ealhhild. *Anglia*, LV, 266–72.

§ 9. STYLE, VOCABULARY AND GRAMMAR

1915 Schücking, L. L. Untersuchungen zur Bedeutungslehre der angelsächsischen Dichtersprache. Heidelberg. Reviews: Binz, *Anglia, Beiblatt*, XXVIII, 193–8; Björkman, *Engl. Stud.* L, 426–7.

1915 Wende, F. Über die nachgestellten Präpositionen im Angelsächsischen. *Palaestra* 70. Berlin. Reviews: Eichler, *Anglia, Beiblatt*, XXIX, 99–102; Franz, *Engl. Stud.* LI, 81–2; Björkman, *Archiv*, CXXXV, 437–9; Schröer, *D.L.Z.* XXXVII, 1455 *etc.*; Ries, *Literaturblatt*, XXXVII, 116–18.

1918 Phoenix, W. Die Substantivierung des Adjectivs, Partizips und Zahlwortes im Angelsächsischen. Dissertation. Berlin. Review: Fischer, *Anglia, Beiblatt*, XXXI, 10–12.

1919 Keiser, A. The influence of Christianity on the vocabulary of Old English poetry. *Univ. of Illinois Studies.* Reviews: Schücking, *M.L.R.* XVI, 176–7; Schöffler, *Anglia, Beiblatt*, XXXII, 55; Klaeber, *Engl. Stud.* LVI, 88–90; Brandl, *Archiv*, CXLVII, 144; Funke, *Literaturblatt*, XLIII, 94–102.

1919 Wolf, A. Die Bezeichnungen für Schicksal in der ags. Dichtersprache. Dissertation. Breslau.

1921 Eismann, A. Der Konjunktiv in Nebensätzen in der ae. Poesie. Dissertation in Typescript. Kiel.

1921 Hübener, G. Das Problem des Flexionsschwundes im Angelsächsischen. *P.B.B.* XLV, 85–102.

1921 Jente, R. Die mythologischen Ausdrücke im altenglischen Wortschatz. Heidelberg. *Anglistische Forschungen*, LVI. Review: Ekwall, *Anglia, Beiblatt*, XXXIV, 133–6.

1922 Glogauer, E. Die Bedeutungsübergänge der Konjunktionen in der angelsächsischen Dichtersprache. Leipzig. *Neue Anglistische Arbeiten*, VI. Reviews: Horn, *Anglia, Beiblatt*, XXXVI, 73–4; Flasdieck, *Engl. Stud.* LVIII, 93–4.

1922 Lussky, G. F. The Verb Forms circumscribed with the Perfect Participle in the Beowulf. *J.E.G.Ph.* XXI, 32–69.

1922 Oroz, R. Lautliche Unterschiede im Vokalismus der Starktonsilben bei den beiden Schreibern der Beowulf-Handschrift. ms Dissertation. Leipzig. Summary in *Jahrb. d. phil. Fak. zu Leipzig*, ii, 28–9.

1923 Janotta, G. Wörterbuch zum Beowulf, sachlich geordnet. ms Dissertation. Rostock. Summary, Rostock, 1923.

1923 Klaeber, F. Eine Bemerkung zum altenglischen Passivum. *Engl. Stud.* lvii, 187–95.

1923 Massey, B. W. A. Compound Adjectives in Shelley and Keats (and Beowulf). *Notes and Queries*, Twelfth Series, xii, 464–8.

1923 Wolff, L. Über den Stil der altgermanischen Poesie. *Deutsche Vierteljahrsschrift für Literaturwissenschaft und Geistesgeschichte*, i, 214–29.

1924 Pfeifer, H. Über die Art der Redeführung in der ae. erzählenden Dichtung, im Heliand und in Layamons Brut. Dissertation in Typescript. Halle.

1924 Spinner, K. Die Ausdrücke für Sinnesempfindungen in der ags. Poesie verglichen mit den Bezeichnungen für Sinnesempfindungen in der altnord., altsächs. und althochdeutschen Dichtung. Dissertation in Typescript. Halle.

1925 Wyld, H. C. Diction and Imagery in Anglo-Saxon Poetry. *Essays and Studies by members of the English Association*, xi, 49–91. Reviews: E. V. Gordon, *Year's Work*, vi, 63–70; Eichler, *Anglia, Beiblatt*, xxxvii, 232.

1929 Buckhurst, H. Terms and phrases for the Sea in O.E. Poetry. *Studies in English Philology, a Miscellany in Honor of Frederick Klaeber*, 103–19.

1929 Magoun, F. P. Recurring first elements in different nominal compounds in *Beowulf* and in the *Elder Edda*. *The same*, 73–8.

1929 Klaeber, F. Eine germanisch-englische Formel: Ein stilistisch-syntaktischer Streifzug. *Britannica, Max Förster zum sechzigsten Geburtstage*, 1–22.

1929 van der Merwe Scholtz, H. The Kenning in Anglo-Saxon and Old Norse Poetry. Utrecht and Oxford.

§ 10. METRE

1911 Kaluza, M. A Short History of English Versification. Trans. by A. C. Dunstan. London. (Old English prosody, 14–126.)

1918 Leonard, W. E. Beowulf and the Nibelungen couplet. *Univ. of Wisconsin Studies in Language and Literature*, ii. Reviews: Klaeber, *Anglia, Beiblatt*, xxxii, 145–8.

1919 Heusler, A. Stabreim. Hoops *Reallexikon*, iv, 231–40.

1920 Bognitz, A. Doppelt-steigende Alliterations-Verse im Ags. Dissertation. Berlin.

1921 Stock, R. Die Verstärkung der Alliteration im Beowulf-Liede. ms Dissertation. Königsberg. Summary in *Inaug. Diss. d. phil. Fak. Königsberg*, 1921.

1923 Routh, J. Anglo-Saxon Meter. *Mod. Phil.* xxi, 429–34.

1925 Greg, W. W. The Five Types in Anglo-Saxon Verse. *M.L.R.* xx, 12–17. Review: E. V. Gordon, *Year's Work*, vi, 75–7.

1925 Heusler, A. Deutsche Versgeschichte mit Einschluss des altenglischen und altnordischen Stabreimverses. Berlin und Leipzig. (Vol. i, 1925; vol. ii, 1927.)

1925 Sievers, E. Zu Cynewulf. *Neusprachliche Studien, Festgabe Karl Luick dargebracht (Die Neueren Sprachen)*. (Contains a statement of Sievers' metrical views. See above, pp. 399–400.)

1928 SCRIPTURE, E. W. Experimentelle Untersuchungen über die Metrik im Beowulf. *Archiv für die gesamte Psychologie*, LXVI, 203–15. Review of this and the next article: Daunt, *Year's Work*, IX, 72–4.

1928 SCRIPTURE, E. W. Die Grundgesetze des altenglischen Stabreimverses. *Anglia*, LII, 69–75.

1929 LEONARD, W. E. Four footnotes to papers on Germanic Metrics. *Studies in English Philology, a Miscellany in Honor of Frederick Klaeber*, 1–13.

1930 BAUM, P. F. The character of Anglo-Saxon verse. *Mod. Phil.* XXVIII, 143–6.

SUPPLEMENTARY BIBLIOGRAPHY TO 1958

The general arrangement and method of the original Bibliography and of the Additions to the Bibliography have been followed as exactly as possible, with one exception. Owing to the immense importance of the archaeological discoveries at Sutton Hoo for the student of *Beowulf* and the stimulus which these have given to the archaeological approach to the poem generally, I have thought it desirable to add a separate section for this field. There are therefore now eleven sections to the Supplementary Bibliography: the ten exactly as before, and an eleventh entitled "Sutton Hoo and Archaeology."

The period covered is that from where the Additions to the Bibliography left off to the present—from 1930–1 to 1957–8. No attempt has been made to include the very rare and unimportant omissions from before 1930 except for one of special significance.

§ 1. PERIODICALS

In addition to those already listed, the following are those more frequently referred to:

E.L.H. = A Journal of English Literary History. Baltimore, 1934 *etc.*

Engl. & Germ. Stud. = English and Germanic Studies. Birmingham University, 1947 *etc.*

English Studies, a Journal of English Letters and Philology. Amsterdam, 1919 *etc.*

Études anglaises. Paris, 1938 *etc.*

Med. Æv. = Medium Ævum, published for the Society for the Study of mediæval Languages and Literature. Oxford, 1932 *etc.*

Neophil. = Neophilologus. Groningen, 1915 *etc.*

Stud. Neophil. = Studia Neophilologica. Uppsala, 1928 *etc.*

2. BIBLIOGRAPHIES

Of recent editions of *Beowulf*, those of Klaeber and of Dobbie (see § 4) include particularly good bibliographies.

Annual Bibliography of the Modern Language Association of America, included in *Pub. Mod. Lang. Assoc. Amer.* Formerly including only works from the U.S.A., since 1955 it has aimed to become completely international.

1940 The Cambridge Bibliography of English Literature, vol. I, pp. 63–8. Cambridge. (Includes, though not very completely, items up to the end of 1938.)

1957 The Cambridge Bibliography of English Literature, vol. V, Supplement, pp. 63–70. Cambridge. (Very efficiently and fully covers work up to 1955, including items omitted from vol. I.)

1941 KLAEBER, FR. A Few Recent Additions to Beowulf Bibliography and Notes, *Anglia*, Beiblatt, LII, 135–7.

1944 KLAEBER, FR. Some Further Additions to Beowulf Bibliography and Notes, *Anglia*, Beiblatt, LIV/LV, 274–80.

§ 3. THE MS. AND ITS TRANSCRIPTS

1932 RYPINS, STANLEY. The Beowulf Codex, *The Colophon*, pt. 10.

1938 SMITH, A. H. The Photography of Manuscripts, *London Mediæval Studies*, vol. I, pt. 2, 179–207. (Important. New light is shed especially on the most illegible pages of the *Beowulf* MS., and there are some very valuable new readings.)

1942 MALONE, KEMP. Thorkelin's Transcripts of *Beowulf*, *Stud. Neophil.* XIV, 25–30.

1949 MALONE, KEMP. The Text of *Beowulf*, *Proc. American Philosoph. Soc.* XCIII, 239–43.

1949 MALONE, KEMP. Readings from The Thorkelin Transcripts of *Beowulf*, *Pub. Mod. Lang. Assoc. Amer.* LXIV, 1190–1218.

1951 The Thorkelin Transcripts of *Beowulf* in Facsimile: edited by Kemp Malone, in the series *Early English Manuscripts in Facsimile*. Copenhagen, Baltimore and London. (Extremely important: good photographic reproductions of photostats of both the Thorkelin copies are preceded by a thorough and very productive study of the methods of transcription and of the types of error most likely.)

1953 SISAM, KENNETH. Studies in the History of Old English Literature. Oxford. (Important here for its inclusion of the article on The Compilation of the *Beowulf* Manuscript.) This volume also reprints the pioneer earlier article from *M.L.R.* XI, listed in the original Bibliography.

1957 KER, N. K. Catalogue of Manuscripts containing Anglo-Saxon. Oxford. (Important: *Beowulf* is dealt with at pp. 281–2 and in its bibliography.)

§ 4. EDITIONS OF BEOWULF AND FINNSBURG

1935 SEDGEFIELD, W. J. Beowulf: third edition revised and partly rewritten. Manchester. (A new study especially of the text, based on a fresh first-hand re-examination of the MS. itself; frequently very free in emendation.)

1936 KLAEBER, FR. Beowulf and the Fight at Finnsburg: third edition revised. Boston. (This, with its later Supplements [see below], remains the most complete and authoritative edition.)

1941 KLAEBER, FR. Beowulf and the Fight at Finnsburg: third edition reprinted, with a Supplement bringing all its parts up to date to the end of 1940.

1951 KLAEBER, FR. Beowulf and the Fight at Finnsburg: third edition reprinted, with a Second Supplement bringing its material up to date to the close of 1950.

1939 LEHNERT, MARTIN. Beowulf, eine Auswahl. Berlin. (Includes only some 1000 lines of the text.)

1949 LEHNERT, MARTIN. Beowulf, eine Auswahl. Berlin. (Second edition.)

1958–9 VON SCHAUBERT, ELSE. Heyne-Schückings Beowulf neubearbeitet, 17 Auflage. Paderborn. (Important: this reprint of the fifteenth edition of 1940 which has been almost entirely destroyed by war includes a thoroughly revised Glossary and Notes, with a very conservative text. The notes especially provide much valuable and new material.)

1948 HOLTHAUSEN, FERDINAND. Beowulf nebst den kleineren Denkmälern der Heldensage, 8. verbesserte Auflage. Heidelberg. (A valuable presentation of the text with some striking emendations: the Notes and Glossary are still in preparation by Professor Heinrich Matthes of Erlangen.)

1953–4 DOBBIE, ELLIOTT VAN KIRK. Beowulf and Judith: vol. IV of The Anglo-Saxon Poetic Records. New York and London. (Though deliberately limited by the plan of its series, it contains new and important textual readings and interpretations.)

1953 WRENN, C. L. Beowulf with the Finnesburg Fragment. London and Boston. (Includes a fairly full and rather literary Introduction, with Glossary, and selective Commentary and Bibliography.)

1958 WRENN, C. L. Beowulf with the Finnesburg Fragment: second edition. London and Boston. (A corrected reprint of the first edition, with a Supplement bringing the material briefly up to date to 1957.)

Most O.E. teaching manuals and readers include some extracts from *Beowulf* with aids to study: but these works have generally been excluded for lack of space.

§ 5. CONCORDANCES ETC.

No concordances have been published in the period under review: but the very full glossary to Klaeber's edition, which lists every occurrence of each word and form, may serve very well for this purpose. The glossary to von Schaubert's revision of the Heyne-Schücking *Beowulf* has similar virtues.

§ 6. TRANSLATIONS

Only those which seem to have some value to the scholar or the literary student are listed.

1934 OLIVERO, FEDERICO. Beowulf. Torino. (An Italian rendering from the text of R. W. Chambers.)

1935 GREEN, A. WIGFALL. Beowulf Literally Translated. Boston.

1940 CLARK HALL, JOHN, and WRENN, C. L. Beowulf and the Finnsburg Fragment, a Translation into Modern English Prose: a new edition of Clark Hall's version (see the original Bibliography), revised by Wrenn, with Prefatory Remarks by J. R. R. Tolkien. London. (Corrects the errors of the earlier edition, and has some very lively and important writing on diction and metre in Tolkien's Prefatory Remarks.)

1950 CLARK HALL, JOHN, and WRENN, C. L. Beowulf and the Finnsburg Fragment, a Translation into Modern English Prose: New ed. completely revised by Wrenn, with Notes and Introduction. (The valuable Prefatory Remarks of Tolkien remain unchanged as in the ed. of 1940.)

1940 KENNEDY, C. W. Beowulf, the Oldest English Epic. New York. (A rendering into alliterative verse by an excellent scholar.)

1945 BONE, GAVIN. Beowulf, in Modern Verse. Oxford.

1949 WATERHOUSE, MARY E. Beowulf in Modern English, a Translation into Blank Verse. Cambridge.

1951 GENZMER, F. Beowulf und das Finnsburgbruchstück, aus dem Angelsächsischen übertragen. Leipzig.

1952 MORGAN, EDWIN. Beowulf: a Verse Translation into Modern English. Aldington (Kent): Hand and Flower Press. (Includes two introductory essays, one of which is a valuable discussion of the art of translating.)

1957 WRIGHT, DAVID. Beowulf, a Prose Translation with an Introduction. London: Penguin Books. (A not unsuccessful attempt to combine satisfactory scholarship with popular appeal in a readable version, with an Appendix on Sutton Hoo and Beowulf.)

§ 7. TEXTUAL CRITICISM AND INTERPRETATION

Inevitably this section must occasionally overlap with § 8, or even with § 9. Any item bearing in part on textual or interpretative matters not found here should therefore be looked for in § 8 or, failing that, in § 9. Where an item is of mixed scope, I could only use my judgment in assigning it to that section to which its preponderating interest seemed to belong.

1931 CRAWFORD, S. J. Beowulfiana, *R.E.S.* VII, 448–50. (Includes discussion of ll. 600 and 1724 ff.)

1931 FURUHJELM, A. A Note on a Passage in *Beowulf*, *Neuphilologische Mitteilungen*, XXXII, 107–9. (Discusses ll. 3066–75.)

1931 HOOPS, J. Zur Bedeutung *Beowulf* 769. *Engl. Stud.* LXV, 177–80.

1931 KLAEBER, FR., and HOOPS, J. Ae "Ealuscerwen" und kein Ende, *Engl. Stud.* LXVI, 1–5.

1931 LYONS, C. P. A Note on *Beowulf* 760, *M.L.N.* XLVI, 443.

1931 SCOTT-THOMAS, H. F. The Fight at Finnsburg: Garulf and the Son of Guthlaf, *J.E.G.Ph.* XXX, 498–505.

1931 SIEVERS, EDUARD. *Beowulf* 3066 ff., *P.B.B.* LV, 376.

1931 WEBER, E. Seelenmörder oder Unholdtöter, *Neuphilologische Monatschrift*, II, 293–5. (Discusses ll. 171–8.)

1932 HOOPS, J. Beowulfstudien. Heidelberg. (Important.)

1932 HOOPS, J. Kommentar zum Beowulf. Heidelberg. (Important: this, together with his *Beowulfstudien* above, provides an outstanding study of the whole poem.)

1932 HOLTHAUSEN, FERDINAND. Zu *Beowulf* v. 3074 f., *Anglia*, Beiblatt, XLIII, 157.

1932 KLAEBER, FR. Eine kleine Nachlese zum *Beowulf*, *Anglia*, LVI, 421–31.

1932 KLAEBER, FR. *Beowulf* 769, *Engl. Stud.* LXVII, 24–6.

1932 KLAEBER, FR. Garulf Guþlafs Sohn im Finnsburgfragment, *Archiv*, CLXII, 1/2, 116–17.

1932 KROGMANN, WILLY. Ae. *scerwan, *Engl. Stud.* LXVI, 346. Also "Ealuscerwen" und "Meoduscerwen," *ibid.* LXVII, 152–3.

1932–3 KROGMANN, WILLY. Ae. "Orcneas," *Anglia*, LVI, 40–2 and LVII, 112, 396.

1932 MALONE, KEMP. "Ecgwela," *Anglia*, LVI, 436–7. (Ingenious explanation of the name at l. 1710 as a kenning.)

1932–3 MALONE, KEMP. Notes on *Beowulf*, *Anglia*, LVI, 436–7. Also *Anglia*, LVII, 218–20 and 313–16.

1932 SCHRÖDER, E. *Beowulf*, *Anglia*, LVI, 316–17.

1932 SEDGEFIELD, W. J. Emendations of the *Beowulf* Text, *M.L.R.* XXVII, 448–51.

1932 WEBER, E. Die Halle Heorot als Schlafsaal, *Archiv*, CLXII, 114–16.

1933 FURUHJELM, A. Beowulfiana, *Anglia*, LVII, 317–20. (Discusses ll. 224, 303–6 and 3074 ff.)

1933 HOLTHAUSEN, FERDINAND. Angelsächsisches Allerlei, *Anglia*, Beiblatt, XLIV, 349–50.

1933 HOOPS, J. "Orcneas," *Anglia*, LVII, 110–11.

1933 IMELMANN, R. *Beowulf* 303 ff. und 3074 ff., *Engl. Stud.* LXVII, 325–39.

1933 IMELMANN, R. *Beowulf* 3074 ff.: Nachprüfung, *Engl. Stud.* LXVIII, 1–5.

1933 KROGMANN, WILLY. Bemerkungen zum *Beowulf*, *Engl. Stud.* LXVIII, 317–19. (On ll. 84 and 850.)

1933 MALONE, KEMP. Beowulfiana, *Med. Æv.* II, 58–64. (Particularly interesting discussions of ll. 304 and 646.)

1933 SEDGEFIELD, W. J. Further Emendations of the *Beowulf* Text, *M.L.R.* XXVIII, 226–30.

1934 BERENDSOHN, WALTER. Healfdenes Vater, *A.f.n.F.* L, 148–56.

1934 HINTZ, H. W. The "Hama" Reference in *Beowulf* 1197–1201, *J.E.G.Ph.* XXXIII, 98–102.

1934 HOLTHAUSEN, FERDINAND. Zu *Beowulf* 457, *Anglia*, Beiblatt, XLV, 19.

1934–5 KROGMANN, WILLY. Ae. "Eolet" (*Beowulf* 224), *Anglia*, LVIII, 351–7. (Further discussed in *Engl. Stud.* LXX, 41 ff.)

1934 MARTIN-CLARKE, ELIZABETH. Beowulfiana, *M.L.R.* XXIX, 320–1. (On ll. 984 ff. and 1357 ff.)

1935 CASSIDY, F. G. Suggested Re-punctuation of a Passage in *Beowulf* (745 ff.), *M.L.N.* L, 88–9.

1935 DU BOIS, ARTHUR E. *Beowulf* 489–90, *M.L.N.* L, 89–90.

1935 DU BOIS, ARTHUR E. *Beowulf* 1107 and 2577: Hoards, Swords and Shields, *Engl. Stud.* LXIX, 321–8.

1935 ELIASON, NORMAN E. "Wulfhliδ" (*Beowulf* 1358), *J.E.G.Ph.* XXXIV, 20–3.

1935 HOLTHAUSEN, FERDINAND. Zum *Beowulf*, *Engl. Stud.* LXIX, 433–4.

1935 HOOPS, J. *Beowulf* 457 f., *Engl. Stud.* LXX, 77–80.

1935 TRAVER, HOPE. *Beowulf* 648–649 Once More, *Archiv*, CLXVII, 253–6.

1936 KLAEBER, FR. Drei Anmerkungen zur Texterklärung, *Engl. Stud.* LXX, 333–6. (Discussion of Garulf son of Guδlaf.)

1937 COLGRAVE, BERTRAM. "Scurheard" (1033), *M.L.R.* XXXII, 281.

1938 BROWN, CARLETON. *Beowulf* and the Blickling Homilies and some Textual Notes, *Pub. Mod. Lang. Assoc. Amer.* LIII, 905–16.

1938 SANDERLIN, GEORGE. A Note on *Beowulf* 1142, *M.L.N.* LIII, 501–3.

1938 VON SCHAUBERT, ELSE. Zur Gestaltung und Erklärung des *Beowulf*-textes, *Anglia*, LXII, 173–89. (Important especially for syntactical points: deals with 1931 b, with Wealhþeow (especially 1169–85), and with absolute participial constructions.)

1939 ANDREW, S. O. Three Textual Cruces in *Beowulf*, *Med. Æv.* VIII, 205–7. (Deals with 648 ff., 1379, and 3074 f.)

1939 HUPPÉ, BERNARD F. A Reconsideration of the Ingeld Passage in *Beowulf*, *J.E.G.Ph.* XXXVIII, 217–25.

1939 KLAEBER, FR. *Beowulf* 769 and *Andreas* 1526 ff., *Engl. Stud.* LXXIII, 185–9.

1939 KLAEBER, FR. A Notelet on the Ingeld Episode in *Beowulf*, *Anglia*, Beiblatt, L, 223–4.

1939 KLAEBER, FR. Beowulfiana Minora, *Anglia*, LXIII, 400–25.

1939 KLAEBER, FR. A Few *Beowulf* Jottings, *Anglia*, Beiblatt, L, 330–2.

1939 KROGMANN, WILLY. Altenglisches, *Anglia*, LXIII, 398–9. (Deals with 3114 f.)

1939 MACKIE, W. S. Notes upon the Text and Interpretation of *Beowulf*, *M.L.R.* XXXIV, 515–24.

1939 MALONE, KEMP. Notes on *Beowulf* IX–XI, *Anglia*, LXIII, 103–12. (Discussion of the Ingeld Episode; also of the forms of proper names in 1176, 1944, 1961, and 2466.)

1939 WHITELOCK, DOROTHY. *Beowulf* 2444–2471, *Med. Æv.* VIII, 198–204.

1940 BROWN, CALVIN S., Jnr. Beowulf's Arm-lock, *Pub. Mod. Lang. Assoc. Amer.* LV, 621–7. (Discusses the fight with Grendel with special reference to ll. 748–9.)

1940 CROSBY, H. LAMAR, Jnr. Two Notes on *Beowulf*, *M.L.N.* LV, 605–6. (Discusses ll. 212 and 216.)

1940 KLAEBER, FR. *Beowulf* 2041 "beah," *Anglia*, Beiblatt, LI, 206–7.

1940 MALONE, KEMP. Time and Place in the Ingeld Episode in *Beowulf*, *J.E.G.Ph.* XXXIX, 76–92.

1941 HOLTHAUSEN, FERDINAND. Zu altenglischen Dichtungen, *Engl. Stud.* LXXIV, 324–8. (Includes discussion of ll. 1107 ff.)

1941 LOTSPEICH, C. M. Old English Etymologies, *J.E.G.Ph.* XL, 1–4. (Discusses l. 224.)

1941 MACKIE, W. S. Notes upon the Text and Interpretation of *Beowulf*: II, *M.L.R.* XXXVI, 95–8.

1941 MALONE, KEMP. Notes on *Beowulf* XII–XIII, *Anglia*, LXV, 227–9.

1941 MALONE, KEMP. Old English "Beagas," *Anglia*, Beiblatt, LII, 179–80.

1941 MERITT, HERBERT. Three Studies in Old English, *American Journal of Philology*, LXII, 331–9. (Includes discussion of MS. "walan" of l. 1031.)

1942 HOLTHAUSEN, FERDINAND. Zur altenglischen Wortkunde, *Anglia*, Beiblatt, LIII, 272–4. (Discussion of l. 1537.)

1942 HOLTHAUSEN, FERDINAND. Zur Textkritik des *Beowulf*, *Stud. Neophil.* XIV, 160. (Deals with ll. 460 ff. and 3168.)

1942 KÖKERITZ, H. Two Interpretations, *Stud. Neophil.* XIV, 277–9. (Deals with *Finnsburg* 5 a.)

1942 WHITBREAD, L. Beowulfiana, *M.L.R.* XXXVII, 480–4.

1943 HOLTHAUSEN, FERDINAND. Zum *Beowulf*, *Anglia*, Beiblatt, LIV/LV, 27–30.

1943 KUHN, SHERMAN M. The Sword of Healfdene (1020), *J.E.G.Ph.* XLII, 82–95.

1943 MEAD, D. S. *Beowulf* II b: "Þæt wæs god cyning," *Explicator*, II.

1943–4 MEYER, W. Zum Finnsburg-Fragment Vers 6–8 a, *Anglia*, Beiblatt, LIV/LV, 125–6.

1943 WOOLF, HENRY BOSLEY. A Note on the Hoard of *Beowulf*, *M.L.N.* LVIII.

1944 ESTRICH, ROBERT M. The Throne of Hrothgar: *Beowulf* ll. 168–169, *J.E.G.Ph.* XLIII, 384–9.

1944 KLAEBER, FR. Zur Texterklärung altenglischer Dichtungen, *Anglia*, Beiblatt, LIV/LV, 170–6.

1944 MEZGER, FRITZ. "On fæder feorme": *Beowulf* l. 21, *M.L.N.* LIX, 113–14.

1945 MALONE, KEMP. Finn's Stronghold, *Mod. Phil.* XLIII, 83–5. (Discusses ll. 1125–7.)

1945 MALONE, KEMP. On Finnsburg 39, *R.E.S.* XXI, 126–7.

1946 BONJOUR, ADRIEN. Weohstan's Slaying of Eanmund (*Beowulf* 2611–2625), *Engl. Stud.* XXVII, 14–19.

1946 SISAM, KENNETH. The Authority of Old English Poetical Manuscripts, *R.E.S.* XXII, 257 ff. Reprinted in his *Studies in the History of Old English Literature* (Oxford, 1953), pp. 29–44. (A most important reassessment of the principles of Textual criticism.)

1948 SPLITTER, H. W. Note on a *Beowulf* Passage (l. 749), *M.L.N.* LXIII, 118–21.

1949 CAWLEY, A. C. Notes on Old English, *Engl. & Germ. Stud.* II, 75–80. (Deals with ll. 163–4 and 1694–7.)

1949 EINARSSON, STEFAN. *Beowulf* 249: "wlite" = Icelandic "litr," *M.L.N.* LXIV, 347. (Discusses in fact l. 250 b.)

1949 LUMIANSKY, R. M. The Contexts of O.E. "ealuscerwen" and "meoduscerwen," *J.E.G.Ph.* XLVIII, 116–26.

1949 MALONE, KEMP. The Text of *Beowulf*, *Proc. American Philosoph. Soc.* XCIII, 239 ff.

1949 WHITBREAD, L. The Hand of Æschere: a Note on *Beowulf* 1343, *R.E.S.* XXV, 339–42.

1950 KLAEBER, FR. Noch einmal *Exodus* 56–58 und *Beowulf* 1408–1410, *Archiv*, CLXXXVII, 71–2.

1950 KLAEBER, FR. Randglossen zur Texterklärung des *Beowulf*, *P.B.B.* LXXII, 120–6.

1951 BOUMAN, A. C. Een Drietal Etymologieën: *Aibr, Eolete, Garsecg,* `Neophil.` XXXV, 238 ff. (Includes discussion of ll. 223 b–226 a.)

1951 KLAEBER, FR. Anmerkungen zum *Beowulf*-Text, *Archiv*, CLXXXVIII, 108–9. (Brief discussion of ll. 473, 867 ff., 982 ff., 1382, 2356, 2372, 2706, 3027, and 3117.)

1951 MALONE, KEMP. A Note on *Beowulf* 2466, *J.E.G.Ph.* L, 19–21.

1951 MEZGER, FRITZ. O.E. "Hamweorðung": *Beowulf* 2998, *J.E.G.Ph.* L, 243–5.

1951 MEZGER, FRITZ. Two Notes on *Beowulf*, *M.L.N.* LXVI, 36–8. (Deals with ll. 253 and 446.)

1951 OCHS, E. Healfdenes Tochter, *Neuphilologische Mitteilungen*, LII, 29–30.

1951-2 SMITHERS, G. V. Five Notes on Old English Texts, *Engl. & Germ. Stud.* IV, 65–85. (Valuable discussions of ll. 12–16 and 303–6, and especially full elaboration of 767–9 and 3074–5.)

1952 DOBBIE, ELLIOTT VAN KIRK. "Mwatide": *Beowulf* 2226, *M.L.N.* LXVII, 242–5.

1952 POPE, JOHN C. Three Notes on the Text of *Beowulf*, *M.L.N.* LXVII, 505–12. (Deals with 1379, 2528 and 3151.)

1952 SPLITTER, H. W. The Relation of Germanic Folk custom and Ritual to "Ealuscerwen" (*Beowulf* 769), *M.L.N.* LXVII, 255–9.

1952 TAYLOR, R. Two Notes on *Beowulf*, *Leeds Studies in English and Kindred Languages*, VII, 5 ff. (Discusses ll. 2444–71 and "Two neglected *Beowulf* Parallels in *Grettissaga*.")

1953 ELIASON, NORMAN E. *Beowulf* Notes, *Anglia*, LXXI, 4, 438 ff. (Discusses 73, 142 a, 168–9, 175–88, 330, 478 b–9, 759 b–65 a, 942 a–6 a, 1030–1, 1355 b–7 a, 1377 b–8 a, 2333–5 a, 2645–6 a: valuable.)

1953 ENGELHARDT, G. J. *Beowulf* 3150, *M.L.N.* LXVIII, 535–8.

1953 GELLING, M. The "Gumstool": *Beowulf* 1952, *M.L.R.* XLVIII, 176–7.

1953 MAGOUN, FRANCIS P., Jnr. "Inwlatide" "onfunde?" *M.L.N.* LXVIII, 540–1.

1953 MALONE, KEMP. A Note on *Beowulf* 377 ff., *M.L.N.* LXVIII, 354.

1953 MATTHES, HEINRICH CHRISTOPH. Beowulfstudien, *Anglia*, LXXI, 2, 148–90. (Three interrelated articles dealing with (*a*) final inflexional syllables, (*b*) the apparent lacuna at l. 62 as linked with the dynastic problem, and (*c*) the problem of Heremod.)

1954 BERRY, F. A Suppressed "Aposiopesis" in the Fight at Finnsburg, *Notes & Queries*, May, pp. 186–7. (Deals with l. 5 of *Finnsburg*.)

1954 COLLINDER, BJÖRN. Beowulfskolier, Festskrift tillägnad Elias Wessén, pp. 16–25. Lund. (Discusses textually ll. 303 b–6 a, 1030–3 a, 1114–18 a, 1144–5, 2155–9, 2249 b–52 a, 2255–7 a, 3069–75 and 3143–8 a: valuable.)

1954 DU BOIS, ARTHUR E. "Gifstol" (168), *M.L.N.* LXIX, 546–9.

1954 FRIEND, J. H. The Finn episode Climax: another suggestion, *M.L.N.* LXIX, 385–7. (Discussion of ll. 1142–7.)

1954 VISSER, F. TH. *Beowulf* 991–992, *Engl. Stud.* XXXV, 116–20.

1954 WOODWARD, R. W. "Swanrad" in *Beowulf, M.L.N.* LXIX, 544–5.

1955 BURCHFIELD, R. W. *Beowulf* 219 "ymb an tid," *M.L.R.* L, 484–5.

1955 LEHMANN, WINFRED PHILIPP. The Finnsburg Fragment l. 34 a: "Hwear-flacra hrær," *Univ. of Texas Studies in English*, XXXIV, 1–5.

1956 CREED, ROBERT P. *Beowulf* 2231 a, *sinc-fæt* (*sohte*), *Philological Quarterly*, XXXV, 206–8.

1956 HOWREN, ROBERT. A Note on *Beowulf* ll. 168–169, *M.L.N.* LXXI, 239–42.

1956 JELINEK, VLADIMIR. Three Notes on *Beowulf, M.L.N.* LXXI, 736–8.

1956 KINLOCH, A. A Note on *Beowulf* 1828 b, *M.L.R.* LI, 71.

1956 ORRICK, ALLAN. "Reðes ond hattres": *Beowulf* 2523, *M.L.N.* LXXI, 551–6.

1956 PIPER, WILLIAM B. The case for "weard scildinga" (*Beowulf* 305 b–306 a), *Philological Quarterly*, XXXV, 202–6.

1957 ISAACS, NEIL D. A Note on *Beowulf* 2570 b–2575 a, *Notes & Queries*, IV, 140.

1957 NIST, JOHN A. Textual Elements in the *Beowulf* Manuscript, *Papers of the Michigan Academy of Science, Arts & Letters*, XLII, 331–8.

1957 POPE, JOHN C. The Emendation "Oreðes ond attres," *Beowulf* 2523, *M.L.N.* LXXII, 321–8.

§ 8. LITERARY HISTORY, DATE AND AUTHORSHIP: BEOWULF IN THE LIGHT OF HISTORY, ARCHÆOLOGY, HEROIC LEGEND, MYTHOLOGY AND FOLKLORE

While some archæological material is included in this section, the more important archæological items dealing with Sutton Hoo and related themes published since 1939 have been placed in a new § 11.

1931 CHAPMAN, C. O. *Beowulf* and *Apollonius of Tyre, M.L.N.* XLVI.

1931 HABER, T. B. A Comparative Study of *Beowulf* and the *Aeneid*. Princeton Univ.

1931 LANGENFELT, GÖSTA. Notes on the Anglo-Saxon Pioneers VII: *Beowulf Problems, Engl. Stud.* LXVI, 236–44.

1932 BERENDSOHN, WALTER. *Hrólfssaga Kraka* und *Beowulf*-Epos, *Niederdeutsche Studien C. Borchling dargebracht*. Neumünster.

1932 KROGMANN, WILLY. Beowulf, *Engl. Stud.* LXVII, 161–4. (Discussion of the name Beowulf.)

1932 O'NEILL, SISTER M. A. Elegiac Elements in *Beowulf*. Washington D.C.

1932 SCHRÖDER, E. Beowulf, *Anglia*, LVI, 316–17. (Discussion of the name Beowulf.)

1932 SCHÜCKING, LEVIN. Das Königsideal im *Beowulf, Engl. Stud.* LXVII, 1–14.

1933 HABER, T. B. *Beowulf* and the *Aeneid, M.L.N.* XLVIII, 207.

1933 MILLS, STELLA M. The Saga of Hrolf Kraki. Oxford: Blackwell. (A good translation.)

1933 SCHRÖDER, E. Nochmals Beowulf = "Bienenwolf," *Anglia*, LVII, 400.

1933 SCHÜCKING, LEVIN. Heldenstolz und Würde im Angelsächsischen: Anhang zur Charakterisierungstechnik im Beowulfepos, *Abhandlungen der philologisch-historischen Klasse der sächsischen Akademie der Wissenschaften*, Band XLII, No. 5. Leipzig. (Valuable.)

1933 SEDGEFIELD, W. J. The Finn Episode in *Beowulf, M.L.R.* XXVIII, 480–2.

1933 WADSTEIN, E. The Beowulf poem as an English National Epos, *Acta phil. Scand.* VIII, 273–91.

1934 BEATY, JOHN O. The Echo-word in *Beowulf* with a Note on the Finnsburg Fragment, *Pub. Mod. Lang. Assoc. Amer.* XLIX, 365 ff.

1934 DICKINS, BRUCE. English Names and Old English Heathenism, *Essays & Studies by Members of the Engl. Assoc.* XIX. London.

1934 DU BOIS, ARTHUR E. The Unity of *Beowulf*, *Pub. Mod. Lang. Assoc. Amer.* XLIX, 374–405.

1934 FISCHER, WALTHER. Von neuerer deutscher Beowulf-forschung: *Germanische Philologie, Ergebnisse und Aufgaben, Festschrift für Otto Behaghel.* Heidelberg. (Surveys the work done on *Beowulf* in Germany since 1900.)

1934 KELLER, W. Beowulf der riesige Vorkämpfer, *Engl. Stud.* LXVIII, 321–38. Also *ibid.* LXIX, 154 ff.

1934 SCHRÖDER, E. Der Name Healfdene, *Anglia*, LVIII, 345–50.

1934 STEFANOVIĆ, SVETISLAV. Zur Offa-Thryðo Episode im *Beowulf*, *Engl. Stud.* LXIX, 15–31.

1934 WEBER, E. Der Germanenglaube im *Beowulf*, *Germanien*, VI. Leipzig.

1935 BERENDSOHN, WALTER. Zur Vorgeschichte des Beowulf. Copenhagen. (A large study of wide scope, highly speculative but often valuably suggestive.)

1935 BOUMAN, A. C. The Heroes of the Fight at Finnsburg, *Acta phil. Scand.* X, 130–44.

1935 DAVIES, C. Beowulf's Fight with Grendel, *Times Lit. Supplement*, Nov. 8th. Cf. *ibid.* Nov. 23rd, and Dec. 14th and 28th.

1935 GIRVAN, RITCHIE. Beowulf and the Seventh Century. London. (Brief and very stimulating lectures on questions of language, historical background, date, folklore, etc.)

1935 GORDON, E. V. Wealhþeow and Related Names, *Med. Æv.* IV, 169–75. (Valuable.)

1935–6 HÜBENER, GUSTAV. *Beowulf* and Germanic Exorcism, *R.E.S.* XI, 163–81. (Highly speculative.) This theory is carried further in *R.E.S.* XII, 429–39 as Beowulf's "Seax," the Saxons and an Indian Exorcism; and again in the *Festschrift für Max Deutschbein* (Leipzig) as *Beowulf*, ein indischer Messerexorzismus und die Sachsen.

1935 KRAPPE, A. H. Der blinde König, *Z.f.d.A.* LXXII, 161–71.

1935 MALONE, KEMP. Healfdene, *Engl. Stud.* LXX, 74 ff.

1936 BRYAN, W. P. The Wægmundings, Swedes or Geats?, *Mod. Phil.* XXXIV, 113–18.

1936 DICKINS, BRUCE. Queen Cynethryth of Mercia, *Proc. Leeds Philosoph. Soc.* IV, pt. I, 54.

1936 MALONE, KEMP. Widsith. London. (An important ed. of the poem, especially for its studies of the proper names.)

1936 MARTIN-CLARKE, ELIZABETH. The Office of Thyle in *Beowulf*, *R.E.S.* XII, 61–6.

1936 SEDGEFIELD, W. J. The Scenery of *Beowulf*, *J.E.G.Ph.* XXXV, 161–9.

1936 TOLKIEN, J. R. R. Beowulf, the Monsters and the Critics, *Proc. Brit. Acad.* XXII. (Exceptionally important: probably the most widely influential critical appreciation of the poem.)

1937 HERBEN, S. J. A Note on the Helm in *Beowulf*, *M.L.N.* LII, 34–6.

1937 KRAPPE, A. H. The Offa-Constantine Legend, *Anglia*, LXI, 361–9.

1937 MALONE, KEMP. Young Beowulf, *J.E.G.Ph.* XXXVI, 21 ff.

1937 MALONE, KEMP. The Burning of Heorot, *R.E.S.* XIII, 462–3.

1937 SHETELIG, H. and FALK, H. Scandinavian Archæology, Translated by E. V. Gordon. Oxford. (Important for the archæological background of the poem.)

1938 HERBEN, S. J. Beowulf, Hrothgar and Grendel, *Archiv*, CLXXIII, 24–30, (Highly speculative but interesting conjectures linking *Beowulf* with the cult of Nerthus described by Tacitus.)

1938 MACKIE, W. S. The Demons' Home in *Beowulf*, *J.E.G.Ph.* XXXVII, 455–61.

1938 SEAL, G. Heorot in Beowulf, *Notes & Queries*, 2 April, p. 245.

1938 WOOLF, HENRY BOSLEY. The Naming of Women in Old English Times. *Mod. Phil.* XXXVI, 113–20. (Includes discussion of some of the *Beowulf* names.)

1939 LAWRENCE, W. W. Grendel's Lair, *J.E.G.Ph.* XXXVIII, 477 ff. (Refutes the views of Mackie in *J.E.G.Ph.* XXXVII.)

1939 MAGOUN, FRANCIS P., Jnr. Zum heroischen Exorzismus des Beowulfepos, *A.f.n.F.* LIV, 215 ff. (Rejects Hübener's theories of *R.E.S.* XI and XII.)

1939 MALONE, KEMP. Hygelac, *Engl. Stud.* XXI, 108–19.

1939 MALONE, KEMP. Swerting, *Germanic Rev.* XIV, 235–57.

1939 SCHRÖBLER, I. *Beowulf* and Homer, *P.B.B.* LXIII, 305 ff.

1940 CALDWELL, J. R. The Origin of the Story of Boðvar-Bjarki, *A.f.n.F.* LV, 223–75.

1940 COOLEY, FRANKLIN D. William Taylor of Norwich and *Beowulf*, *M.L.N.* LV, 210–11.

1940 COOLEY, FRANKLIN D. Early Danish Criticism of *Beowulf*, *E.L.H.* VII. (A useful account of Thorkelin, Rask and Grundtvig.)

1940 GIRVAN, RITCHIE. Finnsburuh, *Proc. Brit. Acad.* XXVI, 327–60. (A new approach to the whole problem of *Finnsburg* in relation to *Beowulf*.)

1940 MAGOUN, FRANCIS P., Jnr. Zu Etzeln burc, Finns buruh and Brunan burh, *Z.f.d.A.* LXXVII, 65–6.

1940 MALONE, KEMP. Ecgtheow, *Mod. Lang. Quarterly*, I, 37–44.

1940 MALONE, KEMP. Freawaru, *E.L.H.* VII, 39–44.

1940 MALONE, KEMP. Hagbard and Ingeld, *Essays & Studies in Honor of Carleton Brown*, 1–22. New York Univ.

1940 NIEDERSTENBRUCH, A. Germanisch-heidnische und Christlich-kirchliche Elemente in *Beowulf*, *Weltanschauung und Schule*, III.

1940 SCHÜTTE, G. Episoderne med Hygelac og Ongentheow, *Danske Studier*, XXXVII, 49–58.

1940 WHITBREAD, L. Grendel's Abode, an Illustrative Note, *Engl. Stud.* XXII, 64–6.

1941 COOLEY, FRANKLIN D. Grundtvig's First Translation from *Beowulf*, *Scandinavian Stud.* XVI.

1941 MALONE, KEMP. Hygd, *M.L.N.* LVI, 356–8.

1941 MALONE, KEMP. Grundtvig as *Beowulf* Critic, *R.E.S.* XVII, 129–38.

1942 BROWN, CALVIN S. On Reading *Beowulf*, *Sewanee Rev.* L.

1942 KLAEBER, FR. Unferð's Verhalten im *Beowulf*, *Anglia*, Beiblatt, LIII, 270–2.

1942 MALONE, KEMP. Grendel and Grep, *Pub. Mod. Lang. Assoc. Amer.* LVII, 1–14. (Relates the Grep episode of Saxo Grammaticus' fifth book to the slaying of Grendel.)

1942 SCHÜTTE, G. Skjoldungsagnene i ny Læsemaade, *Danske Studier*, XXXIX, 81–100.

1942 WHITBREAD, L. Beowulf and Grendel's Mother: Two Minor Parallels from Folklore, *M.L.N.* LVII, 281–2.

1943 BOBERG, I. M. Die Saga von Vermund und Uffe, *Acta phil. scand.* XVI, 129 ff.

1943 BOND, G. Links between *Beowulf* and Mercian History, *Studies in Philology*, XL, 481–93.

1943 BRODEUR, A. G. The Climax of the Finn Episode, *Univ. of California Publications in English*, vol. III, no. 8, 285–362.

1943 BRODEUR, A. G. Design and Motive in the Finn Episode, *Essays and Studies* (*Univ. of California Publications in English*, XIV), 1–42.

1943 GADDE, F. Viktor Rydberg and some *Beowulf* Questions, *Stud. Neophil.* XV (Ekwall Miscellany), pt. 2, 71–90.

1943 LUKMAN, N. C. Skjoldunge und Skilfinge, Hunnen- und Herulerkönige in ostnordischer Überlieferung. Copenhagen.

1943 MALONE, KEMP. Hildeburg and Hengest. *E.L.H.* X, 257–84.

1943 SCHÜTTE, G. Anglian Legends in Danish Traditions, *Acta phil. Scand.* XVI, 233–8.

1945 BOBERG, I. M. Er Skjoldungerne Hunnerkonger?, *Acta phil. Scand.* XVIII, 257–67.

1945 WHITBREAD, L. Three *Beowulf* Allusions, *Notes & Queries*, 17 November, 207–9.

1946 HAMILTON, MARIE. The Religious Principle in *Beowulf*, *Pub. Mod. Lang. Assoc. Amer.* LXI, 309–30.

1946 HULBERT, JAMES R. *Beowulf* and the Classical Epic, *Mod. Phil.* XLIV, 65–75.

1946 SOUTHWARD, ELAINE. The Knight Yder and the *Beowulf* Legend, *Med. Æv.* XV, 1–47.

1947 JOHANSSON, G. Beowulfsagans Hronesnæsse, Lekmannafunderingar angående det gamla Gotland. Göteborg.

1947 SCHÜTTE, G. Offa I Reduced ad Absurdum, *Acta phil. Scand.* XIX, 179–96.

1947 WOOLF, HENRY BOSLEY. Beowulf and Grendel; an Analogue from Burma, *M.L.N.* LXII, 261–2.

1948 MALONE, KEMP. *Beowulf*, *Engl. Stud.* XXIX, 161–72. (A general lecture on the poem.)

1948 TIMMER, B. J. *Beowulf*: the Poem and the Poet, *Neophil.* XXXII, 122 ff.

1948 WOOLF, HENRY BOSLEY. On the Characterization of *Beowulf*, *E.L.H.* XV, 85–92.

1949 BONJOUR, ADRIEN. Grendel's Dam and the Composition of *Beowulf*, *Engl. Stud.* XXX, 4, 113–24.

1949 COOLEY, FRANKLIN D. Contemporary Reaction to the Identification of Hygelac, *Philologica* (*Malone Anniversary Studies*, Baltimore), 269 ff.

1949 MAGOUN, FRANCIS P., Jnr. Danes, North, South, East and West in *Beowulf*, *Philologica* (*Malone Anniversary Studies*, Baltimore), 20 ff.

1949 MAYNARD, W. A. The Fight at Finnsburg, *M.L.R.* XLIV, 228.

1949 WARD, G. Hengest, *Archaeologica Cantiana*, LXI, 77 ff.

1949 WARD, G. Hengest: an Historical Study of his Danish Origins and of his Campaigns in Frisia and in South-East England. London.

1949 WOOLF, HENRY BOSLEY. Unferth, *Mod. Lang. Quarterly*, X, 145–52.

1950 BONJOUR, ADRIEN. The Digressions in *Beowulf*. Oxford: *Mediaeval Monographs* (Blackwell). (Very important: seeks to show the artistic relevance of all digressions to the structure of the poem.)

1950 DONAHUE, C. Grendel and the Clanna Cain, *Celtic Studies*, I.

1950 GENZMER, F. Die scandinavischen Quellen des *Beowulfs*, *A.f.n.F.* LXV, 17–62.

1950 MALONE, KEMP. Notes on *Beowulf*, *Anglia*, LXIX, 3, 295 ff. (A reply to Bonjour's views on "Beowulf's Inglorious Youth" in his The Digressions in Beowulf (pp. 24–7): deals particularly with ll. 2183 b–9.)

1951 BLOOMFIELD, M. W. *Beowulf* and Christian Allegory: an Interpretation of Unferth, *Traditio*, VII, 410–15.

1951 BONJOUR, ADRIEN. *Beowulf* and Heardred, *Engl. Stud.* XXXII, 5, 193–200.

1951 COLGRAVE, BERTRAM. A Mexican Version of the "Bear's Son" Folktale, *Journal of American Folklore*, LXIV, 409 ff.

1951 DONAHUE, C. *Beowulf*, Ireland and the Natural Good, *Traditio*, VII, 263–77.

1951 GIRVAN, RITCHIE. The Mediaeval Poet and his Public, *English Studies Today* (Papers read at the International Congress of University Professors of English in Oxford 1950, ed. G. Bullough and C. L. Wrenn). Oxford. (Deals mainly with *Beowulf*.)

1951 HULBERT, JAMES R. Surmises concerning the *Beowulf*-poet's Source, *J.E.G.Ph.* L, 11–18.

1951 HULBERT, JAMES R. The Genesis of *Beowulf*: a Caveat, *Pub. Mod. Lang. Assoc. Amer.* LXVI, 1168–76.

1951 PETERS, L. J. The Relationship of the Old English *Andreas* to *Beowulf*, *Pub. Mod. Lang. Assoc. Amer.* LXVI, 844 ff. (Emphasizes the importance of shared traditional heroic formulae as opposed to direct influence.)

1951 WHITELOCK, DOROTHY. The Audience of *Beowulf*. Oxford. (Important: three short lectures containing much new material and valuable suggestions.)

1952 BONJOUR, ADRIEN. Young Beowulf's Inglorious Period, *Anglia*, LXX, 4, 339 ff.

1952 BONJOUR, ADRIEN. The Problem of Dæghrefn, *J.E.G.Ph.* LI, 355–9.

1952 ELIASON, NORMAN E. The "Improvised Lay" in *Beowulf*, *Philological Quarterly*, XXXI, 171–9.

1952 GANG, T. M. Approaches to *Beowulf*, *R.E.S.* New Ser. III, 1 ff. (A lively reappraisal of the structure of the poem with some strictures on the views of W. P. Ker and of Tolkien's British Academy lecture of 1936.)

1952 LUMIANSKY, R. M. The Dramatic Audience in *Beowulf*, *J.E.G.Ph.* LI, 545–50.

1952 O'LOUGHLIN, J. L. N. *Beowulf*: its Unity and Purpose, *Med. Æv.* XXI, 1–13.

1953 BONJOUR, ADRIEN. Monsters Crouching and Critics Rampant: or the *Beowulf* Dragon Debated, *Pub. Mod. Lang. Assoc. Amer.* LXVIII, 304 ff. (A reply to Gang's article in *R.E.S.* New Ser. III of 1952.)

1953 DE VRIES, J. Die beiden Hengeste, *Z.f.d.Ph.* LXXII, 125–43.

1953 BRODEUR, A. G. The Structure and Unity of *Beowulf*, *Pub. Mod. Lang. Assoc. Amer.* LXVIII, 1183 ff.

1953 ENGELHARDT, G. J. On the Sequence of Beowulf's "Geogoð," *M.L.N.* LXVIII, 91–5.

1953 LEISI, ERNST. Gold und Manneswert im *Beowulf*, *Anglia*, LXXI, 3, 259–74.

1953 MAGOUN, FRANCIS P., Jnr. The Geography of Hygelac's Raid on the Lands of the West Frisians and the Hætt-ware *ca* 530 A.D., *Engl. Stud.* XXXIV, 160–3.

1953 MOORE, A. K. Beowulf's Dereliction in the Grendel Episode, *M.L.N.* LXVIII, 165–9.

1953 SISAM, KENNETH. Anglo-Saxon Royal Genealogies, *Proc. Brit. Acad.* XXXIX, 287–346. (Important generally, and particularly for the study of the *Beowulf* Danish pedigrees.)

1954 BRODEUR, A. G. Design for Terror in the Purging of Heorot, *J.E.G.Ph.* LIII, 503–13.

1954 BRUNNER, KARL. Why was *Beowulf* Preserved? *Études anglaises*, VII, 1–5.

1954 LAUR, W. Die Heldensage vom Finnsburgkampf, *Z.f.d.A.* LXXXV, 107 ff.

1954 MAGOUN, FRANCIS P., Jnr. Beowulf and King Hygelac in the Netherlands, *Engl. Stud.* XXXV, 193 ff. (A carefully documented reconstruction with the relevant texts printed.)

1954 MALONE, KEMP. Coming Back from the Mere, *Pub. Mod. Lang. Assoc. Amer.* LXIX, 1292–9.

1954 WOOLF, HENRY BOSLEY. Hrothgar, *Louisiana State Univ. Studies*, Humanities Ser. V, 39 ff. Baton Rouge.

1955 KARNEY, JAMES. Studies in Irish Literature and History. Dublin: Institute of Advanced Studies. (Chap. III (pp. 77–128), "The Irish Elements in *Beowulf*," is a speculative attempt to relate *Beowulf* very closely with the Old Irish *Táin Bó Fraich*.)

1955 VAN MEURS. *Beowulf* and Literary Criticism, *Neophil.* XXXIX, 114–30.

1955 PEPPERDENE, MARGARET. Grendel's Geis, *Journal of the Royal Soc. of Antiquaries of Ireland*, LXXXV, 188–92.

1955 ROGERS, H. L. Beowulf's Three Great Fights, *R.E.S.* New Ser. VI, 339–55.

1955 SANDER, GREIF. Gliederung und Komposition des *Beowulfs*. Mainz.

1955 SOUTHERLAND, R. C. The Meaning of *Eorlscipe* in *Beowulf*, *Pub. Mod. Lang. Assoc. Amer.* LXX, 1139–40.

1957 BONJOUR, ADRIEN. *Beowulf* and the Snares of Literary Criticism, *Études anglaises*, X, 30–6.

1957 WRIGHT, HERBERT G. Good and Evil; Light and Darkness: Joy and Sorrow in *Beowulf*, *R.E.S.* New Ser. VIII, I–II. (Valuable.)

1958 FISHER, PETER F. The Trials of the Epic Hero in *Beowulf*, *Pub. Mod. Lang. Assoc. Amer.* LXXIII, 171–83.

1958 NIST, JOHN A. The Structure of *Beowulf*, *Papers of the Michigan Academy of Science, Arts and Letters*, XLIII, 307–14.

1958 SISAM, KENNETH. Beowulf's Fight with the Dragon, *R.E.S.* New Ser. IX, 129–40. (Realistic.)

§ 9. STYLE, VOCABULARY AND GRAMMAR

1932 HULBERT, JAMES R. A Note on Compounds in *Beowulf*, *J.E.G.Ph.* XXXI, 504 ff.

1932 REDBOND, W. J. Notes on the word "Garsecg," *M.L.R.* XXVII, 204–6.

1933 KROGMANN, WILLY. "Gang," *Anglia*, LVII, 216–17. (On the pret. form "gang" in ll. 1009, 1295 and 1316.)

1935 BARTLETT, ADELINE C. The Larger Rhetorical Patterns in Anglo-Saxon Poetry. New York, Columbia Univ.

1936 MARQUARDT, HERTHA. Fürsten- und Kriegerkenning im *Beowulf*, *Anglia*, LX, 390–5.

1937 BATCHELOR, C. C. The Style of the *Beowulf*: a Study of the Composition of the Poem, *Speculum*, XII, 330–42.

1938 BLOMFIELD, JOAN. The Style and Structure of *Beowulf*, *R.E.S.* XIV, 396 ff.

1940 ANDREW, S. O. Syntax and Style in Old English. Cambridge. (Frequent references to passages in *Beowulf*: stimulating but often very individual.)

1940 PIRKHOVER, A. Figurengestaltung im *Beowulf*-Epos. Heidelberg.

1941 HERAUCOURT, W. Figurengestaltung im *Beowulf*-Epos, *Die neueren Sprachen*, XLIX, 170–2.

1941 LOTSPEICH, C. M. Old English Etymologies, *J.E.G.Ph.* XL, 1–4. (Deals with "aglæca," "eolet(e)" and other forms.)

1941 MALONE, KEMP. Grundtvig as *Beowulf* Critic, *R.E.S.* XVII, 129–38.

1942 MERONEY, HOWARD. Old English "ðær" "if," *J.E.G.Ph.* XLI, 201–9. (Discusses ll. 2570 ff.)

1943 WOOLF, HENRY BOSLEY. Subject-verb Agreement in *Beowulf*, *Mod. Lang. Quarterly*, IV, 49–55.

1946 DEROLEZ, R. L. "—and that difficult word, Garsecg," *Mod. Lang. Quarterly*, VII, 445–52.

1948 ANDREW, S. O. Postscript on *Beowulf*. Cambridge. (A really valuable study of syntax and style, though not always linguistically and textually reliable.)

1950–1 FLASDIECK, H. O.E. "Nefne": a Revaluation, *Anglia*, LXIX–LXX.

1951 BONJOUR, ADRIEN. The Technique of Parallel Descriptions in *Beowulf*, *R.E.S.* New Ser. II, 1–10.

1952 BOWRA, Sir MAURICE. Heroic Poetry. London. (Useful for general view of background to style and tone from a comparative standpoint.)

1952 BRADY, CAROLINE. The Synonyms for "sea" in *Beowulf*, *Studies in Honor of Albert Morey Sturtevant*, 24 ff. (Kansas: Univ. of Lawrence.)

1952 WALKER, W. S. The "Brunecg" Sword, *M.L.N.* LXVII, 516–20.

1953 MAGOUN, FRANCIS P., Jnr. Oral-formulaic Character of Anglo-Saxon Narrative Poetry, *Speculum*, XXVIII, 446 ff. (Important.)

1953 SISAM, KENNETH. Dialect Origins of the Earlier Old English Verse, included in his "Studies in the History of Old English Literature," Oxford.

1957 BONJOUR, ADRIEN. *Beowulf* and the Beasts of Battle, *Pub. Mod. Lang. Assoc. Amer.* LXXII, 563–73.

1957 EMERSON, EVERETT H. On Translating *Beowulf*, *South Atlantic Quarterly*, LVI, 369–79.

§ 10. METRE

1924 SIEVERS, EDUARD. Ziele und Wege der Schallanalyse. Heidelberg. (The clearest exposition of Sievers' more individual and solipsistic views.)

1931 ANDREW, S. O. The Old English Alliterative Measure. Croydon.

1941 MALONE, KEMP. Lift-patterns in Old English Verse, *E.L.H.* VIII, 74–80.

1942 POPE, J. C. The Rhythm of *Beowulf*. New Haven: Yale Univ. (Presents a new theory of O.E. metre with the aid of musical notation: very important and influential. This outstanding work also includes a full review of all previous work on O.E. metre, and some most valuable new readings of the text.)

1948–9 BAUM, P. E. The Metre of the *Beowulf*, *Mod. Phil.* XLVI (2 pts.)

1948 KLAEBER, FR. Zum Rhythmus der *Beowulf*-verse, *Archiv*, CLXXXV, 121–4.

1952 SLAY, D. Some Aspects of the Technique of Composition of Old English Verse, *Trans. Phil. Soc.* (London).

1956 LEHMANN, WINFRED PHILIPP. The Development of Germanic Verse Form. Austin: Univ. of Texas. (A stimulating general survey, including Old English.)

1956 SCHAAR, C. On a New Theory of O.E. Poetic Diction, *Neophil.* XL, 301 ff.

1957 LE PAGE, R. B. A Rhythmical Framework for the Five Types, *Engl. & Germ. Stud.* VI, 92 ff. (A stimulating reconsideration of O.E. scansion in modification of the dominant views of J. C. Pope.)

§ 11. SUTTON HOO AND ARCHÆOLOGY

The best general descriptive accounts of the discoveries at Sutton Hoo and their significance are those of Mr R. L. S. Bruce-Mitford: in the *British Museum Quarterly* for 1939, The Sutton Hoo Ship-Burial: a Provisional Guide (Brit. Mus. 1947, reprinted for the second time in 1952), and his Appendix to the third edition of R. H. Hodgkin's History of the Anglo-Saxons, Oxford, 1952. The last-named of these is the best for *Beowulf* study. Valuable articles have appeared on Sutton Hoo frequently in *Antiquity* and in *The Antiquaries Journal*. Of

612   Supplementary Bibliography

especial importance is the series by notable archæologists in *Antiquity*, XIV, for 1940 (pp. 6–87), and *The Antiquaries Journal* for the same year for its pioneer article by Mr C. W. Phillips (pp. 149–202.)

1938 ARBMAN, HOLGER (and others). Vendel i Fynd och Forskning, Skrift med Anledning av Vendelmonumentets Tillkomst utgiven av *Upplands Fornminnesförening*. Uppsala. (After reviewing the Vendel finds which so often parallel items at Sutton Hoo not then known, concludes with an English section on "Vendel in Uppland and the *Beowulf* Poem" by the leading Swedish archæologists of the time.)

1939 KEILLER, A., and PIGGOTT, STUART. The Chambered Tomb in *Beowulf, Antiquity*, XIII.

1948 LINDQVIST, SUNE. Sutton Hoo and *Beowulf, Antiquity*, XXII, 131–40. (Important.)

1949 BRUCE-MITFORD, R. L. S. The Sutton Hoo Ship-Burial: Recent Theories and some Comments on General Interpretation, *Proc. Suffolk Instit. of Archæology*, vol. XXV, pt. I. Ipswich. (Especially important as the most effective and authoritative account, particularly bringing out the historical and archæological evidences on the Geat-Swedish elements in *Beowulf*.)

1950 DAVIDSON, H. R. E. The Hill of the Dragon: Anglo-Saxon Burial Mounds in Literature and Archæology, *Folk-Lore*, LXI, 169 ff.

1950 MARTIN-CLARKE, ELIZABETH. Significant Objects at Sutton Hoo, The Early Cultures of North-West Europe (*H. M. Chadwick Memorial Studies*), ed. Sir Cyril Fox and Bruce Dickins, pp. 107–19. Cambridge. (Particularly interesting on the "Standard.")

1952 GRIERSON, PH. The Dating of the Sutton Hoo Coins, *Antiquity*, XXVI, 83 ff.

1952 BRUCE-MITFORD, R. L. S. The Sutton Hoo Ship-burial, Appendix to the third edition of R. H. Hodgkin's *History of the Anglo-Saxons* (vol. II, 698–734 and notes 749–56). Oxford. (Important: the best short account covering all the major advances made up to its date, and including much that is relevant to the study of both the text and the background of *Beowulf*.)

1954 HAUCK, KARL. Herrschaftszeichen eines Wodanistischen Königtums, *Festgabe Anton Ernstberger* (Jahrbuch für fränkische Landesforschung, XIV), pp. 9–65. Erlangen Univ. (Very full, if at times speculative; includes excellent bibliographical material.)

1954 MAGOUN, FRANCIS P., Jnr. The Sutton Hoo Ship-burial: a Chronological Bibliography, *Speculum*, XXIX, 116–24. (Important: carries the writings on Sutton Hoo (most of which have some bearing on *Beowulf*) to the end of 1952, and is complete.)

1954 SCHRAMM, PERCY ERNST (and others). Herrschaftszeichen und Staatssymbolik, *Schriften der Monumenta Germaniæ Historica*, XIII, 1. Stuttgart. (Important for general background, and for chap. VI by Wilhelm Berges and Adolf Gauert (pp. 238–80) which treats in detail especially of the "Standard" and the "Sceptre.")

1957 HATTO, A. T. Snake-swords and Boar-helms in *Beowulf, Engl. Stud.*, XXXVIII, 145 ff. (Important, especially on l. 1459b and for the boar as a protective symbol.)

1958 BESSINGER, J. *Beowulf* and the Harp at Sutton Hoo, *Univ. of Toronto Quarterly*, XXVII, 148–68.

1958 WRENN, C. L. Sutton Hoo and *Beowulf, Mélanges de Linguistique et de Philologie in Memoriam Fwenand Mossé*. Paris, 1959.

ADDITIONS TO THE SUPPLEMENTARY BIBLIOGRAPHY

The following miscellaneous items came to my notice too late for inclusion at the appropriate places. They are here arranged in order of date and alphabetically, but without regard to subject-matter.

1957 GRABAND, GERHARD. Sutton Hoo, *Zeitschrift für Anglistik und Amerikanistik*, Jahrgang II, Heft 2, 201–9, Berlin.

1958 BLISS, A. J. The Metre of *Beowulf*. Oxford (Basil Blackwell). (Valuable. This is a new, thorough and scientific reconsideration of the Sievers Types.)

1958 KASKE, R. E. *Sapientia et Fortitudo* as a Controlling Theme of *Beowulf*, *Studies in Philology*, LV, 423–56.

1958 LINDQVIST, SUNE. *Beowulf* Dissectus. Uppsala. (An important and provocative setting out of passages (with Swedish translations) of special Scandinavian interest which are held to be the more ancient parts of the poem as against later accretions.)

1958 SALMON, PAUL. Anomalous Alliteration in Germanic Verse, *Neophil.* XLII, 223–42.

1958 STORMS, GODFRID. Compound Names of Peoples in *Beowulf*: a Study in the Diction of a Great Poet, Inaugural Nijmegen University Lecture. Nijmegen and Utrecht.

1958 TURVILLE-PETRE, Mrs J. E. Hengest and Horsa, *Saga-book of the Viking Soc.*, London, XIV, Pt 4, 273–90. (A very speculative suggestion that these heroes were originally only cult-names.)

INDEX

Abbots Morton, "Grindel's pit" near, 305

Abingdon, sheaf-ordeal at, 83–4, 302–3

Adam in West-Saxon and other genealogies, 45 n., 73–4, 198, 314, 316–18, 320–1

Adam of Bremen, 280 n., 339, 340 n., 406

Adamnan, 489

Ælbertus, see Æthelbert

Ælfleda, daughter of Offa II, 240–2

Ælle, king of Deira, 394

Æthelbert (St Ælbertus), king of East Anglia, 37–8, 239–43

Æthelhere, East Anglian king, 511, 514

Æthelred, king of Mercia, 196–7

Æthelred, king of Wessex, 318

Æthelwald, East Anglian king, 514

Æthelwulf, king of Wessex, 78, 201–2, 317–19

Ætla, see Attila

Agathias, 386

Agnar (Agnerus), son of Ingeld, 132–3, 430

Aidan, bishop, 325

Alboin, 272, 281–2, 284–5, 444

Alcester, "Grindel's pit" near, 305

Alcuin, letters of, 22, 38, 123, 332; Life of Willibrord, 289 n.

Aldfrid, king of Northumbria, 325, 489

Aldhelm, bishop, 329, 331–2, 488–9

Alemanni, 91 n., 212–15

Alewih, king of the Danes, 31, 244

Alfred, king of Wessex, 70, 76, 121–2, 293, 317–19, 329, 331–2, 340, 398, 488–9, 506; his translation of Orosius, 402–3; his translation of the Pastoral Care, MSS. of, 295–6

Alfsola, ship-burial of, 69

Ali, see Onela

Aliel (Riganus), 35, 218–25

Allan O'Maut, 298

Almgren, Prof. O., 344 n., 345 n., 416

Amloþi, see Hamlet

Ammianus Marcellinus, 444

Anastasius I, Byzantine Emperor, 511, 517

Andreas, 352–3, 399 n., 530

Andvari, 458

Anganþér, Angantyr, see Ongentheow

Angeln, 31, 51, 70–1, 343, 345–6, 351, 394, 400, 442

Angers, MS. found at, 215

Angles, 10, 18, 45, 53, 98–104, 204, 273, 274 n., 314, 338, 342, 345, 407, 487; kings of, 31–40, 244; genealogy, 314, 316

Anglo-Saxon Chronicle, 8, 11, 17 n., 31, 323, 336; genealogies in, 42 n., 72–4, 76–80, 85–8, 196–8, 200–4, 262, 289, 291, 296, 303, 310–22, 343, 545, 550; Icelandic versions of genealogies, 45 n., 52 n., 313, 315; MSS. and their relations, 312–15

Anglo-Saxons, funeral customs of, 124–5

Annales Lundenses (Annales Esromenses), 17 n., 204, 365

Annales Ryenses, account of Offa, 539

Archaeology, in relation to Beowulf, 124–5, 288, 345–65, 392, 396, 408–19, 433, 445, 507–23

Argos, Homeric, identity of, 423

Arthur, 16, 56 n., 250

Asbiorn, death of, 186–7, 189–90

Asgard, 299

Asser, Life of Alfred, 201–2, 331 n., 312, 315

Atalanta, 39

Aðals, see Eadgils

Athelstan, 269, 348; Charter of, 42–4, 306

Athils, Athislus, see Eadgils

Attila (Atli), king of the Huns, 7, 17 n., 29, 45 n., 99, 243, 275; funeral rites of, 122–5

Attoarii, Atuarii, see Hetware

Aun, burial mound of, 356, 412–18

Ayres, Prof. H. M., on Finn Episode, 258 n., 259 n., 263 n., 266–7, 270, 276 n.

Baba Yaga, 372–3

Bacon, Francis, 271, 422

Baderich, 383–4

Bærings Saga, 460

Baldæg, 316, 321

Baldr, ship-burial of, 68–9

Baldwin Brown, Prof. G., 326, 349 n., 355, 357 n., 359–61

Balham, "Grendel's mire" near, 306

Ballad and epic, relation of, 116, 391–2, 395–400, 471